CRIME AND JUSTICE

LEARNING THROUGH CASES

Third Edition

CAROLYN BOYES-WATSON
SUFFOLK UNIVERSITY

WITH

SUSAN T. KRUMHOLZ
UNIVERSITY OF MASSACHUSETTS, DARTMOUTH

ROWMAN & LITTLEFIELD

LANHAM · BOULDER · NEW YORK · LONDON

D0210034

Senior Editor: Sarah Stanton
Assistant Editor: Carli Hansen
Senior Marketing Manager: Kim Lyons
Interior Designer: Kathy Mrozek

Credits and acknowledgments for material borrowed from other sources, and reproduced with permission, appear on the appropriate page within the text.

Published by Rowman & Littlefield
A wholly owned subsidiary of The Rowman & Littlefield Publishing Group, Inc.
4501 Forbes Boulevard, Suite 200, Lanham, Maryland 20706
www.rowman.com

Unit A, Whitacre Mews, 26-34 Stannary Street, London SE11 4AB, United Kingdom

Copyright © 2018 by Rowman & Littlefield
Second edition 2013. First edition 2003 Pearson Education, Inc.

British Library Cataloguing in Publication Information Available

Library of Congress Cataloging-in-Publication Data Available
ISBN: 978-1-5381-0689-1 (cloth : alk. paper)
ISBN: 978-1-5381-0690-7 (pbk. : alk. paper)
ISBN: 978-1-5381-0691-4 (electronic)

∞™ The paper used in this publication meets the minimum requirements of American National Standard for Information Sciences—Permanence of Paper for Printed Library Materials, ANSI/NISO Z39.48-1992.

Printed in the United States of America

CONTENTS

PREFACE

The study of crime and justice is inherently fascinating to students. One of the pleasures of teaching this subject is the central importance of justice as a foundation to our lives as human beings and as citizens. Few topics elicit such strong opinions rooted in passionate conviction about what is right and wrong. Because the topics studied in this course matter so much to students, teachers have a powerful opportunity to expose students to methods of critical analysis that can influence their thinking throughout their college years and beyond. Yet teaching an introduction to crime and justice class poses unique challenges. Because students come to the material with implicit assumptions, there is a need to stimulate thinking about such fundamental questions as "what is crime?" and "what is justice?" and to encourage students to draw connections between processes within the criminal justice system and the social structure of the broader society. Learning through cases is an effective pedagogy and a popular teaching style for students and provides an accessible strategy for teaching about crime and justice. Cases empower students to think independently and to actively utilize the concepts presented in the chapters.

LEARNING THROUGH CASES

The case study method serves the core learning objectives in each chapter; the narrative form of the case holds student attention and provides historical, sociological, political, and legal context for each case, which provides rich detail for class discussion, analysis, and assignments. For the student, the case is the "hook." Students become *invested* in the case that has been purposely designed to raise critical questions rather than provide answers. As students become engaged in the dramatic narrative, the critical thinking questions invite students to view the administration of justice through "multiple" lenses and to raise critical questions about the meaning of justice in a broad sense and in the events connected to their own lives. Abstract issues of law, criminology, political science, sociology, and criminal justice administration come alive as students grapple with the concrete dilemmas raised by each case. The case study method also creates a lively interactive classroom environment based on discussion and dialogue among students and instructors. Students remain focused and interested in the drama of the cases; are better able to apply the concepts; become active participants in the learning process; and have a deeper understanding of the issues presented in lectures and the text. Students enjoy the class because this approach builds upon what is of most direct interest to the student: the drama of actual people who are facing, reacting to, and "doing" justice.

Crime and Justice: Learning through Cases offers all the tools instructors need to successfully apply the case method approach to a traditional classroom. Key review and study questions provide the basis for critical analysis of the case, and the Check It Out section in each chapter offers material for further investigation.

THE STRUCTURE OF THE CASEBOOK

Each chapter begins with a case elaborated in five to ten pages, followed by a text about twenty to thirty pages in length. Students read the case and have the opportunity for critical consideration and analysis before reading the accompanying chapter. The chapters provide background, concepts, and core knowledge about the justice system. One of the most significant structural changes in the third edition has been to visually integrate the case study and the chapter content into a single, clearly identifiable unit. Review and study questions are designed to assist students in acquiring the core foundation required for an introductory course on the criminal justice system. Key terms and other resource material are also provided to assist in the acquisition of a comprehensive introduction to the criminal justice system.

THE TEXT

Each chapter covers the core knowledge required for an overview of the criminal justice system, preparing students for higher level courses on the justice system.

Thematically, the text emphasizes the process of social change within the criminal justice system. Throughout the text, students are encouraged to see the justice system as a "work-in-progress": the meaning and administration of justice has evolved historically and is continuing to do so, influenced by forces within the broader society. Written in highly accessible, compelling, and concise prose this text adopts a justice studies approach to the criminal justice system suitable for students in a wide range of institutions from community colleges to highly competitive four-year institutions. The central question "what is justice?" is the primary focus. The text analyzes the criminal justice system in the context of our wider issues of social justice and inequality through historical and contemporary analysis and provides full coverage of victims' issues and restorative justice throughout text. Students are encouraged to consider their own role in shaping the future of the criminal justice system. All of the chapters in the casebook focus on the ongoing struggle for equality before the law for all members of American society. Issues of race, class, and gender inequality are raised through multiple cases emphasizing legal and policy developments that have resulted from various social movements.

NEW TO THE THIRD EDITION

Rapid developments in the social and political realms resulted in an expansion of materials in the second edition; we did this by adding several new chapters. Feedback from users of the text has led us to reduce the number of chapters for the third edition while retaining as much of the essential content as possible. For the third edition we have divided the book into five sections, with the chapters evenly distributed (three in each section). The new edition continues to incorporate several topics added to the second edition, including corporate financial crime, governmental crime, the war on drugs, and terrorism. In addition, we have addressed such timely issues as current awareness of police shootings and important social movements, such as Black Lives Matter.

AN OVERVIEW OF THE CHAPTERS

Part I—Exploring Crime and Justice

Chapter 1: Crime, Law, and Justice—Case #1: A Seventeenth-Century Crime Wave: The Salem Witch Trials. This chapter introduces key ideas about crime, law, and due process, while the case invites students to think about the value of due process in the justice system today. Even though the social order and justice system of the seventeenth century bears little in common with the justice system today, the concept of the "witch hunt" remains relevant to the modern context. Students are encouraged in this case to view the familiar rights guaranteed by the Constitution through fresh eyes.

Chapter 2: The Justice Process—Case #2: A "Run-of-the-Mill" Crime. This chapter looks at the overall justice process and emphasizes the importance of discretion within the system. This case demonstrates the reality of discretionary decision-making in all parts of the criminal justice system and many issues that face our legal system when we try to determine guilt or innocence.

Chapter 3: The Struggle for Justice—Case #3: The Scottsboro Trials. This chapter illustrates the persistent gap between rights enjoyed de jure and the de facto practices of the justice system given the inequality within the wider society. The chapter examines the structure of the criminal justice system and illustrates the historical and ongoing political and social forces which seek to achieve equal justice before the law for all citizens.

Part II—Crime and the Law

Chapter 4: Understanding the Crime Picture—Case #4: Can Corporations Commit Murder? The Prosecution of the Ford Motor Company. This chapter looks at types and measurement of crime. It introduces students to all kinds of crime, including those hard to measure and those we rarely think about as crime, such as state and political crimes. By focusing on corporate crime, the Ford case introduces students to the variety of behaviors which constitute crime and to the stereotypes we unconsciously bring to the study of crime.

Chapter 5: Principles of the Criminal Law—Case #5: Accident or Homicide? The Shooting of Yoshi Hattori. This chapter focuses on building an understanding of the criminal law. The case demonstrates the principles of criminal law through a close analysis of the prosecution and defense in a criminal trial. This chapter/case raises questions about racism in the application of the law and its pervasive influence in the determination of the "reasonableness" standard in the criminal law.

Chapter 6: Understanding Victims in the Criminal Justice System—Case #6: Facing the Demons: Making Amends for Drunk Driving. The chapter examines the victims' rights movement, examines victimology, and introduces the idea of restorative justice. The case raises questions about the unique needs of victims and their role in the criminal justice process.

Part III—Policing in a Democratic Society

Chapter 7: Police and the Law—Case #7: Security or Dignity: Rosa at the Border. This case invites students to think about the importance of the Fourth Amendment, and the delicate balance between the needs of security and civil liberties. The chapter content provides an overview of the structure of U.S. law, describing the variety of law enforcement agencies and responsibilities. The chapter also presents a detailed treatment of the impact of the Fourth and Fifth Amendments on policing.

Chapter 8: Policing in the Twenty-First Century: Past, Present, and Future—Case #8: The Thin Blue Line: Rodney King and the LAPD. The King case raises important questions about the relationship of police, particularly urban police, to the citizenry they are dedicated to serve and protect. In this case and the accompanying text, students are invited to think about the conditions within the culture and mission of policing that promote the abuse of authority by those sworn to uphold the law. The chapter also examines the historical origins of police, examines current issues in policing, and looks toward a vision of policing in the new century.

Chapter 9: The Impact of 9/11 on Civil Liberties and Law Enforcement—Case #9, False Patriots: The Oklahoma City Bombing and the Politics of Fear. This case study is about terrorism, and what has come to be referred to as a "home grown" terrorist. The bombing of the Federal Building in Oklahoma City was a precursor to the profound events of September 2001. The content of the chapter focuses on understanding these acts and on the legal and quasi-legal developments that follow in their tracks.

Part IV—Courts and American Justice

Chapter 10: The Structure of the American Judiciary—Case #10: It's Never Too Late for Justice: The Prosecution of Edgar Ray Killen. The Killen case presents a well-known case of violence aimed at civil rights workers in the early 1960s. As we follow the case through the legal system, you will be exposed to concepts such as jurisdiction and appeals. The text covers the overall structure of the state and federal court system and explores the impact of the U.S. Supreme Court decisions on criminal justice policy and practice.

Chapter 11: Trials, Juries, and Judgment—Case #11: America in Black and White: The Celebrity Trial of O.J. Simpson. The chapter looks at the players in the courtroom work group and the formal and informal roles played by each key player. The role of the prosecutor, defense attorney, and judge in "settling" justice raises questions about the fairness of plea negotiations and the continuing advantages of privileged defendants in the informal processes of adjudication.

Chapter 12: The Workings of the Court—Case #12: Bargaining for Justice: *Bordenkircher v. Hayes.* This case explores the reality of adjudication through a close examination of a failed plea negotiation, which results in life in prison for defendant Paul Lewis Hayes. The chapter also looks at the mechanics of the trial process and examines the history and functioning of the modern jury system.

Part V—Punishment and Social Inequality

Chapter 13: The Justice of Sentencing—Case #13: The Crime of Punishment: The Story of Kemba Smith. The Kemba Smith case raises questions about the purpose of sentencing and the goals of punishment. The chapter reviews the goals of punishment, the range of modern sentences, and the issue of capital punishment.

Chapter 14: Inside the Prison World—Case #14: Surviving Time: The Case of Rubin "Hurricane" Carter. This case reveals much about the internal world of the prison and raises many deep concerns about conditions of confinement, inmate subculture, race relations, issues in prison management, and the value of incarceration. The accompanying text reviews the historical origins of the prison, social dynamics inside the prison, and key issues in prison management today.

Chapter 15: Community and Corrections—Case #15: Making Parole in California. This final chapter examines the history of community-based corrections and investigates the role of the community and victims in the future of the justice system.

A WORD ABOUT CASE SELECTION

The cases in this book are not intended to be representative or "typical" of any particular crime or justice event. Cases serve as launching pads for the exploration of broader themes, concepts, or dilemmas. While singular in its details, each case was chosen for its power to raise broad themes for analysis and discussion. Limits of space required a difficult winnowing down of case selection: we chose the cases from the former editions that were best utilized by faculty.

Suggestions for future cases from instructors who have used the text or have developed other cases for their own use will be highly appreciated in future revisions of this book.

ADDITIONAL LEARNING RESOURCES

For instructors, a complimentary Instructor's Manual (including chapter outlines, sample class exercises, and discussion questions) and Test Bank (including multiple choice, short answer, and essay questions) is available. Email textbooks@rowman.com for more information about these materials.

For students, a complimentary open-access web site is available with interactive flash cards of each chapter's key terms, learning objectives, and links to each chapter's Check It Out materials. Visit http://text books.rowman.com/boyes-watson3e to access these materials.

ACKNOWLEDGMENTS

We must begin by thanking Sarah Stanton of Rowman & Littlefield for recognizing the value of the Learning through Cases approach, and for her support on this new edition. Thanks as well to Carli Hansen of Rowman & Littlefield who assisted us as well as Sarah Stanton, in bringing this edition to press.

One of the great pleasures of working on the second and now third edition has been our professional collaboration. We have discovered our personal styles and work habits that make us a terrific team and we look forward to many future collaborations based on the Learning through Cases model.

FOCUS QUESTIONS

- **HOW** do voters think about contending alternatives when they are voting?
- **HOW** does the number of alternatives affect voting?
- **WHAT** considerations contend for attention in the minds of voters? How might they cooperate to support a particular choice?
- **HOW** does voters' identification with a political party affect voting?
- **HOW** do parties and candidates maneuver to gain votes?
- **WHAT** does it mean for voter choice to be meaningful?

In this chapter we present the case of the Salem witch trials. These trials illustrate the challenges in defining what a crime is and in finding a just social response to transgressions. The chapter explains the social construction of crime and deviance, and explores what we mean when we talk about justice.

LEARNING OBJECTIVES

After reading this chapter you should be able to:

- Explain the difference between "crime" and "deviance" and explain why crime is a "social construction."
- Identify a "moral entrepreneur" and explain their role in the Salem witch trials and in the creation of deviance and crime.
- Articulate the difference between a "law" and other types of rules within society.
- Explain the difference between the consensus and conflict theories of law.
- Distinguish between "social control" and "crime control."
- Identify the values underlying the crime control model of justice and the due process model of justice.

Case #1: A Seventeenth-Century Crime Wave: The Salem Witch Trials

Women on trial for witchcraft in a seventeenth-century courtroom.

The year is 1692; the place is a small farming village in Massachusetts. Inside the household of the Reverend Samuel Parris, a small group of young girls—nine-year-old Betty, her twelve-year-old cousin Abigail, and a pair of friends—has spent hours indoors amusing themselves with secretive games of "fortune-telling" and "little sorceries," predicting futures and performing magic on household objects. These obsessions with the occult were inspired by tales told by a West Indian slave named Tituba who worked as a cook in the Parris household. Before long, more girls from the Village had joined in the mysterious club that met in the kitchen of the parsonage during the long dull afternoons.

The master of the household, Reverend Parris was having troubles of his own during this difficult winter. For a new church in the village of Salem he had

recently been appointed minister, a position of great importance and power in the colonial community. But this position was very shaky: only a handful of people within the community had elected to join the new church. Many more refused both to worship at the Village meetinghouse and to pay the taxes to support his salary, and in a recent annual election in October, a majority in the village had voted out of office those who had been responsible for his appointment. The future of Reverend Parris seemed very precarious in the winter of 1692 as the new Village Committee challenged his right to the position of minister and refused to even pay for firewood to warm his hearth.

As winter wore on, the black magic games of the young girls came to the attention of the adults within the Parris household and wider village community. Rumors spread that the girls were meeting in the woods to perform the black magic Tituba had brought with her from her native Barbados. The youngest of the girls was the first to exhibit strange and worrisome behaviors: sudden fits of screaming, convulsions, barking, and scampering about on all fours like a dog. The adult women in the household fretted in muted tones that the afflictions of the child were a malady brought on by the dark forces of witchcraft.

Witchcraft was believed to be a particularly terrifying and horrible crime, not only because it was responsible for evil consequences such as murder, physical torture, or destruction of property, but also because it challenged the supremacy of God in the affairs of human beings. The crime of witchcraft was written into English statutes of law as early as the sixteenth century. The Massachusetts Law of Statutes, likewise, included the crime of witchcraft as a capital offense.

The belief in Satan and his role in the affairs of humans and their evil doings was not confined to hysterical young girls or religious fanatics. On the contrary, the idea that the Devil was real and operated to do malicious things in the affairs of human beings was a widely accepted belief common to most individuals of all social backgrounds and educational levels. It was believed that a person who entered into a covenant with the Devil by signing his book had the power to call Satan to enter his or her body to perform evil doings and deeds to others. By deploying the power of the Devil, the witch was able to act out his or her own petty hates toward other human beings.

At the suggestion of Aunt Mary Silbey who lived in the house, Tituba was asked to prepare the traditional "witches cake," a recipe guaranteed to identify the source of the affliction. By baking a "witches cake"—a recipe which combined rye meal with the child's urine—and feeding the cake to a dog, it was thought that the dog would immediately identify its master, the witch. Before this method of investigation could be completed, however, Reverend Parris called in the town physician, a William Griggs, who examined the girls and proclaimed the chilling news. Malevolent witchcraft was the source of their malady, not any sickness responsive to the cures of medicine: the Devil had come to Salem Village.

The strange behaviors first seen in the Parris household now began to spread like wildfire among the group of girls who attended the secret meetings in Parris's kitchen. Parris and another minister, Thomas Putnam (one of Parris's key supporters and father to Ann Putnam, aged twelve), urged the girls to reveal the names of the individuals responsible for their suffering. "Who are your tormentors?" they asked repeatedly. "Name who is doing this to you!" The girls hesitated, at first, but then named three women: Sarah Good, a local beggar known throughout the village for her nasty temper and bitter tongue; Sarah Osborne, an elderly woman with a dubious reputation; and Tituba, the slave woman herself. On February 29, several men including Putnam traveled to Salem Town to swear out formal complaints charging witchcraft against the three women before the local magistrates. Warrants were issued for the arrest of the three women and an interrogation or preliminary hearing was hurriedly scheduled for the following morning.

All three accused were typical of those found guilty of witchcraft throughout Europe and colonial America. They were marginal, unrespectable, powerless, and deviant in their conduct and lifestyle. Although they lived within the community, they were, in a sense, outsiders viewed with suspicion and disliked by the majority of the community. Sarah Good, at the time of accusation, was both homeless and destitute: she and her husband William had been reduced to begging for shelter and food from neighbors. In her requests for assistance, she had the effrontery to be aggressive and angry, cursing and muttering reprisals to those who refused to offer her charity. Few in the community stood to support her once she was accused; indeed, her husband was one of the first to proclaim that she was, in fact, "either a witch or would be one very quickly."

Sarah Osborne too was an "outsider." Although she possessed an estate from her first husband, she was old, had no children, and had suffered the gossip and disapproval of the community when several years earlier she had cohabited with her second husband for several months before becoming officially wed. The slave women, Tituba, was, of course, a natural target of suspicion and her involvement in the baking of the cake only hardened assumptions that it was she who was acting as an agent of the Devil.

The Investigations

The date for the first hearing to determine if there was sufficient evidence to hand down an indictment for the crime of witchcraft was scheduled to take place the next day at the inn in Salem Village but on the morning of the hearing so many townspeople turned out to witness the proceedings that the venue was changed to the larger meetinghouse to accommodate the agitated and curious crowd. The accusers—the afflicted girls—were seated in the front row as one by one each of the women was brought before the magistrates for questioning. As each of the women came into view, the girls began to exhibit the tortured and tormented behavior in a dramatic enactment of the charge itself. The behavior had frightened their parents, astonished observers, and convinced many skeptical witnesses that they were indeed suffering from an affliction of supernatural causes.

> These children were bitten and pinched by invisible agents; their arms, necks and backs turned this way and that way, and returned back again, so as it was impossible for them to do of themselves, and beyond the power of any epileptic fits, or natural disease to effect. Sometimes they were taken dumb, their mouths stopped, their throats choked, their limbs wracked and tormented so as might move a heart of stone, to sympathize with them.

During the proceedings, as the girls were contorting in dramatic displays of torture and physical agony, the magistrates pressed the women with questions: "Have you made no contract with the devil?" "Why do you hurt these children?" The girls themselves continued to moan and plead for the women, especially Sarah Good, to put an end to their torments. Before long, Tituba had confessed, named the other two as her accomplices, and announced that there were many others in the colony engaged in the conspiracy against the community of

God. While Osborne continued to maintain her innocence, Good eventually accused Osborne and by so doing implicated herself in the eyes of the magistrate. At the end of the interrogation and before a crowded and tightly packed audience composed of the entire village and many from neighboring communities as well, the magistrates ordered all three sent to jail on suspicion of witchcraft to be held there until trial.

The Prosecution

At the religious services the very next day, the fits and afflictions of the young girls continued along with more accusations of witchcraft directed against other women in the community. During the service, twelve-year-old Abigail Williams suddenly began to shout out that she saw an apparition of one of the townspeople in the rafters, a Martha Corey who had publically expressed her own doubts over the whole affair. The next day, Goodwife Corey was arrested to be examined in the presence of their accusers before the magistrate. Within a month, two more "witches" had been identified by the girls and were arrested: Rebecca Nurse and the four-year-old daughter of Sarah Good.

As the snows melted, the intensity of the girls' affliction seemed to increase rather than wane. By the end of April, a total of twenty-eight more people had been accused and charged with the crime of witchcraft. The month of May saw an additional thirty-nine people accused. The town of Andover requested the afflicted girls to come to their village and identify suspected witches among the townspeople. Although the girls did not personally know any of the people accused, they managed to name more than forty persons as witches. By the time of the first trial on June 2, 1692, a total of 160 persons had been publically and legally accused and many of them were languishing in the local jail awaiting trial. These included not only those men and women who were marginal or poor but a large number of men and women of considerable wealth and power, including the former minister of the parish, George Burroughs, who was arrested in his new parish in Maine and transported back to Salem charged with being the master-wizard during the years he had served in Salem Village.

The Trials

The royal governor of Massachusetts had just arrived from England, when he was confronted with the epidemic of witchcraft accusations which had swept through the villages of New England in the preceding four months. Governor Phipps responded to the crisis with swift action appointing a special judicial body known as the Court of Oyer and Terminer which means literally to "hear and determine"; the Massachusetts attorney general was ordered to begin prosecutions; a jury was selected; and on Friday, June 2, 1692, the infamous Salem witchcraft trials began.

The first to appear for a formal trial was Bridget Bishop, an unpopular and widely despised woman who had been held in prison since her indictment on April 18. The evidence against Goodwife Bishop was considerable and many people came forward to provide testimony to support the charge against her. She was accused of causing the death of a child by visiting as an apparition and causing the child to cry out and decline in health from that moment onward. Several men and women testified that she had visited them and afterward they had suffered from strange misfortune or peculiar experiences. The jury returned a verdict of guilty against Goodwife Bishop and she was sentenced to death by hanging. On June 10, 1692, Bridget Bishop was the first to be executed during a public hanging on a rocky hillside forever after known as Witches Hill.

At the second sitting of the court of Oyer and Terminer, the court tried and sentenced to death five more accused witches. A session on August 5 produced six more convictions and five executions, including that of the former parish minister George Burroughs. In September, the court sat two more times, passing a death sentence on six more persons in one sitting and nine more in the final session of the court on September 17. The last executions were held on September 22, when eight persons, six women and two men, were hung at the gallows. A total of twenty-three persons accused of witchcraft died: most by hanging, a few while in jail awaiting trial, and one by being crushed to death from heavy rocks piled upon his prostrate body, an ancient form of execution reserved for those who refuse to testify at all.

The evidence used in the trials was typical of that used to prove the crime of witchcraft but quite different from that used to provide evidence for ordinary murders, assaults, and thefts. The ordinary rules for trial procedures called for two eyewitnesses in a capital offense but in the case of witchcraft the rule was altered because witchcraft was deemed a "habitual" offense. It was sufficient, therefore, that there be two or more witnesses coming forth with testimony about different images or incidents to support the charge of witchcraft.

The most abundant form of evidence came in the form of spectral evidence. These were eyewitness accounts of seeing the image or apparition of the accused. This might be in a dream or in their bedroom at night, or even in a crowded meetinghouse or courtroom. The unique difficulty with spectral evidence was that it was believed that the image might be visible only to those being tormented while completely invisible to others present in the very same room. As long as more than one person came forth with spectral evidence, it was not necessary for them to be "seeing" the same image. The behavior of the girls at the trial provided the most convincing evidence to the jurors since the accusers often described the image of the accused flying on the rafters, or exhibited signs of distress and torment as the accused witch moved her head or arms.

In addition to testimony by witnesses of spectral evidence, there were several other important forms of evidence. Because it was believed that the Devil would not permit a witch to proclaim the name of God or recite the Lord's Prayer without error, there was often a trial by test in which the accused was asked to perform these tasks. Errors, stumbles, or failures of memory were seen as proof they were agents of the Devil. Evidence of "anger followed by misfortune" was another form of evidence. Since the crime of witchcraft was believed to be an instrumental one in which the witch takes out her personal anger against others using the power of Satan, the testimony of those who gave examples of conflict, disputes, or angry outbursts followed by bad fortune was also seen as compelling evidence of the crime of malevolent witchcraft. In the case of Bridget Bishop, five townspeople came forth to accuse her of being responsible for "murdering" a family member. In each instance, evidence was presented of a display of anger on the part of the accused followed sometime afterward by an illness or accident befalling those who had displeased her. A fourth form of evidence came in the search for physical marks on the body of the accused such as moles, warts, or scars which were believed to be "witches teats" or places where the Devil and other evil creatures gained sustenance from the witch herself.

A final form of evidence, and ultimately one of the most compelling, was the freely given confession on the part of the accused. Beginning with Tituba herself, as many as fifty of the accused eventually confessed to their status as witches, and to their involvement in witchcraft in some cases providing elaborate detail and accusing others in the process. During the hearings, as soon as an accused confessed to the crime, the agonized writhing of the girls suddenly and instantly ceased and the girls fell upon the confessed witches with kisses and tearful pledges of forgiveness. None who confessed was brought to trial or hung: the intention of the court was to spare them in order to make use of them in testifying against others in future trials. Only those who continued to proclaim their innocence were made to suffer the spectacle of the trial and the horror of the public execution.

The Aftermath

Between June 10 and September 22, 1692, twenty-four people were executed for the crimes of witchcraft. As the New England fall began to cool the air, an additional 150 people remained awaiting trial in local jails and 200 more formal accusations had been made against others as well. On the part of the judicial authorities, there was a sudden sense of unease about the quality of the evidence used to convict and hang the accused. Anyone might indeed fail to recite the Lord's Prayer with a slip of the tongue, particularly if they are standing before a packed courtroom charged with being a representative of Satan. And legal opinion was plagued by the question that it might be possible for the Devil to present himself in the image of innocent folk as well as those who had struck a covenant with the Devil.

On October 3, Reverend Increase Mather, president of Harvard College delivered an address that claimed that evil spirits might be impersonating innocent men and implied that it was possible the girls themselves were fabricating their afflictions. Mather went on to declare that "it was better that ten suspected witches should escape, than that one innocent person should be condemned."[ii] Many more joined the chorus to object to the fallibility of the court to prove the crime, and the injustice of the proceedings in potentially condemning the innocent based on the unsubstantiated accusations of the inflamed. Within days, the governor had disbanded the court of Oyer and Terminer and replaced it with a court that forbade the use of spectral evidence. The jury acquitted forty-nine of the fifty-two cases it heard; the remaining three had entered confessions but these were given immediate reprieves by the governor. The remaining prisoners were all discharged and a general pardon was issued against all who had been accused in the terrible and most infamous series of trials within our nation's history. Two years after the trials, witchcraft was no longer a legal offense in the colony of Massachusetts Bay.

THINKING CRITICALLY ABOUT THIS CASE

1. Do you believe the accused in the seventeenth-century Salem received a "fair trial"? Why or why not?

2. Why did so many people confess to the crime of which they were accused? What forces might induce innocent people to confess to a crime they did not commit?

3. Consider the powerful statement made by Increase Mather: "It is better that ten witches should escape than one innocent person be condemned." Do you agree with this statement? Why or why not? Would you still agree with this statement if we substituted the crime of murder,

rape, or drug dealing for the crime of witchcraft. Why or why not?

4. Consider the spectacle of the public execution. How do you think you would feel if you were to witness such an event? Would you bring your children to an execution? Why or why not?

5. The term "witch hunt" has moved into our common everyday parlance. What does it mean to you? Give some examples of contemporary "witch hunts" in American society today?

REFERENCES

Case adapted from:

Paul Boyer and Stephen Nissenbaum., Eds. *The Salem Witchcraft Papers: Verbatim Transcripts of the Legal Documents of the Salem Witchcraft Outbreak of 1692.* Vol. 1. (New York: Da Capo Press, 1977).

Kai Erickson, *Wayward Puritans: A Study in the Sociology of Deviance* (New York: Wiley & Sons, 1966).

Richard Weisman, *Witchcraft, Magic and Religion in 17th Century Massachusetts* (Boston: University of Massachusetts Press, 1984).

WHAT IS CRIME?

Through contemporary eyes, it is tempting to dismiss the "crime" of witchcraft as religious superstition. Given our knowledge of science and technology, it is hard for us to believe that those girls were really tormented by witches wielding the dark powers of the Devil. But to people in the seventeenth century, the existence of God, Satan, and their active role in the affairs of human beings was a form of "common sense," a set of beliefs about the world shared by most members of society, rich and poor, educated and illiterate, alike. Sociologists claim that all human ideas, from our basic beliefs about the nature of the physical world, to the rules of social interaction, to our convictions about what is right and wrong, are a product of that human society. Is a rock inhabited by living spirits? Is it composed of tiny particles so infinitesimally small they can never be seen with the human eye? What you believe depends on the society you live in. Beliefs about "reality" are embedded in the cultural beliefs of the entire society: most people (except, perhaps, those who are mentally deranged) accept the **social construction of reality** defined by their culture. Members of every society collectively define and interpret the world around them. This set of shared understandings is what we call culture and is a product of the human interaction.

Like all beliefs within society, **crime too is a social construction**. What we believe to be crime is a result of the beliefs, values, and institutions of our society. While we may no longer believe in witchcraft as a source of harmful conduct, our own beliefs about crime are similarly rooted in our cultural worldview. While it is true that most societies have categories of behavior they refer to as "criminal," it is not true that they identify the same kinds of behaviors as crime. What is crime in one culture is not necessarily a crime in another culture. Moreover, definitions of crime change over time: what is crime today (e.g., the manufacture, sale, and distribution of cocaine) was not so one hundred years ago.

Crime and Deviance

People in our culture who believe in witchcraft or the idea that invisible powers of the Dark underworld cause personal misfortune or illnesses among children are not expressing the social construction of reality taught to most members of a modern industrial society. People who hold the view that illnesses are caused by spells cast by witches using the dark power of Satan are "deviant" in adhering to those beliefs. These ideas no longer form the basis of "common sense" as they did for the people of Salem Village. Those who follow these beliefs form a distinct minority by holding views that are not widely shared.

Sociologists use the term **deviance** to refer to conduct which is contrary to the norms of conduct or social expectations of the group. Not all forms of deviant conduct are considered crimes. We might think a person who believes in the Devil quite odd, and we might not want to associate with that person, hire them as a babysitter, or fully believe their testimony in a court of law, but in our society, to believe in unusual ideas is not a crime. Many other forms of conduct would be considered deviant but not criminal in our society, such as picking one's nose in public, piercing one's nostrils, dying one's hair green, or talking to oneself on the subway.

SOCIAL CONSTRUCTION OF REALITY process by which members of every society collectively define and interpret the world around them.

CRIME AS SOCIAL CONSTRUCTION behaviors defined as crime are the result of the beliefs, values, and institutions of that society.

DEVIANCE conduct which is contrary to the norms of conduct or social expectations of the group.

This style may be deviant, but if it does not violate the law, it is not a crime.

Sociologists have long argued that there is nothing inherently "deviant" about any form of conduct: a behavior is deviant if it is viewed and reacted to as such by others within the society. Kai Erikson, who wrote about the Salem witch trials, suggests, "The term deviance refers to conduct which the people of a group consider so dangerous or embarrassing or irritating that they bring special sanctions to bear against the persons who exhibit it."[1] We need to ask: Who makes the rules? Who identifies the rule-breaker? Who proclaims the violation as a serious threat to the social well-being of the community? According to sociologists, what constitutes "deviance" is the labeling, identification, and successful application of that label to a particular person and their conduct.

Harold Becker coined the term **moral entrepreneurs** to refer to those people who seek to impose a particular view of morality on others within society. Moral entrepreneurs, he believed, are those people who identify certain forms of conduct as particularly dangerous and in need of social control by others within the group. These moral entrepreneurs are often responsible for mobilizing the group against the behavior or for making sure that a law is written against a certain form of conduct. These activists are also able to construct a sense of "**moral panic**" about the threat of this behavior to the well-being of the entire society.

Crime as Legal Construction

As we noted above, not all forms of deviant behavior are crimes. It is also true that not all kinds of crime are really deviant. Some crimes are so commonplace that it would be hard to describe these behaviors as "deviant" at all. An estimated one-third of all Americans cheat on income taxes despite the law. Probably more people violate the speed limits on our nation's highways than observe them; and having sex before marriage may still be illegal in several state criminal codes, but it can hardly be considered deviant according to national polls of premarital sexual behavior.

Both deviance and crime, therefore, are social constructions—that is, they are a product of collective action by individuals within society. What distinguishes the rules of the criminal code from other types of social rules which govern our behavior in society such as the rule that we should eat with a fork, or shake someone's hand when it is extended toward us in friendly greeting? In a sense, the answer is quite simple: crime is behavior that violates the criminal law: without the criminal law there is, literally, no such thing as "crime." It is possible for any behavior to be "transformed" to crime by being written into the criminal code. In many U.S. states, it is a crime for a man to dress as a woman; in some countries, there are criminal laws regulating the acceptable lengths of a woman's skirt; and in Iran, women are prohibited from wearing any clothing other than a full-length robe and a veil which covers both their head and face.

But what makes a "law" different from a social taboo, convention, habit, or custom? Sociologists refer to rules of society as norms. A **norm** is a societal

MORAL ENTREPRENEURS people who identify certain forms of conduct as dangerous to society and mobilize others to exert social control over those who engage in the conduct.

MORAL PANIC shared belief that a particular behavior is significant threat to the well-being of the entire society.

NORM expected behavior for a member of a group within a specific set of circumstances.

expectation of "normal" or acceptable behavior for a member of that group within a specific set of circumstances. Human behavior is deeply rule bound yet many of these rules are never written down nor are they even necessarily verbalized. Yet human beings raised within a given society learn these rules as part of the normal process of growing up within that culture, a process known as **socialization**. Much of the rules we learn through the socialization process belong to the category of rules William Graham Sumner (1840–1910) identified as **folkways**.[2] Sumner studied a wide range of societies and argued that much of human behavior is governed by informal rules beyond the codified criminal code.

Folkways are unplanned but expected ways of behaving within a society. These include telling us what to wear and what is appropriate attire for any given social setting. Take a quick look at your fellow students tomorrow in class and observe the normative nature of the unwritten dress code. Has anyone chosen to come to school in pajamas? Or beach attire? Or evening dress? Considering the fact that most colleges do not have a written dress code, there is a remarkable degree of conformity because we are regulated by informal rules to an even greater extent than we are regulated by formal rules. Folkways include rules about appropriate foods to consume, rituals for making oneself attractive and presentable, manners, etiquette, and so forth. Failure to adhere to the standards of dress, for instance, in your college classroom would probably elicit some odd stares from your fellow classmates, a disapproving comment or two, and a tendency for others to gossip about, or withdraw from, such an odd person. These minor sanctions operate quite effectively (and often unconsciously) to maintain the dress code. Since most human beings tend to avoid ridicule and desire social acceptance, these forms of "punishment" work quite efficiently to enforce social norms.

Mores, according to Sumner, are far more important rules of conduct within all societies than folkways. While failure to comply with a dress code may elicit some negative reactions, failure to conform with a societal more is taken far more seriously by others within that society. A more is a rule that defines not simply what is expected or appropriate, but what is right or wrong. For an adult to wear strange clothing in public may violate a folkway, but wearing no clothes in public violates a more, at least in our culture. The sanctions for failing to abide by a social more are far more substantial than our myriad responses to breaches of social etiquette, manners, or social custom.

How is law different from both mores and folkways? **Laws** are norms which are codified and enforced through the use of coercion backed by the authority of the state. The key element in defining "law" according to Max Weber is that laws are norms which are enforced by specialized institutions that are granted the power to use force to obtain compliance. In order to have law in a modern sense, it is necessary for societies to develop political institutions such as legislatures, governments, courts, law enforcement and penal systems that enact the formal laws of a society enforce compliance with those laws, and punish those who fail to do so. The legal system endows certain individuals within society with the legal right to use physical coercion in order to ensure compliance with the law. These institutions are those agencies and organizations we collectively refer to as the criminal justice system. The institutions of the criminal justice system include the legislature that creates the laws, the police that enforce the law, the

SOCIALIZATION
process of learning the norms, values and beliefs of a given culture.

FOLKWAYS
unplanned but expected ways of behaving within any given culture.

MORES
important rules of conduct within a society which define right and wrong.

LAW
social norms which are codified and enforced through the authority of the state.

courts to adjudicate and interpret the law, and the penal system that provides sanctions to those who are found to have violated the law.

Crime and Morality

Many people assume that crime and morality are two sides of the same coin: a behavior is crime because it is immoral and all immoral behavior is criminal. It is natural to assume that all conduct we think immoral is included in the criminal code and that the criminal law reflects the moral values of the majority of law-abiding American citizens. But the relationship between crime and morality is not as simple as it seems. First, not all conduct that we would agree is immoral is necessarily criminal. For instance, we may think it wrong for a person to refuse to come to the aid of another who has collapsed on the street gasping for breath, but the person who stands and stares or who turns away with a shrug is not committing a crime unless there is a specific legal rule which requires them to assist their fellow citizens and many states do not have such a law within their criminal codes.

It is also possible for governments to write immoral laws. Nazi Germany passed many laws which legalized the theft and murder of innocent citizens because they were Jewish; both South Africa and the United States have had legal systems which sanctioned the cruel and murderous treatment of other human beings because they were nonwhite. Not all immoral or harmful conduct is necessarily criminalized within our society, and not all laws are necessarily moral and just.

What is the relationship between crime and morality? If crime does not reflect our moral values, is it merely a set of legal rules established by the state to regulate conduct? If it is not grounded in our sense of right and wrong, must we obey the law? Do we obey the law simply because the state is powerful and we are afraid of legal sanctions? Are we morally obligated to follow the law even if we believe it is unjust?

Many people argue that law is grounded in a higher set of moral principles: what makes the law a system of justice is that it embraces ideals of right and wrong which are universally agreed upon. This is the idea of **natural law**—the belief that there are agreed-upon standards of right and wrong common to all human societies and ethically binding for all human societies.[3] For some, the precepts of the Ten Commandments, such as the prohibition against murder, theft, and the obligation to be faithful to one's spouse and to honor one's parents, are so fundamental to human societies they believe them to be found in all moral and ethical codes. The idea of natural law says that there are sources of right and wrong above the particular human rules created by particular men and women in any given society.

We find a powerful belief in the idea of a "natural law" across many different societies who believe in many different kinds of gods. In the case of Salem Village, this higher power was God. We find this belief too in our own Constitution. When our founding fathers wrote "And we find these principles to be self-evident" they were stating a principle that the right of all persons to liberty, life, and the pursuit of happiness was a principle established beyond the whims and preferences of human powers reflecting a higher authority governing the affairs of human society. The "Bill of Rights" is based on the "natural law" concepts of John Locke (1632–1704) according to which all men are, by nature, free, equal, and independent. Underlying our faith in the justice of our legal system is a

NATURAL LAW
the belief that law is grounded in a higher set of moral principles universal to all human societies.

foundation of belief in the "natural law" which protects the inalienable "natural rights" of all individuals. According to Thomas Jefferson, the purpose of government is to protect the natural rights retained by the people and it was extremely important that the government itself not be permitted to transgress these rights.

Yet is there really such a thing as "natural law" and if there is, how do we explain the existence of the legal crime of witchcraft in the seventeenth century and its absence today? They too believed in the idea of "natural law" in which the rules of human society were ultimately created by a higher authority—but which society is correct? Concepts of "natural law" upheld ideas to which we would no longer subscribe today, such as the "natural" inferiority of women, blacks, and Native Americans. Theories of "natural law" claiming that there are universal principles of right and wrong found in all societies are also hard to square with the wide range of different ways societies define criminal behavior. All societies condemn killing other human beings but only under some circumstances and only in some types of relationships. In Comanche society, husbands are free to kill their wives and this act is not considered "murder." In our society, the taking of a life in defense of one's own self or one's own property may also not be deemed to constitute the wrong of "murder." Before the Civil War, in the South, a slave owner could legally kill a slave if he or she was engaged in routine discipline. If there is such a thing as "natural law," how can there be such variation between different social groups in how they define rights and wrongs of behavior that is as clearly wrong as murder?

Morality refers to the beliefs about the rightness and wrongness of human conduct. Sociologists have long argued that there is no universal moral code to which all societies adhere. They point out that the belief that behavior is wrong, immoral, or evil is a product of human collective definition making. Crime and morality are a part of a cultural belief system. Like our beliefs about the physical world, moral beliefs are a collective human product.

Crime and Power

If the law does not reflect a natural or divinely inspired order of right and wrong common to all human societies, where does law come from and whose morality does it represent? There are two broad theories that explain the social forces that create the law: one set of theories is based on forces of consensus and another set of theories focuses on conflict as a source of law. The **consensus theory** holds that the law, especially the criminal law, reflects the widely shared values and beliefs of that society.

According to Emile Durkheim, all societies define some conduct as crime: "crime" and its broader category "deviance" are normal parts of any society. People collectively define some conduct as unacceptable, harmful, dangerous, or immoral. Even a "society of saints," according to Durkheim, would define some types of behavior as unacceptable or deviant or criminal. Durkheim stated, "An act is criminal when it offends strong and defined states of the collective conscience."[4] Defining certain conduct as deviant, in Durkheim's view, serves a kind of natural bonding function for any given group, drawing the community together in its mutual disgust at the deviant, affirming the identity of the community while simultaneously defining boundaries of acceptable conduct.

In the consensus model, law reflects the common morality of the social group and it serves a **latent function** of strengthening the social bonds of the group. Kai Erikson, following the consensus model, believed that the Salem witch trials

MORALITY
beliefs about the rightness and wrongness of human conduct.

CONSENSUS THEORY OF LAW
law reflects the collective conscience or widely shared values and beliefs of any given society.

LATENT FUNCTION OF LAW
a by-product of law that defines the identity of and strengthens the social bonds among members of a group.

tightened the bonds of a community undergoing substantial social change. The moral panic instigated by the witch trials was a barometer of the strength of those widely shared moral values. Just as today communities rally against the threat of illegal drugs to "just say no" to the dealers who threaten the safety of their community, the villagers of New England were taking the steps they believed necessary to protect themselves and their families from both physical and moral destruction.

The **conflict theory** of the law argues that law reflects the power hierarchy within any given society. Because societies are composed of diverse groups with different perspectives on moral values (based on race, class, age, gender, religion, ethnicity, region, and so forth), laws will inevitably be shaped by the interests of those who have the most resources to influence the law. Powerful groups shape the law to insure that it reflects their morality and preserves their position of power within society. The law may even be thought of as a tool that enables that group to maintain its position of power over others in the society. For example, laws that declare black men were not really full human beings upheld a social order of white supremacy over nonwhites. Nonwhites, obviously, were not involved in the making of those laws.

Jeffrey Reiman[5] argues that the conflict perspective is relevant to interpreting public attitudes toward serious crimes of violence in our society. Many forms of conduct that cause substantial harm within our society are not "criminalized" by our legal system. When we think of "murder" our first mental image is of a vicious individual who has personally attacked, shot, or knifed another human being. Yet the number of deaths each year from criminal homicide is only a fraction of the number of deaths caused by willful neglect by corporations in the workplace. Reiman asks, "Is a person who kills another in a bar brawl a greater threat to society than a business executive who refuses to cut into his profits to make his plant a safe place to work?"[6] Yet because of the specific way that the law defines homicide, the business executive is not viewed as a criminal and is seen to be pursing legitimate business goals despite the lethal consequences of his or her actions on others within society.

Social norms do not simply "become" crimes through some kind of divine, natural, or automatic process. Rather there is a social process whereby someone or some group creates a law and ensures that it will be enforced. The social construction of criminal law, its application, interpretation, and enforcement by particular social agencies and actors within this society is the business of the criminal justice system. To understand the criminal justice system, we must study the processes whereby laws are made; why some forms of conduct are included in the criminal code and others are not; why some laws are enforced and others are ignored; and why some persons who violate the law are never suspected, arrested, prosecuted, or punished.

Social Control versus Crime Control

Law and the institutions of the criminal justice system are only one type of social control in modern society. Sociologists recognize that the power of formal social control exercised by the law and its agents such as police and the courts is trivial compared to the subtle and awesome power of other sources of social control within society. Law is simply one form of **social control** among many, and arguably, it is far from the most powerful form of social control.

CONFLICT THEORY OF LAW
law reflects the values, beliefs, and interests of powerful elites within any given society and serves to help those in power preserve their position within society.

SOCIAL CONTROL
formal and informal processes that maintain conformity with social norms.

Crime control, unlike social control, is a reactive form of societal control. For the most part, crime control enters the picture only after a criminal violation has occurred. Can the criminal justice system really "control" crime? As we will see in later chapters, criminal justice professionals such as the police or the correctional system cannot address the social conditions within the community that generate serious criminal behavior. Fair and just working of the major institutions within our society, such as the family, the economy, schools, and so forth, creates peaceful communities. Conditions of injustice or unfairness within our communities with endemic poverty, homelessness, drug abuse, unemployment, alienation, boredom are societal conditions that lead to high rates of crime within society. The criminal justice system itself is not designed to address these widespread societal problems.

Reiman believes that the criminal justice system cannot really "control crime" but he goes further to state that the criminal justice system does not even really aim to control crime: the criminal justice system is one that depends upon its own failures for its continued success in society. The more the system fails to reduce crime, the more resources we devote to crime control. Reiman (and many others) point out that if we are serious about controlling crime, we would focus on strengthening the forms of social control in society such as work, family, and community which enhance conformity for positive reasons.[7]

Van Ness and Strong[8] see a more positive role for the criminal justice system. It is the job of the justice system to maintain a just order. The criminal justice system is not simply about crime control but about the creation of a just society. But what do we mean by "justice"? What does a just order look like? What does justice mean to us as Americans? How do we define justice and how do our institutions deliver it to us? Let us return to the tragic summer of 1692 to ask: Was this justice?

WHAT IS JUSTICE?

"Remove justice, and what are kingdoms, but gangs of criminals on a large scale?"

St. Augustine (AD 354–430)

The criminal justice system is not simply about catching criminals or "crime control" but about delivering "justice" in our society. When we talk about the modern criminal justice system, many people ask: Justice for whom? Is obtaining justice for victims of crime within society the system's highest priority? Or are we talking about justice for the person who has been accused? Are all citizens in this country equally subject to the justice process, or are minorities right when they complain that the criminal justice system is a "just us" system which delivers harsh punishment only to those who are poor, young, and powerless. Do all defendants, rich and poor, get an equal chance at "justice for all"? Do all communities get equal protection from the police?

Along with the need to understand what "crime" is, sociologically, we need to understand what "justice" is, substantively and procedurally. Is a process "just" as long as it is "legal"? Is justice something different from the law or is it

CRIME CONTROL
formal and informal processes that respond to violations of legal norms.

only attainable through the rule of law? What do we mean when we talk about "justice"? Do all Americans agree on what "justice" means?

Crime Control versus Due Process Models of Justice

The first question to consider is the relationship between law and justice. When you read the events of those proceedings back in 1694, did you feel that the women and men accused of those crimes were treated "justly"? What makes a process just? Traditionally, the American system of justice has sought a balance between the rights of individuals and the power of the state to respond to crime. The two poles of this delicate balance are referred to as the interests of **due process** and the interests of **crime control**.[9] According to many observers, the due process model of the system competes with the crime control agenda of the system in a more or less constant struggle over the defining notion of justice. Both sets of values are important to our system and are deeply incorporated in the structure of our justice system.

Crime control advocates point out that a society in which no one is free to walk within the streets of their community or dwell within their own home without constant fear of being robbed, mugged, or assaulted by their fellow citizens is not a free society. As President Clinton remarked in his 1994 State of the Union address, "Violent crime and the fear it provokes are crippling our society, limiting personal freedom and fraying the ties that bind us." Women argue that fear of rape forces many women to live according to a restricted "rape schedule" with a substantial reduction in personal freedom for half of the American population.[10] Black Americans who lived in fear of getting lynched by angry white mobs were not really free to walk the streets of their own town or sit at a lunch counter and enjoy a quiet meal.[11] Parents in many urban communities today complain that they are not free in our society if they cannot let their children walk to school or ride a bicycle on the sidewalk without fear of gunfire from rival gangs fighting over drug turf.[12]

If violence is rampant in the streets, no one is free to enjoy the "life, liberty and the pursuit of happiness" promised in the Constitution. Crime control advocates point out that it is the responsibility of an effective government to prevent citizens from terrorizing one another. Efficient and effective enforcement of the law is a basic precondition for a free society.

A competing and equally important notion of freedom centers on the right of the individual to be free from governmental tyranny. The values of due process claim that no one is free in a society where the government can knock on your door whenever it chooses, search your house, and arrest you without answering to a higher authority. This is the basic notion of individual liberty and individual rights. According to this view, no one is really free within society if they must fear the unbridled power of the state to arrest, charge, convict, or punish without adequate protections against the abuse of that power.

Recall that the definition of "crime" is a rule that is enforced by the legal power of the state. The important concept here is "legal power": we grant the state the legal right to use force against us under certain circumstances, that is, when we violate the legitimate laws of the land. But, in our system, we do not give the state carte blanche in the use of force: that force is limited to only the "legal" circumstances. Every police officer on the street, every correctional officer, every judge, and every prosecutor must obey these laws and is not free to use their power in any way they please. These limits are what are known as the rules of "due process."

DUE PROCESS MODEL OF JUSTICE
prioritizes rules of due process which guarantee and protect individual civil liberty and fairness in the enforcement of the criminal law.

CRIME CONTROL MODEL OF JUSTICE
prioritizes the efficient and effective enforcement of the law as a basic precondition for a free society.

From this perspective, the power of the state to control crime must be limited by due process protections for individuals accused of a crime. Without those protections, the unchecked power of the state would threaten the liberty and basic freedom of all citizens. The fundamental value at the heart of due process rules is "fairness." Proponents of a due process model of the criminal justice system remind us that police states such as Nazi Germany enjoyed very low crime rates because there were no rights for citizens; the police had the right to use force in any way they saw fit and while crime was down, the citizens of Germany paid the terrible price of loss of individual liberty. Since we give the state the legal power to use force, we must have protections against the abuse of that power. We grant the power to control crime to the state because we value security as a basic ingredient of freedom but we need the procedures of due process to protect us against the abuse of that legal right by the criminal justice system itself.

Due Process in the Seventeenth Century

Let us closely examine the procedures used in the Salem witch trials in order to better understand our own system of due process. Due process of law in criminal proceedings is generally understood to include the following basic elements: the principle of legality which means that a law is written down which clearly states what the criminal conduct is and what the punishment will be for those who do it; there is some impartial body that will hear the facts of the case; the person who is accused is told what they are accused of and given an opportunity to defend themselves against the charge; at the trial, evidence is heard according to a set of

Individual Rights Guaranteed by the Bill of Rights

A right to be assumed innocent until proven guilty

A right against unreasonable searches of person and places of residence

A right against arrest without probable cause

A right against unreasonable seizures of personal property

A right against self-incrimination

A right to protection from physical harm throughout the justice process

A right to an attorney

A right to a trial by jury

A right to know the charges

A right to cross-examine prosecution witnesses

A right to speak and present witnesses

A right not be tried twice for the same crime

A right against cruel and unusual punishments

A right to due process

A right to a speedy trial

A right against excessive bail

A right against excessive fines

A right to be treated the same as others, regardless of race, sex, religious preference, and other personal attributes fair rules and procedures which places the burden on the state to prove its case against the accused; and if the person is legally found to be not guilty, they are free to return to a complete state of liberty just like any other free citizen.

Most of the rights of the accused are defined in the Bill of Rights. Yet the Salem trials took place almost one hundred years before the framing of the U.S. Constitution. The colonists brought with them from England some important elements of the due process. What elements of due process were present then and which were not in the Salem witch trials?

The **rule of law** is a basic foundation for democratic society in which the exercise of governmental power is legitimated by the institutions of representative government. The crime of witchcraft was codified within the statute books of the Massachusetts Bay colony as early as 1641.[13] The **substantive criminal law**, therefore, specifically defines those actions which are prohibited by the law (or, far less frequently, those which are required), as well as the penalty for violation of the criminal law. Basic to criminal process is the rule of *nullum crimen sine lege* which means "No crime without a law." A fundamental element of fairness is the requirement that citizens have advance warning of the behavior that is unlawful and that these rules be clearly spelled out so that citizens will know what they should not do or what they are required to do.

Procedural criminal law refers to the nature of the proceedings whereby someone is accused, arrested, investigated, tried, and convicted of a crime. While substantive criminal law defines those actions or omissions which are unlawful, the procedural criminal law defines the lawful process for creating, enforcing, and implementing the criminal law. Procedural law defines the rights of an accused person and the protections that exist within the law to guarantee that they will be tried according to legally established procedures. The Magna Carta or Great Charter signed in 1215 by the English monarch guaranteed that "no freeman shall be . . . in any way imprisoned . . . unless by the lawful judgment of his peers, or by the law of the land."[14] Article 1, Section 9 of the U.S. Constitution offers the privilege of the **writ of habeas corpus** to citizens to challenge the legality of imprisonment by state or federal authorities within a court of law. No governmental authority may legally detain or confine an individual if they violate the rules of criminal procedure enshrined in the Constitution.

Adversarial versus Inquisitorial System

Most contemporary observers will notice immediately that a defense attorney did not represent those accused of witchcraft during the trials. The absence of a defense attorney in these trials strikes us as fundamentally unfair. Without an opportunity to cross-examine witnesses and present evidence, there is little opportunity for the accused to question the credibility of those testifying against them. In the seventeenth century, the defendant was required to speak in response to the questions by the magistrate and by the prosecutors, but they were not permitted an attorney to speak, ask questions, or interview witnesses on their behalf. It is the one-sided nature of the trial itself that seems to make the Salem witch trials patently unfair.

The Sixth Amendment to the Constitution guarantees the accused the right to a defense. Although this right was enshrined in the Bill of Rights as of 1791, it was a privilege that was only available to those who could afford to pay for a lawyer in their own defense. As we will see in later chapters, it was not until the

RULE OF LAW
the basic principle that the exercise of governmental power is regulated by laws formulated by legitimate institutions of representative government.

SUBSTANTIVE CRIMINAL LAW
actions which are prohibited or prescribed by the criminal law.

PROCEDURAL CRIMINAL LAW
the lawful process for creating, enforcing, and implementing the criminal law.

WRIT OF HABEAS CORPUS
a petition to the court contesting the legality of imprisonment.

twentieth century that defense counsel became a right for rich and poor alike. In an **adversarial system**, the two sides must be equal if the battle is to be genuinely fair.

But the Salem witch trials did not follow a strictly adversarial model. Like our current crime control efforts against terrorism or drug trafficking, the fight against witchcraft was given the highest priority by the members of the New England communities who feared the loss of security from these dangerous individuals within their communities. The crime of witchcraft was viewed with the same sense of "moral panic" that as we feel about terrorists or drug dealers. Just as we are motivated today to relax many procedural due process protections in order to fight terror and the "war on drugs," the colonists opted to utilize specialized judicial procedures in order to stem the tide of this serious crime wave.

The specialized higher court that heard the witch trials was, in fact, not structured on an adversarial model but followed instead a more inquisitorial structure. The inquisitorial system places the judge in charge of the questioning or fact-finding process. It is the judge who calls forth witnesses and actively examines them. It is the judge who investigates and collects information by calling expert witnesses to the stand. Judges, in short, perform many functions our system typically assigns to the two opposing attorneys. Notice that in the Salem trials, the judges ask questions of the witnesses, victims, and the accused. In the **inquisitorial model**, the presentation of the facts is very one-sided: there is only one truth and the judge is charged with uncovering that truth.

In the adversarial model, the business of presenting the truth is shared by two opposing attorneys. The truth is achieved through a kind of contest between two competing and quite partial views of reality. Each side presents its own facts and interpretation of the facts before an impartial judge and jury who declares one side the "winner" of the battle for truth and one side the "loser." Central to the adversarial system is the concept of advocacy to allow each side to vigorously argue its case before a fair and impartial jury.

Before the adversarial method for determining the truth, there was a method known as trial by ordeal or trial by test. Belief in the truth-finding capacity of such processes rested upon a belief in God. If the accused denied guilt, they would be required to undergo some ordeal such as walking over red-hot coals, or having one's hands plunged into boiling water to retrieve a stone. The guilt was determined by the healing of the skin: it was believed that God would prevent the accused from being scalded if he or she was indeed innocent. Evidence of the burn was evidence of guilt. At the time of the witch trials, trial by test was still a legal method for determining truth: the accused were ordered to recite the Lord's Prayer and any mistake or hesitation in their recitation was believed to be a signal from God.

The Confessions

The Fifth Amendment to the Constitution provides citizens various rights such as the right to a grand jury hearing before being formally indicted; the right to due process of law; and protection against double jeopardy. The most well-known and most important right articulated within the Fifth Amendment is the privilege against self-incrimination. No person accused of a crime can be forced to provide testimony against him or herself. The accused has the right to remain silent before the court: failure to answer questions cannot be used as evidence of one's guilt. At the time of the Salem witch trials, this right was not granted to

ADVERSARIAL SYSTEM
the state and the accused are represented by equal advocates before a neutral judge and jury.

INQUISITORIAL SYSTEM
the state represented by the judge has the power to investigate, interrogate, adjudicate, convict, and sanction the accused.

those accused of a crime. Indeed the worst punishment was reserved for the one man who refused to respond at all to the interrogations during the trial.

The importance of the right to remain silent or privilege against self-incrimination can be seen in the readiness to confess by so many of those accused of witchcraft. The vast majority of those who confessed did so after the first wave of mass hangings. Upon hearing that the magistrates had decided to exempt those who admitted their guilt from execution, the accused acted to save their necks. In the words of one women who tried to retract her confession in order to spare the lives of those she had implicated, "they told me if I would not confess, I should be put down into the dungeon and would be hanged, but if I would confess I should have my life."[15] Her retraction was ignored and those she had implicated were summarily put to death even though she herself was spared.

The framers of our Bill of Rights recognized that the use of threats and torture to force people to confess to crimes makes a mockery of the justice system. Unless the accused is protected against the coerced confessions through the use of physical beatings, deprivation of liberty, or psychological intimation, the right of individual citizens to be free from the arbitrary power of the government simply did not exist.

The Punishment

Nineteen persons were hanged after they were legally convicted of witchcraft; three persons died while being held in jail awaiting trial or punishment; and one person was crushed to death beneath heavy stones for remaining mute during the trial itself. One of the most dramatic differences between the justice system of the colonial period and the justice system today lies in the area of punishment. Although there is much we share in common in the legal process of the courtroom, the legal and social norms around the punishment of criminal offenses are profoundly different between the two societies.

The Eighth Amendment of the Constitution offers to the citizen the protection against "cruel and unusual punishment." But it is important to remember that what was cruel and unusual by the standards of the seventeenth century and by today's standards would be quite different. The colonists brought with them from Europe many forms of the death penalty that we would find repugnant today. Few of us would advocate bringing children to witness the execution of an offender; and few would rest easy if the decaying body of the condemned were hanging in the town square for days after the event. How do we decide what constitutes "cruel and unusual punishment"?

The Supreme Court has ruled that execution itself, for heinous and shocking crimes, does not violate standards of public decency. However, the court has also established that the infliction of unnecessary pain and suffering in the process of execution is a violation of the Eighth Amendment. By today's moral standards, we require the painless execution of those we condemn to die. To our forefathers in the seventeenth century, this would seem as strange as their use of torture and public humiliation does to us today.

THE VALUES OF CRIME CONTROL VERSUS DUE PROCESS

The witch trials in Salem marked the end of an era in our nation's history. Two years after the epidemic, the criminal statute prohibiting the practice of witchcraft was removed from the Massachusetts law. After that fateful summer, no one was ever prosecuted as a witch on U.S. soil again. Why was there such a dramatic shift away from these prosecutions? What did people at the time feel about these events? What lasting impact did these trials have on the criminal justice system?

Today, we have adopted the phrase "witch hunt" to refer to a powerful conspiracy to prosecute individuals without due process and without protections of individual rights. The Salem experience made a lasting impression on the colonists who recognized the awesome power of a judicial system that failed to preserve the rights of those accused of crimes. In the throes of a "moral panic," the citizenry of New England abandoned the values of the due process model in favor of an aggressive campaign of crime control. That delicate balance was severely tipped against those accused of this crime and in their zeal to protect their community from a feared criminal conspiracy, the process of justice swept up many who appeared to have been unjustly accused, convicted, and executed. In the wake of that bloody summer, influential thinkers within New England realized the danger in abandoning the due process protections even when the threat seemed serious and overwhelming.

Increase Mather wrote the following words in a speech in 1692: "It is better that ten suspected witches should escape, than one innocent person be condemned." This statement reflects the values of the due process model. For those who are concerned about the power of government to infringe on the rights and liberties of individual citizens, it is far more important that we ensure against wrongful convictions than we do against wrongful acquittals. It is true that the crime of witchcraft was a serious threat to the communities of New England. They felt about witchcraft the same way that contemporary communities feel about child abuse or terrorism. These are terrible and serious crimes, often hidden from view and often hard to prove in the court of law. We are upset by the thought that persons who are guilty of these crimes are able to use the rules of evidence and criminal procedure to "get off" on technicalities of the law. In our zeal to protect our children and our communities, we may wish these procedural rules be relaxed when faced with a criminal defendant whom we believe to be guilty. At times such as these, when we are fearful, we are far more likely to adopt the values of the crime control model and prefer that the balance of power be tipped in favor of the state to put away those who are a danger to us all.

The values expressed by Increase Mather's statement remain central to the due process model. Substitute the word "child molester" or "terrorist" for the term "witch" and the difficult choice of adopting that position may be more meaningful to modern readers. Protecting the rights of those who may truly be guilty is the only way to insure the rights of those who are innocent. If we desire "perfect" crime control, we would have to relinquish certain rights such as the right to privacy, right to defense attorney, right against self-incrimination, right against unreasonable searches, and so forth. Without these protections, the state would have fewer obstacles in their pursuit of criminals. And it is inevitable that among those who are accused and convicted, some will be innocent of the crime. Without the obstacles that put the burden on the state to prove "beyond a reasonable doubt" that a person is guilty of a crime, many more innocent persons will be swept up in the powerful net of the criminal justice system.

The choice made by the framers of our Constitution is clear. They chose the protection of individual rights and liberties above the ability to limit and control crime. Today we continue to operate a system of crime control that is bound by the law of criminal procedure enshrined in the Bill of Rights. We have a system that pursues the control of crime regulated by due process procedures of the law. As a society, we continue to debate the relative balance of due process and crime control when we are faced with what we perceive as serious threats to our own communities. In the effort to fight the crime of illegal drug trafficking or to prevent the crime of terrorism, we have significantly limited the due process procedures in order to enhance the power of the system to catch, convict, and punish those who are guilty of this crime. For many, the fight against these dangers is well worth the sacrifice of individual liberties. Others see these aggressive crime control strategies as the greater danger unjustly infringing on the liberty of law-abiding citizens, particularly minority citizens.

---

social construction of reality (p. 9)   process by which members of every society collectively define and interpret the world around them.

crime as social construction (p. 9)   behaviors defined as crime are the result of the beliefs, values, and institutions of that society.

deviance (p. 9)   conduct which is contrary to the norms of conduct or social expectations of the group.

moral entrepreneurs (p. 10)   people who identify certain forms of conduct as dangerous to society and mobilize others to exert social control over those who engage in the conduct.

moral panic (p. 10)   shared belief that a particular behavior is significant threat to the well-being of the entire society.

norm (p. 10)   expected behavior for a member of a group within a specific set of circumstances.

socialization (p. 11)   process of learning the norms, values and beliefs of a given culture.

folkways (p. 11)   unplanned but expected ways of behaving within any given culture.

mores (p. 11)   important rules of conduct within a society which define right and wrong.

law (p. 11)   social norms which are codified and enforced through the authority of the state.

natural law (p. 12)   the belief that law is grounded in a higher set of moral principles universal to all human societies.

morality (p. 13)   beliefs about the rightness and wrongness of human conduct.

consensus theory of law (p. 13)   law reflects the collective conscience or widely shared values and beliefs of any given society.

latent function of law (p. 13)   a by-product of law that defines the identity of and strengthens the social bonds among members of a group.

conflict theory of law (p. 14)   law reflects the values, beliefs, and interests of powerful elites within any given society and serves to help those in power preserve their position within society.

social control (p. 14)   formal and informal processes that maintain conformity with social norms.

crime control (p. 15)   formal and informal processes that respond to violations of legal norms.

crime control model of justice (p. 16)   prioritizes the efficient and effective enforcement of the law as a basic precondition for a free society.

due process model of justice (p. 16)   prioritizes rules of due process which guarantee and protect individual civil liberty and fairness in the enforcement of the criminal law.

rule of law (p. 18)   the basic principle that the exercise of governmental power is regulated by laws formulated by legitimate institutions of representative government.

substantive criminal law (p. 18)   actions which are prohibited or prescribed by the criminal law.

procedural criminal law (p. 18)   the lawful process for creating, enforcing, and implementing the criminal law.

writ of habeas corpus (p. 18)   a petition to the court contesting the legality of imprisonment.

adversarial system (p. 19)   the state and the accused are represented by equal advocates before a neutral judge and jury.

inquisitorial system (p. 19)   the state represented by the judge has the power to investigate, interrogate, adjudicate, convict, and sanction the accused.

REVIEW AND STUDY QUESTIONS

1. What does it mean to say, "crime is a social construction"?

2. What is the difference between "crime" and "deviance"? What does it mean to say, "crime is a legal construction"?

3. Explain the distinction between the concept of a "folkway," "more," and a "law." What is the distinguishing feature of a "law"?

4. What is the role of the "moral entrepreneur" in the deviance process? Who was the "moral entrepreneur" in the Salem witch trials? What is the meaning of the concept of a "moral panic"?

5. What is the concept of "natural law"? How does this concept differ from the sociological view that morality is a social construction?

6. Explain the difference between a "consensus" theory of law and a "conflict" theory of law? Discuss the Salem witch trials from each of these theoretical perspectives.

7. Identify forms of social control, other than the law, which operate in society today. Explain the distinction between crime control and social control.

8. What are the greatest threats to individual freedom from the perspective of the crime control model? What are the greatest threats to individual freedom from the perspective of the due process model?

9. Explain the difference between the substantive criminal law and the procedural criminal law.

10. What is the "adversarial" system of justice and how does it differ from an inquisitorial system of justice?

CHECK IT OUT

Websites:

Salem Massachusetts Witch Trials, http://www.history.com/topics/salem-witch-trials

The Salem Witch Museum at http://www.salemwitchmuseum.com/ to learn more about Salem in the seventeenth century.

Witchcraft in Salem Village, http://etext.virginia.edu/salem/witchcraft/ Check this website for access to the detailed information about the victims and the accused. Read narratives of the "examinations" of each of the accused; search rare documents of current debates and dialogues on the crime of witchcraft. Explore historical sites and consult the experts with your questions!

Senator Joseph McCarthy, McCarthyism and the Witchhunt. http://www.coldwar.org/articles/50s/senatorjosephmccarthy.asp Check out this web site on the investigation conducted by Joseph McCarthy at the Cold War Museum.

Wenatchee Witch Hunt: Child Sex Abuse Trials In Douglas and Chelan Counties. http://www.historylink.org/File/7065 Read the story of the largest child abuse case in U.S. history indicting 43 adults on more than 29,000 counts of rape and molestation of sixty children. But are these charges true or is this a miscarriage of justice similar to the Salem witch trials?

Videos:

McMartin Preschool: Anatomy of a Panic. Watch a video with background on the criminal prosecution of the McMartin Day Care, a modern-day version of Salem witch trials. See critique of use of expert testimony and impact of hysteria on criminal process. https://www.nytimes.com/video/us/100000002755079/mcmartin-pre-school-anatomy-of-a-panic.html

When Children Accuse: Sex Crimes, 43 minutes—ABC News What happens when overzealous social workers and investigators coach young children as witnesses in cases concerning accusations of sexual molestation? Are there parallels to the Salem witch trials where 19 people were executed based on the accusations of children?

Available from Films for the Humanities and Sciences at www.films.com

Innocence Lost: PBS documentary about the Little Rascals Day Care Center trial charging a gross miscarriage of justice based on the testimony of children coached by therapists and investigators. http://www.pbs.org/wgbh/pages/frontline/shows/innocence/

Movies:

The Crucible (1996). This is a film starring Winona Ryder and Daniel Day-Lewis with a screenplay written by the original playwright Arthur Miller. Miller fictionalizes the events of 1692 in the invention of an affair between Abigail Williams and John Proctor as a key motive but otherwise presents a historically accurate narrative of the climate and events of the time. *The Crucible* was written and produced in the 1950s as a deliberate effort to criticize the anti-communist "witch hunt" of Senator Joseph McCarthy as he accused hundreds of celebrities and politicians of being communists forcing people to defend their innocence, confess, and name names or risk losing their careers and livelihoods.

NOTES

[1] Kai Erickson, *Wayward Puritans: A Study in the Sociology of Deviance* (New York: Wiley & Sons, 1966), 6.

[2] William Graham Sumner, *On Liberty, Society and Politics: The Essential Essays of William Graham Sumner*, ed, Robert C. Bannister (Indianapolis: Liberty Fund, 1992).

[3] Howard Abadinsky, *Law and Justice: An Introduction to the American Legal System* (Chicago: Nelson Hall, 1995), 5–11.

[4] Emile Durkheim, *Division of Labor in Society* (Glencoe, IL: The Free Press, 1960), 73–80.

[5] Jeffrey Reiman, *The Rich Get Rich and the Poor Get Prison: Ideology, Class and Criminal Justice* (Needham Heights, MA: Allyn and Bacon, 1998).

[6] Reiman, *The Rich Get Rich*, 77.

[7] Elliot Currie, *Confronting Crime: An American Challenge* (New York: Pantheon Books, 1985).

[8] Daniel Van Ness and Karen Heetderks, Strong, *Restoring Justice* (Cincinnati, OH: Anderson, 1997), 63.

[9] Herbert Packer, *The Limits of the Criminal Sanction* (Stanford: Stanford University Press, 1968).

[10] Susan Brownmiller, *Against Our Will: Men, Women and Rape* (New York: Simon & Schuster, 1975).

[11] Randall Kennedy, *Race, Crime and the Law* (New York: Vintage Books, 1998).

[12] John Dilulio, "The Question of Black Crime," *National Affairs* 117, (1994): 3–32.

[13] Richard Weisman, *Witchcraft, Magic and Religion in 17th Century Mass* (Boston: University of Massachusetts Press, 1984), 12.

[14] Theodore F.T. Plucknett, *A Concise History of the Common Law* (London, UK: Butterworth and Co, 1956), 24.

[15] Richard Weisman, *Witchcraft, Magic and Religion in 17th Century Mass* (Boston: University of Massachusetts Press, 1984), 157.

In this chapter we read a case about a robbery, the arrest and prosecution of a young man for that crime, and the many issues that face our legal system when trying to determine guilt or innocence. This chapter provides an overview of the justice processes, from arrest through sentencing, and examines the different decision-making roles within the criminal justice process.

LEARNING OBJECTIVES

After reading this chapter you should be able to:

- Identify the five stages of the criminal justice process; describe the key processes that occur at each stage; and identify the discretionary decisions made by justice professionals at each stage of the process.
- Describe the wedding cake model of the criminal justice system and contrast with the justice funnel model.
- Contrast the assembly line model of justice and compare it to the obstacle course model of justice; identify the values that are associated with each of these models.
- Explain why discretion is central to the justice process and dilemmas are posed by criminal justice discretion.
- Demonstrate the impact of politics on policies of crime control and explain the concept of "expressive justice."

Case #2: A "Run-of-the-Mill" Crime

Terence Garner back home enjoying with his family after serving four years for a crime he did not commit. (McClatchy-Tribune via Getty Images)

It was pretty near the end of an ordinary workday at the Quality Finance Company, a small lending company located on the outskirts of a sleepy town in North Carolina. The manager Charles Woodard was chatting with customer Bertha Miller while secretary Alice Wise focused intently on her computer. "May I help you?" asked the manager in a voice that led Alice to look up sharply from her screen. Two black men loomed over the counter, one tall man wearing a bandana around his face, the other, short, holding a gun to Mr. Woodward's head.

A third man, Keith Riddick, sat outside in the getaway car. The robbery was his idea. He recruited the short man, his cousin named Terrence Deloach, just back after a long stint in prison up North to do it with him. Riddick had tried to dissuade the tall man, Henderson, from joining them. A good kid from a respectable family, Riddick didn't think he had the "heart" to commit armed robbery. But Henderson insisted, so Riddick finally agreed to bring him along for "back-up."

The three drove to the building and waited until most cars left. Riddick parked off to the side in the woods. His instructions to his cousin and Henderson were to go in there, show the gun to get the safe open, and get out. It was supposed to be a simple robbery—in and out. But as it dawned on Bertha what was happening she began to scream. Alice tried to calm her down but with little success. "Please don't kill us!!" Bertha begged. While Henderson busied himself

tying up the women with duct tape, Deloach growled at Woodward to hurry up and get the money.

Suddenly without any warning, Deloach fired his gun at the chest of Alice Wise. Later she distinctly recalled him say, "Should I go ahead and kill the bitch?" She raised her hands to protect herself and he fired again; this time the bullet went through both her wrists before striking her in the forehead.

Outside Riddick panicked when he heard the shots. Then Henderson came running wildly "Let's go! He's shooting people!" Deloach followed and the three piled into the car and sped off with less than a thousand dollars. Henderson was sure Deloach had murdered Alice Wise.

But Alice Wise did not die that day: miraculously she survived the point blank shooting to her chest and head with only the loss of her left eye. Physical wounds, however, are only one kind of injury. For Wise, years later, "Nothing is as I knew it before that day. Nothing." Terrified of crowds and distrustful of people, Wise was unable to pick up the pieces of her life. Like many other victims of violent crime, Wise suffered debilitating symptoms of psychological trauma long after her physical injury had healed.

Getting Caught

Henderson was the first to be caught. Struggling to wrap duct tapes around his victims' wrists, he pulled off his gloves leaving a fingerprint that quickly led law enforcement to his front door. He told authorities all he knew, including the name and address of Keith Riddick and everything he knew about the shooter named Terence. Not knowing his last name, he told them that he was Riddick's cousin from NYC and was staying with his girlfriend. He gave the address and described the apartment where he had picked up and dropped Deloach after the crime. By the time detectives went to pick up Riddick he was gone.

Finding "Terence"

Based on the information from Henderson, detectives from Johnston County set out to find someone named "Terence" living in neighboring Wayne County. They sought assistance from the Wayne County sheriff's office in search of a black male suspect, first name Terence, last name unknown. Captain Jerry Best solicited help from local police who mentioned a Terence Garner whose photograph was in the computer following a recent drug sweep by local housing authority. Although the sixteen-year-old had committed no offense and had no criminal record, his photograph was in the system and a copy of that photo was handed to detectives.

The detectives put that photograph along with several others in front of the manager of the Quality Finance Company. After carefully examining them for a long time, Woodward picked out Terence Garner as the person who had shot Alice Wise. The third eyewitness, customer Bertha Miller, said she only glanced at the gunman because she was so terrified. She did not even look at the photos claiming she would not be able to identify anyone. Alice Wise was still in the hospital recovering from her injuries.

Detectives also checked out the address Henderson had given them where Terence Deloach was supposedly living with his girlfriend. They knocked on the door but when no one answered, they left. Their next stop was twenty blocks away at the home of Terence Garner who was shooting hoops on the court across from his apartment. Seeing the police at his door, Garner rushed over asking if he could be of assistance because his mother was inside sleeping. They told him were looking for Terence Garner. "Yeah that's me." With those words, Garner was placed under arrest. Believing they had found the suspect named Terence who had shot Alice Wise, the detectives never returned to the address given to them by Henderson.

Let's Make a Deal

Three black men had committed the crime at the Quality Finance Company and two black males were now in police custody. But were these the black men who committed the crime? Henderson's fingerprints placed him at the scene of the crime so there was little doubt about him. But Henderson was the first to realize a mistake had been made in the arrest of Garner. Sitting in the visiting room of the local jail, his girlfriend pointed to Garner as "the guy they got for shooting that woman in your case." Henderson was stunned: he had never seen this guy before in his life. He turned to him, "What are you locked up for?" and realized Terence was on the verge of tears right alongside his mother who was already sobbing her eyes out. "They say I shot some woman." Henderson assured him it was all a big mistake. Henderson figured all he had to do was tell the authorities and Garner would be free and clear. "You ain't got to worry about this," he told Garner.

Henderson immediately contacted his defense lawyer and told him that they had arrested the wrong man. Sure his name is Terence but he's not Riddick's cousin, not from NYC, he's 16 not 25, and had absolutely nothing to do with this crime. The only connection was that he was a young black man whose first name was Terence. Henderson wanted his lawyer to get Garner released: "I don't know this kid. They've got the wrong guy."

But his defense attorney was not so keen to carry out the wishes of his client. As his lawyer, his job is to protect Henderson. Officially Terence Garner was his co-defendant in a serious case of attempted murder and armed robbery. He advised Henderson to keep quiet about the mistake fearing that exonerating Garner would place more blame on Henderson. If they couldn't track down Riddick or pin the shooting on this Terence guy, Henderson would be the guy to take the fall. And if Henderson made life difficult for the prosecution, it might lessen his chances for a favorable plea bargain. All in all, he strongly advised Henderson against testifying that Garner was innocent explaining, "You will put yourself in position where it may hurt your cause and hurt my cause." Henderson was shocked at this advice and insisted on testifying they were prosecuting an innocent man.

Meanwhile authorities had located Riddick and extradited him from California where he had fled the night of the crime. Riddick too quickly realized they had locked up the wrong Terence. He told his lawyer,

"I don't know that dude. That's my first time seeing him in my life." But his court-appointed lawyer was even more adamant that it was not in his client's interest to challenge the prosecution's allegation that Terence Garner was the shooter of Alice Wise. Like many defense attorneys, he had a close working relationship with the prosecution. Adversaries in the courtroom but friends in the locker room, they often met over lunch to discuss their cases. While chatting on another case, the investigation of the Quality Finance Company robbery came up. The prosecution was troubled that Henderson was insisting they arrested the wrong guy. By this time, both victims, first the manager, Charles Woodward, and now the shooting victim, Alice Wise, had positively identified Terence Garner as the man who fired a gun on them that day. If Riddick would testify against Garner, the case would be solid for a conviction.

The defense attorney put a stark choice before Riddick: "They're not letting Garner go, so you need to decide—either go down with Garner or go home." If Riddick was willing to provide sworn testimony that Garner was the shooter, his lawyer would be able to get him a deal that would land Riddick with only a brief sentence followed by probation. But that was the only way he could get this deal.

This was an offer Riddick could not refuse. Not only would he benefit from a light sentence, he could avoid snitching on his own cousin. He agreed to get on the stand and provide sworn testimony that Garner was the shooter and he did not have a cousin named Terence from NYC. Now the prosecution felt it had sufficient evidence to go to trial.

The Trial

With Riddick's testimony along with that of the two victims, the case against Garner was extremely strong. Henderson took the stand and tried his best to convince the jury that Garner was innocent. Although he had no motive for lying, the prosecution scoffed at his credibility and claimed he was a liar, pure and simple. They also scoffed at the credibility of Garner's mother, stepdad, and family friend, all of whom testified he was with them at the time of the crime. His mother recalls, "They just laughed at us."

It was one-eyed Alice Wise who provided the most compelling evidence for the jury. In a dramatic statement, Alice took the stand and baldly told the jury, "His face is the last thing that I saw with both my eyes."

It was her certainty, more than any other piece of testimony, that convinced the jury and the judge too that Terence was a guilty man. It did not take long for a jury to convict the now seventeen-year-old Terence Garner. The judge sentenced him to thirty-two to forty-three years in prison.

The Judge

Judge Knox V. Jenkins Jr. is one of the most politically powerful figures in this part of North Carolina. During the trial he felt little sympathy for the accused convinced by Alice Wise's testimony that Terence Garner's was a face she could never forget. During the pretrial proceedings the judge ruled against the defense motions that challenged the process through which Alice Wise had come to identify Terence Garner as the man who shot her.

The way eyewitnesses make identifications of suspects is a complex and challenging part of the criminal procedure process. Alice Wise had twice failed to pick Terence Garner out of a traditional police line-up and a photo array. Yet five months after the crime, when she saw Garner in court for a bail hearing she positively identified him as the shooter. Known as a "show-up" identification in which a witness happens to see a suspect and makes a positive id without any of the protections of a line-up or photo array, these kinds of identifications are notoriously unreliable and often excluded as fair evidence in a trial. Garner's defense attorney filed a motion to suppress the "show-up" identification as evidence but the judge denied the motion. Next the defense filed a motion to allow expert testimony on eyewitness identifications to help the jury understand how inaccurate these identifications may be. The judge denied this motion too.

Judge Jenkins firmly believed Terence Garner was guilty. Like the jury he was convinced by the certainty of the victim Alice Wise. Furthermore, it was his belief that youth like Garner were teen "predators" who needed to be behind bars for a long time. In recent years he had made it his personal mission to crack down on what he saw as a dangerous rise in teenage violent crime. He described this case to a reporter as "run of the mill" but symptomatic of a larger social problem. In the end, it was his insistence that local media cover this case that ultimately saved Terence Garner from serving forty-three years for a crime he did not commit.

The Media

Over the years reporter Glenna Musante had come to know and like the amiable Judge Jenkins. So when he asked her to cover the story of this robbery Musante brought it to her editors at the Raleigh *News and Observer*. They were not too interested: what was so special about a run-of-the-mill armed robbery? No one was killed and the perpetrators were under arrest. No one famous was involved and they could not see an interesting angle to catch the attention of their readers. Why bother to cover such an ordinary crime?

But Judge Jenkins insisted this crime represented a pattern in the community: a wave of crimes committed by violent teens who killed for no reason other than the pleasure of watching someone die. As a favor to an old friend, however, Musante managed to convince her editors to allow her to follow the trial. In one of her first articles about the crime Musante quoted the judge, "These are predators and my responsibility is to protect the public from these people."

To Musante the evidence seemed to fit with this narrative. The testimonies of Riddick, Wise, and Woodward were strong against Garner who seemed to have had no rational motive for shooting Alice Wise. He must be one of these violent teen predators that Judge Jenkins was talking about. His conviction and long sentence was a victory for the justice system and an important step in making the community safer by getting them off the street for a very long time.

Within forty-eight hours of the conviction, however, Musante's cell phone rang with a call from Tom Lock, the district attorney with news that shattered this tidy narrative: "Glenna I think we convicted the wrong person." The headlines in the next day paper reported the astonishing fact that two days after the conviction of Garner, someone else, a man named Terence Deloach, confessed to the crime.

What Happened?

Henderson, whose testimony no one believed during the trial, refused to give up on his quest to clear Garner. While he was being transported to the Wayne County to face prior charges he asked to talk with law enforcement officers there. He told them what he had told detectives from Johnston County: the real shooter was Terence Deloach, Riddick's cousin from NYC still living at this address in Wayne County.

The detectives remembered the investigation they had assisted with nine months earlier and remembered

handing over a photograph of Terence Garner. They called Johnston County and asked if they would check out Henderson's story. Johnson County detectives said no, the case is over with the shooter behind bars. Why re-open a successful case? But detective Jerry Best of the Wayne County sheriff's office was uneasy. Shouldn't they at least check out Henderson's story by going to the apartment where Deloach was supposedly living? If Johnston County detectives wouldn't investigate, they decided to do it themselves.

Everything checked out exactly as Henderson said it would. Deloach was there with his girlfriend who had also assisted in the robbery. They brought both in for questioning and within two hours, Deloach and his girlfriend admitted their roles in the robbery. Deloach, who had a long and violent criminal record, signed a detailed confession of his participation in the robbery, including the shooting of Alice Wise.

Glenna Musante reported these shocking turn of events on the front page of the paper. Everyone expected Garner's conviction to be immediately set aside at hearings scheduled for 9:30 the next day. But by the time of the hearing, Deloach had changed his story. After four hours of interrogation by Johnston County law enforcement, Deloach claimed he had been confused when he admitted to the crime. Now he denied everything. Although there were no audiotapes or transcript of the interrogation, Judge Jenkins accepted the recantation and ruled that the conviction remained valid. He personally continued to believe the right person was behind bars.

Reporter Musante was deeply troubled. She had first started covering the case as a favor to Judge Jenkins. Now the case was getting very complicated. Wayne County detectives testified before Judge Jenkins that Deloach knew too many details about the crime to be making a false confession. Furthermore, he was indeed Riddick's cousin from NYC and had a long history of violent crime. To add to the drama, Bertha Miller, the third eyewitness, now came forward and testified that although she did not have a good visual memory of any of the men there that day, she knew for sure Terence Garner was not one of them. "I practically helped raise him since he was a kid. If it was him, I would have known it."

To the reporter from the Raleigh *News and Observer*, the fact that Terence Deloach suddenly changed his story while in the custody of Johnson County detectives was suspicious. Having closely followed the investigation and trial of this "run-of-the-mill" crime,

Glenna Musante saw too many troubling unanswered questions. How could the district attorney explain the appearance of another Terence who so closely fit the description provided by Henderson? Tom Lock floated a theory that maybe there were four men there that day—two Terences instead of one. The reporter was incredulous: there was no evidence whatsoever to support that idea. That explanation was absurd.

A Second Chance Denied

By now Terence Garner had been behind bars for more than a year. Having been convicted at trial, his only recourse now was to appeal his conviction and request a new trial where a new jury could hear all the additional evidence that was emerging in this case, including Deloach's confession and denial; Bertha Miller's testimony; and the doubts about Riddick's veracity on the stand. The defense attorney representing Garner stood before Judge Jenkins requesting a new trial be granted to determine which of the two Terences shot Alice Wise.

But Jenkins denied the request. Two victim witnesses had already testified that it was Garner: that was good enough for the jury and good enough for Judge Jenkins. The trial had been fair: justice was served. The defense took the case to the court of appeals. They too denied Garner a second trial. A final request to the Supreme Court of North Carolina to review the case was also turned down. Legally this was the end of the line for Terence Garner. With a heavy heart, the defense attorney explained to him and his devastated family that nothing else could be done. The system had spoken: Garner was guilty as charged. The sentence of thirty-two to forty-three years would stand.

The Court of Public Opinion: The Demand for Justice

The story does not end here. Judge Jenkins had invited media coverage for a story about teenage predators. But once turned on, the media spotlight is not so easily shut off. Musante, discouraged by the system's refusal to go back over its tracks, resigned in disgust and turned the story over to a veteran reporter who continued to keep the details on the front page revealing all the disturbing doubts about the truthfulness of this conviction.

A producer from the television news program *Frontline* read the account and began to also ask questions. Within a year, a documentary about the case aired on national television laying out the evidence never heard by a jury in the courtroom. By now, Riddick was out enjoying the light sentence he was given in exchange for testifying against Garner; Henderson was serving thirteen years for his part in the robbery; and Terence Garner was doing hard time. Meanwhile Terrance Deloach had been arrested seven times and was serving a prison sentence for committing another armed robbery on the subway in NYC.

The response to the documentary by the public, especially by citizens of Johnson and Wayne Counties, was overwhelming. The office of the district attorney, courthouse, and sheriff's departments were flooded with phone calls and letters demanding to know why the system would not re-examine the evidence against Terence Garner. Within a month, Judge Jenkins succumbed to pressure and granted Garner's request for a new trial. District Attorney Tom Lock announced that he would not seek another trial explaining he was "no longer convinced beyond a reasonable doubt" that Garner was guilty. Deloach sitting in a NYC jail again confessed to at least two additional witnesses that he was, indeed, the one who shot Alice Wise.

Did the System Work?

After serving four years in prison, Terence Garner was freed and sent home. Surprisingly calm, Terence Garner said he was just happy to be going back to school and resuming his life. Lock told the press that, in the end, the system has worked for Terence Garner. Alice Wise however did not believe the system had worked. In her mind, the system released a man she believes is guilty of shooting her at point blank range. Four years after the crime, Wise has still not recovered from the psychological trauma; the idea that this man walks free in the community is devastating to her.

Mark Montgomery, the defense attorney who worked tirelessly for years to get the system to retry Garner's case, also does not believe the system "worked" in this case. "Terence Garner is free in spite of the system, not because of it. The system would have kept Terence Garner in prison for thirty more years. Public attention derailed the system in this case. It got people to stop and pay attention. . . . Otherwise it was going to be business as usual. Everybody just gave a big yawn: So what else is new. . . . Another black kid in prison. Who cares?"

THINKING CRITICALLY ABOUT THIS CASE

1. District Attorney Lock believed that, in the end, the system "worked." Both Alice Wise, the victim, and Mark Montgomery, the defense attorney, disagreed and felt the system had failed. Which position do you agree with and why?

2. A lot of different players in the justice process had discretion—the ability to choose between different legitimate actions—in this case. Describe the decisions made by the detectives in Wayne and Johnson Counties; the defense attorneys for Henderson and Riddick; and the judge. Do you believe they made the right decisions in this case? Why or why not?

3. Alice Wise believed that Garner was the man who shot her. Why do you think she is so certain?

Should the jury be allowed to hear expert testimony on the reliability of eyewitness identifications? Why or why not?

4. Why did Judge Jenkins invite media coverage in this case? Do you believe that the judge carried out his duties in an impartial manner in this case? Why or why not?

5. What role did the media play in this case? Do you believe this role was constructive? Should the media be more or less involved in the coverage of crime and the justice process?

REFERENCES

Case adapted from:

Frontline: An Ordinary Crime, directed by Ofra Bikel, 2002, Arlington Virginia: Public Broadcasting Service.

Mark Montgomery, "Telling The Story: State v. Terence Garner: A System Gone Awry," in *Trial Briefs*, August 2002.

Jane Ruffin and Adrienne Lu, "Retrial Ruled Out for Garner," *The News and Observer*, June 12, 2002.

Anne Saker, by Will Lyman, "Frontline: An Ordinary Crime," *PBS*, January 10, 2002.

To understand the relationship between formal agencies of the criminal justice system we begin with the use of a flowchart. Only in the game of Monopoly does a player "go straight to jail": cases generally must flow through the system in a particular order. When someone is charged with committing a criminal offense, he or she must be processed through a series of stages: police must first arrest the suspect, whose case is then turned over to the prosecutor for investigation and charging; the accused will be adjudicated guilty or not guilty by the appropriate judicial authorities and if the result is a conviction, only then will a person be turned over to the jurisdiction of the correctional authorities.

Terence Garner and others suspected of committing this crime were brought into the system once arrested by the police. Detectives worked together with the prosecutor's office to build a case to present at trial. The defense attorney and the prosecutors had numerous consultations to determine who would be charged with what offense. Both Henderson and Riddick pled guilty eliminating the need for a trial although Riddick was rewarded with a much less serious charge in exchange for his willingness to testify against Garner. Garner maintained his innocence and therefore went to trial for adjudication before a jury of his peers. During the trial it was Judge Jenkins who made many key decisions that were highly influential in shaping what the jury heard and how they determined Garner's guilt or innocence. The trial phase ended when Garner was convicted and exhausted his judicial appeals.

After conviction, Garner was placed into the custody of the North Carolina Department of Corrections. Under ordinary circumstances Garner would have spent the next thirty years assigned to one facility or another at the discretion of the correctional authorities. His exact release date after having served the minimum thirty years of his judicial sentence would have been determined by a parole board that may or may not have decided to allow Garner to serve the remainder of his sentence under conditional release within the community.

Beyond these formal agencies there are other forces that shape the justice process. The media frames the political climate that impacts lawmakers who write legislation. Public outrage over a particularly heinous crime or gross miscarriage of justice often has an impact on the decisions of the criminal justice system particularly on the decisions of elected officials such as prosecutors, sheriffs, governors, and judges. In this case, media coverage of the case enraged the public who put pressure on judges and prosecutors to exercise their legal discretion to release Garner.

DISCRETION IN THE FIVE STAGES IN THE JUSTICE PROCESS

FIVE STAGES OF THE CRIMINAL JUSTICE SYSTEM
entry, pretrial and investigation; adjudication, sentencing and corrections.

There are **five stages of the criminal justice** decision-making: entry into the system; prosecution and pretrial services; adjudications; sentencing and sanctions; and corrections.[1] Police and prosecutors are the key players in the first stage; prosecutors, defense attorney, judges, and court staff play a predominant role in the second, third, and fourth phases; and correctional staff in prisons, jails, halfway houses, community corrections, probation departments, parole boards, and treatment staff are the primary players in the fifth stage of the justice process.[2]

While the sequence suggests an orderly progression through each of these five stages, the reality is far more complex. At each point in the process, criminal justice personnel make critical decisions in a process known as **selective enforcement of the law**. The exercise of **discretion** is a fundamental reality of the system: from the police officers who first approach a suspect to the attorneys who decide whether and what charge, to the judge who may evaluate the evidence or determine the sentence to the correctional authorities who decide where to classify a prisoner or when a person is ready to return to society. Each individual has a sphere of discretion in deciding how to handle the case.[3]

Does this mean that there are no "rules" or laws guiding the system? Of course not. But the sociological reality is that a human being must always decide whether or not to enforce the law and decide which law applies to the given facts of the case. The law may state that only offenders who express remorse are eligible for a given program but who decides if they are remorseful? Or the law may specify that a given sentence should be applied when a crime is particularly heinous but who evaluates the horrific quality of the offense? There is always an element of human decision-making that must take place in the application and enforcement of the law. Laws do not automatically enforce themselves.

Stage One: Entry into the system

The first stage in the criminal justice process is the detection and reporting of a crime. In order for the legal system to respond to a crime, it is not enough for a crime to have simply taken place: someone, most often the victim, needs to bring that violation to the attention of the authorities. Most crimes are brought to the attention of the justice system when somebody in the community dials 911 to ask for help or to report a crime. Citizens hold a large amount of discretion in the criminal justice process.

For many reasons, citizens frequently do not report crimes to the justice system.[4] It is estimated that only a third to a quarter of crimes are ever reported to the police. Victims may feel ashamed or be too afraid to report a crime fearing ridicule or retaliation by the perpetrator or his friends. They may be fearful of how they will be treated by the system, whether they will be believed or treated with respect. victims' of sexual assault and domestic violence have historically been unwilling to come forward and undergo the traumatic and often degrading process of prosecution. All too often, victims are re-traumatized by a justice system insensitive to victim's needs. Often victims are made to feel they are to blame for their own victimization.

Citizens may be reluctant to report a crime when the offender is a relative, friend, or neighbor. This does not necessarily mean they approve of the criminal conduct but they may be unwilling to get the person in trouble with the law preferring to use other methods to dissuade them from the negative behavior. Citizens who are themselves engaged in illegal activities such as drug dealing, prostitution, or illegal drug use are unlikely to turn to the system when they have been victimized or to cooperate with the police leaving the parties involved to settle matters themselves often through violent means.

The belief that the system can or will do little in response to the crime also influences citizens' decision to report a crime to the police. If a bike is stolen, it may never be reported because the victim thinks it unlikely the police will ever recover the property or catch the perpetrator. Some victims of domestic violence and sexual assault, especially when the perpetrators are intimate partners such as husbands and boyfriends, fear the system will not keep them safe or take their complaint seriously. Crimes may also go unreported because victims are not

SELECTIVE ENFORCEMENT OF THE LAW
when criminal justice personnel enforce some laws and not others or enforce them in some situations and not in other situations.

DISCRETION
the authority to choose between alternative actions.

even aware they have been victimized. Many white collar crimes and corporate crimes go unreported because victims don't know they are being ripped off at the checkout counter or being overcharged through illegal price fixing schemes.

Thus the first layer of discretion in the justice system resides in the public's willingness to report crimes and share information about criminal activity with the police. Police actually rely on citizens to bring crimes to their attention. They also rely on citizens who have been victimized or who have knowledge and information about criminal conduct to serve in court as witnesses or to serve as informants.

The dependence of the justice system on the trust and cooperation of the community is one of the reasons behind the rise of community policing. The greater the mutual respect and trust between the system and the community, the more the citizens will work with the system in the prevention and detection of crime. In many urban communities, citizens are unwilling or afraid to bring information to the police hampering their ability to do their job effectively. In some communities, police try and counter anti-snitching norms with media campaigns that encourage citizens to "Keep Talking."[5]

Police Discretion

When a citizen calls the police to report a crime or make a complaint, the police must decide whether or not to treat that incident as a crime. If police decide to treat a particular incident as a crime, the incident is founded; if they determine that it is not a crime, then it is unfounded. Citizens sometimes think something is a crime when it is not, or the facts of the incident may fail to support the allegation. Even if the incident constitutes crime, police may also consider the crime too trivial to pursue or they may believe the victim is unreliable or unwilling to fully cooperate with a prosecution. The discretionary power of police in the **founding decision** is one of the key stages of the justice process serving a key gatekeeping role in the entire sequence of the judicial process.

The phase of **arrest** and investigation is primarily the responsibility of law enforcement and prosecutors who rely upon citizens as complainants, witnesses, and informers. An arrest is the first step toward prosecution: under some specific conditions this requires a **warrant** or judicial order authorizing police officers to arrest a suspect or to search their premises but in the vast majority of cases, officers are authorized to exercise their own judgment about whether or not there is reasonable cause to believe that the person to be arrested has committed a felony.[6]

Police have a wide range of discretion in how they respond to a citizen whom they believe has violated the law.[7] They may walk away and do nothing[8] or issue a friendly or firm warning; they may insist that the people move along and alter their conduct; they may investigate further by frisking or questioning the suspect; they may collect information such as their phone number or address, look for a record in the computer, search the suspect, transport them to the police station and then release them, or formally arrest them. Police do not and cannot arrest all the violations of the law: we expect police to exercise discretion in their enforcement of the law.

On television, police are often depicted as interrupting a crime in progress but such events are relatively rare. In the case of drug offenses and other so-called consensual or victimless crimes such as prostitution, gambling and drug trafficking, and some forms of white collar crime such as bribery and corruption

FOUNDING DECISION
a decision made by police that a particular incident should be treated as a crime (founded) or not treated as a crime (unfounded).

ARREST
the action of taking a person into custody for the purpose of charging them with a crime.

WARRANT
a writ issued by a judicial officer ordering law enforcement to perform a specific action such as a search or an arrest.

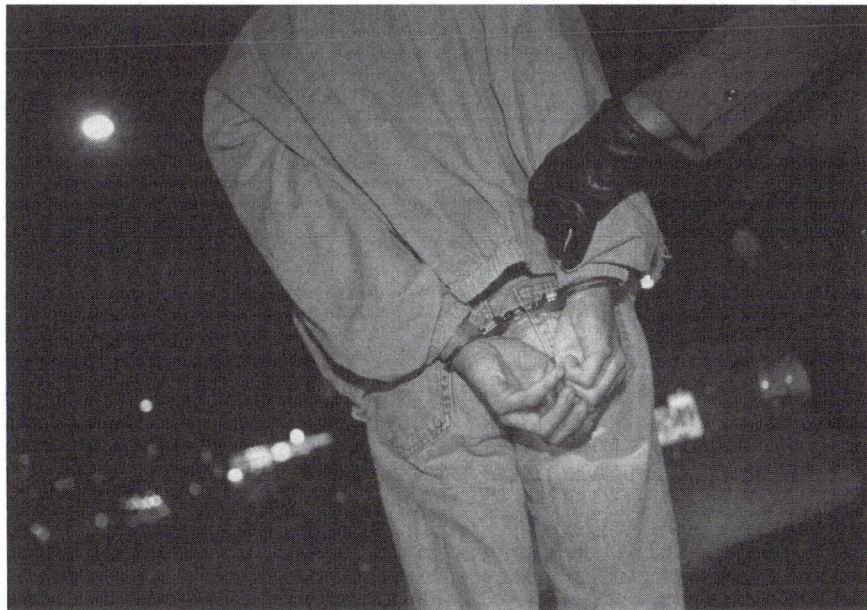

Police are expected to use judgment and discretion in the enforcement of the law and make decisions about the appropriate use of the power of arrest.

of public officials, law enforcement is required to take a pro-active rather than reactive stance toward the detection of crime. To detect those involved in these crimes and to gather evidence for a conviction, police engage in an array of "undercover" strategies to enforce these criminal laws.

Stage Two: Pretrial and Investigation

The second stage of criminal justice processing concerns the charging of the suspect with a specific violation of the criminal law, bail hearings, and other pretrial hearings.[9] These stages are largely the responsibility of the public servant known as the **prosecutor**.[10] The district attorney's office will review the police report and assess the existing evidence to determine the appropriate charge.[11] The prosecution is also responsible for the gathering of evidence against a suspect and for arguing the government's case before the judge and jury.

Prosecutors are the key link between the police and the courts. Early in the process, a consultation may take place between the police and a member of the district attorney's office to decide if the person who has been booked will be released or if formal charges will be filed against the defendant at the arraignment. There may be a decision to offer a "deal" to a suspect in exchange for their willingness to testify as we saw with both Henderson who refused the deal and Riddick who agreed to it.

Just as the police do not arrest all those who have violated the law, prosecutors do not automatically charge all suspects with a crime. Instead, they make decisions about how best to use the resources of their office, what best serves the interests of justice, how much leverage they have in negotiations with the defense, and what they feel they can legally prove in court. Prosecutors may decide not to charge an accused in exchange for their cooperation and testimony in the case against another suspect; or they may decide it is a case they cannot win; or they

PROSECUTORS
a government attorney who instigates the prosecution of an accused and represents the interests of the state at trial.

INITIAL APPEARANCE
the first court processing stage after arrest in which the accused is brought before a judge or magistrate to hear the formal charges.

GRAND JURY
a group of , usually twenty-three, citizens assembled to determine whether sufficient evidence exists to support the prosecution of the accused.

ARRAIGNMENT
a hearing before the court in which the defendant is formally informed of the charges and is required to enter a plea.

PRETRIAL PHASE
the second stage of criminal justice processing where numerous decisions about the trial procedure are adjudicated by the lower court.

BAIL
money or other security placed in custody of the court in order to insure the return of a defendant to stand trial.

RELEASE ON RECOGNIZANCE
a nonfinancial release in which the accused promises to appear in court at the required date.

ADJUDICATION
the process whereby the court arrives at a decision regarding a particular case.

JURY TRIAL
evidence is presented to a panel of citizens who are required to determine the defendant's guilt or innocence of the charges.

believe it is a case that should not be prosecuted. Like the police, prosecutors have wide unreviewable discretion in the decision to charge or not charge a suspect and to determine the precise nature of that charge.

At the **initial appearance**, the accused is brought before a judge and informed of the charges against them. This is also a point in the process where a judge may decide to dismiss the case at this stage if they feel there is insufficient evidence to proceed. The burden of proof lies on the government to present enough evidence to continue to take actions against the accused. It is the responsibility of the judge to make an independent assessment of the evidence and determine if the state has "probable cause" to charge this citizen with a given crime.

In many states for serious felony offenses, the prosecution must present evidence to a grand jury in order to obtain an indictment. The **grand jury** consists of twenty-three citizens who listen to the evidence against the accused gathered by the police and prosecutors. Along with the judge, the role of the grand jury is to evaluate the quality of the proof the state says it has that the accused is likely to have committed the crime. If the grand jury or the judge and believes that the evidence suggests that it is unlikely this person committed this offense, then they may refuse to hand down an indictment or true bill. The **arraignment** is a hearing in which the defendant is informed of the charges and is required to enter a plea.

During this stage, also known as the **pretrial phase**, the prosecution and defense attorney will also present arguments before a judge to make a number of other important procedural decisions such as whether to release the suspect on bail, what evidence will be permissible in the trial, and where the trial will be held. As we see in this case, the decision by Judge Jenkins not to allow the jury to hear defense arguments about the reliability of the eyewitness identification affected the outcome of the case. In many trials, what takes place during the pretrial phase is even more important than what occurs during the trial itself.

Bail, which is taken from the French *baillier* meaning "to deliver or give" is a form of temporary release—it usually involves the posting of some financial security to ensure that the suspect will return to face further trial proceedings. The judge may, however, decide to release a defendant on **ROR or release on recognition** in the belief that the accused may be trusted to return to court at the date of their appointed trial. Alternatively, defendants may be detained at pretrial as well and held without bail if the judge believes that they are likely to attempt to flee before trial or they pose a danger to others.

Stage Three: Determination of Guilt

The third stage of criminal justice processing is the **adjudication** of guilt or innocence before a judge and jury. Although a tiny fraction of cases actually go to trial, this is the most celebrated moment in the justice process when each side is given its opportunity to present the facts and arguments that support their version of the truth. Along with the judge and jury, the principal players are the prosecutor and defense attorneys who each present an argument regarding the defendant's actions, motives, or culpability for the alleged crime. It is the responsibility of the judge to preside over the trial and to ensure that procedures are followed fairly by both sides. If it is a **jury trial** it is the responsibility of the jury to review the facts, hear the evidence presented by both sides, weigh the credibility of the witnesses, and return a verdict of guilty or not guilty. If the trial is a

bench trial with no jury present, the judge will both preside over the trial and make the determination of guilt.[12]

Most convicted offenders enter a guilty plea without going to trial. The decision to enter a guilty plea may be preceded by a formal or informal negotiation between the defense attorneys and the prosecution in which each side agrees to a charge or sentence for the accused. Generally, defendants are advised to plead guilty if their attorneys believe that they will get a less severe punishment for their actions. No defendant has a right to plea bargaining; and any party, including the prosecution, defense, or the judge, may refuse to agree to any particular plea bargain.

Stage Four: Sentencing

The sentencing phase is traditionally the responsibility of the trial court judge. Once a guilty plea or conviction occurs, we rely on the discretion of the judge to determine sentencing.[13] After a guilty **conviction** (either through a trial or through a guilty plea) both the defense and the prosecution may offer a recommended sanction to the judge. The judge is given the final responsibility to determine the specific sentence for this offender bound by the legal range of penalties in the criminal statute. Legislatures set the basic parameters for sentencing in the passing of the laws themselves.[14] In many states and in the federal system, special sentencing commissions have established sentencing guidelines that specify the range of options open to judges for a given type of offense given certain key factors about the offender such as past criminal record, employment status, and other factors.[15]

Sentencing options generally include a suspended sentence, probation, or imprisonment as well as other sanctions such as fines, community service, treatment, or restitution. To assist the judge in making sentencing decisions, the probation department may prepare a pre-sentencing report with relevant information about the offender's family, job history, education, substance abuse issues, and prior criminal involvement.[16] While information about previous criminal convictions is usually excluded from the jury, this information is almost always considered highly relevant for sentencing and is factored into the sentencing decision.

Judges may also take into consideration the particular circumstances of the offender as well as the wishes and impact of the victim when determining the actual sentence for the offender. Judge Jenkins opted for a very long sentence for Terence Garner reflecting his belief that Garner acted with great malice in trying to kill Alice Wise. Historically criminal statutes offered a wide range of penalties for any given offense. Mandatory sentencing statutes, however, severely limit the discretion of the judiciary in the sentencing phase. These laws give judges very little latitude in determining the sentence of convicted offenders. Sentencing guidelines also restrict the sentencing discretion of judges even in offenses not covered by mandatory statutes. Sentencing guidelines were designed to ensure uniformity and fairness in the punishment of similar offenses.[17]

Stage Five: Corrections and Release

Corrections and punishment is the fifth stage of the criminal justice process. The sentence handed down by the courts is carried out by the correctional system. Correctional facilities are run at the county, state, and federal levels and the

BENCH TRIAL
court proceedings in which a judge hears the evidence and determines guilt or innocence.

CONVICTION
the judgment of a court based on the verdict of a jury or judicial officer that the defendant is guilty of the offense charged.

jurisdiction of each of these facilities depends upon the crime and legal status of the offender. In addition to incarceration, there are a variety of sanctions meted out to those who violate the law. For the most serious of crimes and the most serious of offenders, thirty-eight states and the federal government have capital punishment as an option. A decision to punish an offender by taking their life is not made by the judge: the Supreme Court has ruled that to meet constitutional standards a "death jury" must make the decision. Once decided, however, the responsibility to carry out the judicial order of capital punishment falls to the correctional system.

The placement, management, treatment, and release of the convicted offender is the responsibility of the correctional staff.[18] The sentencing judge has no authority over how the sentence is carried out once the offender enters the correctional system. For much of this century, most states and the federal system have given substantial discretion to correction officials to determine the length of time a prisoner actually served within the system. Offenders were required to serve a minimum portion of their sentence and then it was up to the decision-making by the wardens, treatment personnel, social workers, or parole boards to determine where they served and when they were released and under what kind of restrictions or conditions.[19]

For less serious offenders and for first-time offenders, correctional supervision takes place within the community.[20] Probation involves the monitoring of the offender while they remain living within the community. **Probation** almost always carries with it an array of conditions or requirements that must be met by the offender. **Parole** authorities supervise offenders within the community after they have served a portion of their sentence in jail. Standard conditions for both probation and parole include refraining from further illegal conduct, refraining from associating with known criminals, refraining from the consumption of alcohol and regular reporting to the probation officer. It is also common for the condition of probation to include a requirement that the offender attend school, work, or treatment of some kind. It is increasingly common for drug screening to be a routine part of probation and parole supervision to verify that offenders are not using illegal substances.

MODELS OF THE CRIMINAL JUSTICE SYSTEM

To gain a perspective on the nature of the criminal justice system, scholars make use of metaphors that capture and convey important qualities of the system. A metaphor is a figure of speech or an image that describes a phenomenon by analogy or comparison. Metaphors help us to grasp certain realities of the system that are often difficult to comprehend or to even notice. In the sections which follow we will look at four metaphors or "models" which illustrate different but equally significant truths about the system: the criminal justice wedding cake, funnel, assembly line, and obstacle course.

Wedding Cake Model

Scholars have used the imagery of a wedding cake to illustrate an important feature of the criminal justice system.[21] Picture in your mind a glorious multi-tiered confection tall enough to feed five hundred guests. The classic wedding cake comes in several tiers of differing proportions. At the bottom is the largest layer;

PROBATION
a criminal sentence which allows offenders to reside within the community.

PAROLE
conditional release and supervision within the community as part of a criminal sentence.

and each layer after that is substantially smaller with the smallest one crowned with a miniature bride and groom and the most elaborate decorations at the top.

The wedding cake metaphor reminds us that only a few cases are highly visible in the criminal justice system. The Terence Garner case was truly an "ordinary" crime: even the local newspaper was not interested in covering it. The irony of this particular case is that without the insistence by Judge Jenkins that reporters write about it no one beyond his own family and the few professionals who tried to help him prove his innocence would have known anything about this case. It is almost certain that without the media spotlight, Terence Garner would be sitting in a prison cell today instead of a college classroom.

Most cases we follow avidly on the evening news are the exceptions and not the rule. They are sensational because the crime is particularly horrific, the defendants are very wealthy or atypical in some way, or the victims in the case are unusually sympathetic. If the case involves celebrities, even if the charges are mundane, like a drunk driving or simple assault, the process naturally occurs within the limelight. Often these celebrated cases involve lengthy trials with a great deal of media coverage from which best-selling books are written with the names of those involved recorded for posterity.

The Salem witch trials and our next case, the Scottsboro trials, are examples of two important cases from the top of the wedding cake. Today we continue to study these cases to understand the processes of law and justice revealed by those significant episodes in our nation's history. Horrific murder cases involving children, or cases of rape or murder that implicate socially prominent individuals such as the trial of O.J. Simpson (chapter 11), are typical "wedding cake" events. The processing of these cases is complicated, expensive, drawn-out affairs, which does not reflect the ordinary course of events in the criminal justice system. These cases sometimes have lasting impacts on the law and on the conception of due process and equal justice. But we should take care to recognize that the Salem witch trials and the Scottsboro trials were not the typical cases of their era; the **wedding cake model** reminds us that the media, the public, and policymakers rarely pay attention to less sensational cases.

Below the celebrated few are the still relatively rare serious **felony** cases such as rape, murder, and armed robbery. A felony is a broad term which encompasses all offenses serious enough to be punishable by a period of time exceeding one year in state or federal prison. And far more numerous than murder and rape are the much more frequent "ordinary felonies" such as burglaries and auto-thefts where a weapon was not used and no one was threatened or injured, which make up the third tier of the wedding cake.

Most numerous of all, however, are the thousands of **misdemeanors**, petty larcenies, public drunkenness, driving under the influence, vagrancy, and other minor crimes, processed daily through the system, which make up the bottom layer of the wedding cake. The term "misdemeanor" refers to less serious offenses

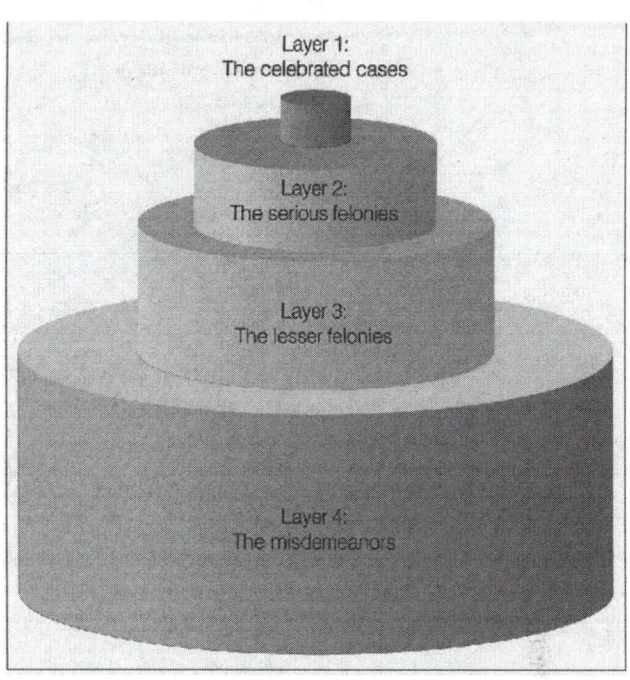

Layer 1:
The celebrated cases

Layer 2:
The serious felonies

Layer 3:
The lesser felonies

Layer 4:
The misdemeanors

The wedding cake model reminds us that the media tends to focus only on celebrated and exceptional cases in the criminal justice system.

WEDDING CAKE MODEL
a model of the justice process which describes the public's and media focus on a few extraordinary and exceptional crimes.

FELONY
an offense punishable by more than one year in state or federal prison.

MISDEMEANOR
a relatively minor offense punishable by fine or up to one year in jail.

500 Crimes Reported
↓
100 Arrests Are Made
↓
65 Cases Considered
For Prosecution
↓
35 Cases Accepted
For Prosecution
↓
30 Indictments Filed
↓
23 Plead Guilty
4 Guilty at Trial
3 Acquitted
↓
27 Sentenced
↓
18 To Prison
9 To Probation

The justice funnel illustrates the impact of discretionary decision-making by justice professionals as defendants are processed through the system.

which are punishable by less than one year or by fines. These stories are never reported in the media for us to read about at all. For most members of the public, the lower layers of the criminal justice wedding cake are completely invisible.

Justice Funnel

The imagery of the wedding cake is like a pyramid with the smallest point at the top and the widest layer at the bottom. The image represents a reality about the system that is often forgotten by the public: namely, that the overwhelming vast majority of criminal incidents are the least serious of offenses despite what we see depicted in the media. The image of the justice funnel illustrates another important reality about the criminal justice system and how it functions. Turn the wedding cake upside down and you have the shape of a funnel with the widest layer at the top and the smallest at the bottom.

The funnel image demonstrates a different but equally important reality about the criminal justice system: the impact of discretionary decision-making by human beings inside and outside the system. The criminal justice system operates as a kind of filtering process: at every stage in the process, some defendants are processed out of the system while others are retained and sent forward to the next stage.

THE JUSTICE FUNNEL a model of the justice process which depicts the impact of discretionary decision-making by criminal justice personnel as they sort and filter defendants through the five stages.

Picture a giant funnel. At the wide opening of the funnel are the millions of crimes that are reported to the police. It is important to recall that only a portion of all the crime that occurs within society is ever reported to the system at all and police will only bring forward for prosecution a portion of those who are arrested. Once formal criminal justice processing begins, the process of attrition continues through later states of justice decision-making. In 2002, for every hundred felony arrests in large urban counties only sixty-five cases were carried forward for prosecution.[22] Of these sixty-five cases, most are convicted through plea bargains, with only a tiny fraction of cases, about three, actually going to trial. The remaining defendants either "dropped out" of the system at the prosecutorial screening stage or were dismissed by the courts.

Assembly Line versus Obstacle Course Models of Justice

These next two metaphors—the image of the system as an assembly line processing criminal defendants the same way that the Ford plant manufactures shiny new cars and the counter-image of an obstacle course full of dead ends, false doors, high walls, and trap floors—offer us two different perspectives on the flow of people through the criminal justice system. Herbert Packer claims there are two competing "models" of the system related to the values of crime control, on the one hand, and the values of due process, on the other.[23]

The crime control agenda wants the criminal justice system to operate as speedily as possible. The quicker the better: when cases are efficiently processed, the net result is more effective crime control since criminals will get the punishment they deserve. Criminals will be less likely to fall through the cracks or get off on technicalities and the end result will be a better, more effective system of crime control. The image is of the production process in a modern industrial factory. The faster the raw material moves along that conveyor belt the better is the system of justice. The ideal is to have defendants processed in an as efficient manner as possible. The **assembly line model** of justice also implies **standardization**. Each person is treated the same through routine processes that are applied regardless of individual circumstances.

The contrasting image of the system that derives from the values of due process imagines the justice process to operate more like the obstacle course designed by army boot camps to challenge raw recruits. At every point along the way, there are blind alleys that dead end, slippery high walls that must be scaled, and sudden chutes which whisk a person out of the system. In this model, processing a criminal defendant through the system requires enormous effort in order to surmount the obstacles intentionally designed to slow down the wheels of justice. By making the state bear the burden of proof and therefore needing to struggle to prosecute a citizen, the end result is a system that protects the truly innocent of wrongful conviction.

This model also implies **individualization** rather than standardization: each person is treated as unique and the specific facts of their case are considered in the fullness of their complexity.

These four models express different perspectives on the justice system. The wedding cake model reminds us that the general public is aware of only the "tip" of the process and that the everyday workings of the justice system may appear quite different to us if we carry only the image of the celebrated few show trials in our mind. The "cattle car" justice processing in the lower courts would surprise

ASSEMBLY LINE MODEL
a model of the justice process which depicts the system processing cases as swiftly and efficiently as possible in a standard manner.

OBSTACLE COURSE MODEL
a model of the justice process which depicts the system as complex and convoluted deliberately difficult to negotiate in order to protect due process rights of the accused.

STANDARDIZATION
the value that each case be treated according to the same rules regardless of individual circumstances.

INDIVIDUALIZATION
the value that each case be treated on the basis of its own unique and specific facts.

many of us who imagine an impassioned courtroom debate for every legal conviction! The "funnel" metaphor tells us a great deal about the everyday working of the system: there are many pathways through the system and, more importantly, backstage decision-making which takes place at many junctures. Justice does not only happen in the dramatic display of the courtroom but also happens in the multitude of everyday decisions on the street, in the station house, in the cramped office, over lunch, in the hall, and even in the bathroom!

Both the "assembly line" image and the "obstacle course" offer two different ways to think about this process. Should the justice system operate quickly and impose standard procedures as much as possible? Should we strive to make the system look like an assembly line? Or is the image provided by the due process perspective a better ideal for the justice process? Do we want each case to be examined on its individual merits and unique qualities? Do we want the wheels of justice to turn slowly and with difficulty so that we can ensure that we are protecting the rights of all our citizens?

THE DILEMMA OF DISCRETION

The "rule of law" expresses an ideal of the American justice system that all citizens will be treated equally before the law. The fair and equal application of the criminal codes of our system is a foundational value of our system. But no law can enforce itself. The public is usually aware only of the awesome responsibility of the judge in determining sentences but the reality is that all of the players in the system including citizens are making choices in the process of "doing justice." The police officer who witnesses a group of kids engaging in a minor act of vandalism must decide if he or she will arrest each of those teenagers or simply issue a warning to them and send them home to their parents. On a practical level, the state police cannot flag down every vehicle that violates the speed limits; instead, the police hope to deter illegal speeding by selectively stopping those who are most flagrant and by occasionally flagging down random vehicles. It is simply impossible for law enforcement or the system as a whole to act with equal force toward all violations of the law.

Nor would that seem to be just. Most Americans want justice personnel to "sort" out those who are minor, first time, and one-time-only offenders from those who are serious or chronic troublemakers. Americans value individualization by the assessment of each case on its own individual merits. There are significant differences between individuals who have committed even the terrible crime of first-degree murder.

Often-times the public assumes that the funnel effect illustrates a "flaw" in the system that needs correcting. But many cases "drop out" of the system precisely because criminal justice personnel are doing their job ethically and correctly. Not every person arrested by the police is guilty of a crime. Not every person charged with a crime is guilty. Nor is it the case that every person who violates the law should be arrested and formally prosecuted by the system. The use of discretion—judgment and wisdom—is an essential element of justice. We expect criminal justice personnel to make discretionary judgments guided by the boundaries set by the law.

On the other hand, we also recognize that giving discretion to criminal justice personnel opens up the possibility of abuse when justice personnel look the other way or use their power to unfairly harass or wrongfully prosecute and convict innocent citizens. The complaint that the justice system is a "just us" system through selective over-enforcement of the law against minority citizens is often the result of the abuse of discretion by law enforcement officers who may use the color of a person's skin as grounds for criminal suspicion. It is possible that criminal justice personnel view citizens of color as more dangerous and less law abiding and therefore are more likely to question them or pull them over for traffic violations. One of the greatest challenges in our system, often referred to as **the dilemma of discretion**, is the need to hold criminal justice system personnel accountable for their discretionary decisions and to institute oversight mechanisms that ensure abuse of discretionary power does not take place.[24]

POLITICS AND CRIME: THE ISSUE OF EXPRESSIVE JUSTICE

The connection between the crime and politics suggests that being "tough on crime" is an important criterion for political success. We have seen politicians from all sides of the political spectrum compete with one another to support tough policies to "express" their moral outrage at the injustice of crime. There is the reason Judge Jenkins wanted the media to cover the trial of Terence Garner: he wanted the public to "see" him pass a tough sentence against a dangerous offender. David Anderson refers to this as the **ideal of expressive justice**[25] in which the use of punishment to express outrage is more important than other ends of the justice system such as rehabilitation, cost, or even public safety. Expressive justice, according to Anderson, values the expression of vengeance over other goals of justice.

Much of the effort has aimed to reduce judicial discretion and parole discretion through passage of laws that require offenders to serve long sentences for their crimes. In California, two highly publicized vicious violent crimes led to the passage of statewide "three strikes and you're out" laws. Two grieving fathers who both lost daughters to violent murderers with long and violent criminal records spearheaded the political battle. The abduction and murder of twelve–year-old Polly Klaas from her own bedroom and the robbery shooting death of eighteen-year-old Kimber Reynolds as she walked out of a restaurant outraged the residents of the entire state of California. The new tough law mandated twenty-five years to life for a third conviction following two prior serious or violent felony convictions. Voters responded to the emotional outrage of these fathers, politicians championed their cause, and the law passed by a landslide in a general election.

But is this the best way to craft the policies that will govern our criminal justice system? In California, the majority of offenders prosecuted as "habitual offenders" do not fit the description of the violent men who murdered Polly and Kimber. Many have committed robberies or drug crimes, both of which are serious offenses but hardly justify lifelong incarceration to protect the public. Is this the best policy for the people of California? Few politicians have been willing to risk their political careers to even pose these questions for public debate.

In recent years bipartisan support has emerged in Congress to reduce the prison population by diverting nonviolent drug offenders as well as youthful offenders to alternatives to incarceration. This shift in attitude among lawmakers is in response to a growing recognition of the high cost of mass incarceration to the taxpayer and to the local community. Increasingly politicians can be heard

THE DILEMMA OF DISCRETION
discretionary decision-making is both essential for justice and creates the possibilities for discrimination and bias in the justice process.

IDEAL OF EXPRESSIVE JUSTICE
the use of heavy and harsh punishments to express moral outrage at the injustice of crime.

rejecting being "tough" on crime in favor of being "smart" on crime by embracing evidence-based alternatives to imprisonment.

The media plays a key role in demanding for vengeance because the media itself does not provide an accurate image of crime in American society. As we will see in the chapters ahead, the image of crime in our news and entertainment media is very different from the reality of crime. What the public fears is often shaped by a mythology of crime generated by the mass media looking to boost their ratings. The media ignores many crimes, and many kinds of criminals, and the public view of safety reflects a distorted understanding of the real risks of criminal conduct.

The tidal wave demanding "expressive justice" also reflects a long-standing neglect within the criminal justice system of the needs and interests of crime victims. Alice Wise was not offered any counseling or therapy by the justice system: she was left on her own to deal with the aftermath of the crime that robbed her of her sense of security and well-being. Often victims are offered only retribution toward the offender, which may or may not help them recover from the trauma of crime. The role of victims in the push for tougher laws may be the result of a system that has allocated resources to the prosecuting offenders while failing to attend to the needs of victims. In later chapters we will also look at the changing role of the victim within the justice process.

---

five stages of the criminal justice system (p. 32) entry, pretrial and investigation; adjudication, sentencing, corrections.

selective enforcement of the law (p. 33) when criminal justice personnel enforce some laws and not others or enforce them in some situations and not in other situations.

discretion (p. 33) the authority to choose between alternative actions.

founding decision (p. 34) a decision made by police that a particular incident should be treated as a crime (founded) or not treated as a crime (unfounded).

arrest (p. 34) the action of taking a person into custody for the purpose of charging them with a crime.

warrant (p. 34) a writ issued by a judicial officer ordering law enforcement to perform a specific action such as a search or an arrest.

initial appearance (p. 36) the first court processing stage after arrest in which the accused is brought before a judge or magistrate to hear the formal charges.

grand jury (p. 36) a group of citizens, usually 23, assembled to determine whether sufficient evidence exists to support the prosecution of the accused.

arraignment (p. 36) a hearing before the court in which the defendant is formally informed of the charges and is required to enter a plea.

pretrial phase (p. 36) second stage of criminal justice processing where numerous decisions about the trial procedure are adjudicated by the lower court.

bail (p. 36) money or other security placed in custody of the court in order to insure the return of a defendant to stand trial.

release on recognizance (p. 36) a nonfinancial release in which the accused promises to appear in court at the required date.

adjudication (p. 36) the process whereby the court arrives at a decision regarding a particular case.

jury trial (p. 36) evidence is presented to a panel of citizens who are required to determine the defendant's guilt or innocence of the charges.

bench trial (p. 37) court proceedings in which a judge hears the evidence and determines guilt or innocence.

conviction (p. 37) the judgment of a court based on the verdict of a jury or judicial officer that the defendant is guilty of the offense charged.

probation (p. 38) a criminal sentence which allows offenders to reside within the community.

parole (p. 38)   conditional release and supervision within the community as part of a criminal sentence.

wedding cake model (p. 39)   a model of the justice process which describes the public's and media focus on a few extraordinary and exceptional crimes.

felony (p. 39)   an offense punishable by more than one year in state or federal prison.

misdemeanor (p. 39)   a relatively minor offense punishable by fine or up to one year in jail.

the justice funnel (p. 40)   a model of the justice process which depicts the impact of discretionary decision-making by criminal justice personnel as they sort and filter defendants through the five stages.

assembly line model (p. 41)   a model of the justice process which depicts the system processing cases as swiftly and efficiently as possible in a standard manner.

obstacle course model (p. 41)   a model of the justice process which depicts the system as complex and convoluted deliberately difficult to negotiate in order to protect due process rights of the accused.

standardization (p. 41)   the value that each case be treated according to the same rules regardless of individual circumstances.

individualization (p. 41)   the value that each case be treated on the basis of its own unique and specific facts.

the dilemma of discretion (p. 42)   discretionary decision-making is both essential for justice and creates the possibilities for discrimination and bias in the justice process.

ideal of expressive justice (p. 43)   the use of heavy and harsh punishments to express moral outrage at the injustice of crime.

REVIEW AND STUDY QUESTIONS

1. Identify the five stages of the criminal justice system.
2. Describe the discretionary decisions made by justice professionals at each stage of the justice process.
3. Describe the role of the citizen in the justice process.
4. Define the term "selective enforcement of the law." Why is selective enforcement of the law inevitable? Why is selective enforcement of the law desirable?
5. Describe the wedding cake model of the justice system. Identify a typical case for each "tier" of the wedding cake. What feature of the justice system is represented by this model?
6. Describe the justice funnel and how it operates. What key feature of the justice system is captured through the use of the "funnel" metaphor?
7. Contrast and compare the "assembly line model" with the "obstacle course model." What values does each of these models represent?
8. What is the dilemma of discretion? What challenges does this dilemma pose for the justice system and our wider society?
9. What is the role of the media in the justice process?
10. What is the ideal of expressive justice? How does it impact the politics of crime control?

CHECK IT OUT

Websites:

Justice Information Center, https://www.ncjrs.gov Visit this JIC site provided by the National Criminal Justice Reference Service to get information about all phases of the criminal justice system: victims, crime prevention, law enforcement, courts, corrections, and criminal justice statistics.

Bureau of Justice Statistics: Criminal Justice System Flowchart, https://www.bjs.gov/content/largechart.cfm

Videos:

Frontline: An Ordinary Crime—See the documentary made by award-winning filmmaker Ofra Bikel which helped to free Terence Garner from a wrongful conviction. Check out the PBS web site to read interviews and transcripts with many of the key people in the case. Available at: http://www.pbs.org/wgbh/pages/frontline/shows/ordinary/

The Making of the 'Three Strikes' Laws, New York Times, Retro Report. This report takes you to the story behind the passage of the three-strikes laws to reveal the tragic story of two fathers' quest for justice and the complex and thorny process through which criminal justice policy is debated, promoted, and championed within the media-saturated world of high-stakes politics. Available at: https://www.nytimes.com/video/us/100000002579045/the-making-of-the-three-strikes-laws.html

NOTES

[1] Bureau of Justice Statistics, *Report to the Nation on Crime and Justice* (Washington, DC: U.S. Department of Justice, 1998), 8–9.

[2] Michael Gottfredson and Donald Gottfredson, *Decision Making in Criminal Justice: Toward the Rational Exercise of Discretion* (New York: Plenum, 1988).

[3] Lloyd E. Ohlin and Frank J. Remington, *Discretion in Criminal Justice: The Tension Between Individualization and Uniformity* (Albany: State University of New York Press, 1993).

[4] M. Greenberg and R. Ruback, "Elements of Crime Victim Decision Making," *Victimology* 10 (1984), 600–616.

[5] "Keep Talking: A Program Fosters Trust Between Youth and Police," *Pittsburg Post-Gazette* (2012) accessed September 26, 2012.

[6] Lloyd E. Ohlin, "Surveying Discretion by Criminal Justice Decision Makers," in *Discretion in Criminal Justice: The Tension Between Individualization and Standardization*, ed. Loyd E. Ohlin and Frank J. Remington (Albany: Suny Press, 1993); Donald J. Black, *Manner and Customs of Police* (New York: Academic Press, 1980).

[7] Laurie Weber Brooks, "Police Discretionary Behavior: A Study of Style," in *Critical Issues in Policing: Contemporary Readings*, ed. Roger G. Dunham and Geoffrey P. Alport (Propsect Heights, IL: Waveland, 1993), 140–164.

[8] Joseph Goldstein, "Police Discretion Not to Invoke the Criminal Process: Low-Visibility Decisions in the Administration of Justice," *Yale Law Journal* 69 (1960).

[9] George F. Cole, "The Decision to Prosecute," *Law and Society Review* 4 (1970), 331–343.

[10] William McDonald, "The Prosecutor's Domain," in *The Prosecutor*, ed. W. McDonald (Beverly Hills, CA: Sage, 1979), 15–52.

[11] Frank Miller, *Prosecution: The Decision to Charge a Suspect with a Crime* (Boston: Little Brown, 1970).

[12] Robert Satter, *Doing Justice: A Trial Judge at Work* (New York: Simon and Schuster, 1990).

[13] Huey Chen, "Dropping In and Dropping Out: Judicial Decision-making in the Disposition of Felony Arrests," *Journal of Criminal Justice* 19 (1991), 1–17; Robert O. Dawson, *Sentencing: The Decision as to Type, Length and Conditions of Sentence* (Boston: Little Brown, 1969).

[14] Andrew von Hirsch and Kathleen Hanrahan, "Determinate Penalty Systems in America: An Overview," *Crime and Delinquency* 27 (1981), 289–316.

[15] Michael Tonry, "The Politics and Processes of Sentencing Commissions," *Crime and Delinquency* 37 (1991), 307–329.

[16] Anthony Walsh, "The Role of the Probation Officer in the Sentencing Process: Independent Professional or Judicial Hack?," *Criminal Justice and Behavior* 12 (1985), 289–303.

[17] Sandra Shane-DuBow, Alice P. Brown and Erik Olsen, *Sentencing Reform in the United States: History, Content and Effect* (Washington, DC: National Institute of Justice, 1985).

[18] Doris Layton MacKenzie and Robert A. Buchanan, "The Process of Classification in Prisons: A Descriptive Study of Staff use of the System," *Journal of Crime and Justice* 13 (1990), 1–26.

[19] Edna Erez, "Dangerous Men, Evil women: Gender and Parole Decision-making," *Justice Quarterly* 9 (1992), 105–126.

[20] Harry E. Allen, Chris W. Eskridge, Edward J. Latesa and Gennaro F. Vito, *Probation and Parole in America* (New York: Free Press, 1985).

[21] Samuel Walker, *Sense and Nonsense about Crime* (Monterey, California: Brooks/Cole, 1985).

[22] Thomas H. Cohen and Brian Reeves, *Felony Defendants in Large Urban Counties, 2002* Department of Justice, Bureau of Justice Statistics (Washington, DC: U.S. Department of Justice, 2006).

[23] Herbert Packer, *The Limits of the Criminal Sanction* (Palo Alto: Stanford University Press, 1968).

[24] Samuel Walker, *Taming the System: The Control of Discretion in Criminal Justice, 1950–1990* (New York: Oxford University Press, 1993).

[25] David Anderson, *Crime and the Politics of Hysteria: How the Willie Horton Story Changed American Justice* (New York: Random House), 14.

In this chapter we explore the goal of the American justice system—equal justice for all. We begin with a case that examines the role of race in the justice process, and illustrates the persistent barriers faced by people of color and women within the justice process. The chapter explains the relationships between state and federal systems, and the role of the Constitution and Supreme Court.

LEARNING OBJECTIVES

After reading this chapter you should be able to:

- Explain the difference between rights that exist de jure and those which exist de facto.
- Describe why the Constitution has been referred to as "Sleeping Beauty."
- Show how the Scottsboro case is an illustration of the "awakening of sleeping beauty."
- Explain the legacy of under-protection and over-enforcement of the law for African Americans.
- Describe the pattern of under-enforcement of the law in the area of male violence against women.
- Identify at least two significant reforms in the criminalization of male violence.
- Present the historical changes to the laws of rape and intimate violence.
- Explain the response of the police and courts to violence against women.
- Describe the role of gender in relation to both crime and victimization.

Case #3: The Scottsboro Trials

Haywood Patterson in the courtroom.

The date was March 25, 1931, the first spring of the deepening economic crisis that came to be known as the Great Depression. The nation's railroads were magnets for drifters, young and old, men and women, black and white, roaming in search of work, shorter breadlines, or simply a place to sleep. A Southern Railroad train heading west through northern Alabama was on its way to Memphis, Tennessee. A group of black youth met up with a band of white boys who challenged their right to be on the train. The argument led to rock throwing and a fistfight in which the losers, the white boys, were thrown from the train at one of its many stopping points. For the black youth still on the train, the departure of the angry boys was the end of the incident. The train chugged on for another forty miles and the boys soon forgot about the scuffle.

As the train rolled into the sleepy station of Paint Rock, a strangely large crowd was assembled at the tiny platform. The sheriff of Jackson County had deputized every male who owned a gun with orders to capture all the Negroes on the incoming train. Dozens of white men armed with pistols, rifles, and shotguns were waiting to meet the train. Standing among them were the white boys who had been thrown from the train. As the black boys emerged from the train, they were immediately arrested by the posse. Nine boys ranging in age from thirteen to nineteen were bound together by a plow line and told they were being charged with assault and attempted murder. They were herded onto an open flatbed truck and transported to a jail in Scottsboro, Alabama, twenty-one miles away.

When they arrived at the jail, the boys were told that the charges were even more serious than assault and attempted murder. Two white women had been riding the train that day and as they got off at the Paint Rock station, they claimed that they had been raped by the boys after the fight. The two women were dressed in men's overalls and had been watching the scene from the sidelines. After the boys were bound and tied into the open truck, one of the women came forward and told the sheriff she and her friend had been raped by the men. The sheriff took the women to the jail and there the two women, Victoria Price and Ruby Bates, identified each of the nine boys as the sheriff lined them up outside their cells in the jail.

For black men in the Deep South in the 1930s, the news that they had been accused of raping a white woman was devastating. An accusation of rape by a white woman against a black man carried with it an almost certain death sentence. As one boy later acknowledged, "I knew if a white woman accused a black man of rape, he was as good as dead."[1] In the world of "he said, she said," the word of a white woman was always accepted before that of a black man and the act of sexual relations between a black male and a white woman was almost always viewed as a form of rape since in the words of a Mississippi editor, no white woman, no matter how depraved or destitute, would ever willingly "bestow her favors on a black man."[2]

As the boys huddled in the cells, they could hear the restless anger from the several hundred white men and boys gathered outside the jailhouse clamoring for traditional southern justice. Lynching was a potent and terrible tool of southern-style "justice." In the decades following the Civil War, white Southerners resisted the idea of formal equality for blacks by exercising a form of terror whose primary tools were the rope and the burning cross. Most vulnerable to vigilantism were blacks who dared to be "familiar" with white woman. Although blacks were lynched for a variety of alleged offenses, the majority concerned accusations of rape against white woman.

Lynching was perceived by many white Southerners, including members of law enforcement, governors, newspaper editors, and other respectable citizens, as a legitimate form of community justice against a serious threat to the social order. They did not trust the State to exact justice and believed that honor demanded direct action on the part of the wronged family to exact revenge through lynching.

By the early 1930s, lynching had slowed to a trickle: fewer than ten lynching victims were reported per year compared to a horrifying rate of more than one hundred black victims per year in the post–Civil War years.[3] There were now many white citizens in the South who disapproved of lynching. They believed that the South should demonstrate its commitment to the rule of law and prohibit this form of private justice. They believed that lynching generated more lawlessness and violence: even in the case of rape, they believed lynching still undermined the rule of law and order.

Luckily for the nine boys held in the jail, those who opposed lynching as a response to violent crime included the county sheriff and the governor of the state of Alabama. By late afternoon a very large crowd had gathered outside the jail; by evening they had cut the wires on the deputy's cars to prevent them from removing the boys to a more secure jail. The sheriff called the governor who ordered the National Guard, which arrived at 11 p.m., with orders to disperse the crowd and guarantee that law, not vigilante justice, would have the final word in this case.

The First Trials

Justice by law came fast and furious. On March 30, all nine boys were indicted for rape by a Jackson County grand jury. One week later, a mere twelve days after their initial arrest, the boys went to trial. The boys were represented, first, by an attorney who arrived in the courtroom stone drunk at 9 a.m. Although he had been paid by black church leaders to represent the boys, the white drunk attorney told the judge he was not really their counsel but only available to offer advice. He admitted that he had not talked to the boys or prepared a case in their defense. The judge then appointed another attorney from the crowd assembled, a local attorney who reluctantly agreed to come forward. Together the two attorneys consulted briefly with the boys and with no investigation or preparation, the trials began.

The four trials lasted only four days, and by April 9 four separate juries had convicted and sentenced eight of the boys to die by electric chair. A mistrial was declared in the trial of the ninth, Roy Wright, who was only thirteen years old, because the jury divided over whether he should be sentenced to death or to life imprisonment. The prosecution had asked for a life sentence because of his age but eleven of the jurors insisted on the electric chair for him as well as the rest and the judge declared a mistrial.

The judge, prosecution, defense attorneys, and jury were all white males. No black man had ever served on an Alabama jury. No women or blacks were even permitted in the courtroom as observers. The packed courtroom consisted of only white men over the age of twenty-one. When the verdict was announced, Haywood Patterson, one of the boys, described the courtroom as "one big white smiling face."[4] When the first verdict came down there was applause and cheers inside the courtroom and a band struck up a tune to the joyous shouts of the enormous crowd of nearly 10,000 gathered outside.

During the trials, the main witnesses were the two women, Ruby Bates and Victoria Price, who described their ordeal in vivid detail. They pointed at the boys and told which one did what to whom and when. They claimed that the boys told them that they were going "to take us north and make us their women or kill us." Others took the stand and testified seeing the boys with the women on the train. Medical testimony confirmed that both women had had intercourse during the time in question although there were no physical signs of beating or abuse. Called to the witness stand during these trials, some of the boys began to accuse one another of doing the crime affirming widespread belief in their guilt. Six denied all knowledge of doing the crime or seeing others do it, but three of them, Norris, Patterson, and Wright, testified that they had seen others commit the alleged acts.

Years later, in an interview, Roy Wright, only thirteen, revealed what had taken place before he testified before the court.

I was sitting in a chair in front of the judge and one of those girls was testifying. One of the deputy sheriffs leaned over to me and asked me if I was going to turn State's evidence, and I said no, because I didn't know anything about this case. Then the trial stopped awhile and the deputy sheriff beckoned to me to come out into another room—the room back of the place where the judge was sitting—and I went. They whipped me and it seemed like they were going to kill me. All the time they kept saying "Now will you tell?" and finally it seemed like I couldn't stand it no more and I said yes. Then I went back into the courtroom and they put me up on the chair in front of the judge and began asking a lot of questions and I said I had seen Charlie Weems and Clarence Norris with the white girls.[5]

Clarence Norris too had been beaten on the night of the first day of the trials. Not surprisingly he turned state's evidence the very next day and testified against the others.

In less than two weeks after being charged with the crime, eight of the nine boys had been tried, convicted, and sentenced to die with an execution date set for less than six months away. The newspapers were full of praise for the halls of justice in the South. They declared "The people of Jackson County have shown to the world that they believe in Justice, regardless of color. . . . Our courts have shown the world that they believe in swift and undelayed justice being meted out." According to another newspaper, the defendants received "as fair a trial as they could have gotten in any court in the world."[6]

A Legal Lynching?

The boys had been spared a lynching by the angry mob but in the eyes of many outside observers, particularly in the North, the trial itself, and the death sentence that followed, was a lynching with a legal face. What was viewed in the South as a success for due process was perceived as a mockery of justice by the rest of the world. Far from an impartial examination of the evidence demanded by the Bill of Rights, the northern newspapers charged racism and abuse. In the wake of the trial, the governor of Alabama, mayor of Scottsboro, and southern newspapers were flooded with mail from around the world demanding the verdict be overturned on appeal. Within days of the verdict, attorneys from the north paid for by the NCCAP, ACLU, and the International Communist Party were

mobilized to come to the boys' assistance. For many in the North, this case symbolized the truth about southern justice, which denied due process to its black citizens despite the nearly sixty years since the passage of the Fourteenth Amendment.

By late spring, these northern attorneys had won a stay of execution for the boys pending appeal to the Alabama Supreme Court. The lawyers based their appeal on the grounds of lack of adequate counsel for the boys, the exclusion of blacks from the jury in Alabama, and the hordes of spectators and press coverage of the case which precluded the possibility of a fair trial. When the Alabama Supreme Court upheld the verdict claiming that the requirements of due process had been met and the boys had had a fair trial, protests were held as far away as Switzerland, France, Germany, and Spain. The attorneys filed and received a second stay of execution pending appeal to the U.S. Supreme Court. The highest court in the land agreed to hear the case in May of 1932.

The First Appeal: *Powell v. Alabama*

On November 7, 1932, by a vote of seven to two, the U.S. Supreme Court overturned the conviction of the first four trials in the famous decision known as *Powell v. Alabama* remanding the cases back to the lower courts for new trials. This was the first time in our nation's history that the Supreme Court set aside a state court's criminal conviction. The ruling was based on the argument that the boys had not been afforded adequate counsel and therefore had been denied due process under the Fourteenth Amendment.

Justice George Sutherland in the majority opinion ruled that a trial without a lawyer or real legal counsel could hardly be considered fair and that the "failure of the trial court to give them reasonable time and opportunity to secure counsel was a clear denial of due process." The boys had been arraigned immediately after the return of the indictments, and at their arraignment the judge did not ask them if they had counsel or if they wished to have counsel appointed. They were given no opportunity to contact their parents or anyone else who might come to their aid. Nor did the presiding judge appoint a specific person to represent them. Instead the judge vaguely appointed the entire defense bar of the small town, seven defense attorneys. According to Sutherland, this was equivalent to assigning no one since no one was obligated to prepare a defense. In fact, it was only moments before the first trial began that the judge specifically appointed an individual attorney to represent the boys.

The majority of the Supreme Court concluded that to accept these guilty verdicts and execute these young men on the basis of this kind of legal process would be equivalent to a legal lynching. Execution without a retrial, according to the Supreme Court, would be judicial murder. The justices ordered a new trial for the boys.

The Second Trial

Samuel Leibowitz was a famous criminal defense lawyer from New York City. He believed his job was to defend anyone who proclaimed their innocence and it was the job of the jury and the judge to determine who was really guilty. His mission was to uphold the presumption of innocence by giving a spirited and zealous defense of his client in a court of law. He agreed to represent the boys pro bono (for free) in the new trial which began March 27, 1933.

During the months leading up to the trial, northern investigators came down and began asking questions, interviewing witnesses, and preparing evidence to defend the boys, a process which had not taken place in the first trial. Almost immediately, the story that came out began to look very different from the one told by the two women in the courtroom. Far from the "flower of southern womanhood" both of these young women were notorious prostitutes, who were raised in poor mill towns where blacks and whites intermingled freely. Both women resided in Chattanooga and had worked in a house of prostitution run by blacks. Both were known to solicit white and black men despite the laws that prohibited this conduct. Ruby Bates had even once been arrested on charges of hugging a black man in public.

Many in the North began to believe that the women claimed to be "raped" to avoid the humiliation or even prosecution when the train appeared in Painted Rock station. A witness came forward testifying that he had seen the women try to sneak away from the posse when they first got off the train in Paint Rock station. They made their accusation twenty minutes after being apprehended by the posse; neither woman had torn clothing or seemed physically or emotionally distraught. White women who solicited sex from black men were subject to the worst kind of social condemnation and even criminal prosecution; as poor white trash, Price and Bates knew they might be thrown in a

jail cell for being hobos and vagrants. They were used to running from the law. For Price and Bates, the trials were the first time they were treated as "virtuous" women in their entire lives.

Samuel Leibowitz began his defense with a pretrial motion that challenged the indictments because they had been handed down by a grand jury of Jackson County which excluded black citizens from serving on juries. If the indictments themselves were a violation of the due process, the whole case might simply be dismissed. The prosecution countered the charge by bringing officials from the election commission to testify that there were no specific laws or rules that excluded black citizens from serving on the jury. Rather blacks were not selected because they lacked the education and character and intelligence to serve on a jury. Despite the fact that there were lawyers, doctors, preachers, and school teachers among the possible black candidates within the county, white officials insisted that the black citizens lack sufficient qualifications to serve on a jury, testifying in court that no Negro in the county had the required sound judgment and "they will nearly all steal."[7] The motion to overturn the indictments was denied by Judge Horton. Jury selection took place and again there were no blacks on the jury because there were no blacks on the jury pool in the county. This fact would serve as the basis for a later appeal to the U.S. Supreme Court.

The star witness for the prosecution, Victoria Price, took the stand to tell her story in a court of law for the fifth time. During the initial trials, the hapless defense attorneys had attempted to raise questions about the character of Victoria Price and Ruby Bates by asking them about their profession and about their previous liaisons with men. However the prosecution objected to every question and these objections were sustained by the judge every time. The court record also showed that the testimony of the doctor was vague and confused but that the defense was so inadequate no objections were raised at the time.

This time star witness Price faced an experienced defense attorney ready and able to challenge the inconsistencies in her story. Like any good defense attorney, Leibowitz had entered the courtroom prepared with investigations into the facts; he had interviewed and subpoenaed witnesses who testified she had not been where she said she was; witnesses testified they had seen her the previous night with men in hobo camp and had seen her board the train in the company of two white men. These two white men were found and they testified that they had been with Price and Bates on the train the night before and had had sexual relations with the women that night.

Leibowitz also called many of the original witnesses and challenged their testimony as to what they had seen forcing them to admit that they had not actually seen the boys with the two girls, that they might have been mistaken in what they saw or were not able to fully see what they claimed to have seen. Finally, he called the boys themselves and allowed them to testify. He pointed out to the jury that at least one of them had been so physically disabled that day he could barely walk, let alone take part in a fight and ravage two women. Others testified that they had fought with the boys but that was all that had happened. None said they had even seen the woman until they arrived at the train station swarming with the posse.

But the most amazing and shocking testimony came from Ruby Bates. At the final moments of the trial, Leibowitz shocked the courtroom by calling her up as a witness for the defense. In an astounding fifteen minutes, Ruby Bates corroborated the testimony of the two white men and completely recanted her earlier testimony. The boys had not raped, touched, or even spoken to her or Victoria Price on that train ride. Victoria had told her to say that to avoid being arrested for vagrancy and crossing the state line with men. It had all been a big lie. To a stunned silence in the courtroom, the defense rested its case.

The prosecution fought back. They claimed that Bates was lying. Ruby Bates had changed her story so we knew she was a liar: she had lied before or she was lying now. Either way she was not to be believed. They said she had been bought with northern "Jew" money who were telling her what to say. The prosecutor claimed that Alabama justice was about to be sold with Jew money from New York. He accused Leibowitz of being a communist and out to undermine the system of law and order in the United States.

The jury returned a guilty verdict with death by electric chair for defendant Haywood Patterson. The jury chose to believe the testimony of Victoria Price over that of the witnesses for the defense. Charges of racism were countered with charges of northern communist influence and Jewish subversion. The attention from around the world in this case was unprecedented. A march on Washington was organized in which thousands of people showed up to see Ruby Bates arm in arm with the mothers of the nine boys

demanding equal justice in the southern courts. In the midst of all the tensions and protests, the courts put the other scheduled trials for the remaining boys on hold.

The defense attorneys made a motion for a new trial for Patterson claiming that they had been denied due process because of the publicity surrounding the trial and the accusations of anti-Semitism made during the trial. The judge from the trial, Judge Horton, agreed to consider the motion on the grounds that the finding of the jury was contrary to the evidence presented in court. Judge Horton cited precedents where a trial judge had overturned the guilty verdict of a jury on the grounds that the jury had been swayed by bias, passion, and prejudice. On examining the testimony given in court, Horton declared a mistrial, overturned the judgment of the jury and ordered yet a third trial for the defendant. Horton hoped that the prosecution would decide not to prosecute for a third trial and the infamous Scottsboro case would end there. Judge Horton was defeated in the next election by an angry southern public who objected to his view that the boys were not receiving a fair trial. The prosecution re-filed an indictment against Patterson and the trials resumed under a new judge, William Callahan, who would preside over the remaining trials for all nine boys.

Judge Callahan made no secret of his opinion that this was a case of northern outsiders interfering with the business of the southern courts. He made no secret of his belief that the boys were guilty as charged. He denied all defense motions for a change of venue. He ruled that evidence presented by the defense to show that the jury rolls had been tampered with to show the presence of blacks on the list was not to be admitted into the courtroom because it would reflect badly on the jury board. He did not allow Leibowitz during the trial to ask questions about Victoria Price's character or her activities prior to boarding the train. He repeatedly cut Leibowitz off during questioning and ruled exclusively in favor of the prosecution.

Not surprisingly, the jury found Patterson guilty for the third time and for the third time sentenced him to die in the electric chair. The other boys were all scheduled for new trials to be presided over by the same judge. Those trials took place quickly and with the same presiding judge came to the same harsh conclusion: guilty as charged with the electric chair as punishment.

The Second Appeal: *Norris v. Alabama*

Again, northern attorneys filed an appeal this time on the basis of the conviction of Clarence Norris. The attorneys appealed to the U.S. Supreme Court asking the court to review the record of the trial claiming that their constitutional right to a fair trial had not been observed. This time the argument they focused on was the widespread and systematic exclusion of black citizens from the jury pool. Leibowitz argued before the court that even though the formal law of Alabama did not exclude blacks from the jury pool, those who were administering the law did.

The Supreme Court agreed that there was ample evidence that blacks had been systematically excluded from the jury rolls and that local officials had forged the jury rolls to conceal this fact. In a unanimous opinion Chief Justice Hughes agreed with the defense position that Negroes had been systematically excluded from the jury rolls of the state of Alabama in violation of the equal protection clause of the Fourteenth Amendment. Even though there was no formal rule, it was evident that not one black man had ever been called to serve on a jury. The conviction of Norris was overturned, and his case was remanded back to Alabama for a new trial.

The Final Round

A new round of trials began for the boys. Most people in the North believed that the state of Alabama would finally give up trying to prosecute these boys especially since the Norris case required at least some representation by blacks on the grand jury and on the trial jury as well. But within seven months after the Supreme Court decision, the district attorney announced he would seek new indictments to be handed down by a new grand jury that included one lone black juror, the first ever to serve in the history of the state of Alabama.

The date is now January 21, 1936; the boys have been held in custody for five years. Haywood Patterson appears for his fourth trial with Victoria Price as the only witness against him. Again the jury found him guilty sentencing him, this time, to seventy-five years in prison instead of the electric chair. Over the next year, four of the remaining boys were also tried, convicted, and sentenced to long prison terms ranging from twenty years to ninety-nine years. Four of the boys who had served six and a half years in jail were freed because they had been so young at the time of the crime, or because they were in such poor health that it seemed pointless to continue to charge them with serious rape and assault charges. They were released on the condition that they never return to the state of Alabama again.

Eventually, the remaining imprisoned boys were given their freedom on parole after serving more than fifteen to twenty years on death row. Although the boys were tried and retried again, they never fully established their innocence although two managed to receive official pardons, twenty to forty five years after the accusation was first made.

Epilogue

The Scottsboro case was famous in its time as a symbol of southern injustice toward African Americans. For many, the repeated guilty verdicts despite the overwhelming evidence that the accusations were a fabrication was confirmation of the reality of the southern legal system in which black citizens were unable to receive a fair trial. For the rest of the world, the trial was a contest between the southern system of racial apartheid and the forces for equal rights. The lasting legacy of the case was the clear indication that the U.S. Supreme Court would seriously enforce the Fourteenth Amendment on the state courts. The Bill of Rights applies to all citizens in all proceedings with any level of government and the Supreme Court gave clear indication that it would overturn convictions if the states did not respect the due process rights of its citizens, black or white.

THINKING CRITICALLY ABOUT THIS CASE

1. What difference did the defense attorney make in the re-trials of the Scottsboro boys? Were these "fair" in your view? Why or why not?

2. The Roman statue of Justicia that often symbolizes the ideal of "justice for all" is a blindfolded goddess holding the scales of justice. Why is the goddess blindfolded? What is that blindfold intended to represent? Can our due process procedures create a system of "blindfolded" justice if the people who administer the laws are not blind to these differences?

3. Why, in your view, did the jury convict the Scottsboro defendants in the second trial despite the new evidence introduced by the competent defense counsel?

4. Do you believe that the outcome of the trials would have been different if there had been substantial representation by black Alabaman citizens in the jury pool? Why or why not?

5. Should the judge have granted a change of venue for this trial? If so, where should the case have been tried? Should it have been tried in the North? Why or why not?

6. After the Supreme Court overturned the original convictions, the district attorney chose to pursue a second series of trials. After the dismissal of the charges at the second trial by Judge Horton, the district attorney elected to pursue a third series of trials. Following the second Supreme Court decision in *Norris v. Alabama*, the prosecutor's office chose to indict the boys for a fourth trial.

A prosecuting attorney has the discretion to dismiss charges against an accused or to continue to pursue them guided by his or her own assessment of the "interests of justice." In your view, should the district attorney have continued to prosecute the boys? Why or why not?

7. What about Ruby Bates and Virginia Price? As prostitutes, do you believe they would have received similar treatment if the accused had been white instead of black? Why or why not?

REFERENCES

Case adapted from:

Lawrence Friedman, *Crime and Punishment in American History* (New York: Basic Books, 1993).

James Goodman, *Stories of Scottsboro* (New York: Vintage Books, 1994).

Michael Maher, "The Case of the Scottsboro Boys," in Lloyd Chiasson, ed., *The Press on Trial: Crimes and Trials as Media Events* (Westport: Greenwood Press, 1997).

The criminal justice system consists of federal, state, and local agencies involved in the control of crime. Together we refer to these agencies as the criminal justice system although the term "system" suggests that there is more coordination among these agencies than there really is. The criminal justice system is a loosely connected series of agencies involved in the definition of, enforcement of, and response to criminal conduct. Decisions made in each of these agencies affect decisions in another agency but there is no single criminal justice system nor is there a single chief or administrator capable of coordinating or streamlining the overall process of crime control.

The criminal justice system is, also, not a static, unchanging system. In fact, the structure of the justice system has changed dramatically over time, is changing today in significant and important ways, and will look quite different in the future. Part of the goal of this text is for students to appreciate some of the important transformations in the criminal justice system and understand some of the forces which are creating change within the system today. The criminal justice system of the seventeenth century has some features in common with our system today but is profoundly different as well. The nineteenth century brought many innovations such as the city and state police forces, the penitentiary and reformatories, systems of probation and parole, and the juvenile justice system. In recent decades, we have seen important changes to the system with the advent of community policing, SWAT teams, community courts and community corrections, drug courts, boot camps, electronic monitoring, day-reporting centers, substance abuse treatment centers, victim advocacy, restorative justice, and other types of innovations which are changing the justice system in our own time.

This chapter will examine one of the key forces for change in the administration of criminal justice: the struggle for equal justice for all members of our society. The Salem witch trials illustrate the fundamental importance of due process protections for individuals facing criminal prosecution by the state. The procedural elements of the criminal law that governs how the law is made and enforced are key to our understanding of justice in our society. We believe that all individuals should be treated fairly by the justice system and that neither the federal government nor the states "shall deprive any person of life, liberty, or property without due process of law." The fair and equal treatment of all persons by the same set of rules is fundamental to our concept of justice based on equal rights for all.

The Scottsboro trial was hailed as a great achievement for equal justice in our society but it took place almost one hundred and forty years after the Bill of

Lynching was used in the South to terrorize blacks and whites to comply with unwritten rules of white supremacy.

Rights was written! Although rights may exist **de jure**, in law, they do not necessarily exist **de facto**, in practice. Many changes within the justice system were the result of political and social action on the part of those within our society who recognized a painful gap between the ideal of equal justice and the reality of the justice process. We refer to this as a "struggle" because it has involved a long and protracted effort to change aspects of a system that denied equal justice to certain segments of society. It is also important for students to recognize that it is a struggle that is ongoing because the ideal of equal justice for all remains an elusive but worthy goal. In this chapter we will see that contemporary social movements, such as the Black Lives Matter (BLM) campaign, which advocates for reform in policing and the criminal justice system are part of a long line of citizens' efforts to create a legal system that truly provides justice for all.

THE STRUCTURE OF THE CRIMINAL JUSTICE SYSTEM

To understand the social process whereby groups within U.S. society have fought for equal rights in the justice system, we must first have a clear picture of the architecture of the justice system. The American structure of government is uniquely complex by design. The founders of our government took seriously the warning issued by Lord Acton in seventeenth century: "Power corrupts and absolute power corrupts absolutely." The structure of the American government divides power between the three branches of government and further segments the power of government through the preservation of four separate levels of government: municipal, county, state, and federal. **Jurisdiction** refers to the legal authority within a given area of law or geographical boundaries or over an aspect of the justice process. In the American system of government, legitimate power is divided into many different jurisdictions to create a much decentralized criminal justice system.

Federalism

The American Revolution instituted a major change in the administration of justice by creating a national system apart from the justice system operating within each state itself. The Tenth Amendment to the Constitution gives states jurisdiction over creating law in all matters not directly concerning the federal government. Violations of federal law are investigated by federal law enforcement and prosecuted in federal courts, whereas violations of state law are handled by state criminal justice agencies. Federal crimes constitute a mere fraction of most criminal offenses; the vast majority of criminal behavior falls within the legal jurisdiction of the state.

The business of criminal justice is overwhelmingly a responsibility of local and state governments with 60 percent of all justice personnel employed at the local level of government. Each state has its own criminal code and its own systems for administering those laws. The **supremacy clause** of the Constitution states that federal law supersedes when the two forms of law conflict. For many crimes, there is a concurrent violation of both state law and federal law: which governmental agency has jurisdiction may depend upon who originally arrested the offender or upon local agreements worked out among the agencies. While each state has a bill of rights in its own constitution individual states cannot reduce the

DE JURE
rights or practices which are established by law.

DE FACTO
rights or practices which exist in fact although not in law.

JURISDICTION
a sphere of legal authority.

SUPREMACY CLAUSE
Article VI, clause 2, of the federal Constitution declares federal law to be the Supreme Law of the Land.

rights of citizens below a minimum set by the U.S. Constitution. States, however, are free to raise the standard for individual rights above those set by the federal Constitution.

Separation of Powers

The **separation of powers** among the judiciary, legislature, and executive branches of government is enshrined in the Constitution reflecting the political wisdom of the founding fathers that sought to prevent the concentration of power in any one branch of government. To create a system of checks and balances, each stage of the criminal justice process comes under a different branch of governmental authority. The authority to make criminal laws is separated from the authority to interpret the law and adjudicate guilt or innocence, which is again separated from the authority to arrest, investigate, and sanction those who are convicted of criminal violations. At each level of government, different branches of government have jurisdiction over different parts of the process.

The power to make law rests principally with democratically elected representatives at all four levels of government: state and national legislatures, along with city and local governments. For the most part misdemeanor and felony laws are created by state and federal representatives while ordinances are created at the town, village, or city level of government. In the South, before the Civil War, blacks were excluded from the process of political participation, as were nonwhites and women. The law of slavery that made it a capital offense for a black man to have consensual sex with a white woman but did not criminalize the forcible sex by a white male with a black woman was written by legislatures composed exclusively of white males.

While the power to make law rests with the legislature, the authority to administer and enforce the law is a responsibility of the executive branch of government. When the boys were initially arrested, they were apprehended by "deputies" of the Jackson County sheriff's department, the legal authority within county government who generally has jurisdiction over law enforcement within its geographical boundaries. The power to "deputize" ordinary citizens to legally use force to apprehend a fellow citizen is held by the legal agents of law enforcement. Their authority is to arrest suspects, gather evidence about their alleged crime, and assist the public prosecutor in presenting that evidence in a court of law.

While law enforcement may use force to apprehend a citizen suspected of a crime, it is not the legitimate authority of law enforcement to determine if that citizen is *guilty* of that crime. The principle of **presumed innocent** until proven guilty is, in fact, a guiding principle for how law enforcement is, ideally, supposed to treat all citizens suspected of a crime.

The only branch of government with the judicial authority to determine legal guilt is the judiciary. It is the job of the judiciary to determine the facts of the case. The boys were accused of committing rape but until they were tried in a court of law according to the rules of evidence and within the bounds of due process, they could not legally be convicted of the crime.

Once a sentence is ordered by the courts the responsibility for carrying out the sentence falls to the correctional system which is a part of the executive branch of government. The custodial responsibility for the boys during the many years they sat awaiting trial and during the time they served their sentences falls on

SEPARATION OF POWERS
the division of the government into three branches: executive, legislative and judicial.

PRESUMPTION OF INNOCENCE
the guiding principle of criminal procedure which places the burden of proof on the state.

the prison system which may be run by municipal, county, state, or federal governments. Usually, individuals convicted of violating a municipal, county, state, or federal law come under the custodial supervision of that legal entity. The boys were held in a county jail awaiting trial initially but were later transferred to the state prison of Alabama. The conduct of their jailers and the conditions of their incarceration are an executive branch responsibility.

Power of Judicial Review

The judiciary is given a unique power to oversee the activities of the other two branches of government. For this reason, unlike the executive and the legislature who are elected by the public and therefore responsive to public opinion, the judiciary for the most part is independent. The appointment of federal judges and Supreme Court justices for life is intended to protect the independence of this branch of government and preserve its capacity to enforce the rule of law on even the most powerful members of society, namely, those within the government itself.

At the pinnacle of the three equal branches of government sits the U.S. Supreme Court that has the power to render acts and decisions of the other two branches null and void if the it determines their actions violate the Constitution. It is the inviolability of the Constitution and the ultimate power of the Supreme Court as the **court of last resort** to interpret the Constitution that creates a unique source of standardization on all fifty states and thousands of local jurisdictions across the land.

The power of **judicial review** means that the courts are able to exercise control over the other two branches of government by insisting that they adhere to the rule of law. No president or governor may place him or herself above the law and the courts are independent of the executive branch to enable it to effectively act as a check on possible abuses of power by individuals within office. Courts may declare laws written by legislatures unconstitutional; they may declare practices of prisons and jail guards of prisoners unconstitutional, they may overturn the decisions of lower courts, and they may declare police behavior as crossing the boundaries of the legitimate and legal use of force. The legal right of the courts to act as a watchdog over the other branches of government has been crucial for the struggle for less powerful groups within our society—minorities, women, children, and poor people—to establish equal rights under the law.

CONSTITUTION AS SLEEPING BEAUTY

The first ten amendments to the Constitution, known as the Bill of Rights, was clearly formulated to regulate only the relationship between the citizen and the federal government. The Constitution was written at a time when the threat of tyranny by the distant king of England was paramount and most colonists were concerned about the threat to their autonomy from a national government. As we have seen, most of the text of the Bill of Rights defines the meaning of due process for the administration of criminal justice.

The Constitution is a living document interpreted anew and made relevant to the changing values and conditions of society. The judiciary is the ultimate interpreter of the Constitution and no governmental authority may violate the

COURTS OF LAST RESORT
the power of the state Supreme Court to be the final interpreter of the state constitution and the power of the U.S. Supreme Court to be the final interpreter of the U.S. Constitution.

JUDICIAL REVIEW
the power of the judicial branch to declare acts of the executive or legislative branch unconstitutional.

laws of the Constitution that may itself be amended only through a congressional majority ratified by a two-thirds majority of the States. Amendments to the U.S. Constitution are extremely rare: between 1800 and 1992, it has been amended less than twenty-seven times.

Until the end of the nineteenth century, the Supreme Court interpreted the Bill of Rights as regulating only the relationships between citizens and the federal government. According to the interpretation of Supreme Court justices in 1833, the Constitution provided citizens no protection against state or local governmental action.[8] The Fourteenth Amendment passed by Congress and state legislatures across the land was a direct response to this narrow judicial interpretation: if the Supreme Court declared that there was nothing in the Bill of Rights that said it pertained to the states, then an additional amendment to the Constitution was needed to protect the civil rights of all citizens in this nation. The Fourteenth Amendment declares that, "No State shall make or enforce any law which shall abridge the privileges or immunities of citizens of the United States; nor shall any State deprive any person of life, liberty, or property, without due process of law; nor deny to any person within its jurisdiction the equal protection of the laws."

The Scottsboro case in the early 1930s marked one of the first times that the federal judiciary enforced the due process requirement of the Fourteenth Amendment by overturning a state court conviction. Although the amendment was passed sixty years earlier, the Fourteenth Amendment was "brought to life" by a new interpretation of its meaning by the Supreme Court beginning with the Scottsboro case. For the first time, the Supreme Court overturned a state court conviction on due process grounds.

The majority opinion in the Powell case stated that the trial in this case violated a sense of fundamental fairness that underlies all the rules of criminal procedure laid out in the Bill of Rights. These are immutable principles of justice that were clearly violated in the trials in Alabama even though they appeared to go through the motions of legal procedure. The **fundamental fairness doctrine** articulated by the Supreme Court in the Scottsboro case states that the U.S. Supreme Court will examine state court processes on a case-by-case basis to be sure that they are substantively "fair."

With the Powell case the Supreme Court also relied upon a different legal doctrine in ruling the trial unconstitutional. The **incorporation doctrine** states that the due process clause in the Fourteenth Amendment includes or "incorporates" all the provisions of the Fourth, Fifth, Sixth, and Eighth Amendments. Because the Fourteenth Amendment says states may not violate "due process," then it must mean that states may not violate all the safeguards in all of these amendments since they define what due process is. While the full incorporation doctrine has never been accepted by the majority of the Supreme Court, over the years the Supreme Court has opted for a system of **selective incorporation** identifying specific elements of each of these amendments that are seen as fundamental to a fair justice process. With *Powell v. Alabama*, the court took the first step in the selective incorporation by establishing that the Sixth Amendment right to counsel, at least in cases where defendants were facing execution, was "incorporated" within the meaning of the phrase "due process of law."

Despite the rulings in the Scottsboro case, the Supreme Court was reluctant to expand the rights "incorporated" into the Fourteenth Amendment and interfere with the state courts during most of the 1930s and 1940s. Beginning in the early

FUNDAMENTAL FAIRNESS DOCTRINE the definition of due process which focuses on the substantive fairness in the application of the law.

INCORPORATION DOCTRINE the legal principle that all the procedural protections of the Bill of Rights applies to state courts under the due process and equal protection clause of the Fourteenth Amendment.

SELECTIVE INCORPORATION the legal principle that only some of the protections in the Bill of Rights apply to state courts under the due process and equal protection clause of the Fourteenth Amendment.

1960s, however, there was an avalanche of rulings by the federal and Supreme Courts that signaled the start of what has been termed the "due process" or "criminal law" revolution. The Supreme Court and other federal courts exercised their power of judicial review to "awaken" other provisions of the Bill of Rights and enforce those provisions on the states relying upon the selective incorporation doctrine.

AND JUSTICE FOR ALL?

The Bill of Rights was added to the Constitution in 1791 to articulate the basic protections for citizens from the powers of the federal government. But in 1791 the privilege of citizenship did not extend to nonwhites or to women. Although the Constitution is based on the "natural law" principle that all men were created equal, the status of personhood was reserved for white males only. Native Americans, blacks, women, and children were all seen as "non-persons" ineligible for the "self-evident" rights afforded to all. Even from the start, the concept of equal rights was based on a form of injustice: the exclusion of whole categories of persons from the status of personhood.

The fundamental bias in the administration of justice can be seen clearly in the Dred Scott case in 1856 when the Supreme Court ruled that Scott could not be considered a citizen because he was a Negro. The justices of the Supreme Court conceded that individual states may choose to grant citizenship for nonwhites but that, as individuals, blacks had no right to claim citizenship because they did not have self-evident rights as persons. In the words of Chief Justice Roger Taney, at the time the Constitution was written, members of the black race were viewed as "altogether unfit to associate with the white race either in social or political relations; and so far inferior, that they had no rights which the white man was bound to respect."[9]

Women too were clearly seen as essentially "different" and "inferior" to men. In a case involving the request of a woman to practice law, the U.S. Supreme Court upheld the state law which prohibited women from admission to the bar claiming that "the paramount destiny and mission of woman are to fulfill the noble and benign offices of wife and mother. This is the law of the Creator."[10] Thus, despite the formal rights granted in the Bill of Rights, the interpretation of that doctrine tolerated and perpetuated profound inequalities between categories of persons within society.

Chief Justice Earl Warren, who some believe played the role of "Prince Charming" to the slumbering Bill of Rights believed the Constitution should be seen as a living document to be interpreted and adapted to the "evolving standards of decency" within society. This has allowed the Constitution to serve as a tool for social change as disadvantaged groups have sought to use the power of the Constitution's words to bring the daily workings of the system in line with the lofty ideals expressed in those documents. It is the architecture of our system of government which grants the power of judicial review to the courts that serves as an enormously valuable avenue for those excluded and oppressed by the system to force some modicum of positive social change.

Not all movements to change the criminal justice system have relied upon the Constitution and the Supreme Court to bring about different laws, policies, and practices. Other movements have changed the attitudes of lawmakers toward certain crimes or certain segments of society. The awareness of child abuse, drunk driving, violence against women, and victims' rights are only a few areas where the efforts of citizens in our society to raise awareness have resulted in significant changes in the law and policies of the justice system.

LEGACY OF RACIAL INJUSTICE FOR AFRICAN AMERICANS

Before the Civil War, the criminal law itself was part of the system of white supremacy and control. States were permitted to write unequal laws that enforced different crimes for whites and blacks. It was a crime for blacks to learn to read, to gather to worship without the presence of a white person, to neglect to step out of the way when a white person approached on a walkway, to smoke in public, make loud noises, or defend themselves or their families from physical assault.[11] Even free Negroes in the slave states were subject to a different set of legal rules: every slave state in the South except Delaware, and several northern states as well, prohibited free Negroes from testifying against whites in court, and many states had laws which prohibited free blacks from meeting with, talking to, or associating with slaves on pain of whipping or worse.

For blacks, the law offered little or no protection from white violence. Actions that were considered criminal when the victim was white were not criminal if the victim was black. The law did not view rape of a female slave as a crime and the use of physical violence against slaves was permissible under the law. The right to use the whip to punish errant slaves was seen as the prerogative of the master and mistress even when that whipping led to the death of the slave so long as the violence was done in the service of discipline. The main check on white violence against black slaves was the economic interest of their owners: as valuable property, slave owners often prosecuted other whites who had "damaged" their property with excessive use of violence.[12]

The end of the Civil War was marked by an extraordinary flurry of legislative activity with the passage of the Thirteenth, Fourteenth, and Fifteenth Amendments to the Constitution. The Thirteenth Amendment outlawed the institution of slavery. Almost immediately many southern legislatures passed discriminatory "Black Codes" which criminalized a wide range of conduct for black citizens only. In Mississippi, for example, it became a criminal offense for a black to make an insulting gesture toward a white. Whites beat or killed African American citizens for such "crimes" as failing to step off the sidewalk, failing to use deferential forms of address, or attempting to vote. The criminal justice system, for the most part, refused to protect blacks against the tidal wave of illegal violence by white citizens and with the absence of slavery there was no longer any "property" interest by white owners to protect the lives of blacks.

The Civil Rights Act of 1866 was written by Congress to abolish these discriminatory criminal codes in the southern states. This act stipulated that all citizens "of every race and color, without regards to any previous condition of slavery or involuntary servitude . . . shall be subject to like punishment, pains and penalties." To further ensure that every local law enforcement officer and court across the land would treat all citizens the same, in 1868 Congress passed the Fourteenth Amendment to the Constitution which obligates the states to bestow upon all persons "the equal protection of the law."[13] The Fifteenth Amendment of

1879 prohibits states from excluding persons from the right to vote on the basis of race. All of these amendments were designed to protect the civil rights of black citizens in the South.

During the period of Reconstruction, many blacks entered into the political offices and participated in the justice system as never before. Blacks were able to serve as jurors, legislators, magistrates, sheriffs, police officers, and even state Supreme Court justices. Supported by the efforts of the federal government and the newly created Department of Justice, there were numerous efforts to prosecute the vigilante terror groups such as the Ku Klux Klan. But by 1877 the forces of Reconstruction fell to the dominance of southern whites who regained power in virtually all legislatures across the South. The end of Reconstruction ushered in fifty long years of segregation, discriminatory laws known as Jim Crow laws and systematic illegal violence against black citizens.

Vigilantism flourished in the South to uphold these laws. Here the sentiment was that the formal law in the postwar period did not reflect the values and morality of white supremacy. Although the South lost the Civil War, the attitudes of the people there did not change. Many in the South felt that the North was imposing laws upon them through the federal government and its constitutional amendments. The Klan organized to enforce the "true" law of the South, the unwritten law of white supremacy. More than 2,500 blacks were murdered in the sixteen years before 1900; between 1882 and 1968 a total of 4,743 people were lynched in the United States, mostly in the Deep South.[14] About two-thirds of the victims were black and one-third were whites.

Lynching was a crime of terrorism and powerful tool of **social control** exercised over whites and blacks alike. This form of violence was carried out to send a warning to whites and blacks to maintain the law of segregation and racial hierarchy in the South despite the changes in the law. It often was used in response to violations of the unwritten codes of color etiquette, when blacks and whites socialized or acted as equals in public. The most egregious crossing of the line concerned the allegation of any kind of sexual interaction between black males and white women. The mob that surrounded the Scottsboro jailhouse that night most certainly intended to use the rope to send the message that sexual relations between the races would be not be tolerated.

Under-Enforcement of the Law

The evidence clearly shows that the criminal justice system did not offer black citizens the type of security against victimization afforded to white citizens. A "culture of impunity" existed within the South when it came to crimes committed by whites against blacks.[15] A white citizen who grew up in the Deep South during 1950s, says: "When I was coming up in Mississippi I never knew it was against the law to kill a black man. I learned that when I went into the army. I was seventeen years old. I thought they were joking."[16] Until federal prosecutions in the 1960s the southern criminal justice system failed to hold anyone accountable for committing vigilante violence. As we will see later in Case #13, it is only in recent years that social activists in the South have begun to pressure the state courts to prosecute crimes committed by whites against both blacks and whites during the civil rights era.

For the most part, until the latter part of the twentieth century, the entire criminal justice system was "lily white": there were no black jurors, no minority police

VIGILANTISM
illegal violence conducted by groups or individuals who believe they are enforcing justice despite the actual content of the law.

LYNCHING
an act of violence used as terrorism and social control typically by vigilantes, and often in the form of hanging.

SOCIAL CONTROL
formal and informal processes that maintain conformity with social norms.

officers, few black lawyers, fewer black judges, no black correctional guards, or probation or parole officers. As Patterson noted when he faced the courtroom, all he saw was "one big smiling white face." Crimes committed by whites against blacks were difficult to prosecute since they depended upon white witnesses, jurors, and prosecutors to enforce these laws.

But the vast majority of criminal victimization, in the past as well as today, occurs within racial groups and the criminal justice system has also failed to respond to criminal victimization *within* black communities. The problem of **under-enforcement of the law** for crimes committed by blacks against other black citizens was noted by Gunnar Myrdal in 1944 in his famous book on the problem of racism within American society. "Leniency toward Negro defendants in cases involving crimes against other Negroes is thus actually a form of discrimination."[17] The criminal justice system has failed to provide minority citizens "equal protection of the law" by not keeping their communities as safe from criminal violence as white communities.

Absence of adequate police protection within the black community continues to be a concern among African Americans today. African Americans are more likely to be victims of violent crime than whites. Rates of robbery are three times as high among blacks and rates of aggravated assaults are twice as high among blacks than among whites.[18] Some people believe that the current epidemic of drugs and violence in the inner city is tolerated only because those most affected are predominantly minority residents of poor inner city communities.[19] Media coverage of crimes continues to vary with the racial status of the victim with the

In 2011 the rate of imprisonment for African American males was nearly seven times the rate for white males, reflecting persistent racial discrimination in the enforcement of the law.

UNDER-ENFORCEMENT OF THE LAW
when the criminal justice system fails to enforce the law and respond to certain kinds of victimization.

media showing relatively little interest in publicizing crimes that involve a black perpetrator and a black victim. When a young white affluent woman was raped in New York City's Central Park in 1989 the case made the front page all across the country. Yet that very same week, in the very same city, there were twenty-eight other cases of sexual assaults, some just as brutal, seventeen of which involved black woman as victims. Most of these cases barely made the back pages of the newspaper.[20]

Over-Enforcement of the Law

Even more controversial than the issue of under-enforcement of black victimization is the belief that the justice system overly polices and excessively punishes minority citizens. For many African Americans, there is a strong conviction that the justice system is a "just us" system bent upon the racially selective pattern of enforcement of our nation's laws.[21] The attitudes of the American public on this subject are profoundly divided by race: a majority of blacks believe that the police and courts discriminate against blacks while an equally large majority of whites do not believe the system treats blacks or whites unfairly.[22] In a 2013 survey 37 percent of whites felt that blacks in their community were treated less fairly than whites, while 70 percent of blacks and 51 percent of Hispanics believed that to be true.[23] Whatever may or may not be true about the racism within the criminal justice system today, it is clear that beliefs among blacks and whites on this subject are divided by race.

The most disturbing evidence of racial discrimination can be found in the racial disparity in the numbers of nonwhite Americans under criminal justice supervision in this county: if current trends continue one in three African American males born in 2011 can expect to go to prison compared to one out of every six Latino males and one out every seventeen white males.[24] In 2012 one in every thirteen black males between the ages of thirty and thirty-four was in prison, compared with one in every thirty-six Hispanic males and one in ninety white males of the same ages. For black non-Hispanic females the rate of incarceration was 2.5 times the rate for white non-Hispanic females and 1.4 times higher than the rate for Hispanic females.[25]

Other data show evidence of persistent forms of discrimination in the policing of minority communities particularly for drug offenses,[26] the incidents of police shootings[27] and police brutality,[28] jury selection,[29] and the application of the death penalty.[30] Scholars who study the criminal justice system today are divided on this issue with some believing that the evidence of discriminatory patterns in arrest, conviction, and sentencing of black defendants is clear and convincing[31] while others argue that apart from the existence of occasionally racist individuals, the evidence shows that the system treats blacks and whites alike, given the difference in the pattern of offending between the two groups.[32] Researchers differ on whether or not the racial disparity exists primarily because of discriminatory laws such as the only recently reduced disparity in penalties for crack cocaine versus powder cocaine; the activities of the police on the inner city streets or nation's highway through racial profiling; bias in the backroom prosecutorial discretion in plea bargaining or in judicial sentencing and parole decision-making. The majority of researchers conclude that bias exists within all stages of the criminal justice system.

Race is also compounded by the influence of social class.[33] The experience of privileged criminal defendants who enjoy the advantages of skillful defense attorneys and other hidden advantages of class operates to influence the outcome of the justice process. The criminality of the streets rather than the criminality of the suites remains the dominant target of the justice system. The legacy of black unemployment concentrated in heavily policed urban spaces has led to a spiraling cycle of criminality and social disorganization within poor minority communities.[34]

To a certain extent, middle-class black Americans who reside within integrated neighborhoods do not experience the same levels of victimization from crime and excessive policing as poor minority citizens. Attitudes about fairness and fear of police also vary over both race and class: middle-class African Americans and middle-class Hispanics who reside in more affluent, predominantly white neighborhoods are less fearful of the police and skeptical about fairness than blacks and Hispanics who reside in poorer minority neighborhoods.[35] On the other hand, minority citizens, regardless of class, are subject to greater levels of police surveillance—driving along our nation's highways or arriving at the airport—because of the color of their skin and middle-class minority citizens who reside in predominantly minority neighborhoods share many of the same attitudes toward police as poor minority citizens.

Mass Incarceration and Disproportionate Minority Contact

While the United States constitutes about 4.4 percent of the world's population, this country houses 22 percent of the world's incarcerated population.[36] Throughout this text, we will examine the myriad of factors that contribute to the United States having the highest incarceration rate in the world. It is important to recognize that this has not always been the case: for most of this century, the U.S. incarceration rate was no higher, and sometimes lower than that of Canada, Japan, England, France, and other similar European nations. Our rate of incarceration began to rise at the very end of the1970s and increased rapidly during the "get tough" era of the 1980s and 1990s and has remained high into the first decade of the twenty-first century.

The disproportionately large number of minority citizens involved in the criminal justice system has also increased along with the numbers of people confined by the system. The reasons for this disparity is an important theme through this book as we examine the discretionary decision-making of thousands of players within the criminal justice system from the police on the street, to the prosecutors, defense attorney and judges, to legislators, governors, and parole boards. Researchers and policymakers have used the acronym DMC or **Disproportionate Minority Confinement** to refer to the high levels of racial and ethnic minorities behind bars; now the preferred term is **Disproportionate Minority Contact** to refer to the more accurate reality that minorities are over-represented at all stages of the criminal justice process, not just within the prison system. Minority citizens are more likely to be stopped and questioned by police, searched, arrested, held without bail, convicted, as well as more likely to be sent to jail as punishment.

A New Jim Crow Era?

One consequence of the staggeringly high levels of involvement of minority citizens in the criminal justice system is that being convicted and incarcerated has

DISPROPORTIONATE MINORITY CONFINEMENT
it refers to the high levels of racial and ethnic minorities behind bars relative to their numbers in the population.

DISPROPORTIONATE MINORITY CONTACT
it refers to the over-representation of minorities at all stages of the criminal justice process.

serious consequences for one's status in society during and after incarceration. Convicted felons are treated as second-class citizens and subject to a system of legalized discrimination that restricts an ex-offender's right to vote, access to housing, education, and employment. One prominent critic argues the criminal justice policies have created a legal environment similar to that created by **Jim Crow** laws of the South.[37] Despite the 2008 election of Barack Obama as the nation's first African American president a large percentage of African Americans today are legally treated as second-class citizens because of their status as convicted felons. For Michele Alexander, the criminal justice system operates to uphold a "racial caste system" in which people of color are legally discriminated against within our society.

> Today a criminal freed from prison has scarcely more rights and arguable less respect than a freed slave or a black person living "free" in Mississippi at the height of Jim Crow. . . . The "whites only" signs may be gone but new signs have gone up—notices placed in job applications, rental agreements, loan applications, forms for welfare benefits, school applications and petitions for licenses, informing the general public that "felons" are not wanted here.[38]

The Thirteenth Amendment to the Constitution, enacted in 1865 state that "Neither slavery nor involuntary servitude *except as punishment for crime whereof the party shall have been duly convicted*, shall exist within the U.S." The exception—that those who are convicted of crimes may, indeed, be treated as slaves—has created a "loophole" that allows the re-establishment of a lesser form of citizenship for millions who have been convicted of a crime.

A Crisis of Legitimacy

That Justice is a blind goddess
Is a thing to which we black are wise;
Her bandage hides two festering sores
That once perhaps were eyes.[39]

This poem was written by black poet Langston Hughes in 1932 to help raise money for the defense of the Scottsboro boys. The poem expresses profound skepticism about the fundamental fairness of the system toward African Americans. A basic belief in the fairness of our system underlies the legitimacy of the law and the institutions of the criminal justice system. If the system is widely perceived as unfair and unequal, this generates a crisis of legitimacy that undermines respect for the law.[40] Research has found that belief in the fairness of the process of legal system is one of the primary motivations for obeying the law itself.[41] When people feel the system of laws and how they are enforced is fair, they are less likely to violate the law. The criminal justice system too depends on cooperation and support of citizens as witnesses, victims, members of the jury, and voters. Therefore it is essential to pay attention to the tensions within our society that undermine faith in the fairness of our justice system.

There is a long history of urban unrest worldwide, including in American cities, where citizens take to the streets, often peacefully but at times violently, to express their discontent, rage, and despair over conditions of inequality within the society. Deep anger over issues of persistent poverty, joblessness, unemployment, discrimination, inadequate housing, education, health care, and services

JIM CROW
state and local laws passed in the aftermath of the Civil War that reinforced racial segregation, marked by the concept of "separate but equal."

is at the core of this discontent. But the most common grievance that pushes citizens into the streets to express their anger is the issue of police brutality. More than any other root cause, police encounters with minority citizens that are perceived to be racist and unfair have led to the eruption of widespread social protest and riots. The police are the public face of the criminal justice system and when the police behave professionally and within the bounds of the law, citizens tend to respect the law. When citizens encounter police who violate the law or use excessive force to uphold the law, the result is often cynical and negative attitudes toward the entire criminal justice system and the fairness of the legal system itself.

The phrase "black lives matter" began as a poignant phrase on Facebook. Activist Alicia Garcia reacted to the 2013 acquittal of George Zimmerman in the shooting death of an unarmed teenager named Trayvon Martin. On Facebook she wrote, "We don't deserve to be killed with impunity. We need to learn to love ourselves and fight for a world where black lives matter."[42] The phrase "black lives matter" struck a nerve among those concerned about police violence toward African Americans and three activists founded an organization called BLM which quickly grew to dozens of chapters across the country. The chief demands among activists in the BLM movement have been to stop police brutality toward African American citizens; to end excessive and hostile policing practices within African American communities; and to make police more accountable to the communities they serve.

In August 2014, the shooting death of Michael Brown, an unarmed eighteen-year-old in Ferguson Missouri, at the hands of police, sparked nationwide protests amplifying the phrase "black lives matter" as a unifying sentiment impelling thousands of citizens into the streets in cities across the country to protest police brutality toward minority citizens. The protests that began in Ferguson continued over the subsequent deaths of African Americans during arrests or while being held in custody. These include Eric Garner in Staten Island, Tamir Rice in Cleveland, Freddie Gray in Baltimore, Laquan McDonald in Chicago, Alton Sterling in Baton Rouge, Louisiana, Philando Castile in Minnesota, and Sandra Bland in Houston, Texas. More names get added to this list each week as the media continues to report on this explosive issue.

In each city after an incident occur, thousands of protesters were met by armed police often in riot gear, which was filmed by television cameras. Most protests concluded peacefully with a handful of arrests for protesters who throw rocks or loot stores. In Dallas, Texas, however, on July 7, 2016, at the close of a peaceful BLM rally, a hidden sniper deliberately shot and killed five police officers, wounding nine others. The shooter, a former army reservist, was reportedly angry over the deaths of African Americans at the hands of the police. This violence fueled a counter-movement among law enforcement and their supporters using the phrase "all lives matter" or "blue lives matter."

Throughout this text we will consider the impact of the criminal justice policies and its relationship to the structure and systems of inequality within our society. The term "prison industrial complex" refers to the network of private and public interests that operate and benefit from the **mass incarceration** of U.S. citizens from the phone companies, to health care, to food services that contract with the prison system to the many industries that utilize prisoner labor to produce goods and services. When the financial interests of large corporations become more influential in shaping criminal justice policy than the needs of

MASS INCARCERATION it refers to the rapid increase in incarceration in the United States between 1970s and 2010, resulting in record high numbers of Americans in jails and prisons.

citizens and community, then the system is no longer serving the needs of the community or the interests of justice. Race, class, gender, and corporate status are all important bases of privilege and power that also have shaped our system of laws and how they are enforced within society. Our next section continues to examine injustice by examining the legacy of gender injustice and the struggle to achieve equal protection of the law for women.

THE LEGACY OF GENDER INJUSTICE

When Haywood Patterson looked out to see one big smiling white face in the courtroom it was the smiling face of a white *man*. Imagine being a woman sitting in the dock facing a roomful of men. Until 1870, women were barred from practicing law and serving on juries, and did not have the right to vote until 1920. It was as late as 1975[43] that the Supreme Court ruled that excluding women from juries was a violation of the Sixth Amendment. Nor did women have a significant presence in policing or corrections until recent decades and even now there remains considerable gender discrimination within policing, corrections, and the legal profession.

Historically the law has also failed to protect women from serious victimization by males in society, particularly in crimes of violence and sexual assault committed within the context of intimate relationships. Even today, seeking justice often requires that women publicly reveal the most intimate aspects of their lives to a group of strangers, who impartially access and evaluate their words.

In this section we examine the legacy of gender inequality that has undermined equal protection of the law for women as victims of intimate and domestic violence. We also look at the progress women have made in becoming employed within the occupations of the criminal justice system. It is important to recognize too that the influence of gender roles in contemporary society has had significant impact on men as well as women. Men commit crime in far greater numbers than do women, and are victims of violence far more often than women. As we will see throughout out this text, men constitute 93 percent of those who are incarcerated for crime; men are also the dominant personnel within the criminal justice system particularly in the professions of policing and corrections. At the close of this section we briefly examine the influence of the dominant view of masculinity prevalent within American culture on the dynamics of crime and the administration of justice.

THE UNEQUAL STATUS OF WOMEN

The formal law deriving from centuries of common law tradition embodied a serious bias against women especially in the marital relationship. Just as the law failed to criminalize routine violence by whites against blacks, so too was the criminal law silent on the use of violence by men against their lawful wives. Just as the master held the legal authority to use violence to discipline his slaves so too did the father possess the right to use violence against his wife and children. The law did not recognize women as independent adults: according to the legal doctrine of **coverture**, the wife's legal status was subsumed under her husband's

COVERTURE
the wife's legal status was subsumed under her husband's identity as a citizen.

identity as a citizen. She did not have the right to own property or to control her own resources once she had legally joined in marriage.

Denied the vote until 1920, women had no voice in shaping the law of rape or domestic violence. Even after the passage of the Nineteenth Amendment, women continued to be excluded from participation on juries and full access to participation in the justice system until recent decades. Beginning in the 1970s, however, women have used the laws against discrimination and sexual harassment to challenge barriers to female employment in occupations within the criminal justice system such as policing and corrections. Major changes in the criminal law have also occurred as the feminist movement mobilized around the area of legal reform to fully criminalize male violence against women and to end the "blame the victim" attitudes which excused men from full responsibility for their actions by focusing on the allegedly provocative actions of the victim. The two key areas of criminal justice reform started by the women's movement were in rape and domestic violence.

THE UNDER-ENFORCEMENT OF MALE VIOLENCE AGAINST WOMEN

The de facto practice of under-enforcement of male violence against women parallels the experience of blacks who suffered from a failure of the justice system to criminalize violence of whites against blacks. The common law doctrine regulating the use of violence by husbands to discipline their wives was known as the **rule of thumb**: the use of physical force was not a form of criminal assault unless the husband made use of a stick that was thicker than a human thumb. In the United States statutory law did not take wife beating seriously: a law written in Maryland, for example, makes it only a misdemeanor for a man to "brutally assault and beat his wife."[44] Assaults that were not "brutal" were, of course, perfectly legal.

Even when the laws prohibited violence within the home, the informal attitude of the justice system prevented enforcement of those laws. In an infamous decision in *State v. Oliver* in 1874, a judge acknowledged that it was barbaric for husbands to beat their wives but that the courts were not interested in meddling in the affairs that take place within the home. "In order to preserve the sanctity of the domestic circle, the Courts will not listen to trivial complaints . . . it is better to draw the curtain, shut out the public gaze, and leave the parties to forgive and forget."[45]

The courts and police failed to respond to the violence against women unless it was an attack by a stranger; the violence that took place within the home was simply considered not the business of the justice system. Men were tacitly seen as exercising their right to discipline their wives or it was seen as a private matter, a domestic disturbance that should be properly settled by the parties themselves. Police who responded to a call in these cases were told to calm the parties down and mediate the disagreement.[46] Judges repeatedly lectured women who brought charges against their husbands to "not waste the court's time";[47] prosecutors refused to bring rape charges if they felt the victim would not be a sympathetic or credible witness to a jury; defense attorneys attacked the character and sexual history of victims; and police treated women who turned to the system with suspicion and callous disrespect. For many women, the experience with the criminal

RULE OF THUMB
the common law doctrine regulating the use of physical force by husbands against their wives.

justice system was one of secondary victimization where they found themselves to be blamed for their own victimization.

Sexual assault between husbands and wives especially was not brought to the system at all because women were seen as having legally consented to sexual relations at the time of consenting to marriage itself. Historically, husbands were granted immunity in state legal codes from the crime of rape committed against their spouse. Rape was defined as forcible sexual act upon a woman "other than a wife." Husbands, simply, could not be prosecuted for raping their wives since these acts were not criminalized.

Reforms in the Law of Rape

Sexual violence against women, the crime of **rape**, was subject to a systematic pattern of selective enforcement throughout our nation's history. The degree of seriousness and even the criminality of the act depended far more on the status of the victim and the offender than on the crime itself. As we have seen, black women were never perceived as genuine "victims" of rape. But this "double standard" was also true of women who were divorced or sexually active, or whose dress, behavior, or occupation meant they were less than virtuous.[48] The law of rape demanded that a woman charging rape prove her virtue in the trial. It was often the women's sexual history and character that was on trial when a charge of rape was being prosecuted in a court of law.

The law also required women to show evidence of actual resistance. Thus, when women failed to show signs of physical violence and struggle, they were seen as having consented to the act. The legal burden was on the victim to show she had resisted the actions of the man. If the accused in the Scottsboro case had been white men, this case would never have gone to trial since women like Ruby Bates and Victoria Price would hardly have been considered worthy victims given their social status and neither woman had signs of physical injury to support their claim of rape.

The law of rape changed in important ways during the latter part of the twentieth century, largely due to the efforts of feminists who believed women's safety was not being adequately addressed. Starting in the 1970s, **rape shield laws** were passed by most states barring evidence of past sexual activity at trial and prohibiting the media publication of the identity of rape victims. The extent of the prohibitions varies by state, but generally forbid the defense from attacking a victim's sexual history or reputation. Numerous exceptions to the law exist, again varying from state to state, that allow evidence of prior sexual history with the defendant and also allow evidence of prior false accusations.[49]

The first case to bring criminal rape charges against a spouse was in the state of Oregon in 1978. In a particularly vicious case a man was charged with the rape of his wife and despite a long history of abuse, he was found not guilty of the rape.[50] The public response to this case however brought about changes in the Oregon statutes that removed the exemption for husbands from the crime of rape. Now the crime of **spousal rape** exists in all fifty states although the actual prosecution for the crime remains relatively rare.

Most states now have laws that are **gender neutral** and include rape in a range of behaviors identified as sexual assault. Unlike most of the states, the FBI continues to limit their definition of **forcible rape** as the carnal knowledge of a female forcibly and against her will. Today rape remains a highly underreported

SEXUAL ASSAULT
verbal, visual, or any other kind of assault that forces a person to join in unwanted sexual contact or attention, including rape, inappropriate touching, voyeurism, exhibitionism, incest and sexual harassment.

RAPE
forced or coerced sexual assault, usually intercourse.

RAPE SHIELD LAW
laws that bar the introduction of evidence about a victim's prior sexual conduct.

SPOUSAL OR MARITAL RAPE
rape of one's spouse.

GENDER NEUTRAL
modern rape laws do not specify gender, applying to either male or female victims.

FORCIBLE RAPE
unlawful sexual intercourse with a female without her consent and against her will.

crime largely because of the shame for victims and the continued social attitudes that blame women for male violence toward them.

Though women's rights activists made advances in society's understanding of rape and in the legal definitions of rape, there are still many contested issues; chief among these remains the issue of consent and force. State laws, however, continue to require evidence of **consent**. In the crime of **statutory rape**, consent is not relevant because the victim is too young to give legal consent. To prove non-statutory rape, however, the prosecution must be able to prove the absence of consent. Proving that something didn't happen is always complex, and for that reason it is rarely required in criminal cases. For instance, if someone steals your wallet, there is an assumption in the law that you did not consent. In the case of rape there is no such assumption, and proving lack of consent often comes down to the only two people present—the accuser and the accused.

This is where the issue of force becomes relevant. If there is evidence of force, such as bruises or visible external injuries, then there is an assumption that there was not consent. Some have even suggested that this is the only type of "real" rape. Victims of rape where secondary injury is not visible would challenge this presumption. They believe they have indeed been the victims of "real rape" even if they did not sustain additional injuries: the rape itself is the injury. In other violent crimes, robbery for example, the law does not require that the victim show evidence of injury in order to prove that he or she was subject to the threat of force. In these crimes, it is understood that the victim would not willingly consent to theft. In the crime of rape, however, there is the challenge of proving the absence of consent.

The issue of consent is also a challenge for the prosecution of rapes that occur within the context of casual acquaintances. Known as **date rape** this category of crime is one of the most common forms of rape. Date rape was brought to the public's attention in 1985 with the publication of Dr. Mary Koss's research findings in *Ms.* magazine that revealed the scope and severity of rape by acquaintances.[51] She found that one in four of the women surveyed was the victim of rape or attempted rape and that 84 percent knew their attacker.

Date rape has been a subject of continued focus, especially on college campuses where there is evidence that one in five college women are raped during their college years.[52] The attention to this issue has been extensive, including focused research by the Department of Justice and the Center for Disease Control. In 1990 President George H.W. Bush signed into law the Cleary Act. Named after a nineteen-year-old who was raped and murdered in her residence hall, the act requires that every institution of higher education collect and report data about a range of crimes committed on campus. Despite the attention to this issue, fewer than 5 percent of college women who are the victims or rape or attempted rape report it to police.[53]

Women on college campuses have mobilized protests to raise awareness about the prevalence of sexual assault on college campuses. A survey commissioned by the Association of American Universities in 2015 found 27 percent of female college seniors reporting some level of unwanted sexual contact during their college years often involving the use of alcohol.[54] Reforms have led to a significant reformulation of the legal definition of consent. Replacing the idea that "no means no" is a requirement that both parties to a sexual act now seek affirmative consent. Affirmative consent requires an actual statement of "yes" rather than the absence of a "no." In California and New York, all colleges and universities

CONSENT
positive cooperation in act or attitude.

STATUTORY RAPE
sexual activities with someone not capable of giving consent, typically because they are too young to give legal consent.

DATE RAPE
non-consensual intercourse where the victim knows the attacker socially.

that receive state financial aid are required by law to adopt a standard in which consent is voluntary, conscious, and affirmative.

In 1994 the federal government enacted the Violence against Women Act (VAWA),[55] establishing the Office of Violence against Women in the Department of Justice providing support for research into causes and patterns of violence, the development of model prevention programs, and a range of victim services. Some examples of programs funded by VAWA are CASA for Children, a program that allows juvenile court judges to assign volunteers to work one on one within the child welfare system to secure services for young victims of abuse and neglect; specialized law enforcement departments that include rape-crisis or domestic violence advocates; medical training for sexual assault response teams; and coordinated response teams that create collaborative networks of advocates, police, prosecutors, and court personnel. The VAWA was reauthorized by Congress in 2000, 2005, and 2012.

Intimate Violence and Domestic Violence

The area of **domestic violence** is another key focal point of social reform within the criminal justice system brought about by the political action of women. Beginning with the battered women shelter movement in the early 1970s, women began organizing to provide safe havens for women victimized by violent partners. By 1989, there were 1,200 shelters or safe homes across the nation.[56] Women activists also fought for state legislation authorizing judges to issue **domestic violence restraining orders**, also known as civil protective orders, and no contact orders in response to the complaints of the victim. There are no national data tracking restraining orders, nor do state data distinguish between restraining orders requested by intimate partners from restraining orders for other reasons, so the actual numbers are unclear. There is evidence, however, that the request for restraining orders has increased since they were first identified as a valuable tool in restricting domestic abuse.

Studies on the effectiveness of restraining orders have a range of conclusions. For example, while one study found that physical abuse declined from 68 percent to 23 percent if victims maintain the order other studies have found that maintaining the order had no discernable impact on the level of abuse.[57] A recent research study had more optimistic results finding that restraining orders stopped the violence for half of the women surveyed, and reduced the violence and abuse experienced by the other half.[58] The same study recognized that police enforcement can be the weak link in the effectiveness of a restraining order. Though the actual usefulness of such orders in preventing future violence remains contested, there is evidence that victims who receive protective orders feel less vulnerable.[59]

As noted above, the law is only as effective as its enforcement by police. The first law requiring police to make an arrest in the case of domestic assault came in 1977.[60] By the early 1990s most jurisdictions recommended arrest in instances of domestic assaults; by 1992 arrest was mandatory in fourteen states.[61] **Mandatory arrest** grew as a trend in policing domestic violence in the aftermath of a highly publicized study that found those who were arrested had lower rates of recidivism than those who were simply advised of their violation or removed from the scene.[62] Though the results were widely accepted by the media as well as many police departments, researchers raised a number of concerns, including

DOMESTIC VIOLENCE a pattern of violence and/or abuse used by one person against another in an intimate relationship such as marriage or dating.

DOMESTIC VIOLENCE RESTRAINING ORDERS legal remedies created for abused women which can be sought at the discretion of the complaining party to prohibit or restrict contact with an abusing spouse or partner.

MANDATORY ARREST a policy requiring police to make an arrest in the case of an allegation of domestic violence.

the methodology of the study, interpretation of the results, and the generalizability of the results. In response to these concerns the National Institute of Justice funded several replication studies, which produced a range of results. Two of the studies found there was no significant difference in recidivism based on police response.[63] One study found that arrest was the most effective intervention for those who had no prior police contacts.[64] Yet another study found that a range of factors punctuated by race and class determined the usefulness of arrest.

So what conclusions can be drawn? Sherman suggests: (1) arrest reduces the incidence of domestic violence in some cities, but increases it in others; (2) arrest reduces domestic violence among employed people, but increases it among the unemployed; and (3) arrest reduces domestic violence in the short run, but can increase it over the long run.[65] All of these findings reinforce the idea that offenders are most likely to be deterred if they have a **stake in conformity**, or a reason beyond the threat of punishment to be law-abiding.

Even with all the research and the resulting changes in the laws, some police are reluctant to intervene. Police officers often adhere to traditional ideas of gender roles and therefore continue to view domestic violence as a family matter. Some police do not see intervening in domestic relationships as legitimate police work while others feel that domestic cases pose the great risk to their own safety, even though research studies have shown this to be a myth.[66]

Within the courtroom, women have advocated for reform of the law of self-defense to include criteria that fit the conditions under which women are threatened by the men in their intimate life. The "Battered Woman's Defense," as it has come to be known, has been used in cases where women are prosecuted for killing or assaulting their intimate partner.[67] To understand this defense it is necessary to have a basic understanding of battering. Battering is not just physical abuse, but "a pattern of coercive behaviors used to intimidate and manipulate the victim for the purpose of gaining and maintaining control. This pattern of violence takes place in a [what has been called a] confused climate of intimacy and love mixed with hope, fear, isolation, and intimidation."[68]

The violence typically follows a pattern called the **cycle of violence**.[69] One day the perpetrator is full of vicious threats while the next day these are followed by tearful apologies. While this cycle persists, the victim doesn't know what to believe. Eventually anyone in this situation might stop trusting her own instincts and at some point manifest **learned helplessness**, a clinical term that describes the point at which victims believe they are entirely powerless to change their situation.

Even among advocates there is disagreement whether it is meaningful to label these patterns as **Battered Women's Syndrome**. Some argue that it is necessary for juries to understand why women do not simply leave abusive partners long before an incident of lethal violence occurs. Others argue, however, that it portrays women as mentally challenged or deranged when the reality is quite different. Critics of the battered women's syndrome argue that women remain in the relationship because they accurately perceive that their life will be in greater danger should they attempt to leave. Research supports this showing that a woman's risk of a lethal attack by her husband actually increases as she takes steps to end the relationship.[70] The isolation and disempowerment associated with battering relationships, fear of losing custody of their children, fear of violence toward children, and the basic inequality between men and women are also factors that help explain why women remain in abusive relationships.

STAKE IN CONFORMITY
when a person is subject to social controls such as employment or marriage they are believed to have an increased interest in complying with society's rules or laws.

CYCLE OF VIOLENCE
a pattern of behaviors experienced in abusive relationships that moves from tension, to action, to apology or remorse.

LEARNED HELPLESSNESS
the point at which a victim of domestic abuse believes they are entirely powerless to change their situation.

BATTERED WOMEN'S SYNDROME
a constellation of symptoms similar to those experienced by someone with post-traumatic stress.

WOMEN IN THE CRIMINAL JUSTICE SYSTEM

One of the obstacles preventing justice for women as victims has been the exclusion of full female participation in the criminal justice system itself: as legislators, jurors, attorneys, judges, police officers, and correctional officers. As noted earlier, there were no woman lawyers before 1870s and women were barred from participation on juries until well into the twentieth century. Today the picture looks quite different. By the year 2012, women made up approximately half the nation's law students.[71] The first woman to be appointed to the U.S. Supreme Court, Sandra Day O'Connor, has since been joined by three additional female justices: Ruth Bader Ginsburg, Sonia Sotomayor, and Elena Kagan. Sotomayor is also the first Latina to serve as a Supreme Court justice. Women have had a small presence on urban police forces since the early twentieth century: the first female police officer was in Portland, Oregon, in 1905; by 1914, the LA police force had eight policewomen.[72] In the twenty-first century women comprise 13 percent of police officers across the country,[73] while in local departments the percent of women remains below 10 percent.[74]

Women continue to face substantial obstacles toward achieving equal status and participation within the predominantly male occupations of the criminal justice system. Yet women were not permitted to work as patrol officers until the 1960s, and there were no female sergeants in the entire nation until a successful lawsuit was won against the New York City police department in 1965. Progress for women as workers in the justice arena has been erratic. By 2011 women represented 26 percent of correctional officers, and 31.5 percent of lawyers,[75] yet women's presence in law enforcement, especially in local police departments, has actually been declining.

Although there is far greater equality and diversity within the field of criminal justice today than in the past, women and minorities still find it necessary, at times, to use the laws against discrimination to struggle for equal participation in the administration of justice. In policing and corrections, women have used the equal opportunity law to challenge the barriers to hiring and promotion and a workplace environment that is often hostile to women.

MASCULINITY, CRIME, AND JUSTICE

When we look at the arrest rates for crimes, almost any crime, but especially crimes involving acts of aggression or violence, the contrast between the number of males arrested and convicted and the number of females arrested and convicted is striking. Men commit homicides at nine times the rate women do.[76] In general men are arrested for about 75 percent of all reported crimes.[77] Ninety-three percent of those behind bars are men.[78] Simply put, males constitute the overwhelming majority of convicted criminals. Why does such a disparity occur?

In the past twenty-five years criminologists have begun the study of masculinity in a search for these answers. **Masculinity** is a term that describes all the gender characteristics assigned to males within a society. In our culture some of these characteristics are strength, control, power, and the suppression of emotion in favor of rationality. As early as 1957, theorists were aware that the socialization of gender roles was a major factor contributing to male behavior within society. It would take a few decades for criminologists to examine the

MASCULINITY
all the gender characteristics assigned to males within a society.

ways in which masculinity contributes to criminal behaviors. The burden of these cultural stereotypes shapes how men behave. Within American culture, men are taught to see aggression as a way to solve problems; to never back away from a fight; to feel responsible for the protection of women and children; and to use fists instead of language to express emotions. The dominant view of gender roles for men or the ideal of masculinity embraces aggression as highly normative behavior for males.

We can begin with the crime of assault. From the time a boy is young he is likely taught that the proper response to a threat or an actual blow is to hit back; to do less would be to brand him as "less" than a real man. Often this lesson comes from parents, both mothers and fathers, that teach male children to "stand up for themselves" physically. This is also clearly the lesson learned on the schoolyard. Boys and girls alike learn behaviors from their peers. And so boys learn that fighting is not only sanctioned, but is required. As individuals grow into adolescence the opportunity for group interaction increases, and limits of acceptable behavior are defined and hardened. Boys learn that control, strength, and forcefulness are valued, equally on the street and in our society. These values are constantly reinforced. Theorists refer to this as **hegemonic masculinity**, or the cultural ideal.

The potential negative impact this masculine ideal has on women is most evident in instances of rape and intimate violence, both of which are acts of power, determined to display and maintain control over the bodies of women. We also see the impact of these cultural norms on the barriers to women's full participation in the male-dominated occupations of policing and corrections where the presence of female personnel is viewed as a threat to the masculine identity of the occupation itself. Women who seek to climb the ranks to higher positions of authority in these fields often face a climate of harassment and discrimination intended to make the workplace a hostile environment for women. There exists, the critique is that the workplace culture of policing and corrections is also shaped by norms of hegemonic masculinity that are often counter-productive for the effective administration of justice. One question to consider is whether the administration of justice will change as more women enter into criminal justice occupations.

INTERSECTIONALITY: THE IMPACT OF RACE, CLASS, AND GENDER

Throughout this text, as we consider the impact of race, class, and gender on the criminal justice process, a final point is the need to see how these factors combine to influence outcomes.

Sociologists refer to **intersectionality** to assert that all of these characteristics collude or intersect when we try to understand the influence that social structures have on our lives. The theory of intersectionality reminds us that the influence of race, class, and gender combines in complex ways. Poor white males are more likely to be convicted of the crimes they commit than white males from a more privileged social class. But class shapes the types of crimes they commit: regardless of race, poor males commit different types of crimes from middle-class males. Yet the rate of incarceration for poor black males far exceeds the rate for poor white males.

HEGEMONIC MASCULINITY
the cultural ideal of masculine gender characteristics.

INTERSECTIONALITY
a variety of demographic characteristics, such as race, gender, and sexual identity, that collude or intersect when we try to understand the influence that social structures have on our lives.

The victimization rate for men and women is also affected by the combined influences of race and class. Consider, for example, the likelihood of being a victim of homicide. For most middle-class Americans the risk of dying from homicide is well below other factors such as disease or accidental injuries. And across the population the risk is much higher for males than it is for females. However, for young black men and women living within poor communities, homicide is a leading cause of death for both sexes.[79] Sociologists use the term **multiple marginalities** to refer to the combined impact of low status in more than one aspect of identity.

In examining the impact of gender or race on outcomes in the criminal justice, it is necessary to consider the intersection or combination of all these key factors that make up an individual's life chances within society. As we explore the criminal justice process we will pay attention to the how these factors—race, class, gender—and also age—affect the discretionary decision-making that shapes the justice process and the outcomes of the process of different groups within society.

MULTIPLE MARGINALITIES
the combined impact of low status in more than one aspect of identity.

---

de jure (p. 56) rights or practices which are established by law.

de facto (p. 56) rights or practices which exist in fact although not in law.

jurisdiction (p. 56) a sphere of legal authority.

supremacy clause (p. 56) Article VI, clause 2, of the federal Constitution declares federal law to be the Supreme Law of the Land.

separation of powers (p. 57) the division of the government into three branches: executive, legislative, judicial.

presumption of innocence (p. 57) guiding principle of criminal procedure which places the burden of proof on the state.

judicial review (p. 58) the power of the judicial branch to declare acts of the executive or legislative branch unconstitutional.

courts of last resort (p. 58) the power of the state Supreme Court to be the final interpreter of the state constitution and the power of the U.S. Constitution to be the final interpreter of the U.S. Constitution.

fundamental fairness doctrine (p. 59) the definition of due process which focuses on the substantive fairness in the application of the law.

incorporation doctrine (p. 59) the legal principle that all the procedural protections of the Bill of Rights applies to state courts under the due process and equal protection clause of the 14th amendment.

selective incorporation (p. 59) the legal principle that only some of the protections in the Bill of Rights applies to state courts under the due process and equal protection clause of the 14th amendment.

vigilantism (p. 62) illegal violence conducted by groups or individuals who believe they are enforcing justice despite the actual content of the law.

lynching (p. 62) an act of violence used as terrorism and social control typically by vigilantes, and often in the form of hanging

social control (p. 62) formal and informal processes that maintain conformity with social norms.

under-enforcement of the law (p. 63) when the criminal justice system fails to enforce the law and respond to certain kinds of victimization.

disproportionate minority confinement (p. 65) refers to the high levels of racial and ethnic minorities behind bars relative to their numbers in the population.

disproportionate minority contact (p. 65) refers to the over-representation of minorities at all stages of the criminal justice process.

Jim Crow (p. 66) state and local laws passed in the aftermath of the Civil War that reinforced racial segregation, marked by the concept of "separate but equal."

mass incarceration (p. 67) refers to the rapid increase in incarceration in the United States between 1970s and 2010, resulting in record high numbers of Americans in jails and prisons.

coverture (p. 68) the wife's legal status was subsumed under her husband's identity as a citizen.

rule of thumb (p. 69) common law doctrine regulating the use of physical force by husbands against their wives.

sexual assault (p. 70) verbal, visual, or any other kind of assault that forces a person to join in unwanted sexual contact or attention, including rape, inappropriate touching, voyeurism, exhibitionism, incest, and sexual harassment.

rape (p. 70) forced or coerced sexual assault, usually intercourse.

rape shield law (p. 70) laws that bar the introduction of evidence about a victim's prior sexual conduct.

spousal or marital rape (p. 70) rape of one's spouse.

gender neutral (p. 70) modern rape laws do not specify gender, applying to either male or female victims.

forcible rape (p. 70) unlawful sexual intercourse with a female without her consent and against her will.

consent (p. 71) positive cooperation in act or attitude.

statutory rape (p. 71) sexual activities with someone not capable of giving consent, typically because they are too young to give legal consent.

date rape (p. 71) non-consensual intercourse where the victim knows the attacker socially.

domestic violence (p. 72) a pattern of violence and/or abuse used by one person against another in an intimate relationship such as marriage or dating.

domestic violence restraining orders (p. 72) legal remedies created for abused women which can be sought at the discretion of the complaining party to prohibit or restrict contact with an abusing spouse or partner.

mandatory arrest (p. 72) a policy requiring police to make an arrest in the case of an allegation of domestic violence.

stake in conformity (p. 73) when a person is subject to social controls such as employment or marriage they are believed to have an increased interest in complying with society's rules or laws.

cycle of violence (p. 73) a pattern of behaviors experienced in abusive relationships that moves from tension, to action, to apology or remorse.

learned helplessness (p. 73) the point at which a victim of domestic abuse believes they are entirely powerless to change their situation.

Battered Women's Syndrome (p. 73) a constellation of symptoms similar to those experienced by someone with post-traumatic stress.

masculinity (p. 74) all the gender characteristics assigned to males within a society.

hegemonic masculinity (p. 75) the cultural ideal of masculine gender characteristics.

intersectionality (p. 75) a variety of demographic characteristics, such as race, gender, and sexual identity, that collude or intersect when we try to understand the influence that social structures have on our lives.

multiple marginalities (p. 76) the combined impact of low status in more than one aspect of identity.

REVIEW AND STUDY QUESTIONS

1. Explain the difference between rights which exist *de jure* and those which exist *de facto*.

2. What is the meaning of "separation of powers" and how does it operate to balance authority within the criminal justice system?

3. What is the "power of judicial review"? How was it used in the Scottsboro case?

4. Why have people referred to the Constitution as Sleeping Beauty?

5. What are the "fundamental fairness" doctrine and the "incorporation doctrine"? Explain how these legal theories have impacted the struggle for justice in the United States.

6. Describe the pattern of under-enforcement of the criminal law for black citizens. Why is this a form of racial discrimination?

7. What does it mean to say that lynching was used as a tool of social control by whites over black citizens?

8. What does Michelle Alexander mean when she says today's criminal justice system is the new Jim Crow?

9. Why does racism within the administration of justice challenge the legitimacy of our legal system?

10. Describe the pattern of under-enforcement of the criminal law in the area of male violence toward women.

11. How is rape used as a tool of social control by men over women?

12. Identify two reforms that have increased prosecution of males who commit violence against women.

13. Describe the law of consent and discuss why it is so important in the prosecution of rape. Do you think proving the absence of consent should be removed as a requirement in rape cases? Do you believe affirmative consent on college campuses is an effective policy?

14. What is mandatory arrest and why is it controversial?

15. Describe the legal change that you believe has had the greatest impact on women's victimization. Why?

16. What characteristics in men put them most at risk of being victims of crime? At risk of being perpetrators of crime?

17. Give an example of how intersectionality, or multiple aspects of one's identity, impacts treatment by the criminal justice system. Explain.

CHECK IT OUT

Websites

Famous American Trials, www.jurist.org. Learn more about the trial and events surrounding this case. Read transcripts of testimony made by key witnesses in each of the trials. Review the evidence and the judge's rulings. Read newspaper editorials of the time and check out an unpublished report written in 1931 by female reporter Hollace Ransdell about attitudes toward poor white women in Alabama.

Southern Poverty and Law Center, web site at http://www.splcenter.org/. It is an organization founded in 1971 to win equal rights for poor people and minorities.

Center for Court Innovation, http://www.courtinnovation.org/topic/procedural-justice. On this site you will find links to interviews, publications, and videos relevant to the role of process in achieving justice.

VAWA: Violence Against Women Office Homepage, www.ovw.usdoj.gov. Check out the VAWA home page to learn about the Violence Against Women Act of 2000 and the statewide strategies to criminalize and prosecute violence against women.

National Center for Women and Policing, http://womenandpolicing.com/. This site features a history of women in policing since 1905, along with current statistics, news items, and career planning resources.

National Women's Law Center, http://www.nwlc.org/. The National Women's Law Center offers information on a range of legal issues that relate to women, including a range of equality concerns, health care, poverty, and judges and the courts.

Videos:

Scottsboro: An American Tragedy. Check out the PBS web site accompanying the documentary about Scottsboro. See timelines, maps, and biographies of Victoria Price, Ruby Bates, Samuel Liebowitz, and others. Use this site to explore themes about race in America in 1930s; lynching in America and attitudes toward Jews, blacks, and women. Available at: http://www.pbs.org/wgbh/amex/scottsboro/

Lynching: Postcards from a Heinous Past. A documentary which features picture postcards from the period which create a grim chronicle the gross inhumanity and public spectacle of lynching. Available from Filmakers Library; www.filmakers.com

A Portrait of Domestic Violence, http://time.com/68989/video-a-portrait-of-domestic-violence/

Movies:

To Kill a Mockingbird (1962). This fictional classic film starring Gregory Peck is set in a southern town and closely parallels the real-life events of the Scottsboro trials.

Mississippi Burning (1988). This contemporary film portrays the first successful civil rights conviction won against a white defendant accused of murdering black civil rights workers in a southern court with an all-white jury in Mississippi.

13th (2016). This critically acclaimed documentary provides an in-depth look at the prison system in the United States and how it reveals the nation's history of racial inequality. It was nominated for Best Documentary in the 2017 Academy Awards.

NOTES

[1] James Goodman, *Stories of Scottsboro* (New York: Vintage Books, 1994), 5.

[2] Goodman, *Stories of Scottsboro*, 21.

[3] Lawrence Friedman, *Crime and Punishment in American History* (New York: Basic Books, 1993), 191.

[4] James Goodman, *Stories of Scottsboro* (New York: Vintage Books, 1994), 6.

[5] Goodman, *Stories of Scottsboro*, 97.

[6] Michael Maher, "The Case of the Scottsboro Boys," in *The Press on Trial: Crimes and Trials as Media Events,* ed. Lloyd Chiasson (Westport: Greenwood Press, 1997), 105.

[7] Maher, "The Case of the Scottsboro Boys," 110.

[8] *Barron v. Baltimore,* 32 U.S. (7 Pet.) 243 (1833), 70.

[9] *Scott v. Sanford,* 19 How. 393, 410 (1857), 7,66,67,68.

[10] *Bradwell v. Illinois,* 16 Wall. 130 (1873), 7.

[11] Randall Kennedy, *Race, Crime and the Law* (New York: Vintage Books, 1997), 76.

[12] Lawrence Friedman, *Crime and Punishment in American History* (New York: Basic Books, 1993), 86.

[13] Friedman, *Crime and Punishment,* 85.

[14] Randall Kennedy, *Race, Crime and the Law* (New York: Vintage Books, 1997), 42.

[15] Howard Ball, *Justice in Mississippi: The Murder Trial of Edgar Ray Killen* (Lawrence Kansas: University of Kansas Press, 2006), 10–11.

[16] Ball, *Justice in Mississippi,* 10.

[17] Gunner Mrydal, *An American Dilemma: The Negro Problem and Modern Democracy* (New York: Harper Brothers, 1944), 551.

[18] Marc Mauer, "Addressing Racial Disparities in Incarceration," *The Prison Journal* 91 (2011), 89.

[19] Robert Staples, "Black Male Genocide: A Final Solution to the Race Problem in America." in *Reading Racism and the Criminal Justice System,* ed. David Baker (Toronto: Canadian Scholar Press, 1994), 57–69.

[20] Randall Kennedy, *Race, Crime and Law* (New York: Vintage Books, 1998), 72.

[21] Kennedy, *Race, Crime and Law,* 115.

[22] "Nation Seeing Simpson Case in Black and White," *The Associated Press,* October 1, 1995; Mark Whitaker, "Whites v. Blacks," *Newsweek,* October 16, 1995; Michael C. Dawson, Riaz Khan and John Baughman, *Black Discontent: Final Report on the 1993–94 National Black Politics Study* (University of Chicago: Center for the Study of Race Politics and Culture, Working Paper No. 1, 1996).

[23] "Vast Majority of Blacks View Criminal Justice System as Unfair," (Pew Research Center, 2013); http://www.pewresearch.org/fact-tank/2014/08/12/vast-majority-of-blacks-view-the-criminal-justice-system-as-unfair; retrieved November 28, 2016.

[24] Marc Mauer, "Addressing Racial Disparities in Incarceration," *The Prison Journal* 91 (2011), 88.

[25] The Sentencing Project, "Facts About Prisons and People in Prison," January 2014. http://www.sentencingproject.org/wp-content/uploads/2015/12/Facts-About-Prisons.pdf; retrieved December 4, 2016.

[26] Michael Tonry, *Malign Neglect: Race, Crime and Punishment in America* (New York: Oxford University Press, 1995).

[27] Arnold Binder and Lorie Fridell, "Lethal Force as a Police Response," *Criminal Justice Abstracts* 16.2 (1984), 250–280; James J. Fyfe, "Blind Justice: Police Shootings in Memphis," *Journal of Criminal Law and Criminology* 73 (1982), 707–722; William A. Geller and Michael S. Scott, *Deadly Force: What We Know* (Washington, DC: Police Executive Research Form, 1992).

[28] Kenneth Adams, "Measuring the Prevalence of Police Abuse of Force," in *And Justice For All,* ed. William A. Geller and Hans Toch (Washington, Police Executive Research Forum, 1995); Anthony M. Pate and Lorie Fridell, *Police Use of Force* 2 (Washington Police Foundation, 1993); Albert Reiss, "Police Brutality– Answers to Key Questions," *Transaction* 5 (1968), 10–19.

[29] David Cole, *No Equal Justice: Race and Class in the American Criminal Justice System,* (New York: The Free Press, 1999), 101–131; Hiroshi Fukari, Edgar W. Butler and Richard Krooth, "Where Did Black Jurors Go? A Theoretical Synthesis of Racial Disenfranchisement in the Jury System and Jury Selection," in *Reading Racism and the Criminal Justice System,* ed. David Baker (Toronto: Canadian Scholars Press, 1994), 87–97; Hiroshi Fukurai et.al., *Race and the Jury: Racial Disenfranchisement and the Search for Justice* (New York: Plenum, 1991).

[30] David Baldus, George Woodworth and Charles A. Pulaski, *Equal Justice and the Death Penalty: A Legal and Empirical Analysis* (Boston: Northeastern University Press, 1990); William Bowers, "The Pervasiveness of Arbitrariness and Discrimination Under Post-Furman Capital Statutes," *The Journal of Criminal Law and Criminology* 74 (1983), 1067–1100.

[31] Coramae Richey Mann, *Unequal Justice: A Question of Color* (Indiana: Indiana University Press, 1993); Steven Donziger ed., *The Real War on Crime: The Report of the National Criminal Justice Commission* (Washington, DC: National Center on Institutions and Alternatives, 1996), 99–129; Marc Mauer, *Young Black Americans and the Criminal Justice System: Five Years Later* (Washington, DC: The Sentencing Project, 1995); Jerome Miller, *Search and*

Destroy: African American Males in the Criminal Justice System (Cambridge: Cambridge University Press, 1996).

[32] William Wilbanks, *The Myth of a Racist Criminal Justice System* (Monterey: Brooks/Cole, 1987); Donald Black and Albert Reiss, "Police Control of Juveniles," *American Sociological Review* 35 (1970), 63–77; Donald Black, "The Social Organization of Arrest," *Stanford Law Review* 23 (1971), 63–77; Samuel Walker, Cassia Spohn and Miriam DeLone, *The Color of Justice: Race, Ethnicity and Crime in America* (California: Wadsworth Publishing, 1996).

[33] Darnell Hawkins, ed., *Ethnicity, Race, and Crime* (Albany, New York: Suny Press, 1995); James W. Wilson, *The Truly Disadvantaged* (Chicago: University of Chicago Press, 1987).

[34] Troy Duster, "Crime, Youth Unemployment and the Black Urban Underclass," *Crime and Delinquency* 33.2 (1987), 300–316.

[35] Amie M. Schuck, Dennis P. Rosenbaum and Darnell F. Hawkins, "The Influence of Race/Ethnicity, Social Class and Neighborhood Context on Residents' Attitudes Towards the Police," *Police Quarterly* 11 (2008), 496–519.

[36] Michelle Ye Hee Lee, "Does the U.S. really have 5% of the world's population and one quarter of the world's prisoners?" *Washington Post* (April 30, 2015).

[37] Michele Alexander, *The New Jim Crow: Mass Incarceration in the Age of Colorblindness* (New York: The New Press, 2010).

[38] Alexander, *The New Jim Crow*, 138.

[39] Langston Hughes, *Scottsboro Limited: Four Poems and Play in Verse* (New York: Colden Stair Press, 1932).

[40] Lawrence Bobo and V. Thompson, "Unfair by Design: The War on Drugs, Race and the Legitimacy of the Criminal Justice System," *Social Research: An International Quarterly* 73 (2006), 445–471.

[41] Tom Tyler, "What is Procedural Justice: Criteria Used by Citizens to Assess the Fairness of Legal Procedures," *Law and Society Review* 22 (1988), 103.

[42] Jessica Guyan. "Meet the Woman who coined #Black Lives Matter," *USA Today* (March 4, 2015).

[43] *Taylor v. Louisiana*, 419 U.S. 522 (1975).

[44] Lawrence Friedman, *Crime and Punishment in American History* (New York: Basic Books, 1993), 429.

[45] James Ptacek, *Battered Women in the Courtroom: The Power of Judicial Responses* (Boston, MA: Northeastern University Press, 1999), 3.

[46] Eva Buzawa and Carl G. Buzawa, *Domestic Violence: The Criminal Justice Response*, ed., (Thousand Oaks, California: Sage, 1996).

[47] James Ptacek, *Battered Women in the Courtroom: The Power of Judicial Responses* (Boston, MA: Northeastern University Press, 1999).

[48] Susan Estrich, *Real Rape* (Cambridge: Harvard University Press, 1987); Julie Horney and Cassia Spohn, "The Influence of Blame and Believability Factors on the Processing of Simple and Aggravated Rape Cases," *Criminology* 34 (1996), 135–62.

[49] Michelle J. Anderson, "Understanding Rape Shield Laws, Excerpted from, Chastity Requirement to Sexuality License: Sexual Consent and a New Rape Shield Law," *George Washington Law Review* 70 (2002).

[50] "Rape Trial: Not Guilty," *Lawrence Journal* (1978) accessed September 22, 2012.

[51] Mary Koss, "Hidden Rape: Sexual Aggression and Victimization in the National Sample of Students in Higher Education," in *Violence in Dating Relationships: Emerging Social Issues*, ed. M.A. Pirog-Good and J.E. Stets (New York, Praeger, 1988), 145–168.

[52] Bonnie S. Fisher, Francis T. Cullen and Michael G. Turner, "The Sexual Victimization of College Women," (Department of Justice: Bureau of Justice Statistics, 2000), NCJ 182369; accessed September 22, 2012.

[53] Fisher et al., "The Sexual Victimization of College Women."

[54] David Cantor et.al., *Report on the AAU Campus Climate Survey on Sexual Assault and Sexual Misconduct* (Rockville, MD: Westat). 2015. Download at https://www.aau.edu/uploadedFiles/AAU_Publications/AAU_Reports/Sexual_Assault_Campus_Survey/AAU_Campus_Climate_Survey_12_14_15.pdf

[55] Title IV, sec. 40001–40703 of the Violent Crime Control and Law Enforcement Act of 1994, H.R. 3355.

[56] James Ptacek, *Battered Women in the Courtroom: The Power of Judicial Responses* (Boston, MA: Northeastern University Press, 1999), 46.

[57] "Practical Implications of Current Domestic Violence Research: For Law Enforcement, Prosecutors and Judges," *National Institute of Justice* (2009) accessed September 22, 2012.

[58] TK Logan and Robert Walker, "Civil Protective Orders Effective in Stopping or Reducing Partner Violence," *Carsey Institute*, Policy Brief No. 18 (2011) accessed September 22, 2012.

[59] "Practical Implications of Current Domestic Violence Research: For Law Enforcement, Prosecutors and Judges," *National Institute of Justice* (2009) accessed September 22, 2012.

[60] Joan Zorza, "Must We Stop Arresting Batterers?: Analysis and Policy Implications of New Police Domestic Violence Studies," *New England Law Review* 28:4 (1994), 929–990.

[61] Eva Buzawa and Carl G. Buzawa, *Domestic Violence: The Criminal Justice Response*, ed., (Thousand Oaks, CA: Sage, 1996).

[62] Lawrence W. Sherman and Richard A. Berk, "The Specific Deterrent Effects of Arrest for Domestic Assault," *American Sociological Review* 49 (1984), 261–72.

[63] Franklyn W. Dunford, David Hunizinga, and Delbert S. Elliot, "The Role of Arrest in Domestic Assault: The Omaha Police Experiment," *Criminology* 28 (1990), 183–206; J. David Hirschel and Ira W. Hutchinson, "Female Spouse Abuse and the Police Response: The Charlotte, North Carolina Experiment," *Journal of Criminal Law and Criminology* 83 (1992), 73–119.

[64] Paul C. Friday, Scott Metzgar, and David Walters, "Policing Domestic Violence: Perceptions, Experience, and Reality," *Criminal Justice Review* 16 (1991), 198–213.

[65] Lawrence W. Sherman, Douglas A. Smith, Janell D. Schmidt, and Dennis P. Rogan, "Crime, Punishment, and Stake in Conformity: Legal and Informal Control of Domestic Violence," *American Sociological Review* 57 (1992), 680–90.

[66] Shannon Meyer and Randall H. Carroll, "When Officers Die: Understanding Deadly Domestic Violence Calls for Service," *The Police Chief* 78 (2011), 24–27.

[67] Lenore Walker, *The Battered Woman* (New York: Harper Collins, 1980).

[68] Diane Wetendorf, "The Impact of Police-Perpetrated Domestic Violence," in *Domestic Violence by Police Officers*, ed. Donald C. Sheehan (Washington, DC: U.S. Department of Justice, 2000).

[69] Lenore Walker, *The Battered Woman* (New York: Harper Collins, 1980).

[70] Barbara J. Hart, "Assessing Whether Batters will Kill," *National Coalition Against Domestic Violence* (1988).

[71] "Quick Takes: Women in the Law in the U.S.," *Catalyst* (2012) accessed September 26, 2012.

[72] Lawrence Friedman, *Crime and Punishment in American History* (New York: Basic Books, 1993).

[73] "National Center for Women and Policing," Feminist Majority Foundation, accessed September 18, 2012, http://womenandpolicing.com/

[74] Lynn Langton, *Women in Law Enforcement, 1987–2008* (Department of Justice: Bureau of Justice Statistics, 2010), NCJ 230521.

[75] "Women in the Labor Force: A Databook," *Report 1034* (Department of Labor: Bureau of Labor Statistics, 2011).

[76] Alicia Cooper and Erica Smith, "Homicide Trends in the United States, 1980–2008," *Office of Justice Programs* (Department of Justice: Bureau of Justice Statistics, 2011), NCJ 236018.

[77] "Uniform Crime Reports," *Federal Bureau of Investigation* (2010), Table 42.

[78] Judith Green and Kevin Pranis, "The Punitiveness Report: Part I: Growth Trends and Recent Research," Institute on Women & Criminal Justice (2004) accessed September 19, 2012.

[79] "Surveillance for Violent Death-National Violent Death Reporting System, 16 States, 2007," Centers for Disease Control and Prevention, Surveillance Summaries (2010) accessed September 26, 2012.

FOCUS QUESTIONS

- **HOW** do voters think about contending alternatives when they are voting?

- **HOW** does the number of alternatives affect voting?

- **WHAT** considerations contend for attention in the minds of voters? How might they cooperate to support a particular choice?

- **HOW** does voters' identification with a political party affect voting?

- **HOW** do parties and candidates maneuver to gain votes?

- **WHAT** does it mean for voter choice to be meaningful?

In this chapter the case presents the dramatic prosecution of the Ford Motor Company for the crime of negligent homicide. The case illustrates the challenges of proving a crime occurred within the rules of evidence especially dealing with corporate crime. The chapter content describes different categories of crime and how we measure and assess seriousness of different types of crime within society.

LEARNING OBJECTIVES

After reading this chapter you should be able to:

- Describe the three key methods used to gain an estimate of crime and identify the main limitations of each of these methods.
- Explain why the incidence of white collar crime is relatively invisible in our society and identify methods used to measure white collar crime.
- Identify the main forms of violent crime and property crime and identify the specific crimes that comprise the Total Crime Index.
- Explain the term "victimless" crime and describe key methods for measuring these forms of behavior.
- Explain the "dramatic fallacy" of violent crime.
- Describe the image of crime depicted in our news media and popular entertainment and the impact those images have on our crime policies.

Case # 4: Can Corporations Commit Murder? The Prosecution of the Ford Motor Company

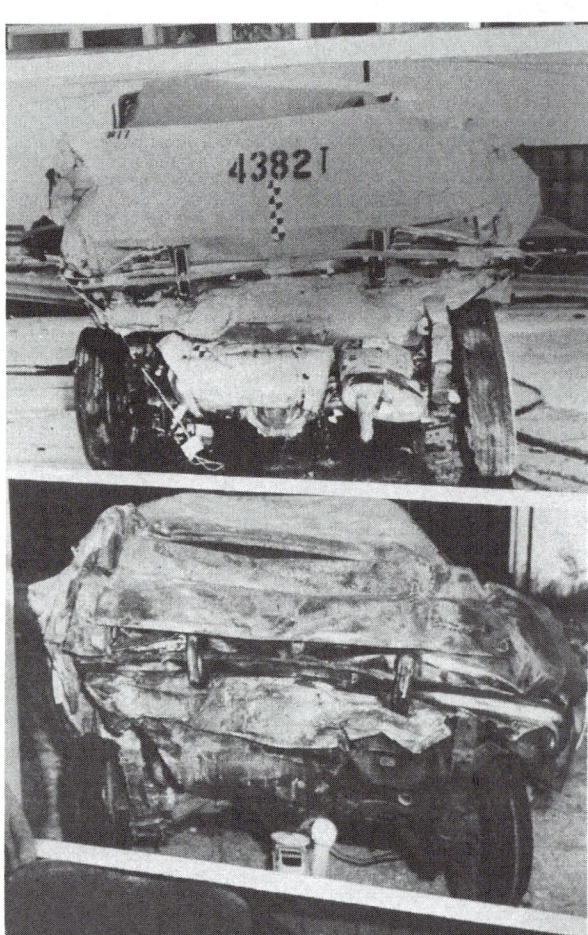

The Ford Motor Company was aware of a defect in the design of the Pinto fuel tank that sparked lethal fires in minor collisions. (Associated Press)

Terry Shewmaker, a thirty-year-old assistant district attorney, had just arrived home from work when he received a call from a local television station. A terrible automobile accident had just claimed the lives of two girls and a third teen, critically burned, had barely clung to life. Was the DA's office planning to file criminal charges against the driver of the other car? After checking with the sheriff's office to get the facts, Terry phoned his boss, Michael Consentino, a conservative district attorney in a highly conservative county in rural northern Indiana. Consentino instructed him to treat the accident as a potential homicide. By the end of the following day, the driver of the van that had rear-ended the vehicle was arrested on charges of

possessing pills believed to be amphetamines found inside his van.

But the driver, Robert Duggar, was never charged. Instead, one month later, an Indiana grand jury agreed with the evidence presented by the prosecution that the real culprit in the crash was the Ford Motor Company, manufacturer of the 1973 Pinto driven by the three teens. The indictment charged that Ford Motor Company's "reckless disregard for the safety of other persons" caused the fire that killed the girls. The Ford Motor Company through the acts and omissions of its agents "did recklessly design and manufacture a certain 1973 Pinto" likely to incinerate upon rear-end impact. Furthermore, the company failed to "repair and modify said Pinto" and "knowingly permitted the Pinto to remain on the highways and roadways of Elkhart County."

A letter from the Ford Motor Company informing the victims' family that the Pinto was being recalled for safety reasons arrived six months after the accident. For the first time in U.S. history a major corporation was criminally charged with reckless homicide for manufacturing and then failing to recall a dangerous consumer product.

What Happened on Highway 33?

Judy and Lyn Ulrich along with their cousin Donna set out from their home on a summer evening at 5:30 p.m. to play volleyball at a Baptist church about twenty miles away. The used 1973 Pinto was Judy's high school graduation present from her parents. Traveling along Highway 33, the girls stopped for gas. Continuing with a full tank, they discovered they had left the gas cap on the roof of the car when it flew across the road. To retrieve it, Judy slowed down, turned on her flashing lights and made a U-turn to the other side of the road. Unable to get off the road because of an eight-inch kerb, Judy pulled over as much as possible. Meanwhile Robert Duggar was traveling in that lane in a Chevy van. He had just reached down to retrieve his cigarettes which had fallen to the floor when he looked up to see the Pinto only ten feet ahead of his vehicle. He slammed on his brakes but there was little he could do to avoid a collision. The van rammed into the rear of the Pinto and an instant later the Pinto burst into flames.

Albert Clark was also driving down Highway 33 that day. In fact, moments before the crash, he turned to his wife and yelled, "Watch out! There's going to be an accident" (Cullen and Maakestad, 1987, p. 145). Seconds later he and his wife watched in horror as the car exploded into a ball of flames. Clark later said it was like the napalm bomb explosions he had seen in Vietnam. Clark and another bystander succeeded in pulling the badly burned Judy out from the driver's seat. With third-degree burns over 95 percent of her body, she died eight hours later. Lyn and Donna were burned beyond recognition trapped inside an inferno where the temperature of the fire was over 1,000 degrees.

Why Ford?

At first it seemed likely that Robert Duggar would be the target of criminal prosecution. Twenty-one years old, he had a record of traffic violations including speeding and running a stop sign which had led to suspension of his driving license. Inside the van, investigators found marijuana, rolling papers, two half-empty bottles of beer, and a bottle of pills. The initial arrest was based on the mistaken belief that the pills were illegal amphetamines when in fact they were caffeine pills.

But there were other troubling facts about the crash that pointed suspicion away from Duggar. State trooper Neil Graves had seen a lot of car crashes during his six and half years on the force. By the time he arrived about an hour after the accident, firefighters had extinguished the flames. Graves was the first to look inside to the backseat of the Pinto to see the charred remains of the two girls. He was horrified at what he saw and he wondered how such a minor accident could cause such destruction. Witnesses reported that the speed differential between the two cars was only about 30 miles per hour. When Graves looked inside the passenger compartment he smelled and saw gasoline splashed all around the interior of the car. Looking at Duggar's van further convinced him that something else might be at fault here. The van had only a cracked headlight and a dented front grill. What appeared to be a fender-bender in one car had resulted in a lethal inferno in the other.

Like many other Americans, Graves had read about problems with the Ford Pinto. There was extensive media coverage of an ongoing consumer safety investigation into small compact cars spearheaded by consumer activist Ralph Nader. Nader's recently published book *Unsafe at Any Speed* had increased public pressure on the government to stiffen safety regulations for automobiles. The auto industry argued that such regulations would undermine their competitiveness already under assault from Japanese and German automakers. They were lobbying hard with the federal government to limit safety regulations on the industry.

The Pinto had been Ford Motor Company's response to the challenge of cheap foreign imports. Designed to cost under $2,000 the Pinto was rushed through production in almost half the normal time period. By the date of the accident, the Pinto was among the best-selling American cars. Yet concerns about the safety of the car were growing louder. Although the National Highway Safety Transportation Board/(NHSTB) had recently set new standards to protect against fuel leakage in the event of rear-end collisions, the regulations did not require Ford to recall the nearly two million vehicles already out on the road.

Media reports in 1976 stated that there was a problem in the gas tank of the Pinto and Ford both knew about it and refused to fix it despite having the technology to do so. *Washington Post* reporters claimed that repositioning the fuel tank would only cost Ford a few dollars per car. Another investigative report by the magazine *Mother Jones* provided even more detail about the internal decision of Ford to knowingly sell a car that had a defect likely to cause it to explode into flames after rear-end collisions at relatively low speeds. The defect was the placement of the gas tank only six inches from the rear bumper. When hit from behind, it was highly likely that gas would spill out and this gushing gas was easily ignitable by a random spark from the road or steel in the car.

The investigative reporter from *Mother Jones* had acquired internal company documents that claimed that Ford's own crash tests resulted in a ruptured fuel tank over forty times. The documents also showed that their engineers knew several ways to fix it. Yet Ford did nothing. Why? According to the reporter, internal company documents outlined a routine cost-benefit analysis comparing the expense of a recall with the cost of settling lawsuits with future victims. At about $11 per vehicle, the cost of the recall would total $137 million. This figure was compared with the estimated cost of an anticipated 180 deaths, 180 serious burn injuries, and an estimated 2,100 burnt-out vehicles. The total cost estimate of settling the injury claims would be approximately 49.5 million. Based on the analysis it was more cost effective to leave the cars on the highway and settle with the victims later.

The public outcry grew louder as civil lawsuits brought by individual victims produced even more documents which showed Ford's own crash tests revealed this problem before the first car was ever sold. Juries began to award damages to victims and added punitive damages in amounts never seen before. More lawsuits and class action suits were filed in states across the country. Then in 1978, the National Highway Traffic Safety Administration announced public hearings into the safety defects in the Pinto and other small vehicles where the company would have a chance to present its own evidence. They warned the company that they had independent reports from crash tests that demonstrated significant leakage in the Pinto vehicle at low-speed collisions compared to other small vehicles that did not have this defect. In response the Ford Motor Company finally, and at long last, announced that it would send out recall notices to owners. The first of the official recall notices went out in September, too late for the three Ulrich girls from Indiana.

By the time that Michael Consentino was considering if criminal charges should be filed for the tragedy that occurred on Highway 33, there were many in the press expressing the view that the Ford Motor Company had callously put profits ahead of the lives and safety of their customers. The task Consentino faced was to consider whether or not a crime had been committed, and if so, who specifically should be charged with committing the crime. Obviously the executives, engineers, and managers who made decisions within the Ford Motor Company were the human beings responsible for the design of the Pinto and the decision to not recall the vehicle. But would it be possible to prosecute these individuals? Could Consentino actually gather sufficient evidence to establish the culpability of these individuals none of whom would willingly turn over information and none of whom resided anywhere near Elkhart County, Indiana? This seemed an insurmountable challenge against building a case against specific individuals.

Instead Consentino took a different approach. Consentino filed charges against the Ford Corporation itself charging the Ford Motor Company with reckless homicide, a charge that required only that he prove the company acted recklessly when any reasonable person would have or should have known that such behavior would result in lethal harm.

Can Corporations Commit Murder?

Consentino filed criminal charges against the Ford Motor Company. But does it make legal sense to say

Ford had committed a crime? Who is the Ford Motor Company? The challenge of applying criminal statutes to corporations faces two key obstacles. First, the corporation is only a "person" in legal terms. Corporations acquired the legal status of "personhood" through a decision to grant rights of citizenship, largely property and due process rights, to collectivities such as the church or companies dating back to the Middle Ages. With this legal status, the corporate entity itself could own property, enter into a contract with another person or company, or make a claim in court. The corporation was a kind of fictional person, granted the same legal rights afforded to natural or real persons.

Over time, particularly during the nineteenth and twentieth centuries, the courts began to increasingly use the civil law rather than the criminal law to hold corporations liable for their conduct vis-à-vis employees, customers, and the public. Corporations were gradually held to a higher standard of care for the operation of railroads, for selling of safe foods, safe products, and workplace safety. Through civil law corporations have been held liable when their conduct causes injury through the payment of compensatory and punitive damages.

Many courts, however, rejected the use of criminal statutes against corporate conduct for the simple reason that the corporation was not an actual person. Statutes that defined criminal homicide as the unlawful killing of one person by another were interpreted literally as requiring that the perpetrator be an actual human being. A second obstacle is that the criminal law rests on the concept of the actor who has a certain state of mind known as criminal intent. How could a corporation who is only a person on paper possess the mens rea, or intent, necessary to commit a crime? And how could Ford be sent to jail? There is no physical body to put behind bars. While it might be possible to hold real humans such as Lee Iacocca, the chairman of the company or the engineers who designed the Pinto criminally liable, it made no sense legally to charge Ford itself with a crime. Ford's first motion to dismiss the trial repeated the long-held legal opinion that it legally impossible to treat a corporation as a "person" in the context of the criminal prosecution.

So why did Michael Consentino, a small-time local county prosecutor, believe he could and should file criminal charges against the Ford Motor Company? A recent revision of the Indiana Penal Code had made clear to Consentino and to other legal experts he consulted that the state legislature intended the new criminal statute of reckless homicide to include acts committed by corporations, both public and private. Because the statute was so new, there was no case law interpreting the statute. Nonetheless Consentino depended on the definition within the Indiana Penal Code that explicitly stated that the word "person" means "a human being, corporation, partnership, unincorporated association or governmental entity." He also relied on another section of the code which also explicitly stated that "a corporation, partnership, or unincorporated association may be prosecuted for any offense, it may be convicted of any offense only if it be proved that the offense was committed by its agent acting within the scope of his authority."

On February 2, 1979, six months after the death of the three girls, a superior court judge denied Ford's motion to dismiss and ruled that the indictment was sufficient. As Consentino said, "As far as the law is concerned a corporation can be indicted for homicide."

The Trial: David versus Goliath

Consentino may have won the pre trial skirmishes with the corporate giant but the battle had only just begun. Like David versus Goliath, the lowly county part-time prosecutor who worked for a salary of less than $25,000 was facing one of the most skillful, talented, and well-resourced defense teams imaginable. The corporate team from the Ford Motor Company may have lost the battle to keep the state from criminally prosecuting the company but they were far from losing the war. They set out to do all they could to prevent the conviction of their client.

In the typical criminal trial, the defendant is represented by a public defender whose resources are outmatched by those of the prosecution. But when the criminal defendant is a major U.S. corporation, the tables are turned. Ford took no chances when it hired a 185-member law firm from Chicago to develop its legal strategy. When it looked inevitable that the case would go to trial, Ford also hired one of the nation's most talented defense attorneys well known for his ability to charm a jury and build rapport with a judge. Meanwhile, on the side of the prosecution was a tiny staff and even tinier budget. To compensate Consentino recruited several law professors and a cadre of dedicated law students willing to donate their time and energy for free.

Like all experienced trial attorneys, Defense Attorney Neal knew that the key to a trial was a sympathetic jury and friendly judge. To achieve this Ford won a change of venue far away from Elkhart County where the accident occurred. The trial moved to a small town 55 miles away imposing a significant financial burden on the already cash-starved prosecution team who would need to spend scarce dollars on local lodging and gasoline. But even more consequential was the defense decision to hire a local attorney to join their team. He was not only a prominent local lawyer in the town but also the office mate and close friend of the presiding judge thus ensuring a host of friendly rulings over the course of the trial.

The Prosecution and Defense

Consentino may have triumphed in many of the pretrial proceedings but one of his defeats shaped the contours of the case he was able to present at trial. The defense had argued that because the Indiana statute enabling corporations to be liable for reckless homicide had passed into law only two years ago, any actions of the company prior to that date were not legally actionable. Because the design, manufacture, and testing of the Pinto occurred before the law was written, none of this behavior could be subject to the law without violating the constitutional prohibition on the post-facto application of the law. The defense moved to dismiss the trial.

The judge agreed with the defense but noted that the failure of Ford to recall and repair the defective vehicles occurred after the passage of the law. Thus the prosecution, in making its case at trial, was only allowed to present evidence about the failure of Ford to make the recall. The voluminous evidence that had been gathered by investigative journalists about decisions to manufacture the Pinto despite knowledge of the defect along with evidence of numerous in-house crash site tests showing cars bursting into flames would not be presented to the jury unless the judge decided to allow it as background information. During the trial Consentino tried to convince the judge to permit him to enter evidence of events surrounding the manufacture and design of the car but the judge refused.

Another roadblock for the prosecution was the need to get original documents from the company to avoid claims that these were forgeries. In a civil trial defendants are required to turn over potentially relevant evidence. But in this case, the judge reminded the prosecution of the corporation's Fifth Amendment privilege against self-incrimination. Like any criminal defendant, Ford could not be compelled to assist the state to convict them and exercised its "right to remain silent" by refusing to turn over any internal documents.

Probably the most damaging evidentiary ruling made against the prosecution was the refusal to allow any photos of the incinerated bodies to be shown to the jury. The defense argued that since they agreed the girls died from the burn injuries there was no point in showing these highly disturbing images to the jury. The judge agreed and ruled that no oral, documentary, physical, or photographic evidence of the victims and the manner of their death could be submitted at trial. Without those photos, the emotional power of the case, namely, the moral outrage that Ford had put profits ahead of lives was severely diminished. An angry Consentino complained, "Ford has sanitized the state's case."

Nonetheless the main argument Consentino made was that Ford knew it had an unsafe product out on America's roadways and it failed to take the necessary steps to recall and repair this product. The reason was profit, pure and simple. He attempted to prove that this crash would not have resulted in deaths unless the car itself was unsafe. The prosecution had eyewitnesses testify that the crash appeared to be no more than a fender-bender and yet the car suddenly burst into flames. A doctor testified that there were no internal injuries indicative of a major impact: all three girls died from the burns but were otherwise free of physical injuries. Finally, he presented as much evidence as the judge would allow that showed that the Ford Motor Company was aware of these defects when it first began marketing the vehicle, continued to sell it, and was slow to issue a recall, all in order to protect and preserve profits.

The defense strategy was to raise reasonable doubt in the mind of the jury about who or what really caused the death of the three girls on Highway 33. They reminded the jury that Robert Duggar was not standing trial for his role in the accident. In his closing statement, Neals warned the jury not to blame businesses for the irresponsible drivers on the road. They also blamed the presence of eight-inch kerbs which prevented the car from fully pulling onto the shoulder of the road. The defense also put numerous executives and engineers from Ford on the stand who testified that they drove model 1973 Pintos themselves and purchased them for their wives and children.

But the crowning argument for the defense was to raise reasonable doubt about the speed differential between the two vehicles at the time of accident. They argued that in fact the speed differential between the two vehicles was much greater than prosecution witnesses claimed it to be. To bolster that argument, the defense put two witnesses on the stand who testified that they had spoken with Judy Ulrich in her dying hours in the hospital. Both witnesses reported her dying declaration that her car had been stopped when it was hit from behind. Despite several eyewitnesses from the prosecution claiming that both cars were moving at the time of impact, this testimony raised the possibility that the van hit the car at a much higher speed of fifty miles per hour that would have been sufficient to rupture fuel systems on many other car models not just the Pinto.

The prosecution entered substantial rebuttal evidence but had difficulty challenging the witnesses from the hospital that repeated the statement made by the dying girl that her "car was stopped" at the time of the crash. One final blow to the prosecution came with another unfriendly ruling from the judge that disallowed testimony from a former Ford employee that the company had rigged numerous crash tests to make it appear they met federal standards. The defense argued that it was too late in the process to enter new evidence and on matters of procedure, the judge agreed.

The Verdict and Aftermath

After twenty-nine days of testimony, the jury took four days to deliberate. At first, the jury was divided 8–4 in favor of acquittal. By day four, it came down to a single holdout who believed Ford was guilty. At the end of the fourth day, he capitulated stating that although he still believed they were guilty, the evidence the jury saw did not prove it beyond a reasonable doubt. The outcome of the trial was a crushing blow to the hard working prosecution team. It fell even harder on the Ulrich family who supported the prosecution in the hope that something positive would come of the horrific tragedy that took three beloved girls.

Despite the lack of a conviction, both the prosecutor and the family, however, have taken comfort in the fact, observed by many, that this path-breaking trial forever changed the landscape of the American criminal justice system. Although they didn't win, they did succeed in putting the Ford Motor Company on trial for homicide. This trial forever changed the assumption that corporations are immune from criminal prosecution.

THINKING CRITICALLY ABOUT THIS CASE

1. Do you agree with Michael Consentino's decision to bring criminal charges against the Ford Motor Company? Why or why not?

2. In your view, was this a fair trial? Why or why not? What elements were fair in your view and which were unfair?

3. If the Ford Motor Company had been found guilty of reckless homicide, who should have been punished for their actions? What do you believe is the appropriate punishment when a company is found to make reckless decisions that endanger the lives of the public?

4. Michael Consentino believed that this trial would make large corporations realize that boardroom decisions might be scrutinized by twelve of their fellow citizens in a jury. Do you think that this possibility has a deterrent effect on the behavior of major corporations? Why or why not?

5. Do you believe that it is important to hold corporations criminally responsible for their conduct? Why or why not?

6. Do you believe this trial offered "justice" for the victims? Why or why not?

REFERENCES

Case adapted from:

Francis T. Cullen and William J. Maakestad, *Corporate Crime Under Attack: Ford Pinto Case and Beyond* (New York: Anderson, 1987).

Mark Dowie, "Pinto Madness" *Mother Jones Magazine*, Sep/Oct, 1977.

Becker, Jipson and Bruce "State of Indiana v. Ford Motor Company," *American Journal of Criminal Justice*, 26(2) (2002).

Russell Mokhiber, *Corporate Crime and Violence: Big Business Power and the Abuse of the Public Trust* (San Francisco: Sierra Club Books 1988).

Gary T. Schwartz, "The Myth of the Ford Pinto Case," *Rutgers Law Review* 43 (1991).

The Ford Motor case is a classic "top of the wedding cake" case. It is exceptional in almost every respect: the defendant is rich whereas the vast majority of criminal defendants are dirt poor. The crime was one committed by a corporation—though there were individual board members who made the decisions that resulted in the deaths, their names were never in the public eye. No one responsible touched the weapon (the car) nor did they come in contact with the victim. In fact the time and distance between the act and the result was so great it could have gone unrecognized. This case is atypical because despite the wealth and resources of the Ford Motor Company, a determined prosecutor saw that this case got prosecuted. More typical was the failure to convict. The top of the wedding cake refers to exceptional cases that prove the rule: these are not the typical crimes to be processed by the justice system and these were not the typical criminal defendants.

The commission of crime is a phenomenon that crosses boundaries of social class, age, race, and gender: it is not the specialty of only the young and the poor. But who gets labeled a "criminal" by the justice system and which defendants end up inside the system is influenced by dynamics of class, race, and gender. People like Terence Deloach, not companies like Ford, are the typical offenders in the criminal justice system. Most criminal defendants are young; male, not highly educated, working class or lower class, and disproportionate to their numbers in the population people of color.

This chapter gives an overview of how crime is categorized, measured, and studied and offers a "snapshot" of different types of crime. Students will learn that we are better at studying and keeping official records of crimes of the street versus crimes of the boardroom. We are also better at policing and prosecuting certain segments of the American population rather than other segments. This systemic bias is reflected in the overall crime picture.

This chapter also takes a closer look at the images we as a society hold about the typical nature of crime. How does the "image" of crime in the news and entertainment media compare with the crime picture derived from official data and social science research? We contrast the picture of crime that comes into our living room every night with the picture produced by social science data. What is the relationship between the images we consume in the media and the reality of crime?

Getting the Crime Picture

Crime is hard to measure. Like most forms of deviant behavior, the people who do it try to conceal their activities from others in order to avoid the negative response typically associated with all forms of deviant behavior. For a variety of reasons, a great deal of crime goes unreported to official sources and much crime that is reported to the police is never entered into the official record. Despite all the ways we have to measure crime, there is one certainty agreed upon by all criminologists: we can only estimate the amount of crime that actually exists. Far more crime exists than we will ever be able to count or measure. The unknown amount of crime in society is referred to by criminologists as the **dark figure of crime**.

There are three key sources of information about crime: the official statistics of crimes known to the police collected by the FBI; victimization surveys which collect information directly from citizens about their own victimization; and

DARK FIGURE OF CRIME
crimes that do not become part of the official police record.

self-report studies which ask citizens to voluntarily report about their own criminal conduct. Each of these measurement devices misses an element of the picture: by examining all three for any given type of crime, we are able to fill in the gaps and piece together an approximation which is more reliable than if we used only a single source. Even so, there are certain types of crimes that are not likely to appear on the radar screen with these measurement tools and we still recognize that the dark figure of crime remains a shadowy unknown.

The Uniform Crime Reports[1]

In 1920, the International Association of Chiefs of Police (IACP) realized the need for national statistics on crimes reported to the police. By 1930, Congress was authorized to collect this information and the task was delegated to the FBI who adopted the format developed by the IACP.[2] Today, the **Uniform Crime Reports** (UCR) compiles data from thousands of police agencies across the country.

The UCR divides crime into two main categories: **Part I offenses and Part II offenses**. Part I offenses are considered to be the more serious offenses and consist of eight crimes: murder and non-negligent manslaughter; forcible rape; robbery; aggravated assault; burglary; larceny-theft; motor vehicle theft; and arson. These are so-called "headline" crimes: those that we conventionally think of when we think of crime, especially when we think of violent crime.

Until June of 2004, the FBI reported crime through the use of summary data. The **Total Crime Index** is the sum of all Part I offenses known to the police during a given period of time. The **Violent Crime Index** is the sum of all Part I violent offenses (homicide, forcible rape, arson, and robbery) or "crimes against persons"; burglary, auto-theft, larceny, and arson, constitute the **Property Crime Index**. The decision was made to discontinue the use of these indices in 2004 because of the distortion of high-frequency categories: for example, the high number of aggravated assaults drives the Violent Crime Index up concealing the rates for more serious but less common crimes of rape or homicide. Because each index was always driven by the highest offense category the index was not an accurate reflection of the crime picture.

Part II offenses contain twenty-one other less serious crimes, including status offenses, which are those acts that violate the juvenile code but are not crimes if committed by an adult such as violating curfew or running away from home.

The FBI reports data in several different formats: arrest data, crimes reported, and clearance rates. The **crime rate** is calculated by dividing the number of crimes reported to the police by the total population and then multiplying by 100,000. A crime rate is expressed as the number of crimes per unit of population that allows for a more accurate indication of increases and decreases in crime over time or for comparisons between jurisdictions with different population densities, say comparing the rates in Kansas City to New York City. Obviously there will be more crime in cities with many more people: the crime rate allows us to compare the level of crime over different historical time periods and across locations to gain a more accurate picture.

Clearance rates for these eight offenses are also collected. According to the UCR, an offense that is clear is one for which "at least one person is arrested, charged with the commission of the offense and turned over to the court for prosecution."[3] The proportion of crimes reported which are cleared by an arrest

UNIFORM CRIME REPORTS
the collection and dissemination of national data on crimes known to the police and arrest operated by the FBI.

PART I OFFENSES
crimes designated by the FBI as most serious.

PART II OFFENSES
crimes designated by the FBI as less serious.

TOTAL CRIME INDEX
the sum of Part I offenses reported in a given place for a given period of time.

VIOLENT CRIME INDEX
the sum of four Part I violent offenses (homicide, forcible rape, robbery, aggravated assault) reported in a given place for a given period of time.

PROPERTY CRIME INDEX
the sum of four Part I property offenses (burglary, larceny, auto-theft, and arson) reported in a given place for a given period of time.

CRIME RATE
the number of crimes known to the police for a given year divided by the population for that year and multiplied by 100,000.

CLEARANCE RATE
the proportion of crimes that result in arrest.

is the clearance rate. In 2015 the clearance rate for the violent crime of homicide is the highest at 61.5 percent and the lowest for robberies at 29.3 percent. Among property crimes, a mere 19.4 percent of property crimes were cleared by an arrest: 21.9 percent of larcenies resulted in an arrest but only 12.9 percent of burglaries and 13.1 percent of motor vehicle thefts reported resulted in an arrest.[4]

Criminologists have long criticized the focus on these eight crimes which are overwhelmingly crimes committed by the poor.[5] Crime data which serve as the official statistics for the rising or falling amount of crime in society do not include the twenty-one offenses listed in Part II category. Thus, the burglary committed by the young male is recorded in the official crime rate, whereas the embezzlement committed by the older middle-class employee is not. The crimes of the middle class and the well-to-do, such as insurance fraud, Medicaid fraud, filing inaccurate tax statements, insider trading, and price fixing, never appear in our official crime statistics.

Data on Part I offenses are also made available to the public in the form of **"crime clocks"**[6] which show how often each of these crimes are committed if they were spread evenly over a twenty-four-hour period. In 2015, there was one violent crime every 26.3 seconds and one property crime every 3.9 seconds.[7]

This graphic portrayal of crime in our society distorts our understanding of crime in our society. The crime clock seems to suggest that these terrible crimes are constantly occurring random events happening to all Americans. If the clock tells us that one robbery occurs every 20 minutes, it is natural for citizens to fear predatory violence from strangers everywhere and at any time.

In reality, this is very far from the truth. Crimes are concentrated in certain neighborhoods, at certain times of the day and year and among certain categories of victims. Most crime is not random but highly predictable. Violent crimes occur in certain kinds of social spaces, such as outside bars, at certain times of the day, such as closing time, and most often between people who know each other.

Limitations of the UCR

While the UCR is a major source of statistics for crime in the United States, it is a serious error to suppose these data provide a perfect picture of crime. As noted in chapter 3, a large percentage of crime is not reported to the police. Furthermore, official crime statistics focus almost exclusively on the violent and property crimes of the poor. The vast majority of corporate crimes, such as price fixing, environmental crimes, and tax fraud, are committed by those from the upper echelons of society yet we do not broadcast a crime clock which measures how often and how costly such behavior is to the American public.

Another important drawback in these data is that the UCR is a direct measure of the activity of the police and citizens and only an indirect measure of crime. In some cases, what appears to be a "crime wave," or dramatic increase in the rate of a particular crime, may be a change in the recording of crime by law enforcement. In the 1970s, the institutionalization of 911 systems in many cities resulted in a dramatic rise in reporting to police but did not reflect an increase in the actual incidence of crime itself.[8] Burglary rates may rise because insurance companies require police reports for filing a claim: thus if more property is insured, more crimes will be reported. Again, this is not measure of an actual increase in burglaries but a change in reporting behavior itself. Changes in computer

CRIME CLOCK
a form of display used in the UCR to illustrate the annual ratio of specific crimes to fixed time intervals.

technology, police practices, or the willingness of victims to report crime will affect crime data that appear in the UCR.[9]

The UCR is also hampered by other sources of inaccuracy. The data are a summary entered monthly by each police department and some jurisdictions do a better job than others in providing the data in an accurate and timely fashion. Police however do not always officially record the crimes that are reported to them. There may be many reasons for this, including pressure from politicians to reduce crime. Because crime data are often used as a measure of effectiveness of law enforcement and politicians there may be an incentive to manipulate crime statistics by systematically failing to record serious crimes.[10] This occurred in Atlantic City where a city audit found police failed to record 22,000 reports of crime in 2002.[11] In 2012, researchers in New York City surveyed 2,000 retired police officers and also confirmed that police routinely downgraded crimes to lesser offenses and discouraged victims from filing complaints to make crime statistics look better in their jurisdiction.[12]

The Hierarchy Rule is another source of distortion in the UCR. The UCR allows for the recording of only one crime, the most serious, per incident. Thus, if a robbery and rape were committed in a single incident, only the rape would appear in the official statistics and the robbery would not be recorded. The descending order of crimes in the index indicates the seriousness of the offense; thus forcible rape is considered the more serious offense compared to robbery. However, if arson occurs with either a violent or a property crime, both crimes are reported in the UCR. Since many incidents actually involve multiple criminal offenses, this method fails to provide an accurate method of reporting.

The National Incident-Based Reporting System (NIBRS)

In 1987 the Department of Justice began implementation of a new system for recording criminal statistics to replace the UCR and address some of its short-comings. Known as the **National Incident-Based Reporting System,** the NIBRS records a standard complement of information on twenty-four different types of crime. The most important improvement of the NIBRS over the UCR is recording of far more data on each crime allowing for far greater detail about crime. For each incident, specific details about the offense such as whether it involved weapons or drugs and the type of losses sustained by the victim and specific characteristics about the offender and the victim such as age, gender, and race are recorded.

The NIBRS adds an updated definition of rape that includes both male and female victims compared with the UCR that only includes data when females are reported as rape victims. The NIBRS does not use the Hierarchy Rule so all crimes are reported as offenses within the single incident. The NIBRS also includes reporting on crimes committed with computers, which provides greater coverage of white collar offenses. Finally while the UCR reports on two broad categories of Violent Crimes and Property Crimes, the NIBRS adds a third category called Crimes Against Society which includes more comprehensive coverage of drug-and narcotic-related offenses.[13]

The NIBRS collected its first data in 1991 but adoption by the entire 18,000 police departments across the nation has been static since 2012. One major reason for this is that the NIBRS is paperless and requires a department to have an up-to-date computerized records management system. The original goal was for

NIBRS OR NATIONAL INCIDENT-BASED REPORTING SYSTEM new system for recording criminal statistics to replace the UCR based on twenty-four types of crimes with expanded data on victims and offenders.

the NIBRS to replace the UCR. As of 2015 thirty-two states had been certified to report the NIBRS to the FBI, yet only about one-third of U.S. law enforcement agencies participated. Because they believe the quality of reporting under NIBRS is far superior to the traditional reporting system, the FBI is working closely with law enforcement and the public toward the goal of moving "to a NIBRS only data collection by 2021."[14]

Victimization Surveys

The second key source of information we have on the extent of crime is the **National Crime Victimization Surveys** (NCVS) conducted by the U.S. Census Bureau and published by the Bureau of Justice Statistics annually. Every year approximately 160,000 people are drawn from a nationally representative sample covering approximately 90,000 households. These same people are interviewed twice a year for three years. In addition to the household survey, the NCVS also conducts surveys within twenty-six of the nation's largest cities and surveys of business victimizations. Statistics are published as research briefs called "Crime and the Nation's Households" and "Criminal Victimization," and annual reports entitled *Criminal Victimization in the United States.*

Victimization surveys ask individuals to report on their own victimization experiences within the previous six months. Individuals are asked about crime they or members of their household have experienced during this time period and whether or not these events were reported to the police. The NCVS requests information about all index crimes except murder, kidnapping, arson, and victimless crimes. The survey also collects data about the age, race, sex, marital status, income, and educational level of victims, and minimal information about offenders such as age, race, sex, victim-offender relationship, the time and place of the crime, injuries or losses sustained, and weapons used. The NCVS has recently begun to ask questions regarding victimization that takes place in the workplace as well as at home.

The interview process for the NCVS is designed to help respondents recall and report on experiences that they have forgotten, overlooked, or found difficult to talk about. Screening questions conducted over the phone or face to face ask people to think about times when they have been threatened or attacked at home or school even by people they know or members of their family. Often victims do not think of these incidents as "crimes" and would not think to report them if they were not directly asked by the interviewer.

The data obtained from victims clearly demonstrate that the UCR undercounts crime. The first survey conducted in 1972 found the ratio between unreported crime and "crimes known to the police" to be as high as five to one in some American cities.[15] In 2015, 52 percent of all violent crimes and 45 percent of what NCVS classifies as serious violent crimes that were reported in victimization surveys went unreported to the police for a variety of reasons. The highest percentage of unreported crimes was for household theft (71%) and rape or sexual assault (69%). The lowest percentage (30%) was for motor vehicle theft probably reflecting the requirement that car owners file a police report in order to receive compensation from insurance companies.[16*]

NATIONAL CRIME VICTIMIZATION SURVEY
an annual survey of 100,000 people age 12 and older to determine the nature and extent of their victimization of crime administered by the U.S. Census Bureau.

VICTIMIZATION SURVEYS
surveys that ask people whether they have been victims of crime during a given period of time.

---

* 2015 appears to be an anomaly, as the rate of unreported motor vehicle thefts is typically about 17 percent.

Limitations of the NCVS

Just as the UCR has limitations, so too does the NCVS. First of all, victimization surveys do not measure all crimes. The NCVS also does not request information about victimless crimes, such as prostitution, drug use, or pornography. Like the UCR it does not collect data on the white collar crimes of embezzlement, price fixing, or bribery. Furthermore, many victims of consumer fraud or corporate crime do not even realize that they are victimized and so would not be able to reveal this information on the surveys even if they were asked.

Additionally, there is the problem of memory, accuracy, and honesty. Asking people about what happened to them in the past always raises questions about the quality of their memory particularly with respect to the characteristics of the offenders. Since participation is voluntary, some people may be eager to talk while others are unwilling to do so. It is not possible to know the extent to which people will underreport or exaggerate incidents that happen to them.[17] Victims of domestic violence may be afraid to report crimes committed by their spouses especially since it is possible that person may in the house or present while the interview is being conducted. Finally, although the NCVS sample is quite accurate with respect to representing the American population that resides within households, there are still significant categories of American citizens who are not included in the survey such as those who are homeless, in prison, or in the military.

Self-Report Surveys

The third and final method of measuring crime is voluntary reports by offenders themselves. These are known as **self-report surveys** because they ask individuals to reveal crimes they have committed and to report whether or not these crimes were brought to the attention of the police. Self-report surveys were originally developed in the 1960s when criminologists began to interview inmates inside prison about the number of times they committed crime without getting caught. Researchers were astonished at the enormous amount of crime undetected by the justice system. The focus of much of this research was to assess if there were important differences between those individuals whose crimes were detected by the system and those who remained unknown to the justice system.

The first nationwide self-report survey was the **National Youth Survey** that began by interviewing a group of 1,725 adolescents in 1976 about their delinquent activity. These youth were interviewed annually between 1978 and 1981 and four more times as adults until 1993. The survey asked respondents about their involvement in a wide range of activities including misdemeanor offenses such as vandalism and minor assaults to drug offenses to serious felonies including arson, assault and battery, robbery, attempted rape, and assault with intent to kill. The data revealed that although most youth engaged in minor forms of delinquency, a relatively small group of highly active chronic offenders accounted for a large amount of the self-reported delinquent conduct.[18]

Self-report instruments remain a major source of data on the illegal use of drugs and other relatively minor forms of criminal conduct. The **High School Senior Survey** sponsored by the National Institute of Drug Abuse surveys a representative sample of high school seniors about drug and alcohol use and their attitudes and values toward these behaviors. These surveys help to track patterns in drug behavior and attitudes over time among adolescents and other specific populations.

SELF-REPORT SURVEYS surveys that ask people whether they have committed crimes during a given period of time.

NATIONAL YOUTH SURVEY A longitudinal survey of adolescents interviewed each year from 1978 to 1981 and then four more times as adults through 1993.

HIGH SCHOOL SENIOR SURVEY an annual survey of a representative sample of high school seniors which asks questions about use of drugs and alcohol, and attitudes and values toward these behaviors conducted by the National Institute of Drug Abuse.

Limitations of Self-Report Data

The limitations of these data are similar to the victim surveys: Are people accurate and truthful when they report the number of crimes they may have committed? Do some young people exaggerate the extent of their involvement in crime? Do others fail to report what is most serious? In the early years of self-report studies, the surveys tended to focus on lower-level crimes on the assumption that respondents will not be likely to accurately provide information about more serious crimes. Critics argued that this underestimated the seriousness of juvenile crime and later surveys were amended to include more questions about more serious criminal behavior.

Another important limitation of self-report data can be found in the samples themselves that are often not representative of a wider population. Self-report data from incarcerated offenders may not reflect the activities of criminals who are smart or skillful enough to operate without detection. Only when samples are representative can we use data to generalize with any degree of confidence. The National High School Senior Survey uses a representative national sample of high school seniors making it possible to make reliable generalizations based on these data about the behavior of high school seniors across the country. But even this sample fails to include adolescents who have dropped out of school or those who are chronically absent from school, both categories of youth likely to engage in heavy criminal and drug use activity. Thus, despite its extreme usefulness, it is important to bear in mind that the survey cannot be used to make accurate inferences about the behavior of all adolescents of this age group.

The Measurement of White Collar Crime

The term **white collar crime** was originally coined by criminologist Edwin Sutherland to refer to crime committed by "respectable" persons. Sutherland defined white collar crime as crimes committed by "a person of respectability and high social status in the course of his occupation."[19] Not all white collar crimes, however, are committed in the course of one's job: white collar crimes include tax fraud, fraudulent claims on insurance or workers' compensation, check forgery, counterfeiting, and swindling through business schemes. The FBI defines white collar crime as "those illegal acts which are characterized by deceit, concealment, or violation of trust, and which are not dependent upon the application or threat of physical force or violence. Individuals and organizations commit these acts to obtain money, property, or services; to avoid the payment or loss of money or services; or to secure personal or business advantage."[20]

We can further classify white collar crime into two broad categories. Crimes committed through one's occupation are known as "**occupational crime**" which includes the crimes committed by the employees wearing mechanics' overalls as well as the managerial employee in the starched white shirt. The common bond between these two is the use of one's job or occupation to commit crime for personal advantage. **Corporate crime** refers to the criminal conduct of employees of a firm carried out to benefit the corporation.[21] The Ford Motor Company case was a perfect example of this type of crime. Both of these are forms of economic crimes: illegal acts committed by nonphysical means involving concealment or guile to obtain money or property. As noted below, white collar crime is not necessarily nonviolent: just as a robber's attempt to obtain property may result in

WHITE COLLAR CRIME
a general term which encompasses crimes committed by "respectable" persons.

OCCUPATIONAL CRIME
offenses committed by persons acting in their legitimate occupational roles.

CORPORATE CRIME
criminal conduct of employees of an organization committed for the benefit of the organization.

violence, so too do many forms of white collar crime result in death and injury even though the goal was to obtain greater profits.

Organized crime[22] is essentially an illegal business that provides illegal goods or services to the public. The illegal business enterprise relies heavily upon personal violence, fear, and corruption and is also known as syndicated crime. Although people often think of the Italian Mafia as synonymous with organized crime, almost every ethnic group and nationality has been represented by criminal syndicates at some point in time. Today new ethnic gangs operate large-scale businesses that control the illegal drug market. Chinese, Dominican, Puerto Rican, Colombian, and African American are just a few of the ethnic groups who have formed syndicates operating in these markets.

Unlike street crime, crimes of the boardroom are under-examined and under-counted in our society. There is no equivalent agency to the FBI's UCR that collects and reports data on the frequency and extent of many white collar crimes beyond embezzlement, fraud, and forgery/counterfeiting. Much of white collar crime comes under the jurisdiction of regulatory federal agencies such as the Securities and Exchange Commission, the Internal Revenue Service, Postal Inspections Service, or Environmental Protection Agency rather than state and local law enforcement that reports data through the UCR or NIBRS. There are virtually no government-sponsored official counts of the number of offenses known to the police or the number of white collar offenders prosecuted every year.[23]

Partly, this absence reflects the fact that white collar crimes are often undetected. Paper trails are hard to follow and there are few mechanisms for policing illegal financial activities. Often, victims themselves are unaware they have been ripped off or harmed. This is particularly common in crimes against consumers who acknowledge a price hike but have no idea that it is the result of illegal collusion or other anti-competitive practices by corporations. And it is particularly true for the harms caused by the exposure to dangerous toxins and carcinogens that cause death and disease in their victims over long periods of time.

Researchers, however, have used criminal and civil court records and the records of agencies such as the Securities and Exchange Commission, Environmental Protection Agency, or Internal Revenue Service is to compile data on the extent of white collar crime. The consistent result is that criminal and administrative violations are quite common among many large corporations. Beginning in 1949 with Sutherland, researchers have found that many corporations are repeat offenders: that is, despite getting "caught" and paying fines, these corporations continue violating the law again and again.[24] A study of the nation's 500 largest corporations found that 23 percent—almost one in four—had been the subject of criminal or civil action for serious misconduct in the previous ten years.[25]

Victimization surveys for white collar victims are relatively new. Recently this method has been used to ask a random sample of citizens about their own exposure to fraudulent activities. The National Public Survey on White Collar Crime was designed by the National White Collar Crime Center to measure the public's experience with these crimes, including victimization rates and perceptions of the seriousness of white collar crime compared to other kinds of crime.[26] To date, surveys have been conducted twice—in 2005 and 2010. In 2010 a random sample of 2,503 households were asked about their experiences with mortgage fraud, credit card fraud, identity theft, unnecessary home or auto repairs, price misrepresentation, and losses occurring due to false stockbroker information, fraudulent business ventures, and internet scams within the past twelve months.

ORGANIZED CRIME
an illegal business which provides illegal goods and services to the public.

Results show 24 percent of households and 17 percent of individuals surveyed had been victims of one of these crimes within the previous year but only 11 percent reported any of these offenses to any crime control agency. Attitudes among those surveyed found that respondents believed white collar crimes to be as serious or slightly more serious than, traditional street crimes. Particularly troubling were crimes committed by higher status offenders in positions of trust such as doctors, lawyers, or accountants or crimes committed by corporations. A majority of respondents believed that white collar criminal activity was a contributing factor to the economic crisis of 2008 and nearly half believed that the government was not devoting sufficient resources to fighting white collar crime.

THE CRIME PICTURE

In this next section, we will attempt to give students a snapshot vision of the distribution of criminal conduct within the United States. There are many ways to categorize crime: violent, property, organized, sexual, white collar, corporate, juvenile, domestic, organized, political, and more. What follows below is a basic division of crime into four broad categories: crimes of violence; property crimes; victimless crimes; and **state crimes**.

The Great Crime Drop in America

The big picture of crime trends in the United States shows a fluctuating pattern of crime that has seen a dramatic decline for the past twenty years. Between 1991 and 2015, the homicide rate decreased by 50 percent, from a high of 9.8/100,000 in 1991[27] to a low of 4.9/100,000 in 2015.[28] Property crimes have also declined continuously during this period in every single category from a high of 5,140/100,000 in 1991 to 2,487/100,000 in 2015, an overall decline of 48 percent.

The historical pattern during the twentieth century shows the United States has witnessed periodic crime waves when crime, both violent and property crimes, rose and then fell. During the 1920s crime rose and then declined beginning in 1934 and remained relatively low until the end of the 1950s. Beginning in the 1960s crime rates start to rise again and climb steadily for three decades until 1991 when we start to see a continuous decline that has lasted for twenty-five years.[29] The overall crime rate in 2015 is the same as it was in the 1960s. Homicide rates have been below 5/100,000 since 2010, the lowest rates since 1964.[30]

Crime however is not evenly distributed across the population. Rather it is concentrated both geographically, that is, within particular spaces in society, and demographically, among different segments of the population. The rise of crime during the 1960s, 1970s, and 1980s was highest in the major urban centers where rates of violent crime tripled or quadrupled and within cities, the worst crime rates are concentrated within low-income minority neighborhoods.[31] Similarly the decline in crime that has occurred within major cities across the country is less extensive within certain geographical spaces within the city.

STATE CRIMES
illegal acts committed by governments and other public authorities in violation of domestic and international law.

The Violent Crime Picture

Most Americans fear violent crimes in public opinion surveys; citizens report their concern about the threat of violent crime. Yet the vast majority of crime in American society is not violent. As we will see even more clearly in the last section of this chapter, popular entertainment and our news media vastly overrepresent violent crime. Understanding the distinction between violent and nonviolent crime is critical for understanding the nature of crime and crime policy in American society.[32]

The U.S. crime rate compared to other nations is not extraordinarily high: in fact, some countries such as Australia and Canada actually have higher rates of victimization for some types of crimes. Spain has a higher robbery rate than the United States and the robbery rate in the United States is roughly equal to the rate in many European countries such as the United Kingdom and Italy. The crime of assault is roughly equivalent in the United States as it is in Australia and Canada and many European countries.[33]

The main area where the pattern in the United States departs from that in these other nations is the area of **criminal homicide**: it is in the crime of lethal violence that the American picture radically departs from other advanced industrial nations. Homicide is the killing of one human being by another: if it is not legally justifiable or excusable (see chapter 5), it is a criminal homicide. Criminal homicide is usually divided into two categories: murder and manslaughter and each of these is divided further by degrees of seriousness. In 2015, there were just over 15,000 homicides in the United States.[34]

The U.S. homicide rate still exceeds that of most advanced industrial democracies: in 2015, the U.S. rate at 5.0/100,000[35] reveals our nation as a far more violent place compared to other English-speaking developed countries such as England/Wales at 1/100,000, Australia at .95/100,000, and Canada at 1.73/100,000. If we change our point of reference and compare the United States to the poorer, developing world, particularly those in Latin America and Africa, the United States appears to have lower levels of violence than these nations. And there are a few countries, such as those with major drug trafficking economies, such as Colombia (36/100,000), Honduras (87/100,000), and Mexico (20/100,000), where the homicide rate greatly exceeds the U.S. homicide rate.[36]

For the whole of the U.S. population, homicide is the fifteenth leading cause of death, far below many other causes such as heart disease, cancer, and automobile accidents.[37] But the risk of being a victim of homicide is not distributed evenly across the population. Gender, race, and age are factors that greatly influence the chance of becoming a victim. Most offenders and victims of lethal homicide are males between the ages of eighteen and thirty-four. Among young males between the ages of fifteen and twenty-four we see that intentional homicide is the second leading cause of death after accidents. If we look at the data by gender, race, and age, we see that, in 2013, intentional homicide is the leading cause of death for both male and female African Americans between the ages of twenty and thirty-four.[38]

According to the Uniform Crime Reports Expanded Homicide Data of murders for which relationships were known in 2014, 43 percent were committed by people—neighbors, friends, relatives, or acquaintances—known to the victim. The largest group is acquaintances but this category also includes 14.3 percent of victims killed by a family member.[39] Violence erupts in the course of the relationship itself: an argument between brothers, an argument at a bar among acquaintances, a fight between a husband and a wife. Most lethal crimes are not the result of a robbery, rape, or mugging from a stranger but arise out of non-criminal contexts, such as a personal argument, a clash of egos, or a perceived insult or slight. The not very dramatic truth is that "murder is in general the tragic result of a stupid little quarrel."[40] The two factors which most contribute to a lethal outcome are the closeness of a loaded gun and the distance of a well-equipped emergency room.

CRIMINAL HOMICIDE
the unlawful killing of one human being by another.

The UCR defines **forcible rape** as unlawful sexual intercourse with a female forcibly and without her consent.[41] This reflects traditional definitions of rape that require the following elements: 1. sexual intercourse, 2. by a male with a female other than his wife, 3. against her will and without consent, and 4. by force or threat of force or while she is unconscious. Common law specified that the woman must be a person other than the individual's wife. Forty-nine states now have specific statutes that allow prosecution of a husband for raping his wife. Some states also now have specific statutes that criminalize the rape of a male by a female and other states have sexually neutral statutes that criminalize the forcible penetration of male victims as well as female victims.

Rape is the least reported of all violent crimes partly because of the tacit acceptance of male violence against women and partly because of the shame, stigma, and difficulty in successful prosecution of these crimes that are rarely witnessed by others. Rape is a seasonal crime with the highest incidence rates in the hot summer months from June through August. Most rapes are committed by an acquaintance, relative, friend, or partner of the victim betraying a trust embedded in an ongoing relationship.

Since the 1970s, feminist activists have achieved substantial changes in the criminal justice response to victims of rape. Improved methods of responding to victims through rape-crisis centers, victim advocates, police sensitivity training, hospital emergency room rape counselors, and other kinds of innovations have greatly increased the likelihood that women who are victims of rape will be willing to report that crime to the police. The first comparison between the UCR and the NCVS survey in the late 1960s found that only one-quarter of rapes were reported to police.[42] Data from the National Crime Survey suggest that women are slightly more willing to report rape than thirty years previously: in 2015, 31 percent of rapes that were reported in the victimization survey were also reported to the police.[43]

FORCIBLE RAPE
unlawful sexual intercourse with a female without her consent and against her will.

ROBBERY
the felonious taking of money or goods from another person through the threat of force and violence.

ASSAULT
the intentional attempt or threat to physically injure another.

AGGRAVATED ASSAULT
the intent to commit serious bodily injury.

BATTERY
the non-lethal culmination of an assault.

Robbery is the felonious taking of money or goods of another from his person or in his presence and against his will, through the threat of force and violence. Robbery, armed or not, is a crime against a person because of the direct face-to-face contact and threat to the victim. Purse-snatching and pick pocketing are not considered robberies but are classified under larceny-theft. Robbery is primarily an urban offense; after assault, robbery is the most common violent crime. Perpetrators arrested for robbery are overwhelmingly male (85%), under the age of 25 (59%), and black or African American (56%).[44] Second to individuals, typical victims of robberies are gas stations, convenience stores, and banks. In 2015, firearms were used in 41 percent of all robberies and knives in about 8 percent.[45,46] In one-fifth of the robberies where a gun was used, the gun was actually discharged during the commission of the crime.

Assault refers to the intentional attempt or threat to physically injure another. **Aggravated assault** refers to the intent to commit serious bodily injury, including murder, rape, or robbery; simple assault refers to the intent to do less serious harm. **Battery** refers to the actual culmination of the injury (provided it is not lethal in which case it would constitute an act of homicide). Assault and battery therefore refer to the inflicted injury coupled with the intent to inflict that injury. Aggravated assault is the largest category of crimes against persons or violent crime. In 2015, 64 percent of violent crimes were aggravated assaults.[47] The vast majority of assaults do not result in serious harm or injury: these are incidents where one person hits another or verbally threatens another person. Although it is considered a violent offense, only three out of every hundred arrests for this crime result in any injury to the victim.[48]

Violence and White Collar Crime

White collar crime is often conceived as inherently nonviolent. This is a false characterization of the consequences of white collar crime which often have lethal effects on their victims. Consider the Ford Pinto case.[49] A faulty design of the subcompact vehicle was detected well in advance by the designers at Ford. Recognizing that the fuel system was easily ruptured in a minor collision, the company elected to continue to sell the vehicle despite the fairly certain prediction that it would result in several hundred deaths. The decision was made based on a cost-benefit analysis that showed the cost of recalling the vehicle to be greater than the projected cost of settling lawsuits with future victims. The company made a terrible miscalculation in its assessment of the cost of killing innocent consumers: in the lawsuits that followed the deaths of young people in the Pinto, judgments of fines against the company far exceeded the anticipated profits.

But as we saw, the criminal prosecution of the executives who willingly put profits ahead of consumers' lives is difficult to achieve under the current criminal statutes. The paradox of white collar violence is that a human being who would never harm another person on a face-to-face basis may nonetheless make knowing corporate decisions which may wound or kill. The Pinto case is not an exception. It is estimated that the annual death rate from white collar crime including

Whites collar crime, very costly and often violent, is overlooked and under-enforced by the criminal justice system.

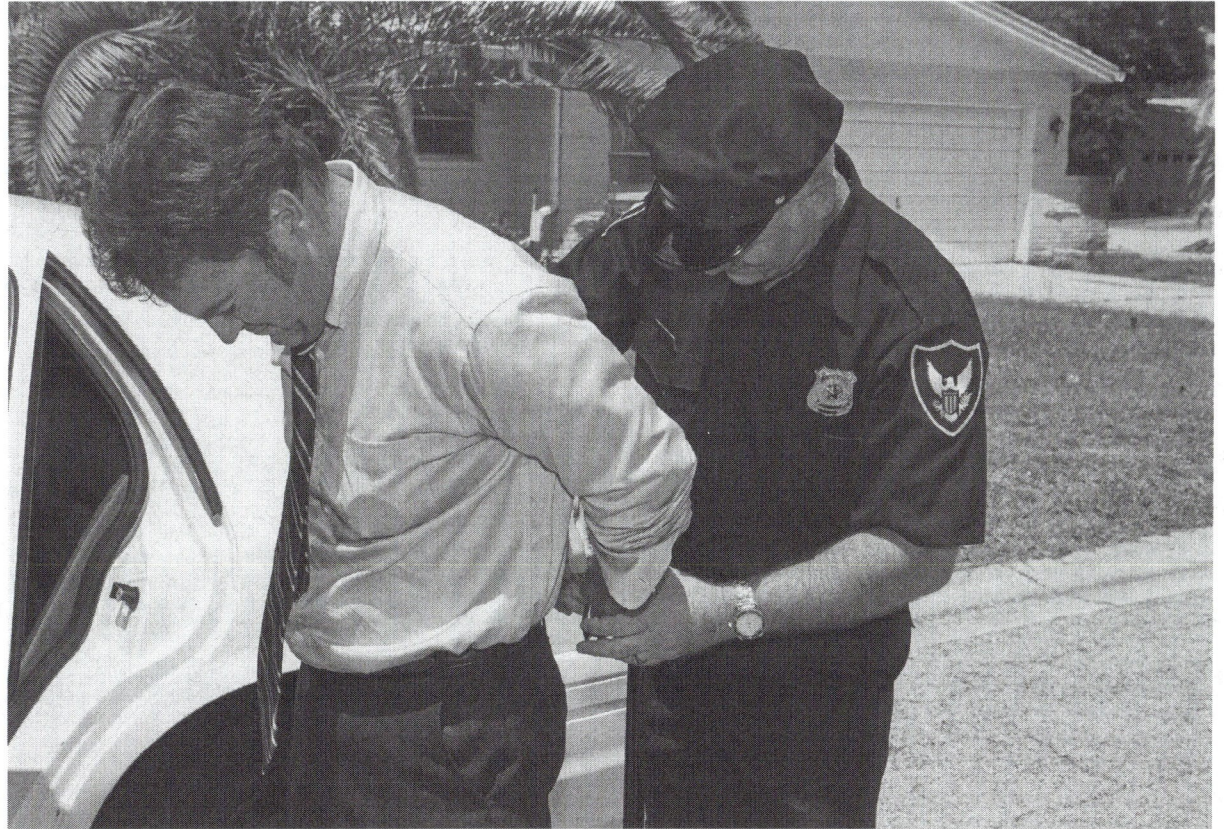

faulty products, medical quackery, violations of safety and health codes, illegal toxic dumping, and other forms of environmental pollution far exceeds the annual death rate from person-to-person homicides. Much of this violence is what Ralph Nader referred to as "postponed violence."[50] The consequence of illegal actions may be experienced by victims years, sometimes generations, after the act is committed. Illegal dumping of toxic materials may result in severe birth defects, cancers, and other illnesses for residents, detectable only decades after the events take place.

The Property Crime Picture

The vast majority of felonies, however, are not crimes against persons but are, in fact, crimes against property. Property crimes that constitute the index offenses include burglary, larceny-theft, motor vehicle theft, and arson. Part II property crimes include forgery and counterfeiting, fraud, embezzlement, buying and receiving stolen property or fencing of stolen property, and vandalism.

Burglary most often involves the breaking and entering of a personal or commercial property most often when no one is present on the premises. Daytime burglary in residences is far more common than nighttime burglaries. Burglars, unlike those who commit assaults, are usually unknown to their victims and the clearance rate for solving these crimes is quite low at 12.9 percent in 2015.[51] The average loss in a burglary in 2015 is $2,316.[52] **Larceny** is simply another name for theft. Some states distinguish between grand larceny and simply larceny involving losses below a set dollar amount such as 250 dollars. Larceny does not involve other kinds of thefts using forgery, fraud, or technology such as computers or the internet. Larceny is the most frequently reported index crime; the average value of items stolen in 2015 was about $929.[53] Bear in mind that most minor thefts are probably never reported to the police.

Arson and motor vehicle theft are the two remaining index property crimes. Motor vehicle theft is a $4.9 billion annual crime[54] that like burglary has a relatively low clearance rate: 13.1 percent in 2015.[55] Many cars are quickly disassembled and sold on to chop shops to be stripped of their parts. Arson data include only those fires that are known to have been willfully or intentionally set: those of unknown or suspicious origin are not included in the data. In 2015, the average dollar loss per instance of known arson was $14,182.[56]

Victimless Crimes

Victimless crimes are often referred to as consensual crimes and included in the statutes as crimes against public order, morality, or safety. Under English common law, such activities were not criminalized; instead activities such as fornication outside of marriage or adultery were handled by ecclesiastical courts since the Church was the clear arbiter of sinful behavior. In the colonies, however, the early settlers were successful in infusing the state with the legislative authority to enforce common morality.

Crimes against public order typically have no specific complaining victim who feels sufficiently injured to enter a complaint to the authorities. Consensual crimes are illegal acts in which the parties participate willingly usually involving the sale or exchange of an illegal good such as a controlled substance; or services, such as prostitution, gambling, pornography, or illicit sex. Most states within

BURGLARY
the trespass through breaking and entering of a personal or commercial property with the intent to commit a crime.

LARCENY
the taking and carrying away of personal property of another with intent to deprive them of the property permanently.

ARSON
the willful or malicious burning or attempt to burn any dwelling, building, vehicle, or personal property.

VICTIMLESS CRIMES
illegal activities that involve willing participants, such as drug use, prostitution, and gambling.

the United States continue to have statutes that prohibit and punish fornication, adultery, and illicit co-habitation.

It has long been debated whether these types of offenses can genuinely be considered "victimless crimes." Victims may be those community members who are forced to suffer the negative consequences of public drunkenness, wanton sexual conduct, illegal drug markets, and their associated violence. Victims are also those who suffer from the negligent behavior of those addicted to drugs or gambling such as the neglected children or impoverished families. These crimes are also seen as offense to standards of public decency and morality because such behavior undermines standards of conduct and promotes values that are contrary to the community norms. The "victims" of once-called victimless crimes, therefore, also include those within the community who experience a reduction in moral values within their community.

Although President Nixon declared a "war on drugs" as early as the 1970s, the real growth in federal and state budgets to prosecute drug crimes began in the late 1980s when media attention on the nation's "drug problem," particularly the use of crack cocaine, skyrocketed. In chapters 9 and 13 we look at the war on drugs and its impact on law enforcement, sentencing, and incarceration.

The data on the extent of illegal drug use principally come from two key self-report surveys: *Monitoring the Future Project* gathered by the University of Michigan's Institute for Social Research which collects data on secondary school student's involvement in delinquent activities and the household data collected by the *National Institute of Drug Abuse* surveying drug use among the American household population aged twelve and over. According to the 2013 survey results, drug use has been increasing. The survey estimates that 9.4 percent of Americans used illegal (or what they call illicit) drugs in the past thirty days, compared to 8.3 percent in 2002.[57] They attribute most of the increase to marijuana use, an increase that might be explained by the growing perception that marijuana should no longer be illegal. And while drug use is highest among people in their late teens and twenties, the largest increase is among adults aged fifty to sixty-four.[58] Among high schoolers, the use of illegal drugs other than marijuana is at the lowest level, 14.3 percent among twelfth graders, in the history of the survey.[59]

The sampling limitations of these two major self-report surveys help to explain a different pattern seen in two other sources of information about drug use. One is the **DAWN** or **Drug Abuse Warning Network** that relays information about drug overdoses and deaths in emergency rooms. These data show an increase in drug-related admissions in the same time period that we see a steady decline in those wider surveys. The second source is the **DUF** or **Drug Use Forecasting** data reports on routine urinalysis screens of people arrested by the criminal justice system. Like the DAWN data, the DUF shows by high patterns of heavy drug use by people arrested by the criminal justice system even for non-drug-related offenses.

State and Political Crimes

The legal definition of crime declares these acts as "crimes against the state." But what about when crimes are committed *by* the state?[60] Like corporate crime and white collar crime, the illegal acts of the government are not given much conscious attention when we talk about crime or crime control. Abusing legal authority has far reaching harm on society by eroding public confidence in

DAWN/DRUG ABUSE WARNING NETWORK a program which compiles data on drug overdoses and deaths reported within hospital emergency rooms.

DUF/DRUG USE FORECASTING a Department of Justice program which compiles data on drug use by people arrested in selected cities.

those institutions we have entrusted with the power in our society. Crimes of corruption committed by police, correctional officials, judges, and other public authorities undermine the legitimacy of the law itself.

As a culture, we hear a great deal more about crimes of individual violence than we do about the crimes of mass violence otherwise referred to as **genocide**. Ironically, a person is more likely to be brought to "justice" if he or she kills only one person than if they are responsible for the death of hundreds, thousands, or even millions of innocent people. Crimes of the powerful are generally far more destructive than the routine crimes committed by the powerless.

Genocide is not a crime in a legal sense since it is not found in the codes of statutes and other legal doctrines. Typically, crimes waged against entire peoples by states—crimes such as civilian massacres, genocides, and other forms of mass killings—are not criminalized by a body of law. The history of the European world-wide imperialism and colonialism is one of the most extreme cases of genocide, of both peoples and their culture and way of life. Before the seventeenth century, the presence of European soldiers on the continent of the Americas led to the death of between sixty and eighty million Indians destroying the advanced civilizations and cultures of the Incas, Brazilians, and other sophisticated civilizations. From the perspective of the Europeans, the indigenous populations were seen as "subhuman" and therefore not true "victims" of unjust violence. In North America, the destruction of the native cultures and tribes continued well into the twentieth century. Africans were forcibly removed from their native lands and kidnapped into slavery and submission: again, these crimes were committed by governments who acted without any regard for the fundamental human rights of the victims.

Victims of these types of violence and injustice are often without recourse other than to appeal to international intervention based on principles of international law and declarations of human rights. Generally, citizens find it easier to see foreign governments as violating the law than to view their own government's action in this light. The mass beatings, murders, and arrests carried out by the Chinese government against student demonstrators in June 1989 were widely condemned within this country as illegal and in violation of international laws of human rights.

American history is full of examples of similar forms of illegal conduct carried out by the U.S. government against its own citizens engaged in legitimate and legal political protests. As recently as the 1960s and the 1970s, the FBI conducted illegal surveillance, burglary, mail tampering to disrupt the activities of the Black Panther group and the American Indian Movement. In 2013 a low-level CIA contractor by the name of Edward Snowden revealed information about extensive U.S. spying, from bugs in EU offices to "continent-wide surveillance" in Latin America to collections of text messages across the globe. Americans were especially shocked to learn that the National Security Agency was collecting phone and email communications by and between American citizens.[61]

Included in the category of state crime are also criminal violations of the law by professionals within the criminal justice system. When police officers abuse their legal authority to use coercive force by beating a black suspect, it is an example of state criminality particularly when such conduct is widespread within a police force and tacitly condoned by the administration. When prison guards beat prisoners or deny them basic human needs such as adequate food or sanitation, agents of the state are engaged in the abuse of authority recognized as criminal conduct in violation of both U.S. and international laws.

GENOCIDE
an international crime consisting of specific acts of violence committed with intent to destroy, in whole or in part, a national, ethnic, racial or religious group.

Still in its infancy, the concept of war crimes or the existence of **human rights** which are inviolable by any political entity speaks to the need to hold individuals and nations accountable for the crimes perpetrated by the government against their own citizens and the citizens of other nations.[62] Included within the conception of crimes against humanity are **crimes of omission** where governments fail to provide decent opportunity for jobs, housing, education, and political rights for its citizenry.[63]

The crime of **terrorism** is a **political crime** defined by its motive to influence political policy or public opinion rather than for the purpose of financial gain or personal vengeance. The FBI defines terrorism as "the unlawful use of force or violence against persons or property to intimidate or coerce a government, the civilian population, or any segment thereof, in furtherance of political or social objectives."[64] Before 1993 most terrorist attacks committed against U.S. citizens occurred on foreign soil directed at military personnel, U.S. embassies, or international flights. The bombing of the World Trade Center by Islamic terrorists in 1993 marked the first major attempt at a domestic target. The car bomb planted in the parking garage of the twin towers left six people dead and injured one thousand people. In 1995, members of a right-wing extremist group in the United States planted a massive truck bomb in a federal building in Oklahoma City that killed 166 and injured hundreds more. Up until this time, this was the largest terrorist attack on American soil.

On September 11, 2001, that event was eclipsed by an even more lethal terrorist crime when four airliners were hijacked and deliberately flown into high-profile targets in New York City and Washington, D.C. Two of the planes were deliberately crashed into the twin towers of New York City's World Trade Centers, a third was crashed into the Pentagon, and a fourth was headed for the White House or Congress before it was thwarted by passengers and forced to crash in a field in Pennsylvania. In chapter 9, we examine the extent and impact of terrorism and the challenge of policing and preventing terrorism.

UNDERSTANDING THE SYMBOLIC PICTURE OF CRIME

The final section of this chapter examines how Americans "imagine" and "talk" about crime in everyday life. It is tempting to talk about the "crime" problem in the United States as if "crime" is a single form of behavior. Most Americans think of only certain types of crimes and certain "images" when they talk about "crime." Researchers believe that more than 90 percent of American adults have engaged in behavior that, if prosecuted, would result in a criminal conviction but few of us look upon our neighbors, teachers, and friends as "criminals." Usually we are not thinking about members of a board of a major corporation when we use the word "criminal." Women and men who are wealthy, well educated, and well dressed hardly fit most people's mental image of a convicted criminal.

Although crime constitutes all of these diverse forms of conduct when we refer to the "crime problem" we often are speaking in a kind of coded language to represent a particular type of crime and a particular type of the offender. The concept of "crime" therefore takes on a symbolic meaning in our culture to represent our fear of the "dangerous people, places, and classes." Sociologists refer to the transformation of a neutral term such as crime into a sacred symbol as the

HUMAN RIGHTS the concept that there are basic inalienable rights universal to all people by virtue of their humanity.

CRIMES OF OMISSION failure of governments to provide decent opportunities for housing, education, jobs, and citizenship rights for its citizenry.

TERRORISM the use of unlawful force or violence against a target to create fear or coercion for the purpose of obtaining some political concession or reward or other goal.

POLITICAL CRIMES illegal acts committed against the government or other public authorities.

process of **reification**. Our culture has a tendency to "reify" the term "crime." When we speak about the "crime" problem as if it is a single type of behavior, we reify crime. We turn a legal category of behavior into a symbol with powerful, but often unspoken meaning.

The Image of Crime in the Mass Media

The source for most Americans' mental pictures about crime derives from the images broadcast into the living rooms each evening and those splashed across the headlines each morning. Crime has increasingly become a dominant theme both within the "news" media that purports to inform citizens about the important events of the current times and in the "entertainment" media that offers amusement and distraction. Both of these genres devote disproportionate attention to a very narrow definition of the "crime problem." News programming, popular television and film content, and a host of so-called "reality-programs" offer the American media consumer a very distorted, one-sided, and racist picture of crime.

Crime in the News

The coverage of crime in the news media has been boosting sales since the advent of daily newspapers in the nineteenth century. By the turn of the century, reporters on major city newspapers began to specialize in the coverage of the crime beat devoted to police reports and court cases. Once radio and then television entered the picture, the need to create a dramatic story of great interest to a fickle audience intensified and heightened attention focused on the most sensational and gory of crimes.[65]

In recent decades, crime has continued to dominate our news media. Despite the decline in violent crime since the 1990s, the coverage of crime has increased by more than 400 percent.[66] This trend has been exaggerated by the rapid growth of news-only television stations such as MSNBC, CNN, and Fox News. And while crime coverage has dropped from 29 percent of the local news in 2005 to 17 percent in 2013, coverage on the network morning and primetime shows increased from 8 percent in 2007 to 14 percent in 2013.[67]

Although more than nine property crimes occur for every one violent crime, only 4 percent of crime news stories depicted instances of nonviolent crime. And those violent crimes that were reported were more likely to be ones that were committed by strangers than by acquaintances or intimates. Coverage of domestic violence and date rape were also less likely than cases involving predatory strangers. Studies have shown that media coverage focuses most attention on crimes where white females are victims and tend to ignore victimization of young men of color who are most often the victims of violent crime.

Crime as Entertainment

REIFICATION
the transformation of a neutral word or concept into a sacred and powerful symbol.

Most Americans form their opinion about the nature of crime and the crime problem not only from the news but also from entertainment media such as cop shows and movies. What is the image of crime that dominates our entertainment media? That is an easy question to answer. It is overwhelmingly crimes of violence, particularly, murder and rape. The world of television and movies is astonishingly more violent than the real world. Despite the fact that homicide is less than 1 percent of the major crime total, the National Coalition on TV Violence reports that the average U.S. child will view an average of approximately 500,000 murders on television by the age of sixteen. On prime time television, the rate of homicide is 1,000 times greater than it is on our streets.[68]

One of the consequences of this distorted picture of crime and justice is to influence people's perceptions and fear of crime in their own lives. The more people watch television, the more they develop what George Gerbner calls the **mean world syndrome** or the belief that the world is really full of predators lying in wait to assault total strangers for no reason other than pure malice.[69]

The fear of crime often outweighs the actual risk of victimization especially for the most violent crimes. Measures of public fear about risk of crime indicate that people's perception of what is likely to happen to them is shaped by how much and how often they watch television than by their own personal experience or that of their friends and neighbors. Watching about a terrible crime on the evening news makes people feel as if it has happened in their own backyard even if the crime took place half way across the country. The more lurid the crime, the more likely it will be broadcast in communities across the nation.

As a consequence of media-driven fear, people often alter their behavior by staying off the streets at night and avoiding interaction with strangers. This may be good news for the private security industry but it has the negative effect of undermining social life within public places. Abandonment of public spaces eventually may lead to an increase in street crime since empty streets mean less chance of detection. To an extent, fear can become a self-fulfilling prophecy.

MEAN WORLD SYNDROME
the belief that the world is full of predators waiting to assault innocent strangers.

dark figure of crime (p. 92) crimes that do not become part of the official police record.

Uniform Crime Reports (p. 93) the collection and dissemination of national data on crimes known to the police and arrest operated by the FBI.

Part I Offenses (p. 93) crimes designated by the FBI as most serious.

Part II Offenses (p. 93) crimes designated by the FBI as less serious.

Total Crime index (p. 93) the sum of Part I offenses reported in a given place for a given period of time.

Violent Crime index (p. 93) the sum of four Part I violent offenses (homicide, forcible rape, robbery, aggravated assault) reported in a given place for a given period of time.

Property Crime index (p. 93) the sum of four Part property offenses (burglary, larceny, auto-theft, and arson) reported in a given place for a given period of time.

crime rate (p. 93) the number of crimes known to the police for a given year divided by the population for that year and multiplied by 100,000.

clearance rate (p. 93) the proportion of crimes that result in arrest.

crime clock (p. 94) a form of display used in the UCR to illustrate the annual ratio of specific crimes to fixed time intervals.

NIBRS or National Incident-Based Reporting System (p. 95) new system for recording criminal statistics to replace the UCR based on twenty four types of crimes with expanded data on victims and offenders.

National Crime Victimization survey (p. 96) an annual survey of 100,000 people aged 12 and older to determine the nature and extent of their victimization of crime administered by the U.S. Census Bureau.

victimization surveys (p. 96) surveys that ask people whether they have been victims of crime during a given period of time.

self-report surveys (p. 97) surveys that ask people whether they have committed crimes during a given period of time.

National Youth Survey (p. 97) A longitudinal survey of adolescents interviewed each year from 1978 to 1981 and then four more times as adults through 1993.

High School Senior Survey (p. 97) an annual survey of a representative sample of high school seniors which asks questions about use of drugs and alcohol, and attitudes and values toward these behaviors conducted by the National Institute of Drug Abuse.

white collar crime (p. 98) a general term which encompasses crimes committed by "respectable" persons.

occupational crime (p. 98) offenses committed by persons acting in their legitimate occupational roles.

corporate crime (p. 98) criminal conduct of employees of an organization committed for the benefit of the organization.

organized crime (p. 99) an illegal business which provides illegal goods and services to the public.

state crimes (p. 100) illegal acts committed by governments and other public authorities in violation of domestic and international law.

criminal homicide (p. 101) the unlawful killing of one human being by another.

forcible rape (p. 102) the unlawful sexual intercourse with a female without her consent and against her will.

robbery (p. 102) the felonious taking of money or goods from another person through the threat of force and violence.

assault (p. 102) the intentional attempt or threat to physically injure another.

aggravated assault (p. 102) the intent to commit serious bodily injury.

battery (p. 102) the non-lethal culmination of an assault.

burglary (p. 104) the trespass through breaking and entering of a personal or commercial property with the intent to commit a crime.

larceny (p. 104) the taking and carrying away of personal property of another with intent to deprive them of the property permanently.

arson (p. 104) the willful or malicious burning or attempt to burn any dwelling, building, vehicle, or personal property.

victimless crimes (p. 104) illegal activities that involve willing participants, such as drug use, prostitution, and gambling.

DAWN/Drug Abuse Warning Network (p. 105) program which compiles data on drug overdoses and deaths reported within hospital emergency rooms.

DUF/Drug Use Forecasting (p. 105) Department of Justice program which compiles data on drug use by people arrested in selected cities.

genocide (p. 106) an international crime consisting of specific acts of violence committed with intent to destroy, in whole or in part, a national, ethnic, racial or religious group.

political crimes (p. 107) illegal acts committed against the government or other public authorities.

human rights (p. 107) the concept that there are basic inalienable rights universal to all people by virtue of their humanity.

crimes of omission (p. 107) failure of governments to provide decent opportunities for housing, education, jobs, and citizenship rights for its citizenry.

terrorism (p. 107) use of unlawful force or violence against a target to create fear or coercion for the purpose of obtaining some political concession or reward or other goal.

reification (p. 108) the transformation of a neutral word or concept into a sacred and powerful symbol.

mean world syndrome (p. 109) the belief that the world is full of predators waiting to assault innocent strangers.

REVIEW AND STUDY QUESTIONS

1. What is the dark figure of crime? Describe the three key methods used by criminologists to gain a reasonable estimate of this figure? Give examples of each method.

2. Describe the limitations of each of the three key methods of measurement.

3. Describe the methods to measure white collar crime. Why is white collar crime relatively invisible in our society?

4. What is a "victimless" crime? What are the rationales for prohibiting consensual activities such as prostitution, gambling, pornography, or drug use?

5. Describe the key difference between the crime picture in the United States and the crime picture in other major European and North American industrial democratic nations. How does the "crime clock" distort our understanding of crime?

6. What is the dramatic fallacy of violent crime? In what sense may corporate crime be "violent crime"?

7. What is "state" crime? What is "political" crime? How do they differ from other kinds of crime?

8. What is the process of reification? How does this process occur in the construction of the portrait of the "typical criminal" in American society?

9. Describe the image of crime depicted within our news and entertainment media. How does this reflect the statistics collected through the measures described above?

10. What is a "racial hoax" and how are these false claims supported by the media portrayal of crime in our society?

CHECK IT OUT

Websites

Federal Bureau of Investigation, http://www.fbi.gov. The FBI website will lead you to the UCR; ten most wanted criminals; FBI case reports, major investigations, and more.

Sourcebook of Criminal Justice Statistics, Online http://www.albany.edu/sourcebook/. This site provides data on all aspects of criminal justice in the United States. Check out the Section on Statistics for the Distribution of Known Offenses which provides summary statistics from all the major sources for criminal data covered in this chapter.

Bureau of Justice Statistics, https://www.bjs.gov. Check this site out for information, statistics, and publications about crimes, criminal offenders, and incarceration in the United States.

Crimes of Persuasion and other white collar crimes, http://www.crimes-of-persuasion.com/. This informative site gives an overview of white collar and organized crime involving telemarketing, investment, and other types of fraud. It has links to many sites on white collar investigation and prosecution.

The National Center for Victims of Crime, http://www.ncvc.org/. Check this site out for all kinds of information about victims.

Human Rights Watch, http://www.hrw.org. Human Rights Watch is the largest human rights organization based in the United States. It provides a wealth of information on human rights abuses around the globe. Click on World Report 2011 to see details and check out the section on the United States which includes information about over-incarceration and race, prison conditions, police brutality, and the death penalty.

Videos

Violence: An American Tradition—55 minutes. From the violent repression of Native Americans through vigilantism and the contemporary epidemic of domestic violence, this documentary explores recurring patterns of violence within American society. Available from Films for the Humanities and Social Sciences at www.films.com

Crime in the Suites—24 minutes. This documentary examines the phenomenon of white collar crime through profiling two notorious white collar criminals and a victim of a scam who lost his entire pension for retirements to illustrate the harmful impact of these crimes and the absence of corporate ethics. Available from Films for the Humanities and Social Sciences at www.films.com

Killing Screens: Media and the Culture of Violence—40 minutes. This video presents the research of George Gerbner which demonstrates the negative effects of media violence through desensitization to real violence and encouragement of real violence. Available from Insight Media at www.insight-media.com

Movies:

Wall Street (1987). A classic Hollywood portrayal of a corrupt ethical culture which promotes and rationalizes illegal conduct among the highest echelons of the financial industry.

Class Action (1991). The fictional Hollywood film is about a lawsuit concerning injuries caused by a defective automobile. The suit takes on a personal dimension because the injured plaintiff's attorney, Jedediah Tucker Ward discovers that the automobile manufacturer's attorney Maggie Ward is his estranged daughter. The central premise of the film is roughly analogous to the controversy surrounding the Ford Pinto.

Clockers (1995). A Spike Lee film which portrays young black men and their chronic involvement in the drug trade and violence of street life.

Enron: The Smartest Guys in the Room (2005). A documentary regarding Enron's employee choice to use corrupt business practices to protect the company. Greed, drama, and damage control all brought together in real life make this the biggest white collar crime to date.

NOTES

[1] Federal Bureau of Investigation, *Crime in the United States – 1999* (Washington, DC: U.S. Government Printing Office, 2000).

[2] Albert Morris, "What Are the Sources of Knowledge About Crime in the U.S.A.?," *United Prison Association of Massachusetts* 15 (1965).

[3] Federal Bureau of Investigation, *Crime in the United States – 2005* (Washington, DC: U.S. Government Printing Office, 2006).

[4] Federal Bureau of Investigation, *2015 Crime in the United States,* https://ucr.fbi.gov/crime-in-the-u.s/2015/crime-in-the-u.s.-2015/offenses-known-to-law-enforcement/clearances/national-data; retrieved October 31, 2016.

[5] Gregg Barak, *Integrating Criminologies* (Boston: Allyn and Bacon, 1998), 32.

[6] Federal Bureau of Investigation, *Uniform Crime Reports* (Washington, DC: U.S. Government Printing Office, 1998).

[7] Federal Bureau of Investigation, *2015 Crime in the United States,* "Crime Clock," https://ucr.fbi.gov/crime-in-the-u.s/2015/crime-in-the-u.s.-2015/resource-pages/crime-clock; retrieved October 31, 2016.

[8] Peter Moskos, *Cop in the Hood: My Year Policing Baltimore's Eastern District* (Princeton: Princeton University Press, 2008), 99.

[9] Steven R. Donziger, ed., *The Real War on Crime: The Report of the National Criminal Justice Commission* (New York: Harper Collins, 1996), 4.

[10] D. Seidman and M. Couzens, "Getting the Crime Rate Down: Political Pressure and Crime Reporting," *Law and Human Behavior* 8 (1974), 327–343.

[11] Wes Smith, "Report: Atlanta Hushed Crimes," *Orlando Sentinel* (February 21, 2004), A1.

[12] Wendy Ruderman, "Crime Report Manipulation Is Common Among New York Police, Study Finds," *New York Times* (June 28, 2012) A19.

[13] Federal Bureau of Investigation, *National Incident-Based Reporting System: General Information,* http://www2.fbi.gov/ucr/faqs.htm

[14] "NIBRS Overview." FBI:UCR. https://ucr.fbi.gov/nibrs-overview; retrieved February 4, 2017.

[15] "Criminal Victimization in the United States–1977," *Law Enforcement Assistance Administration* (Washington, DC: U.S. Government Printing Office, 1979).

[16] Jennifer L. Truman and Lynn Langton, "Criminal Victimization, 2015," (Washington, DC: Bureau of Justice Statistics, NCJ 250180, October 2016). https://www.bjs.gov/content/pub/pdf/cv15.pdf; retrieved December 7, 2016 and February 4, 2017.

[17] J. Levine, "The Potential for Crime Overreporting in Criminal Victimization Surveys," *Criminology* 14 (1976), 307–331.

[18] Franklyn W. Dunford and Delbert S. Elliott, "Identifying Career Offenders Using Self-Reported Data," *Journal of Research in Crime and Delinquency* 21 (1984), 57–86.

[19] Edwin H. Sutherland, *White-Collar Crime: The Uncut Version* (New Haven: Yale University Press, 1983), 7.

[20] Federal Bureau of Investigation, *White Collar Crime: A Report to the Public* (Washington, DC: Government Printing Office, 1989).

[21] Marshall Clinard and Peter Yeager, *Corporate Crime* (New York: The Free Press, 1980).

[22] Jay Albanese, *Organized Crime in America* (Cincinnati: Anderson Publishing, 1996).

[23] Stephen M. Rossoff, Henry N. Pontell and Robert Tillman, *Profit Without Honor: White Collar Crime and the Looting of America* (New Jersey: Prentice Hall, 1998), 12.

[24] Edwin Sutherland, *White-Collar Crime: The Uncut Version* (New Haven: Yale University Press, 1983).

[25] Kelly Orr, "Corporate Crime: The Untold Story." *U.S. News and World Report* 6 (September 6, 1982), 25–29.

[26] Rodney Huff, John Kane and Christian Desilets, *The 2010 National Public Survey On White Collar Crime* (Washington, DC: National White Collar Crime Center, 2010).

[27] Federal Bureau of Investigation, *Crime in the United States by Volume and Rate per 100,000 Inhabitants* (Washington, DC: U.S. Government Printing Office, 2010).

[28] Federal Bureau of Investigation, *Crime in the United States by Volume and Rate per 100,000 Inhabitants* (Washington, DC: U.S. Government Printing Office, 2015).

[29] William E. Stuntz, *The Collapse of American Criminal Justice* (Cambridge: Harvard University Press, 2011), 27–28.

[30] Federal Bureau of Investigation, Crime in the United States: 2015. (Washington, DC: 2016). https://ucr.fbi.gov/crime-in-the-u.s/2015/crime-in-the-u.s.-2015; retrieved February 4, 2017.

[31] Stuntz at 245.

[32] Franklin E. Zimring and Gordon Hawkins, *Crime is Not the Problem: Lethal Violence in America* (New York: Oxford University Press, 1997), 3–6.

[33] Steven Donzinger, ed., *The Real War on Crime: The Report of the National Criminal Justice Commission* (New York: Harper Collins, 1996), 10.

[34] Federal Bureau of Investigation, Crime in the United States: 2015. (Washington, DC: 2016). https://ucr.fbi.gov/crime-in-the-u.s/2015/crime-in-the-u.s.-2015; retrieved February 4, 2017.

[35] Federal Bureau of Investigation, Crime in the United States: 2015.

[36] Retrieved from http://www.nationmaster.com/country-info/stats/Crime/Violent-crime/Intentional-homicide-rate

[37] "Center for Disease Control and Prevention" U.S. Department of Health and Human Services http://www.cdc.gov/nchs/fastats/homicide.htm

[38] "Leading Causes of Death by Age Group for Black Men in the United States" http://www.cdc.gov/men/lcod/2013/Blackmales2013.pdf

[39] Federal Bureau of Investigation, Crime in the United States – 2014. (Washington, DC: U.S. 2015.) https://ucr.fbi.gov/crime-in-the-u.s/2014/crime-in-the-u.s.-2014/offenses-known-to-law-enforcement/expanded-homicide; retrieved February 4, 2017.

[40] Marcus Felson, *Crime and Everyday Life* (Thousand Oaks, CL: Pine Forge Press, 1998), 3.

[41] American Law Institute, *Model Penal Code*, 213–213.6.

[42] Presidents Commission on Law Enforcement and Administration of Justice, *Challenge to Crime in a Free Society* (Washington, DC: Government Printing Office, 1967).

[43] Jennifer L. Truman and Lynn Langton, "Criminal Victimization, 2015," (Washington, DC: Bureau of Justice Statistics, NCJ 250180, October 2016). https://www.bjs.gov/content/pub/pdf/cv15.pdf; retrieved December 7, 2016 and February 4, 2017.

[44] Federal Bureau of Investigation, Crime in the United States: 2015. (Washington, DC: 2016). https://ucr.fbi.gov/crime-in-the-u.s/2015/crime-in-the-u.s.-2015; Retrieved February 4, 2017.

[45] Federal Bureau of Investigation, *Crime in the United States* (Washington, DC: U.S. Government Printing Office, 2010), Table 321.

[46] Federal Bureau of Investigation, Crime in the United States: 2015. (Washington, DC: 2016). https://ucr.fbi.gov/crime-in-the-u.s/2015/crime-in-the-u.s.-2015; retrieved February 4, 2017.

[47] Federal Bureau of Investigation, Crime in the United States: 2015. (Washington, DC: 2016). https://ucr.fbi.gov/crime-in-the-u.s/2015/crime-in-the-u.s.-2015; retrieved February 4, 2017.

[48] Steven R. Donzinger, ed., *The Real War on Crime: The Report of the National Criminal Justice Commission* (New York: Harper Collins, 1996), 12.

[49] Francis T. Cullen, William J. Maakaestad and Gray Cavaender, *Corporate Crime Under Attack: The Pinto Case and Beyond* (Cincinnati, OH: Anderson Publishing Co. 1987).

[50] Stephen M. Rossoff, Henry N. Pontell and Robert Tillman, *Profit Without Honor: White Collar Crime and the Looting of America* (New Jersey: Prentice Hall, 1998), 81.

[51] Federal Bureau of Investigation, Crime in the United States: 2015. (Washington, DC: 2016). https://ucr.fbi.gov/crime-in-the-u.s/2015/crime-in-the-u.s.-2015/tables/table-25; retrieved February 5, 2017.

[52] Federal Bureau of Investigation, Crime in the United States: 2015. (Washington, DC: 2016). https://ucr.fbi.gov/crime-in-the-u.s/2015/crime-in-the-u.s.-2015/offenses-known-to-law-enforcement/burglary; retrieved February 5, 2017.

[53] Federal Bureau of Investigation, Crime in the United States: 2015. (Washington, DC: 2016). https://ucr.fbi.gov/crime-in-the-u.s/2015/crime-in-the-u.s.-2015/offenses-known-to-law-enforcement/larceny-theft; retrieved February 5, 2017.

[54] Federal Bureau of Investigation, Crime in the United States: 2015. (Washington, DC: 2016). https://ucr.fbi.gov/crime-in-the-u.s/2015/crime-in-the-u.s.-2015/offenses-known-to-law-enforcement/motor-vehicle-theft; retrieved February 5, 2017.

[55] Federal Bureau of Investigation, Crime in the United States: 2015. (Washington, DC: 2016). https://ucr.fbi.gov/crime-in-the-u.s/2015/crime-in-the-u.s.-2015/tables/table-25t; retrieved February 5, 2017.

[56] Federal Bureau of Investigation, Crime in the United States: 2015. (Washington, DC: 2016). https://ucr.fbi.gov/crime-in-the-u.s/2015/crime-in-the-u.s.-2015/tables/arson_table_2_arson_by_type_of_property_2015.xls; retrieved February 5, 2017.

[57] National Institute of Drug Abuse, Drug Facts: Nationwide Trends. (Washington, DC: 2015). https://www.drugabuse.gov/publications/drugfacts/nationwide-trends; retrieved February 5, 2017.

[58] National Institute of Drug Abuse, Drug Facts: Nationwide Trends.

[59] National Institute of Drug Abuse, Drug Facts: Nationwide Trends. (Washington, DC: 2015). https://www.drugabuse.gov/publications/drugfacts/monitoring-future-survey-high-school-youth-trends; retrieved February 5, 2017.

[60] Gregg Barak, "Toward a Criminology of State Criminality" in *Crimes by the Capitalist State: An Introduction to State Criminality*, ed. Gregg Barak (Albany, NY: Suny Press, 1991), 3–18.

[61] BBC News, "Edward Snowden: Leaks that Exposed the US Spy Programme." January 17, 2014. http://www.bbc.com/news/world-us-canada-23123964; retrieved February 5, 2017.

[62] Stanley Cohen, "Human Rights and Crimes of the State: The Culture of Denial," *Australian and New Zealand Journal of Criminology* 26 (1993), 97–115.

[63] Stuart Henry, "The Informal Economy: A Crime of Omission by the State," in *Crimes by the Capitalist State: An Introduction to State Criminality*, ed. Gregg Barak (Albany, NY: Suny Press, 1991), 253–267.

[64] Federal Bureau of Investigation, *Terrorism in the United States – 1995* (Washington, DC: U.S. Government Printing Office, 1997), 2.

[65] Katherine Beckett and Theodore Sasson, *The Politics of Injustice: Crime and Punishment in America* (Thousand Oaks, CA: Pine Forge Press, 2000), 75–77.

[66] Beckett and Sasson, *The Politics of Injustice*, 77.

[67] Mark Jurkowitz, Paul Hitlin, Amy Mitchell, Laura Santhanam, Steve Adams, Monica Anderson and Nancy Vogt, "The Changing TV News Landscape," Pew Research Center's Project for Excellence in Journalism. http://www.stateofthemedia.org/2013/special-reports-landing-page/the-changing-tv-news-landscape/; retrieved February 5, 2017.

[68] Beckett and Sasson, *The Politics of Injustice*, 102.

[69] George Gerbner, *Television and Its Viewers: What Social Science Sees* (Santa Monica, CA: Rand, 1976).

In this chapter we begin with the case of a man who claimed he acted to defend his home and family in the shooting death of a young man. We explore the trial and the reactions of the victim's family to the laws and the trial process. The chapter presents the legal elements of a crime, definitions of crimes and criminal defenses, as well as an exploration of the issue of guns raised by the case.

LEARNING OBJECTIVES

After reading this chapter you should be able to:

- Identify and define the five material elements of crime.
- Explain the difference between: murder, manslaughter, felony murder, and vehicular homicide.
- List the principles of defense including the idea of affirmative defenses and describe the different between defense of excuse and defense of justification.
- Identify and describe the five elements required to prove self-defense.
- Explain the "reasonable person standard" and how it might introduce bias into the legal process.

Case #5: Accident or Homicide? The Shooting of Yoshi Hattori

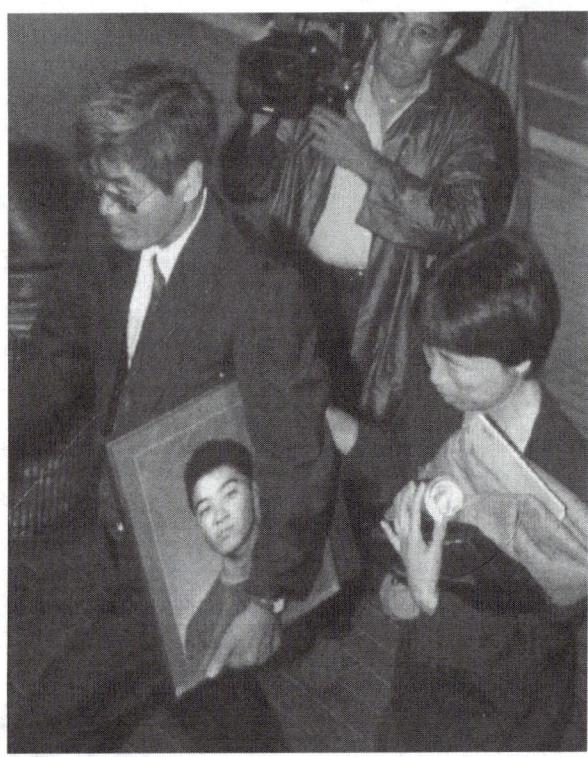

Masaichi and Mieko Hattori, parents of the victim Yoshi Hattori, carry a framed photograph of their son with them as they enter the courtroom. (Associated Press)

It was Saturday night, October 17, 1992, fourteen days before Halloween. In their modest brick ranch home on a quiet treeless street, Rodney Peairs, 30, and his wife, Bonnie, were just sitting down to a supper of grits and eggs with their two children when the doorbell rang. Not expecting visitors, Bonnie gets up to peer through the curtains of the window. Unable to see clearly, she goes to the side door of the house and opens the door a crack. Almost immediately she slams the door shut and with rising panic in her voice shouts, "Rodney, get your gun!" Rodney bolts to the bedroom closet to fetch his .44 caliber Magnum pistol fitted with a night hunting scope which he keeps fully loaded alongside his shotgun, rifle, and two pellet guns.

What frightened Bonnie Peairs was the sight of two sixteen-year-old boys, one a Japanese exchange student, the other a local boy, who had rung the doorbell expecting to be welcomed to a Halloween party actually taking place five doors down the street. Yoshi Hattori was dressed in a white tuxedo jacket in an attempt to imitate John Travolta; Webb was in ordinary clothing with bandages wrapped around his head to imitate an accident victim. Driving through an unfamiliar neighborhood to a classmate's Halloween party, the boys had mistakenly transposed the numbers of the address: instead of number 3131, they had arrived at number 1313. The house was festively decorated with a large Happy Halloween banner stretched across the front window so they figured they had come to the right place. Walking up to the front door, they rang the doorbell expecting to be greeted by their friends. They saw someone peer out a curtain and when Bonnie Peairs opened the carport door, Webb started to speak, saying "Excuse me. . ." only to be answered by Bonnie's slammed door.

Webb and Yoshi, then, turned to leave walking back to their car when they heard the carport door re-open. This time it was Rodney carrying a long-barreled and powerful gun pointed directly at the two boys. Yoshi, turned and skipped back toward Rodney, arms out at his sides in a dancing motion, repeating a gleeful refrain, "We're here for the party!" Rodney assumed a crouch position and yelled, "Freeze!" but Yoshi kept moving forward. Rodney shot him in the chest from about five feet away.

The entire sequence of events took less than two minutes. No words were exchanged other than the one sentence uttered by Yoshi, "We're here for the party" and the one word of warning uttered by Rodney Peairs, "Freeze!" Webb, standing only a few feet away, saw a man point a large gun at his friend, heard him shout "freeze," then saw his friend collapse. Rodney shut the door and locked it while Webb screamed for help. Alarmed by the sound of the gunfire and the cries for help, a neighbor called the police. Twenty-five minutes later, Yoshi was declared dead from one fatal shot to his heart.

The Judicial Process

The sheriff who arrived on the scene did not arrest Rodney Peairs or his wife Bonnie that night. According to his later testimony, the officers believed, "He was not a criminal. It was an accident." In Louisiana state law, a property owner has the right to use lethal force to defend his property from invaders or to compel someone to leave his property. In 1983, an amendment to the state code known as the "shoot the burglar" law permits residents to justifiably kill someone they believe to be an intruder if they are within four walls of a residence.

Was Rodney Peairs acting in defense of his family, life, and property as permitted by law? Or did Rodney Peairs commit a crime when he shot and killed Yoshi Hattori? In the minds of the law enforcement officers who arrived on the scene that night, the answer was obvious. Rodney Peairs, a meat-cutter at a local supermarket, was a family man protecting his property from what he believed was a lethal threat. They did not take him into custody that night nor did they seek a warrant for his arrest in the following days.

But the district attorney's office took a different view of the matter. The district attorney convened a grand jury seeking to indict Rodney Peairs on a criminal charge of negligent homicide. According to the district attorney, Rodney Peairs acted negligently when he fired his .44 caliber weapon point blank at Yoshi Hattori. Owners of firearms have a special duty to operate these weapons with care: although they did not believe that Rodney Peairs had the desire to kill Hattori and they did believe he had been genuinely frightened by his wife's fear and by the unusual behavior and appearance of the two boys that night, they argued, nonetheless, that he acted with a degree of carelessness that was criminal. Prosecutors believed that Rodney should be held criminally liable for the death of Yoshi Hattori because of his failure to operate his firearm with sufficient care and diligence. The grand jury agreed and Rodney Peairs was indicted for negligent homicide.

The case attracted enormous publicity largely because of the interest taken in the case by the Japanese public.[1] While the killing of Americans by firearms is relatively commonplace, in Japan these events rarely happen even among the criminal underworld. With a population half the size of America, densely crowded on a tiny series of islands, there are less than a hundred deaths from guns per year and most of these occur among organized crime gangs. Compare this to the 12,000 American deaths each year from handguns alone and you may appreciate how shocking the death of Yoshi Hattori was to the Japanese public. Almost immediately, the case became a national media attraction in Japan.

In this kind of atmosphere, jury selection is always a delicate affair. Both sides presented potential jurors with elaborate questionnaires that asked the typical questions required of jurors. In addition, each attorney was permitted to ask questions specific to this case. The defense grilled potential jurors about their attitudes toward gun control and about the right of a person to defend their property against invasion by intruders. The questionnaire asked potential jurors if they were members of crime-watch groups; "What do you believe needs to be done to lower the crime rate?" "how many people owned guns?" "who potential jurors felt was their greatest hero?" "have you ever experienced unannounced visitors at your home, i.e. girl scouts selling cookies, charitable organizations, persons looking for directions, etc.?" From the answers to these types of questions, attorneys for each side argued that certain jurors were prejudiced against the case from the outset. Most of these arguments were made by the defense since the law gives the defense a greater number of opportunities to strike potential jurors. In this case, the final jury that was seated consisted entirely of Louisiana citizens who believed in the right to gun ownership, the right to keep a gun at home, and the right to use a gun to protect one's family and property.

At the trial, there was little disagreement between the defense and the prosecution as to the "facts" during those fateful two minutes. The case hinged upon the interpretation of those facts and what was in the mind of Rodney Peairs and whether this was a reasonable state of mind for any common citizen confronted by the same set of circumstances. The law of self-defense does not require an individual to be "correct" in the perception that he or she is facing a lethal threat. The law simply requires that the person act as any reasonable person would act faced with a similar set of circumstances. Would any "reasonable person" have come to the conclusion that he and his family were about to be subject to an invasion of their home? Did Rodney Peairs act as any reasonable person would have done to defend his family from a lethal threat?

According to the argument presented by the defense, Rodney Peairs acted reasonably, justifiably shooting and killing Yoshi Hattori given his perception in those seconds prior to the shooting. He was, in fact, wrong in those perceptions, and he is terribly sorry for the tragic mistake, but he acted legally and justifiably on the information he had at the time. Alarmed by his wife's cries and claiming never to have heard her so frightened, Rodney perceived Yoshi and Webb as invaders who were threatening his family. Rodney Peairs gave a verbal warning and Yoshi failed to heed his warning to stay back and "freeze." It was dark and Rodney thought the camera in his hand was a weapon. Yoshi was moving erratically, waving his arms about, and Rodney feared Yoshi might grab his own weapon from his hand. According to the defense attorney, Peairs acted as any reasonable person would have when he killed Hattori. He acted in self-defense. "I had no choice," Peairs testified on the stand. "I want the Hattoris to understand that I'm sorry for everything."[2]

The prosecution rejected the view that Peairs's reaction was a reasonable one under the circumstances. The prosecution argued that Peairs had many alternatives to the lethal use of his firearm. He was well-armed when he peered out the carport window and a phone stood at his elbow in the kitchen to call the police. The yard, carport, and street were brightly lit so he could clearly see what the boys were doing. In fact, when he looked out the window, the boys had already turned and were leaving the house. They rang the doorbell just once. They did not loiter or linger about the house. They did not peer into the windows, ring the doorbell again, jiggle the doorknob of the house, try to open the door, or break into the carport door. There was no legitimate reason for Rodney Peairs to open his door and confront the boys with his gun. Even after issuing his warning, Rodney could have retreated into his house and locked the door instead of firing his gun. According to the prosecution, Peairs was guilty of the illegal discharge of a firearm. There was no justification for the firing of his weapon that night. Peairs made several bad decisions that night and deserves to be held responsible for them. "Otherwise," said the district attorney, "anyone who comes by your house, you could kill them. You don't need a reason."[3]

The jury deliberated for less than three hours. Then they returned a unanimous verdict of not guilty. The twelve-person, all-white jury found that Rodney Peairs acted in self-defense when he killed Yoshi Hattori when he rang the wrong doorbell on Saturday night at 8 p.m. in the evening.

The Victims' Perspective

Stories about crimes rarely chronicle the experience of those who are most affected by the crime itself, namely, the victim and their families. In the case of homicides, the survivors of the victim are often the last to be notified about almost every development in the criminal case. The Haymakers, parents of Webb and Yoshi's "host" parents in the United States, gave the parents of Yoshi Hattori the grim news of their son's death. Masaichi Hattori, an engineer with an auto-parts manufacturer, and his mother, Mieko, a homemaker, flew to

Louisiana where the Haymakers tried to comfort and explain the incomprehensible to these parents and to their entire nation. Why was their son killed? What had he done to provoke such a lethal response? Why would someone shoot an unarmed young man? What were the Peairses thinking that they were so frightened by the mere presence of strangers outside their front door?

These were questions the Haymakers were at a loss to answer. Like many victims, the Hattoris sought answers to understand the reason for their son's death. They sought to understand the behavior and motives of their son's killer. But like all victims, they were prevented from asking any direct questions of the defendants. During the months leading up to the trial, the Hattoris were denied any direct contact with the Peairs. No letter of regret, remorse, sympathy, or expression of sorrow ever came from Peairs or his wife directly to the Hattori family.

The Hattoris took their son home to be buried in Japan. The funeral was a major media event in Japan.[4] Thousands of mourners showed up to pay their respects to the Hattoris. There were flowers, bouquets, and messages from all over Japan including expressions of sympathy from Japan's major companies, the Foreign Ministry, and the U.S. government. The Prime Minister of Japan called on Washington to change its gun ownership laws. There was, however, no sign of flowers or message sent from the man and woman directly responsible for the death of the sixteen-year-old boy.

The Hattoris returned to the United States several times over the next year as the criminal proceedings against Rodney Peairs churned forward. Like most victims, they felt compelled to be present, to hear, and witness the proceedings even though little new information or insight was offered to them. Hundreds of spectators showed up at the courtroom and in the throng the parents of the victim were given little attention, finding it difficult to even find a seat among the crowd. At each hearing and for every day of the trial, Mr. Hattori sat impassively listening as the defense painted an unflattering portrait of his son's behavior that night. They described Yoshi as "erratic," "kinetic," and even "bizarre."

Were these truthful? Is truth what takes place in a courtroom? Not necessarily. The job of the defense is to present the facts in a light most favorable to his or her client's interests. In this case, it was in the interest of Rodney Peairs that the actions of Yoshi be presented as menacing in order to convince the jury that Peairs was reasonable to be afraid of him and therefore acted legally in discharging his weapon. For grieving members of the victim's family, such a zealous defense makes attending the trial a painful and difficult experience in which they are made to feel as if their son, not the defendant, was to blame.

From the witness stand, Rodney Peairs testified that he felt deep regret over the incident. He stated in court that he was sorry but that he felt he had no choice but to shoot Yoshi. Beyond that testimony in the trial, Peairs made no attempt to contact the parents of the boy by letter, telephone, or face to face. In Japanese culture this failure to acknowledge personal responsibility to the victim's family is unthinkable. In Japan, an expression of sincere and deep apology is an expected response in the wake of such a violent act.

For the victims, the long silence from Peairs was as incomprehensible and painful as the adversarial trial itself. Told that it would not be possible to interact with Peairs directly while criminal proceedings were in progress, the Hattoris believed they were finally going to hear directly from Peairs at a meeting scheduled after the acquittal. But it was not Rodney or his wife who showed up on Monday morning to the meeting, but the lawyer who continued to speak for his client and defend his actions as "justifiable."

Even more painful for the Hattoris were the shouts of victory and celebrations that erupted when the jury returned the verdict of "not guilty." For the Japanese the American-style adversarial system which focuses all the attention on the "battle" of the trial and declares one side the "winner" and the other the "loser" was a mockery of their understanding of justice. Many were stunned by the conduct of the courtroom scene in which spectators cheered and made the V sign for victory even while the parents of Yoshi sat nearby watching the spectacle.

The Civil Trial[5]

Shortly after the verdict in the criminal trial, the Hattoris announced that they were bringing a civil suit of wrongful death against Peairs. The money, they said, was of no interest to them. But they intended to bring this suit because "they wanted the U.S. judicial system to say their son's death was a wrongful death."[6] For the Hattoris, it was important for them to have the justice system confirm that a wrong had been done when their son was killed. According to their lawyer, Mr. Moore, they filed a civil suit because they wanted "to show that what happened was not right."

The civil law differs from the criminal law in at least one important way. A civil trial is subject to a lower standard of proof than a criminal trial because the penalties are about making financial reparations rather than inflicting punishment on the defendant. While a defendant who loses a civil case may be required to pay damages, they cannot be punished by being sent to jail.

In the civil trial, a Baton Rouge trial court found Peairs guilty of wrongful death and ruled that he and his insurance company jointly owed the Hattoris $653,077. The state district court judge rejected the defense's argument that Peairs thought that Yoshi Hattori was a lunatic threatening to invade his home and harm his family stating that "There was no justification whatsoever that the killing was necessary to save himself or his family. . . . There was absolutely no need to the resort of a dangerous weapon."[7] Peairs was ordered to pay $85,000—the maximum allowed under state law—for the youth's pain and suffering, $275,000 each to his parents for the wrongful death, and about $18,000 to cover funeral expenses.

Peairs appealed the decision arguing that Hattori had been partially responsible for the incident and that therefore the amount should be reduced. This argument was rejected by the appeals court. Later the Louisiana Supreme Judicial Court denied a writ filed on behalf of Rodney Peairs leaving the judgment against him to stand. The insurance company, Louisiana Farm Bureau Mutual, paid the 100,000 it was responsible for in the policy while Peairs is technically responsible for paying the remaining $550,000.

The Hattoris knew from the outset that Peairs was unlikely to ever repay the money. The civil trial was not about money. The Hattoris were seeking the symbolic statement from the justice system that what Peairs had done was neither reasonable nor right. The Hattoris offered a statement following the first civil verdict that stated: "We are satisfied to finally find out with whom the responsibility belongs." Mrs. Hattori also went on to say, "Although the verdict was in our favor, the hole in my heart will always be there forever. . . . Please decrease the number of handguns as much as possible." After Peairs had exhausted all appeals, his lawyers argued that he was totally broke, having lost his job at the supermarket and his home and was living in a trailer park working as an auto mechanic.

The Gun Control Campaign

The Hattoris announced that they would be willing to forgo the judgment against Peairs if he would give them the gun he had used to kill their son. Emiko Hattori said, "No matter how much financial compensation we are awarded, it is not equal to the loss of our son. Though the lawsuit has not yet been settled, we plan to negotiate with Peairs' representative. We hope to use the gun as a symbol of the gun control movement."[8] The money they received from the insurance company was already being used to sponsor a U.S. gun control award in memory of their son. The Hattoris have donated all that they received to a foundation established in their son's name for reform of American gun control laws.

Like many survivors of murder, for the Hattoris the biggest question is why? Rodney Peairs was not a killer or murderous criminal. The Hattoris along with many of their fellow countrymen struggled to comprehend the mindset of the Peairses that led to the violent death of their son. Yoshi's mother wrote in an open letter to the major Japanese newspapers shortly after the acquittal: "When an innocent child is shot by mistake and the guilty party is let off scot-free, we can only conclude that such a society is sick." The most obvious culprit in this terrible tragedy was the ubiquity of guns in every American household. To their mind, the true cause of their son's death was the overwhelming presence of guns in so many American homes.

Like many survivors, the Hattoris needed to do something constructive with their grief. Yoshi's mother explained that their son had always hoped to do something positive in the world, so in his place, they would speak out against the use of guns in American society. Within months of the shooting, by the time of the first pretrial hearing on the case, the Hattoris had begun a petition drive, signed by 800,000 Japanese citizens urging the newly elected President Clinton to push for more stringent gun control laws. In the petition written by the Hattoris the parents clearly placed the blame for their son's death in the American laws that permit people to own guns. For this family, like many survivors of murder, an outlet for grief is to turn their pain into activism that will prevent future tragedies. Few families can accept the idea that their loved one's death is without some value or benefit to the world.

In the petition the Hattoris wrote: "The thing we must really despise, even more than the criminal, is the American law that permits people to own guns. We know many fine Americans, but we feel a fierce anger that these Americans have let their country become a place where people must walk the streets in fear."[9] Over the next year, the Hattoris collected more than 1.8 million signatures on that petition from Americans and from Japanese. They presented this petition to President Clinton at the White House on November 22, 1995, the day that would have been Yoshi's eighteenth birthday.

THINKING CRITICALLY ABOUT THIS CASE

1. Who are the members of the criminal justice system who had "discretion" in this case? How did the police, prosecution, and defense defend the interests of justice in their exercise of discretion?

2. If the job of the jury is to determine what was "reasonable," how important is the composition of the jury for making these decisions? Can we agree on a single standard for "reasonable" conduct?

3. Was this "justice" for the family of the victim? Why or why not?

4. Do you believe that race played a factor in this case? Did it influence the fear experienced by Bonnie and Rodney Peairs? Did you believe the issue of race influenced the decision of the jury?

5. Why was it important for the victims to meet with Rodney and Bonnie Peairs? Do you believe that such a face-to-face meeting should have been arranged? What about the adversarial process that was disturbing to the victim's family?

6. Do you think Peairs should honor the request of the victims and hand over the gun used to kill their son to serve as a symbol in the fight for gun control? Why or why not? Why was this important to the victims?

7. Even though he has been acquitted by the criminal system, Rodney Peairs was found liable by the civil law system. Which verdict do you believe is more just? Do you believe that Peairs "owes" restitution to the victim's family? Why or why not?

REFERENCES

Case adapted from:

Peter Applebome, "Verdict in Death of Student Reverberates across Nation," *The New York Times*, May 26, 1992.

Christan Cheakalos, "Culture Clash Plays Out in Louisiana Hearing Set Today In Shooting Death," *The Atlanta Journal and Constitution*, January 7, 1993.

Christopher Cooper, "Japan Tunes In as Trial in Teen's Slaying Begins," *The Times-Picayune,* May 19, 1993.

Christopher Cooper, "Slain Student's Father Hears Killer's Version," *The Times-Picayune*, May 23, 1993.

Christopher Cooper, "Teen's Friend Recounts Shooting: Seeing the Gun Was Puzzling," *The Times-Picayune,* May 21, 1993.

M. Hattori and M Hattori v R. Peairs, B. Peairs and Louisiana Farm Bureau Mutual Insurance Company. No. 95 CA 0144 (La.App. 1 Cir, 10/06/95); 662 So2d 509.

"No Justification Whatsoever," *St. Louis Dispatch*, September 21, 1994.

Adam Nossiter, "Student's Trust in People Proved Fatal," *The New York Times*, October 23, 1992.

Adam Nossiter, "Judge Awards Damages in Japanese Youth's Death," *The New York Times*, September 16, 1994: The *Washington Post,* "Japanese Students Parents Want Death Gun Destroyed," September 18, 1994.

T. R. Reid, "Angry Japan Lays to Rest Students Shot to Dead in U.S.; Slaying Sparks Criticism of Gun Laws," *The Washington Post,* October 27, 1992.

T. R. Reid, "Japanese Media Disparage Acquittal in 'Freeze Case': Commentators See America as Sick Nation," *The Washington Post*, May 25, 1993.

T. R. Reid, "Ruling Softens Japan's Image of Violent U.S. After Monetary Award...'There is a Sense of Justice in America After All,'" *The Washington Post*, September 19, 1994.

David E. Sanger, "After Gunman's Acquittal, Japan Struggles to Understand America," *The New York Times*, May 25, 1993.

Joan Treadway. "Parents Turn Grief into Anti-Gun Effort," *The Times-Picayune*, October 6, 1996.

That Yoshi Hattori's death had been caused by the firing of a lethal weapon by Rodney Peairs is an undisputed fact in this case. No one denies that Peairs's act of firing his weapon was responsible for the death of Hattori. But has Peairs committed a crime? Although we know that Peairs was physically responsible for killing Hattori, the purpose of the trial is to determine if he is legally responsible. This is the important distinction between **factual guilt** and **legal guilt**. A person may be factually guilty of killing another person yet nonetheless be found legally "not guilty" for a variety of reasons. Legal guilt may only be determined through the legal proceedings of the criminal law.

Criminal liability[10] refers to the degree of blameworthiness assigned to the defendant as a result of the legal proceedings of adjudication. Once liability is established through the mechanisms of due process, the state can determine the appropriate sanctions. The purpose of the trial is to establish the degree of criminal liability, if any at all, of the defendant. Criminal liability or blameworthiness may be reduced or even entirely eliminated (as it was in this case), if the defendant has legal justification or excuse for his actions.

THE MATERIAL ELEMENTS OF CRIME

As we saw in chapter 1, a foundation of due process in our system of criminal law is the presumption of innocence. Unless the state can prove a person committed a specific crime "beyond a reasonable doubt" to an impartial judge or jury, the citizen cannot be convicted of a crime. No one accused of a crime must "prove" his or her innocence before a court of law; the burden rests on the accusers to produce the evidence that convicts the defendant. What does the state have to prove? This depends upon the specific crime as it is written in the specific statute or body of law. The substantive portion of the criminal code spells out the specific behaviors that are prohibited or, in less common circumstances, the specific behaviors that are required.

There are five elements common to almost all criminal statutes: 1. the element of **actus reus** which requires that there must have been an action or failure to act on the part of the defendant; 2. the guilty mind or **mens rea** element which requires that there must have been a conscious mental decision to commit the act; 3. the concurrence requirement which states that the harmful act and the guilty mind must occur simultaneously; 4. the requirement that these acts must have resulted in an identifiable harm to the victim and/or society; and, finally, 5. the requirement to prove that the action was the genuine cause of the harm to the victim and/or society. Let us examine each of these elements in turn.

Actus Reus

The first requirement of criminal liability is known as the **human conduct rule**. The actus reus requirement states that a crime must be an act. In the Western tradition of law, we hold people accountable for their deeds, not their thoughts. We prohibit conduct, not ideas, fantasies, beliefs, or thoughts: no one can be punished for simply thinking about committing a crime—there must be behavior which puts thought into action.

Speech is a form of action. For example, talking to someone about hiring them to kill one's spouse may seem to be "merely speech." Yet the act of speaking

FACTUAL GUILT
guilty based upon the facts, though not necessarily legally guilty.

LEGAL GUILT
proof of criminal liability beyond a reasonable doubt by admissible evidence within a court of law.

CRIMINAL LIABILITY
the degree of blameworthiness assigned to the defendants is a result of legal adjudication.

ELEMENTS OF THE CRIME
the five key elements common to almost all criminal statutes which must be proven within a court of law beyond a reasonable doubt according to the rules of criminal procedure and evidence to establish legal guilt.

ACTUS REUS
the physical element of the criminal act

MENS REA
the mental element in crime or criminal intent or the guilty mind.

HUMAN CONDUCT RULE
the requirement that some human action is required for criminal liability; thought is not sufficient.

satisfies the actus reus element and the person who hires a killer is criminally liable for crime of solicitation, and for the consequences of those words, that is, homicide. If a person yells "fire" in a crowded theater sparking a panicked stampede, they may be liable for the injuries that result. Similarly, threatening to harm may result in an arrest and criminal prosecution. Solicitation, conspiracy, and threat are all forms of criminal conduct that prohibit certain forms of speech that causes harm in society.

The "human conduct rule" distinguishes between "doing" and "being." The courts have interpreted the actus reus element to mean that criminal law may not penalize a person simply for "being" a prostitute, an addict, or a thief. The distinction between a state of being and a form of conduct was tested in the case of *Robinson v. California*[11] in which a California statute declared it a criminal offense for a person "to be addicted to the use of narcotics." The constitutional question was whether the statute violated the "human conduct rule" by punishing someone for a state of being rather than for a specific action. The Supreme Court reversed the ruling of the California court on the principle that although the state had the right to prohibit and impose criminal sanctions for the "acts" of manufacture, sale, possession, and use of narcotics it could not punish an individual for "being" an addict.

The actus reus element also contains within it the requirement that an action be voluntary. A person who is forced to act by another or if a person's actions are involuntary reflexes caused by stimuli beyond their control, they would not be held criminally responsible. Actions undertaken during sleep or under hypnosis would also not be considered criminal even if they resulted in substantial harm to others and/or violated the criminal law.

The criminal code not only punishes acts that violate the law but also, in less frequent circumstances, punishes a failure to act in those instances where the law requires a person to act. In this case, it is the omission to act that is criminally liable. A most obvious example is the requirement that all citizens file and pay taxes: failure to do so may be a criminal act. Parents and guardians, lifeguards, military personnel, doctors, child care workers are some of the special categories of individuals who may be held criminally liable if they fail to take certain actions such as providing for the well-being of their children, taking steps to save a drowning person's life or reporting a suspected case of child abuse to the police. For example, a parent may be prosecuted for involuntary manslaughter for failing to obtain medical care for their child if the untreated illness results in that child's death.

In the case of Rodney Peairs, the law of Louisiana requires certain forms of action from gun owners similar to the kind of care required of people who operate motor vehicles.[12] Criminal negligence may exist when a person fails to exercise a reasonable standard of care. In Peairs's case, the district attorney argued that a reasonable person would have waited and observed Hattori's conduct from inside the house before shooting the gun; or they would have phoned the police; or fired a warning shot into the air. Failing to take these cautionary steps makes Peairs criminally liable for Hattori's death.

Mens Rea

The state-of-mind element is so fundamental to our concept of criminal responsibility that it is an essential element of criminal conduct. The term "literally" means "guilty mind" and refers to the mental state of the person when they committed the action. It is not enough to simply know who physically carried out a harmful action to satisfy our concept of criminal responsibility; we must also find out if they intended to do the harm. In the Western legal tradition, there is a fundamental notion that people should be held responsible for actions they voluntarily, willfully, and knowingly commit. We distinguish between actions which are purposeful, planned, or malicious and those that are unintentional, involuntary, or accidental. In justifying this distinction, Oliver Wendell Holmes, a famous Supreme Court justice, observed, "Even a dog distinguishes between being stumbled over and being kicked."[13] Mens rea does not refer to "**motive.**" Motive refers to the reasons a person commits a particular action whereas mens rea refers to the conscious awareness of the outcome or consequences of their conduct.

When a person acts with pre-mediated intent we consider their criminal liability or responsibility to be greater than when a person acts on the spur of the moment, out of fear or anger, or simply because of neglect. We punish more severely the mental state in which a person plans out a crime in advance and then implements that plan "in cold blood." This phrase refers to the deliberate and clear conscious intention on the part of an individual to carry out this act. This is the mental state most criminal codes refer to as "**first degree**" and it is the most serious type of criminal conduct for which we reserve our most severe penalties.

Specific intent is the thoughtful and conscious intention to perform a specific act in order to achieve a particular result. If Rodney Peairs had seen Yoshi coming up the drive, told his wife and children he was "going to kill the guy," and gone and fetched his gun in order to do so, his conduct would be clearly seen as intentional and purposeful. A specific intent crime means that the person consciously desired a particular outcome. Specific intent crimes are usually referred to as "first-degree" crimes because in addition to the action itself, there is evidence that the person intended a specific outcome.

A lesser evil state of mind is that which is referred to as **general intent**. General intent is often inferred from the behavior or conduct itself. When a person breaks and enters a home, it is it concluded from this conduct that he had the general intent to commit larceny. However, if the offender had showed evidence of planning that crime in order to steal from the person there, they may be charged with first-degree larceny because they had a specific intent to deprive the owner of the property. The latter crime in which the conduct is accompanied by strategic planning and preparatory actions is seen as more serious than the conduct in which intent is more or less formed on the spur of the moment.

Individuals are also held criminally responsible for their conduct when they don't have a particular intention to commit these acts. **Criminal negligence** refers to unconscious reckless conduct. In these cases, a person may not have known that they were acting recklessly but *they should have known*. Even if they did not intend the circumstances or the results and did not realize they were endangering others, it was their responsibility to be diligent and if there are harmful consequences they may be held criminally responsible for those consequences. Thus, the mother who leaves a very young child unattended in the bathtub may be found criminally negligent if the child subsequently drowns.

The legal doctrine of **constructive intent** refers to cases in which actors don't intend harm but their conduct violates basic standards of responsible conduct. These are cases of reckless conduct or negligent conduct. **Criminal recklessness** is to knowingly create a high risk of harm to others. The wrongdoer may not

MOTIVE
reason a person commits a particular action

FIRST DEGREE
a premeditated, deliberate, and clear conscious intention on the part of an individual to carry out a homicide

SPECIFIC INTENT
the thoughtful and conscious intention to perform a specific act in order to achieve a particular outcome.

GENERAL INTENT
state of mind inferred from the behavior or conduct itself to commit the act.

CRIMINAL NEGLIGENCE
unconscious creation of high risk of harm.

CONSTRUCTIVE INTENT
the actor doesn't intend harm but their conduct violates basic standards of responsible conduct.

CRIMINAL RECKLESSNESS
knowing creation of high risk of harm to others.

intend to harm someone or desire to harm someone but nonetheless, they know that they are acting in such a way as to place others at grave risk. For instance, leaving a loaded gun on a table is reckless conduct. While the individual may not intend or want a child to pick up the gun and fire it at someone else, if they do, it is the gun owner who is criminally liable for the consequences. Although they did not mean to cause this outcome, they nonetheless knowingly acted recklessly by leaving the loaded gun where a child could pick it up.

Strict liability statutes[14] hold persons criminally liable for their actions regardless of whether they acted with intent, knowingly, recklessly, or negligently. There are relatively few of these types of statutes within the American criminal law. Traffic violations and crimes such as statutory rape are examples where the mental state of the defendant is irrelevant to the criminal statute. Even if a person is unaware of the speed limit and does not knowingly violate the speed limit, the law permits the conduct to constitute the offense regardless of the mens rea of the actor.

Legal Definitions of Criminal Homicide[15]

We can gain understanding into the importance of the mens rea of a crime when we examine the range of criminal statutes that prohibit the taking of human life. Depending upon one's state of mind, or criminal intent, knowledge, purpose, awareness, and perception, a person factually guilty of killing another human being may be legally innocent or criminally responsible to varying degrees of seriousness.

Homicide is the killing of one human being by another. There are three basic types of homicide: **justifiable**, **excusable**, **and criminal**. As we will see later in the chapter, justifiable homicides are cases where the law permits killing such as in the military, or as the defense successfully argued in the Peairs case, a killing to protect one's self, family, and property. Excusable homicides are cases where the act is not considered criminal because it is accidental or the person is not acting voluntarily or with their full mental capacity. The remaining forms of killing fall within the category of criminal homicide.

Murder versus Manslaughter

There are two broad types of criminal homicide: murder and manslaughter. **Murder** is the unlawful killing of a human being with malice. There are two main categories: first degree and second degree. First degree requires premeditation which is defined, practically speaking, as a period of time for reflection between the time the intent was formed and the time the act was committed. If a person purchased some poison, for example, and later put it in someone's food, that period in between was time when they had the opportunity to reflect on their actions and sufficient evidence that they willfully chose to pursue the act of killing.

Second-degree murder is killing with malice but without premeditation. Malice does not necessarily refer to hatred of the victim or particular state of viciousness. Rather the concept refers to the state of mind in which the person intentionally acts to kill or harm another. In this sense it is similar to the idea of specific intent in which the person purposefully and intentionally acts to harm another.

Felony murder is a specific subset of murder most closely associated with first-degree murder. Felony murders are those acts of killing which result from an intention to commit a different felony altogether. Thus, if a person is robbing a

STRICT LIABILITY STATUTES
crimes for which one may incur liability without fault or intention.

HOMICIDE
the killing of a human being by the act, procurement or omission, of another human being.

JUSTIFIABLE HOMICIDE
homicide that is permitted under the law either through self-defense, necessity, or through the execution of a public duty.

EXCUSABLE HOMICIDE
homicide that is committed by persons without legal liability for their conduct or in a manner that the criminal law does not prohibit, for example, accidentally.

CRIMINAL HOMICIDE
the unlawful killing of one human being by another.

MURDER
the killing of one human being by another with malice or premeditation

SECOND DEGREE
committing a homicide with malice but without premeditation

FELONY MURDER
if a death occurs during the commission of a felony, the person committing the primary offense can also be charged with first-degree murder.

convenience store and kills someone in the course of committing that felony, they are guilty of murder regardless of whether the killing was intentional, reckless, negligent, or accidental. It is, in a sense, a form of strict liability in which the person is held fully responsible for their actions and the mens rea for the act is of no consequence legally. All the state must prove is that they had the mens rea to commit the felony itself.

Manslaughter is a lesser form of criminal homicide. All forms of manslaughter are unlawful killings without malice. Generally there are two broad types: **voluntary manslaughter** and **involuntary manslaughter** that also often includes forms of criminal negligence. Voluntary manslaughter is often referred to as a "crime of passion." This is because voluntary manslaughter is an intentional killing usually in the context of an intense quarrel or sudden fit of rage or passion. Voluntary manslaughter rests upon the notion that the killer was, to some extent, provoked by the circumstances, that they formed the intent to kill in response to that provocation (and not before, as in first-degree murder), that they acted in the heat of passion, that they had no time to cool off and think more clearly about their actions.

Involuntary manslaughter encompasses acts of criminal homicide in which the mens rea of the defendant is one of recklessness or negligence. Unlike the other forms of criminal homicide, involuntary manslaughter generally does not entail the intentional desire to cause the person lethal harm. Rather the individual acted with gross negligence that involves a willful and conscious disregard of the safety of others and of one's duty to take care to protect the safety of others. **Vehicular homicide**, which is a separate count in many states, specifically identifies the operation of a motor vehicle in a reckless manner.

In Peairs's case, there is no doubt as to the actions Rodney Peairs took that fateful evening in October. The key evidence to determine the issue of criminal liability was evidence concerning the mental state of Mr. Peairs during those two minutes when he fetched his gun, aimed it at Yoshi, and pulled the trigger. Did Mr. Peairs form a plan in his mind to kill Yoshi Hattori? Did he lure Yoshi to his house? Did he desire the death of this boy? Did he have an evil state of mind such that he wanted to kill any stranger or person who came to his front door? Was he terrified of his life and trying to protect his family? Was he acting on impulse with reckless and thoughtless disregard for the safety of his fellow citizens?

The charge of negligent homicide required the district attorney to prove to the jury that Rodney Peairs failed to meet the standard of care expected to be maintained by a reasonably careful man under like circumstances. Both the prosecution and defense relied upon the **reasonable person standard** to convince the jury of their argument. The prosecution argued that Mr. Peairs failed to act prudently when he fired on Hattori. The defense claimed that any reasonable person in Peairs's shoes would have believed they were in imminent danger of home invasion by Hattori. The job of the jury was to decide which course of action was "reasonable" in these circumstances.

Concurrence

The element of **concurrence** is the requirement that a given act and a given state of mind occur at the same time. In order for the crime to occur, there must be evidence that the act and the state of mind were happening together. If one precedes the other, the requirements of the criminal law have not been met. For example, if Billy threatens to kill his brother at one point in time, and two weeks later, reconciles with him, goes on a hunting trip and accidentally kills

MANSLAUGHTER
the unlawful killing of a human being without malice or premeditation.

VOLUNTARY MANSLAUGHTER
the unlawful killing of a human being without malice which is done intentionally upon a sudden quarrel or in the heat of passion.

INVOLUNTARY MANSLAUGHER
an unintentional killing for which criminal liability is imposed.

VEHICULAR HOMICIDE
the killing of a human being by the operation of a motor vehicle by another in a reckless manner likely to cause the death of, or great bodily harm to, another.

REASONABLE PERSON STANDARD
the circumstances as they appeared to the defendant would have created the same beliefs in the mind of an average, normal, sensible human being.

CONCURRENCE
the simultaneous coexistence of an act in violation of the law and a criminal intent.

his brother, the earlier state of mind cannot be coupled with the later act. The relevant state of mind is that which is present at the time of the act itself. The act must be propelled forward by the state of mind.

Causation[16]

The fourth requirement for a crime to occur is that the actus reus or the action be the cause of a harm. To prove that a particular crime occurred, therefore, it is necessary to demonstrate, not only that a harm occurred, but also that the actions of the defendant caused the harm itself. In the case of Rodney Peairs it is not a difficult element to prove. Yoshi Hattori's death was clearly the result of the bullet that was fired from Peairs's gun.

Yet in some cases, the element of **causation** can be very complex and difficult to establish. Consider the case of Gary Wall. Gary was stabbed in the stomach by his roommate Daniel. Gary was transported to the hospital, treated for the stab wound, and released. He died three days later from internal bleeding. Daniel was charged with second-degree murder. But at the trial, a jury found him guilty only of assault. They did not find him criminally liable for Gary's death. Why? The defense argued that it was the failure of the surgeon who examined Gary but who did not realize that the knife that had penetrated his liver actually caused the death. It was the doctor's criminal negligence that was the actual cause of death, not the initial stabbing by Daniel.

The element of causation uses a **"but for" standard** to determine criminal liability. Had Gary not been taken to the hospital he surely would have died from those stab wounds and Daniel would have been fully responsible for his death. In that set of circumstances the charge of second-degree murder would have likely held against Daniel. But in this case, there was an intervening cause, the treatment by the doctor. The actions (or failure to act in this case) by the doctor reduced Daniel's liability to a lesser offense. But for the mistreatment of the doctor, Gary would have lived.

The principle behind the element of causation is whether or not it is fair to hold the accused accountable for a harm that occurred. Suppose Marty punches Sam in the nose with what would have been a non-lethal blow except for the fact that Sam is a hemophiliac who bleeds to death as a result. Is Marty liable for Sam's death under these circumstances even though he didn't know about Sam's condition? The legal rules of causation would say yes by applying the "but for rule." But for Marty's blow, Sam would not have died. A preexisting condition such as Sam's illness does not excuse Marty from criminal responsibility for the harm caused by his actions.

The guidelines for causation are that unless there is an unforeseeable intervening cause, criminal liability falls to the primary actions that set a chain of events in motion. If Sandy chases Bobby with a bat into the street where Bobby is struck by a car and killed, the "but for rule" would hold Sandy responsible for that outcome since Bobby getting hit by a car was reasonably foreseeable given his being chased into traffic by Bobby wielding a weapon. However, if Bobby was being chased in a field and was struck by lightning and killed, Sandy would not be liable for that outcome since he could not have reasonably foreseen that sequence of events, that outcome of events.

The Resulting Harm

A central principle of criminal law is that conduct that is criminalized is inherently harmful both to specific victims and to the wider society itself. For many

CAUSATION
a causal link between an actor's conduct and a harm.

"BUT FOR" STANDARD
a standard for determining causality which holds that "but for" the conduct of the accused, the harm in question would not have occurred.

crimes, this is relatively easy to see: murder, rape, robbery, fraud, and theft are clearly harmful to those who are directly victimized and clearly create the type of society which undermines everyone's ability to live with security and harmony. Understanding the impact on the quality of life within the community is one of the reasons we criminalize the "attempt" to commit crimes. Even though these are instances where an act is not carried out so there is no individual harm suffered, it is understood that the purpose of the law is to discourage those forms of conduct within the wider public. Therefore, it is just as important to punish "attempts" as those actions that are successfully carried out.

It is important, however, to realize that the issue of criminalization, that is, whether or not a particular conduct ought to be prohibited or required by the criminal law, is a matter of social policy and legislative debate. The general issue of **harm** is not debated within a court of law that is concerned with the application of the existing law to a particular set of events. The criminalization of certain consensual activities such as drug use, prostitution, gambling, or pornography enters into law through political debates about the harmfulness of this conduct for the wider community.

PRINCIPLES OF DEFENSE

Now let us turn to the job of the defense counsel in a court of law. Due process requirements of our legal system require that the prosecution's case be met by an equally vigorous case presented by an attorney for the accused. A criminal defense is the presentation of evidence and arguments in a court of law by the attorney representing the defendant to show why the defendant is not criminally liable for the charges. The job of the defense attorney is to defend their client to the utmost of their ability within the ethical boundaries set down by the legal profession.

Because of the basic presumption of innocence of the accused, the burden falls on the prosecution to affirmatively prove its case against the accused. One key defense strategy is to demonstrate that the prosecution has failed to provide evidence to convince a jury beyond a reasonable doubt. Is it possible there is an alternate explanation for the prosecution's conclusions? Is it possible a witness is not telling the truth? Is it possible a witness is mistaken in what they saw or recall? A powerful role for the defense attorney is to test the strength of the prosecutor's evidence and to raise "reasonable doubt" in the mind of the jury or judge.

A second strategy for the defense is to challenge the due process requirements that should have been met by the state. Often referred to as "technicalities," these are key elements of the rights of the accused fundamental to the protection of the rights of all citizens. Was the defendant informed of his or her rights by the arresting officer? Did the officers have a warrant when they searched the trunk of the car? Was the accused afforded competent counsel for their defense? Was jury selection fair and unbiased? One of the responsibilities of the defense attorney is to ensure that the laws of criminal procedure are not violated in any particular case.

Affirmative Defenses

In both of these defense strategies, testing the prosecution's case and challenging the due process procedures followed by the state, there is no requirement on the part of the defense to prove their arguments beyond a reasonable doubt. Their job is to raise enough doubt to undermine the certainty needed for a conviction.

HARM
loss, disadvantage, or injury to victim.

Juries are instructed as to the meaning of the "beyond a reasonable doubt standard" and are told that if they have "reasonable doubt" then they should allow the "benefit" of that doubt to go to the defendant.

When the defense chooses to argue self-defense, or claims an alibi or claims the defendant is mentally ill, the burden of proof switches from the prosecution to the defense in most jurisdictions. **Affirmative defenses** are subject to the same "reasonable doubt" standard as the prosecutions effort to convict. In Peairs's case, the defense counsel had to "prove" to the jury beyond a reasonable doubt that Peairs was acting in accordance with the legal requirements of justifiable homicides when he killed Yoshi Hattori.

There are three main categories of affirmative defenses. The first is known as the **defense of alibi.** This simply means that the accused is not guilty because they were somewhere else at the time the crime was committed and evidence of their whereabouts will be presented in court. Both defenses of justification and defenses of excuse are also known as affirmative defenses because they require the defense to prove their version of events beyond a reasonable doubt.

Defenses of Justification

Defenses of justification make the claim that the defendant was morally justified in their choice of conduct because they are avoiding a harm that was greater than the one committed. In the Rodney Peairs case, when faced with a choice between two evils, permitting his home to be invaded by a dangerous stranger or killing Hattori, Peairs chose the lesser of two evils. The typical forms of justification are self-defense including defense of others and property; execution of public duty and necessity.

The execution of **public duty** permits the legal use of force in the service of a lawful arrest or apprehension. Thus law enforcement can claim the public duty defense if they are accused of assault and battery on a citizen during the course of an arrest. The use of force is only lawful if the person is resisting arrest and if the arrest itself is a lawful one. The **necessity justification** is generally used in the face of extreme threats from nature. If a person is stranded in a blizzard and therefore forced to break and enter a home for shelter, they may claim the defense of necessity.

The concept of **self-defense** is based on a widely recognized principle that every person has an inherent right to defend themselves against an unlawful attack and that the person who harms or even kills an attacker does not so much as intend to take another's life as seeks to preserve one's own. The use of force to defend oneself has been extended to include the protection and preservation of the lives of others who appear to be in imminent danger.

The use of lethal force is generally not permitted in the defense of property alone although if the trespasser is armed then the threat of force may justify a lethal response to protect property. In Louisiana state code, the law permits the use of lethal force to remove a person from one's home regardless of whether or not that person is armed in an amendment known as the "shoot the burglar" clause. In Louisiana, justifiable homicide includes an action taken against a person who is attempting to make an unlawful entry into a dwelling and is justified if it is necessary to compel the intruder to leave the premises.

The five main elements for a defense of self, others, or property are as follows. First there is the reasonableness standard. There has to be a reasonable perception such as that any other "reasonable" man or women faced with the same

AFFIRMATIVE DEFENSES
a category of defense raised by the defendant's counsel who had the burden of proof to prove beyond a reasonable doubt.

DEFENSE OF ALIBI
a legal defense in which a defendant claims to be in a different location when the crime was committed.

DEFENSES OF JUSTIFICATION
a category of legal defense in which the defendant admits committing the act in question but claims it was necessary to avoid some greater evil.

PUBLIC DUTY
a defense that claims the defendant was lawfully exercising their authority at the time the act was committed.

NECESSITY JUSTIFICATION
a defense to a criminal charge that claims it was necessary to commit some unlawful act in order to prevent or avoid a greater harm.

SELF-DEFENSE
a defense to a criminal charge based on a person's inherent right to self-protection and to reasonably defend oneself from unlawful attacks.

circumstances would come to similar conclusions. Rodney Peairs claimed that he and his wife believed the boys were about to invade their home and that Hattori was going to grab his gun and kill him and his family. Peairs claimed these were reasonable inferences based on Hattori's appearance and behavior during those few minutes preceding the shooting.

The law also requires one believes oneself to be in imminent danger. This requirement is designed to prevent the claim of self-defense in situations where someone is acting in retaliation or to forestall a future attack. Both of these cases, where a person might harm someone because "they deserve it" or "to get them before they get me," are not lawful and do not meet the requirements for self-defense. Thus, the law requires that only dangers which are likely to occur within a short period of time to be considered as legitimate grounds for a claim of self-defense.

Third, it is necessary that the harm itself must be unlawful. Defendants cannot claim self-defense when they are responding to the use of force by law enforcement engaged in a lawful use of coercive force. The fourth element in the classic self-defense argument is that response is equal to the threat of force. The law generally does not permit a threat from fists to be met with a firearm. Peairs testified that he believed Hattori was armed mistaking the camera that hung around his neck for a weapon.

The final requirement is that the force is used as a last resort although only a few state laws actually require a "retreat rule" upon those who claim self-defense. Under these circumstances, if there is a retreat option, then the decision to use force is not seen as a form of defense but as a form of offensive action subject to criminal liability.

The one universal exception to the retreat rule is so-called "castle" exception. A man's home is his castle according to the sixteenth-century jurist Sir Edward Coke. No man must be forced to "retreat" from his home, business, or car. For this reason, there are special considerations given to the protection of one's own property: under those circumstances, the individual need not flee from one's home but may stand his ground and use force to get another to leave. This is the theory behind the "shoot the burglar" rule in Louisiana. The relevant clause in the statute for "justifiable homicide" in Louisiana[17] reads "A homicide is justifiable when . . . the person committing the homicide reasonably believes that the use of deadly force is necessary to prevent the entry or to compel the intruder to leave the premises. . . . The homicide shall be justifiable even though the person committing the homicide does not retreat from the encounter."

In recent years numerous states including Florida have expanded on this common law doctrine by adopting statutes that permit the use of deadly force when someone is confronted anywhere where they have a legal right to be. Known as "stand your ground" laws these statutes permit the use of force including deadly force if a person reasonably believes this is necessary to prevent death or great bodily harm to themselves or others or to prevent commission of a felony greatly expanding the scope of justifiable homicides in those states. The "stand your ground" laws gained national attention in 2012 when George Zimmerman, on neighborhood watch duty in Sanford, Florida, shot and killed an unarmed teenager named Trayvon Martin. Zimmerman was subsequently charged with second-degree murder and ultimately found not guilty in Martin's death. The jurors stated they found the law applicable in this case.

GUNS AND VIOLENCE

The battle over gun control and the right to bear arms raises important questions about the limits of crime control and the right of citizens for self-protection. The number of registered firearms in the possession of individuals in America has risen nearly tenfold, from 147,484 in 2005 to 1,426,211 in 2015.[18] In 2010 as many American citizens were killed by guns as by automobile accidents; about a third of these deaths was the result of criminal homicides.[19] As we see in the case in chapter 2, the prevalence of handguns in the United States turns many run-of-the-mill crimes, such as assaults, thefts, and robberies, into potentially lethal events. Guns account for approximately two-thirds (67%) of homicide deaths each year in the United States.[20] This is one of the key reasons many citizens cite for owning a weapon: to protect themselves against criminals with guns.

Yet there are high levels of risks associated with gun ownership. In 2015 there were more than 36,000 firearm deaths in the United States—the majority of these (over 60%) were self-inflicted deaths or suicides; 36 percent were homicides; and 4 percent accidental, unintentional, or legal killings. In 2015 an average of fifty-eight Americans committed suicide each day.[21] Unlike homicide, suicide rates are much higher in rural areas where there is a higher presence of guns in the household: states with higher rates of gun ownership also have higher rates of suicide.[22] Accidental deaths from firearms are also most likely to occur inside a household with guns: two-thirds of all accidental deaths with guns occur inside the home, about half involve victims under the age of twenty-five, and most are inflicted by a family member, usually an older brother or cousin.[23]

While mass killings make the headlines, most firearm homicides are individual killings, typically a dispute or conflict between people who know one another that escalates into a lethal outcome due to the presence of a firearm. Between 1966 and 2016 there were 127 mass shootings, events in which four or more people were killed by a lone shooter (two shooters in three instances). These shootings resulted in 874 deaths.[24] In the year 2014 alone there were 8,124 individual homicides committed with a firearm.[25] The rate of firearm homicides is higher in the south and west, where there are more guns, and in urban areas, where the rate of all crime is generally higher. Homicide with a gun has been the leading cause of death for African American males, aged fifteen to nineteen, since 1969.[26]

The Peairs case involves the use of guns for self-protection and shows us the tragic result when an innocent teenager is mistakenly assumed to be a lethal threat. Our nation has a long tradition of upholding the right of individuals to protect themselves, their family, and their property, particularly within the home. Yet the greatest danger for women and children comes from an intimate partner, especially in homes with a firearm. Both examples illustrate the challenges in the regulation of responsible gun ownership for self-protection.

The percentage of households with guns has fallen to nearly a forty-year low; a 2016 poll found that 36 percent of households in the United States have a gun. This is a positive change as the presence of a firearm in the home increases the likelihood of homicide, suicide, and accidental death in that home. Children in the United States are thirteen times more likely than children in other wealthy nations to be killed by a firearm.[27] And a woman who lives in a house with a gun is three times more likely to be a victim of homicide than a woman who does not. Yet we must wonder, with the number of guns in possession of Americans increasing tenfold in the past decade, where are all those guns?

Within the last two decades, the ownership of military-style weaponry by citizens has raised additional concerns and debates about gun regulation, particularly sparked by a series of tragic mass murders by mentally unstable individuals with access to semiautomatic weapons and high-capacity magazines. The school shootings in Columbine, Virginia Tech, and Sandy Hook Elementary School, or Marysville, Washington, along with the senseless rampages in the Aurora movie theater, a Tucson parking lot, an Orlando nightclub, and the Ft. Lauderdale airport, to name but a few, have raised the temperature on current debates on gun control. The case in chapter 9 on the Oklahoma bombing offers a glimpse into an extremist gun subculture within the United States, associated with gun shows and a militia movement that views the right to bear arms as protection not against criminals with guns, but against the government itself.

Defenses of Excuse

Excuses admit that the action committed by the defendant was wrong and violated the criminal law but argue that special circumstances absolve them of legal responsibility for their actions. There are a number of conditions or individual characteristics that excuse criminal liability. These include mistake of law and fact; age; duress; entrapment; intoxication; insanity; diminished capacity; and mental and biological syndromes.

Ignorance of the law is generally not considered a valid legal defense but under very rare circumstances, a defendant may successfully argue that he or she made a reasonable effort to understand or learn what a law is and was honestly mistaken in their understanding of the law. **Mistake of fact** is a much more common excuse. In this circumstance, the defendant honestly misinterprets the facts of the situation and therefore does not have the mens rea of the crime even though they may have committed the criminal act. For instance, suppose you attend a party and pick up a coat that looks exactly like your own and go home with it. Although you have committed the act of larceny, you did not intend to steal the coat and your honest mistake is a valid defense against the charge. Of course, if your own coat was wool and the one you left with was mink, you would have a hard time convincing a jury or judge of your mistake.

The mistake of fact excuse was, in fact, a significant part of the defense of Rodney Peairs. Peairs claimed he mistook Yoshi Hattori for an intruder and he mistook the camera in Yoshi Hattori's hand for a weapon. In the dark and with all the confusion, Peairs argued that he believed Hattori to be armed and that he made a mistake of fact in assessing the danger to his home and family. No doubt this was an important part of the defense strategy in convincing a jury that Peairs's response was reasonable under the circumstances. Indeed, a crucial element of the mistake of fact defense is the reasonable standard: a reasonable mistake is one that would be made by any typically competent person faced with the same set of circumstances.

The **defense of duress** exists because we do not wish to punish people for actions they are forced to commit against their own free will. Recall the "human conduct rule" in which the criminal law only punishes actions that are voluntary. The defense of duress claims that the defendant was not criminally responsible for their conduct because they were coerced by the use or threat of unlawful force by another person. Thus, a bank teller who turns over money to a robber holding a gun is not guilty of embezzlement nor is the airline pilot who veers off course

IGNORANCE OF LAW
a lack of knowledge of the law or the existence of the law

MISTAKE OF FACT
a defense claiming an error or misunderstanding of fact or circumstances resulting in an act that would otherwise not have been undertaken.

DEFENSE OF DURESS
a defense to a criminal charge that the defendant was forced to act against one's will.

in response to the commands of the terrorist guilty of the crime of hijacking. However, the defense of duress cannot be used if the person willingly placed oneself in the situation where he would be subject to pressure to act illegally. Thus this defense is not available to a person who willingly joins a gang and then later claims that the gang forced him to commit crimes against his will.

Although being in an intoxicated state of mind diminishes the actor's capacity to form mens rea, a claim of intoxication is generally not regarded as an effective defense. At most, **voluntary intoxication** may lessen criminal liability by, for example, allowing the defense to argue that a charge of first-degree murder should be lessened to second-degree murder since the high level of intoxication undermined the defendant's capacity to form a specific intent to kill, the mental state required for a first-degree conviction. Otherwise, most states are very wary about permitting intoxication to be used as a criminal defense. The area of exception is claim of **involuntary intoxication**. Intoxication may be a legal defense if the substance was introduced into the person's body without his or her consent or without the knowledge that the substance would cause intoxication. Someone who has consumed punch spiked with LSD or by following medical advice may be excused from liability for his or her actions directly related to the intoxication such as driving under the influence or illegal drug use.

Under English common law, the **defense of infancy**[28] held that children under the age of seven were incapable of rational thought and planned action and therefore could not be held criminally responsible for their conduct. For centuries, the criminal liability for children between the ages of seven and fourteen was determined on a case-by-case basis depending upon the severity of the offense and the individual facts of the case. In the nineteenth century, most states wrote juvenile statutes that established a legal age of maturity somewhere between the ages of sixteen and twenty-one. Today most states continue to specify a blanket age of adulthood somewhere around fifteen and sixteen although all states have mechanisms whereby younger juveniles who commit serious crimes may be held fully responsible for their crimes in adult court. For the most part, children who commit crimes are subject to the authority of the juvenile court on the theory that they are not as fully capable as adults in recognizing the wrongfulness of their conduct and in making fully responsible choices between legal and illegal conduct.

Entrapment[29] refers to the inducement of a citizen into crime by law enforcement officers. The argument is that without the temptations set up by the "sting" operation, the citizen would have remained law-abiding since they did not seek out the illegal opportunity on their own. Entrapment most often occurs in the enforcement of laws against so-called victimless crimes. The standard used by the courts to determine entrapment is whether or not the person demonstrated a predisposition toward committing the crime before the government agents set him or her up for the "sting" operation.

The **defenses of insanity**,[30] **diminished capacity**, and various "syndromes" all exist to refer to the mental state of the accused at the time of the crime. This category of defenses is based on the widely accepted legal principle that only those who are of sound mind can be put on trial, held responsible for their actions, and punished for their actions. The insanity plea has a long history in Western criminal law but is rarely used and rarely successful as a defense. When defendants are successful in convincing the jury that they were, indeed, mentally ill at the time they committed their crime, they are likely to be confined to a mental hospital for the criminally insane. John Hinckley, for example, attempted to

VOLUNTARY INTOXICATION intoxication that is the result of willful personal choice.

INVOLUNTARY INTOXICATION intoxication that is not willful.

DEFENSE OF INFANCY a defense that claims that individuals below a certain age should not be held criminally liable for their actions by virtue of their young age.

ENTRAPMENT the inducement of an individual to commit a crime not contemplated by him or her.

DEFENSES OF INSANITY an affirmative defense seeking to prove a mental state that prevents an individual from comprehending the nature and consequences of actions or from distinguishing right from wrong.

DIMINISHED CAPACITY an affirmative defense that an individual could not have developed the requisite intent; usually resulting in conviction on a lesser offense.

assassinate the former president Ronald Reagan in an attempt to gain the attention of actress Jodie Foster. At his trial, Hinckley was found not guilty by reason of insanity. He remains, however, confined to a maximum-security hospital and is likely to remain there for the rest of his life.

The term "insanity" is a legal term, not a medical one. It is not synonymous with the term "mental illness." It is entirely possible for a person to have a mental illness and still have the sufficient mens rea to commit a crime. All jurisdictions in the United States require that a defendant be mentally competent in order to stand trial as a basic principle of due process. Defendants who are incapable of understanding the proceedings against them or in assisting in their own defense are legally incompetent to stand trial.

A related set of recent defenses rests on the mental condition of the defendant at the time of the crime. Syndromes[31] such as the battered women's syndrome, urban survival syndrome, Vietnam vet syndrome,[32] child abuse syndrome, fetal alcohol syndrome, rape trauma syndrome,[33] post-traumatic stress disorder,[34] and PMS syndrome[35] are all recognition of specific pressures on individuals in particular circumstances which might influence their behavior to such an extent as to be a kind of compulsion on their behavior. The use of these syndromes as defenses of excuse are rarely successful and leave many people uneasy because they imply that people can point to harms done to them to "excuse" their own behavior. A legal excuse generally requires a force so powerful that it truly undermines the voluntariness of the act or the mental awareness of the actor. Despite the growing use of these syndromes, as in the Menendez trial in California, in which two brothers claimed to be victims of child abuse as the legal excuse for murdering their parents, these defenses are not convincing juries that these experiences absolve them of moral and legal responsibility for their own behavior.[36]

The battered women's syndrome,[37] as we have discussed in chapter 3, is an exception that has been used to augment a defense of justification, namely self-defense, rather than a **defense of excuse**. Battered woman's syndrome or the more gender neutral battered person's syndrome began with the publication of Lenore Walker's book *The Battered Woman* in 1980. Walker argued that women who had been victims of chronic abuse for years by their batterer develop common psychological characteristics which she calls "learned helplessness." This psychological understanding helps juries to believe that it may be "reasonable" for women to believe they are unable to simply leave their batterer to escape serious harm or eventual death. This syndrome has been used to assist in the argument of a self-defense in cases where women have killed their husbands even though at the time of the killing he did not pose an imminent threat or lethal threat to them.[38] The killing may have occurred when the men are sleeping or not during an episode of violence or when they are unarmed and it has been difficult for women to argue that they acted as a reasonable person would have done in those circumstances. The battered women's syndrome asks the jury to judge the defendants, actions according to the criterion of a "reasonable battered woman."[39]

This raises the question of whether a jury of men can adequately judge the reasonableness of that woman's conduct who has been beaten, raped, tortured, humiliated, and threatened by the man in her life for years. What is "reasonable" conduct under those circumstances?

DEFENSE OF EXCUSE
a category of legal defense in which the defendant claims a personal condition at the time of the act that excuses them from criminal liability under the law.

In Peairs's case, the defense argued that Peairs acted as any reasonable man would have done. Yet for many observers, especially for the entire nation of Japan, it is inconceivable that shooting a young, unarmed stranger within seconds of opening your front door is reasonable conduct. For many observers the perception that this was a potentially lethal home invasion was far from a reasonable belief based on the factual circumstances. Some believe, in fact, that the Peairs's reaction was fundamentally racist attributing danger to Yoshi because he was Asian. But, as in every case, the determination of the "reasonable" standard is made by the twelve men and women on the jury. And in this case, the individuals in that jury box were peers of Rodney Peairs, men and women from Louisiana who believed in the right of gun ownership and the right to use that gun to protect one's home from danger. More importantly, the jury shared the same beliefs about what appeared dangerous to Bonnie and Rodney Peairs. For the jury, the Peairses' conduct, that night, was reasonable.

IS RACISM "REASONABLE"?

The jury's decision in the Peairs case raises thorny issues about the influence of racism on the criminal justice system.[40] Would the defense have been as successful at portraying young white Webb Haymaker as "crazy" or "bizarre" or been able to convince the jury that an unarmed sixteen-year-old boy ringing a doorbell at 8 p.m. was a menace so "frightening" and "scary" that it put Rodney Peairs in desperate fear of a lethal home invasion? Would the jury have been as quick to see the couple's terror as "reasonable" and Peairs's split second decision to fire point blank as "reasonable" if the victim had been a local white teenager rather than a foreign exchange student? Would the courtroom have erupted in applause at the verdict if the Haymakers had been the parents of the victim rather than a quiet Japanese couple?

Americans have a long history of hatred, prejudice, and distrust of people of Asian ethnic background.[41] Since the late nineteenth century, there has been discrimination against various immigrants from Asian countries beginning with the Chinese Exclusion Act of 1880. During World War II, Americans of Japanese descent were forcibly removed from their home and interned within camps even though no similar actions were taken against citizens of German or Italian descent whose status as Americans was never officially questioned. No matter how many generations Asian Americans have been citizens of this country, they are still viewed through a racial lens which identifies them as "foreigners" and not true Americans.

Negative stereotypes of all Asians as the "Japs," "Chinks," the "yellow peril," or the "gooks" our country fought in Vietnam are widely held by Americans citizens. In the Peairs trial, the defense attorney told the jury that Yoshi was acting in a menacing aggressive fashion, "like a stranger invading someone's home turf." This tapped into these perceptions of Asians as "the enemy" threatening their security and safety. For the Peairses the "foreign-ness" of Yoshi was the quality they noticed above all else: when asked to describe what she saw that night, Mrs. Peairs responded during the trial, "I guess he appeared Oriental. He could have been Mexican or whatever." Mrs. Peairs screamed at her husband to get his gun because she saw someone who was foreign: Oriental or Mexican; it didn't really matter. She was terrified by his ethnic difference.

Watch tower at the Manzanar Japanese internment camp in California.

The law of self-defense requires that the belief and the action be reasonable. In this case, the jury shared the defendant's view that Yoshi's foreign appearance was sufficient to generate such fear. They also agreed that the action Peairs took—firing his weapon point blank at the young man's chest—was also "reasonable." Yet, as Judge Brown ruled in the civil trial, Peairs had many alternate courses of action that night that were "reasonable": he could have stayed in the house and called the police; he could have simply let the boys leave; he could have fired a warning shot in the air from the doorway of his house.

In this case, we must ask ourselves the painful question if the loss of life of a "foreign boy" was easier for the jury to accept than if the loss had been of a young white boy. Research consistently shows that juries are more sympathetic when the victim is from the same class and racial and social background. Research on prosecutors seeking the death penalty also indicates that more serious punishments are sought when the victim is white. Was Yoshi's life devalued because he was non white?

The reality of racism presents a great dilemma for the legal system's reliance upon the discretionary decision-making of citizens who carry with them all the biases and stereotypes of the society. Racial stereotypes affect all people, including prosecutors, judges, and jurors. Particularly troubling is the question of whether the "reasonableness" standard means that it is acceptable to act on irrational and emotional prejudices against people who look different. Rodney and Bonnie Peairs may be typical of the residents of Baton Rouge, Louisiana, in their perception that minorities, Asians or Mexicans or African Americans, are inherently dangerous. But the real question is whether this is "reasonable" according to the law. Should the law uphold these racist views simply because they are widespread? A typical belief is not necessarily a reasonable one even if it is shared by a large group of people. If this were true, then the view of German citizens that Jews were the source of all evil in their country and deserved to die should be deemed "reasonable" simply because it was shared by the majority of the citizenry.

In later chapters we will return to some of the questions about the composition of the jury and its capacity to make decisions that are fair and just. We can see here that the legal system cannot separate itself from the society in which it operates. Can we achieve "justice" in a society where there is systemic injustice and racial bias? Are there reforms that we can institute that will help to the "struggle for justice" to achieve greater fairness for all regardless of their gender, race, or social class? Do we need to move beyond the adversarial system and examine alternate forms of justice in order to imagine a system that can deliver "justice for all"?

---

factual guilt (p. 122)   guilty based upon the facts, though not necessarily legally guilty.

legal guilt (p. 122)   proof of criminal liability beyond a reasonable doubt by admissible evidence within a court of law.

criminal liability (p. 122)   the degree of blameworthiness assigned to the defendants is a result of legal adjudication.

elements of the crime (p. 122)   the five key elements common to almost all criminal statutes which must be proven within a court of law beyond a reasonable doubt according to the rules of criminal procedure and evidence to establish legal guilt.

actus reus (p. 122)   the physical element of the criminal act.

mens rea (p. 122)   the mental element in crime or criminal intent or the guilty mind.

human conduct rule (p. 122)   the requirement that some human action is required for criminal liability; thought is not sufficient.

motive (p. 124)   a reason a person commits a particular action.

first degree (p. 124)   a premeditated, deliberate, and clear conscious intention on the part of an individual to carry out a homicide

specific intent (p. 124)   the thoughtful and conscious intention to perform a specific act in order to achieve a particular outcome.

general intent (p. 124)   state of mind inferred from the behavior or conduct itself to commit the act.

criminal negligence (p. 124)   unconscious creation of high risk of harm.

criminal recklessness (p. 124)   knowing creation of high risk of harm to others.

constructive intent (p. 124)   the actor doesn't intend harm but their conduct violates basic standards of responsible conduct.

strict liability statutes (p. 125)   crimes for which one may incur liability without fault or intention.

homicide (p. 125)   the killing of a human being by the act, procurement or omission, of another human being.

justifiable homicide (p. 125)   homicide that is permitted under the law either through self-defense, necessity or through the execution of a public duty.

excusable homicide (p. 125)   homicide that is committed by persons without legal liability for their conduct or in a manner that the criminal law does not prohibit, for example, accidentally.

criminal homicide (p. 125)   the unlawful killing of one human being by another.

murder (p. 125)   the killing of one human being by another with malice or premeditation

second degree (p. 125)   committing a homicide with malice but without premeditation

felony murder (p. 125)   if a death occurs during the commission of a felony, the person committing the primary offense can also be charged with first-degree murder.

Manslaughter (p. 126)   the unlawful killing of a human being without malice or premeditation.

involuntary manslaughter (p. 126)   an unintentional killing for which criminal liability is imposed.

voluntary manslaughter (p. 126)   the unlawful killing of a human being without malice which is done intentionally upon a sudden quarrel or in the heat of passion.

vehicular homicide (p. 126)   the killing of a human being by the operation of a motor vehicle by another in a reckless manner likely to cause the death of, or great bodily harm to, another.

reasonable person standard (p. 126)   the circumstances as they appeared to the defendant would have created the same beliefs in the mind of an average, normal, sensible human being.

concurrence (p. 126)   the simultaneous coexistence of an act in violation of the law and a criminal intent.

causation (p. 127)   a causal link between an actor's conduct and a harm.

"but for" standard (p. 127)   a standard for determining causality which holds that "but for" the conduct of the accused, the harm in question would not have occurred.

harm (p. 128)   loss, disadvantage, or injury to victim.

affirmative defenses (p. 129)   a category of defense raised by the defendant's counsel who had the burden of proof to prove beyond a reasonable doubt.

defense of alibi (p. 129)   a legal defense in which a defendant claims to be in a different location when the crime was committed.

defenses of justification (p. 129)   a category of legal defense in which the defendant admits committing the act in question but claims it was necessary to avoid some greater evil.

public duty (p. 129)   a defense that claims the defendant was lawfully exercising their authority at the time the act was committed.

necessity justification (p. 129)   a defense to a criminal charge that claims it was necessary to commit some unlawful act in order to prevent or avoid a greater harm.

self-defense (p. 129)   a defense to a criminal charge based on a person's inherent right to self-protection and to reasonably defend oneself from unlawful attacks.

ignorance of law (p. 132)   a lack of knowledge of the law or the existence of the law

mistake of fact (p. 132)   a defense claiming an error or misunderstanding of fact or circumstances

resulting in an act that would otherwise not have been undertaken.

defense of duress (p. 132)   a defense to a criminal charge that the defendant was forced to act against one's will.

voluntary intoxication (p. 133)   intoxication that is the result of willful personal choice.

involuntary intoxication (p. 133)   intoxication that is not willful.

defense of infancy (p. 133)   a defense that claims that individuals below a certain age should not be held criminally liable for their actions by virtue of their young age.

entrapment (p. 133)   the inducement of an individual to commit a crime not contemplated by him or her.

defenses of insanity (p. 133)   an affirmative defense seeking to prove a mental state that prevents an individual from comprehending the nature and consequences of actions or from distinguishing right from wrong.

diminished capacity (p. 133)   an affirmative defense that an individual could not have developed the requisite intent; usually resulting in conviction on a lesser offense.

defense of excuse (p. 134)   a category of legal defense in which the defendant claims a personal condition at the time of the act that excuses them from criminal liability under the law.

REVIEW AND STUDY QUESTIONS

1. Define the five material elements of crime.

2. What is the human conduct rule and why is it an important principle to prove in determining criminal liability?

3. Explain how *mens rea* or the state of mind influences the seriousness of the crime.

4. Explain the differences between key types of criminal homicide: murder, manslaughter, felony murder, and vehicular homicide. How is the "intent" different in each form of criminal homicide?

5. Explain the element of concurrence. Why is it an important principle for establishing criminal liability?

6. What is the principle of causation? Explain the "but for" standard of causation.

7. What is an affirmative defense? How does affirmative defense differ from traditional defense strategies?

8. What is a defense of justification? What is a defense of excuse? How are these two defenses different from one another? Give examples of each type of defense.

9. Name the five elements required to prove self-defense.

10. What is the "reasonable person standard"? How does this raise the possibility of bias in the criminal justice decision-making?

CHECK IT OUT

Websites

Criminal Law and Criminal Justice Resources, http://www.law.northwestern.edu/library/research/topics/criminallaw/ is a good source for state and federal criminal codes as well as legal decisions.

Videos

The Shot Heard Around the World—67 minutes. It is a documentary produced and directed by award-winning filmmaker Christine Choy about the shooting of Yoshi Hattori; the issue of guns; prejudice: and the criminal justice system. Available on YouTube or from CAAM, http://www.law.northwestern.edu/library/research/topics/criminallaw/

Who Killed Vincent Chen?—82 minutes. An award-winning documentary also by Christine Choy of the murder of twenty-seven-year-old Chinese American man, Vincent Chin, in Detroit and the criminal trial of Ron Ebens, a Chrysler Motor foreman, who was given a suspended sentence and a small fine for the brutally violent crime. Academy Award nominee for the Best Documentary in 1989. Available online or visit https://www.vincentwhofilm.com

When Women Kill—47 minutes. A powerful award-winning documentary of three battered women on why they killed, confronting the issue of male violence and female self-defense. This film puts violence against women in legal and historical context including a critique of the battered women's syndrome as a legal defense. Available online or from HBO.

Abused Women Who Fought Back: The Framingham Eight—44 minutes. This documentary tells the dramatic story of eight women imprisoned for killing a spouse or partner. Each claimed battered women's syndrome as a defense. The program explores both sides of the issue including prosecutors and family members of victims who believe the defense has gone too far. Available from FilmsMediaGroup https://www.vincentwhofilm.com

Guns: An American Way of Life and Death—22 minutes. ABC News anchor Ted Koppell explores the love-hate relationship of American society with firearms and contrasts the U.S. attitudes, laws, and violence with our near neighbor Canada through interview with police chiefs from both countries. Available from FilmsMediaGroup https://www.vincentwhofilm.com

Movies

Anatomy of a Murder (1959). Otto Preminger directed this realistic study of an Army lieutenant accused of murdering a bartender who allegedly raped his coquettish wife. The surprise, though, is the stupendous performance in the role of the judge by real-life lawyer Joseph Welch, who represented the Army in the McCarthy hearings. The plot skips nimbly through a thicket of ethical dilemmas involved in representing a murder defendant. It was inspired by an actual case and adapted from a novel written by a Michigan Supreme Court judge.

NOTES

[1] Christopher Cooper, "Japan Tunes in as Trial in Teen's Slaying Begins," *The Times-Picayune*, (May 18, 1993), A1; T.R. Reid, "Japanese Media Disparage Acquittal in 'Freeze Case'; Commentators See America as Sick Nation," *The Washington Post*, (May 25, 1993), A14; Christina Cheakalos, "Culture Clash Plays out in Louisiana Hearing Set Today in Shooting Death," *The Atlanta Journal and Constitution*, (January 7, 1993), A-3; T.R. Reid, "Angry Japan lays to Rest Student Shot Dead in

U.S; Slaying Sparks Criticism of Gun Laws," *The Washington Post,* (October 27, 1992), A1.

2 Christopher Cooper, "Slain Student's Father Hears Killers Version," *The Times-Picayune,* (May 23, 1993), A1.

3 Christopher Cooper, "Teen's Friend Recounts Shooting: Seeing the Gun was Puzzling," *The Times-Picayune,* (May 21, 1993), A1.

4 David E. Sanger, "After Gunman's Acquittal, Japan Struggles to Understand America," *The New York Times,* (May 25, 1993), A-1.

5 *M. Hattori and M. Hattori v. R. Peairs, B. Peairs and Louisiana Farm Bureau Mutual Insurance Company.* No. 95 CA 0144 (La.App. 1 Cir, 10/06/95); 662 So.2d 509.

6 T.R. Reid, "Ruling Softens Japan's Image of Violent U.S.; After Monetary Award. 'There is a Sense of Justice in America After All'," *The Washington Post,* (September 18, 1994), A29.

7 "No Justification Whatsoever," *St. Louis Dispatch,* (September 21, 1994), 6-C; Adam Nossiter, "Judge Awards Damages in Japanese Youth's Death," *The New York Times,* (September 16, 1994), A-12.

8 "Japanese Student's Parents Want Death Gun Destroyed," *The Washington Post,* (September 18, 1994), A20; Joan Treadway, "Parents Turn Grief into Anti-Gun Effort," *The Times-Picayune,* (October 6, 1996), B1.

9 T.R. Reid, "Angry Japan Lays to Rest Student Shot Dead in U.S; Slaying Sparks Criticism of Gun Laws," *The Washington Post,* (October 27, 1992), A1.

10 Jerome Hall, *General Principles of Criminal Law* (Indianapolis: Bobbs-Merrill, 1960).

11 *Robinson v. California,* 82 S.Ct. 1417 (1962).

12 Criminal negligence exists when, although neither specific nor general criminal intent is present, there is such disregard of the interest of others that the offender's conduct amounts to a gross deviation below the standard of care expected to be maintained by a reasonably careful man under like circumstances. LA. R.S. 14:12 (2000).

13 Oliver Wendall Holmes, *The Common Law* (Boston: Little, Brown and Company, 1881).

14 Kenneth W. Simons, "When is Strict Liability Just?" *Journal of Criminal Law and Criminology* 87 (1997), 1075–1137.

15 American Law Institute *Model Penal Code* Section.

16 H. L. A. Hart and A. M. Honore, "Causation in the Law," *Law Quarterly Review* 72 (1956), 58–90.

17 La. R.S. 14:20 (2000).

18 "Data and Statistics." Bureau of Alcohol, Tobacco, and Firearms and Explosives, https://www.atf.gov/resource-center/data-statistics; retrieved February 4, 2017.

19 Matthew Miller, Deborah Azreal, and David Hemenway. "Firearms and Violent Death in the United States," in *Reducing Gun Violence in America,* ed. David W. Webster and Jon S. Vernick (Baltimore: John Hopkins University Press, 2013).

20 Alexia Cooper and Erica L. Smith, "Homicide Trends in the United States, 1980–2008," in *Patterns and Trends* (Washington, D.C.: U.S. Department of Justice, 2011).

21 "Health, United States, 2015."(Washington, D.C.: U.S. Department of Health and Human Services, May 2016). https://www.cdc.gov/nchs/data/hus/hus15.pdf#019; retrieved February 4, 2017.

22 Sabina Tavernise, "To Reduce Suicide rates, New Focus Turns to Guns," *New York Times,* February 13, 2013.

23 Miller, Azreal, and Hemenway, "Firearms and Violent Death in the United States," 5.

24 Bonnie Berkowitz, et.al, "The math of mass shootings," *The Washington Post,* (July 27, 2016). Retrieved at https://www.washingtonpost.com/graphics/national/mass-shootings-in-america/; December 3, 2016.

25 U.S. Murders by Weapon Type from "Crime in the U.S., 2014" (Washington, DC: U.S. Department of Justice, 2015) Retrieved from https://www.quandl.com/data/FBI/WEAPONS11-US-Murders-by-Weapon-Type;, December 3, 2016.

26 "Promising Strategies to Reduce Gun Violence," NCJ 173950.

27 Miller, Azreal, and Hemenway, "Firearms and Violent Death in the United States."

28 Sanford J. Fox, "Juvenile Justice Reform: A Historical Perspective," *Stanford Law Review* 22 (1970).

29 Paul Marcus, "The Development of Entrapment Law," *Wayne Law Review* 33 (1986).

30 Henry J. Steadman, Margaret A. McGreevy and Joseph P. Morrisey, *Before and After Hinckley: Evaluating Insanity Defense Reform* (New York: Guildford Press, 1993); Norval Morris, *Insanity Defense* (Washington, DC: National Institute of Justice, 1979).

31 Stephen J. Morse, "The 'New Syndrome Excuse Syndrome'," *Criminal Justice Ethics* (1995), 3–15.

32 John R. Ford, "In Defense of the Defenders: The Vietnam Vet Syndrome," *Criminal Law Bulletin* 19 (1983), 434–443.

33 A. Burgess and L. Holmstrom, "Rape Trauma Syndrome," *American Journal of Nursing* 131 (1974), 981–986; P. Giannelli, "Rape Trauma Syndrome," *Criminal Law Bulletin* 33 (1997), 270–279.

34 Judith Herman, *Trauma and Recovery* (New York: Basic Books 1992).

[35] "Not Guilty Because of PMS?," *Newsweek,* (November 8, 1982).

[36] Alan Dershowitz, *The Abuse Excuse* (Boston: Little, Brown and Company, 1995).

[37] Lenore Walker, *The Battered Woman Syndrome* (New York: Springer, 1984).

[38] P. Ewing, *Battered Women Who Kill: Psychological Self-defense as Legal Justification* (Lexington, MA: D.C. Heath, 1987).

[39] C. Gillespie, *Battered Women, Self Defense and the Law* (Columbus, OH: Ohio State University Press, 1989).

[40] Cynthia Kwei Yung Lee, "Race and Self Defense: Toward a Normative Conception of Reasonableness," *Minnesota Law Review* 81 (1996).

[41] Pat K. Chew, "Asian Americans: The 'Reticent' Minority and Their Paradoxes," *William and Mary Law Review* 36 (1994).

In this chapter the case tells the story of a woman killed by a drunk driver. We learn about her family's anger, the driver's remorse, and their meeting together to bring healing for both sides. The chapter examines the unique and complex role of the victim in our criminal and legal systems.

LEARNING OBJECTIVES

After reading this chapter you should be able to:

- Describe the sense in which the criminal justice system is "offense-focused" and "offender-driven."
- Explain the process of "victim-blaming" and the process of "secondary victimization."
- Identify key victim rights that are currently guaranteed in most state and federal jurisdictions.
- Be able to identify the symptoms of post-traumatic stress disorder.
- Define restorative justice and explain the difference between retributive and restorative justice.

Case #6: Facing the Demons: Making Amends for Drunk Driving

With a blood alcohol level two times the legal limit, Susanna Cooper drifted across the center line and crashed into the car driven by Elaine Myers Serrell, killing her instantly.

Elaine Serrell Myer's routine was to drive home at night after her evening accounting class on the empty rural roads in the state of Washington.[1] The fifty-seven mile trip usually took about an hour while at home her husband David dozed off as he waited up for the sound of her car in the driveway. On April 27, 1993, he awoke with a start at 1 a.m. and knew immediately something was wrong. The sound of footsteps on the porch brought him to the front door where a state trooper and two friends stood to break the terrible news. Two hours earlier at approximately 11 p.m. his wife of 27 years had been killed in a head-on collision on a deserted stretch of highway near Skamokawa, Washington. The driver of the vehicle, Susanna Kay Cooper, lay in critical condition in the hospital. Driving a 1991 Mazda, she had drifted across the center line and smashed into Elaine's 1984 Nissan. Both cars had been completely demolished and the damage had been so great there was slim hope that Susanna, a single mother of two young children, would survive.

A Girls Night Out

Susanna had spent the evening drinking peppermint schnapps at a friend's house. They persuaded her to stay for dinner to give the liquor time to wear off but later did not recall thinking Susanna was too drunk to drive when she left the house. Apparently Susanna herself thought she was too drunk to drive because witnesses say she stopped at a roadside tavern to use the bathroom; she tried to get a ride from someone else to avoid getting back behind the wheel. In the end, Susanna made the fateful decision that would change the lives of so many. When the ambulance reached the emergency room Susanna's blood alcohol level measured twice the legal limit for the state of Washington.

The Devastation of Crime

In the wake of Elaine's death, despair enveloped the extended family of Elaine Serell. Elaine had been a vibrant and vital person central in the lives of many of her friends and family. She was known for her radio show on rainforest gardening, for the sweater vests made of wool that she dyed, spun, and knitted, and for her pottery. She was beloved by her parents, her three sisters and their husbands, and three young nieces. The day they planned her funeral would have been the twenty-seventh wedding anniversary of a couple who had been high school sweethearts. The funeral filled a local community hall to overflowing with hundreds whose lives were touched by Elaine and her generous spirit.

In the weeks and months that followed, David was so crushed by his loss he was barely able to function. He recalls that at that time if he were to have met the person who wrenched his beloved wife from him, he believed he was capable of killing her with his own hands. The parents of Elaine were also deeply damaged by the violent loss of their daughter. Elaine's father became so withdrawn and depressed that Elaine's mother felt when she lost her daughter she may have lost her husband as well. The nieces so close to Elaine struggled to return to normal but found they could not function: their school grades dropped and their nights were interrupted by bouts of crying and nightmares.

In the aftermath of such a tragedy, like many other victims, the family of Elaine suffered the rage, grief, bitterness, and helplessness so common among survivors of violence and trauma. Elizabeth, Elaine's sister, recalls the frustration and the anger and in the hopes of assuaging some of that rage she began to attend Mothers against Drunk Driving (MADD) meetings to connect with other victims in her situation.[2] She found that she was not alone in her feelings of bitterness and rage especially when she learned that the driver, Susanna, had been convicted of drunk driving once before four years earlier.

Susanna Survives

At first it seemed likely that Susanna would die from injuries she sustained in the crash. During those months of her hospitalization, Elizabeth found herself wishing Susanna would live to feel the full horror of her actions hoping she would emerge blind as a lifelong punishment for the pain and suffering she had brought to them. When the family learned that the driver was going to survive the crash, they felt mixed emotions. But when they also learned that Susanna was considering pleading not guilty to the charge of vehicular homicide, their sorrow turned to acid rage. Elaine's mother referred to the driver as a "human weed that ought to be pulled up."

It was Peter, Elaine's father, who from the depths of his depression remembered a lecture he had attended about victim-offender mediation or reconciliation. According to the speaker Marty Price, victims are able to come face to face with the people who have harmed them. Victims tell the truth about their loss and what was done to them, and then request some form of restitution from the offender. These programs are designed to help offenders truly understand the suffering they have caused and offer them some opportunity to right the wrong in a way that is meaningful to those who have been hurt.

Elaine's father was motivated to consider this type of process by an insight provided by Aileen, Elaine's ten-year-old favorite niece who visited the wreckage of the car only a day or so after the accident. It was Aileen who noticed that in the minivan driven by Susanna

there were children's toys. Peter suddenly remembered Aileen's remark about there being toys in the car and he realized that the monster who took his own child's life is herself a mother of two small children. This struck Peter deeply.

Like so many survivors of violence, it was crucial for Peter to see that Elaine's death served some positive purpose. Susanna had been convicted once before of drunk driving and even now, despite killing Elaine and nearly ending her own life, she was claiming that it was "just an accident." He saw that it was very possible, even if she was convicted of vehicular homicide, she would do her time in jail, return home, and continue to drink and drive raising children who would themselves follow in her footsteps. The ugly cycle of harm would churn on and the loss of his beautiful daughter would count for nothing in this world. That thought was more than the eighty-year-old father could bear. He decided that although he himself would never forgive her for taking his child, he did not want to see two small children raised by a mother who continued to be an alcoholic in denial. Peter called the man he heard lecture about mediation, Marty Price, to ask about the possibilities for meeting with the person who was responsible for the death of his daughter in the hopes that, at least, maybe something worthwhile would come of it.

Marty Price agreed to meet with Peter and the rest of his family to discuss the possibility of mediation. Unlike the majority of mediation cases that involve crimes of theft and vandalism, mediation in cases of serious violence requires lengthy preparation for both victims and offenders before they are genuinely ready to meet each other face to face.[3] Marty Price knew that it was important for all of the family members to have the opportunity to seriously reflect about and think about the idea of meeting the person responsible for killing Elaine. Peter called with the intention that he alone would meet Susanna but Marty Price, as an experienced mediator, knew that such a meeting could tear apart even the closest of families. Peter agreed that he would not proceed with the mediation unless his wife Kathleen was prepared to join him.

The Start of Healing Journey

Most of the other family members were skeptical about the idea. David, Elaine's widower, did not believe that he would be able to contain his anger and hate in meeting with the offender. Elizabeth, Elaine's sister, asked,

"Why would I want to meet the woman who had taken away someone I loved?" Both were willing to come together to a family meeting to talk about the mediation. There the mediator asked the family to share their pain, discuss the impact of their loss, and to brainstorm about what they want from the offender. During the emotional meeting, he asked them to think about the requests they might make of her which would in some meaningful way address their loss. That meeting would be the start of healing journey for the family.

One commitment they all wanted most from the driver is the promise that she will never drink and drive again and that she will use her terrible crime to prevent others from doing the same. Elizabeth realized when she attended MADD meetings that if Susanna were simply sent to jail without undergoing some kind of treatment for alcoholism, there was little to stop her from driving drunk again once she was released. The MADD meetings were full of tales of drunk drivers who had served jail time only to return to the same old patterns when they were out in society.

Secondly, the family realized they wanted Susanna to take responsibility for being a good mother to her children: they wanted to know that the children would be cared for and raised to be positive members of society. They wanted this to be a turning point in her life and for Elaine's loss to be offset by a positive gain for those two young lives.

The more the family talked, the more various members of the family began to feel that they would like to participate in the mediation. Even David was moved to the point where he felt he could be present and he even suggested that it was important for Susanna to have someone there to support her so she would not need to face them all alone. After several months of these family meetings, it was David who proposed that if they were to meet Susanna she should bring "someone who cares about her to sit next to her and hold her hand."

Ultimately, Peter and Kathleen, Elaine's parents, her husband, David, two sisters, Elizabeth and Barbara, and their spouses, and Aileen, Elaine's favorite niece, were all present at the mediation meeting with Susanna. Another sister from out of state joined the meeting by speaker phone. Susanna herself was accompanied by her defense attorney and a close friend.

Susanna's Journey: Denial and Self Pity

Susanna spent three months in intensive care and recovery in a nursing home. When she learned in the hospital that she had crossed the center line and caused the death of someone else, she simply wanted to die. But medical science saved her life and as she slowly recovered physically, she came to the realization that she had to face up to what she had done.

When she was finally able to leave the hospital, Susanna was arraigned and charged with vehicular homicide. The Serrell family attended the arraignment and found themselves filled with anger when her court-appointed attorney entered a plea of "not guilty" in response to the charges. Like so many victims who suffer the agonies of the criminal justice process, the standard defense strategy to deny all legal guilt felt emotionally devastating for family members who want the offender to fully admit and acknowledge what they have done. In November of 1993, Susanna herself decided to admit legal responsibility and entered a guilty plea to the charge of vehicular homicide. A date for the sentencing hearing was set and the family asked Marty Price to arrange for the mediation meeting to take place before the sentencing hearing so the family could have input into Susanna's sentence.

The mediation team contacted the defense attorney for Susanna and explained the desire of the victim's family to meet with Susanna. The defense attorney agreed to discuss the idea with Susanna. The next step was for the mediation team to meet with Susanna to prepare her for the mediation with the Serrell family.

At the first two-hour interview, Susanna acknowledged what she had done to the Serrell family but spent most of her time talking about her own physical suffering and her own concerns for her family and her future. Like many offenders, Susanna was shielded from the full impact of the pain she had caused the Serrell family. She had never met them, never knew Elaine, and had no concept of the full horror and suffering she had caused. Like so many offenders, her own pain and troubles were far more real to her. And quite naturally, her attention was focused on what lay in store for her.

Marty Price prepared Susanna by asking her to think about Elaine's family and how they have been affected; he asked her to think about what she could say to them or what she thinks they might want from her. The purpose of these preparatory meetings was to assist Susanna in opening herself up to empathizing with the pain of her victims.

More troubling to the mediator, however, was the refusal on Susanna's part to admit that she was an alcoholic. She explained that she was not a problem drinker and that what she drank that night was fairly normal among all her friends and family. She admitted that her father drinks too much, but she believed she herself did not have a serious problem with alcohol. The mediator explained that it was very important to the Serrell family that Susanna deal with her drinking problem and the first step, in their view, was for her to get an alcohol abuse evaluation. If Susanna was to remain in denial about her drinking, the mediation could not proceed and nothing more could be achieved.

Acknowledgment and Responsibility

By the second meeting with Susanna, the mediation team felt she had "changed." Somehow she had come to an understanding of what she is responsible for and had let go of the denial and defensiveness she had wrapped so tightly around her in the first meeting.

Susanna had obtained the alcohol evaluation the family had asked for and this led her to some soul searching of her own. She learns from the evaluation that she is considered to be in the beginning to intermediate stages of alcoholism. She learns that the "normal" habits of her family and friends were both abusive and dangerous to others and to themselves. "It's normal to get drunk in my town. That's all there is to do. I thought it was normal to go out with my girlfriends and drink. We went out almost every weekend and some weeknights. Now I know that it's not normal. I wish that what happened to me would wake up those people, but it hasn't. They don't think it can happen to them."

During this period, Susanna had the opportunity to read the victim-impact statement written by members of the family. The victim-impact statements described what the loss of Elaine has meant in their lives and Susanna had time to process the enormous consequences of her actions. Elizabeth's statement, in particular, was very powerful in its clear presentation about what Elizabeth would need from Susanna if she were to ever forgive her for what has happened.

Betty wrote:

Forgiveness is not something which I believe is my obligation to bestow unilaterally, but it can be earned. The perpetrator must show the five R's: recognition, remorse, repentance, restitution and reform. Recognition means admitting that what she did was wrong, and that she is responsible for the wrongdoing and all of the negative consequences that follow from it. (If she is in jail, she recognizes that it is because she drove drunk, not because the prosecutor or the judge was mean or unfair to her. If she is in pain, she recognizes it is because she drove drunk, not blaming it on the lack of pain medicine or lack of medical science's ability to fix her as good as new.) Remorse means that each time she thinks of the wrong she did, she regrets that she did not make a better choice. It is a repeated rehearsal of how she wishes she had done it differently, how she would do it differently if given another chance. Repentance is when a deep remorse leads to a firm resolve to do better in the future. Restitution cannot be direct in this case—there is no way that she can provide a wife for David or a sister for me. The only restitution she can make is a lifelong commitment to a daily effort toward making the world a better place for her having survived the crash. She is not required to complete the job of repairing the world, but she must not be excused from starting and continually working at the job. Reform means that she must create a new form of herself—to emerge as a sober person, a thoughtful and considerate person, a contributor. If she can do all these, I can forgive.

The Mediation

On January 17, 1994, eight months after the accident, Susanna and the Serrell family were ready to meet. Twelve people assembled in a small hotel conference room in Oregon. The Serrell family sat nervously awaiting the arrival of Susanna, her lawyer, and her best friend. When the family first laid eyes on Susanna, they saw a small, frail, gaunt young woman, clearly terrified of encountering the family of the person whose life she had ended.

The mediators allowed Susanna to speak first. She began to speak only to be overwhelmed with sobs. Knowing her words were hopelessly inadequate, she nonetheless struggled to express her sorrow and apologies. She eventually controlled her emotions enough to state at least the start of what needed to be said.

Each of the family members was given an opportunity to talk about the crash and what the loss of Elaine meant to them. Susanna sat quietly and listened intently to it all, weeping silently as she heard the words of loss knowing there was nothing she could do or say to make it right. She sat and listened as David described the loss of his lifelong partner, his companion, and love of his life. She sat and listened as he said, "In the end, my world will never again be right, and I will always have to live knowing the horror of Elaine's death." She listened as Elaine's mother expressed her resentment and loss of not only her daughter but also her husband.

The family was also given the opportunity to ask for answers to questions which were important to them. For instance, Elizabeth wanted to know about Susanna's thoughts the night she made the decision to drive drunk. "What were you thinking that night? Why did you do it?" Susanna explained that she had no memory of that night or the entire week before the crash. Aileen asked her to describe what she thought when she learned that someone had been killed in the crash. Again, Susanna dissolved in tears communicating her genuine horror and remorse at what she had done.

The mediation lasted five hours. The agreement reached by everyone required Susanna to attend AA meetings and victim-impact panels while in prison; it required Susanna to write letters to her children weekly while in jail and to write to Peter as well to provide updates on her progress; she also agreed to find ways to speak out against drunk driving in the community when she was released; and to complete her General Education Diploma, take parenting classes, and give 10 percent of her income for the rest of her life to charity. The family agreed to present the mediation contract to the judge at the upcoming sentencing hearing.

A Shared Journey of Healing

At that meeting, an extraordinary transition took place. The victims and the offender, in the words of Marty Price, "became allies in the healing of each other." The day after the mediation, David wrote in his journal, "What a wonderful effect of last night's mediation—I have regained my brightness and vigour." He felt like a renewed man, able to walk with energy and to focus on the affairs of his life. Elizabeth reported feeling a great sense of relief: the tension that had been weighing on her had vanished, she let go of vengeance and felt ready to find enjoyment in life once more.

At the sentence hearing, all of the parties shared with the judge the agreement reached during the mediation. The judge agreed that Susanna's willingness to meet with the family was evidence of her own rehabilitation. Nonetheless, because of her prior conviction, the judge felt compelled to order the maximum sentence under the state's mandatory sentencing guidelines. Susanna was sentenced to thirty-four months in state prison.

In the months that followed, the family petitioned the governor to reduce the sentence, but the petition for clemency was denied. After serving twenty-one months in jail, Susanna was paroled and began to speak out at MADD panels telling her story; she also spoke at high school driver education classes and agreed to have her real name and story published in the largest daily newspaper in Oregon. The story received national coverage. In the years that followed, the Serrells and Susanna went public again and again with their story including on a national television show.

Aftermath

One year after her death, the family held a memorial service for Elaine where they dedicated a headstone with an engraving that celebrated the way she led her life. With that ceremony, the Serrell family felt a shift from mourning how Elaine died to a celebration of how Elaine lived. Years later, the Serrell family and Susanna remain in close contact with each other. The letters between Susanna and Peter began as progress reports but developed into a genuine ongoing correspondence. Aileen even exchanged letters with Susanna while she was in prison. The two families have appeared together on national television and at conferences to share their story of hope and healing. Susanna remains committed to keeping her promise to the Serrell family to remain sober, attend community college, and continue to openly and honestly tell her story to others in the hope that it will prevent the same tragedy from repeating itself in the lives of other human beings.

THINKING CRITICALLY ABOUT THIS CASE

1. How did a face-to-face meeting between Susanna and the Serrell family change both of these parties' feelings about the crime that had taken place? Should such face-to-face meetings be encouraged by the criminal justice system? Why or why not?

2. The Serrells wanted input into the sentencing. Do you feel this is appropriate? Should victims have a significant input into the sentencing process? Why or why not?

3. Is healing victims an important part of "justice" in your view? What is the responsibility of the justice system to the healing process for victims?

4. Why was the future conduct of Susanna and the safety and well-being of her children important to the Serrell family? Why would victims who have lost a loved one be concerned for the future?

5. Why was preparation important for the process of bringing the offender and victims together in this case? What are the possible dangers if the two had not been prepared to meet one another face to face?

6. Consider the five "Rs" Betty felt were necessary for forgiveness. Do you believe that Susanna Cooper would have achieved any of these goals without the experience of mediation? What was gained through the mediation process for Susanna?

REFERENCES

Case adapted from:

Florangela Davila, "Finding Peace Eye to Eye," *Seattle Times,* March 11, 1996, p. B1.

Spencer Heinz, "Coming Home: a Life Lost and a Life Saved," *The Sunday Oregonian,* December 31, 1995; retrieved June 6, 2002, from Victim-Offender Reconciliation Program Information and Resource Center, www.vorp.com/articles/lifesave.html

Elizabeth S. Menkin, "Life After Death," *San Jose Mercury news, West Magazine,* 1994; retrieved June 6, 2002, from Victim-Offender Reconciliation Program Information and Resource Center, www.vorp.com/articles/lifeaft.html

Elizabeth S. Menkin with Lori K. Baker, "I Forgave My Sister's Killer," *Ladies Home Journal,* December 1995; retrieved June, 2002 from Victim-Offender Reconciliation Program Information and Resource Center, www.vorp.com/articles/forgave.html

Marty Price, "The Mediation of a Drunk Driving Death: A Case Development Study," June 7, 1994; retrieved June 6, 2002, from Victim-Offender Reconciliation Program Information and Resource Center, www.vorp.com/articles/lifeaft.html

The institutions of the criminal justice system are designed to handle people who violate the law. Whether arresting, prosecuting, defending, punishing, or treating them, the primary focus of the agencies that make up the system is persons who commit crime. The justice system as a whole is **offender-focused**.[4] Until recently, virtually no justice personnel were focused on protecting the rights, meeting the needs or delivering "justice" directly to the people victimized by crime.

The criminal justice process focuses on the relationship between the defendant and the state. The defendant is accused of violating the law and the state makes its case against the accused. The adversarial process is well demonstrated by the justice process in the Peairs case. The prosecution's vigorous arguments were matched by equally zealous arguments on the part of the defense. The jury sat and listened to the two attorneys presenting quite different portraits of Peairs's behavior that night. The prosecution presented the picture of a man who was unnecessarily aggressive and reckless. The defense focused on the behavior of Hattori, painting a picture of his behavior that night as weird, bizarre, and erratic. Each side had its supporters in the courtroom. When the jury returned a verdict of "not guilty," the friends and family of the Peairses cheered and gave the V sign for victory.

But what about the victims? Did anyone attempt to meet the needs of Yoshi Hattori's parents who had lost their only child? Was this justice for them? What is the meaning of "justice" for victims of crime? What were the victim's needs in this case and how did the system meet or fail to meet those needs? Should the criminal justice system attempt to meet the needs of victims? What is the role of the victim in the criminal justice system?

The Serrell family's involvement with Susanna Cooper is not typical of the criminal justice response to a drunk-driving homicide. In the criminal justice system, the state is seen as the "victim" of the crime: the prosecutor acts in the name of the individual victim, in this case the deceased, and the wider public. Although the Serrell family was clear in their preference for a kind of justice that involved restitution, remorse, repentance, and reform, the state sought a different kind of justice that required imprisonment for Susanna.

This chapter looks at the experience of victims, the changes within the criminal justice process that altered the role of victims over time, and the current efforts to restore the rights of victims in the justice process. We will also look at the different understandings of justice in the traditional system that focuses primarily on punishment and treatment of offenders, and other understandings of justice that focus on restoration and restitution of victims and communities. We examine alternate visions of justice rooted in pre-Western and non-Western societies and explore the rise of restorative justice within the contemporary justice system.

OFFENDER-FOCUSED all the resources, policies, and personnel of the justice system are devoted to activities which concern the person who is accused of or has been convicted of violating the law.

THE DECLINE OF THE VICTIM IN THE JUSTICE PROCESS

Prior to the modern era, victims played a leading role in the resolution of criminal matters[5]. Victims, and more frequently, their extended family or clan, used their own resources to extract reparations and avenge an aggressor. Early legal systems prioritized the need for offenders to settle directly with victims and their families. Many societies developed elaborate systems of compensation that were paid by the offender and offender's family directly to the victim or victim's family. The emphasis was on a direct obligation from the offender to the victim. The central goal of justice was to make victims whole.

State-centered justice begins when centralized authorities, first the church and then the royal courts, define crime as primarily an offense against the authority of these powerful institutions rather than a harm to individuals within the community[6]. In Europe, by the mid-thirteenth century, the concept of "crime" was re-defined to refer to a violation of the "King's peace." The origin of the word "felony" comes from the Norman word for "breach of faith": a felony was a violation of a subject's loyalty to the king. To violate the "Kings Law" by committing theft against one's neighbor was now viewed as an act of treason against the king himself. By that reasoning, the offender now owed reparations to the monarch rather than the victim.

A system of fines paid to the court king gradually replaced the system of compensation paid to victims: instead of restitution being paid directly to the victim whose horse was stolen or purse robbed, a fine was paid to the court. The king's magistrates and lawyers determined what law was violated and what fine was deserved. As early as the thirteenth century, revenues from criminal fines accounted for almost one-sixth of the royal income. In medieval England, all the property owned by a person convicted as a "felon" became the property of the king and his lords. By "owning" crime, the monarch gained power and riches. If retribution was deemed necessary, the king's soldiers and executioners meted out physical punishment upon the offender. In place of private vengeance, the public executioner staged a spectacle that punished an offender in the name of the king usually in full view of the community.

By the modern era, the person who had actually been harmed by the criminal offense gradually disappeared from the justice process except in their role in reporting the crime to the authorities and testifying in the case that the state brings against the offender. Offenders lost all notion of direct accountability to the victim for the harm inflicted and instead became embroiled in a defensive strategic battle against the state in a court of law. For victims, "justice" came to be served exclusively by the knowledge that offenders are being punished by the state.

This transformation from a victim-oriented system of justice based on the community to an offender-focused system of justice run by the government has taken place over a period of centuries. In colonial America at the time of the Salem witch trials, victims still conducted their own investigations, paid for warrants to have sheriffs make arrests and hired private attorneys to indict and prosecute. If convicted of a crime, the offender was required to repay the victim three times the amount they stole or damaged. The adoption of the Bill of Rights signaled a shift toward state-centered justice and by the nineteenth century the role of the public prosecutor had expanded to exercise powers and responsibilities previously exercised by victims and the community.

THE FIELD OF VICTIMOLOGY

The field of criminology is generally considered to be over 200 years old originating with the work of European scholars who began the first serious scientific study of people who violate the criminal law. The field of *victimology* dates only as far back as the 1940s[7]. **Victimology** is now recognized as the scientific study

STATE-CENTERED JUSTICE
when crime is defined as primarily an offense against the authority of these powerful institutions rather than a harm to individuals within the community.

VICTIMOLOGY
the scientific study of the physical, psychological, and financial harm people suffer because of crime and the handling of crime by the criminal justice system itself.

of the physical, psychological, and financial harm people suffer because of crime and the handling of crime by the criminal justice system itself.[8]

Early victimologists focused on the victim-offender relationship, the vulnerability of different groups such as the elderly or women to crime, and the relative risk factors that contribute to the likelihood a person might become a victim of crime. Victimologists examined the victim-proneness of different groups to crime in order to identify preventative steps individuals and communities might take to reduce or avoid crime.[9] As we saw in chapter 4, much of the information we have about the "dark figure of crime" comes from victimization surveys. Research also paid careful attention to analyzing the role victims themselves played in criminal event.[10] The concept of **victim-precipitation**[11] refers to behavior such as walking alone at night, or frequenting certain types of bars, using drugs and alcohol, confrontational language, and so forth, which increases the likelihood of criminal victimization.

The research on victim-precipitation was criticized in recent decades as contributing to a widespread societal attitude of **victim-blaming.**[12] "Blaming the victim" for being vulnerable to crime is a deep-seated American attitudinal response to crime. Victimization is an experience of weakness and this is often perceived as a shameful experience within a culture which values power and control. Because all of us fear victimization, we psychologically look for ways to hold the victims responsible for what happened to them. We claim they were "stupid" to be out alone late at night, for carrying cash in their wallets, leaving windows open, or wearing provocative clothing. This attitude helps us to feel more secure and falsely assures us it won't happen to us as long as we are "careful" and don't make those same mistakes. Being a victim of crime is a loss of control and all of us seek to maintain the belief that we are in control of our fate.

As members of our culture, victims themselves often share these beliefs. Most of us consciously or unconsciously believe in a "just world" where people deserve what happens to them: victims as well as offenders are on the receiving end of societal attitudes which blames individuals for the bad things that happen to them. One of the most common responses among victims is to blame themselves for being victimized. "If only I hadn't walked down that street . . . if only I had locked my windows. . . ." "If only" forms of thinking often torment victims long after a crime has taken place. Victims experience shame about being a victim and are often reluctant to talk about their experience with others. And when they do choose to talk about it, their response is often met with the judgmental response of those around them.

SECONDARY VICTIMIZATION BY THE CRIMINAL JUSTICE SYSTEM

VICTIM-PRECIPITATION behavior of individuals that increases the likelihood of criminal victimization.

VICTIM-BLAMING the responsibility for the crime is shifted from the perpetrator to the victim.

Crimes that terrorize take many forms, from aggravated assault to petty thievery. But one crime goes largely unnoticed. It is a crime against which there is no protection. It is committed daily across our nation. It is the painful, wrongful insensitivity of the criminal justice system toward those who are the victims of crime. . . . The callousness with which the system again victimizes those who have already suffered at the hands of an assailant is tragic.

Senator John Heinz, sponsor of the Omnibus Victims Protection Act passed by Congress, 1982.[13]

The victims' rights movement has called attention to the insensitive and callous treatment by the justice system and lobbied for more resources and rights for victims of crime. (Getty Images)

The anger and resentment of victims has been fueled by the neglect they experienced within the criminal justice process itself. Victims, particularly those who suffered the serious crimes of violence, often find they experienced a **second victimization** at the hands of an insensitive and callous justice system.[14] Police routinely question victims without any thought to their psychological or emotional state often misinterpreting their anxiety and confusion as dishonesty or lack of credibility. Victims are told that if their injuries are not life threatening, their injuries are "not serious," no support or assistance is available to accompany a terrified victim back home or to assist with cleaning up of a ransacked room or apartment. If victims are required to go to the hospital, no one in the justice system offers them a ride, some extra clothing, a cup of coffee, or a sympathetic ear to help them through this stressful experience.

Rape victims, in particular, often have found themselves treated like the guilty party by male officers who view them with suspicion and mistrust particularly when they do not fit the stereotype of the "worthy" victim. Prosecutors often refuse to charge a defendant if they feel the victim will not make a credible witness because of how she was dressed, where she worked, what she had drunk, or what her relationship was with the man accused of rape.

Although the prosecutor represents the interests of the victim, it is also the prosecutor's job to win the case for the state. Victims are only one of several constituencies district attorneys seek to satisfy in making decisions about any particular case. In determining what to charge or whether to dismiss or reduce the charges, district attorneys must consider many factors beyond the victim's wishes such as the limited resources of the office, the chances of winning a conviction, the credibility of the victim and witnesses, and the interests of the community and the system in prosecuting this crime. Prosecutors may be interested in using the defendant as an informant or key witness in other cases or they may believe the defendant is a good candidate for diversion or other alternatives. Typically, prosecutors are neither trained nor organized to assist victims, explain the process to them, or meet their emotional, financial, or physical needs.

SECONDARY VICTIMIZATION callous and insensitive treatment by the criminal justice system which inflicts additional psychological harm and emotional trauma on victims.

As a result, victims are routinely mistreated and misinformed by the system. They may be ordered to show up to testify at a hearing forcing them to take time off from work (without pay), provide their own transportation and babysitting only to find themselves sitting on a bench for hours waiting for a hearing which has been postponed until a later date. During this time they may even find themselves seated next to the defendant or surrounded by his family and friends. No one appears to inform them of the process, offers them assistance, or apologizes for their time. This dismal and painful experience re-occurs repeatedly as the case grinds slowly and torturously through months of pretrial hearings.

At the trial itself, victims may find that truth is far from the genuine outcome. The story heard by the jury in the courtroom is shaped by the opposing attorneys, the rules of evidence, and what arguments the judge believes the law will allow. Not all the available evidence may be presented to the jury since it may be suppressed for due process reasons. Skillful defense attorneys will also make use of cross-examination to raise reasonable doubt in the jury's mind casting negative innuendo on the witnesses including the victim. In the courtroom, the rape victim, as often as not, finds herself placed on trial and her own sexual past used as evidence against her.[15]

Recall the defense's subtle portrayal of young Yoshi as a kind of crazed bizarre freak. The defense sought to suggest that Yoshi himself was to blame for Rodney's decision to fire his gun. For Yoshi's parents, who were forced to sit in the back of the courtroom, and who sometimes had trouble even finding a seat during the trial, this treatment is painful and terribly unjust. For people who have been injured by crime, this treatment is a second victimization.

The Victims' Rights Movement

In the 1970s and 1980s, several social movements contributed to a more politicized and empowering approach to victims and their role in the criminal justice system.[16] Victims began to form organizations to protest the poor treatment they received by the justice system and the wider society.[17] Organizations such as MADD formed by Cindy Lightner to advocate for the needs of victims, and the activities of two fathers of murdered daughters in California who fought for three-strikes legislation for violent offenders, are examples of activist victims groups which joined with law enforcement groups to lobby for tougher sentencing laws and other reforms.

The women's movement was a second social movement that greatly contributed to the resurgence of concern, respect, and attention paid to victims by the justice system. Feminists attacked the pervasive leniency toward men who victimized their wives and girlfriends. Victims of rape and domestic violence joined forces with feminists to make the justice system more sensitive to victims, to counter the powerful victim-blaming attitudes of the justice personnel and to provide institutional support, safety, and counseling for victims of male violence. The first rape-crisis center was established in 1972 in Berkeley California and Washington D.C. and the first "safe" house for battered women followed shortly thereafter in 1974 in St. Paul, Minnesota.[18]

The women's movement fought against the tacit presumption that violence against wives was not "real" crime and won successful societal battles in attitudes toward these crimes and in the procedures for prosecuting these crimes. Women who did not struggle against rapists were routinely depicted in court as consenting, even though they may have submitted in sheer terror recognizing the likelihood of being killed by the rapist. Activists fought to change the legal criteria for rape that required signs of resistance to prove the element of forcible rape. The feminist movement increased awareness of the domestic and sexual violence against women and promoted a number of changes within the law and justice system, including the hiring of victim's advocates for rape victims, awareness training for law enforcement and rape shield laws to protect the past sexual history of the woman from being on trial.

Empowerment of Victims in the Criminal Justice System[19]

Before the **victims' rights movement**, victims had little or no input into the sentencing process. Unless the victim was called as a material witness, there was no right of the victim to be heard in the courtroom. Victims and their families were often not permitted in the courtroom out of fear that their presence would prejudice the jury against the accused and provoke a mistrial. Sometimes judges warned victims to display no outward signs of emotion or they would be removed from the courtroom despite the fact that defendant's family often prominently displayed emotions in support of their loved one. Even more disturbing was the denial of a direct voice to articulate the impact of the crime and how it had affected them. Victims had to rely upon prosecutors to describe how they felt and the losses they had suffered.

The establishment of a right to make a **victim-impact statement** to the court was an important gain for the victims' rights movement. Victims demanded the opportunity to be heard in the courtroom at the time of sentencing. While defendants had the opportunity to present information about themselves and to humanize themselves for the jury, victims felt that they were unfairly silenced and excluded from the process that did not allow them to talk about how they had been harmed. Victims groups lobbied hard for victims to have the right to make a victim-impact statement to the judge at the time of sentencing[20]. Some states now require such a statement before sentencing can take place while others offer the victim the right to make a statement if they so choose. The victim-impact statement provides an account of the loss sustained: financial, emotional, and physical—articulated in the victim's own words. In some jurisdictions, this statement is incorporated into the pre-sentence report prepared by probation; in others, the victim is permitted to read the statement directly to the judge at the time of sentencing.

Victims' rights groups also fought for the establishment of **victim witness and advocacy programs**[21] to assist victims in a host of ways in the criminal justice system. These programs, in some states as part of the district attorney's office, in others separate offices, provide an advocate for the victim to accompany them to hearings and trial, to monitor the court process and provide them updates and information about the proceedings and to assist them in preparing their victim-impact statement. Victim's advocates may also set up separate waiting spaces for victims so they are isolated from defendants and the general public and offer basic useful information about the location of the court and other practical issues. Finally they may provide assistance in the application for victim compensation and other forms of restitution available for victims.

Victims have also fought for the **right to be notified** by the system when an offender was being released on parole and for the right to attend the parole hearing and to make a formal statement before the parole board. During the 1970s and

VICTIMS' RIGHTS MOVEMENT
a social movement started in the 1970s to increase awareness of victims' issues and to advocate for the right of victims in the criminal justice process.

VICTIM-IMPACT STATEMENT
a report to the sentencing judge listing the effects of the crime on the victim.

VICTIM WITNESS AND ADVOCACY PROGRAMS
an organized program with specialized personnel housed within district attorneys' offices or victims assistance agencies who assist victims throughout the justice process.

NOTIFICATION RIGHTS
the right of victims to be informed of key decisions and hearings related to their cases, such as plea agreements, parole hearings, or early release decisions.

1980s, many victims groups along with other law enforcement interests lobbied against parole as an unwarranted form of leniency for offenders and many states and the federal government responded by reducing the use of parole release. Legislation in most states now grants victims the right to be present at parole hearings and to submit written or oral opinion on whether or not it should be granted to the offender. In some states, restitution to victims is a mandatory requirement for parolees.

Another significant achievement of the victims' rights movement has been the establishment of state-funded **victim compensation funds** in all fifty states. These funds offer repayment to victims of serious crime for medical expenses, mental health services, and lost wages. Although some are funded out of general revenues or taxpayers, increasingly these programs are funded from fines and surcharges levied on persons convicted of misdemeanors or felony offenses. It is not necessary for an assailant to be caught and convicted for a victim to be repaid but the victim must report the crime to the police and be fully cooperating with the authorities in the investigation in order to be eligible for compensation.[22]

Finally, victims groups also organized themselves into greater support groups for each other to overcome the "wall of silence" surrounding victims and to reduce some of the shame and blame that falls on victims of crime in our society. Work with victims has increased our understanding of the long-term psychological impact of crime and of the healing process for victims to restore them back to equilibrium.

UNDERSTANDING THE PSYCHOLOGICAL TRAUMA OF CRIME

The impact of crime upon victims extends far beyond the financial and physical losses inflicted by the offender. Recall the difficulty Alice Wise faced in trying to "come back to normal" years after the crime. Even in the case of property crimes, research demonstrates that there is often a chronic and long-term psychological impact on crime victims. Crime undermines the basic sense of security in the world. It undermines the sense that the world is a "safe place." Mistrust, anxiety, fear, loneliness, and anger are lasting emotional states often compounded by a sense of anxiety that the offender will return or had acted deliberately against them, watching them, and might be planning to return.

In interpersonal crime, such as rape or assault, the psychological trauma is even more severe. The research on the experience of rape victims as well as victims of domestic violence has contributed to our broader understanding of the psychological trauma of all types of victimization. Psychologists have found that many victims of serious crime suffer from **post-traumatic stress disorder (PTSD)** that has a profound impact on their lives long after the crime has taken place.[23] Judith Herman[24] has studied the victims of sexual violence who suffer similar psychological symptoms as people who are exposed to violence during war. Herman argues that what earlier physicians termed "shell shock" is now understood to be PTSD brought on by exposure to the traumatic violence of war.

In the short term, exposure to severe violence leads to a physiological response of hyper-arousal. The body reacts with shortness of breath, increased respiration, extreme anxiety, and feelings of terror and helplessness. For many victims of rape, the immediate response may appear like cooperation but is in fact a psychological state of profound terror. This psychological state may be re-triggered in the victim, days, months, or even years after the crime occurred, by stimuli

VICTIM COMPENSATION FUNDS
money collected by the state from criminal fines and awarded to victims for medical bills, counseling, and to compensate for financial losses.

POST-TRAUMATIC STRESS DISORDER
a set of psychological symptoms suffered by some victims in response to the trauma of the crime.

that remind the victim of the original incident such as a particular time of day, or spatial cue, sound, or smell. Many victims also experience physical symptoms of sleep disorders, stomach problems, muscle spasms, and other dysfunctions. Negative effects often last for months and may persist for years as victims continue to experience depression, anxiety, anger, guilt, and shame.

For family members of murder victims, the psychological harms are profound and lasting. Losing a loved one to a violent killing is not the same experience as losing a loved one to an accidental death. Family members of murder victims are often completely neglected by the system especially when they have little to offer as witnesses in the case. The psychological impact of the crime often destroys marriages and creates a lasting psychological pain that is hidden from the wider society. Family members of murder victims suffer from the intense shame, loneliness, social isolation, anger, guilt, and frustration that is so common among all victims.

Healing and Justice

The study of victims has only begun to offer insight into the emotional and psychological healing process for victims of crime. Judith Herman has studied the healing process for victims of sexual violence. The first requirement for healing is safety: victims need to feel safe and in control of their own immediate environment. Too often well-meaning family and friends are tempted to tell a victim what he or she "needs" to do. This has the unintended consequence of further undermining the victim's sense of autonomy and retards the healing process.

As part of the process of dealing with the pain of crime, victims often have many questions about the crime and the person who committed it. There is a need to "re-live" the event, to re-construct it in the attempt to understand it. The Serrell family responded to the loss of Elaine in a number of ways that are quite common among many survivors of violence. First of all they felt a need to understand why this crime occurred. It was important to the family to ask Susanna why she drove that night, to try and understand what she was thinking, and what had caused her to take the actions she did.

The Hattori family also sought answers to these same questions in trying to understand why Rodney Peairs owned several firearms and why he was so quick to use them against their unarmed and innocent son. One of the key needs for victims in the wake of crime is answers to the question of why: why me, why my house, why were you carrying a gun, what was going on in your head at the time, and so forth. Victims often feel a need to understand the motives of the offender and what about his or her life would help them make sense of this terrible injury.

By seeking answers to questions, victims are seeking the *meaning* of the injury. This is an attempt to restore some sense of moral order in the wake of actions that undermine their previous beliefs in morality and justice. The need for understanding is related to our need for control: unless we can make sense of what happens, we are powerless to steer our own course in the world. Humans require understanding in order to feel we can exercise meaningful control in our lives. Victims of burglaries, assaults, robberies, and rapes express the same basic need to understand why: why were they chosen? What was in the mind of the offender? Who is this person who would do such a thing? What motivated them to do it? Oftentimes there are very specific and painful questions that victims feel a need to ask such as what happened in the last few minutes of their loved one's life, did they suffer, and if they uttered any last words what were they.

Survivors Missions

The Serrell family gains enormous solace from the knowledge that Susanna Cooper is not out on the streets drinking and driving again. The idea that she would return to the nation's highways unchanged and possibly inflict future tragedies on other families or bring harm to her own young children was more than the family of Elaine could bear to contemplate. In the aftermath of the crime, victims often seek to take some kind of action that will make a positive difference in the future. Victims may become active in lobbying for new laws, for resources to study crime, for harsher punishment for offenders, or for assistance for other crime victims. Victims find meaning in these **survivors missions** that seek to help others who may be in the same position or which prevent others from going through what they experienced.[25] It is important to them to feel that their loved one did not die in vain.

Victims need to regain control over their lives in the wake of crime. Because crime represents a profound loss of control, it is extremely important for victims to be active in the response to the crime. As we will see below, the criminal justice system excludes victims and makes them passive bystanders in the justice process itself. They are not decision-makers, do not take action, and are generally not consulted by the professionals who take action against the offender. Thus many victims channel their energies into "justice" through social action such as lobbying for tougher sentencing laws, or gun control, or the death penalty. This type of action gives meaning to their loved one's death and gives victims an outlet for participation that is not possible within the current justice system.

In the mid-1980s, Candy Lightner, the mother of a teenage girl killed in an automobile crash, by a drunk driver with two previous drunk-driving convictions and out on bail on a third charge, founded the organization Mothers against Drunk Driving. MADD became a powerful lobbying organization that changed both the laws on DUI (Driving Under the Influence) and public attitudes toward this crime.[26] MADD established drunk-driving awareness programs and pioneered a form of restitution in which victims tell their story to offenders and offenders go public with their stories to help to prevent future tragedies. MADD also helped to promote increased penalties for drunk driving, including laws such as the automatic loss of a driver's license and mandatory prison sentences such as the one served by Susanna Cooper in the state of Washington.

The efforts by the Hattoris to pass gun control laws is another example of a survivor mission as is the lobbying of Polly Klaus's father for three-strikes legislation in California, and efforts by the Serrell family to see that some good would come from Elaine's death. In each these cases, the victims and survivors of crime became involved in social movements and action to prevent others from becoming victims in the future. Although each of these victims may not agree on the strategy of prevention with some lobbying for harsher punishment and others lobbying against it, all became active as a result of their victimization.

AN ALTERNATIVE VISION OF JUSTICE: RESTORATIVE JUSTICE

The Serrell family sought a very different kind of justice than the one that the state offered to them by sentencing Susanna Cooper to jail for 36 months. What the Serrell family wanted has been termed **restorative justice**.[27] The type of

SURVIVORS MISSION sustained efforts by victims to bring about positive legislative or social change that will prevent re-occurrence of the crime to others or will assist victims in dealing with the trauma of crime.

RESTORATIVE JUSTICE a response to crime that seeks to restore the well-being of victims and the larger community while promoting responsible and productive behavior in offenders.

| TABLE 6.1 | Retributive Justice V. Restorative Justice |

Retributive Justice Asks These Questions	Restorative Justice Asks These Questions
1. What law was broken?	1. What was harmed?
2. Who did it?	2. What is needed to repair the harm?
3. What punishment do they deserve?	3. Whose responsibility is it to provide repair?

justice meted out by the criminal justice system by inflicting punishment on the convicted offender is referred to as **retributive justice.** These two understandings of justice are beginning to compete with one another in the contemporary justice system as more and more victims seek alternatives to the traditional justice response.

According to Howard Zehr the retributive model of justice focuses on three key questions: What law was broken? Who broke it? What punishment do they deserve? Much of the time and energy of the traditional justice system involves obtaining an accurate and fair answer to these three questions through arrest, investigations, collection of evidence, the trial process, and the imposition of sentencing. In the retributive model the "work" of the justice process is done by professionals. Justice professionals protect the legal rights of the accused, determine legal guilt within the boundaries of due process, and ensure public safety and justice for victims and the community through the imposition of fair punishment and opportunity for appropriate rehabilitation. As we have noted before, the traditional response to crime overwhelmingly focuses on the offender.

A restorative response to crime focuses on three very different questions: Who has been harmed by the crime? What is needed to repair the harm? Whose responsibility and obligation is it to offer this repair? In this vision of justice, the victim and the losses sustained by the crime are the primary focus and victims themselves are put back into a role of central importance. The first question puts focus upon the direct and indirect victims of the crime. Often a criminal act harms not only the immediate victim of the crime but also the spouse and children, may suffer psychological trauma from the crime. The community may also be affected by a crime as neighbors may fear walking down the street or choose to withdraw or move in order to feel safe within their neighborhood. In the Serrell case, the family used the opportunity at the victim-offender mediation to articulate exactly how all of them—her husband, parents, siblings, and nieces—were affected by the death of Elaine.[28]

The second question in a restorative response seeks to figure out what is needed to help restore or repair the harm. As Elizabeth stated, in the case of a homicide, it is not possible to literally provide wholeness. Elizabeth acknowledges that Susanna cannot "provide a wife for David or a sister for myself." But the family did articulate what, in their view, would provide restoration. In this case, the family wants Susanna to change her ways and devote her life to

RETRIBUTIVE JUSTICE
a response to crime that seeks to inflict punishment on offenders in just proportion to the seriousness of the offense.

preventing drunk driving by having the courage to share her story truthfully and in public. Just as in the pre-Western times, repair is often not an exact return to a prior state but rather a mutual agreement about what can be done to make amends for a past injury.

Who is responsible for doing this repair is the third key concern in a restorative response. Here the role of the offender is also quite different in restorative justice than it is in a retributive system. In the traditional system, punishment is imposed upon an offender who must passively be made to suffer for their crimes. The offender is acted upon rather than taking actions themselves. In a restorative system, offenders, like victims, are more directly involved. Susanna is asked to meet directly with the people she harmed, an encounter that is as difficult for offenders as it is for victims. Susanna must listen to the real and painful consequences of her criminal negligence and she must live with the full knowledge of what she took from this family. Susanna is also charged with taking positive action for the rest of her life to make up for this loss. Unlike the traditional system, which asks only that an offender sit in jail for a duration of time, the restorative system asks what an offender can do to make the victim and the community whole again.

The Hattoris' painful experience with the American justice system derives in part from the contrast between the Japanese system which operates on more restorative principles. The use of apology and direct acknowledgment of wrongdoing is highly prevalent within the Japanese system. For many victims, one of the deepest injuries of the traditional system comes from the absence of any expression of remorse, regret, or moral responsibility on the part of the offender. The insight of the restorative justice movement is that the traditional adversarial system discourages those who are accused of crimes to step forward and fully admit their guilt. The conscientious defense attorney advises their client to remain silent, allow the attorneys to negotiate the legal charge, and let the matter be handled by the legal professionals. The unintended consequence is often that victims and offenders are denied an opportunity for honest accountability, remorse, and future reconciliation.

The restorative justice movement has emerged within modern Western societies beginning in the 1970s and a variety of restorative justice programs and practices are beginning to be implemented within traditional justice systems. Beginning in the 1970s, there was a rediscovery of the victim and the use of **restitution** as a means to compensate victims for their loss.[29] The first **victim-offender reconciliation** programs[30] also emerged in the 1970s bringing the two parties together as a basis for genuine healing and reconciliation. Several states have embraced a return to the goal of restitution, accountability to communities through community service, and the use of restorative principles in the traditional system, particularly for juveniles and less serious offenses.[31]

Practices within restorative justice have also been influenced by non-Western justice traditions that are being incorporated in the Western system. In New Zealand, the traditional practices of the Maori tribe use a model of family group conferencing to bring victims, offenders, and their families together instead of the adversarial court process dominated by legal professionals. In 1989, the juvenile system in New Zealand adopted the **family group conferencing** model for all juvenile cases except those involving first-degree murder and sexual assault.

The restorative justice movement is still quite small but it is impacting all parts of the criminal justice system.[32] In some communities, the police are involved in

RESTITUTION
a criminal sanction in which offenders repay victims for their crime or provide work service to the community or the victim.

VICTIM-OFFENDER RECONCILIATION
programs which bring victims and offenders in a face-to-face dialogue to discuss the impact of the harm and to negotiate restitution by the offender to the victim and the community.

FAMILY GROUP CONFERENCING
a form of restorative justice originating in New Zealand in which offenders, victims, and their respective families meet under the authority of the justice system to discuss the impact of the harm and negotiate accountability by the offender to the victim and the community.

experiments using the family group conferencing model to deal with young, first-time offenders. In other jurisdictions, offenders can be referred to community panels for restorative probation. These panels bring victims and offenders together, seek to show offenders how they have harmed victims and the community and develop ways to make amends to those they have harmed.

There are also experiments making use of the Native American peacemaking circles in the sentencing and disposition of cases within Canada and the United States. [33] Many schools within the United States have also begun to adopt restorative practices in place of exclusionary discipline through suspensions and expulsions.

---

offender-focused (p. 150) all the resources, policies, and personnel of the justice system are devoted to activities which concern the person who is accused of or has been convicted of violating the law.

state-centered justice (p. 151) when crime is defined as primarily an offense against the authority of these powerful institutions rather than a harm to individuals within the community.

victimology (p. 151) the scientific study of the physical, psychological, and financial harm people suffer because of crime and the handling of crime by the criminal justice system itself.

victim-precipitation (p. 152) behavior of individuals that increases the likelihood of criminal victimization.

victim-blaming (p. 152) the responsibility for the crime is shifted from the perpetrator to the victim.

secondary victimization (p. 153) callous and insensitive treatment by the criminal justice system which inflicts additional psychological harm and emotional trauma on victims.

victims' rights movement (p. 155) a social movement started in the 1970s to increase awareness of victims, issues and to advocate for the right of victims in the criminal justice process.

victim-impact statement (p. 155) a report to the sentencing judge listing the effects of the crime on the victim.

victim witness and advocacy programs (p. 155) an organized program with specialized personnel housed within district attorneys' offices or victims assistance agencies who assist victims throughout the justice process.

notification rights (p. 155) the right of victims to be informed of key decisions and hearings related to their cases, such as plea agreements, parole hearings, or early release decisions.

victim compensation funds (p. 156) money collected by the state from criminal fines and awarded to victims for medical bills, counseling, and to compensate for financial losses.

post-traumatic stress disorder (p. 156) a set of psychological symptoms suffered by some victims in response to the trauma of the crime.

survivors mission (p. 158) sustained efforts by victims to bring about positive legislative or social change that will prevent re-occurrence of the crime to others or will assist victims in dealing with the trauma of crime.

restorative justice (p. 158) a response to crime that seeks to restore the well-being of victims and the larger community while promoting responsible and productive behavior in offenders.

retributive justice (p. 159) a response to crime that seeks to inflict punishment on offenders in just proportion to the seriousness of the offense.

restitution (p. 160) a criminal sanction in which offenders repay victims for their crime or provide work service to the community or the victim.

victim-offender reconciliation (p. 160) programs which bring victims and offenders in a face-to-face dialogue to discuss the impact of the harm and to negotiate restitution by the offender to the victim and the community.

family group conferencing (p. 160) a form of restorative justice originating in New Zealand in which offenders, victims, and their respective families meet under the authority of the justice system to discuss the impact of the harm and negotiate accountability by the offender to the victim and the community.

REVIEW AND STUDY QUESTIONS

1. Define the field of victimology.

2. In what sense is the criminal justice system "offense-focused" and "offender-driven"?

3. What is the process of "victim-blaming"? Why is this a common psychological reaction to victimization in our culture?

4. What is "secondary victimization"? Give examples where this might take place within the criminal justice system.

5. What are "victims' rights" in the criminal justice process? Why are these important to victims? How do victims' rights address the problem of secondary victimization?

6. How do victims' rights differ from offenders' rights for due process? Are victims' and offenders' rights in competition with one another? Why or why not?

7. What are the symptoms of PTSD? How can the criminal justice system respond effectively to the needs of victims with PTSD?

8. What is a "survivors mission"? Why is such a mission important for victims?

9. Define retributive justice. What are the three questions Howard Zehr believes are central to retributive justice?

10. Define restorative justice. What are the three questions Howard Zehr believes are central to restorative justice?

11. Compare the role of the victim in restorative justice and retributive justice.

CHECK IT OUT

Websites

National Organization for Victim Assistance, https://www.trynova.org. Links for victims of crimes and those interested in helping.

Victim-Offender Mediation Association, http://www.voma.org. Check out the web site of the Victim-Offender Reconciliation Program Information and Resource Center (VORP) to learn more about these programs across the country. Read more articles by mediator Marty Price and check out the many resources and links available at this site.

Office for Victims of Crime, http://www.ojp.usdoj.gov/ovc. U.S. Department of Justice site with information about crime victims and resources for crime victims. Check out the Victims Assistance and Compensation programs in your state!

Parents of Murdered Children (PMOC), http://www.pomc.com/. This organization is dedicated to providing support and services for families and friends of those who have died by violence. The organization promotes emotional support for parents, family members, and friends dealing with acute grief and assistance in dealing with the criminal justice system as well.

Restorative Justice Online, at http://www.restorativejustice.org. A service of the Centre for Justice and Reconciliation of the Prison Fellowship International. Check on the online tutorial about restorative justice, the interviews and annotated bibliographies of material on restorative justice, and the links to action sites around the world.

Center for Restorative Justice and Peacemaking, at www.cehd.umn.edu/ssw/RJP/default.asp. Excellent web site with tons of information about victim-offender mediation, conferencing, and the use of restorative justice within the United States.

Victim Offender Reconciliation Programs (VORP) Information and Research Center, at http://www.vorp.com. Click here to learn more about the VORPS and how they are being used extensively in the criminal justice system and the community.

Videos

Restorative Justice Mediation Video—60 minutes. This video includes the ABC broadcast, *Restoring Justice*, which documents the victim-offender mediation between the Serrell family and Susanna Cooper, among other stories. To order, go to www.vorp.com/video.html

Victim Impact: Listen and Learn—57 minutes. Produced by the Dept. of Justice Office for Victims of Crime. Watch at https://www.youtube.com/watch?v=_ghpl4vDZ3s

NOTES

[1] Spencer Heinz, "Coming Home: A Life Lost and a Life Saved," *The Oregonian* (December 31, 1995); Florangela Davila, "Finding Peace Eye to Eye," *Seattle Times* (March 11, 1996), B1; Elizabeth S. Menkin, "Life After Death," (Seattle, WA: VORP Information and Resource Center, 1998–2000).

[2] Elizabeth S. Menkin and Lori K. Baker, "I Forgave my Sister's Killer," *Ladies Home Journal* (1995).

[3] Marty Price, "Some Observations and Principles for Victim Offender Mediation in Cases of Seriously Violent Crime," Paper presented at *International Conference of the Victim-Offender Mediation Association* (Manitoba, Canada: June 7, 1994).

[4] Robert B. Coates, Boris Kalanj and Mark S. Umbreit, *Victim Meets Offender: The Impact of Restorative Justice and Mediation* (Monsey, New York: Willow Tree Press,1994).

[5] Stephen Schafer, *Victimology: The Victim and His Criminal* (Reston, Virginia: Reston Publishing Company, 1977), 5–32.

[6] Daniel Van Ness, *Crime and Its Victims* (Downers Grove, Illinois: Intervarsity Press, 1986), 61–83.

[7] H. Von Hentig, "Remarks on the interaction of perpetrator and victim," *Journal of Criminal Law, Criminology and Police Science* 31 (1941), 303–309; B. Mendelsohn "The Victimology," *Etudes Internationales de PsychoSociologies Criminelle* (1956), 23–26.

[8] Andrew Karmen, *Crime Victims: An Introduction to Victimology* (Pacific Grove, CA: Brooks Cole, 1990).

[9] R. Block, "Victim-offender dynamics in violent crime," *Journal of Criminal Law and Criminology* 72 (1981), 743–761; R. Black and Wesley Skogan, "Resistance and non-fatal outcomes in stranger-to-stranger predatory crime," *Violence and Victims* 1 (1986), 241–254.

[10] M. Wolfgang, "Suicide by means of victim precipitated homicide," *Journal of Clinical and Experimental Psychopathology and Quarterly Review of Psychiatry and Neurology* 20 (1959), 335–349; Andrew Karmen, "Victim Facilitation: The Case of Auto Theft," *Victimology* 4 (1979), 361–370; Susan Estrich, *Real Rape* (Cambridge, UK: Cambridge University Press, 1986).

[11] R. Silverman, "Victim Precipitation: An Examination of the Concept" in *Victimology: A New Focus,* eds. I. Drapkin and E. Viano (Lexington MA: D.C. Heath, 1974), 99–110.

[12] Ryan William, *Blaming the Victim* (New York: Vintage Books, 1971).

[13] J. Heinz, "On Justice to Victims," *New York Times* (July 7, 1982), A19.

[14] M. Symonds, "The 'Second Injury' to Victims," *Evaluation and Change* 7 (1980), 36–38.

[15] G. Hackett and G. Cerio, "When the Victim Goes on Trial," *Newsweek* (January 18, 1988), 31.

[16] Robert Elias, *Victims of the System: Crime Victims and Compensation in American Politics and Criminal Justice* (New Brunswick, New Jersey: Transaction, 1983).

[17] Lawrence Friedman, "The Crime Victim Movement at its First Decade." *Public Administration Review* 45 (1985), 790–794.

[18] Andrew Karmen, *Crime Victims: An Introduction to Victimology,* (Pacific Grove, CA: Brooks Cole, 1990), 5.

[19] "New directions from the Field: Victims' Rights and Services for the 21st Century," *National Institute of Justice* (Washington, DC: U.S. Department of Justice, 1998).

[20] David Hellerstein, "The Victim-Impact Statement: Reform or Reprisal?," *American Criminal Law Review* 27 (1989), 390–434.

[21] Andrew Karmen, "Towards the Institutionalization of a New Kind of Justice Professional: The Victim Advocate," *The Justice Professional* 9 (1995), 1–16.

[22] T. Miller, M. Cohen and B. Wiersema, *Victim costs and consequences: A new look,* (Washington, D.C.: U.S. Department of Justice, 1996).

[23] T. Williams, "Post-Traumatic Stress Disorder: Recognizing it, Treating it," *NOVA Newsletter,* (February 1, 1987).

[24] Judith Herman, *Trauma and Recovery* (New York: Basic Books), 207.

[25] Herman, *Trauma and Recovery,* 207–211.

[26] M. Thompson, "MADD Curbs Drunk Drivers," *Victimology* 9 (1984), 191–192.

[27] Howard Zehr, *Changing Lenses* (Pennsylvania, Herald Press, 1990); Daniel Van Ness and K. Strong, *Restoring Justice* (Cincinnati, OH: Anderson, 1997).

[28] Martin Wright, "The Impact of Victim-Offender Mediation on the Victim," *Victimology* 10 (1985), 630–646.

[29] Charles Abel and F. Marsh, *Punishment and Restitution: A Restitutionary Approach to Crime and the Criminal* (Westport, CT: Greenwood Press, 1984); R. Barnett, "Restitution: A New Paradigm of Criminal Justice," in *Assessing the Criminal: Restitution, Retribution and the Criminal Process,* eds. R. Barnett and J. Haagel (Cambridge MA; Ballinger, 1977), 1–35.

[30] Robert Coates, "Victim-Offender Reconciliation Programs in North America: An Assessment," in *Criminal Justice, Restitution and Reconciliation,* eds. Burt Galaway and J. Hudson (Monsey, New York: Willow Tree Press, 1990), 125–134; Mark Umbreit and D. Greenwood, *National survey of victim-offender mediation programs in the United States* (Washington, DC: Office of Victims of Crime, 1998).

[31] "National Directory of Restitution and Community Service Programs," *Office of Juvenile Justice and Delinquency Prevention* (Washington DC: U.S. Department of Justice, 1998).

[32] "Restorative Justice Fact Sheet," *National Institute of Justice: Office of Victims of Crime* (Washington D.C.: U.S. Department of Justice, 1997).

[33] Kay Pranis, "Victims in the Peacemaking Circle Process," *The Crime Victims Report* 3 (September 15, 1999).

FOCUS QUESTIONS

- **HOW** do voters think about contending alternatives when they are voting?
- **HOW** does the number of alternatives affect voting?
- **WHAT** considerations contend for attention in the minds of voters? How might they cooperate to support a particular choice?
- **HOW** does voters' identification with a political party affect voting?
- **HOW** do parties and candidates maneuver to gain votes?
- **WHAT** does it mean for voter choice to be meaningful?

In this chapter the case of Rosa Montoya focuses on the challenges of policing the border, and tells a story of one woman's encounters with law enforcement in our nation's airports. The chapter examines the composition of law enforcement and the legal framework that governs the actions of police.

LEARNING OBJECTIVES

After reading this chapter you should be able to:

- Articulate the difference between the concepts of "authority" and power and describe their relevance for the use of force by police in our society.
- Describe the structure of U.S. law enforcement.
- Explain private security and how it differs from public security.
- Understand the application of the Fourth and Fifth Amendments to police work.
- Identify the forms of proof associated with stop and frisk; arrest; and searches.
- Explain the exclusionary rule and describe its intended purpose in our justice system.
- Understand the Miranda rights and explain why these rights are an important protection of the Fifth Amendment.

Case #7: Security or Dignity: Rosa at the Border

Passengers entering the United States are subject to heightened scrutiny by U.S. Customs and Border Protection along with other federal law enforcement agents.

A Suspicious Passenger

On her arrival at Los Angeles International Airport, a groggy Rosa Elvira Montoya de Hernandez[1] walked stiffly down the airport corridor after the ten-hour flight from her home in Bogota, Colombia. It was after midnight and her high heels shoes pinched her swollen feet. She waited on the long line for immigration control to show her passport to the officer behind the glass booth. Rosa didn't realize it but several pieces of information about her had already raised the suspicions of the customs inspector.

Probably the biggest strike against Rosa was her arrival on Avianca Flight 080, a direct flight from the largest source city for the worldwide cocaine drug trade. All passengers who arrive on international "high-risk flights" from places such as Bogota, Peru, Bolivia, Mexico, Jamaica, or Nigeria are subject to greater scrutiny than the roughly 70 million international passengers who pass through U.S. Customs annually. Customs officers receive information from specialized investigative units of customs agents called Passenger Analytical Units (PAU), which analyze the passenger list of the flight to identify known drug traffickers or terrorists. Inspectors also access the Advanced Passenger Information Systems that provides information on passengers about to arrive in the United States and tracks any connecting flights a passenger may have made from another destination. The passenger list may be processed through the Interagency Border Inspection system, which includes the combined databases of Customs, the Immigration and Naturalization Service, the Department of State, the FBI's National Crime Information Center, and twenty-one other federal agencies. "People would be surprised how much we know about them and where they have been even before they step off the plane," says Robert Kelly, Commissioner of U.S. Customs.[2]

In Rosa's case it was not high-tech information from the NCIC or PAU system that raised the inspector's alarm: it was her passport showing she had made at least eight trips between Bogota and either Los Angeles or Miami in the previous two years. It was also her response to the routine questions posed by Customs Inspector Serrato about the reasons for her visit. In broken English, Rosa explained she had come to Los Angeles to do some "shopping," was visiting no one in particular but vaguely planned to find a room at "a Holiday Inn" and travel around by taxi. Her pattern of behavior fit the classic profile of a drug smuggler, probably carrying drugs somewhere inside her body.

Serrato signaled to Rosa to come to a "secondary" customs desk for further questioning by an agent who spoke Spanish and for a search of her luggage and belongings. Rosa said she had come to LA to purchase goods for her husband's clothing store back in Bogota. That was the purpose of the $5,000 in cash in $50 bills in her purse. She planned to go to J.C. Penney and K-Mart to buy goods and produced some old receipts and fabric swatches displayed in a photo album to confirm her story. But Rosa had no hotel reservations, no scheduled appointments, no credit cards, and no checks with her name or the name of her husband's business. Inside her small suitcase were several changes of clothing, odd because they were heavy and not suitable for a stay in sunny Los Angeles. Apart from the high-heeled shoes on her feet, there were no additional pairs of shoes in the suitcase. When asked how and where she purchased her ticket, Rosa could not remember.

The inspectors believed Rosa was a balloon swallower: a drug courier who swallows balloons, usually condoms filled with narcotics, and transports them for a fee. After allowing the drugs to pass through her system, Rosa would deliver them to a contact and return home on the next available flight. The anonymous contact would hand her a ticket just as they suspected someone had done for this flight.

Body cavity smuggling is a very risky and desperate business: people have died from choking on the balloon or from a massive overdose if the balloon leaks or bursts internally flooding their system with a lethal quantity of narcotics. Then, of course, there is the risk of being apprehended by law enforcement: the penalty for drug smuggling is more than ten to twenty-five years in jail. This kind of smuggling is usually carried out by people with few choices in life: they are desperate to escape the misery of poverty or they are doing it to protect a loved one from violence by the drug traffickers back home.

The Strip Search

A terrified Rosa was escorted to a private area and two female customs inspectors were called in to perform a pat-down and strip search in a back room in the airport. A pat-down or frisk is a physical inspection of the person's external body: a female agent runs her hands all over the suspect's body, including her breasts, abdomen, crotch, and buttocks. The strip search requires the suspected smuggler to remove all her clothing, bend over, and spread her buttock cheeks for visual inspection. A suspect is also required to open her legs and have the inspectors examine her vaginal area visually. These so-called personal searches are done at the discretion of

the customs officers based on a "reasonable suspicion" that the person is carrying concealed drugs on or in their body. In Rosa's case, the pat-down revealed what the inspector reported as a "firm" abdomen. The strip search revealed Rosa was wearing two pairs of elastic pants with paper towel lining the crotch area. No actual contraband was discovered by the personal search.

At this point in the investigation, the U.S. Customs inspectors were uncertain about how to proceed with Rosa. They strongly suspected she was a drug smuggler but they had not found any drugs yet. The next level of search involves the examination of the suspect's body cavities by medical personnel, the taking of an X-ray at the hospital or a monitored bowel movement in which the person is required to defecate in the presence of one or more customs inspector. Customs inspector Talamantes informed Rosa that he suspected she was carrying drugs inside her alimentary canal and asked her consent to be X-rayed at a local hospital. Rosa shook her head claiming she was pregnant. The inspector offered to conduct a pregnancy test before administering the X-ray. At first, Rosa consented but when the officers walked in the room and started to handcuff her in order to transport her to the hospital, she crossed her arms in front of her chest and shook her head, "You are not going to put those on me. That is an insult to my character." The customs inspector asked his supervisor to request a court order forcing her to go to the hospital but the supervisor decided that there was not sufficient evidence to convince a judge to sign such an order.

At this point, the inspector offered Rosa two choices: either she was to be sent back to Bogota on the next available flight or she would have to remain in detention until she had produced a bowel movement thus proving that she was not carrying drugs in her abdomen. They would not permit her to enter the country suspecting that she was carrying drugs inside her body. Rosa chose to leave on the next flight. But another flight was not available for many hours and the inspectors told her she must remain in the detention room and could not leave until she had excreted by squatting over a wastebasket under the supervision of the two female officers in the room. De Hernandez responded, "I will not submit to your degradation. I'd rather die."

An Illegal Detention?

Rosa remained locked in the room for almost 24 hours under the watchful supervision of three different sets of female officers while customs officials supposedly tried to find her a flight out of the country. They tried to place her on a flight via Mexico City but since she lacked a Mexican visa, the request was refused. As she sat and waited, Rosa refused to drink or eat. She sat in the chair clutching her purse and weeping, repeatedly asking permission "to call my husband and tell him what you are doing to me." Every time someone entered the room, Rosa took out the two small photographs of her children and begged them to let her contact them, call her husband, or call an attorney. After about 12 hours, Rosa was strip-searched again, "to ensure the safety of the surveilling officers." The search revealed no new information.

A change of shift brought a new inspector on duty who immediately sought a court order to force Rosa to have a pregnancy test, X-ray, and body cavity examination. The warrant summarized all the suspicious circumstances of Rosa's visit to Los Angeles: the absence of plans, her frequent trips, the cash in her purse, lack of clothing for a visit, the firmness of her abdomen, and the extra pair of underwear she was wearing. In addition, the warrant included the fact that Rosa had refrained from going to the bathroom during all these hours of detention, refused any drink or food, and had shown signs of extreme abdominal discomfort during that time.

A federal magistrate issued the order just before midnight of the next evening. A hysterical Rosa was handcuffed and transported to the hospital where a rectal examination indicated the presence of a cocaine-filled balloon. At about 3:15 a.m., Rosa was formally placed under arrest and advised of her Miranda rights. During the course of the next four days, Rosa excreted a total of 88 balloons containing 528 grams of 80 percent pure cocaine hydrochloride.

A Violation of the Constitution?

In federal district court, Rosa's attorney requested a suppression hearing arguing that the evidence resulting from the rectal examination, namely the 88 balloons filled with cocaine, had been obtained illegally and therefore was inadmissible as evidence. The argument centered upon the length of Rosa's detention and the failure to seek a court order in the early stage of her detention. They believed that once the pat-down and strip search failed to produce demonstrable evidence of drug smuggling, Rosa should have been released or deported. If the inspectors wished to detain her further

and/or submit her to a more intrusive investigation of an X-ray or rectal examination, they would need to obtain a search warrant by convincing a judge that the evidence against her, namely, the firmness in her abdomen, her clothing, and the peculiarities of her travel plans constituted probable cause that she was an alimentary canal smuggler. According to defense attorneys, U.S. Customs investigators illegally detained Rosa in order to gather incriminatory information against her.

The district court judge disagreed and denied the motion to suppress. Evidence was submitted against Rosa that she was convicted at a bench trial on various narcotics charges.

On appeal, a majority of the Ninth Circuit Court of Appeals took a different view of the legality of the evidence.[3] In the opinion of the Court of Appeals, the customs inspectors, at the time they detained Rosa, did not have a "clear indication" that she was an alimentary canal smuggler. They clearly had a reasonable suspicion that she was carrying drugs in her body and that suspicion gave them the grounds to pat-down, strip search, and detain her for the length of time it took to complete that investigation. After the strip search revealed no drugs or hard evidence of drugs, however, the inspectors were in violation of the Fourth Amendment when they continued to detain her in order to collect more evidence against her.

Acknowledging that it is a difficult job to secure our borders and recognizing the tough choice facing U.S. Customs officers who clearly believed Rosa would be conveying drugs into the country if they released her, the Ninth Circuit judges nevertheless felt that it was the job of the judiciary to make that tough decision. "These cases suggest that when in doubt the customs officers should present their information to a magistrate and permit that judicial officer to exercise judicial discretion in striking the delicate balance between human rights and the practical necessities of border security."[4] The Ninth Circuit Court of Appeals overturned the conviction of Rosa Montoya de Hernandez.

A Reasonable Balance in Favor of Security?

But the Supreme Court took yet another view of the matter agreeing with the district court and reinstating Rosa's original conviction. In a 7–2 decision, the majority of the Supreme Court argued that no one disputed that the original strip search was perfectly legal based as it was on the grounds of "reasonable suspicion."

A U.S. Customs officer using his or her training and experience reviews the totality of the circumstances and has a strong hunch that a person may be engaged in drug smuggling. On the basis of that hunch, he or she had the legal power, at the border, to pat-down the individual or force that person to remove his or her clothes for visual inspection. They do not need to be right in their suspicion, just reasonable.

But alimentary canal smuggling presents a greater challenge to law enforcement officers charged with policing our borders. The strip search is usually a sufficient method to detect drugs concealed in the body cavities of the rectum or vagina but the use of the digestive tract to conceal drugs cannot be detected without the use of X-rays, forced bowel movements, or invasive examinations. Officers are caught in a Catch 22: they cannot obtain a court order without some evidence beyond "reasonable suspicion" and they cannot obtain this evidence without a court order. In the view of the Supreme Court justices, it is necessary to lower the standard of evidence needed to justify searches in order to detect this particular form of smuggling.

That it is humiliating to endure a monitored bowel movement is also not the fault of law enforcement but is a direct result of the chosen method of smuggling. The only logical solution, according to the majority opinion, is to permit inspectors to act based on reasonable suspicion and permit them to "search" those spaces, that is, body cavities via X-ray, forced excretions, or rectal and vaginal examinations. Given the high public priority of preventing drugs from entering the country, the balance between private and public interests favored this intrusion on the individual based on an articulable or reasonable suspicion.

"A Disgusting and Saddening Episode[5]?"

Justice Brennan and Justice Marshall strongly dissented from the majority opinion of the Supreme Court calling this case "a disgusting and saddening episode" at our nation's borders. To grant to all customs officials patrolling our borders the right to determine if someone should be forced to submit to the most intrusive searches of their most private and intimate parts of the body is a flagrant violation of the intent and the spirit of the Fourth Amendment. That these intrusions were described as "limited" struck these justices as outrageous. Being forced to defecate in front of strangers in order to "prove" your innocence is a profoundly degrading and humiliating experience.

According to the dissenting justices, the issue is this: "Does the Fourth Amendment permit an international traveler, citizen or alien, to be subjected to the sort of treatment that occurred in this case without the sanction of a judicial officer and based on nothing more than the 'reasonable suspicion' of low-ranking investigative officers that something might be amiss?" The majority opinion had answered this question in the affirmative stating that it was necessary to allow law enforcement officers the flexibility to conduct investigations based on experienced hunches. This is, in fact, the only way to uphold the government's interest in protecting the borders from this kind of drug smuggling.

But the dissent pointed out that the vast majority of those who are detained and subjected to these kinds of searches are totally innocent. Most of the time, "reasonable suspicions" turn out to be wrong. In theory, the intrusions based on low-level suspicions are relatively harmless so that the trade-off is worthwhile; weighed against the benefit of finding people carrying concealed weapons in the street or conveying drugs into the country, this "inconvenience" is easily worth the cost of stopping innocent citizens for brief questioning or pat-downs.

But to Justices Brennan and Marshall there is nothing "harmless" or "trivial" about being brought to a back room of an airport for a strip search or being forced to defecate in a wastepaper basket in front of strangers. And it was hard to imagine anything more degrading and humiliating than being handcuffed and taken to hospital for a forced X-ray or rectal exam.

The dissenting justices expressed concern that this degree of power in the hands of U.S. Customs agents would lead to the harassment of innocent people by unscrupulous or incompetent Customs officers. Would this power be abused, intentionally or unintentionally? Would some people be subject to these humiliating searches based on their skin color, dress, ethnicity, class, or age?

I do not imagine that decent and lawabiding international travelers have yet reached the point where they "expect" to be thrown into locked rooms and ordered to excrete into wastebaskets, held incommunicado until they cooperate, or led away in handcuffs to the nearest hospital for exposure to various medical procedures all on nothing more than the "reasonable" suspicions of low-ranking enforcement agents. In fact, many people from around the world travel to our borders precisely to escape such unchecked executive investigatory discretion. What a curious first lesson in American liberty awaits them on their arrival.[6]

Ten years after Rosa's case was decided a story broke on the front pages of the nation's major newspaper describing the thousands of innocent travelers, most of them American citizens, strip-searched at our nation's airports and customs stations. In 1997 and 1998, data from a government GAO study[7] reported that U.S. Customs had conducted searches of approximately 93,764 international travelers ranging from pat-downs to strip searches to forced laxatives. Out of all those subject to pat-down searches, only 3 percent had revealed the presence of drugs. For the almost 3,000 individuals who were strip-searched, 77 percent were innocent. And for the almost 1,000 during those two years who were forced to be X-rayed, 69 percent were found to be innocent travelers who happen to fit the criteria of "reasonable suspicion" for alimentary canal smuggling.

The GAO study was ordered in the wake of a broader public discussion and outrage over the widespread police practice of racial profiling and the use of the police power to stop, question, and search minority Americans on the nation's streets, highways, and airports. President Clinton ordered U.S. Customs to keep track of airport searches in order to document the race and gender of people who were stopped. The GAO study confirmed a racial bias in who was likely to be subject to a search by a U.S. Customs agent: black women were nine times more likely than white women to be X-rayed and 73 percent more likely than white women to be strip-searched. The term flying while black[8] was coined by the media to describe what critics claimed was widespread targeting of minorities as objects of "reasonable suspicion" based on the color of their skin.

THINKING CRITICALLY ABOUT THIS CASE

1. In your view was the detention and body cavity search of Rosa a "reasonable balance" between liberty and crime control or a "disgusting and saddening episode"? Explain why you agree with the majority or the dissenting opinion in this case.

2. Rosa De Montoya de Hernandez is not an American citizen. Yet the Supreme Court has held that the "aliens" on American soil are, nevertheless, guaranteed due process by the Fourteenth Amendment. Do you believe that non-citizens should be entitled to equal protection under the U.S. Constitution? Why or why not? If aliens must obey our laws when they are in the country should they also be entitled to protections afforded by the law? Why or why not?

3. How does this case illustrate the trade-off between liberty and crime control? Why is the "protection of the innocent" in conflict with the "pursuit of the guilty"?

4. In striking a balance between individual liberty and crime control, the judiciary makes a determination about the potential threat of the crime weighed against the level of intrusion on individual liberty. In your view, did the Supreme Court strike an appropriate balance given the threat of alimentary canal drug smuggling? Why or why not?

5. What are the trade-offs between civil liberties and threats posed by terrorism? Would you support the reduction in civil liberties in order to detect and apprehend terrorists? Why or why not?

6. The search of a passenger's luggage and person is considered to be a "trivial" loss of liberty. Is this true in your opinion? Do you consider a strip search a minor intrusion on liberty? Why or why not? Is any loss of liberty "trivial"? Why or why not?

7. Should law enforcement be permitted to use travelers' ethnic or racial identity as a factor supporting reasonable suspicion? Why or why not?

REFERENCES

Case adapted from:

Lisa Bekin, "Airport Drug Efforts Snaring Innocents Who Fit Profiles," *New York Times*, March 20, 1990.

Cathy Harris, *Flying While Black: A Whistleblower's Story*, (Los Angeles: Milligan Books, 2001).

Nelson Erik-Lars, "Changing the profile at Customs," *Daily News*, October 15, 2000.

Montoya De Hernandez v United States 473 U.S. 531; 105 S. Ct. 3304 (1986); 731 F2d 1369 (1984).

U.S. General Accounting Office, *U.S. Customs Service: Better Targeting of Airline Passengers for Personal Searches Could Produce Better Results*, GAO/GGD-00-38, March 2000.

The case of Rosa de Montoya de Hernandez illustrates the dilemma of policing in a free society.[9] As the dissenting justices noted, one of the reasons people come to America is to be free from powerful governments who can act against citizens and non-citizens without justification or restriction. In Nazi Germany, there was very little crime but there was also very little liberty: police could knock on people's doors at any hour, for any reason, search the premises, and arrest whomever they suspected of wrongdoing. In many countries around the world, non-citizens suspected of illegal activity may be detained without access to counsel or the guarantee of a right to a fair trial. American values embedded in the Constitution uphold the principle of individual liberties and high standards of fairness for citizens and non-citizens alike.

Yet it is also true that Americans rely upon the powers of law enforcement to protect our right to live in an orderly society. Freedom depends upon a degree of order. If U.S. Customs agents permit Rosa to enter the country to sell drugs, our freedom is impaired by the lawlessness and disorder created by the drug trade. Citizens forced to huddle behind closed doors to avoid a volley of bullets between rival drug gangs are hardly living in a free society. Most Americans find detention without trial and unexplained "disappearances" behind the closed doors of the authorities without access to counsel or contact with the outside world to be repugnant. But most Americans also recognize the need to weigh this evil against the magnitude of threat stemming from the illegal conduct whether it is smuggling of illegal drugs or the intention to commit violent acts of terrorism.

Airport security body scan.

The question for the American justice system is: How do we strike the balance between liberty and order? Where do we draw the line? The jurisprudence of the American criminal law is constantly re-evaluating the latitude law enforcement needs to ensure the safety and security of American society. Should U.S. Customs be permitted to conduct body cavity searches on the basis of reasonable suspicion in order to interdict illegal drugs? Is the threat of international terrorism worth the suspension of habeas corpus rights for those who are detained for questioning? Should law enforcement legally use a person's racial or ethnic appearance as grounds for legitimate suspicion? In the pursuit of international terrorists, should the police be permitted to question or investigate Muslim Americans on the basis of their religion and ethnicity alone? In order to reduce street crime, should young black males be subject to higher levels of suspicion on our city streets or nation's highways than other citizens?

This chapter looks at the overall structure of American law enforcement and the legal rules that regulate the relationship between officers of the law and the citizens whom they "protect and serve." Unlike countries such as Japan, China, and many Western European nations, the United States does not have a single national police force[10] or centralized structure of law enforcement. Instead there are over 19,000 different agencies employing more than 800,000 people responsible for the enforcement of the laws of this nation. The five major types of law enforcement agencies are municipal police departments; sheriff's departments; state police; federal law enforcement agencies; and special police forces limited to particular localities such as schools, parks, or airports. Some of these agencies are tiny with less than ten officers; others are huge complex bureaucratic organizations employing tens of thousands of police and civilian workers. Some are highly specialized focusing only on the specific area of law enforcement, whereas others have a broad mandate to perform a wide array of functions for a particular community.

The dilemma of policing in a free society varies for different segments of the law enforcement community. At our borders, Homeland Security agents have a narrow responsibility to protect our nation's borders and are granted greater powers to detain and search people and goods entering our borders to fulfill that responsibility. Within our borders, "calling the cops" is usually motivated by a desire for someone with authority to solve a problem that a citizen cannot: a drunk who won't leave the restaurant; a husband who is threatening his wife; a loud party that refuses to quiet down.[11] Under appropriate circumstances police can lawfully stop citizens, ask them questions, physically restrain them, forcibly remove them, transport them against their will, deprive them of the liberty, deliberately inflict pain, and take their life. Public police have broad discretion about how to use their legal authority to respond to the myriad of problems they must deal with every day.

But in all cases, the power held by law enforcement is not without limits and these limits are defined by law. A basic principle of a democratic society is that the police are accountable to use their power and perform their job within the bounds of the law. Law enforcement officers possess an awesome degree of legitimate **authority** to use coercive force. The distinction between power and authority is an important one. Possession of a gun gives the user **power** over others. In the exercise of power, "might makes right." Authority is specific form of power characterized by a shared sense that the use of power is legitimate. In the

AUTHORITY
a specific form of power which is seen as legitimate by those subject to it.

POWER
the ability to affect the behavior of others, with or without the use of force.

exercise of authority, "right makes might." In a democratic society, only when police power is exercised lawfully, the use of force is legitimate.[12]

THE STRUCTURE OF U.S. LAW ENFORCEMENT

The United States has the most complex law enforcement structure in the world. Most people do not think of U.S. Customs inspectors as members of law enforcement but Inspector Talamantes is one of 36,863 U.S. Customs and Border Protection (CBP) agents, among 120,000 full-time federal law enforcement employees who are a small subset of the approximately 926,000 employees across the land who can be found in municipal police departments, state police forces, highway patrols, county sheriff's departments, campus security, special police forces, or one of over a hundred federal law enforcement agencies.[13]

Although each agency may have its own sphere of law enforcement responsibilities, there are also overlapping responsibilities with rivalries, competition, and territorial disputes between agencies. Different segments of policing emerge historically at different points in time and for different reasons. In addition to the complex structure of public law enforcement, there is also a burgeoning private security industry which provides policing services to corporations and private individuals as a for-profit service. The number of personnel employed in the private policing industry is higher than the number employed in public policing: in 2009 just over 1 million personnel were employed by private security firms compared to just over 830,000 employed within public sector policing.[14]

Local Law Enforcement

City police departments are, in a sense, the most important component of American law enforcement. In 2013 there were 12,326 local police departments in the United States employing 605,000 full-time employees, 477,000 of whom were sworn officers.[15] Municipalities may be large cities, small towns, or villages that are authorized to hire, organize, train, fund, and operate their own police forces. These can range vastly in size and scope: more than half of the police departments across the country employ fewer than 10 officers and two-thirds employ more than 100. At the other end of the spectrum are the large city police departments such as New York City, Houston, Chicago, Detroit, and Los Angeles who employ 20,000 or 30,000 officers and a small army of civilian employees who perform such functions as crime analysis, record keeping, computer operations, communications, personnel, public relations, and legal support. Cities spend more than any other state or local unit of government for police protection.

Of all levels of law enforcement, municipal agencies have the broadest scope of authority to maintain public order within the community. The duties of the municipal police officer range from dealing with the ordinary nuisances of everyday life such as traffic control, medical emergencies, public drunkenness, and lost animals to responding to extraordinary events of homicide, public catastrophes, and private traumas within citizen's homes. More than any other officer of the law, the local police officer performs a sweeping peacekeeping and service function for the community and therefore confronts the myriad of social problems which plague modern society. As we will see in later chapters, police officers interact closely with the life of the community and must balance conflicting functions of crime control, service, and order maintenance.

County Law Enforcement

The office of the sheriff is the oldest law enforcement position in the United States brought to the colonies from England as the person appointed by the king to collect taxes, administer justice, and enforce the king's laws. Today, sheriffs are elected public officials whose agencies are responsible for law enforcement in the counties in which they function. Sheriff departments run county jails, serve civil papers such as court-ordered liens or eviction notices, transport prisoners to and from courts, serve as the officers of the county court, and are responsible for housing detainees awaiting trial. In 2013, there were 3,012 sheriff's offices in the United States employing 351,904 full-time personnel.[16]

As an elected official (only Hawaii and Rhode Island do not hold elections for the position of sheriff), the sheriff is more politician than law enforcement professional. Sheriff's departments are also independent of civil service control and executive branch accountability. The jurisdiction of the sheriff's department is established by state law and generally circumscribed by the municipal boundaries of the cities within the county. About 90 percent of sheriff's departments have primary responsibility for criminal investigation within their jurisdiction although in densely populated eastern cities, they stay out of the affairs of the municipalities. In the southern and western states, sheriff's departments are much more powerful and serve as the chief law enforcement agencies in the county.

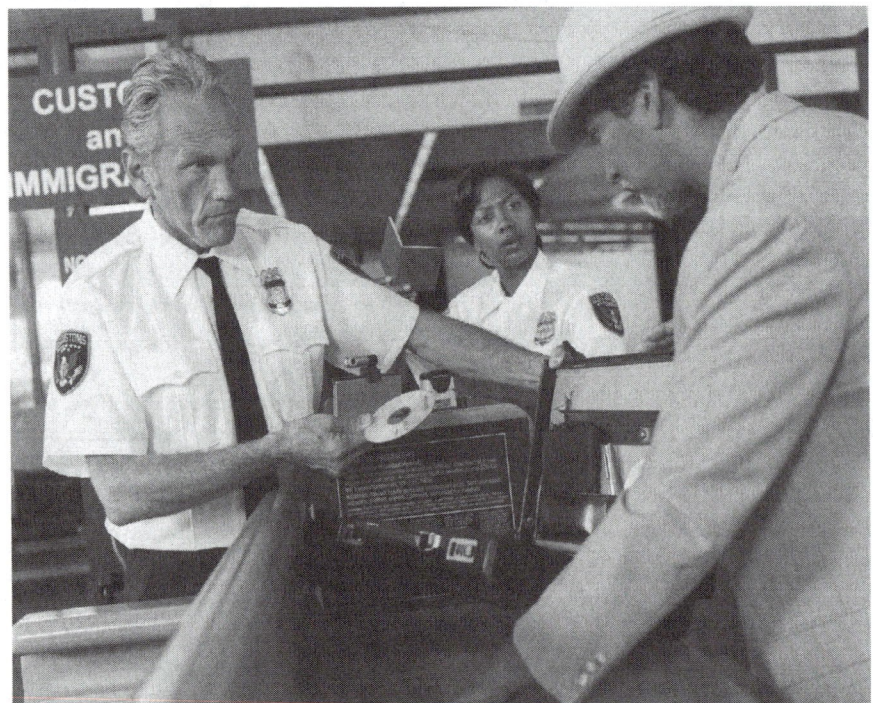

Transportation Security Administration agents have legal authority to search and detain people and goods entering U.S. borders.

State Police and Highway Patrols

The first statewide law enforcement agency was the Texas Rangers initially formed in 1835. Most state police were formed in the early twentieth century in response to the charges of corruption, inefficiency, and political partisanship of municipal and county police. The first state to institute a modern state police force was Pennsylvania in 1905 in response to the massive coal strike of 1902. The advent of the automobile and the building of the nation's first highway in 1921 necessitated the development of a statewide police force on the nation's highways.

Today there are fifty state police agencies (highway patrols or public safety agencies) in the United States. State police departments maintain law and order throughout the state especially in the regions with sparse population unable to afford their own police forces. State police departments generally also operate highway patrols which regulate the state highways but they may also maintain helicopter fleets for traffic, criminal, and medical matters and forensic laboratories, narcotics divisions, fire investigations, and auto-theft divisions. Highway patrols have more limited authority focusing primarily on the regulation of traffic and limiting their activity to the patrol of the state and federal highways.

Federal Law Enforcement

About 9.3 percent or approximately 120,000 full-time sworn officers work for one of 73 federal law enforcement agencies charged with enforcing more than 4,100 federal laws.[17] Federal agencies can only enforce federal laws although they routinely assist and cooperate with state and local law enforcement. Congress has historically been reluctant to create a "superforce" or national police: most federal law enforcement agencies are highly specialized units designed to enforce particular bodies of law passed by Congress. Federal police do not typically perform the peacekeeping or service functions commonly performed by local police agencies.

The largest federal police agency is now the Department of Homeland Security (DHS) with approximately 46 percent of the department employed to provide police response and patrol, immigration and customs, including 36,863 employed by the U.S. CPB.[18] The second largest federal law enforcement agency is the Department of Justice, employing 40,000. The U.S. Customs and U.S. Marshals Service are the oldest, both established in 1789.

The **Homeland Security Act of 2002** that established the DHS was the most massive reorganization of the federal law enforcement bureaucracy since 1947 when President Truman consolidated all three branches of the military into the Department of Defense.[19] In 2016 the DHS has over 240,000 employees and a budget that exceeds 64 billion dollars.[20] Twenty-two separate federal agencies were combined under the new department including the U.S. CBP, the U.S. Secret Service, U.S. Immigration and Customs Enforcement (ICE), U.S. Citizenship and Immigration Services, Federal Emergency Management Agency (FEMA), and the U.S. Coast Guard. New federal agencies were also created such as the Transportation Security Administration, which federalized responsibility for aviation security as well as other transportation systems. The responsibilities of DHS include five key areas: preventing terrorism and enhancing security; securing and managing our borders; enforcing and administering immigration laws; safeguarding and securing cyberspace; and ensuring resilience to disasters.[21]

HOMELAND SECURITY ACT OF 2002 massive reorganization of federal law enforcement, creating the Department of Homeland Security.

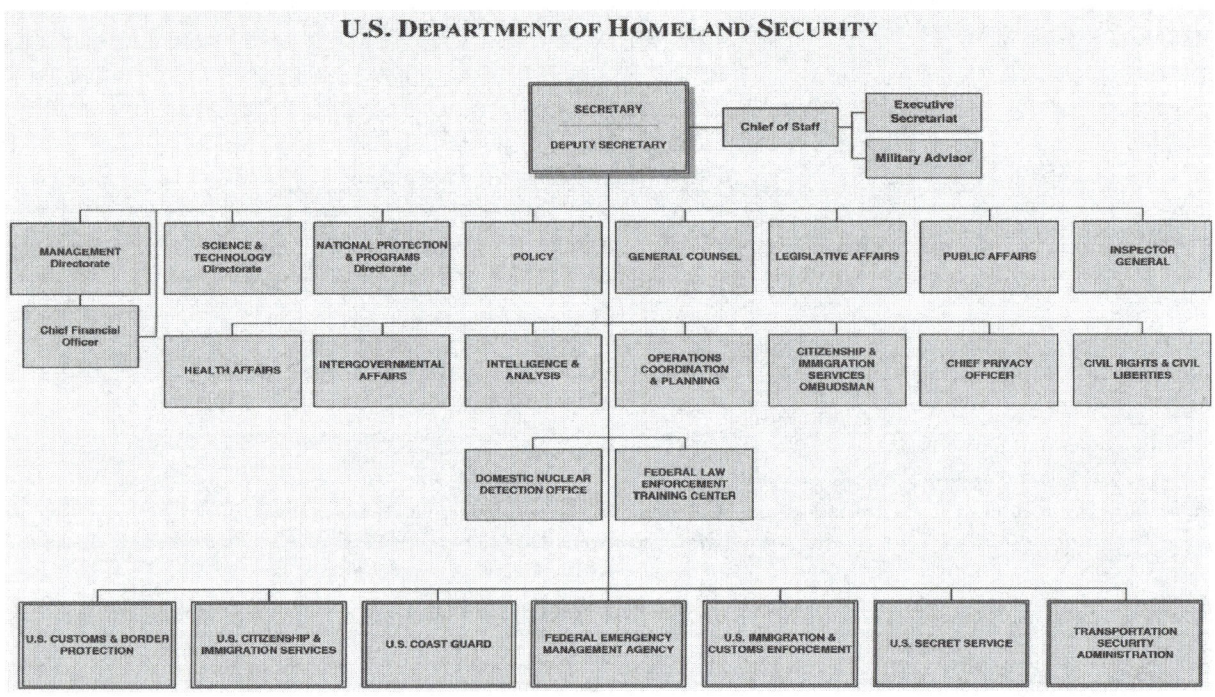

Organizational chart for the U.S. Department of Homeland Security.

The FBI under the Department of Justice is probably the best known law enforcement agency in the country and possibly in the world. It originated in 1870 as the investigative arm of the Department of Justice. In the early days, the agency hired private agents from the Pinkerton Agency or borrowed men from the Secret Service rather than hire its own agents. President Theodore Roosevelt wanted the agency to hire its own agents to enable the DOJ to enforce the anti-trust laws against big business but Congress refused to authorize the president's request for a separate police force fearful of a "secret police" which might be used to investigate members of Congress. In 1908, Congress reluctantly authorized a modest beginning when it established the Bureau of Investigation with thirty-five agents focused primarily on business and bankruptcy fraud.

The agency expanded over the years primarily by identifying "public enemies" that generated a sense of urgency, which pressured lawmakers to authorize growth in the agency.

In 1924, J. Edgar Hoover was appointed to head the agency, a post he held until his death in 1972 at age 77. By 1935, when the agency name was changed to the Federal Bureau of Investigation, Hoover had transformed the agency into an elite general crime-fighting agency. He established a national fingerprint identification file, a crime laboratory, the Uniform Crime Reports, and the FBI National Academy. Hoover also created the "image" of the FBI agent as the heroic "G-man" fighting underworld mobsters, kidnappers, and bank robbers.

By the time of Hoover's death, however, the public image of the FBI had been tarnished by public exposure of the surveillance activities of the FBI against lawful American citizens and legitimate American organizations including members of Congress.[22] Harassment, infiltration, wiretapping, mail tampering, and other forms of illegal surveillance sullied the image of the elite crime-fighting unit. The FBI's counter-intelligence program COINTELPRO was terminated in 1972 in the wake of a political outcry over the extent of domestic surveillance on American citizens.[23]

Today 35,890 FBI employees staff fifty-six field offices across the country.[24] This includes 13,890 special agents. After the events of 9/11, however, the FBI came under serious criticism by Congress for its failure in intelligence and counter-terrorism.[25] Although some legislators wanted to place the FBI within the DHS, the director of the FBI successfully argued that it was more efficient to reform the agency than to try and create a whole new domestic intelligence agency. As a result the FBI shifted its top priority from law enforcement to intelligence and counterterrorism. About one-quarter of all FBI agents are currently assigned to counterterrorism. Another significant change in the FBI is the setting of the policy agenda from Washington, D.C, rather than by individual field offices.

Law enforcement activities of the bureau are concentrated on white collar crimes, drug offenses, arson, civil rights violations, and violent serial offenders. In addition, the FBI operates the UCR and the National Crime Information Center, which supports law enforcement investigations across the country and around the world.

Private Security Industry

Private police have long co-existed with public police. The first private security company was founded by Allan Pinkerton in 1850 to protect the property of the railroads and to fight on the side of businesses during periods of major industrial labor conflicts. For the most part, private security as a for-profit industry has grown to meet the needs of businesses. Major private corporations such as Pinkerton, Wells Fargo Co., and Wackenhut provide equipment and technology such as alarm systems, closed-circuit television, video cameras, electronic gates, armed couriers, bodyguards, undercover investigators, and security personnel.

Private security guards are not granted the same degree of authority as publicly sworn officers: in most states guards cannot detain suspects or conduct searches without consent. Some states require special licenses and some states grant security personnel the authority to make felony arrests. There are no federal laws governing the private security industry; in twenty-nine states no training is required; in twenty-two states there is no need of licensing; and in sixteen states no background check is required.[26] In short, the vast majority of private security personnel are neither licensed nor trained. One key trend is the moonlighting of sworn public officers as private security personnel during off-duty hours although some departments have regulations to limit the kind of employment officers can accept.

In recent decades, the growth of the private security industry has included the provision of security for upper income residential areas through gated communities and upscale apartment and condominium security services and especially for campus security on the nation's universities and colleges. Many state laws afford campus police similar powers to public police especially at state institutions. Spending for private security outstrips spending for public law enforcement by as much as 70 percent.[27] Even the government spends more on the hiring of private labor to perform police-related functions than it does on public police.[28] The result is a privatization of security and pseudo-public space as gated communities, shopping malls, and other retail spaces are closely regulated by private security leaving public spaces more vulnerable and less secure.[29]

As we examine the legal limitations on public police in the next section, it is important to recognize that the constitutional rules, which constrain the authority of public law enforcement in its treatment of American citizens, do not apply to the actions of private security officers if they are not sworn peace officers. The legal rights of private security derive primarily from the property rights of owners who hire them to protect their lives and property. Therefore private police can engage in surveillance and searches without the legal restrictions placed on public law enforcement as long they are performing these duties on private property at the request of the owner. As citizens of course private security are subject to all civil and criminal laws especially laws against false arrest, assault and battery, harassment, and civil rights violations.

POLICING AND THE LAW

The right of the people to be secure in their persons, houses, papers, and effects, against unreasonable searches and seizures, shall not be violated, and no warrants shall issue, but upon probable cause, supported by oath or affirmation, and particularly describing the place to be searched and the persons or things to be seized.

(Fourth Amendment, U.S. Constitution)

The Fourth Amendment states that all coercive action on the part of the government against the lives, property, liberty, and privacy of individuals requires some "reasonable" grounds or evidence to justify that action. The amount of factual information depends upon how coercive the action is but the principle remains the same: to infringe on a citizen's right to be let alone, officers must have some kind of evidence that a crime has occurred or is about to occur. When officers operate outside the boundaries of the law in their efforts to enforce the law, they undermine the wider societal belief in the legitimacy of the law itself.

The rule of thumb for the standard of proof states simply that the greater the intrusion on the individuals liberty, the greater the degree of proof required.[30] The Bill of Rights presumes that each citizen essentially has a basic and fundamental

PREPONDERANCE OF THE EVIDENCE
the standard for determining legal liability in civil trials requiring a certainty of more than 50 percent of defendant's guilt.

TABLE 7.1	Standards of Proof
Intrusion on Liberty	Level of Proof Required
Stop and frisk	Reasonable suspicion
Arrest	Probable cause
Search	Judicial affirmation of probable cause
Felony indictment	Grand jury affirmation of probable cause
Civil penalty imposed	**Preponderance of evidence**
Criminal penalty imposed	Beyond a reasonable doubt

TABLE 7.2	Structure of U.S. Public Law Enforcement		
Federal	**State**	**County**	**Local**
Treasury Department	Highway patrol	County coroners	Municipal police departments
Alcohol Tobacco & Firearms	Fish and Wildlife Agencies	Marine Patrol Agencies	Campus Police
Internal Revenue Service	State Police	Sheriff's Departments	Transit Police
U.S. Customs Service	State Park Services		Coroner or Medical Examiner
U.S. Secret Service	State University Police		Housing Authority Agents
U.S. Mint, Police	State Bureaus of Investigation		
Federal Law Enforcement Training Center	Weigh Station Operations		
	Port Authorities		
Department of Justice			
Federal Bureau of Prisons			
Drug Enforcement Agency			
Federal Bureau of Investigation			
U.S. Marshal's Office			
Immigration and Naturalization Service			
Department of Transportation			
U.S. Coast Guard			
U.S. Postal Services			
Postal Inspections Service			

(continued)

TABLE 7.2	*(Continued)*
Department of the Interior	
U. S. Park Police	
National Park Service	
Bureau of Indian Affairs, Office of Law Enforcement	
U. S. Fish and Wildlife Service, Division of Law Enforcement	
Washington, D.C.	
Metropolitan Police Department	

Source: Adapted from William A. Geller and Norval Morris, "Federal and Local Police," in *Thinking about Police*, 2nd ed., ed. Carl Klockars and Steven Mastrofski (New York: McGraw-Hill, 1992); Brian Reeves, *Federal Law Enforcement Officers* (Washington, DC: Bureau of Justice Statistics, 1997).

"right to be let alone." In order to intrude upon that sphere of liberty, the state must have some kind of justification or proof.

The Pendulum Swing between Liberty and Order

Until the 1960s, the courts took a "hands-off" attitude toward enforcing the Bill of Rights in the state and local law enforcement. As we saw in the Scottsboro case, despite the existence of formal rights in the Constitution, in practice there was little attempt to enforce those rights in the daily operations of the thousands of police agencies across the land. Led by the former California prosecutor, Chief Justice Earl Warren, judicial decisions during the 1960s and 1970s established specific criteria regarding the delicate balance between liberty and order with a tendency to place limits on the lawful power of law enforcement.[31]

In the 1980s and 1990s the Burger Court followed by the Rehnquist Court had shifted the balance toward the legitimate power of law enforcement to intrude upon liberty of citizens. As we see with the decision in Rosa's case, the rationale for the expansion of police power has been based on the need to aggressively enforce the nation's drug laws. The tactics and strategies used by law enforcement to fight the war on drugs have led to a rollback in the civil liberties of the American citizen. The burden of this rollback of civil liberties has fallen, as we will see later in the chapter, disproportionately on minority citizens who are subject to routine searches and stops in their homes, on our city streets, highways, and airports.[32]

Since the events of 9/11 there has also been a reduction in the scope of civil liberty to allow for greater counterterrorism surveillance and intelligence

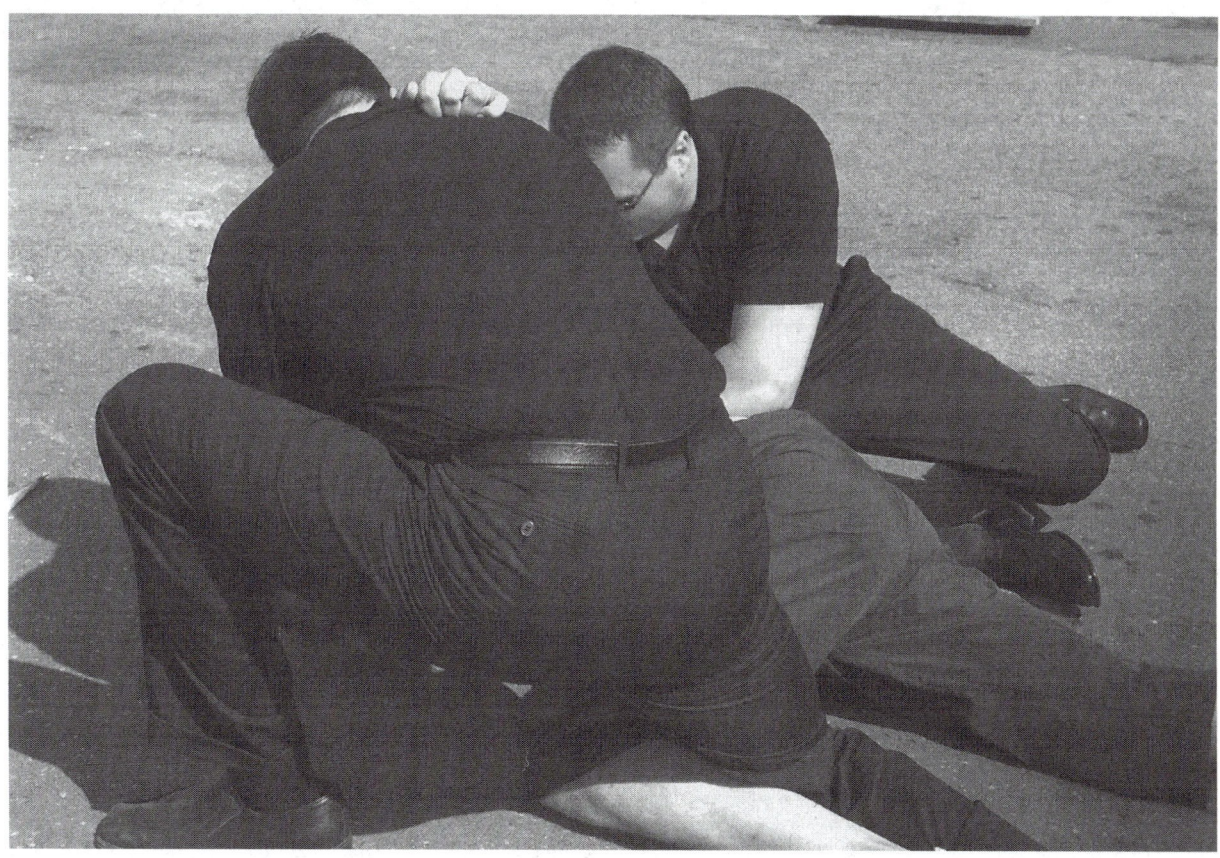

gathering in order to prevent potential acts of terrorism. The Roberts Court has signaled a willingness to uphold the principle of habeas corpus for the detention of people suspected of engaging in terrorist activities. On the other hand, there have been significant legislative changes that increase the level of police surveillance for national security purposes. This enhanced surveillance has increased for all Americans to some degree, especially in the use of air transportation but still falls disproportionately on specific groups such as Muslim Americans. We look more specifically at the impact of these changes on the relationship between police and U.S. citizens when we examine the policing of terrorism in chapter 9.

Police possess the authority to stop, question, and frisk citizens they reasonably suspect are engaged in criminal activity, but many believe police routinely abuse this authority in the inner city by targeting young men of color for searches.

Stop and Frisk

Where does the power of the police to intrude upon citizens' liberty "begin" so to speak? When a citizen is walking along a city street, window shopping, for example, or simply walking down the street, can a police officer stop that person and ask them questions about where they are going and what they are doing? Can police legally frisk them for weapons or illegal drugs?

The ruling case regulating this aspect of police authority is *Terry v. Ohio*[33] decided in 1963. In Cleveland, Ohio, Detective Martin McFadden observed two men conversing on a street corner periodically peering into a particular store window. Convinced they were casing the store in order to rob it, McFadden approached the men, identified himself as a police officer, asked for their names,

STOP AND FRISK a technique used by police to "pat-down" a person suspected of being armed or in possession of the instrumentalities of crime.

and spun one of them, Terry, for a pat-down on the outside of his clothing. The search revealed concealed weapons and the men were arrested. Both were convicted and Terry was sentenced to one to three years in a state penitentiary. Terry appealed the conviction arguing that Detective McFadden did not have probable cause for the arrest because the guns were obtained in an illegal search. There was no reason to conduct the search in the first place and the guns that were found should be suppressed as illegal evidence.

The Supreme Court agreed to hear the case and ruled that the detective was acting lawfully. In *Terry v. Ohio*, the Supreme Court established the principle that even for a stop to ask questions, police must have some level of legitimate suspicion, which the court defined as "reasonable suspicion that a crime is afoot." The liberal Warren Court asserted that police could not simply decide to stop or frisk a citizen arbitrarily: the Fourth Amendment applies even to the questioning and pat-down process regardless of whether or not it leads to an arrest. Such an intrusion interferes with the basic dignity of the citizen and like all intrusions it requires a standard of proof, albeit, a new lower standard known as **"reasonable suspicion."**

The reasonable suspicion standard, which is the basis for strip searches at our nation's airports, is an extremely open-ended standard as we have seen in the case of Rosa. Under this basis law enforcement at the border may engage in strip searches and even body cavity searches on the basis of reasonable suspicion.

The courts have also upheld a wide array of behaviors such as being in a high-crime neighborhood, acting evasive toward the police, being a known gang member or drug user or associating with a known gang member or drug users as sufficient to justify a "Terry" stop. Technically the "frisk" is done for the protection of the police officer who is authorized to do a pat-down pursuant to questioning. Although the Terry stop and frisk is not intended to be used for evidentiary searches, if drugs, weapons, and other forms of illegal contraband are found on a person in the course of these searches, this evidence has been ruled as acceptable to the courts.

Even without probable cause, a police officer may perform a limited automobile search based on reasonable suspicion.

The Basic Law of Arrest

The power to "arrest" is the power to "seize" a citizen, transport them against their will and detain them overnight. Technically, an arrest occurs whenever a person's freedom to leave is curtailed by a law enforcement officer. If a reasonable person believes that they are "not free to leave" then they have been arrested. Because Rosa was at the border, she could be legally detained without being arrested.

According to the Fourth Amendment, **probable cause** is needed to back up an arrest: probable cause are facts which would lead a reasonable officer to believe the person arrested has committed, is committing, or is about to commit a crime. If we think of proof as a continuum from a baseless suspicion at one end ("I don't like his face") to absolute certainty at the other ("I saw him do it"), probable cause is located somewhere in the middle. It is more than a mere hunch, more than "reasonable suspicion" but far less than the certainty of **beyond a reasonable doubt.**

Most arrests are **warrantless arrests**: that is, they are based on the police officer's assessment that the facts are sufficient to provide probable cause to believe the person committed or is about to commit a felony. Information that

REASONABLE SUSPICION
reliable facts that a person has been or is about to commit a crime.

PROBABLE CAUSE
facts are reliable and generate a reasonable belief that a person has committed, is committing, or is about to commit a crime.

BEYOND A REASONABLE DOUBT
the standard of proof necessary for a conviction in criminal trials; the highest possible standard.

WARRANTLESS ARRESTS
an arrest made without first seeking a warrant based on probable cause and permissible under specified circumstances.

satisfies probable cause is quite broad. Obviously if a police officer actually sees a person committing a crime there is sufficient probable cause. Otherwise the requirement usually allows for an overall assessment of the **totality of the circumstances**. While each piece of information alone might not satisfy probable cause, when put together, they will create a reasonable set of facts to justify an arrest. Facts that contribute to probable cause include physical flight by the suspect upon being approached, suspicious conduct, a tip from a reliable informant, previous criminal record on the part of the suspect, and physical clues such as footprints or fingerprints.

Entering a private home to arrest a person is another matter altogether and generally requires an **arrest warrant** that has been authorized by a judge or magistrate. Unless there is an emergency and the officer is in "hot pursuit" of a fleeing suspect following them into a private residence, the law requires officers to obtain a warrant before entering private homes to arrest suspects. Because of a long-standing tradition that protects the sanctity of the home against intrusions by the law, **judicial affirmation of probable cause** is required to knock on a person's door and place them under arrest.

Searches

Until 1967, the courts traditionally viewed the Fourth Amendment as protecting certain places—such as private property owned by the suspect. The right to be secure in one's own home has deep roots within Anglo-American law harkening back to the sixteenth century when the man's home was seen as his "castle." In *U.S. v. Katz,*[34] the FBI placed a wiretap on the outside of a public telephone booth from which Katz, a bookmaker, was conducting his illegal gambling business. The U.S. Supreme Court ruled that the Fourth Amendment protects "people not places": what a person knowingly exposes in public is not protected by the Fourth Amendment but what he seeks to keep private is. Katz's personal telephone calls, even if he is using a public phone, are protected by the Fourth Amendment and the government should have obtained a search warrant in order to place a wiretap on the public phone booth.

A **search warrant** is authorized based on the facts and circumstances that would lead a reasonable officer to believe that the places or persons searched will yield the things or persons to be seized. The Fourth Amendment requires that a search warrant be specific as to the location to be searched and what is being looked for. A search warrant is not intended to give law enforcement the right to go searching for whatever illegal evidence they may find: the warrant must describe the places to be searched and state what they expect to find there. A "**no knock**" warrant authorizes police officers to enter a certain premises without first knocking and announcing their presence or purpose prior to entering the premises. These warrants have become common in the "war on drugs" and through the use of SWAT teams to execute warrants.

The warrant is generally accompanied by an affidavit or sworn statement by the officer about the facts and circumstances that make up probable cause. When the magistrate or judge issues the warrant, he or she has "affirmed" the officer's belief that there is probable cause. This was precisely what the U.S. Customs officers failed to obtain in the early stages of the search of Rosa de Montoya de Hernandez. They feared that a judge would not agree there

TOTALITY OF CIRCUMSTANCES
while each piece of information alone might not satisfy probable cause, when put together, they will create a reasonable set of facts to justify an arrest.

ARREST WARRANT
a written order, based on probable cause and issued by a judge or magistrate, commanding that the person named on the warrant be arrested by the police.

JUDICIAL AFFIRMATION OF PROBABLE CAUSE
judicial review and agreement with the facts establishing probable cause for an arrest or search.

SEARCH WARRANT
an order issued by a judge and signed by a police officer indicating where the search will take place and what is expected to be found in the search.

NO KNOCK
warrant is: a warrant that allows officers to enter a property without notifying residents immediately prior to such entry.

was probable cause to do a body cavity search and they would be required to release Rosa.

The use of electronic surveillance remote from the person or places that are being searched poses a serious challenge to the courts in interpreting the Fourth Amendment within the context of twenty-first-century technology. The use of telephones, cell phones, the internet, and GPS devices offers the possibility for the government to monitor the communication activities of citizens without their knowledge or awareness. The USA Patriot Act passed in response to the threat of terrorism expands the legal use of many forms of electronic surveillance such as the monitoring of internet searches, cell phone communications, and telephone calls; global positioning satellite devices also allow police to follow movements of cars or people from a remote location. In 2012, in *U.S. v. Jones*[35] the Supreme Court unanimously ruled that the use of GPS tracking devices placed on an automobile constitutes a legal "search" under the Constitution requiring a court-ordered warrant.

Warrantless Searches

There are a variety of circumstances where searches are permitted without a judicial warrant. In fact, the vast majority of searches conducted by law enforcement every day are more likely to fall within these "exceptions" than those that require judicial approval.

When police arrest a suspect, they are permitted to conduct a limited search for concealed weapons or to prevent evidence from being destroyed. **Searches incident to a lawful arrest** are probably the most common kinds of police searches. The purpose of this search is to protect the safety of the arresting officers.

A **consent search** is simply one in which law enforcement asks permission and the citizens willingly agrees to allow the police to conduct the search of their person, home, or personal effects. People can, and do, voluntarily give up their right against unreasonable searches and seizures and cooperate with a search. With consent, there is no issue of a violation of the Fourth Amendment unless the courts find that the consent was not truly voluntary. Unlike the so-called Miranda rights, police are not required to inform citizens that they have the right to withhold their consent although it is the policy of some law enforcement agencies such as the FBI to inform suspects that they have the right to withhold their consent.

The issue of voluntariness is a critical one: Do citizens really understand that they are free to say "no" when they are asked for their consent? Should the police be required to inform citizens that they have the right to withhold their consent as we do in the process of informing them of their right to remain silent when they are arrested? In an airport detention, if the authorities are refusing to allow a person to leave, can we really say that their consent to an X-ray or some other procedure is "voluntary"?

We have already seen the **border exception** to the warrant requirement. In 1977 the Supreme Court ruled that all persons entering the country are subject to routine searches without probable cause.[36] Travelers entering into the country may have their luggage and persons searched by law enforcement without the need to meet a probable cause standard. Ironically, had Rosa been legally arrested she would have been entitled to far more rights including the right to an attorney

SEARCH INCIDENT TO A LAWFUL ARREST search of persons immediately after an arrest specifically for the purpose of seizing weapons or evidence.

CONSENT SEARCH warrantless search conducted when the party to the search provides voluntary and intelligent consent to law enforcement.

BORDER EXCEPTION all persons, citizens and non-citizens, may have their luggage and persons searched by law enforcement without probable cause.

and the right to make a phone call. The dissenting justices argued that people who are detained at the border are extraordinarily isolated and at the mercy of the law enforcement officers who have the legal power to detain them on the barest of suspicions until they prove that they are innocent of the crime of which they have been accused.

The **plain view exception** states that police may lawfully seize items—weapons, stolen property, drugs—that are in plain sight, plain hearing, plain smell, or plain touch. Provided that the officers are where they have a legal right to be, for example, standing on public sidewalk, if they can smell, hear, or see evidence of illegal material with their ordinary senses, even if it is inside a building, the plain view exception permits them to enter and legally seize those items. If they are using high-powered telescopes or mechanical hearing devices, this exception would not apply.

In recent years, police have relied on "pretextual stops" to conduct warrantless searches especially on the nation's roads and highways.[37] Routine traffic stops for some minor infraction are used as a pretext for searching the vehicle for other contraband such as weapons or drugs. In 1996 the Supreme Court upheld this practice as constitutional in *Whren v. United States*[38] stating that as long as there is probable cause to suspect a minor traffic violation has occurred police may conduct a search and seize whatever contents may be illegal inside the vehicle. Critics argue that this gives police a nearly unlimited power to search almost any vehicle since traffic violations are so common. Again, as we see with searches at our nation's airports, these practices are routinely combined with racial profiling and so are more commonly used against minority citizens than white citizens Fifth Amendment, U.S. Constitution.

The Fifth Amendment and the Law of Interrogation

No persons shall be held to answer for a capital or otherwise infamous crime, unless on a presentment or indictment of a Grand jury, except in cases arising in the land or naval forces, or in the Militia, when in actual service in time of War or public danger; nor shall any person be subject for the same offence to be twice put in jeopardy of life or limb; nor shall be compelled in any criminal case to be a witness against himself, nor be deprived of life, liberty, or property, without due process of law; nor shall private property be taken for public use, without just compensation.

Interrogation has been defined by the U.S. Supreme Court as any behavior by the police "that the police should know are reasonably likely to elicit an incriminating response from the suspect." One of the central purposes of law enforcement is to gather information about the guilt of the suspect. At the same time, the Fifth Amendment states that "no person shall be compelled to be a witness against himself in any criminal case." Freely given confessions on the part of criminal suspects are legitimate evidence in any court of law but coerced confessions are not. Remember the suspects in the Salem witch trials? Most of them confessed to being guilty even though they were innocent to avoid being hanged or burned at the stake. The purpose of the Fifth Amendment is to protect citizens from being intimidated into making false confessions.[39]

The first significant case to impact police interrogations was *Brown v. Mississippi*[40] decided in 1936. In the investigation of the murder of a white man, the "confessions" of three black suspects were extracted by a series of physical beatings,

PLAIN VIEW EXCEPTION
the rule that any evidence police can see or hear in plain view when they are where they have a legal right to be is admissible in court even without a legal warrant or probable cause.

INTERROGATION
explicit questioning or actions by law enforcement that may elicit an incriminating statement from a suspect.

whippings, and hangings by a rope from police interrogators. When they finally "confessed," they were all three duly convicted of murder. The convictions were upheld by the Mississippi Supreme Court despite a full admission of the beatings by a deputy who testified that they were "not too much for a Negro." The U.S. Supreme Court overturned the conviction stating that it was difficult to imagine a process of interrogation more "revolting" to a sense of justice than physical torture, terror, and beatings.

In addition to physical coercion, the U.S. Supreme Court has also prohibited methods of psychological coercion used by law enforcement to induce suspects to confess. The U.S. Supreme Court ruled that defendants cannot be tricked into making a confession. If the officer tells the suspect they will arrest his family, or he will lose his job, or his family will be kicked out of their apartment, the resultant confession is rendered illegal, because the officer had used threat and deception.

These standards are difficult to enforce because interrogations are made behind closed doors usually only with the police and suspect present. Only Minnesota and Alaska require that police record all interrogations. Otherwise, no one really knows what goes on in interrogation rooms. The 1965 ruling in *Miranda v. Arizona*[41] attempted to solve this dilemma by ensuring that defendants have "read their rights" and are given the opportunity to demand the presence of an attorney *before* going into the interrogation room.

Ernesto Miranda was arrested on charges of suspected rape and abduction. He was positively identified by the victim and signed a confession stating he committed the crime. The U.S. Supreme Court overturned his conviction because he was never advised of his right to an attorney during his interrogation. In their ruling the Court outlined the procedural safeguards law enforcement must take to ensure a legal confession.

These are what are now known as **Miranda rights.** As soon as law enforcement has taken a particular individual into custody, typically at the moment of the arrest, the defendant must be informed of his or her Fifth and Sixth Amendment rights. Specifically, the Miranda ruling requires that the suspect be informed 1. of their right to remain silent; 2. that anything they say can and will be used against them by the government; 3. that they have the right to have an attorney present during interrogations; and 4. that if they cannot afford an attorney, the government will appoint one on their behalf.

In addition, the Court has ruled that if the suspect states the desire to remain silent, the interrogation must cease at that point. If no attorney is present, the government must prove that a suspect voluntarily waived their rights and the prosecution may not use the defendant's decision to remain silent as evidence against them at trial. Finally, any evidence obtained in interrogation that violates these procedural rules will be deemed inadmissible at trial.

The Miranda decision angered and concerned the law enforcement community who felt that the balance had tipped way too far in favor of the rights of suspects. Law enforcement feared that in a post-Miranda world there would be few confessions and police hands would seriously be tied in pursuing investigations and in obtaining voluntary confessions. Almost forty years of experience has shown, however, that it has had little impact on the power of police. Miranda has not been as effective in protecting the rights of suspects as people had hoped it might be. Data show that the number of voluntary confessions is about the same after Miranda as before it was enacted: only about 20 to 25 percent of suspects refuse to allow police questioning without an attorney present. The vast majority

MIRANDA RIGHTS
warnings that explain the rights of an arrestee which police are required to recite at the time of arrest or prior to interrogation.

of suspects are relatively unsophisticated and waive their rights. Many people have serious doubts that most suspects understand the significance of these rights. Once a suspect has waived their rights, law enforcement is free to use the same manipulative and deceptive tactics of interrogation that led to the Miranda decision in the first place.

The experience of Rosa in the backroom of an airport demonstrates the terror of being detained by the police without anyone to advocate on one's behalf. The Supreme Court recognized the profound imbalance of power when a suspect sits alone in an airless interrogation room disconnected from the outside world. Recalling the nation's experience with coerced confessions, they sought to provide protection for suspects by inserting the right to have someone present who would balance and protect the rights of the lone individual against the awesome power of the state. Unfortunately the Miranda rights only "work" for those who are educated or experienced enough to utter the words, "I want to see a lawyer" when the police deliver the warnings.

On the other hand, the courts recognize the importance of interrogating a suspect particularly to obtain crucial and time-sensitive information about ongoing criminal activity that threatens public safety. A 1984 Supreme Court ruling allows law enforcement to delay reading a suspect their Miranda rights for a limited time under circumstances where public safety is an issue. New guidelines issued under the Obama administration give the law enforcement extended time for interrogation before issuing suspects in domestic terror cases their rights.

The Exclusionary Rule: Putting the Teeth in the Fourth and Fifth Amendments

In the first chapter we referred to the Constitution as a "sleeping beauty" whose power was "awakened" hundreds of years later by the interpretation of Supreme Court judges. The impact of court rulings on the day-to-day conduct of the police requires some kind of enforcement mechanism. That mechanism is the **"exclusionary rule"** which bars the use of illegally seized evidence in court proceedings. The **"fruit of the poisoned tree doctrine"** states that any evidence which derives from an illegal search should also be excluded as evidence. Once one step in the process is determined to be an illegal violation of due process rights, all the subsequent parts of the investigation are also "tainted" by the violation and are inadmissible in court.

Mapp v. Ohio[42] made the exclusionary principle applicable to criminal prosecution at the state level. In Cleveland, Ohio, Dolly Mapp who ran a boarding house was suspected of harboring a fugitive wanted in a bombing, part of an ongoing battle between rival bookmakers. When Ohio police officers arrived, Mapp demanded to see their search warrant and refused them entry. They waved a piece of paper at her which was most likely not a warrant and proceeded to force their way in to search her apartment. They found three dirty books in a trunk in the basement and charged and convicted Mapp with possession of obscene materials.

In 1961 the U.S. Supreme Court overturned her conviction using the Fourteenth Amendment principle that no state shall "deprive any person of life, liberty, or property, without due process of law; nor deny to any person within its jurisdiction the equal protection of the laws." Because the police should have had a warrant to search her apartment and did not, the evidence seized in the

EXCLUSIONARY RULE
the constitutional prohibition of the use of illegally obtained evidence in court.

FRUIT OF A POISONOUS TREE DOCTRINE
evidence obtained through other illegally obtained evidence, inadmissible because it is tainted by the illegality of the initial search, arrest, or confession.

search, the pornographic books, was inadmissible which rendered her conviction unsupportable by any legal evidence.

The point of the exclusionary rule is to require police to obey the laws of the Constitution when conducting investigation, searches, and interrogations of criminal suspects. In theory, the threat that evidence will be excluded and cases will fall apart should make police more concerned and careful about following legal procedure in how they conduct their investigations. Critics argue that the exclusion of evidence at trial does not directly affect police who are not responsible for prosecutions so it rarely influences their behavior. The exclusionary rule does however affect the strategy of defense attorneys who focus more on the conduct of police in preparation of a criminal defense.

Recent decades have relaxed the impact of the exclusionary rule by the creation of what is called the **good faith exception** for cases where police conduct illegal searches through honest error rather than intentional action. In *U.S. v. Leon,* the Supreme Court conceded that the magistrate had been wrong to issue the search warrant; they reasoned that the police were acting in good faith in conducting the subsequent search and whatever was found at that time was admissible in court. The so-called "good faith exception to the exclusionary rule" has emerged as a major avenue for police to continue to submit evidence even when significant errors are made as long as it can be shown that these were not intentional errors.[43]

DEBATING THE ISSUE OF RACIAL PROFILING

The practice of **racial profiling** refers to the use of race (or other group characteristics like ethnicity or gender) as part of the criteria that make up "reasonable suspicion that crime is afoot." Group characteristics such as race, ethnicity, or gender are often empirically associated with the commission of crime. In theory, the use of race as a part of a profile is a "neutral" practice since any ethnicity or racial group may be part of a particular empirical pattern of criminal behavior. When U.S. Customs identified Rosa as a potential suspect for more careful investigation they were using her race and ethnicity as part of a fact pattern, which signifies reasonable suspicion.

The balance between the power of police to enforce the law and the freedom of citizens to be "left alone" is constantly debated and always shifting. In a society which values equal rights for all its citizens, basic fairness requires that both protection of the law against crime and restrictions of liberty be equally distributed among all citizens. The equal protection clause of the Fourteenth Amendment states that no one should be deprived of equal protection of the law based on race, gender, religion, or ethnicity: the trade-off between liberty and crime control therefore should be the same for all groups within American society. The dilemma raised by racial profiling is the question of equality: Are some segments of American society (minority citizens and especially young black males), subject to significantly fewer civil liberties than those enjoyed by all Americans and guaranteed by the Constitution?

Defenders of racial profiling believe that, used properly, group characteristics such as race and ethnicity are legitimate and effective tools of law enforcement. Bernard Parks, the African American chief of the LAPD gives the following example in support of the use of profiling as a legitimate tool for law enforcement.[44]

GOOD FAITH EXCEPTION
exception to the exclusionary rule in which evidence obtained by police acting in good faith with a search warrant issued by a judge is admissible even though the warrant is ultimately found invalid.

RACIAL PROFILING
the use of a group characteristic such as race, gender, or ethnicity as a part of the evidence that constitutes reasonable suspicion that a crime has occurred.

In the city of Los Angeles, there is a problem in some neighborhoods of violent crime against jewelry salespeople. The predominant suspects in these crimes are Colombians. Police have not found Mexican Americans, blacks, or whites to be involved in the commission of this particular pattern of criminal activity within this local area. Parks believes that if police officers see six Colombians milling about in front of the Jewelry Mart, officers should have reasonable suspicion to stop and question them.

Using this logic, the courts have ruled that law enforcement may use race and ethnicity as legitimate criteria as part of a criminal profile as long as race or ethnicity are not the sole criteria used. In the decision to subject Rosa to a strip search, her ethnicity as a Colombian woman was only one element of suspicion along with her travel plans, method of purchasing her ticket, past travel pattern, and so forth. Used in concert with other factors, the courts claim that race is a legitimate tool in the detection of crime. According to the courts, the fact that crime is committed disproportionately by specific racial or ethnic groups within society is simply an unpleasant fact which cannot be ignored, "We wish it were otherwise, but we take the facts as they are presented to us, not as we would like them to be."[45]

Critics of racial profiling argue that racial profiling unfairly targets the vast majority of minorities who are innocent and law-abiding citizens and subjects them to unfair and excessive police scrutiny. They argue that the courts underestimate the harm which results when our legal system says that it is legal for police to be suspicious of a citizen because they are black, Mexican, or Colombian. The courts claim that stopping and questioning a person on the highway or briefly detaining a traveler entering the country for questioning is "quite limited" in its intrusiveness. But, according to minority critics, to live under a cloud of generalized suspicion from law enforcement simply on the basis of one's race or ethnicity is a profound intrusion on a person's civil liberty.

When racial profiling is widely used, being stopped and questioned by the police is not a one-time event for citizens of color as it may be for white citizens.[46] And it won't matter if they are innocent of any wrongdoing when they are stopped and questioned by the police because the next time they are driving down the highway or walking down the street, a different police officer will stop them and question them, not because of what they are doing or not doing but because of their race. Critics argue that even if race and ethnicity are useful as tools of law enforcement, it comes at the cost of alienating the minority community who quickly begin to resent and distrust the justice system.

After the terrorist attack of September 11, the debate about racial profiling shifted from African Americans to the targeting of Arab and Muslim Americans for police investigation and suspicion. Despite the earlier bombing beneath the World Trade Center in 1993, the Oklahoma City bombing in 1995, and the pipe bomb at the Olympic Games in Atlanta in 1996, the threat of violent terrorism on American soil was not on the forefront of most citizens' minds until the catastrophic strike on the World Trade Center which caused the death of more than 3,000 people. In the aftermath of the crisis, the threat of violent terrorism has sought many to seek to erode constitutional protections of civil liberties for more than twenty million alien residents living within the United States and for thousands of Muslim Americans who fit the physical profile of a terrorist.

For some, the use of ethnicity and religion as part of a profile of reasonable suspicion is sensible given the magnitude of the threat and what is known about previous terrorist profiles. For others, reliance upon ethnic, religious, and racial characteristics by law enforcement undermines the values of American society and threatens the foundation of American justice as a system of equality for all. We take a closer look at the tension between security and liberty and its implications for policing in a free society in chapter 9.

authority (p. 174)   a specific form of power which is seen as legitimate by those subject to it.

power (p. 174)   the ability to affect the behavior of others, with or without the use of force.

Homeland Security Act of 2002 (p. 177)   massive reorganization of federal law enforcement, creating the Department of Homeland Security.

preponderance of the evidence (p. 180)   the standard for determining legal liability in civil trials requiring a certainty of more than 50 percent of defendant's guilt.

stop and frisk (p. 183)   a technique used by police to "pat-down" a person suspected of being armed or in possession of the instrumentalities of crime.

reasonable suspicion (p. 184)   reliable facts that a person has been or is about to commit a crime.

probable cause (p. 184)   facts are reliable and generate a reasonable belief that a person has committed, is committing, or is about to commit a crime.

beyond a reasonable doubt (p. 184)   the standard of proof necessary for a conviction in criminal trials; the highest possible standard.

warrantless arrests (p. 184)   an arrest made without first seeking a warrant based on probable cause and permissible under specified circumstances.

totality of circumstances (p. 185)   while each piece of information alone might not satisfy probable cause, when put together, they will create a reasonable set of facts to justify an arrest.

arrest warrant (p. 185)   a written order, based on probable cause and issued by a judge or magistrate, commanding that the person named on the warrant be arrested by the police.

judicial affirmation of probable cause (p. 185)   judicial review and agreement with the facts establishing probable cause for an arrest or search.

search warrant (p. 185)   an order issued by a judge and signed by a police officer indicating where the search will take place and what is expected to be found in the search.

No knock (p. 185)   warrant is: a warrant that allows officers to enter a property without notifying residents immediately prior to such entry.

search incident to a lawful arrest (p. 186)   search of persons immediately after an arrest specifically for the purpose of seizing weapons or evidence.

consent search (p. 186)   warrantless search conducted when the party to the search provides voluntary and intelligent consent to law enforcement.

border exception (p. 186)   all persons, citizens and non-citizens, may have their luggage and persons searched by law enforcement without probable cause.

plain view exception (p. 187)   the rule that any evidence police can see or hear in plain view when they are where they have a legal right to be is admissible in court even without a legal warrant or probable cause.

interrogation (p. 187)   explicit questioning or actions by law enforcement that may elicit an incriminating statement from a suspect.

Miranda rights (p. 188)   warnings that explain the rights of an arrestee which police are required to recite at the time of arrest or prior to interrogation.

exclusionary rule (p. 189)   the constitutional prohibition of the use of illegally obtained evidence in court.

fruit of a poisonous tree doctrine (p. 189)   evidence obtained through other illegally obtained evidence, inadmissible because it is tainted by the illegality of the initial search, arrest, or confession.

good faith exception (p. 190) exception to the exclusionary rule in which evidence obtained by police acting in good faith with a search warrant issued by a judge is admissible even though the warrant is ultimately found invalid.

racial profiling (p. 190) the use of a group characteristic such as race, gender, or ethnicity as a part of the evidence that constitutes reasonable suspicion that a crime has occurred.

REVIEW AND STUDY QUESTIONS

1. Describe the "dilemma" of policing in our society. Why is this a dilemma for societies that value the individual's "right to be let alone"?

2. Define the concept of authority. How is it different from power? Explain the difference between the exercise of authority and the use of power by police within society?

3. Describe the structure of U.S. law enforcement. Where are most police personnel employed?

4. What is the rule which guides police use of coercive force?

5. Explain the roles and responsibilities of private security and compare these with the roles and responsibilities of public security.

6. What is the proof needed to stop and frisk? What is the proof required for an arrest?

7. Describe those circumstances when a warrantless search is legally permissible.

8. What is the exclusionary rule and what is its intended purpose within our legal system?

9. Describe the ruling which established the Miranda rules. Explain the purpose of the ruling and why Miranda is an important protection for the privilege against self-incrimination.

10. Outline the arguments for and against racial profiling. Is racial profiling a legitimate law enforcement tool in your view? Why or why not?

CHECK IT OUT

Websites

U.S. Customs Service, https://www.cbp.gov. Learn more about the U.S. Customs and its anti-drug, smuggling, and many other law enforcement responsibilities.

Supreme Court, http://www.uscourts.gov/multimedia/podcasts/Landmarks/mappvohio.aspx. Go to this web site and listen to a podcast on *Mapp v. Ohio* and *Miranda v. Arizona* to read summaries of the case and the majority and minority Supreme Court opinions.

SCOTUSblog, http://www.scotusblog.com. The Supreme Court of the United States blogs. Keep up to date with the goings on at the Supreme Court.

Directory of Law Enforcement Agencies, http://www.usacops.com/. Calling itself the most popular law enforcement web site, this site offers an online directory for links to federal, state, and local agencies. Click on your state and city to view the web page for your local law enforcement agencies. Check out the websites for the federal law enforcement too.

The FBI Home Page, https://www.fbi.gov. The official web site of the FBI with links to crime information, data, and other law enforcement agencies.

Drug Enforcement Administration (DEA), https://www.dea.gov/index.shtml. Click onto this web site to learn more about drugs, drug policy, and strategies of federal drug law enforcement.

Department of Homeland Security (DHS), https://www.dhs.gov. To learn more about the DHS visit their web site.

Videos

Need to Know: Crossing the Line—PBS—25 minutes. This reports on the alleged abuses of undocumented immigrants by U.S. Border Patrol agents and officers. Correspondent John Larson investigates massive overcrowding of detainment centers and mistreatment including physical abuse, sexual assault, and even torture. Available at http://www.pbs.org/wnet/need-to-know/video/need-to-know-july-20-2012-crossing-the-line-part-2/14271/

Racial Profiling and Law Enforcement: America in Black and White—41 minutes. ABC news anchor Ted Koppel and correspondent Michel McQueen look at the issue of Driving While Black from the victims, viewpoint and then from the viewpoint of the law enforcement. Available from Films for the Humanities and Sciences www.films.com

A Conversation with Police on Race | Op-Docs | *The New York Times*—7 minutes. In this short documentary, former officers share their thoughts on policing and race in America. https://www.youtube.com/watch?v=5Funraox29U

NOTES

[1] *United States v. Montoya De Hernandez* 473 U.S. 531; 105 S. Ct. 3304. (1985).

[2] Nelson Erik-Lars, "Changing the Profile at Customs," *Daily News*, (October 15, 2000), 43.

[3] *United States v. Montoya De Hernandez* 473 U.S. 531; 105 S. Ct. 3304. (1985).

[4] *United States v. Montoya De Hernandez.*

[5] *United States v. Montoya De Hernandez.*

[6] *United States v. Montoya De Hernandez.*

[7] "U.S. Customs Service: Better Targeting of Airline Passengers for Personal Searches Could Produce Better Results," *U.S. Government Accountability Office* (2000).

[8] Harris Cathy, *Flying While Black: A Whistleblowers Story* (Los Angeles, CA: Milligan Books, 2001).

[9] Herman Goldstein, *Policing in a Free Society* (Cambridge, UK: Ballinger, 1977).

[10] Obi N. Ignatius Ebbe, *Comparative and International Criminal Justice Systems: Policing, Judiciary and Corrections* (Boston, MA: Butterworth Heinemann, 1996); David H. Bayley, *Forces of Order: Police Behavior in Japan and the United States* (Berkeley, CA: University of California Press, 1976).

[11] Egon Bittner, *The Functions of the Police in Modern Society: A Review of Background Factors, Current Practices and Possible Role Model* (Chevy Chase, MD: National Institute of Mental Health, 1970).

[12] Jerome H. Skolnick and James J. Fyfe, *Above the Law: Police and the Excessive Use of Force* (New York: Free Press, 1993).

[13] Brian Reaves, "Federal Law Enforcement Officers, 2008," *Bureau of Justice Statistics* (Washington, DC: U.S. Department of Justice, 2012).

[14] "Annual National Occupational Employment and Wage Estimates for 1997 through 2009," *Bureau of Labor Statistics* (Washington, DC: U.S. Department of Labor, 2010); Kevin Strom, Marcus Berzofsky, Bonnie Shook-Sa, Kelle Barrick, Crystal Daye, Nicole Horstmann and Susan Kinsey, *Private Security Industry: Review of the Definitions, Available Data Sources, and Paths Moving Forward* (Triangle Park, NC: RTI International, 2010).

[15] Brian Reaves, "Local Police Departments, 2013: Personnel, Policies and Practices," *Bureau of Justice Statistics* (Washington, DC: U.S. Department of Justice, 2015).

[16] Reaves, Local Police Departments, 2013.

[17] Brian Reaves, "Federal Law Enforcement Officers, 2008," *Bureau of Justice Statistics* (Washington, DC: U.S. Department of Justice, 2012).

[18] "U.S. Department of Homeland Security," www.dhs.gov/ and www.dhs.gov/xabout/structure/

[19] Jonathan R. White, *Terrorism and Homeland Security* (Belmont CA: Wadsworth, 2009).

[20] "Budget-in-Brief FY 2016," Department of Homeland Security, https://www.dhs.gov/publication/fy-2016-budget-brief

[21] "U.S. Department of Homeland Security," www.dhs.gov/

[22] Tony Poveda, *Lawlessness and Reform: The FBI in Transition* (Pacific Grove, CA: Brooks/Cole, 1990).

[23] Susan N. Herman, *Taking Liberties: The War on Terror and the Erosion of American Democracy* (New York: Oxford University Press, 2011).

[24] Brian Reaves, "Federal Law Enforcement Officers, 2008," *Bureau of Justice Statistics* (Washington, DC: U.S. Department of Justice, 2012).

[25] "Final Report of the National Commission on Terrorist Attacks Upon the United States," *The 9/11 Commission Report* (New York: W.W. Norton & Co, 2004).

[26] Mimi Hall, "Private Security Guards," *USA Today* (January 23, 2003), 1A.

[27] "Private Security: Patterns and Trends," *Bureau of Justice Statistics* (Washington, DC: National Institute of Justice, 1991).

[28] Marcia Chaiken and Jan Chaiken, *Public Policing–Privately Provided* (Washington, DC: National Institute of Justice, 1987).

[29] Clifford D. Shearing and Philip C. Stenning, eds., *Private Policing* (Newbury Park, CA: Sage, 1987).

[30] Wayne R. LaFave and Jerold H. Israel, *Criminal Procedure* (St Paul, MN: West, 1985).

[31] Criminal Law Reporter, eds., *The Criminal Law Revolution and Its Aftermath (1960–1977)* (Washington, DC: Bureau of National Affairs, 1972).

[32] David Cole, *No Equal Justice: Race and Class in the American Criminal Justice System* (New York: The New Press, 1999), 218.

[33] *Terry v. Ohio*, 392 U.S. 1 (1968).

[34] *Katz v. United States*, 389 U.S. 347 (1967).

[35] 565 *U.S. v. Antoine Jones*, (2011).

[36] *Ramsey v. United States,* 431 U.S. 606 (1977).

[37] David Cole, *No Equal Justice: Race and Class in the American Criminal Justice System* (New York: The New Press, 1999), 34–41.

[38] *Whren v. United States* 116 S. Ct. 1769 (1996).

[39] Leonard W. Levy, *Origins of the Fifth Amendment: The Right Against Self-Incrimination* (New York: Oxford University Press, 1968).

[40] *Brown v. Mississippi* 297 U.S. 278 (1936).

[41] *Miranda v. Arizona,* 384 U.S. 436 (1966).

[42] *Mapp v. Ohio* 367 U.S. 643 (1961).

[43] William J. Mertens and Silas Wasserstrom, "The Good Faith Exception to the Exclusionary Rule: Deregulating the Police and Derailing the Law," *Georgetown Law Journal* 70 (1981).

[44] Randall Kennedy, "Racial Profiling Usually Isn't Racist: It can help stop crime and it should be abolished," *The New Republic* (September 13, 1999).

[45] *U.S. v. Weaver,* as cited in R. Kennedy.

[46] *U.S. v. Weaver.*

In this chapter the case explores the beating of Rodney King by the LAPD and legal trials of the LAPD. This case illustrates the challenges in drawing the line between legal and extra-legal violence and barriers to the prosecution of police misconduct. The chapter describes the evolving role of police, the realities of police work, and the relationships between police and the communities they serve.

LEARNING OBJECTIVES

After reading this chapter you should be able to:

- Describe the rules that regulate the use of lethal force by police.
- Explain why a code of silence exists within policing and why a "blue curtain" separates police from civilians.
- Explain the concept of the "working personality" within police and describe what features of police work contribute to this working personality.
- Illustrate the military model of policing and discuss the impact of the model on the incidence of police brutality.
- Explain why the modern police was invented in the cities of the nineteenth century.
- Describe the problem of patronage and corruption in nineteenth-century policing.
- Discuss the key elements of professionalism in policing and the impact of technology and militarization on police-community relations.
- Identify the three key functions of policing.
- Describe the philosophy of community policing and its impact on contemporary policing.

Case #8: The Thin Blue Line: Rodney King and the LAPD

The infamous videotape of police beating Rodney King broadcast on a local television news station. (Time & Life Pictures/Getty Images)

The Videotape that Started it All

Most people today recognize the name of Rodney King and know about the acquittal of the four LAPD officers who were videotaped beating him that sparked four days of some of the worse rioting in our nation's history. Most people too recall King's eloquent plea, "People . . . can we all get along?"[1] broadcast over the nation's airwaves in an attempt to stop the violence and destruction. But no one would have heard of Rodney King or even known of his beating if it weren't for George Holliday, who captured the incident on video footage and supplied that tape to the local news station the following Monday morning. The video was aired for the first time that night on the local evening news, picked up by CNN and broadcast nationwide by early Tuesday morning. By Wednesday, the videotape had become an international news sensation broadcasting the "truth" about police brutality against blacks in America.

On March 3, 1991, George Holliday was awakened by the sound of police sirens and the whirr of a police helicopter hovering above his apartment. Holliday stood out on his second floor balcony and saw a ring of police cars surrounding a large black man with his hands on the roof of a white Hyundai. He grabbed his new camcorder which was fully loaded and ready to be used the next morning at the LA marathon and began to tape the next nine minutes and twenty seconds of action in the street below.

The first thirteen seconds of the tape were somewhat blurry as Holliday shifted his position to get a better view. Later, these crucial seconds would be edited out of the version aired on the local television news station only to re-appear when the tape was shown as evidence in the trial of the four police officers. Those thirteen seconds along with the full nine minutes and twenty seconds of the entire tape would be painstakingly analyzed and viewed by the jury. Widely seen as the best evidence for the prosecution of the officers, the tape would come to serve as a key piece of evidence for the defense as well.[2]

What Happened that Night[3]

The start of the incident took place far from the corner outside of Lake View Terrace apartments. On the evening of March 2, Rodney King was watching basketball and drinking malt liquor in the home of his childhood friend Bryant Allen and his friend, Freddie Helms. No one can remember why the three decided to go out for a drive but a little past midnight, they got into King's Hyundai and headed for a park where King used to go night fishing with his father. King sped along Interstate 210 singing to loud music on the radio while Helms fell asleep in the front seat. Allen alone in the backseat saw the headlights of the California Highway Patrol car and heard its sirens as it clocked the speeding vehicle at 80 miles per hour. Later Allen would testify that King seemed to just get "stuck" on driving and ignored the sirens and his pleas to stop. King testified at the federal trial in 1993 that he knew a DUI conviction would automatically revoke his parole. "I was scared of going back to prison and I just kind of thought the problem would just go away."

Melanie and Tim Singer, both California Highway Patrol officers, were partners in work and marriage. At 12:30 a.m. on March 3, Melanie Singer began a high-speed 7.8 mile pursuit of King's speeding vehicle. Ignoring the flashing lights and sirens of the patrol car, King went faster reaching speeds of nearly 115 mph on the freeway and continuing at speeds of 80–85 mph on the residential streets. Tim Singer radioed for help and they were soon joined by a car from the Los Angeles Unified School District and several LAPD patrol cars. King ran a red light to the intersection of Van Nuys and Foothill Boulevard and came to a halt near the entrance of the Hansen Dam Park blocked by a pickup truck that had pulled over when the driver heard the approaching sirens. The Hyundai was now surrounded by five patrol cars including three LAPD cars while a LAPD helicopter hovered overhead shining a spotlight down on the scene.

One LAPD car held officers Lawrence Powell and Timothy Wind, the other officers Theodore Briseno and Rolando Solano. Sergeant Stacey Koon arrived in the third car alone. The LAPD officers drew their guns and took cover behind the car doors. More cars arrived and by the end of the incident, there were a total of twenty-five law enforcement officers on the scene including fourteen LAPD officers. These officers became known as "bystander" officers: none assisted in the arrest and none took any action to stop or interfere with the arrest.

Using a hand-held microphone Tim Singer ordered the occupants of the car to get out and surrender. Realizing they could not hear him over the din of the helicopter and other noise, Singer left his car and verbally shouted commands to the car occupants. Allen and Helms complied but King remained in the driver's seat. Tim Singer began to handcuff the two on the ground while Melanie Singer continued to verbally order King to get out the car.

King slowly began to emerge, struggling with his seatbelt, smiling at the officers, waving at the helicopter overhead. King did a little dance, talked gibberish, and went down on his hands and knees patting the ground. Sergeant Koon was in his car preparing an electric stun gun known as the Taser to subdue King who appeared to be drunk or on drugs and was clearly not cooperating. Melanie Singer continued to shout at King to put his hands where she could see them and lie down on the ground. King made another strange gesture putting his hands on his buttock and shaking them in the officer's direction. Singer continued to repeat her orders and King finally complied by placing his hands on the roof of the car. At this point, Singer drew her gun and began to approach King, gun in hand, in order to cuff him. When she was five or six feet away, she heard Sergeant Stacy Koon order her to "Stand back. Stand back. We'll handle this." Looking back, Singer saw the stripes on his uniform and respecting rank relinquished the arrest to the LAPD.

According to Koon, LAPD training teaches officers never to approach a suspect resisting arrest with a drawn gun, a dangerous move which gives the suspect a chance to wrestle the gun away from the officer. Koon ordered all his officers to return their guns to their holsters and then ordered Powell, Briseno, Wind, and Solano to "swarm" King by jumping on his back trying to cuff King at the same time but King pushed them off of his back with a powerful gesture that allegedly frightened the officers. The officers later testified that King was an extremely large and powerful man, clearly "buffed out," most likely from a stay in prison, whom they believed to be on PCP, a drug which made him "immune" to pain and "like a monster."

Koon shot the Taser at King twice, hitting him first in the chest and then in the back. King groaned and collapsed but once more rose to his feet. Facing Powell with his arms outstretched, in Powell's recollection, King "charged him" although King would later testify that he was in tremendous pain from the Taser shots and he had it in his mind to "run toward the hills, the park area" and that he ran in the direction of Powell with his hands up in the air so the officers could see he did not have a gun and would not shoot him. From down on the ground, a man's voice can be heard on the tape, probably Allen saying "You're gonna get shot, you're gonna get shot."

It was exactly at the point that King rushed toward Powell with his arms in the air that George Holliday began shooting his video camera. The first three seconds captured that precise movement but the next ten seconds were blurry as Holliday jostled the camera to get into a good position. The remaining tape captured the next 80 seconds during which time Rodney King is hit in the face with a metal baton, collapses on the ground and is being beaten by batons and kicks until he cries out "please stop" and is handcuffed by Officer Powell. What the tape shows and what the public saw over and over again was a videotape showing three officers kicking and beating a man clearly on the ground surrounded by almost twenty-five law enforcement officers including a helicopter hovering overhead, who stood by and watched.

King passed out from the beating and awoke in the ambulance on the way to the hospital. Holliday's videotape showed the LAPD had double-handcuffed him and hog-tied him by fastening the cords from his feet to his hands. They dragged the unconscious King to the car with his face on the ground. King suffered a broken cheekbone, multiple fractures on the right side of his face, lacerations on his forehead, a fracture of his right leg, and multiple bruises and abrasions on his torso and legs. King recalled feeling like a "crushed can." [4] Although no one can say for absolute certainty it is estimated that in less than a minute and half King was hit with the metal batons more than thirty-one times.

The Impact of the Videotape

Holliday's first response on Sunday morning was to call the Foothill police station and tell them about the videotape but they were not interested in the tape. Next, Holliday phoned CNN's Los Angeles bureau but no one was there to take his call. On Monday morning, Holliday took the tape down to the local news station that immediately viewed the tape and edited for the evening news. Out of courtesy the news station sent a copy to LAPD headquarters and gave them notice it will be aired on the evening news and reported as an incident of "white LAPD officers beating a black motorist."

The fallout from the showing of the videotape was immediate and explosive. On March 5, the FBI opened an investigation, Chief Daryl Gates, head of the LAPD, pledged an inquiry and the mayor of LA, Tom Bradley, announced that appropriate action would be taken against the officers.[5] On March 6, Rodney King was released from jail with District Attorney Reiner stating that there was insufficient evidence to prosecute him. On March 7, Gates informed the public that the officers involved would be prosecuted. By March 8, fifteen officers who were on the scene were suspended and the DA convened a grand jury to seek indictments against several officers. The American Civil Liberties Union (ACLU) took out a full page ad in the *LA*

Times targeting Daryl Gates and demanding that he be fired. The ad blazoned the question: "Who do you call when the gang wears a blue uniform?" The mayor of Los Angeles immediately ordered a high-level independent investigation of the LAPD to be headed by Warren Christopher which swiftly echoed the mayor's demand for Gates's resignation.[6]

The Criminal Prosecution

Four LAPD officers were indicted by a grand jury on a total of eleven felony charges. Sergeant Koon and Officers Lawrence Powell, Timothy Wind, and Theodore Briseno were all accused of assault with a deadly weapon and assault under the color of authority. Koon and Powell were also charged with filing false police reports because in the subsequent reports there had been no mention of the blows to Rodney King's head nor that he was lying on the ground for most of the time he was being beaten.

Lawrence Powell was in the most serious trouble: he was shown on the tape hitting Rodney King more than twenty times. There was also evidence that afterward he had gloated about the incident, evidence that he openly expressed racist opinions about blacks. Sergeant Koon never touched King except to fire the Taser, but as the supervising officer he was responsible for the actions of the officers and had accepted responsibility claiming the incident was a "controlled and managed use of force" within the bounds of LAPD policy and the law. Officer Theodore Briseno was shown on the tape taking only one action that was potentially criminal: at one point, Briseno stomps King in the neck area. Briseno claims he did this in order to protect King from blows coming from Powell's baton. Briseno believed that Powell was out of control and his actions were designed to get King to stay down so that Powell would stop hitting him with the metal baton. Finally, Timothy Wind, a new recruit to the LAPD, was the least criminally liable, shown hitting King with the baton but only on his legs and torso.

The Change of Venue

In retrospect, many observers believe the most crucial battle between the prosecution and the defense occurred long before the spectacle of the trial. The Fifth Amendment gives criminal defendants the right to be "tried by a jury of their peers and in the place where the crime was committed." Defendants, however, have the right to request to move the location if they can demonstrate they will not receive a fair trial in the place where the crime was committed because the jury, selected from that location, will not be fair minded. Defense attorneys claimed that constant airing of the videotapes and the publicity concerning the findings of the Christopher Commission made it impossible for their clients to receive a fair trial in any courtroom in Los Angeles County.

Change of venue requests are rarely honored in the California courts: only two had ever been granted in the previous twenty-five years. The judge refused the defense motion agreeing with the prosecution that the King beating was so renowned that there was nowhere it could be moved to that would be insulated from the worldwide publicity given to the infamous videotape. But the appellate court panel disagreed citing the intense political nature of the case, and in a decision that shocked the prosecution, ordered the change with the precise location for the trial to be selected by the trial judge.

It was the precise location chosen by the trial judge, Stanley Weisberg, that most likely affected the outcome of the trial. For reasons no one quite understands (although many suspect it has to do with proximity to his own home), Weisberg chose a brand new courtroom in the sunny city of Simi Valley located sixty miles northwest of downtown LA, home to thousands of LAPD officers who commute each day from the safe streets of quiet suburbia to work the gritty streets of central Los Angeles. The selection shocked prosecutors and delighted the defense. Weisberg could not have selected a more favorable location for finding jurors likely to be sympathetic to the defense. In 1991, only 1.5 percent of the population of Simi Valley was black.[7]

Of the seven men and five women chosen to serve, all were white except for one Latino and one Asian; all were middle class; all had law enforcement background or connections; they were an average age of fifty-five; and all shared very positive attitudes about the police in general and the LAPD, in particular. The jury was seated on March 2, 1992, just one day before the anniversary of the beating of Rodney King.

The Trial

The most critical piece of evidence in the trial was clearly the videotape. If it weren't for that objective record it is likely no one would ever have known about

what happened to Rodney King. He might have filed a civil suit but he was too drunk to remember and in most of these kinds of cases, pitting the word of LAPD officers against that of complaining citizens, especially those with a criminal record, is a lost cause. The videotape provided an objective and permanent record. Most people believed the trial would be an open and shut case. The images spoke for themselves: this was the use of excessive force by white officers against a defenseless black man cowering and lying on the ground.

But the most powerful piece of evidence for the prosecution turned out to be the most powerful piece of evidence for the defense as well. One of the reasons was the missing thirteen seconds which had been edited out of the original media version aired by KVTA station on its first showing of the evening of March 3. The first three seconds show Rodney King upright and moving toward Lawrence Powell. The defense claimed King was "charging" Powell, which justified self-defensive force on his part. Unlike the media version, which begins with King on the ground, the jury was shown the full 83 seconds of tape to support the defense argument that the officers were responding to the aggressive actions by King himself.

The Prosecution's Case: Out of Control and Excessive

The prosecution's case centered upon urging the jury to "trust your eyes" and believe what you see on the videotape. The lead prosecutor Terry White did not try and deny that King had led the officers on a high-speed chase, or that he was drunk, or that he was, at first, resisting arrest. White hammered home the point that what we see on the videotape is the excessive use of force: Powell, in particular, was "out of control" hitting Rodney King in the face and head, continuing to beat him even after he was on the ground and lying still. White presents eyewitness testimony from Melanie and Tim Singer, the only two law enforcement officers on the scene that night who testified for the prosecution, who saw Powell hit King in the face, in their opinion an unauthorized and excessive use of force. The prosecution presented evidence of the reports filed by Koon and Powell which failed to accurately portray what happened claiming that King was upright and resisting arrest, that they successfully "swarmed" him to cuff him rather than beat him incessantly while he was lying on the ground.

The prosecution's case included testimony from emergency room doctors and nurses about the extent of King's injuries and the taunting attitude displayed by Powell and other officers in the emergency room. In addition, there were computer messages and other LAPD communications from Powell boasting about the incident. Less than twenty minutes after the beating, Powell radioed a partner claiming "I haven't beaten anybody this bad in a long time" and short bursts of laughter erupt on the tape from an excited Powell as he calls for an ambulance to come to the scene.

The prosecution rested its case without calling Rodney King himself to the stand. The decision was hard for the team to make: they knew the jury would want to hear from King himself and that the jury needed to see him as a human being rather than the huge monster portrayed by the police. But they feared King would lose his temper on the stand and appear unsympathetic to a mostly-white middle-class jury. They were also concerned that King's recollection of the facts that night kept shifting and that he was not truthful about what happened. At first King did not recall any racial slurs and then he did; at first he said he was not speeding and then he admitted that he was. Worried that King could do more damage than good, the prosecution announced it would not call Rodney King. Many in the media interpreted this decision as a signal of the confidence by the prosecutorial team in the quality of the evidence presented thus far. Most people outside the courtroom assumed that the videotape was so damning it wasn't necessary to put King on the stand.

The Defense's Case: The "Reasonable Officer" and the Thin Blue Line

There were four separate defense attorneys representing each of the four defendants. The request for separate trials had been denied early in the process. The key defense strategy shared by three of the four defendants was simple: the officers had acted based on the "reasonable" perception that King was a dangerous felony suspect, on the "reasonable" perception that he was on PCP and therefore extremely aggressive and immune to pain, and on the "reasonable" perception that he was potentially dangerous because he was un-searched and might be armed.

According to the defense it was Rodney King who was "in control" of events that night. The officers were professionally and responsibly reacting to his conduct: it was his choice to get drunk, to lead law enforcement on a high-speed chase, to refuse to pull over, to resist the lawful attempt by officers to cuff him and arrest him. If he had simply obeyed commands like Allen and Helms did, there would have been no need for the use of force. The force that was used was reasonable, necessary, and in compliance with their training and LAPD policy.

Koon, as supervising officer, testified that he was completely in control of his officers that night and their conduct was consistent with LAPD policy on how to subdue a combatant and aggressive suspect. Koon openly acknowledged that the incident was brutal and violent but admitted that, at times, police work is brutal and violent. He reiterated his position that his main motive that night was to place King under arrest without the use of lethal violence. He followed his training, by ordering his officers to holster their weapons, to use the "swarm" technique, by using the Taser and by using the metal batons. All of these actions were executed in a "managed and controlled" manner with the goal of subduing King. As soon as he went into "compliance mode," the violence stopped.

Lawrence Powell was the defendant with the most physical brutality and unprofessional conduct to explain and justify. He testified in his own defense about his state of mind that night. Like the other officers, he believed King was on PCP and therefore immune to pain, oblivious to instruction and capable of extreme violence. He had also experienced King's great physical strength and observed his strange behavior. Powell claimed he was "terrified" and "in fear of his life" believing that King might rush him, overpower him, and grab his weapon.

In was with that state of mind that Powell, acting in self-defense, struck King above the neck. According to LAPD policy and the law, the only time that baton blows are permissible to the head is for the purpose of self-defense. Powell's attorney Michael Stone also argued that the injuries on Rodney King's face were caused by a fall to the pavement rather than the blows from Powell's baton. As part of his defense, Stone presented medical testimony that asserted it was possible that the fall caused King's injuries and on cross-examination of the prosecution medical experts, Stone got them to admit that they could not be absolutely certain the injuries were caused by Powell rather than the fall.

Police Solidarity for the Defense

A central part of the defense strategy was to use LAPD experts to analyze the videotape frame by frame and show that the actions of the officers were in accordance with the policies of the LAPD. The jury saw the videotape dissected over and over. The defense put on three expert witnesses all of whom testified that in their expert opinion this was a controlled and managed use of force. The star witness for the defense was LAPD use-of-force expert, Charles Duke, who explained that it was LAPD policy to have officers use batons to subdue a suspect resisting arrest. He confirmed Koon's testimony that Koon had appropriately chosen to use the Taser and ordered his officers to use the batons rather than point a gun at King. The defense claimed that Koon's professional police work most likely saved Rodney King's life (or, possibly, the life of another officer on the scene) who was at extreme risk of being shot and killed if guns had been used as a means of force.

The prosecution too put a use-of-force expert on the stand to argue that this was not a legitimate use of excessive force, but his credentials and testimony were weak compared to the experts who testified for the defense. The prosecution had tremendous difficulty finding a use-of-force expert who would testify against the LAPD officers despite the fact that many experts agreed that the use of force on the videotape was excessive. In the months leading up to the trial, the prosecution searched in vain for someone from the LAPD willing to testify. Even nationally recognized experts from other police departments or in the private sector refused to testify in this case. Three experts finally agreed and all three backed out by the time of the trial. Although each privately believed this was excessive force, none was willing to say so at the most notorious police trial of the century. Even Chief Daryl Gates, fearing personal liability, refused to testify at the trial despite his forthright statements in the media.

The prosecution tried to recruit an LAPD sergeant, Fred Nichols, who was in charge of the physical training and self-defense section of the LAPD Police Academy at the time of the incident.[8] Nichols had testified before the Christopher Commission that he believed the officers had used excessive force. He told this to Internal Affairs officers and to the grand jury who indicted the four officers. But by the time of the trial, Nichols had lost his job at the police academy and had been re-assigned to a desk job. Out on "stress leave" he wanted nothing to do with the King case. The DA's office subpoenaed him but he fought the subpoena claiming he was suffering from a stress-related disability. In the hearing before the judge, the prosecution claimed that Nichols was lying to get out of testifying. The judge ruled that the prosecution could not prove this and excused him. Later Nichols explained that he knew it looked like he was inventing a story to avoid testifying but said, "To be honest with you, I'm not concerned about appearance. I'm concerned about my well-being."

Fourteen officers who were "bystander" officers that night all testified for the defense. The only eyewitnesses to testify for the prosecution were the California Highway Patrol officers Melanie and Tim Singer. Each and every one of the officers who witnessed the scene testified that, in their opinion, the actions of the officers that night were "reasonable" under the circumstances. None of the officers would "break ranks" and condemn the actions of their fellow officers that night.

Benedict Briseno

Only one officer crossed the line of solidarity and many believed he did so only to protect himself from criminal prosecution. Officer Theodore Briseno, a thirteen-year veteran, was charged with excessive use of force for a single stomp to King's neck with his boot. On the night of the incident, Briseno had complained to his partner, Solano, as they left the scene that Powell had been totally "out of control" and that Koon had badly mismanaged the arrest. Solano repeated these statements to the Internal Affairs investigators and the damning statements made by Briseno that night were on record. At the trial, Briseno testified that Powell had struck a blow to King's face which he believed was accidental but once he was down on the ground, Powell continued to swing and beat him with blows directed at his head. He testified that he believed that it was possible that Powell was going to beat King to death and he put his foot on King's left shoulder to try get King to stay down so Powell would stop.

In the eyes of the LAPD, Briseno was a traitor. Indeed, they labeled him Benedict Briseno. Officers who refused to provide any information to prosecutors or the media about the past conduct of the other three officers on trial were eager to come forward with details about Briseno with rumors about domestic problems and physical abuse of his spouse and with details concerning a previous discipline for use of excessive force.

Two LAPD officers testified in the trial that Briseno was lying hoping to absolve himself by putting the blame on Powell and Koon.

Closing Arguments

At closing arguments, Terry White urged the jury to again look at the tape and "believe your eyes." No one is above the law, he said, not even the LAPD. And it is up to you, the jury, to say, enough is enough. The defense pushed another line. They urged the jury to put themselves in the shoes of the police officers out there every day protecting the good citizens of Simi Valley from the dangerous criminals like Rodney King. They are the "thin blue line" that keeps their children and homes safe but they are humans, with fears and hopes. They do a tough job to keep the good citizens safe from the bad element: they deserve our gratitude and respect. They were just doing their job.

The Verdicts

The jury deliberated for seven days for a total of thirty-two hours. In their deliberations, the jury decided quickly to acquit Wind, Briseno, and Koon and focused most of their deliberations on Powell. Ultimately, the minority who held out to convict Powell of assault under the color of authority caved in and voted with the majority. To a shocked and hushed courtroom, the foreman announced the not-guilty verdicts on all counts for all four defendants.

Prosecutor Terry White had told the jury to "trust their eyes" and believe what they saw. But it appears the jury relied on the interpretation of the LAPD experts about what they were seeing on the tape. The jury clearly had been heavily influenced by the unity of opinion by the LAPD witnesses at the incident and use-of-force experts. As one juror commented, "In my opinion, it's not right or morally acceptable to beat any human being, but if LAPD policy has determined its right in certain circumstances, we had to go with that and we did."

The Riots

In the immediate wake of the verdicts, the political climate in LA was tense but calm. No one knew it at the time but it was the kind of calm that precedes a terrible storm.[9] No one expected the storm because no one expected the non-guilty verdict. And no one quite imagined the rage stored up in the derelict and impoverished neighborhoods of South Central LA, least of all the LAPD, whose mission it was to "protect" that city, its people, and its property.[10]

On Wednesday morning, April 29, the day the verdicts were to be announced, the police station at 77th street, right in the heart of the worst poverty zone of South Central LA, received the first of series of anonymous phone calls threatening violence in the streets. Mostly these phone calls were ignored. But when Lt. Moulin, the watch commander for the station, heard the verdicts announced on television at 2 p.m. he began to get worried. A twenty-year veteran of the LAPD, he personally believed the officers were guilty of excessive force. In his view, the criminal justice system had let down the people of LA and now he was scared that they were going to burn the city down. Little did he know how right he was.

By 3:20, five minutes after the verdict was announced, angry crowds had gathered outside the station. Crowds also gathered where King had been beaten and outside the Parker Center, headquarters for the LAPD. At 3:43 the first emergency call to the LAPD came when a man threw a brick at a passing truck and missed. Shortly after 4 p.m. five young black men bought some malt beer from a Korean-owned store and began to hurl the bottles at the glass door shattering it. Another was aimed at the store owner's son hitting him in the head. "This is for Rodney King," one of them yelled. The riot, one of the deadliest in the nation's history, had begun.

By now police cars in all parts of the city became targets for rocks and bottles. By 5:43 p.m. Lt. Moulin ordered all police officers to retreat out of the area back to the station house fearing for his officers' safety who were hugely outnumbered by the crowd. The LAPD headquarters was surrounded by a crowd throwing rocks, bottles, uprooted plants, and chunks of concrete from broken roadways. An unoccupied guard shack and several vehicles were set on fire; City Hall, the *LA Times*, and the Criminal Courts buildings were broken into and attacked by rioters. By 10 p.m. forty-seven major fires blazed in the city. Firefighters were attacked trying to respond while the LAPD was nowhere to be found.

The riot lasted from Wednesday to Monday.[11] On Thursday, the worst day of the rioting, more than twenty people died; another ten were killed on Friday, with nine more over the weekend and six more on Monday. As the world watched in horror, whites, Asians, and

Latinos were dragged out of their vehicles and beaten, attacked and murdered, on the streets, in broad daylight, filmed by television helicopters hovering overhead. Eight hundred and sixty-two structures were destroyed by fire. Almost 2,000 Korean American–owned businesses were looted and destroyed. By Friday, May 1, the governor of California requested federal assistance and 3,500 troops and Marines were sent to LA. By Sunday a combined force of 13,000 including National Guard; military; and federal, state, and local agencies was mobilized to bring order to the city.

The Federal Trial

After the acquittals in the state prosecution of the defendants, it was the federal government's turn to argue that what had happened to Rodney King was not within the bounds of the law. The federal trial began on February 25, 1993, only ten months after the riots. In *U.S. v. Stacey C. Koon* the four officers were accused of the federal crime of violating the civil rights of Rodney King.

In this trial, the prosecution learned from the mistakes of Terry White and his team.[12] The venue remained in downtown Los Angeles, a location as unfavorable to the defense as the Simi Valley had been for the prosecution. There were two black jurors. The prosecution put King on the stand so the jury could see him as a human being rather than a PCP-crazed monster. And this time, the federal government had the benefit of a LAPD use-of-force expert who testified that the actions of Officer Powell were in violation of the LAPD policy.

The verdicts were announced at 7 a.m. on Saturday April 17, just two weeks short of the anniversary of the other announcement which had set LA on ablaze. When the convictions of Koon and Powell were announced, celebration and joy erupted in the streets of South Central LA.

And Justice for None

Prosecutors requested the maximum sentence for Koon of nine to ten years and the maximum for Powell of seven to nine years. The defense too submitted a sentencing recommendation requesting probation or prison terms of less than one year for each of the defendants. They also asked that no fines be required since both men had lost their jobs and were financially devastated by the costs of their legal defense. Judge

Davies wrote a 54-page memo to explain his reasons for reducing the sentence of both defendants to only thirty months in prison. He also refused to require fines stating that both officers could hardly afford to pay and that both had suffered the loss of their livelihoods and reputations as a result of this conviction.

The reaction to the sentences was divided along racial lines: among African Americans the sentence was another "travesty of justice" and yet another example of the "just us" system of punishment which treats whites with leniency when their victims are black. Among LAPD police officers and their supporters, the imposition of prison time was an outrage: from the point of view of the police, Koon and Powell were trying to do their job as best they could. The last thing they deserve is to be put in prison with the very criminals they are sworn to fight every day.

A Persistent Divide?

The Los Angeles riot of 1992 after the RK verdict was not the first time an American city erupted in violence in response to perceived racial injustice at the hands of law enforcement. Nor was it the last. In 2015, the death of Michael Brown, an unarmed eighteen-year-old boy at the hands of the police, led to a fresh round of citizen protest under the banner of the Black Lives Matter campaign. Like the LA protests, widespread police brutality proves to be the match that lights the fire. In the twenty-first century, the Black Lives Matter movement continues the protests of the LA riots in 1992; the Watts riot of 1962; and many others that preceded it as minority citizens demand equal and fair treatment by the criminal justice system especially by the police. Again a racial divide separates views of white citizens who tend to side with police from the views of black citizens who, regardless of class and social background, have a similar experience of police hostility and disrespectful treatment by law enforcement.

THINKING CRITICALLY ABOUT THIS CASE

1. In the immediate aftermath of the beating, the head of the LAPD police union said, "I don't think Rodney King was beaten because of his race. But I also don't think what happened to King would have happened to a white man." Do you agree with this statement? Why or why not?

2. Should the videotape have been aired on the media? Why or why not? What is the role of the media in monitoring the actions of law enforcement?

3. Should the officers have been tried in South Central LA or in Simi Valley or in some other location? In a case such as this, is it possible to obtain a fair jury? Why or why not?

4. What should Daryl Gates have done to respond to the King beating when the videotape was first aired on national television? What steps should he have taken in response to the videotape?

5. The riots were sparked by the verdict in the first King trial. What other factors accounted for the violence of those four days? What steps can the LAPD take to ensure riots such as these won't happen in the future? What steps can the city take to ensure riots such as these won't happen in the future?

6. The LAPD officers felt they had been unfairly punished for trying to "do their job." They lost their livelihoods, reputation, and life savings in the subsequent trials and publicity. Having to also serve jail time seemed unjust in the eyes of law enforcement personnel of the LAPD. On the other hand, minority citizens of South Central LA felt the officers were given exceptionally lenient sentences. Thirty months in prison is well below the recommended sentence for their crime. What do you think? What would have been a just punishment for Koon and Powell?

REFERENCES

Case adapted from:

Nancy Abelmann and John Lie, *Blue Dreams: Korean Americans and the Los Angeles Riots* (Cambridge, MA: Harvard University Press, 1995).

Lou Cannon, *Official Negligence: How Rodney King and the Riots Changed Los Angeles and the LAPD* (New York: Random House, 1997).

Warren Christopher et al., *Report of the Independent Commission on the Los Angeles Police Department,* July 9, 1991.

Robert Deitz, *Willful Injustice: A Post-O. J. Look at Rodney King, American Justice and Trial by Race* (Washington, DC: Regnery, 1996).

Jerry Gray, "In Police Brutality Case, One Videotape but Two Ways to View It," *The New York Times,* December 13, 1991.

Gibbs Jewell Taylor, *Race and Justice: Rodney King and O. J. Simpson in a House Divided,* (Jossey-Bass, 1996).

"Los Angeles Chief Assailed by Mayor," *The New York Times,* April 3, 1991.

"Los Angeles Policemen Acquitted in Taped Beating: Storm of Anger Erupts," *The New York Times,* April 30, 1992.

D. M. Osborne, "A Defense Turned Inside Out," *American Lawyer Media,* April 20, 1993.

Carl E. Pope and Lee E. Ross, "Race, Crime and Justice: The Aftermath of Rodney King," *The Criminologist 17* (1992).

Riots in LA: The Blue Line Surprised, Police React Slowly as Violence Spreads," *The New York Times,* May 1, 1992.

William Robert Gooding, ed., *Reading Rodney King: Reading Urban Uprising* (New York: Routledge, 1993).

Mike Sager, "Damn! They Gonna Lynch Us," *Gentlemen's Quarterly,* October 1991.

"Simi Valley Journal: Town Too Feels Eyes of Nation for Trial," *The New York Times,* February 22, 1992.

"Violence and Racism are Routine in Los Angeles Police, Study Says," *The New York Times,* July 10, 1991.

This chapter examines the role and mission of public police within our society. Why was urban policing first developed? What is the relationship of police to politics and to the community? Who do police serve and to whom are they accountable? This chapter also examines the institutional and organizational features of policing which promote and shape the encounters between police and the citizens, especially minority citizens, police are hired to "protect and serve." Stacey Koon testified that sometimes "police work is brutal and violent."[13] Like the military, the police are an institution which authorizes the use of force by their agents in the pursuit of legitimate organizational goals. Police are society's agents of coercion; therefore, the use of force is an inevitable part of the police function. Yet, as we pointed out in chapter 7, that force is only legitimate when it operates within the constraints of the law. When police systematically step outside those boundaries and engage in unfair and illegal violence, citizens protest and rebel. In this chapter we ask, why do police engage in extra-legal violence? And how do we effectively police the police themselves?

We close the chapter by examining current trends in policing, especially the community policing movement. For some observers, community policing is a passing fad that ends when the federal dollars to support it are used up. For others, community policing represents a progressive philosophy and the most creative force for change within contemporary policing.[14] It is both a return to the past and a step forward into the future. We consider the strengths and weaknesses of community policing and evaluate its value in providing a model for policing a diverse society in the future.

ORIGINS OF POLICING

Before the nineteenth century, there was no police force in the modern sense.[15] Traditional village communities, in England and in colonial America, relied upon ordinary citizens to assist to maintain order and peace in the community. In England, a community system known as the **frankpledge** required that every male above the age of twelve join the **tything**, a group of ten able-bodied men sworn to deliver to court any neighbor who committed a crime. Ten tythings were under the supervision of a constable appointed by the local nobleman. A hundred of these were grouped into shires under the leadership of a "shire reeve" or sheriff who was appointed by the local land-owner representing the king.

Over time this system evolved into a structure consisting of a sheriff, constable, and watchman. The sheriff's duties included collecting taxes, apprehending criminals, serving subpoenas, and appearing in court. The sheriff was paid a fee for each task. Both the constable and the watch were unpaid positions served on a rotating basis by able-bodied male citizens. The main purpose of these jobs was to maintain order and protect the peace of the community. Their tasks included reporting fires, arresting or detaining suspicious persons, walking rounds at night, and raising the **hue and cry** if there was a serious threat to the community.

The investigation of crime was largely up to the victim or to a private system of the **thief-takers** who offered these services for a fee.[16] As a form of bounty hunting, the thief-taker would recover stolen property or find the culprit and deliver him or her to a magistrate for a price. In the 1700s, one of England's most

FRANKPLEDGE
a system of law enforcement in medieval societies where every male member of the community over the age of 12 was bound by a pledge to keep peace and assist in delivering offenders to court.

TYTHING
In Anglo-Saxon law, an association of ten families bound together by a frankpledge.

HUE AND CRY
an old English call for assistance in the pursuit of felons.

THIEF-TAKERS
eighteenth-century mercenaries who offered to pursue felons for a fee.

notorious criminals ran a "thief-taking" operation stealing from victims and then taking a fee to "return" their property to them!

Sir Robert Peel and London "Bobbies"[17]

By the nineteenth century, this system of policing had collapsed. The rise of capitalism and the impact of the Industrial Revolution dramatically altered economic and social conditions and relationships and the old system of policing proved inadequate to deal with the social chaos brought on by rapid social change.[18] Between 1750 and 1820, the population of London doubled in size. Along with this growth came enormous civil disorder in the streets as newly arriving migrants from the countryside flooded the cities in search of work living

The London Bobbies were the first modern police force in the world created to deter crime through preventative patrol and keep citizens safe on the streets of the city.

in the cramped squalor of the city's poor districts. Food riots, wage protests, street fighting, and crime became intolerable for the city's wealthier residents. The city streets and highways became increasingly unsafe from robbers, muggers, pickpockets, thieves, and burglars.

Sir Robert Peel, the then home secretary of Britain, developed the idea of a modern police force that would patrol the streets to prevent crime and reduce public disorder in the street. Convincing Parliament that he was not proposing the creation of a new kind of army which would give the government power over its own people proved to be a difficult task. Parliament opposed Peel's proposal for decades. In the end, however, crime and disorder forced residents of the city of London to try Peel's proposal. In 1829, the London Metropolitan Police Act created the world's first full-time uniformed police force.

The primary purpose of the police force was to be a preventative presence on the city streets. To have a deterrent effect, policemen were supposed to be visible and omnipresent. Peel chose an extremely high hat for police and purposefully selected men to serve who were exceptionally tall. The idea of **preventative patrol** was that through continuous patrolling of a fixed beat the "**Bobbies**" would ensure that city streets would again be safe for law-abiding citizens to walk about without fear of being mugged or assaulted.

Peel was sensitive to the concern that police might resemble an army with its power targeted at citizens themselves. Although Peel chose to design his new organization with a quasi-military style with rank designations and hierarchical

BOBBIES
the nickname for the first formal municipal police unit in London founded by Sir Robert Peel.

PREVENTATIVE PATROL
the use of continuous and visible walking of public streets by police in order to deter crime.

Police routinely perform an array of service functions for the community, including emergency medical assistance.

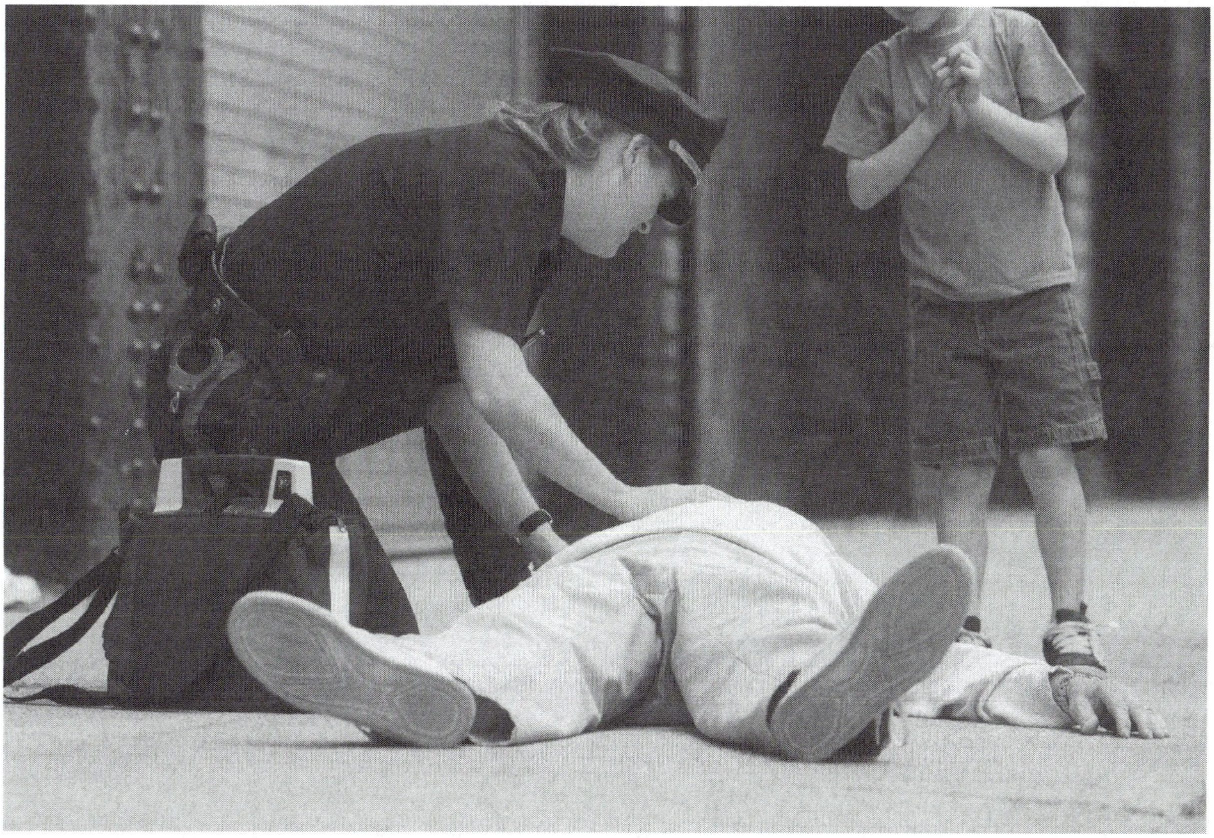

forms of command and control, he was careful to distinguish his "Bobbies" from soldiers in the king's army. He clothed the men in blue instead of the military red; he did not allow them to carry guns and insisted that they behave in a polite and restrained manner. Peel understood that the legitimacy of the newly created institution of public law enforcement depended upon the principle that police always acted within the bounds of the law. To establish their authority, police would need to behave in a lawful manner reassuring the citizenry that they were there to protect them from crime, not to control or dominate them.

Peel put forth his philosophy of policing in nine core principles that remain profoundly relevant to the challenges of modern policing.[19] Foremost among these principles is the emphasis on prevention of crime and disorder rather than use of force and punishment after crime has occurred. The second key idea is the importance of the respectful treatment of the public at all times. Police, in Peel's view, depended on the approval and cooperation of the public and the way to secure that was to demonstrate "absolutely impartial service to the law." Nor should police usurp the role of the judiciary in adjudicating guilt or inflicting punishment. Physical force was to be used only as a last resort and with the minimum level required. To Peel, the ultimate measure of effective policing was the prevention of crime, not the "visible evidence of police action." Above all, the creation of a peaceful city was the shared duty and responsibility of police and citizens alike.

Early American Police

Cities of the United States were experiencing the same problems of rapid growth, rampant street crime, and civil disorder as London.[20] The population of New York City, for example, mushroomed from 33,000 in 1790 to 150,000 in 1830. Much of the disorder arose from conflicts between rival ethnic groups as new arrivals came in search of employment and clashed with already established groups. Conflict and violence also erupted in U.S. cities, especially in the North, along racial lines.

Like the British, Americans did not like the idea of an armed force patrolling the streets with the power to use force against citizens. It brought to mind the hated British army. Americans were extremely suspicious of giving the government power over its citizens. Many were afraid a police force would act at the command of rival politicians and most citizens disliked paying taxes to fund their salaries.

But growing disorder in the streets pressed the need for some kind of force to maintain order. The first police force of six officers emerged with the establishment of a day watch in Boston in 1838. By the start of the Civil War in 1861, Boston, New York, Baltimore, Philadelphia, New Orleans, and Chicago consolidated a day watch and night watch under a single police chief modeled after Metropolitan Police in London.[21]

Patronage and Corruption

Just as people feared, police of the nineteenth century were very much under the control of local politicians.[22] Police were a part of the political machinery with police officers selected on the basis of their loyalty to the ward boss. Political parties controlled the mayor's office which in turn controlled access to jobs in the city services such as the fire department, schools, courts, and police. These well-paid jobs were handed out as rewards for loyalty to party activists. In some cities, a job as a police officer or a promotion within the force could be bought for a fee paid to the political party in office. On election day, the entire police force would be dismissed and replaced with new officers loyal to the party in power.

The function of the nineteenth-century police department was quite broad and focused on being an all-purpose service agency for the city.[23] Police ran ambulances, handled licensing of businesses, provided services for the poor, took in lost children and the homeless. Patrol was the heart of police work but there was little professionalism or supervision of the patrol officer on the streets. This set the stage for corruption as police on the street profited from the selective enforcement of laws against gambling, saloons, prostitution, illegal prize fighting, and other activities. Police ran protection rackets demanding fees from businesses; police also looked the other way for pickpockets and thieves in exchange for a share in the proceeds.

Citizens were highly ambivalent about the police. They were viewed as political hacks rather than public servants and people who were arrested often fought back. Police were a part of the ethnic conflicts, not above them. Whichever ethnic group had control of the political power within the city had control of the police. Clashes between the police and groups of citizens led the police adopting firearms.

TWENTIETH-CENTURY POLICING IN THE UNITED STATES

By the end of the nineteenth century, there was a movement to create a truly professional police force independent of local political control.[24] The Progressive movement made up of middle-class reformers sought to take the corruption out of city government. Reformers believed that police should be selected on the basis of ability and receive formal training. They argued that the broad array of services performed by the police should be handled by other agencies and police should deal with crime alone.

The Progressives had little success in actually transforming police. Systemic corruption particularly in the big cities of the industrial northeast and mid-west continued to be bastions of **patronage** and profit-driven corruption. In 1929, President Herbert Hoover appointed the first national commission to report on the state of the American criminal justice system. Headed by the former attorney general George Wickersham, the National Commission on Law Observance and Enforcement, popularly known as the **Wickersham Commission**, published fourteen volumes on the criminal justice system in 1931.[25] The eleventh volume, entitled "Lawlessness in Law Enforcement" garnered most of the attention from the public with its systematic and thorough documentation of police brutality and abuses of authority across the country. Near the end of Prohibition, in 1931, the level of corruption was so great in Chicago that a blue ribbon commission suggested that the only way to clean up the force was to fire all 4,000 officers and start from scratch.[26]

George Kelling and Mark Moore characterize the early period of policing until about 1930 as the political era of policing in which patronage and political considerations dominated big city police organizations. The police performed a wide range of services for the local community but their primary role was to serve the political interests of the local bosses. Systemic corruption and brutality flourished largely unchecked within a highly decentralized police structure.

PATRONAGE
a form of corruption in which the political party in power awards jobs and promotion in policing is given out as return for loyalty and favors to politicians.

WICKERSHAM COMMISSION
a panel of national experts convened in 1929 to conduct the first comprehensive national report on the criminal justice system. Evidence of systematic corruption and abuses within policing in the Wickersham Report generated public support for reform.

Professionalism: A Master Trend

From 1910 to 1960, another more successful movement to adopt a professional model for police was led by a series of influential police chiefs such as Richard Sylvester from Washington, D.C., O.W. Wilson in Wichita, Kansas, and August Vollmer of the Los Angeles Police Department. The central goal of **professionalism** was to separate policing from politics.

August Vollmer[27] was chief of the Berkeley police force, in Berkeley, California. Vollmer believed police officers should be experts in their field; that police departments should be independent of political influences and should use technology, science, and efficient administrative practices in their work.[28] Vollmer was the first police chief to recruit college students and create college-level police education.

Impact of Technology

By the 1960s, the patrol car, two-way radio, and telephone had profoundly altered urban policing and relationships with the community.[29] Before the automobile, most city police departments assigned officers to regularly walk specific streets on the same beat to ensure familiarity with the residents. The use of automobiles for preventative patrol, however, removed officer's direct contact with citizens and placed officers behind the glass of a rolling vehicle. Driving slowly down the street distanced officers from the people on the streets. Isolated in their cars with the windows rolled up, police no longer developed face-to-face relationships with the residents and business owners.

The two-way radio, telephone, and institutionalization of the rapid response 911 system put the patrol car at the beck and call of citizens who demanded an urgent response from the police. With mobile command and control units, supervisors could more carefully monitor the movements of the officers via the two-way radio and mobilize them to different locations of the city. Success became measured by the speed of the arriving patrol car rather than the personal contacts made by the cop on the street corner.

In the twenty-first century, technological innovation continues to impact police practice and relationships with citizens. The use of crime mapping enables police to more effectively analyze geographical and spatial crime data and effectively deploy resources where crime is more likely to occur. The use of global positioning system (GPS) also opens new possibilities for surveillance, intelligence, and tracking of suspects.

The spread of cell phones with built-in cameras has also altered the citizen-police relationship by giving citizens the capacity to record police-citizen encounters with far more accuracy and sophistication than the crude videotape made by George Holliday in 1992. Bystanders, suspects, and witnesses are now able to record an incident and post it directly on social media for dissemination to the public. These postings go viral and have been a major incitement for protests against police brutality. Many police departments now recognize the need to maintain an accurate recording of police-citizen encounters as a way to protect both the public and the officers. This is possible through body camera technology worn by officers to provide a continuous visual and auditory recording of all interactions with the public. In the wake of the high-profile incidents recorded by citizens' cell phones, many urban police departments are exploring the use of

PROFESSIONALISM
the master trend in twentieth-century policing which sought to separate policing from politics through civil service examination, education, training, and bureaucratization.

this technology and many citizen groups are including this in the demand for greater police accountability.

The Militarization of Policing

The 1960s were an era of huge social unrest and conflict. Crime rose dramatically during these two decades: the violent and property crime index climbed steadily during these years to peak in 1979. Urban unrest also erupted in cities across the nation often sparked by incidents of police brutality. In August 1965, a five-day riot in Watts, Los Angeles, led to the deaths of thirty-four people, with a thousand more injured; in 1966 Detroit, a riot ended with forty-three deaths; and following Martin Luther King's assassination in 1968, rioting broke out in over 120 cities.

In 1965 President Johnson created the President's Commission on Law Enforcement and Administration of Justice which appointed several task forces to study crime and the administration of justice and to understand the riots which erupted in so many of the inner cities between 1964 and 1968.[30] These task forces identified the underlying causes of the riots to be the rampant racism, inequality, poverty, and discrimination within the nation's black communities. Unemployment, discrimination in jobs and housing, inadequate social services, and unequal justice were the primary factors to blame for both rising crime and social unrest.

While recognizing the need to address the "root causes" of crime and social unrest, the Commission also promoted the concept of waging a federally funded "war on crime" using technology paid for by federal dollars. The Omnibus Crime Control and Safe Streets Act of 1968[31] created the Law Enforcement Assistance Administration (LEAA), a federal bureaucracy to develop new devices, techniques, and approaches in law enforcement and provide funds and assistance to states for adopting these technologies and strategies. The LEAA became the agency within the federal government to promote the new war on crime.[32] LEAA money supplied many police departments with the basic physical infrastructure of car radios, high-tech dispatch systems, and mobile command and control centers. LEAA grants also funded more sophisticated **para-militarization** of policing in specialized SWAT (Special Weapons and Tactics) units, technologically advanced helicopters, infra-red technology, and computer communications technology.[33] To black inner city residents of neighborhoods with LA, Detroit, New York, Boston, Chicago and other major cities, the patrol cars moving slowly around their city streets, resembled the rolling fortresses of an occupying army generating tremendous conflict between the minority community and the police.

The LEAA was officially defunded in 1982 but the federal programs it spawned include the National Institute of Justice, the National Institute of Corrections, the Bureau of Justice Statistics, and the Office of Juvenile Justice Delinquency Prevention, all of which continue to shape policing and criminal justice through federal funding.

George L. Kelling and Mark H. Moore refer to the era of American policing between 1930 and 1980 as the Reform Era when the strategic goals of crime control through rapid response, patrol, and centralized command and control systems were dominant strategies in major police departments.[34] Higher levels of professionalization and independence from political control were achieved through formalization and bureaucratization. The main drawback of these reforms was pervasive alienation between the police and the community, particularly, among those living in urban minority neighborhoods.

PARA-MILITARIZATION
the use of military equipment, tactics, and weapons in policing.

Two key developments have led to further increases in the militarization of policing during the 1990s and into the first decades of the twenty-first century. The first is the war on drugs, a national policy that has involved a major transfer of military technology, expertise, and strategy through federal programs that have armed and trained local police departments through coordinated efforts of the war on drugs. During the 1990s SWAT teams became commonplace in police departments and have been heavily utilized in drug and weapon enforcement. Although originally created for extraordinary events such as hostage situations, military-style SWAT raids have been primarily used to execute search warrants in homes for drugs mainly within poor communities of color.[35]

The war on terror, which is the focus of chapter 9, is the second development that has shifted policing away from a community-based model toward increasing militarization. Today the DHS is the major federal agency providing funding for military-grade technology and technical assistance to local law enforcement.

Diversity in Policing

Until the 1970s, most American police forces were almost entirely all male and all white even in communities such as Los Angeles and New York with large Hispanic or African American populations. Title VII of the federal 1964 Civil Rights Act prohibits discrimination on the basis of race, creed, color, sex, or national origin with regard to compensation, terms and conditions, or privileges of employment. In 1972, Title VII was amended to apply to state and local government employees including police officers motivating many minorities and women to attempt to enter into occupations previously closed to them.

Minorities and women who did join the police force faced substantial discrimination and blocked opportunities for advancement. Tom Bradley, the first black mayor of the city of LA, began his career as a LAPD officer in 1940.[36] At that time, black patrol officers were required to have black partners: whites refused to work with blacks. Black officers were forced to serve in a segregated unit known as the Black Watch. Even though Vollmer and Parker had instituted civil service examinations for promotion, black officers still experienced discrimination. Even when they did well on the written portion of the exam, they were invariably rated low on the oral interviews or by their white supervisors. With little hope for promotion within the racist institution, many ambitious black police officers like Mayor Bradley left policing to seek other opportunities as lawyers, judges, or politicians.

In the twenty years from 1972 to 1992, black representation in policing had come to almost equal the percentage of African Americans within the U.S. population as a whole. More recently there is concern that minorities in general are underrepresented in police departments. When compared with census data, blacks are underrepresented in their local police departments by 6.4 percent, while Hispanics are underrepresented by 10.8 percent.[37]

These percentages do not tell the full story. African Americans remain significantly underrepresented in the upper ranks of police administrations despite some notable achievements within individual police departments such as the appointment of Willie Brown in the wake of the Rodney King incident. And further, the proportion of minority police is much higher in large cities than it is in small city police departments. In the city of Ferguson, Missouri, for example, two-thirds of the residents are black but there are only three black officers on a force of fifty-one officers.[38] This racial mismatch between the racial composition of the community and the composition of the police force is a common pattern in small police departments across the nation and is widely seen as a factor which contributes to distrust of the police by minority citizens.

The situation for women within policing is less encouraging than it is for male racial and ethnic minorities.[39] In 1910, Alice Stebbins Wells became the first female police officer in the LAPD. Female officers, being responsible only for women and children, were often viewed as "mothers with badges." In the 1970s, women accounted for about 2 percent of all sworn officers with most of the women in clerical positions. By 1990, the Police Foundation found that women made up 10.1 percent of the total number of officers in departments functioning under court orders to increase their proportion of women officers.[40] In 2009, 11.7 percent of sworn officers were women although women were 61 percent of the civilian workforce within law enforcement.[41] By 2013, women still constitute only about 13 percent of the force in larger big city police departments. The main obstacle for women in policing comes from the negative attitude of male police officers and the stress of sexual harassment and discrimination on the job.

UNDERSTANDING POLICE MISCONDUCT

The pattern of conduct, which leads to brutal and violent treatment of citizens even by the few, permeates the entire organization of American policing itself, not

Aggressive police behavior.

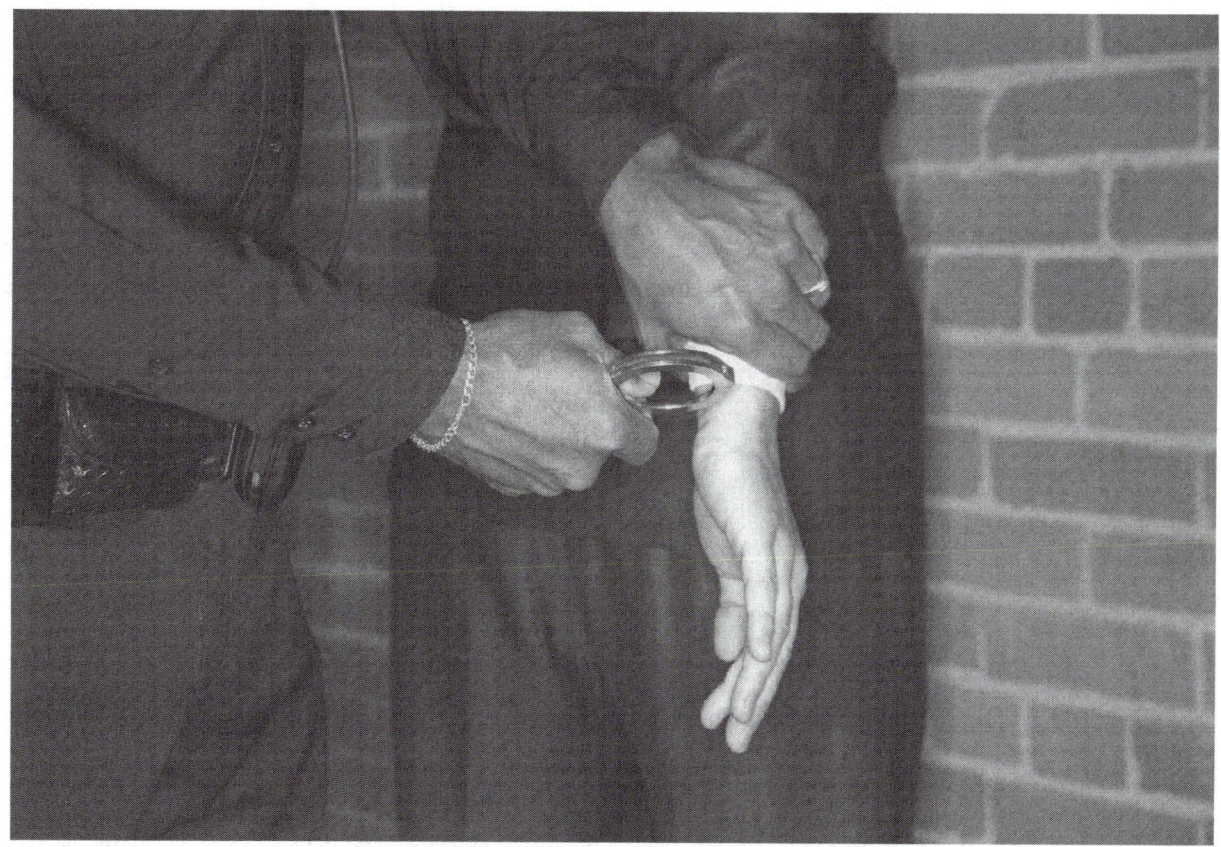

just one particular department or one isolated group of individuals. The sociological causes of this behavior are found in the characteristics of police work, the organization of policing, and the mission police define for them rather than in any of the individual personality characteristics of police officers themselves.

Police brutality is one form of police misconduct, which also includes corruption, crime, and other abuses of power.[42] **Corruption** in the profession of policing has been an endemic problem since the start of modern policing in the nineteenth century.[43] The temptation toward illegal conduct ranges from accepting free doughnuts and coffee from the local shopkeeper to the systemic operation of organized crime rings under the shield of the police badge. Beginning in the 1930s with the Wickersham Commission[44] investigating the LAPD, periodic investigations reveal pervasive and wide-ranging illegal conduct among police officers. In 1993 the Mollen Commission unearthed evidence of extensive drug dealing among the NYPD. In 2011, the Justice Department investigation into the New Orleans Police Department uncovered corruption and dysfunction in nearly every facet of the department, including use of excessive force, discrimination against minority citizens, and a failure to investigate many serious crimes especially sexual assault.[45] This misconduct is routinely protected by the infamous code of silence among all police.

The lowest level of corruption involves the acceptance of small favors such as free meals or coffee from local establishments. This is often related to corrupt patterns of selective law enforcement in which the wrongdoings are routinely overlooked or ignored. Police officers are often in a position to engage in opportunistic theft: in the course of a search they may pick up and pocket some of the stolen jewelry or money; or they may confiscate and keep cash or drugs they find.

On a wider scale, police have operated protection rackets and organized systems of bribe taking to withhold law enforcement or to use it selectively at the request of a paying customer. The Knapp Commission investigating the NYPD in 1973 distinguished between **grass eaters**, or police who occasionally accepted bribes, and **meat eaters**, or police who were systematically engaged in bribery and intimation for financial gain.[46] The association with the criminal underworld creates an enormous opportunity for officers to take part in the illegal profit-making. This is particularly true in the enforcement of laws against alcohol, drugs, and other kinds of vice. The huge flow of cash involved in this business and the multitude of opportunities to take advantage of the trade and cash in on the profits result in the widespread participation of officers in illegal businesses.

Finally, in addition to these forms of crime for profit are the abuses of police power through the systematic denial of due process, harassment, perjury in court, and tampering with evidence. Included with abuses of power are also abuses of the use of force: the illegal use of police violence, which includes illegal violence toward suspects and citizens, torture, and unjustifiable homicides. Often referred to as "curbside" justice, police use illegal violence as a form of social control teaching those they think deserve it a "lesson" through the abuse of power.

Regulating the Use of Force

Police training involves instruction in decision-making around the use of appropriate levels of coercion. These are, of course, merely guidelines. The ultimate decision lies in the police officer's own "intuitive grasp of situational exigencies."[47] In other words, the officer must read the dynamics of a rapidly changing and unpredictable set of circumstances and make a split second decision about the

POLICE BRUTALITY
the unlawful use of physical force by officers in the performance of their duties.

POLICE CORRUPTION
misconduct by police officers through illegal activities for economic gain including the acceptance of payment for services, non-enforcement of the law in exchange for payment, and active participation in criminal activities.

GRASS EATERS
police officers who accept payoffs for rendering police services or who look the other way when police action is called in exchange for goods and services.

MEAT EATERS
police officers who actively and systematically solicit bribes or conspire with criminals in criminal activity.

appropriate conduct.[48] Nevertheless, police departments generate policies and training to officers in the levels of force appropriate to different types of situations.[49] The first "show of force" in an encounter between the police and citizens is the mere presence of the police officer on the street. By possessing the right to use force, police *threaten* that use of force by their very presence. Beyond mere presence is the use of verbal commands by police officers to order a citizen to slow down, move along, or in some way change their conduct. Police officers may approach a citizen or use their siren to pull them over, politely request to see their driver's license, or respectfully ask them questions about their purpose in the neighborhood. While the request may be in a polite tone, the underlying reality is that the exchange is a command, which the citizen is not free to refuse. Police officers may use a command tone of voice and more overtly order a citizen to show their license or raise their arms.

Beyond verbal commands, the first level of physical force is a series of techniques called firm grips. Officers are trained in the use of various forms of body holds such as gripping the elbow of the suspect or bending their head as they are placed in the patrol car under arrest. These firm grips are techniques for controlling the body of the subject without causing pain or injury. At a higher level are various techniques for inflicting pain in order to compel a citizen to physically comply with an officer's order. These "come along" or "pain compliance" holds such as hammerlocks, wristlocks, and finger grips are means for subduing a suspect who is resisting arrest. "Swarming" a suspect falls within this level of force.

In the LAPD, one of the departmentally approved upper body holds taught to officers was the carotid chokehold.[50] The carotid chokehold involves the cutting off of the flow of blood to the brain for the purpose of inducing unconsciousness. This technique had been used by the LAPD in minor traffic incidents or on unruly teenagers as a relatively low-level use of force. Just prior to the Rodney King incident, the carotid chokehold had been upgraded from a form of pain compliance to a form of deadly force in response to a series of deaths which resulted from the application of this technique.

In the influential expert testimony offered by Charles Duke, the LAPD use-of-force expert, Duke stated that he believed that the recent ban on this technique as a means to control a suspect resisting arrest had created a more dangerous situation by forcing the use of far more aggressive levels of force.[51] Without the choice to use this method, officers were forced to rely upon the next level of force, so-called impact techniques that in the opinion of the use-of-force expert inflicted far greater and more lasting injuries on the suspect.

Impact techniques include the use of kicks, batons, chemical sprays, or stunning electronic weapons. The point of these techniques is to subdue a combative suspect without resorting to life-threatening means such as guns. This was the key defense offered by Stacey Koon and supported by the LAPD defense experts: the use of the batons and stun gun were departmentally approved uses of force at a level below the use of **lethal force**. Koon testified that he himself would have administered the carotid chokehold and was prepared to do so if King had not finally submitted to the blows of the baton. As a form of lethal force, Koon was following appropriate procedure by relying first on the use of impact techniques such as the baton and the Taser before moving to a higher level.

In the testimony in the trial, Duke analyzed the videotape frame by frame to show that each action by the officers was in response to a continued aggressive response on the part of Rodney King. Melanie Singer, Koon, Powell, and others issued verbal commands ordering King to lie down on the ground. Ignoring

IMPACT TECHNIQUES techniques for use of coercive force designed to subdue a combative suspect without resorting to lethal force.

LETHAL FORCE a force likely to cause death or great bodily harm; also known as deadly force.

their order, they then used baton swings and the Tasar to force King to comply. Duke testified that as long as Rodney resisted being handcuffed, the officers were required to use their batons in appropriate ways to inflict pain and injury to compel King to comply.

When Is Lethal Force Justified?

Until about 1960, most American states relied upon the common law doctrine otherwise known as the **fleeing felon doctrine**: if a person suspected of committing a felony fled, then an officer was permitted to use deadly force to stop them. The fleeing felon doctrine originated in English common law when all felony offenses were punishable by death. The use of lethal force for apprehending misdemeanor suspects was not permissible under common law. This rule was adopted in the United States even though few felonies within the American legal code are capital crimes and even though the distinction between the severity of felonies and misdemeanor offenses has hugely diminished. By the 1960s, many states and mainly big city police departments had adopted statues and regulations which permitted officers to use lethal force only if the suspect is armed or dangerous.

In 1985, the fleeing felon doctrine was declared unconstitutional in the Supreme Court case of *Tennessee v. Garner*.[52] In this case, a fifteen-year-old unarmed boy was chased by officers as he ran from a house. As he escaped by climbing over a chain link fence, the pursing officer shot him in the back. The Supreme Court ruled that the use of deadly force against a fleeing felon is justified only when it is necessary to prevent the escape of a suspect for whom there is probable cause to believe he or she poses a significant physical threat to the officer or to others.

Police jurisdictions have varying rules regarding the appropriate use of lethal force to apprehend a suspect. The use of deadly force by police officers is authorized in all jurisdictions for the purposes of self-defense. If police perceive themselves to be in lethal danger they are not required to meet the force with equal force but are permitted to use whatever level of force necessary to protect their own lives.

While Koon was attempting to make use of lethal force as a last resort, Lawrence Powell was shown on the tape striking King in the face and head. The use of the baton above the neck is authorized by LAPD regulations only under those circumstances that justify the use of lethal force. Powell testified at the trial that he was in "fear of his life" believing that King was sufficiently strong to take his weapon from him and use it against him. Powell testified that he was acting in self-defense when he struck King in the face as he charged him.

This means that the mindset of police during the encounter with a citizen is the most important legal factor for a jury to consider when deciding if lethal force is justifiable. As we saw with the Rodney King trial, jurors are instructed not to consider if a "reasonable person" might be in fear of their life but rather if a "reasonable police officer" might conclude it is necessary to use force to protect their own lives. In a trial, this means that jurors are likely to give more weight to the opinion of police experts who testify as to what is reasonable for a police officer to believe to be true. When police testify that they were in fear for their lives, juries tend to accept this assertion.

FLEEING FELON DOCTRINE
a now-defunct law enforcement rule which permitted officers to shoot a suspected felon attempting to flee from a lawful arrest.

When Citizens Are Killed by Police

In 2014, the FBI reported that 444 civilians were killed by a police officer in the line of duty: all but one through use of a firearm. This is an increase from

378 justifiable homicides committed by law enforcement in 2008.[53] However, in 2015, the *Washington Post* newspaper set out to record every instance in which a citizen died at the hands of the police within a single year using public records to log every on-duty fatal shooting by the police including the race of the victim. The results were more than double the number recorded in the official data by the FBI. As of December 24, 2015, with six days left in the year, 965 citizens had been shot and killed by law enforcement. This is nearly twice as many as the official records report. The director of the FBI admitted the flaw in the official data explaining that reporting to the FBI is voluntary and less than half of the nation's 18,000 police departments report incidents to the FBI resulting in a serious undercount in official data.[54]

One burning question is whether or not minority suspects are subjected more to the use of lethal force by police than non-minority suspects. The current Black Lives Matter campaign is the most recent expression of the widespread perception that law enforcement has a double standard when it comes to respect for the lives of white and black citizens. Research evidence shows that minority citizens are justified in their concern. Milton et al. found that 70 percent of the suspects shot by the police in seven major cities were black even though blacks make up only 39 percent of the population.[55] In some jurisdictions, black suspects were between five and thirteen times more likely than white suspects to be killed by the police.[56] In 2015, one study found that the probability of getting shot by the police when a suspect is unarmed is 3.49 times higher for blacks than for whites.[57] In Memphis, Tennessee, where Edward Garner was shot under the fleeing felon rule, research found that police shot and killed thirteen unarmed African American suspects as compared to one white suspect who was unarmed and not assaultive.[58] Researchers have posed the question of whether this may be attributed to the reality of racial discrimination and the fact that police have "two trigger fingers"—one for whites and one for African Americans and Hispanics.[59]

An alternate explanation for the racial disparity in victims of police shootings is the disproportionate involvement of minority suspects in violent crime and in the prevalence of the use of guns by minority suspects.[60] When the situational circumstances such as the nature of the crime, high-crime area, and use of guns are controlled for, then the disparity between white and black victims disappears in several studies.[61] Research has also found that the race of the police officer does not influence the likelihood of using lethal force: white, African American, and Hispanic officers are equally likely to fire weapons when assigned to certain high-crime precincts.[62]

Evidence also suggests that the use of lethal force toward suspects from all racial groups significantly declines when more restrictive policies regulating use of force are adopted by the police department. The rate of deaths caused by police use of lethal force varies widely across different jurisdictions. Analysis of the racial disparity in police shootings under more restrictive policies suggests that these rules reduce the number of African Americans shot by the policing suggesting that more permissive policies open the door for racial discrimination in the split-second decisions by police, at least in some cities.[63] The racial disparity between black and white victims from police shootings has declined substantially under the more restrictive policies of the post-Garner era.[64] One conclusion to draw from this research is that the effect of racial discrimination has diminished under departmental policies that limit officer discretion in the use of lethal force. The remaining racial disparity that still exists may be explained by the disparate involvement of minorities in more serious violent crimes.[65] A counter-trend, however, is the adoption of aggressive military tactics associated with military weapons and equipment that increases the use of excessive force within targeted minority communities.[66]

Explaining Police Violence

The simplest explanation for police violence points to the excesses of a few "aberrant" individuals. These so-called "rotten apples" spoil the reputation of the vast majority of law enforcement officers who conduct themselves within the bounds of the law. According to the **rotten apple theory,** the key to understanding what happened outside Van Dam Park that night lies in the personality and character of Lawrence Powell.

Indeed, there is much evidence to support this idea. Many who knew Powell described him as "immature," "cocky," and "unprofessional." In his first years as a police officer, Powell earned a reputation among his peers that was less than flattering. According to one black LAPD officer, "He treated everybody like crap. He always had his hand on his gun. We could be ordering a soda, talking to the lady at the register, and he would have his hand on his gun. We call it badge-heavy."[67]

By the time of the King incident, Powell had accumulated a record of incidents in which he was accused of improper conduct or excessive force in the interactions with citizens. Only five months earlier, Powell had been reprimanded for striking a handcuffed prisoner with a flashlight. In an earlier incident, Powell had struck a suspect breaking his elbow. The victim filed an excessive force lawsuit that had been settled out of court. And only two weeks before the King arrest, three black students from San Fernando Valley College filed a complaint against Powell who forced them to lie on the ground, handcuffed them while he made racially derogatory remarks.

When Daryl Gates publically declared that this incident was an "aberration," he implied that this conduct was not the fault of the policies, practices, management, or structure of the LAPD as a whole, but acts of isolated individuals who should be removed from the force.[68] But does this explanation really fit the pattern of facts regarding the LAPD and its relationship with the minority community? In 1990, the year before the King beating, the city paid out more than $11.3 million in lawsuits and settlements in LAPD-related litigation. In fact, each year the city pays out many millions to settle lawsuits alleging police misconduct. Considering that most cases of police misconduct never result in the filing of actual lawsuit, these settlements represent the mere tip of the iceberg of LAPD misconduct. The cold reality is that this behavior is far too widespread and far too common to be attributed to a "few bad apples." Furthermore most of these "bad apples" have repeatedly violated the rights of citizens and were neither punished nor removed from the force but were instead tolerated and protected by their fellow officers.

ROTTEN APPLE THEORY
a theory that extra-legal violence by police is the result of few excessively aggressive individuals, or "rotten apples," who spoil the reputation of police as a whole.

The "Working Personality" of the Police Officer

Another possible explanation for the pervasiveness of police brutality is that police officers are more likely than ordinary citizens to be aggressive, cynical, or authoritarian in personality and temperament.[69] One theory is that policing attracts individuals with a tendency toward pessimistic views about human nature and a predisposition toward authoritarian attitudes. Yet research studies on the personality characteristics of recruits to the police academy reveal that the typical police recruit does not differ from the average person in terms of these personality traits.[70] While the typical recruit may be the type of person who is more likely to be idealistic and more of an "adrenaline" junkie than an office type, people attracted to policing are not otherwise particularly aggressive, suspicious, or authoritarian. Indeed, many police departments use personality tests to screen out aberrant personalities.[71]

What researchers have found, however, is that a **working personality** among police officers emerges through being on the job itself. Police have one of the strongest vocational subcultures of any occupational group. Occupations such as doctors, clergy, and the military also tend to be "24 hour a day" identities: people in these occupational roles see their job as a defining identity for "who they are" even when they are not at work. Jerome Skolnick argues that the "working personality" of the police officer develops through the shared experience of being a cop on the street.[72]

The experience of being a patrol officer is shared by all levels of the police hierarchy. This common experience shapes the outlook of all police officers simultaneously creating a strong bond between officers and opening an enormous gulf between police and civilians. In the trial, the most important credentials of expert witnesses were their experience as streetwise police officers. The prosecution witness in the Rodney King trials was easily discredited for his lack of experience as an officer on the street. Even the lawyers defending the police had experience as cops before they went to law school. More than any other credentials, the ability to empathize with the uniquely demanding position of the police officers on the street generates respect and trust from other police officers. This attitude even infected the jury who found the testimony of experienced officers more credible than those who lacked street experience.

Police Subculture: Danger and Authority

The source of the "working personality" therefore lies in certain features of police work itself.[73] The element of danger in policing means that police are trained to be suspicious of civilians in society. Most of us operate with certain stereotypes regarding who might be a threat to us on the street: we notice what aspects of a person's appearance and behavior that signal to us a potential threat. Many people in our culture, for example, see young black males as more likely to be a danger to them than an elderly white woman: we might cross the street to avoid passing that person or avoid going down a street where a group of people who fit this description are gathered.

While citizens pay attention to **symbolic assailants** in order to avoid danger (i.e., cross to the other side of the street or leave the party), the police officer is expected to pay attention in order to face and suppress the danger. Police develop a list of subtle signals to identify "symbolic assailants" or people who pose a potential threat.[74] The identification of Rodney King as a "duster" (someone on PCP) and an ex-con were inferences officers made based on his appearance and his behavior. Both these cues communicated to the officers an inference about how King might behave and the potential threat he represented to the officers. To civilians jumping to these conclusions seems fundamentally unfair, but for police, failing to make inferences can be both dangerous and unprofessional.

The second key element of the police work that affects the personality of the police officer is the possession of authority over others within society.[75] Police

WORKING PERSONALITY
the effect of daily police work on officers' view of the world characterized by cynicism and suspicion. The key features of police work to generate this view are the response to danger and the obligation to exercise authority.

SYMBOLIC ASSAILANTS
working stereotypes of citizens likely to pose a potential threat to police officer's safety used informally by police in their interactions with citizens on the street.

protect citizens against danger but they are also charged with the responsibility of enforcing many laws of public order that most citizens violate at some point in their lives even if in relatively minor ways. Citizens resent police who stop them for speeding tickets or who come by their house at the request of a neighbor to ask them to turn down the music at a party. Police officers often feel a sense of social rejection from civilians even when they are off duty. Police officers come to feel most at home in the company of other police officers particularly when their own conduct may be less than in perfect accordance with the law.

The Blue Curtain: Us versus Them Mentality

The sense of danger and authority associated with police work leads police officers to isolate themselves from civilians and to develop an "us" versus "them" mentality. Police generally feel that the public resents their authority, does not understand how difficult their job is or what it entails and is fickle in its support for police. Older officers often teach younger officers that it is best to avoid socializing with civilians. As a result, police often come from "police families," marry into police families, choose to live near, and socialize with, other people in law enforcement. In a sense, police officers construct an invisible **blue curtain** between themselves, their families, and the rest of society.[76]

It is this peculiar reality of policing that helps to explain the enormous consequence of moving the King trial to a community like Simi Valley. The members of jury were very likely to be predisposed to the belief that the media and politicians were unfair to the police and did not really understand what it is like to be an officer out there on the streets. Police often feel that citizens, especially minority citizens, view them as the enemy. The conviction that the public is ungrateful and uncaring about the risks police endure every day shows through in the closing arguments of Defense Attorney Michael Stone. These are the people who put their lives on the line every day so that ordinary civilians may enjoy peaceful lives. Chasing Rodney King and placing him under arrest is a difficult and dirty job: it is easy to condemn the action of the police officers from the safety of your living room watching the videotape on the television. For police families, however, it is a different matter to be in the moment, facing a potential assailant whose behavior and conduct suggest you may be facing grave danger.

Code of Silence

The working personality of the police officer leads to a sense of distrust of civilians, a pattern of social isolation from other civilians, and an intense reliance upon the connections to fellow police officers. The norms of the police subculture of loyalty, obedience, and solidarity then provide the foundation for the **code of silence** which prevents officers from criticizing their fellow officers to civilian outsiders. The code of silence is a powerful feature of all police subcultures and one that makes it very difficult to regulate police misconduct. On May 12, 1991, a guest editorial appeared in the *LA Times* demanding the resignation of Chief Daryl Gates for denouncing the beating as an "aberration."[77] The editorial was written by Sergeant Stacey Koon. The unwritten code of the LAPD required senior personnel to support their officers to the outside world and be loyal to their version of the truth. Senior officers who failed to "back up their street cops" were seen as traitors of the norms of solidarity and loyalty.

BLUE CURTAIN
social isolation of police and their families from civilians in society

CODE OF SILENCE
the unwritten norm to support fellow officers by not revealing problems and illegal conduct to outsiders.

The code of silence is rigorously enforced by other police officers in their treatment of those who violate the code and betray fellow officers. The treatment of Briseno and Nichols illustrates the kind of shunning treatment, demotion from jobs, willingness to inform about ones faults, the slander, and general cold treatment. While no officer came forward to talk about Powell's past record of misconduct, many were willing to talk about Briseno and it appears that many officers were even willing to commit perjury to punish his treachery. On a more fundamental level, police officers fear if they violate the code, fellow officers will fail to "watch their backs" out on the street.

These features of police work help us to understand why police forces are so tolerant of the "rotten apples" within their organization. Valuing solidarity above all else and operating with the strong belief that civilians do not understand or appreciate the realities of police work, police departments routinely fail to correct the misconduct that takes place within their ranks. The "thin blue line" serves as a thick blue curtain between the police and rest of society. The bystanders at the King incident may very well have had private feelings about the actions of Lawrence Powell but they also very likely believed in the importance of protecting their fellow officers from the world of citizens who do not understand the difficult line police are forced to walk every day.

Racism, Deference, and Demeanor

One of the key reasons Rodney King may have been beaten that night was because he symbolically challenged the authority of the police by his behavior. Rodney King was grinning, waving at the helicopter, jiggling his buttocks, and talking gibberish during this period. Even though King was on the ground and may not have represented an actual physical threat to the safety of the officers, research shows that police officers are more likely to beat an individual, even one who is handcuffed, if they are still demonstrating a degree of symbolic resistance to the authority of the police.[78]

Respect for authority is crucial for police out on the street. Because police are suspicious of symbolic assailants, they maintain their authority by demanding that citizens display signs of respect. For the police, a show of disrespect is a danger sign signifying an individual who may be willing to use force against them. Research shows that police often use unnecessary force when they believe that their authority is being challenged.

The sensitivity of police to signs of disrespect is exacerbated within minority communities where relations between police and the community are extremely tense and mutually suspicious. From their perspective, police believe that the minority communities are among people who do not accept the legitimacy of their authority. This heightens the tendency for some officers to be especially aggressive in their use of force in order to maintain that authority. Being tough and using violent tactics against symbolic assailants like young black males hanging out on a corner is one strategy for forcing respect. Constantly displaying their ability to use force is one method used to command respect on the streets.

Paradox of Coercive Power[79]

Yet there is a profound irony in this approach to maintaining authority. Respect and fear are two different attitudes toward people in power. The **paradox of**

PARADOX OF COERCIVE POWER
the more a person in authority uses power, the more they lose authority to use power.

coercive power is that the more you use your power, the more you lose your authority. Police authority depends upon careful use of force within the bounds of the law. While at times it is necessary to use force to maintain authority, the excessive use of force by police undermines their legitimate authority to use force on the street. The more police behave in a heavy-handed fashion in their encounters with citizens on the street, the more they sow the seeds that undermine their authority in the long run.

The distinction between power and authority is an important one for understanding the enormously delicate relationship between citizens and the police as they encounter one another on the street. If American citizens do not accept the legitimate right of police to tell them what to do, for example, when approaching an intersection, then the job of the police standing there in the middle of the street is extremely dangerous and fundamentally impossible. If every citizen resisted the authority of the police, then all the police would have to draw upon would be whatever power they possess which is no match for the greater power of citizens to oppose them. This is the situation the LAPD found themselves to be in during those first hours and days of the riot out there on the streets among thousands of citizens refusing to obey their authority. Under these circumstances, the police retreated for their own safety.

The more police rely upon the use of force on the street, the more they are resented, hated, and seen as "just another gang out on the street." Hated cops are not safe cops.[80] And because police are not seen as individuals, officers like Lawrence Powell, who choose to instill fear rather than respect, create unsafe streets for all police. When people begin to resist the authority of the police on a large scale, as happened as soon as the riots began, the power of the police is overwhelmed by the much greater power of the citizens in the community. The police no longer held the upper hand in terms of power and were forced to retreat for their own safety until the arrival of reinforcements from the military.

WAR MODEL OF POLICING

From its inception in the nineteenth century, municipal police organizations have adopted a quasi-military style of organization with chains of command, ranks, divisions, platoons, squads, and details. Military language and metaphors pervade the culture and function of public policing; since the 1970s waging a "war on crime" is the central metaphor governing the crime control function and the mission of the police. Yet the military model and mission may be dysfunctional for the real work of public policing and may contribute to the incidence of violence on the part of police.

Probably more than any other police department in the nation, the LAPD had embraced a "war model" of policing since the early 1950s. William Henry Parker, chief of the LAPD for over twenty years, promoted an image of the LAPD as an elite commando force fighting the forces of evil in the city.[81] It was Parker who came up with the concept that the LAPD was the "thin blue line" protecting the "good" citizens of Los Angeles, mostly white, from the bad criminals, mostly Mexican, Asian, or African American.

Daryl Gates rose through the ranks of the LAPD under William Parker. Gates too was steeped in the military model of policing. He had earned promotions for developing the SWAT team, a heavily armed tactical unit designed to respond to street militants and hostage situations. The SWAT team was deployed in conflicts with the militant Black Panthers in the late 1960s and early 1970s. Lawrence Powell had served in the prestigious CRASH (Community Resources against Street Hoodlums) unit that suppressed gangs using aggressive military-style tactics.

The **military model of policing**, however, lends itself to excessive use of force. In a war situation, violence against the enemy is normative: acting with restraint in the face of the enemy is foolish and soldiers are trained to use whatever means necessary to destroy the enemy. In public policing, force is supposed to be used only as a last resort and only to bring a suspect to justice, not to vanquish them or eliminate them. The military use of force and the public police use of force are fundamentally different from one another.[82]

Cops as Soldiers

Patrick V. Murphy, former police chief of Syracuse, Washington, D.C., Detroit and New York City, in his autobiography claims that the primary role of police in society is to "keep the peace and maintain order in a sophisticated, humane, and Constitutional way."[83] This is very different from the job of the soldier in war: which is to destroy the enemy as efficiently as possible. Soldiers are not trained to resolve a situation with the minimum force possible.[84] The military is a top-down hierarchy in which all the important decisions are made at the top of the organization. The commander in chief decides whether to go to war, where to wage the battle, how many troops should be deployed, and what tactics to use. Down the line, discretion is increasingly diminished until we reach the private who is told their job is not to "reason why" but to "do or die."

In policing, the frontline police officer on the beat holds most of the decision-making authority to decide to use force or not in countless discretionary and fluid encounters with citizens on the street. Should they arrest a person or warn them? Talk to the drunk or wrestle them into the patrol car? Defuse the angry argument between two males by arresting them or joking with them? Frisk the suspicious teenage or let them walk on by? In policing, it is the person at the bottom of the chain of command who holds the "non-negotiable discretion" to decide if force should be used, when, where, and how much.

Citizens as Enemies

In a war, the enemy is clearly defined. In the context of policing, the enemy is often claimed to be the "criminal" or in Koon's vocabulary "scum." But criminals are not easily distinguishable from ordinary citizens. Remember, most U.S. citizens violate the law at some point in their lives so technically most citizens may come under police scrutiny. But only a tiny fraction of citizens commit serious and dangerous crime. How can police tell the "bad guys" from the "good guys"?

The war mentality makes it extremely easy for police to use the outward signs of race and class to identify the so-called enemy. Police rely upon stereotypes, profiles, and typifications to decide who is "friend" and who is "foe." This means that black people become targets of police surveillance, investigation, and harassment since they are seen as part of the "enemy class." For the vast majority of law-abiding minority citizens, this kind of treatment is a deep insult and source of great injustice.

Furthermore, it is important to remember that people who violate the law are not the equivalent of foreign "enemies" devoid of civil rights. By law, a criminal

MILITARY MODEL OF POLICING
the use of the military metaphor for the structure and mission of policing.

suspect remains entitled to full protection of the Constitution until they are duly convicted in a court of law. It is not the job of the police to act as vigilantes delivering street justice to people they deem to be guilty. Even once they are convicted, criminals are still American citizens. They may be criminals, they may have committed violent acts but they are not enemies to be destroyed. The mentality, which is functional in the context of war, is highly dysfunctional for professionals in the criminal justice system who should never treat suspects or convicted criminals as "enemies" to be destroyed. They remain their fellow citizens, guilty, or not guilty.

Getting the Job Done?

The ultimate flaw in the military model of policing is that crime is not "battle" or "war" that police can "win." The source of crime lies within the dynamics of the wider society: in the structure of opportunity, in the lines between legal and illegal ways of making money and in the moral values and norms of the entire culture. Police enter into the picture late in the game once the law has been violated. Police may be able to catch individual criminals but the police cannot solve the problems of inner city violence driven by poverty, structural unemployment, teenage pregnancy, systemic racism, and other societal forces.[85] Police can no more control crime than they can control the movement of the tides.

Telling police officers that they should fight a war on crime or drugs is putting police in a no-win situation that can breed cynicism and frustration. Out on the street, day after day, many realize that their efforts at arresting an endless stream of offenders are essentially futile. One person arrested and placed behind the walls will be replaced by another on the street in a matter of minutes. When asked how effective police are in controlling the drug trade, one experienced narcotics officer answered, "We are like a gnat biting on a horse's ass."[86]

RETHINKING THE MISSION OF THE POLICE

A great deal of unnecessary violence and illegal violence therefore can be linked to our failure to accurately understand the job of policing in our society. The war model of policing establishes unrealistic expectations for police, which in turn, breeds cynicism, corruption, violence, and mistrust between the police and the community. It drives an ever-deeper wedge between those who are the victims of police abuse, namely poor minority communities, and those who are insulated from such treatment. It is hard for white citizens in suburban communities to comprehend the resentment toward the police simmering within black America. As we saw in the previous chapter, privileges of class do not shield even middle-class and upper-class minorities from the "criminalization of blackness" by the police. Whether driving, flying, or walking while black (or Latino or Asian depending upon where you live), police target "visible" enemies in trying to fight crime. This treatment by police alienates law-abiding citizens and undermines their willingness to cooperate with the criminal justice system in the detection and prosecution of criminal behavior.

But the heaviest burden falls upon those who bear the disadvantages of both race and class. Poor minority communities like that in South Central LA suffer from the social conditions that breed crime. They are both the victims of crime within their own neighborhoods and victims of ineffective and brutalizing military tactics of a police force that too often does more harm than good for the community it is paid to protect and serve.

Image versus Reality

In the mythology of policing, officers are valiant or heroic "crime fighters" who risk their lives every day to get dangerous criminals off the streets. But the reality of policing is far from this dramatic and exciting fiction we enjoy so much on our video screen and in detective novels. Policing is not nearly as dangerous an occupation as it appears to be in popular fiction. In 2011, forty-eight law enforcement officers including federal, state, and local officers were feloniously killed in the line of duty.[87] This rate is only slightly higher than the homicide rate for the entire population: the chance an officer will be killed by a criminal is about the same as it is for everyone else. Police are more likely to die from an accident or suicide than felonious homicide. Other occupations such as farming, construction, and mining are far more dangerous than policing. Police officers rarely discharge or fire their weapons: in New York City, guns are fired in only one out of every 352 encounters with criminal suspects.[88]

Although fiction portrays police as solving crime, the simple truth is that most crimes are not reported to the police and police are not hugely successful in solving even the small percentage of crimes that are reported. Because most crime suspects cannot be identified, many crimes go unsolved. In the United States about half of reported crimes result in an arrest. This is higher for homicides where the clearance rate is about 64 percent and very low for crime such as auto-theft where the clearance rate is less than 12 percent.[89] Also less than one-third of all police work is spent in criminal law enforcement. The typical law enforcement officer rarely makes a felony arrest. Patrol is the heart of modern police work. Sixty-five percent of all police officers in the United States are assigned to patrol work.[90] Police officers drive slowly around in the cars essentially waiting for the radio dispatcher to send them on a call for service. Contrary to the view on television, patrol work is quite boring: most of the time is spent waiting for something to happen. More than 90 percent of police work is a reactive response to a call for service or assistance. Probably the most self-generated police work involves the stopping of motor vehicles that violate traffic laws.

James Q. Wilson identified three key functions of the police.[91] The first is peacekeeping or **order maintenance function** that is achieved through patrolling the streets and keeping things under control. The second is the **service function.** This type of police work involves dealing with problems and people in society that no one else wants to deal with such as the homeless or mentally ill and a host of concerns; the third function is the detection and apprehension of those who violate the law. **Crime control** is the third distinct function of modern police work.

Empirical data reveal that the bulk of police work involves performing either the order maintenance or human service function. Studies repeatedly find that somewhere between 15 percent and 25 percent calls to police concern criminal matters.[92] Police most often deal with situations where there has been no violation of criminal law but there is a need for some kind of assistance or intervention such as loud parties or radios, drunken or lost individuals, rowdy teenagers, kids turning on a fire hydrant, a truck illegally parked blocking a driveway, a car alarm which is stuck, traffic accidents, medical emergencies, drunks, suicides, animals that are out of control, lost children, barking dogs, and people who are stuck or the mentally ill. The list goes on and on. Citizens call upon the police for help in all sorts of situations, most of them non-criminal in nature. The police seem to function as a kind of all-purpose 24-hours-a-day social service agency.

ORDER MAINTENANCE FUNCTION
to maintain peace and order, handle disputes, deal with troublemakers, and keep the public spaces free from disorder.

SERVICE FUNCTION
to provide assistance with a wide array of social problems.

CRIME CONTROL FUNCTION
detection and apprehension of law violators.

Preventative Patrol and Rapid Response

The concept of the modern police force is built upon the notion of preventative patrol. The assumption is if we increase police patrol, crime will go down; if we take officers off the street, crime will go up. Periodically researchers have tested this theory to see if it actually works. In one study, conducted in the mid-1950s, carried out by the New York City police department, many more foot patrols were added in one precinct. During the four months of the experiment, mugging, burglaries, and auto-thefts fell. These data were used to justify an enormous increase in the number of police officers in New York City within the next twenty years.

Yet along with the rise in the number of police officers out on the street was a steady increase in the crime rate during the next twenty years. This raised many questions about the relationship between patrol and crime commission. Another study in New York City subway system conducted in the 1970s found that increasing patrols between the hours of 8 p.m. and 4 a.m. reduced amount of crime. But researchers found a corresponding increase in the amount of crime taking place after 4 a.m. Crime was simply displaced to another time or place where patrols were less heavy.

The most ambitious study to look at the preventative power of patrol was conducted in 1973 in Kansas City.[93] The goal of the **Kansas City experiment** was to test the proposition that preventative patrol had a deterrent effect on crime and made citizens feel safer. Fifteen police beats were divided into three matched groups. The first group, chosen randomly, was the control group where patrol patterns stayed normal. The second group was the "pro-active patrol" beats. The number of cruising cars was increased two to three times the normal volume. In the third beat, the so-called **reactive patrol** strategy, there was no preventative patrol at all. Police cars went out into the community only in response to calls from citizens for help. Researchers interviewed businesses and individuals before and after for their perception and fear of crime; and reviewed victimization reports and official statistics on crime before and after the experiment.

The results were startling to everyone. After a whole year, it was found that there was no difference at all among the three areas in the official crime rate, rate of victimization, level of citizen fear, or degree of satisfaction with the police. The only slight difference was that citizens in the pro-active beats perceived that crime had gone up largely because they saw many more police cars in the community and assumed the reason was that crime had gotten worse. The results from this study, and other work on policing, have led many to question the value of traditional-style patrol, particularly when it is done in police cars.

Responding to the studies of the 1970s showing that regular motor patrols have little impact on crime, police departments have experimented with other models of patrol. **Saturation patrolling** or **problem-oriented patrolling** targets particular locations or "hot spots" where crime is known to take place.[94] The aim is to enormously increase the police presence in very specific locations. Like the subway experiment, these strategies are quite effective but only in the short run because they cannot be maintained indefinitely.

Another strategy is to disrupt markets for criminal activity through an active police presence without trying to arrest the criminals themselves. This is used most often to regulate prostitution and drug dealing activity within a specific public location in the city.[95] Police may combine enforcement crackdowns with a pattern of surveillance that is designed to make business impossible by scaring

KANSAS CITY EXPERIMENT
a 1973 experiment which compared the deterrent effect of three different modes of police patrol.

REACTIVE PATROL
a police patrol model in which police respond only when there is a call for assistance.

SATURATION PATROLLING
increased police presence in "hot spots" known to have high amounts of criminal activity. Also known as problem-oriented patrolling.

PROBLEM-ORIENTED POLICING
the identification, analysis, and solution of the source of a crime problem in cooperation with the community.

away customers for the illegal business. Uniformed officers may be stationed to conspicuously write down license plates of customers looking to purchase sex or drugs. This has the positive benefit of making the neighborhood much safer for the law-abiding residents although the activity will resume as soon as the presence is withdrawn.

Research conducted in the 1970s and 1980s also questioned the effectiveness of the **rapid response** approach to police calls for service.[96] The 911 system emphasized the ability of police to arrive on the scene in as short a time as possible but the evidence shows that reducing the time the police takes to get to crime scene has no impact at all on improving the likelihood that the criminal will be apprehended. Citizens tend to measure police responsiveness by the amount of speed with which they arrived on the scene after placing a call. Yet, in most cases of theft, by the time the victim has discovered the loss, the offender is long gone. Arriving quickly may make a victim feel better, but it doesn't make much of a difference to the investigation of the crime. Even when there is a confrontation between a victim and suspect, victims generally take as long as twenty minutes before they phone the police. Even with the quickest possible response, by the time police have arrived, the offender can no longer be followed or caught by law enforcement.

The really critical ingredient in successful criminal investigation is the quality of the information provided by the victims and witnesses, which identifies the offender and provides the evidence needed to make a successful legal prosecution.[97] Police need a description, name, address, or a license plate number. Most successful criminal investigations depend upon the identification of a likely suspect by citizens; rarely do police identify a suspect based on an investigation. Typically, police investigate and collect evidence about a suspect identified for them by a member of the community.

The Promise of Community Policing

For its many supporters, the concept of **community policing** holds the most promise for re-inventing public policing and reforming the institution to better serve the needs of the community as we enter the twenty-first century. The U.S. Department of Justice's Community Oriented Policing Services office defines community policing as "a philosophy that promotes organizational strategies, which support the systematic use of partnerships and problem-solving techniques, to proactively address the immediate conditions that give rise to public safety issues such as crime, social disorder, and fear of crime."[98]

The key concept of community policing is that by building partnerships with the community and addressing the conditions that give rise to crime, police have an opportunity to abandon the futile and dangerous "war making" approach to crime in favor of a peace making model which relies upon cooperation, trust, and mutual respect between police and the community. Community policing, in some respects, is a move "back to the future" by making a conscious effort to put police back out onto the street corner in direct contact with the citizens they serve.

The widespread and growing movement to institute community policing represents a third wave of reform similar to the advent of professionalism partly because it is so diverse. There is no single theory or model of community policing. Rather it is a loose set of concepts and a host of strategies and approaches. Some departments have adopted community policing strategies in a comprehensive plan while others are implementing pieces of the strategy.

RAPID RESPONSE
an urgent response system of policing based on citizen use of 911, two-way radios, and mobile command and control units.

COMMUNITY POLICING
a pro-active policing strategy which relies upon problem-solving in close collaboration with the citizens within the community.

Advocates of community policing urge police to patrol on bikes and foot instead of cars in order to form strong relationships with citizens in the community.

There are many within policing and within the wider community who are skeptical about community policing or are professionally opposed to it as a crime control strategy. Traditionalists within policing believe community policing is nothing more than the current fad, which will fade when the federal dollars that fund it are gone. These officers do not support community policing because they are firm believers in the classical approach to policing. There are also those within the minority community who believe that the so-called strategy of community policing is nothing more than a wolf dressed in sheep clothing. The continuation of military-style tactics, undercover surveillance and so-called "broken windows" style of policing amounts to an all-around war-like assault on the young men of the minority communities. Community policing, in this view, is merely a public relations campaign by a more sophisticated police organization trying to control the public outcry when its aggressive tactics "get out of hand."

Quality of Life Policing

The **broken windows theory of crime** was developed by George Kelling and James Q. Wilson in an influential article which appeared in *The Atlantic Monthly* in 1982.[99] Kelling and Wilson argued that mere police presence in radio cars or even on the street is not sufficient to make citizens feel safer. It is necessary for police to take a more pro-active approach in dealing with minor crime, vandalism, and other negative "**quality of life**" issues within poor

BROKEN WINDOWS THEORY OF CRIME minor crimes such as vandalism and graffiti are early signs of a neighborhood in decline which lead to more serious criminal conduct in that location.

QUALITY OF LIFE POLICING aggressive enforcement of public nuisance laws.

neighborhoods. Police should take the lead in cleaning up the graffiti, broken windows, burnt-out cars, piles of garbage, broken street lights, or abandoned vacant lots because these signs of neglect signify an "unsafe" neighborhood. These so-called "trivial" physical signs along with the public disorders of teens hanging out, loud swearing, panhandling, or loud music are signs of a neighborhood which is beginning to decay. When these problems are ubiquitous, law-abiding citizens feel unsafe and they abandon the neighborhood by moving away, if they are able to, or by staying indoors, if they are not. Before long, the neighborhood has attracted far more serious criminal activity and has become a "high-crime" location. As on officer put it, "if you see garbage all around you, you begin to act like garbage."

New York City under the leadership of newly appointed police commissioner William Bratton embraced the strategies of quality of life policing with a vengeance. Newly elected mayor Rudy Giuliani vowed to implement a "zero-tolerance policy" for minor "quality of life" violations such as jumping turnstiles in the subway, panhandling, kids who were truants from school, homeless people sleeping under bridges or in doorways, and the "sequeegee operators" who frightened suburban drivers stopped at a traffic light by cleaning their windshield and asking for payment in return. Police were instructed to take these crimes seriously and arrest those who were engaged in them. As often as not, an arrest would turn up an outstanding warrant or parole violation, which would lead to a stint in jail.

At the same time, the rate of serious crime fell dramatically in New York City. According to the broken windows theory, attention to trivial crimes will impact more serious crime. During these same years, the rate of serious crime also fell dramatically in New York: by 1998 the city had its lowest murder rate in thirty-eight years. That trend has continued and even accelerated since 2008 in most major cities across the United States. Giuliani and Bratton were quick to take credit for the decline in NYC and even fought over which of them was really responsible for it. But in truth, the decline in serious crime is a widespread pattern which predates the rise of quality of life policing and is linked to an array of factors.[100] Any single police intervention cannot significantly impact the commission of crime according to most criminologists and in many cities the fall in crime began in 1992 long before any reforms in police strategy were implemented.

Community-Police Partnerships

The community policing movement identifies two key reasons police need stronger bonds with the community. The first rationale is that police need the community in order to successfully apprehend and prosecute people who commit crime. Without information, cooperation, trust, and support from the community, the police are nothing more than the rolling fortresses of an occupying army cut off from access to any quality information about crime.

The second reason police need to develop close ties with the community is even more important. According to David Bayly, policing is based on a big untruth: police work *even at its most effective* cannot control crime. The power to genuinely prevent, and therefore reduce, crime does not lie within the power of the police at all. The police respond to crime after it has already occurred. "They have been shutting the barn door after the horse has escaped."

This fundamental reality puts police in a difficult situation: they are being asked to "fix" something without having the tools to do the job. One option, according to proponents of community policing is for the police to be more pro-active in partnering with the community to deal with the problems that generate crime. While police cannot do the work alone, police can collaborate with schools, human services, politicians, businesses, and other agencies to address solutions that help to correct the underlying problems. Most crime is highly predictable: kids who are out of school and unsupervised by responsible adults will be committing crime before too long. Police can either wait for it to happen and then arrest them or decide to run midnight basketball leagues or other sports programs, which will keep kids who are on the streets anyway, out of trouble. This is the difference between a pro-active versus reactive approach to policing.

Community policing is a response to the dilemma of policing in a free society. As we have seen, the modern police force was, to a significant extent, the creation of a state-run armed force to keep peace in the public streets. The key threat came from collective unrest due to ethnic and social inequality. In the twentieth century, the institution of policing has found itself increasingly under attack from the public in its role as coercive force. The requirements of a democratic society demand that police not wage "war" against citizens or behave like an occupying army within enemy territory. White middle-class America is largely shielded from this source of tension while minority communities suffer from both rampant crime and a destructive and ineffective military style of policing that isolate police from the very communities they are supposed to protect and serve.

As community police officers, police can take the lead in partnering with the community and other social services to assess the needs of the community, diagnose, and understand the causes of crime and other forms of social disorder, helping to develop strategies to address those causes. They may not be the ones to implement all of those strategies since many of them involve services and interventions that should be provided by others agencies and groups but police can advocate for these interventions and help the community understand the link between negative conduct and these problems. Activists within the Black Lives Matter campaign believe that police officers need to have a fundamental shift in how they see their role as public servants.[101]

Yet there are significant pressures on law enforcement to abandon the community-based model envisioned by Sir Robert Peel and championed by local police chiefs across the country. The war on terror is the topic of the next chapter in this unit on law enforcement. This national agenda leads to an approach to policing more heavily shaped by military tactics, mentality, and technology. Sir Robert Peel did not believe that the military was a model for the modern police force, yet police departments today are facing conflicting pressures from citizens who want greater collaboration with police, and from federal programs seeking to enlist local law enforcement to serve as soldiers in the protection of national security.

frankpledge (p. 207)   a system of law enforcement in medieval societies where every male member of the community over the age of 12 was bound by a pledge to keep peace and assist in delivering offenders to court.

tything (p. 207)   In Anglo-Saxon law, an association of ten families bound together by a frankpledge.

hue and cry (p. 207)   an old English call for assistance in the pursuit of felons

thief-takers (p. 207)   eighteenth-century mercenaries who offered to pursue felons for a fee.

Bobbies (p. 209)   the nickname for the first formal municipal police unit in London founded by Sir Robert Peel.

preventative patrol (p. 209)   the use of continuous and visible walking of public streets by police in order to deter crime.

patronage (p. 211)   a form of corruption in which the political party in power awards jobs and promotion in policing is given out as return for loyalty and favors to politicians.

Wickersham Commission (p. 211)   a panel of national experts convened in 1929 to conduct the first comprehensive national report on the criminal justice system. Evidence of systematic corruption and abuses within policing in the Wickersham Report generated public support for reform.

professionalism (p. 212)   the master trend in twentieth-century policing which sought to separate policing from politics through civil service examination, education, training, and bureaucratization.

para-militarization (p. 213)   the use of military equipment, tactics, and weapons in policing.

police brutality (p. 216)   the unlawful use of physical force by officers in the performance of their duties.

police corruption (p. 216)   misconduct by police officers through illegal activities for economic gain including the acceptance of payment for services, non-enforcement of the law in exchange for payment, and active participation in criminal activities.

grass eaters (p. 216)   police officers who accept payoffs for rendering police services or who look the other way when police action is called in exchange for goods and services.

meat eaters (p. 216)   police officers who actively and systematically solicit bribes or conspire with criminals in criminal activity.

impact techniques (p. 217)   techniques for use of coercive force designed to subdue a combative suspect without resorting to lethal force.

lethal force (p. 217)   a force likely to cause death or great bodily harm; also known as deadly force.

fleeing felon doctrine (p. 218)   a now-defunct law enforcement rule which permitted officers to shoot a suspected felon attempting to flee from a lawful arrest.

rotten apple theory (p. 220)   a theory that extralegal violence by police is the result of few excessively aggressive individuals, or "rotten apples," who spoil the reputation of police as a whole.

working personality (p. 221)   the effect of daily police work on officers' view of the world characterized by cynicism and suspicion. The key features of police work to generate this view are the response to danger and the obligation to exercise authority.

symbolic assailants (p. 221)   working stereotypes of citizens likely to pose a potential threat to police officer's safety used informally by police in their interactions with citizens on the street.

blue curtain (p. 222)   social isolation of police and their families from civilians in society

code of silence (p. 222)   the unwritten norm to support fellow officers by not revealing problems and illegal conduct to outsiders.

paradox of coercive power (p. 223)   the more a person in authority uses power, the more they lose authority to use power.

military model of policing (p. 225)   the use of the military metaphor for the structure and mission of policing.

order maintenance function (p. 227)   to maintain peace and order, handle disputes, deal with troublemakers, and keep the public spaces free from disorder.

service function (p. 227)   to provide assistance with a wide array of social problems.

crime control function (p. 227)   detection and apprehension of law violators.

Kansas City experiment (p. 228)   a 1973 experiment which compared the deterrent effect of three different modes of police patrol.

reactive patrol (p. 228)   a police patrol model in which police respond only when there is a call for assistance.

saturation patrolling (p. 228)   increased police presence in "hot spots" known to have high amounts of criminal activity. Also known as problem-oriented patrolling.

problem-oriented policing (p. 228)   the identification, analysis, and solution of the source of a crime problem in cooperation with the community.

rapid response (p. 229)   an urgent response system of policing based on citizen use of 911, two-way radios, and mobile command and control units.

community policing (p. 229)   a pro-active policing strategy which relies upon problem-solving in close collaboration with the citizens within the community.

quality of life policing (p. 230)   aggressive enforcement of public nuisance laws.

broken windows theory of crime (p. 230)   minor crimes such as vandalism and graffiti are early signs of a neighborhood in decline which lead to more serious criminal conduct in that location.

REVIEW AND STUDY QUESTIONS

1. Why was the modern police force "invented" in the first part of the nineteenth century? How did the concept of the police force differ from that of the military force?

2. Describe the problems of patronage and corruption in nineteenth-century police forces. In what ways do professionalism reforms reduce these kinds of problems within policing?

3. Describe the impact of technology on the methods of policing, on the effectiveness of patrol, and on relationships between the police and the community.

4. What is the purpose of preventative patrol? What evidence do we have today that patrol "works" to prevent crime? Describe the Kansas City experiment. What does this research suggest about the most effective use of police personnel? Describe the different strategies of patrol and discuss the relative advantages of each type of patrol.

5. What are forms of police misconduct? How widespread is this behavior within policing?

6. What is the "fleeing felon doctrine"? Why was it declared unconstitutional in *Tennessee v. Garner*?

7. Describe the evidence concerning the disproportionate shootings of minority citizens. How has the pattern changed since the 1970s? What does the evidence suggest about the role of racism in the use of lethal force against minority suspects?

8. What are the code of silence and the concept of the "blue curtain"? Why do researchers believe these develop as features of police subculture? How does the culture of policing contribute to the problem of police brutality?

9. What is the "working personality" of police officers? What are the origins of this set of attitudes and values?

10. Describe how the military model of policing may contribute to the prevalence of police brutality.

11. In what way is the metaphor of cops as soldiers inaccurate for modern policing?

12. What is the paradox of coercive force? How does the use of force undermine police authority to use force?

13. What do police really do and how does this contrast with the "image" of policing? What are the three functions of policing? Which is most important in your view and why?

14. What is community policing? Do you support the image of police as "problem-solvers"? Why or why not? In your view, is community policing the latest fad or an important and lasting trend in police reform?

15. What is the status of minorities and women in modern policing? What steps, if any, would you advocate to increase the diversity of police?

CHECK IT OUT

Websites

Shielded from Justice: Police Brutality and Accountability in the U.S., http://www.hrw.org/reports98/police/. Report by Human Rights Watch on police brutality in fourteen major U.S. cities, including LA, New York, Chicago, Detroit, and Boston. Read the Christopher Commission

Report and the Furman Report on brutality and racism in the LAPD and the St. Clair Commission Report on the Boston police department. See data and reports from each major city.

Police Foundation, http://policefoundation.org/. Click on the National Center for the Study of Police and Civil Disorder founded after the LA riots. Check out reports on police use of force, civil disorders, and community policing. The Police Foundation is a major think tank on innovative ideas in policing hoping to serve as a catalyst for new developments in policing.

Videos

The Rodney King Beating (Full Version)—9 minutes 40 seconds. The original video shot from the balcony of George Holliday is now available for viewing in its entirety at https://www.youtube.com/watch?v=sb1WywlpUtY

The Rodney King Incident: Race and Justice in America—57 minutes. A documentary which interviews all key participants including Rodney King, the police officers, former chief Daryl Gates, and trial prosecutors demonstrating complex divergent views of this case. Can be viewed at: https://www.youtube.com/watch?v=SqGR-B58V2fM&feature=youtu.be

How do we bridge the divide among Americans over race and justice? – Part 2—8 minutes. This PBS video explores how race affects our understanding of justice. http://www.pbs.org/newshour/bb/bridge-divide-among-americans-race-justice/

Behind the Blue Wall: Police Brutality—50 minutes. The documentary details the killing of Amadou Diallo and the brutal assault on Abner Louima by the NYPD. It covers commentary by police leaders and community and civil rights advocates on the issue of police violence. Currently available online at http://www.hollywood.com/tv/behind-the-blue-wall-police-brutality-59488097/

Movies

Serpico (1973). Starring Al Pacino in the true story of Frank Serpico, this film portrays the powerful subculture of the NYPD and its treatment of whistleblowers from within its own ranks. Pacino was nominated for an Academy Award for his performance in this drama.

NOTES

[1] Lou Cannon, *Official Negligence: How Rodney King and the Riots Changed Los Angeles and the LAPD* (New York: Random House, 1997), 346.

[2] Jerry Gray, "In Police Brutality Case, One Videotape but Two Ways to View it," *The New York Times* (December 13, 1991), B7.

[3] Mike Sager, "Damn! They Gonna Lynch Us," *Gentlemen's Quarterly* (1991); Jerome Skolnick and James Fyfe, *Above the Law: Police and the Excessive Use of Force* (New York: The Free Press, 1993), 1–22; Lou Cannon, *Official Negligence: How Rodney King and the Riots Changed Los Angeles and the LAPD* (New York: Random House, 1997), 20–43.

[4] Lou Cannon, *Official Negligence: How Rodney King and the Riots Changed Los Angeles and the LAPD* (New York: Random House, 1997), 45.

[5] "Los Angeles Chief Assailed by Mayor," *The New York Times* (April 3, 1991).

[6] "Violence and Racism are Routine in Los Angeles Police, Study Says," *The New York Times* (July 10, 1991); Warren Christopher et al., *Report of the Independent Commission on the Los Angeles Police Department* (July 9, 1991).

[7] "Simi Valley Journal: Town too feels eyes of nation for Trial," *The New York Times* (February 22, 1992).

[8] Lou Cannon, *Official Negligence: How Rodney King and the Riots Changed Los Angeles and the LAPD* (New York: Random House, 1997), 237–239.

[9] Seth Mydans, "Los Angeles Policemen Acquitted in Taped Beating: Storm of anger Erupts," *The New York Times* (April 30, 1992), 1.

[10] "Riots in LA: The Blue Line Surprised, Police React Slowly as violence spreads," *The New York Times* (May 1, 1992).

[11] Nancy Abelmann and John Lie, *Blue Dreams: Korean Americans and the Los Angeles Riots* (Cambridge, MA: Harvard University Press, 1995); William Robert Gooding, ed., *Reading Rodney King: Reading Urban Uprising* (New York: Routledge, 1993).

[12] D. M Osborne, "A Defense Turned Inside Out," *American Lawyer Media* 20 (1993), 1.

[13] *The Rodney King Case: What the Jury Saw.* (CourtTV. [S.l.]: MPI Home Video, 1992).

[14] Jerome H. Skolnick and David H. Bayley, *The New Blue Line* (New York: Free Press, 1986).

[15] Harold T. Amidon, "Law Enforcement: From the Beginning' to the English Bobby," *Journal of Police Science and Administration* (1977), 355–367; Wilbur R. Miller, "Cops and Bobbies, 1830–1870," *Journal of Social History* (1975), 81–101.

16 Andrew T. Scull and S. Spitzer, "Social Control in Historical Perspective: From Private to Public Responses to Crime," in *Corrections and Punishment*, ed. David F. Greenberg (Beverly Hills, CA: Sage, 1977), 265–286.

17 Thomas A. Critchley, *A History of Police in England and Wales, 900–1966* (London, UK: Constable, 1967).

18 Allan Silver, "The Demand for Order in Civil Society: A Review of some Themes in the History of Urban Crime, Police and Riots," in *The Police: Six Sociological Essays*, ed. David Bordua (New York: Wiley, 1967), 1–24.

19 Peter Moskos, *Cop in the Hood: My Year Policing Baltimore's Eastern District* (Princeton, NJ: Princeton University Press, 2008), 199–200.

20 Roger Lane, "Urban Police and Crime in Nineteenth Century America," in *Crime and Justice: A Review of Research*, eds. Michael Tonry and Norval Morris (Chicago: University of Chicago Press, 1992), 1–50.

21 Lawrence Friedman, *Crime and Punishment in American History* (New York: Basic Books, 1993), 69–71.

22 Samuel Walker, *Popular Justice: A History of Criminal Justice* (New York: Oxford University Press, 1980), 61–65; Wilbur Miller, "Cops and Bobbies, 1830–1870," *Journal of Social History* (1975), 81–101.

23 Eric H. Monkkonen, *Police in Urban America, 1860–1920* (New York: Cambridge University Press, 1981).

24 Samuel Walker, *Popular Justice: A History of Criminal Justice* (New York: Oxford University Press, 1980), 127–145.

25 Walker, *Popular Justice*, 173–174.

26 Jerome H. Skolnick and James Fyfe, *Above the Law: Police and the Excessive Use of Force* (New York: The Free Press, 1993), 129.

27 Nathan Douthit, "August Vollmer, Berkeley's First Chief of Police and the Emergence of Police Professionalism," *California Historical Quarterly* 54 (1975), 101–124.

28 A. Vollmer and A. Parker, *The Police and Modern Society* (San Francisco: University of California Press, 1936).

29 Samuel Walker, *Popular Justice: A History of Criminal Justice* (New York: Oxford University Press, 1980), 189–190.

30 "The Presidents Commission on Law Enforcement and Justice Administration," *The Challenge of Crime in a Free Society* (Washington, DC: Government Printing Office, 1967).

31 The Omnibus Crime Control and Safe Streets Act of 1968, Public Law 90–351, 90th Congress, June 1968, 18 U.S.C., Sec.2518.

32 U.S. Department of Justice, *The LEAA: A Partnership for Crime Control* (Washington, DC: U.S. Government Printing Office, 1976).

33 Christian Parenti, *Lockdown America: Police and Prisons in the Age of Crisis* (New York: Verso, 1999), 21–23.

34 George L. Kelling and Mark H. Moore, "From Political to Reform to Community: The Evolving Strategy of Police" in *Community Policing: Rhetoric or Reality*, eds. Jack Green and Stephen D. Mastrofski (New York: Praeger Publishers, 1991).

35 ACLU https://www.aclu.org/report/war-comes-home-excessive-militarization-american-police. (2014).

36 Lou Cannon, *Official Negligence: How Rodney King and the Riots Changed Los Angeles and the LAPD* (New York: Westview, 1999), 70–72.

37 Mike Maciag, "Where Police Don't Mirror Communities and Why It Matters," *Governing* (August 28, 2015) http://www.governing.com/topics/public-justice-safety/gov-police-department-diversity.html; retrieved November 29, 2016.

38 U.S. Department of Justice, EOC, Advancing Diversity in Law Enforcement. https://www.justice.gov/crt/case-document/file/900761/download. (2016).

39 Donna C. Hale and C. Lee Bennet, "Realities of Women in Policing: An Organizational and Cultural Perspective," in *Women, Law and Social Control*, eds. Alida V. Merlo and Joycelyn M. Pollock (Boston: Allyn and Bacon, 1995), 41–54.

40 Susan Martin, *On the Move: The Status of Women in Policing* (Washington, DC: Police Foundation, 1990).

41 "Police Employee Data: Crime in the United States - 2009," *Federal Bureau of Investigation* (Washington, DC: U.S. Department of Justice, 2010), Table 74.

42 Herman Goldstein, *Police Corruption: A Perspective on Its Nature and Control* (Washington, DC: Police Foundation, 1975).

43 Samuel Walker, *Popular Justice: A History of Criminal Justice* (New York: Oxford University Press, 1980), 161–183; Lawrence Friedman, *Crime and Punishment in American History* (New York: Basic Books, 1993), 360–362.

44 "Report on Lawlessness in Law Enforcement," *National Commission on Law Observance and Enforcement* (Washington, DC: United States Government Printing Office, 1931).

45 Jonathan Schwartz, "New Orleans Police Mired in Scandal, Accept Plan for Overhaul," *New York Times* (July 24, 2012), A1.

46 "Grass-eaters and Meat-eaters: Police Corruption in New York City," reprinted in *Legal Process and Corrections*, eds. Norman Johnston and Leonard D. Savitz (New York: Wiley, 1982), 26–34.

47 Egon Bittner, *The Functions of the Police in Modern Society* (Chevy Chase, MD: National Institute of Mental Health, 1970).

48 William A. Geller and Kevin J. Karales, *Split-Second Decisions* (Chicago: Chicago Law Enforcement Study

Group, 1981); James J. Fyfe, "The Split-Second Syndrome and Other Determinants of Police Violence," in *Violent Transactions*, eds. Anne Campbell and John Gibbs (New York: Basil Blackwell, 1986).

[49] Jerome Skolnick and James J. Fyfe, *Above the Law: Police and the Excessive Use of Force* (New York: Free Press, 1993), 37–43.

[50] *City of Los Angeles v. Lyons*, 461 U.S. 95, 105 1983; David Cole, *No Equal Justice: Race and Class in the American Criminal Justice System* (New York: The New Press, 1999), 161–165.

[51] Lou Cannon, *Official Negligences: How Rodney King and the Riots Changed Los Angeles and the LAPD* (New York: Random House), 100–105.

[52] *Tennessee v. Garner* 471 U.S. 1 (1985).

[53] "Justifiable Homicide by Weapon, Law Enforcement, 2005–2009," *Crime in the United States, 2009, Expanded Homicide Data* (Washington, DC: U.S. Government Printing Office, 2000), Table 14.

[54] Kimberly Kindy, M. Fischer, J. Tate and J. Jenkins, "A Year of Reckoning: Police Fatally Shot Nearly 1000," *Washington Post* (December 15, 2015). http://www.washingtonpost.com/sf/investigative/2015/12/26/a-year-of-reckoning-police-fatally-shoot-nearly-1000/

[55] Catherine Milton, J.W. Halleck, J. Lardner and G.L. Albrecht, *Police Use of Deadly Force* (Washington, DC: Police Foundation, 1977).

[56] Paul Takagi, "Death by Police Intervention," in *A Community Concern: Police Use of Deadly Force*, eds. R.N. Brenner and M. Kravitz (Washington, DC: U.S. Government Printing Office, 1979).

[57] Ross C.T., "A Multi-Level Bayesian Analysis of Racial Bias in Police Shootings at the County-Level in the United States, 2011–2014," *PLoS ONE* 10. 11 (2015), e0141854. doi:10.1371/journal.pone.0141854.

[58] James J. Fyfe, "Blind Justice: Police Shootings in Memphis," *Journal of Criminal Law and Criminology* 73 (1982), 707–722.

[59] James J. Fyfe, "Reducing the Use of Deadly Force: The New York Experience," in *Police Use of Deadly Force* (Washington, DC: Government Printing Office, 1978), 29.

[60] John S. Goldkamp, "Minorities as Victims of Police Shootings: Dis-proportionality and Police use of deadly force," *Justice System Journal* 2 (1976), 169–183.

[61] Arnold Binder and Peter Scharf, "Deadly force in Law Enforcement," *Crime and Delinquency* 28 (1982), 1–23; Mark Blumberg, "Race and Police Shootings: An Analysis in Two Cities," in *Contemporary Issues in Law Enforcement*, ed. J. Fyfe (Beverly Hills, CA: Sage Publication, 1981); Jerry Sprager and David J. Giacopassi, "Memphis Re-visited: A Reexamination of Police Shootings after the Garner Decision," *Justice Quarterly* 9 (1992), 211–225.

[62] James Fyfe, "Who Shoots? A look at Officer Race and Police Shooting," *Journal of Police Science and Administration* 9 (1981), 367–382.

[63] Jerry Sprager and David J. Giacopassi, "Memphis Re-visited: A Reexamination of Police Shootings after the Garner Decision," *Justice Quarterly* 9 (1992), 211–225.

[64] William A Geller and Michael S. Scott, *Deadly Force: What We Know* (Washington, DC: Police Executive Research Forum, 1992); Lawrence W. Sherman and Ellen G. Cohn, *Citizens Killed by Big City Police, 1970–1984* (Washington, DC: Crime Control Institute, 1986).

[65] Samuel Walker, Cassia Spohn and Miriam DeLone, *The Color of Justice: Race, Ethnicity and Crime in America* (Belmont, CA: Wadsworth, 1996), 95.

[66] ACLU. *War Comes Home: Excessive Militarization and the American Police*. Downloaded https://www.aclu.org/report/war-comes-home-excessive-militarization-american-police. (2014).

[67] Lou Cannon, *Official Negligences: How Rodney King and the Riots Changed Los Angeles and the LAPD* (New York: Random House), 81.

[68] Daryl F. Gates and Diane K. Shah, *Chief: My Life in the LAPD* (New York: Bantam, 1993).

[69] Arthur Niederhoffer, *Behind the Shield: The Police in Urban Society* (Garden City, New York: Anchor Books, 1967).

[70] Richard S. Bennett and Theodore Greenstein, "The Police Personality: A Test of the Predispositional Model," *Journal of Police Science and Administration* 3 (1975), 439–445; Raymond Cochrane and Anthony J.P. Butler, "The Values of Police Officers, Recruits and Civilians in England," *Journal of Police Science and Administration* 8 (1980), 205–211; Bruce N. Carpenter and Susan M. Raza, "Personality Characteristics of Police Applicants: Comparisons Across Subgroups and with Other Populations," *Journal of Police Science and Administration* 15 (1987), 10–17.

[71] George Pugh, "The California Psychological Inventory and Police Selection," *Journal of Police Science and Administration* 13 (1985), 172–177; Robert D. Meier, Richard E. Farmer and David Mazwell, "Psychological Screening of Police Candidates: Current Perspectives," *Journal of Police Science and Administration* 15 (1987), 210–215.

[72] Jerome Skolnick, *Justice Without Trial: Law Enforcement in a Democratic Society* (New York: Wiley, 1975), 42–70.

[73] Skolnick, *Justice Without Trial*, 54.

[74] John Van Maanen "The Asshole" in *Policing: A View from the Street*, eds. Peter K. Manning and John Van Maanen (Santa Monica CA: Goodyear 1978), 221–238.

[75] Jerome Skolnick, *Justice Without Trial: Law Enforcement in a Democratic Society* (New York: Wiley, 1975), 44.

[76] William Westley, *Violence and the Police: A Sociological Study of Law, Custom and Morality* (Cambridge, MA: MIT Press, 1970), 226.

[77] Stacey C. Koon, "Its Time for Gates to Step Down," *Los Angeles Times* (May 12, 1991).

[78] Albert J. Reiss Jr., "Police Brutality: Answers to Key Questions," *Transaction* (1968).

[79] William Muir Jr., *Police: Streetcorner Politicians* (Chicago: University of Chicago Press, 1977), 59–100.

[80] Jerome Skolnick and James Fyfe, *Above the Law: Police and the Excessive Use of Force* (New York: Free Press, 1993), 96.

[81] Samuel Walker, *Popular Justice: A History of Criminal Justice* (New York: Oxford University Press, 1980), 211–212.

[82] Egon Bittner, *Aspects of Police Work* (Boston, MA: Northeastern University Press, 1990).

[83] Jerome Skolnick and James Fyfe, *Above the Law: Police and the Excessive Use of Force* (New York: Free Press, 1993), 115.

[84] Egon Bittner, *Aspects of Police Work* (Boston, MA: Northeastern University Press, 1990), 47.

[85] William Julius Wilson, *The Truly Disadvantaged: The Inner City, the Underclass and Public Policy* (Chicago: University of Chicago Press, 1987); L. J. D. Wacquant and William J. Wilson, "The Cost of Racial and Class Exclusion in the Inner City," *Annals of the American Academy of Political and Social Science,* (1989).

[86] Jerome Skolnick and James Fyfe, *Above the Law: Police and the Excessive Use of Force* (New York: Free Press, 1993), 132.

[87] "Crime Statistics Management Unit, LEOKA Program," *Federal Bureau of Investigation* (Washington, DC: U.S. Department of Justice, 2010), Table 330; "Statistical Abstract of the United States," *U.S. Census Bureau* (Washington, DC: Department of Commerce, 2012), 208.

[88] William A. Geller and Michael S. Scott. *Deadly Force* (Washington, DC: Police Executive Research Forum, 1992).

[89] Federal Bureau of Investigation *Crime in the United States – 2005*, http://www.fbi.gov/ucr/05cius/offenses/clearances/index.html

[90] David Bayley, *Policing for the Future* (New York: Oxford University Press, 1994), 16.

[91] James Q. Wilson, *Varieties of Police Behavior* (Cambridge, MA: Harvard University Press, 1968).

[92] David Bayley, *Policing for the Future* (New York: Oxford University Press, 1994), 17.

[93] George Kelling et al., *The Kansas City Preventative Patrol Experiment: A Summary Report* (Washington, DC: The Police Foundation, 1974).

[94] Lawrence W. Sherman and David Weisburd, "General Deterrent Effects of Police Patrol in Crime 'Hot Spots': A Randomized Controlled Trial," *Justice Quarterly* 12 (1995), 625–648; Christopher Koper, "Just Enough Police Presence: Reducing Crime and Disorderly Behavior by Optimizing Patrol Time in Crime Hot Spots," *Justice Quarterly* 12 (1995), 649–672.

[95] David Weisburd and Lorraine Green, "Policing Drug Hot spots: The Jersey City Drug Market Analysis," *Justice Quarterly* 12 (1995), 711–735.

[96] U.S. Department of Justice, *Response Time Analysis: Executive Summary* (Washington, DC: U.S. Government Printing Office, 1978); George L. Kelling and David Fogel, "Police Patrol- Some Future Directions," in *The Future of Policing*, ed. Alvin W. Cohn (Beverly Hills, CA: Sage, 1978), 166–167; David Bayley, *Policing for the Future* (New York: Oxford University Press, 1994), 6.

[97] Peter Greenwood, Jan Chaiken and Joan R. Petersilia, *The Criminal Investigation* (Lexington MA: D.C. Heath, 1977); John Eck, *Solving Crimes: the Investigation of Burglary and Robbery* (Washington, DC: Police Executive Research Forum, 1982).

[98] Kate Abbey-Lambertz and Joseph Erbentraut, "The Simple Strategies that can Fundamentally Change how Communities View Police," *Huffington Post* (July 07, 2016).

[99] James Q. Wilson and George Kelling, "Broken Windows," *Atlantic Monthly* (March, 1982), 29–38; George Kelling and Catherine M. Coles, *Fixing Broken Windows* (New York: Martin Kessler Books, 1996).

[100] Gordon Witkin, "The Crime Bust," *U.S. News and World Report* (May 25, 1998), 28–33.

[101] Kate Abbey-Lambertz and Joseph Erbentraut, "The Simple Strategies that can Fundamentally Change how Communities View Police," *Huffington Post* (July 07, 2016).

In this chapter you will read a case about terrorism, and what has come to be referred to as a "home grown" terrorist. The bombing of a federal building in Oklahoma City was a precursor to the profound events of September 2001. The content of the chapter focuses on understanding these acts and on the legal and quasi-legal developments that follow in their tracks.

LEARNING OBJECTIVES

After reading this chapter you should be able to:

- Define terrorism.
- Explain what motivates terrorists to action.
- Describe the role the U.S. Constitution plays in our response to terrorism.
- Describe the impact that the U.S. response to terrorism has had on our systems of law and justice.
- Explain the conflicts between liberty and security.

Case #9: False Patriots: The Oklahoma City Bombing and the Politics of Fear

The Oklahoma City National Memorial at the site of the Alfred P. Murrah building to honor the memory of the 168 victims who died in the bombing.

On April 19, 1995, 168 people, including 21 children, perished in the massive collapse of the Alfred P. Murrah Federal Building in Oklahoma City. Just before 9 o'clock on an ordinary workday when most people were still settling at their desks sipping their morning coffee, a Ryder truck packed with nearly seven thousand pounds of explosives parked strategically at the drop-off spot near the entrance of the building. Exactly At 9:01, according to plan, a lit fuse reached its destination. The force of the explosion equivalent to three tons of TNT annihilated half of the building. Some died instantly incinerated in the blast and firestorm that followed while others were crushed beneath the rubble, eviscerated by flying glass, or fell to their deaths as floors collapsed beneath them. Five hundred and nine people sustained horrific injuries trapped beneath mounds of red-hot twisted metal and concrete. It took days for rescuers to pull the living and the dead out of the steaming wreckage. Of the twenty-one babies and toddlers in the America's Kids day care center situated just thirty feet from the entrance, only six survived.

The bomber, twenty-six-year-old Timothy McVeigh, was less than two blocks away when the bomb went off. The force of the blast lifted him a full inch off the sidewalk and he was forced to bob and weave as glass from surrounding buildings showered around him. He climbed into his yellow Mercury and drove deliberately just under the speed limit away from Oklahoma City. At 9:10 a.m. eight minutes after the bombing, McVeigh was heading in the opposite direction to the screaming fire trucks, police cars, and running pedestrians rushing toward the billowing smoke and yellow dust of the fiery inferno.

By 11 a.m. that morning McVeigh was in the custody of the Noble County Jail in the small town of Perry in the neighboring state of Kansas. A state trooper had pulled him over for a missing license plate and arrested him for carrying a concealed weapon without a permit. McVeigh was charged with four misdemeanor offenses and held in the county jail awaiting an appearance before a judge. While McVeigh sat in the county jail, the news of the Oklahoma bombing blared from every available radio and television. This was the worst attack on American soil since the bombing of Pearl Harbor and everyone was glued to media. It seemed obvious to most observers that this was the work of foreign terrorists from somewhere in the Middle East looking to instill fear by targeting a federal building in the nation's heartland. No one dreamed that the polite, lanky young man with military-style buzz-cut hair would have any connection to this horrific act.

It was a fluke that McVeigh was still in custody, when authorities realized who it was they were looking for. Under normal circumstances, McVeigh would come before the county judge within twenty-four hours of his arrest and most likely had been released without bail given the minor charges and his status as a first-time offender. But because the calendar was unusually busy county authorities held him an extra night. By Friday morning, federal agents had traced the rental of the Ryder truck and were typing up arrest warrants for a suspect named Timothy McVeigh, along with two accomplices, Terry and James Nichols. A routine check of his name in the National Crime Information System brought up his arrest less than two hours after the bombing eighty miles north of Oklahoma City. A phone call to the county jail confirmed that he was still sitting in cell awaiting his court appearance: no one could believe this unassuming young man was the Oklahoma bomber.

Who Was Timothy McVeigh?

There is very little that is exceptional about the boyhood of Timothy McVeigh. Born in Buffalo, New York, to working-class parents, Tim was the middle child and only son of Bill and Mickey McVeigh. Physically small for his age, Tim had an uneventful childhood marred only by the separation and eventual divorce of his parents. Tim remained living with his father, a hardworking and mild-mannered man, who found it hard to connect with his son who did not share his passion for baseball and golf. Tim's close relationships were with his younger sister Jenny, who idolized him, and his grandfather, who taught him to shoot at a young age and gifted him his first rifle.

By all accounts, Tim was a well-behaved and intelligent student, who nonetheless failed to find any real connection with school. When he graduated from high school, he tried a local college for a few semesters but abandoned it as too "boring." He bounced between jobs working mainly as a security guard but his real passion was guns. He spent all his free time shooting, buying guns, and reading about them. He even purchased a small tract of remote land with a friend so he could conduct target practice without complaints from concerned neighbors.

As part of his growing interest in guns, Tim subscribed to numerous gun magazines. The more he read, the more he became interested in the ideas that were promulgated through these publications. Increasingly

Tim talked with friends and family about the idea of survivalism: the idea that each person needs to be self-sufficient and protect oneself and one's family without relying on assistance from the government. Increasingly he talked about the looming threat of government laws restricting the right of citizens to bear arms.

One book more than any other captured his imagination. *The Turner Diaries* is a work of fiction published in 1978 by William Pierce, a former official with the American Nazi party. The hero of the novel is Ed Turner, a gun enthusiast, who reacts to ever-tighter gun laws by blowing up the FBI building in Washington D.C. with a truck bomb. Pages of the book were in an envelope in the yellow Mercury along with other similar literature and McVeigh had sent excerpts to his sister Jenny in the days just before the bombing to help her understand his mission.

In 1988, Tim suddenly decided to enlist in the Army where he met Terry Nichols and Michael Fortier, two of the men who would later join him in the execution of the Oklahoma plot. In his two years in the Army, McVeigh found himself to be well suited to the disciplined life of a soldier. He loved the order, the sense of mission, and the intensity. More than anything else he loved working with firearms. He excelled in the work of being a soldier, became a firearms expert and top gunner and was rapidly promoted to sergeant. After a successful combat tour in Desert Storm, McVeigh was tapped as a recruit to the elite Special Forces unit. But after only a few weeks at the training camp, he backed out of the program. Shortly afterward, McVeigh, who many expected to pursue a career in the military, abruptly quit and returned home to his old job as a security guard.

For the next three or four years McVeigh would become increasing adrift from his family and childhood friends traveling from gun show to gun show periodically living with Terry Nichols and his wife in Montana, with James Nichols on his farm in Michigan, or with Michael Fortier and his family in Arizona. He supported himself doing odd jobs, selling literature at gun shows and serving as a "straw buyer," someone willing to purchase guns for people who could not or would not put their own names on the requisite paper work. He occasionally came home to Buffalo to see his father but kept most contact with his younger sister with whom he shared his growing belief in the threat of a government takeover of individual's right to bear arms. Jenny McVeigh did not always understand what her big brother was talking about but she loved him and thought he was brilliant. Just before the bombing, McVeigh wrote her a letter in which he explained that he was no longer interested in mere "propaganda": he told her it was time for him to move to the "action stage" and that he was planning something "big."

Why Did He Do It?

The date of the bombing—April 19, 1995—is key to understanding the logic behind this act of mass murder. The date is significant for three different reasons. First and foremost the date is the second anniversary of the tragic end of a disastrous federal gun raid on the Branch Davidian religious sect just outside Waco, Texas. On the first day of the raid, a shootout left six Davidians and four federal agents dead; fifty-one days later, on April 19, 1993, federal law enforcement agents ended the standoff using military tanks to fire canisters of tear gas into the compound. This barrage eventually ignited a fire killing seventy-six people inside, including twenty-four children. Timothy McVeigh twice visited the compound to show his support for the Davidians and watched the conflagration with Terry Nichol as it was broadcast on national television.

April 19 is significant for another reason. Ten years earlier on that date another federal raid took place on a group called the Covenant, Sword, and Arms or CSA. Part of a loose coalition of organizations known as the Patriot movement, the leaders of this group were working on a plot to blow up the Alfred P. Murrah Federal Building in Oklahoma City. They had targeted the building because it housed numerous federal agencies, including, most significantly, the ATF, DEA, and FBI and seemed to have only minimum security. They were seeking a target that would kill lots of people because they believed a high "body count" was necessary to make the government sit up and take notice. This plan was never executed because the compound was raided before the bomb could be built: the date of the FBI led raid on the CSA was April 19, 1985, ten years to the day of the Oklahoma City bombing.

A third reason that this date had meaning is that one of the leaders of another Patriot underground group called The Order (after the fictional account in *The Turner Diaries*) was scheduled to be executed on that day. This group believed that 1984 was going to be the year of the Second American Revolution; so starting in September of 1983, they began committing bank robberies and other crimes to purchase land for training camps. They bombed a synagogue and carried out the first of several planned assassinations. Wayne Snell was convicted of murdering a Jewish radio talk show host. He had been sentenced to death and the date of his execution was set for April 19, 1995, the day of the Oklahoma City bombing.

A final clue to the "logic" behind the bombing is the T-shirt McVeigh was wearing on the day of the bombing. On the back of the shirt is an image of a tree with drops of blood dripping from its branches. Superimposed over the tree is a quotation by Thomas Jefferson: "The tree of liberty must be refreshed from time to time with the blood of patriots and tyrants." On the front of the shirt are the words, "Sic Semper Tyrannis," which means "Thus ever to tyrants." These were the words uttered by John Wilkes Booth when he assassinated Abraham Lincoln in 1865. It was McVeigh's favorite T-shirt.

In the immediate aftermath of the bombing while most experts were speculating that foreign terrorists were responsible, the significance of April 19 was immediately apparent to Special Agent Clinton R. Van Zandt of the FBI's Behavioral Science Unit in Quantico, Virginia. Having served as the lead negotiator at the Waco debacle, he was well aware what the anniversary of the tragic fire would mean to the members of the Patriot Militia movement. When asked by his supervisor to provide a profile of the Oklahoma City terrorists, Van Zandt made no mention of the Middle East. He told his supervisor, "You're going to have a white male, acting alone or with one other person. He'll be in his mid-twenties. He'll have military experience and be a fringe member of some militia group. He'll be angry at the government for what happened at Ruby Ridge and Waco." His supervisor was not convinced, "We're thinking it's more of a Third-World terrorist type."

The Hidden World of the Far-Right Militia Movement

In the first half of the 1990s, there was an explosive growth in citizen militias and insurgent anti-government groups that coalesced around the issue of gun rights and used the national network of gun shows as a venue for recruiting and organizing. With his passion for guns, military training, and seething anger at the government, Timothy McVeigh was in the right place at the right time to be tapped as an eager and talented member of the Patriots.

The ideological roots of the Patriot movement harken back to earlier conflicts within American society and to other social movements both on the right and left sides of the political spectrum. To fully understand, it is necessary to look back to the era at the end of World War II in the 1950s and 1960s when fear of the Soviet Union and its quest for world domination captured the political imagination of many American citizens. For many including Senator Joseph McCarthy and President Richard Nixon, the greatest danger to the United States came from those working to subvert the United States from inside American society. The belief led to the infamous anti-communist crusades to cleanse government, academia, Hollywood, and business of anyone with "communist sympathies."

For many on the right, the civil rights movements of the 1960s was really part of the international spread of communism and leaders like Martin Luther King Jr. were merely "pawns" or "fronts" for the Communist Party seeking world domination. The goal was to sow the seeds of racial division and discord within American society in order to take control of our government. As early as 1961, armed militias calling themselves the Minutemen (after the U.S. revolutionaries) espoused violent action using arms to resist the federal government. There groups overlapped and intermingled with the resurgence of the Ku Klux Klan in the Deep South already resentful of the federal government's support of the civil rights movement. In 1957, when the governor of Arkansas called on the National Guard to protect blacks attending all-white schools in Little Rock, many saw this as proof that the federal government was part of the conspiracy to impose a federal dictatorship on the South.

Of particular significance was the ideological rejection of the authority of the federal government itself especially its legitimate right to exercise taxation authority over individual citizens. This movement questioned the constitutional authority of the federal government to levy taxes and enforce federal laws. Some even went so far as to deny the legitimacy of any law enforcement officer above the level of county or sheriff's office. The resulting mix of ideas was a toxic brew that bundled resentment against the federal government's income tax with racists' fears of a "negro revolution" to enslave whites bankrolled by "Jewish bankers" seeking to impose a single world order headed by the United Nations.

During the 1980s, the movement gained adherents from the rural Farm Belt in places like Idaho, Michigan, and Iowa when thousands of family farms struggling under unsustainable debt were forced to declare bankruptcy and sell off in farm auctions. Encouraged by favorable agricultural policies, small farmers had taken out loans to buy equipment and expand production but then got caught in a financial bind when China and India expanded their own production of grain. Prices fell and the U.S. government refused to subsidize them. Terry Nichols was one of these small farmers. Unable to continue the family business he joined the military in his late thirties after being forced to sell his farm. Like many others, he bitterly blamed the federal government, who refused to come to their aid, and the greed of bankers, who foreclosed on loans. Nichols, like many other farmers, became highly sympathetic to the arguments of the Patriot movement.

A final piece of the ideological puzzle and one most important for understanding the motives of Timothy McVeigh and others, who bombed the Murrah Building in 1995, is the growth of military-style policing in both state and federal law enforcement during the 1990s. McVeigh and others believed that the U.S. government was engaging in acts of "war" against its citizens and they attributed this development to a sinister conspiracy designed to "disarm" and "enslave" white Christians under a One World government. The threat of a war waged by the government against its citizens was made all the more plausible by changes that were taking place within the structure of federal and state law enforcement.

The "War" on Drugs and the Militarization of U.S. Policing

Since President Nixon, the use of the term "war" was a powerful rhetorical device for garnering support for crime control. Nixon declared a "war on crime" and the Reagan-Bush administrations expanded that even further with the "war on drugs." Starting with the Reagan administration, however, there was a shift from the mere words of war to the actual deployment of the U.S. military in domestic law enforcement and the militarization of policing tactics, training, and equipment. This began primarily in the area of drug enforcement but over time expanded to weapons enforcement and terrorism.

After the end of the Cold War, there was a declining rationale for a huge federal defense budget to maintain forces around the world. Rather than reduce defense spending the Reagan and then later the Bush administrations recruited the military to assist in various domestic law enforcement agendas. Primary among these was the war on drugs. Reagan lobbied Congress to amend nineteenth-century laws that prohibited military involvement in domestic law enforcement and began to increasingly use military personnel in the war on drugs. In 1986 Operation Alliance brought together the FBI, DEA, ATF, INS, U.S. Customs, Border Patrol, Coast Guard, U.S. Marshals Service, Secret Service, National Guard, and the Department of Defense in an unprecedented effort to coordinate the war on drugs. This same apparatus would later provide a key role in assisting the ATF on its gun raid at Waco, Texas. Not surprisingly, this raid was structured like a military assault using high-tech military equipment, such as tanks, assault weapons, snipers, and tear gas.

Aggressive enforcement of drug laws did not galvanize the Patriot movement but once the same approach was applied to the enforcement of gun laws, this apparatus was viewed as a significant assault on the freedom of U.S. citizens. Under President Reagan and then President Clinton, gun laws began to prohibit the use of military-style assault weapons by citizens. Both the passage of the Brady Bill in 1991 and the 1994 Crime Control Act banning assault weapons were seen by the gun rights networks as an attempt to disarm American citizens. The use of military-style policing strategies developed in the realm of drug enforcement in the enforcement of gun laws fed into the existing belief that the government was going to war against its citizens. The gun raids at Ruby Ridge and Waco, Texas, solidified this perception that the government was the enemy of the people.

William Pierce's novel, *The Turner Diaries* written in 1978 was a kind of bible and organizing manual for many in the movement, including Timothy McVeigh. For years, McVeigh urged anyone he knew to read the book and often handed out copies to complete strangers. In the plot of the novel, the federal government passes a law, the Cohen Act, which outlaws the possession and sale of weapons by citizens as a prelude to subjugate white citizens in a dictatorship called the New World Order. The government makes use of paramilitary police teams to confiscate all weapons in military-style gun raids. The hero Turner uses guerilla tactics, including blowing up a federal building using a truck bomb made from fertilizer.

The rallying cry of the book, which appears on the blurb on the back cover and is repeated endlessly in gun magazines is, "What are you going to do when they come to take your guns?" McVeigh believed, "The government is trying to eliminate all private gun ownership in this country . . . they want to rob us of our guns; strip us of all firearms. It's not going to happen without a fight. If the government wants to use overwhelming force, then we will meet it with overwhelming force. We have the right to defend ourselves against all enemies foreign or domestic."

To McVeigh and others in the Patriot movement, the government's enforcement of gun laws through the use of paramilitary style of policing was evidence of a deeper plot to disarm the U.S. citizen. For them, the use of the military against its own citizens was grounds for armed resistance. As they plotted to blow up the Murrah Building they saw themselves as Patriots of the Second American Revolution.

The Criminal Prosecution of McVeigh and Nichols

Within only two hours of the bombing, the FBI had the names of two American citizens, both former U.S. soldiers, in their investigation. The breakthrough came because a piece of the Ryder truck, the rear axle had been catapulted a full city block away from site. Unscathed the axle had the CVIN or confidential vehicle number stamped on it. This hidden identifier is crucial in the tracking of stolen vehicles and led investigators to the rental location in Junction City Kansas where McVeigh had rented it two days earlier. McVeigh had used an alias but agents dispatched to the site got a composite sketch from the clerk. This sketch was immediately broadcast on national television. Taking the sketch door to door agents quickly came upon the motel where McVeigh had registered for two nights while he assembled the bomb inside the truck. The manager of the motel confirmed that he had been driving a Ryder truck. Here McVeigh had registered under his own name and had also listed the Nichols family farm in Decker, Michigan, as his home address which led investigators to Terry and James Nichols.

Meanwhile another witness came forward with crucial information that led authorities to McVeigh. A fellow security guard in Buffalo, Carl E. Lebron Jr., had spent many nights listening to McVeigh's rant about the government and its threat to U.S. citizens. Like everyone else, McVeigh tried to convince Lebron to read *The Turner Diaries* and talked ceaselessly about the need for violent action against the federal government. When Lebron saw the police sketch on CNN, he went straight to the FBI with all he knew about McVeigh.

On August 10, four months after the bombing, a federal grand jury handed down an indictment against McVeigh and Terry Nichols accusing them of using a weapon of mass destruction to "kill and injure innocent persons and damage the property of the United States." The federal trial *U.S. v. Timothy J. McVeigh* started on April 24, 1997.

The prosecution's case against McVeigh and his co-conspirator Nichols depended on the strong evidence that he had purchased the ingredients to make the fertilizer bomb in the days and weeks before the bombing; his rental of the Ryder Truck; his former accomplice Fortier and his wife's testimony about the planning of the operation; and the testimony of his sister who reluctantly testified about his anti-government views and turned over his letters referencing the "big action" he was planning in the month of April.

While McVeigh insisted to his defense team that he alone planned and carried out this operation with the assistance of only Nichols and Fortier, the defense wanted to present evidence that this was not the true and suggest to the jury that FBI had failed to fully investigate all possible suspects once they apprehended McVeigh and Nichols. This defense strategy was curtailed, when the judge refused to allow the defense to enter evidence that suggested that McVeigh and Nichols were only a small part of the larger conspiratorial network of actors.

The remaining argument by the defense was that evidence in the prosecution's case was merely circumstantial. Although he had no alibi for that morning, the defense argued that simply because McVeigh was found to be nearby wearing ear plugs and an offensive T-shirt did not prove beyond a reasonable doubt that he committed the bombing. Furthermore having incendiary literature in one's car was not itself a crime and did not prove he actually acted on that literature.

The jury disagreed with the defense. On June 2 McVeigh was found guilty of all eleven counts against him. In a capital trial, a jury decides guilt and innocence and then qualification for the death penalty in two separate proceedings. In the first trial, his defense attorney vigorously claimed McVeigh was innocent; in the penalty phase of the trial, the defense attorney fully admitted McVeigh had committed the bombing but tried to argue that McVeigh committed this act because he was trying to defend the ideals of his country. The jury did not find this rationale mitigated his culpability for his actions. Two weeks later, on Friday, June 13, the jury handed the death penalty for his crime.

At the sentencing, the judge permitted McVeigh to make a statement. Everyone expected him to express some kind of regret but McVeigh had no sympathy or remorse for his victims whom he coolly regarded as "collateral damage" in an act of war. His statement was intended to justify his actions by blaming the government for declaring war on citizens in the first place. His statement was a single quotation from a Supreme Court justice Louis Brandeis, "Our government is the potent, omnipresent teacher. For good or ill, it teaches the whole people by its example." Without any further explanation, that was all McVeigh said to his victims and to the American public.

McVeigh instructed his attorneys not to appeal his death sentence: he had always expected to sacrifice his life for this cause. Timothy McVeigh was executed by lethal injection on June 11, 2001 three months to the day before 9/11.

On December 23, 1997, Nichols was found guilty of conspiracy and involuntary manslaughter and sentenced to life in prison without parole. Michael Fortier too was convicted for failing to warn the government about the plot and sentenced to twelve years in federal prison. Yet there are many who firmly believe that it is highly unlikely that Timothy McVeigh was capable of carrying out an operation of this magnitude with only two accomplices. Experts now feel strongly that by claiming to have acted alone, McVeigh was protecting a wider network of domestic terrorists active within our borders.

Who Won?

From the outset McVeigh admitted to his defense team that he carried out the bombing but he did not want his defense attorneys to enter a guilty plea on his behalf. Like most terrorists, McVeigh wanted to use his day in Court to get his message to the public. He asked his lawyer to use the defense of "necessity" so he could claim that he was forced to take action against a government that had declared war on its citizens. He wanted to convince the American public of the righteousness of his actions.

Rather than seeing McVeigh as the self-sacrificing soldier he believed himself to be, however, the American public reserved its compassion for the victims. Two acts of Congress had to be passed to accommodate the needs of an unprecedented number of victims to attend the trial. The first allowed victims to serve as witnesses and remain in the courtroom during the proceedings. Up until that point federal law did not allow witnesses to hear proceedings for fear it would influence their testimony. The mother of a young woman killed in the blast fought for victims' right to be present. The second law allowed the trial to be broadcast to Oklahoma City to accommodate the large number of victims who wanted to attend.

In the end, the public rejected McVeigh's view of himself as a patriot. Rather than seeing McVeigh as the revolutionary hero he thought himself to be, most Americans viewed him as a "baby killer" and a coward. When President Clinton referred to the bombing as the ultimate act of cowardice McVeigh was infuriated. In closing arguments to the jury, the prosecutor echoed the president, "Our forefathers didn't fight British women and children. They fought other soldiers. They fought them face to face, hand to hand. They didn't plant bombs and run away wearing ear plugs." In the court of public opinion, McVeigh experienced the ultimate failure: if his goal was to win hearts and minds of the American public to feel sympathy for his political cause, this act of terror was a complete failure. The Oklahoma bombing marked a decline of the right-wing militia movement, as even supporters turned away in disgust at the naked brutality of terrorist violence.

THINKING CRITICALLY ABOUT THIS CASE

1. What makes this a crime of "terrorism" in your view? How is this crime different from other acts of mass murder? Explain your answer.

2. Do you believe that this case was successfully handled by the criminal justice system? Why or why not? Did the trial hurt or help the victims in your view?

3. Many people believe that there were others who assisted McVeigh in this case. Should the government have utilized military-style interrogations to force McVeigh to reveal any other co-conspirators? Why or why not?

4. Timothy McVeigh was upset at the government's use of military force against its citizens at Waco, Texas. Why? He believed these actions justified his behavior. Do you agree? Why or why not?

5. Do you believe that Timothy McVeigh deserved the death penalty? Why or why not?

6. Timothy McVeigh viewed his victims as "collateral damage" in an act of war. Where did he learn to think that way? What did McVeigh mean when he stated, "The government is the teacher, for good or ill." Does this justify his conduct in your view? Explain your answer.

7. What steps do you believe should be taken to prevent crimes in the future?

REFERENCES

Case adapted from:

Stephen Jones and Peter Israel, *Others Unknowns: The Oklahoma City Case and Conspiracy* (New York: Public Affairs, 1998).

Lou Michel and Dan Herbeck, *American Terrorist* (New York: HarperCollins Publishers Inc., 2001).

Stuart A. Wright, *Patriots, Politics, and the Oklahoma City Bombing* (New York: Cambridge University Press, 2007).

THE CRIME OF TERRORISM

Timothy McVeigh believed the bombing of the Alfred P. Murrah Building would change the course of history. Little did he know that his act of political violence would be instantly forgotten in the wake of another act of terrorism exactly three months after his execution on June 11, 2001. Forever known by the date "9/11," the events of September 11, 2001, would shake the confidence of an entire nation, destabilize the global balance of power, instigate two costly American-led wars and initiate the greatest restructuring of the American government since the founding fathers drafted the U.S. Constitution.

This chapter examines the crime of **terrorism**—the debates about what it actually means and patterns of terrorist acts within American history and around the world. The most important focus of the chapter will be on the U.S. response to terrorism by governments and citizens since 9/11. How has the U.S. response to terrorism changed our institutions of law and justice? Has it led to a reduction in freedom or an increase in security that guarantees our freedom? What is the balance between security and liberty and which is the greatest danger: the threat of terrorism or an overzealous effort to prevent it within a free and open democratic society?

TERRORISM
the unlawful use of force or violence against a target to create fear or coercion for the purpose of obtaining some political concession or reward or other goal.

Known as the Tribute in Light, eighty-eight searchlights at the site of the destroyed World Trade Center create two vertical columns of light every year in remembrance of the September 11 attacks.

Defining Terrorism

To a certain extent, terrorism is an act that lies in the "eye of the beholder." Political violence is often labeled as "terrorism" by the opposing side in a conflict.[1] The saying "one man's terrorist is another man's freedom fighter" points to an important element of the crime of terrorism, namely its character as being politically motivated. The citizens who fought against British soldiers at the time of the American Revolution were committing acts of politically motivated violence against the legal government of the English crown. To the British, these were acts of illegal violence against the legitimate authority of English law; to the revolutionaries these were acts of war in a struggle for political power. In this context, both sides view the moral righteousness of the violence from different perspectives: labeling an action as "terrorism" inescapably makes a value statement that expresses moral disapproval of that action. No one who believes their cause is just labels themselves a "terrorist."

One important distinction can clearly be made: all terrorist actions violate the criminal code of established legal systems. The U.S. Code of Federal Regulations (28 C.F.R. Section 0.85) defines terrorism as "the unlawful use of force or violence against persons or property to intimidate or coerce a government, the civilian population or any segment thereof, in furtherance of political or social objectives." All terrorist acts are also criminal acts. Timothy McVeigh was convicted of eleven violations of Title 18 of the U.S. Code, including the use of weapon of mass destruction to commit murder; conspiracy to commit murder using a weapon of mass destruction; destruction by explosives; and four counts of first-degree murder. While most crimes are not acts of terrorism, all terrorists commit crime.[2]

So what makes a criminal act an act of terrorism? There are several distinguishing characteristics of terrorist crimes.[3] First is the motivation for the action. Terrorism involves the illegal use of force against people or property for political purposes. Terrorism is crime committed for a cause. Other analysts point out that with terrorist crimes, the victims are chosen for their symbolic value. The direct victim serves as a means to send a message to a different audience. This message may be to publicize a point of view as when animal rights activists blow up a chicken farm to call attention to the abusive treatment of animals. Or it may be to instill fear among a population by attacking mass transit systems, busy shopping streets, or bustling nightclubs. The act may be intended to force specific actors to take certain actions such as the release of political prisoners or withdrawal of military personnel from a particular location. Whatever the intended purpose, the victims of violence are typically chosen for their symbolic value in communicating some desired message to another audience.

Terrorist acts also differ from many criminal acts by being a planned activity committed for purposes other than personal gain. Terrorists often finance their operations by committing crimes such as armed robberies prior to an act of violence. McVeigh did this when he arranged for the robbery of a wealthy gun collector. But the purpose of the robbery was not to enrich himself. Terrorists are committed to an ideology or set of beliefs that forms the rationale for the crime; they are not committing these crimes to put money in their pockets.

Terrorists typically are part of a larger movement of some kind. Even when an individual acts alone, they view themselves as part of a group with a higher purpose. The act is neither impulsive nor opportunistic. They have generally created a plan and moved through some kind of disciplined set of acts toward the fulfillment of that plan. An act of terrorism therefore typically involves more people than those who carry out the final act. There are others who may have not committed a particular act but are involved in planning, financing, training, and logistics behind it.

Terrorists: Who Are They?

There is really no single profile of a "terrorist." There are as many **profiles** as there are different kinds of groups with different agendas seeking to use violence to further their political agenda or beliefs. There are, however, clear profiles of individuals within these specific groups.[4] Consider how accurate the FBI was in producing a description of the likely suspect in the Oklahoma City bombing only minutes after the attack: as a young rural white male, ex-soldier, gun enthusiast, McVeigh fit the profile for an attack on a federal building on the anniversary of the Waco fire. To make an accurate profile for any given act of terror, experts need a deep level of understanding of the sociological characteristics and political agendas of particular terrorists group. When developing a profile the unit of analysis should be a particular group and its cause, not terrorists in general.

Yet those who engage in terrorism do share some broad characteristics. Prior to committing the act, terrorists tend to be disconnected from mainstream society and other sources of social approval and social support. Like McVeigh they are often unmarried young males or if married, it is to someone within the group as well. The group has become the defining part of their life. The group itself tends to be highly insular from others within the society and is motivated by a strong sense of injustice or grievance.[5]

This injustice is the basis for a sense of mission and also for a mythology or story that explains what has happened in the past and provides a vision for a better future. For McVeigh, like many others in his movement, *The Turner Diaries* and other futuristic novels provide a powerful set of ideas that clearly divide the world into good and evil with an "us" versus "them" mentality. While specifics vary from group to group, all terrorist organizations have some kind of narrative that defines the enemy and provides a shared language and worldview for those within the group.

One element in the wave of terrorism associated with the recent rise of **militant jihadism** has been the willingness of individuals to knowingly and intentionally sacrifice their lives in the operation itself. Suicide terrorism has been a factor in many different political conflicts in history. It is a particularly effective tactic because the attacker is able to maneuver without concern for their self-protection. The events of 9/11 in which hijackers deliberately crashed planes into specific targets could have not happened unless individuals were willing to lose their lives in the process of the attack.

Terrorism in Historical Context

Terrorism is not a new phenomenon.[6] The history of terrorism is bound up with the complex histories of political conflicts around the world. The word "terrorism" itself was coined in 1789 in the wake of the French Revolution by British observers.[7] Edmund Burke called the massive number of executions of formerly powerful members of the nobility and church by the new government a **reign of terror** and those carrying out these executions "terrorists."

During the course of the nineteenth century as different groups struggled against autocratic European governments the term "terrorist" came to refer to

PROFILING
a tool used by law enforcement to narrow offender characteristics to assist in prevention or apprehension.

MILITANT JIHADISM
a term used to describe a movement claiming to be rooted in Islam and perceived to be devoted to the destruction of "the west."

REIGN OF TERROR
coined by Edmund Burke, the term described the massive number of executions of formerly powerful members of the nobility and church by the new government in the aftermath of the French Revolution; the source of the term "terrorism."

groups who were challenging governmental authority rather than upholding it. These were sometimes radical political groups trying to achieve a more egalitarian society who tended to choose important political or military personnel for assassination. The invention of dynamite toward the end of the nineteenth century was a breakthrough in enhancing the power of individuals and small groups to make bombs to throw at targets. In Europe and the United States **anarchist** groups sought to challenge military and capitalist power through what they termed **propaganda by deed** by tossing bombs at important figures in public places.[8] The tactics of these myriad groups differed from modern terrorism in that they did not target ordinary civilians to achieve their objectives.

In the nineteenth and twentieth centuries, the use of terrorist tactics in political struggles against established governments took place in the context of anticolonial movements and struggles for national independence and sometimes civil war. **Nationalists** tended to see themselves as unconventional soldiers fighting for the fellow countrymen. In many contexts it is not possible to distinguish terrorism from guerilla warfare in which a weaker force relies on nontraditional strategies to attack a more powerful military force. Contemporary military theorists point out that in the twenty-first century, established military forces are fighting an asymmetrical form of warfare—a tactic of the weak against a much stronger adversary in which the aim is to leverage a small amount of violence to generate a much greater level of fear.[9] Publicity is essential since the point is to generate far greater damage by instigating reactions on the part of the adversary. Most terrorists see themselves as unconventional soldiers fighting a far more powerful enemy.

Terrorism in U.S. History

Throughout U.S. history various domestic political groups have turned to terrorist tactics to achieve their political aims. Lynching is a powerful form of terrorism violence and was used by right-wing groups like the Ku Klux Klan since emancipation of the slaves to terrify both whites and blacks in the South.[10] The purpose of lynching a victim who was accused of violating norms of **white supremacy** (i.e., whistling at a white woman; failing to step aside when a white person passed on the street; becoming educated; exercising the right to vote) was to send a message to a wider audience. The climate of fear and intimidation was intended to force people to conform to the code of white supremacy. This tactic was highly effective in maintaining the racial hierarchy in the South despite the formal changes in the law.

In the 1960s, left-wing political activists also turned to terrorist tactics to send a political message to a wider audience.[11] More active in Europe and Latin America than in the United States, some of these groups committed targeted violence, focusing largely on the symbols of state power like law enforcement or symbols of capitalist power. In Europe much of the violence involved kidnapping of prominent businessmen or politicians. To a great extent none of these left-wing groups attempted to influence politics by targeting the general public.

While most left-wing groups in the United States were based in the urban centers, right-wing groups tended to be based in rural communities and draw their followers from small towns and rural regions in the West and South. Groups on both the left and right often funded their operations by committing other crimes particularly armed robberies. By the 1980s, left-wing activism in the United States had diminished down to single-issue activists fighting for specific

ANARCHIST
a political philosophy that rejects the state and opposes hierarchy.

PROPAGANDA BY DEED
actions, including tossing bombs at important persons in public places, used by anarchists in the nineteenth century to bring attention to their cause.

NATIONALISTS
unconventional soldiers fighting for fellow countrymen.

WHITE SUPREMACY
the belief that "white" people are superior to other races.

causes such as the Animal Liberation Front or **eco-terrorists** who use violence to draw public attention to practices they feel are immoral and unjust. Right-wing extremist groups such as those that spawned the Oklahoma City bombing remain far more extensive and active in the current U.S. political context than left-wing groups.

The FBI currently divides domestic terrorism into three broad categories to reflect the current political landscape: the activities of right-wing extremist groups like those who planned the Oklahoma City bombing; single-issue groups such as animal rights activists, eco-terrorists, or anti-abortion extremists; and lone-wolf individuals who are disconnected from any organized group.[12]

On April 15, 2013, two bombs went off near the finish line of the Boston Marathon, killing 3 spectators and wounding more than 260 other people. While the damage was substantial, the weapons used were two primitive explosives. This attack proved to be a lone-wolf attack by two brothers, nineteen-year-old Dzhokhar Tsarnaev and his older brother twenty-six-year-old Tamerlan Tsarnaev, who was killed in a shootout with police. Although the Tsarnaevs spent part of their childhoods in the former Soviet republic of Kyrgyzstan, investigators concluded that the two brothers planned and carried out the attack on their own. Timothy McVeigh maintained that he planned and executed the bombing with only minor assistance from Nichols and Fortier, but many experts are skeptical about this assertion. While smaller operations might be carried out by lone wolves, large operations such as the Oklahoma City bombing or 9/11 require extensive personnel providing logistical support, financing, and expertise.[13]

Osama Bin Laden and al Qaeda

The specific origins of al Qaeda, the terrorist organization responsible for the attacks on 9/11, lie in the declining years of the Cold War and the Soviet-Afghanistan war.[14] To oppose Soviet expansion, the United States dedicated billions of dollars to support the ragtag Afghan rebel forces, largely local tribal fighters joined by the **mujahideen**—or holy warriors—essentially Muslim young men from across the Middle East and North Africa who came to overthrow a hated foreign power. When the Soviets withdrew in 1989, Americans too abandoned the region leaving a war-torn Afghanistan to continuing chaos and strife among the remaining warring tribal groups.

Many young men came to fight from across the Middle East including a twenty-three-year-old Osama Bin Laden. Born in Saudi Arabia to a wealthy construction executive, Bin Laden dropped out of college to join the fight in Afghanistan forming and leading his own guerilla unit. As the son of a wealthy family, Bin Laden brought his own funds but soon became active in raising additional funds once American support disappeared. al Qaeda at first was focused on trying to bring order to Afghanistan by imposing Islamic Law but later adopted a broader agenda targeting the economic power and influence of the West, especially the United States.

The victory in Afghanistan of a tiny force of guerilla fighters against the Soviet military was interpreted as a triumph of good over evil: if a ragtag army of dedicated Muslims could drive out a superpower it had to be a victory awarded by God. Bin Laden began to call for a return to greatness by a people who saw themselves as dominated by a succession of foreign masters throughout their history. He sought to restore the pride of a people who had been exploited by secular rulers who collaborated with the West and destroyed the previous greatness of Muslim civilization.

ECO-TERRORISM
people who use violence to draw public attention to practices related to animal welfare or the environment that they believe are immoral and unjust.

MUJAHIDEEN
Muslim holy warriors.

Specific grievances of al Qaeda against the United States included the presence of military bases in Saudi Arabia, the boycott against Iraq after the first Gulf War, and American support of the state of Israel, but the jihadist agenda was motivated by a deep-seated economic and political discontent among millions within the region. The deteriorating social conditions within these countries produced millions of young men skilled and educated but unable to find meaningful work and build a life for themselves. Under these circumstances, a few become susceptible to the call of radical jihadists to join the cause. Millions more are broadly sympathetic to a set of ideas that blame these dire conditions on the corruption of internal rulers and the complicity of the West in supporting them.

Starting in 1992, Osama Bin Laden made numerous public announcements directed at radical Muslims to take action against Americans, first against those stationed in Saudi Arabia and then later against Americans anywhere, civilian or military.[15] Like the militia movement, the jihadist movement is composed of many different groups with local agendas and grievances rooted in specific conflicts. They do not all share the same agenda or goals. Bin Laden's call to focus jihadist efforts on the United States created a common cause uniting these groups against a common enemy.

On February 26, 1993, a truck bomb parked in the underground garage of the World Trade Center carved a hole seven stories high in the building killing six people and injuring over a thousand. Those responsible for the plot were followers of the jihadist movement and quickly apprehended and successfully prosecuted. In 1998, the U.S. embassy in Nairobi, Kenya, was destroyed by a truck bomb killing twelve Americans and several hundred Kenyans. In October 2000, a Naval destroyer, the U.S.S. Cole stationed off the coast of Yemen was hit by a boat laden with explosives. Seventeen members of the ship's crews were killed in the suicide attack. Osama Bin Laden planned and directed this attack and assisted to some degree in others.

The Events of 9/11

For most Americans the events of September 11, 2001, are all too well known. Early that morning, a total of nineteen men boarded four flights departing from three cities on the east coast bound for the city of Los Angeles.[16] Two of the planes were departing from Boston's Logan airport, one was leaving from Dulles airport in Washington D.C., and one from Newark airport in NYC. All were bound for the city of Los Angeles fully loaded with fuel for the transcontinental trip, a total of 11,400 gallons. The plan was to hijack the planes and use them as guided missiles to attack targets on the ground in NYC and Washington D.C. As the world would soon find out, the plan was wildly successful.

At 8:46 American airlines flight 11 was flown into the North Tower of the World Trade Center; at 9:01 the second Boston flight, United Airlines 175, crashed into the South Tower of the WTC; at 9:37 American Airlines Flight 77 flew at top speed of 530 miles per hour into the Pentagon; and the fourth plane, United 73, had been aiming for the White House or Capitol but resistance by passengers on the flight forced the hijackers to crash the plane into an empty field in Pennsylvania at 10:02, only twenty minutes away from Washington D.C. Air defense strategies of the FAA and the military system NORAD were prepared to respond to a hijacked aircraft headed to an unknown destination but were not prepared for a **suicide mission** that intended to convert the passenger jets into lethal guided missiles.

SUICIDE MISSION
a task that is so dangerous that the person performing the act is not expected to survive.

Fifty-six minutes after the impact of United Airlines 75, the South Tower of the WTC collapsed into itself killing all civilians and emergency first responders who were inside; 29 minutes later the North Tower collapsed killing all those on the upper floors and below, including the chiefs of New York Fire Department and the Superintendent of Port Authority police, who were directing the rescue operation from the lobby of the building. Two thousand nine hundred and seventy-three people died at the WTC, the Pentagon, or as passengers on one of the four crashed airliners. This was the largest loss of life as a result of a hostile attack on American soil.

The U.S. Military Response to 9/11

The remainder of this chapter is devoted to an analysis of the U.S. response to 9/11 and how that response has changed the structure of our government and institutions of law and justice. First we examine the military response to 9/11 and then turn to changes in the legal system, including the structure of U.S. intelligence and law enforcement in the wake of 9/11.

The national and international response to 9/11 was overwhelming. The sympathy of the world was with the American people as the full impact of the devastating attack was broadcast around the globe. Within hours of the attack President Bush declared to his advisers that the United States was "at war." Although little was known about who was responsible, national security advisers believed correctly that this was the work of Islamic terrorists, probably al Qaeda, based in one of the nations known to provide safe haven for these organizations. The known bases of operation were Afghanistan, Pakistan, Sudan, Libya, Yemen, Cuba, and possibly Iraq. At 8:30 p.m. on the evening of September 11, G.W. Bush addressed the nation and the world with the warning, "We will make no distinction between the terrorists who committed these acts and those who harbor them."[17]

An immediate demand to turn over Osama Bin Laden and his co-conspirators was made to the Taliban government in Afghanistan. The Taliban government refused, and sixty days later, the United States launched a military offensive called Enduring Freedom in Afghanistan that was widely supported by the international community. The plan was swiftly successful in toppling the Taliban and eliminating al Qaeda's base of operations in that region. Bin Laden was nearly captured but he and other top leaders escaped to the mountains of Pakistan. Most analysts believe that Bin Laden's ability to direct operations was hampered by the removal of his sanctuary in Afghanistan. However, he continued to provide inspiration, direction, and coordination for the jihadist movement as he eluded capture for the next ten years. He remained at large until 2011, when he was killed in a secret U.S. raid on his compound in Pakistan conducted by U.S. Special Forces and authorized by President Obama.[18]

The success of the early Afghanistan operation was a sharp contrast to the failure of the second war on Iraq launched by the Bush administration. The first Afghan operation had the broad support of the international community. Two years later when the Bush administration launched a second military offensive against Iraq, the United States lost much of that sympathy and support. Many questioned any link between Saddam Hussein and acts of terror directed at the United States: no evidence of a connection has ever been verified, and the allegation that Hussein harbored weapons of mass destruction in violation of international law proved to be false.

Some analysts argue that the invasion of Iraq has reinvigorated the jihadist movement by generating a new set of grievances and common cause against the United States. The term "**jihad**" has both a broad religious meaning to all Muslims who practice the faith of Islam and a more specific meaning to those who are engaged in a political violence. For most Muslims the term "jihad" refers to an internal journey of purification and to the willingness to carry arms to defend your community. To militants the term refers to an offensive holy war committed against both Muslims and non-Muslims who oppose the restoration of a fundamentalist Islamic regime.[19]

Although formal U.S. engagement in Iraq ended in 2010, there is little evidence that global jihadist terrorism has been "defeated." The war on Afghanistan has also not ended as U.S. operations there revived Taliban forces to fight against the U.S.-backed government. While international opinion believes the first invasion was an effective use of the military, both the invasion of Iraq and the continued operation in Afghanistan have far fewer supporters both within the United States and abroad. The war in Iraq and Afghanistan may have spurred many young men to join the insurgency, just as the Soviet occupation of Afghanistan had for an earlier generation of militants in the 1980s.

Changes in U.S. Law in Response to 9/11

Many observers have noted that each time the United States has suffered a terrorist attack there is a restriction on the civil liberties of U.S. citizens. This was true in the wake of the Oklahoma City bombing when President Clinton signed anti-terrorism legislation to increase the capacity of the FBI to engage in counterterrorism and enhance federal penalties for the crime.[20] The U.S.A. **Patriot Act** was passed in October 2001, just six weeks after 9/11, and was reauthorized in 2006.[21]

The main goal of the Patriot Act is to enhance the ability of the government to collect intelligence inside the United States by removing the "wall" or legal prohibition on information shared between national intelligence and law enforcement agencies.[22] The U.S.A. Patriot Act expands the powers of law enforcement intelligence gathering and the power of the executive office in important ways. Specifically, it allows law enforcement and intelligence systems to share non-criminal information about individuals both foreign and domestic. It requires private companies such as banks, internet service providers, and telephone companies to share data with the FBI and allows the FBI to seize the material if it deems it a threat to national security. It places employees under nondisclosure orders preventing them from revealing ongoing surveillance.

The act also requires libraries to provide the FBI with records of patron's reading and internet searches and forces educational institutions to release records of foreign students. The law gives federal law enforcement the right to monitor internet searches and keep tabs on individual searches for information and to infiltrate religious organizations for the purpose of intelligence gathering. The government can also conduct wiretaps on any phone calls between the United States and foreign countries without a warrant in the hope of gathering information.

Finally, the Patriot Act gives the president the authority to designate organizations as **terrorist organizations** without any public process or oversight from the courts or Congress. Once designated as a terrorist organization, assets are frozen and seized; and anyone who makes a charitable contribution to that organization even if for totally unrelated purposes may be subject to criminal prosecution as a **material supporter** of a terrorist organization.

JIHAD
an internal journey of purification and the willingness to carry arms to defend your community.

PATRIOT ACT
an act of Congress passed in the immediate aftermath of the September 11 attacks, the main goal of which is to enhance the ability of the government to collect intelligence inside the United States by removing the "wall" or legal prohibition on information shared between national intelligence and law enforcement agencies.

TERRORIST ORGANIZATIONS
organizations designated by the president, pursuant to the authority of the Patriot Act, as funders or supporters of "terrorism."

MATERIAL SUPPORTER
anyone who makes a charitable contribution to an organization designated as "terrorist organization."

Criminal versus National Intelligence

Legally and operationally there is an important difference between **criminal intelligence** and **national security intelligence**.[23] As we have seen throughout this text, the Bill of Rights protects the right of U.S. citizens to be free of surveillance, intrusion, and interference by the government, state or federal, unless there is individualized suspicion that they have committed some kind of illegal activity. Under the Fourth Amendment, law enforcement personnel cannot collect criminal intelligence without reasonable suspicion or probable cause. The police must have evidence that a crime is taking or about to take place and the person is engaged or about to engage in crime, and generally they must present that information to a neutral judge who issues a warrant before information can be gathered, analyzed, or stored.

National security intelligence, by contrast, is preventative in nature and is designed to be ongoing and clandestine. The information gathered is often completely unrelated to any criminal activity and entirely legal. Intelligence analysts talk about "connecting the dots," suggesting that casting a wide net allows for detection of hidden relationships and connections among individuals, legal groups, and potential terrorist groups. This involves continuously gathering data on people's daily activity, finances, shopping, socializing, and most importantly, their political and religious activities and beliefs.

This intelligence gathering flies in the face of the right of U.S. citizens to live freely without interference from their government. One of the founding principles of American democracy is the right of citizens to be free to practice their religion, to express their views, and to associate with others unless there is some evidence that they are violating the law. This basic principle defines how law enforcement and the prosecutors are allowed to gather information about citizens: the warrant requirement of the Fourth Amendment requires some evidence of wrongdoing and the verification by the courts before law enforcement is allowed to violate the privacy of a citizen for ongoing surveillance.

THE ROLE OF LAW ENFORCEMENT IN THE WAR ON TERROR

In chapter 7 we described the creation of the Department of Homeland Security (DHS) as the most radical restructuring of the federal government since the end of World War II. The DHS also asks local, county, and state law enforcement to be active in the war on terror by gathering and sharing potentially suspicious information. According to a *Washington Post* investigative report, 3,984 federal, state and local organizations are now involved in counterterrorism: 934 of which are new agencies created in response to 9/11.[24]

On September 9 one of the pilots for the hijacked airliner out of Newark was stopped for speeding in Maryland as he was headed north on I-95. The state trooper ran his license plate through the local police database and sent him on his way. This missed opportunity is one of the motivations behind the creation of massive infrastructure of intelligence gathering designed to funnel information from local law enforcement into national databanks operated by the FBI. This information is collected and stored in 72 **fusion centers** located across the country run by the DHS.[25] These centers gather and store information collected by local police who fill out SARS or **suspicious activity reports** on citizens.

CRIMINAL INTELLIGENCE law enforcement surveillance of those believed to have engaged in illegal activities, typically responding to such activities; constrained by the Fourth Amendment requirements of reasonable suspicion or probable cause.

NATIONAL SECURITY INTELLIGENCE preventative clandestine surveillance by the government designed to gather information about potential threats to national security.

FUSION CENTERS centers across the country, administered by the Department of Homeland Security, where information is collected and stored.

SUSPICIOUS ACTIVITY REPORTS any report of individual suspicious activity reported to Homeland Security by a citizen or local police; also referred to as SAR.

This involves activity such as taking photographs of public buildings, drawing maps or any other kind of "suspicious behavior" around public facilities. They may also be from undercover police attending religious meetings or other group activities. These files are secret and remain within the database indefinitely.

The ACLU and other civil rights organizations point out that there is almost no oversight on whose information is being held and how that information might be used in the future.[26] Not surprisingly activists opposed to the war in Iraq were among the first to be subject to surveillance and harassment despite their first amendment rights to express dissent. Citizens organized around climate change and peace activists opposing government policies have also appeared within the database although like most secret intelligence, subjects do not know they are being monitored until they are arrested.

The history of the U.S. domestic intelligence has shown that when law enforcement is given the responsibility to eavesdrop on U.S. citizens for national security purposes, the government engages in significant violations of the political freedom of American citizens.[27] In the 1930s, the FBI was given the responsibility for domestic intelligence gathering for national security purposes under the direction of J. Edgar Hoover. Although the Central Intelligence Agency was created for this purpose at the end of World War II, the FBI continued to conduct domestic spy operations during the 1950s and 1960s. The **COINTELPRO** unit of the FBI was abruptly shut down in 1972 in the wake of discoveries that the FBI had been amassing a dossier on a huge number of domestic political individuals and organizations for decades.

This new responsibility of **counterterrorism** for local law enforcement also involves the use of ethnic and racial profiling, which conflicts with basic freedoms of American society. The recent exposure of a NYPD surveillance program on Muslim Americans is an illustration of the dilemma posed by law enforcement engaging in domestic national intelligence.[28] Beginning in 2002, in cooperation with the CIA, the NYPD used undercover officers to engage in covert monitoring of Muslim neighborhoods, mosques, and businesses. Police argue they targeted these individuals based on "legitimate leads" and not on the basis of racial profiling. Nonetheless, many Muslim Americans feel they no longer are entitled to the same rights to privacy that other Americans citizens enjoy.

If federal, state, and local law enforcement agencies are included in the mission of national defense, they are being asked to collect information having no relation to criminal investigations or activity. This is an enormous dilemma for a democracy—to gather information about potential terrorism is to ask police to monitor citizens for their religious and political beliefs and not for their criminal behavior.

Some critics question if collecting information on citizens is the most effective way to prevent terrorism. Despite the elaborate system of surveillance created after 9/11, it has been ordinary citizens who have detected most of the foiled plots since 9/11. The plan to detonate a truck bomb in New York City was thwarted by street vendors; the so-called Christmas Day bomber who tried to board a plane wearing explosives in his underwear was turned in by his father, who was aware that his mentally unstable son was preparing to do something he thought might be harmful to others.[29] Jonathan White argues that old-fashioned police-community relationships in which ordinary citizens have positive and trusting relationships with law enforcement is more likely to generate useful preventative intelligence than the massive and expensive system of data surveillance established by the DHS.[30]

COINTELPRO
an FBI program in the 1950s and 1960s that engaged in, often illegal, infiltration and disruption of domestic political organizations.

COUNTERTERRORISM
a government tactic for responding to terrorist threats.

The effectiveness of traditional criminal investigation and prosecution can be clearly seen in the apprehension of McVeigh and his co-conspirators within hours of the incident itself and the successful conviction and punishment. Many more individuals have been successfully charged and prosecuted in the criminal courts for the crime of terrorism, including the bombing of the World Trade Center in 1993 and the Boston Marathon bombing in 2013. Between 2001 and 2007, a nationwide study of prosecutions examined a specific set of 257 defendants charged with terrorism related violations in the United States and found federal prosecutors achieved a conviction rate above 90 percent.[31] In the Boston Marathon bombing, Dzhokhar Tsarnaev was indicted while still in the hospital on thirty charges relating to homegrown terrorism, including use of a weapon of mass destruction and malicious destruction of property resulting in death. He was found guilty on all charges on April 8, 2015, and the following month sentenced to death.

Some critics believe that the U.S. criminal courts are unable to conduct an effective response to terrorism given the possibility of acquittal; the sensitivity of evidence which may compromise national intelligence; and the possibility that terrorists will use the trial to publicize their political views. Others disagree pointing out that the courts are well equipped to handle sensitive intelligence; have successfully convicted and punished terrorists many times; and the sympathies of the public are far more likely to be with the victims, thereby reducing the courtroom as a platform for spreading their political message.

DEBATING THE "WAR" ON TERROR

The use of the military force as a primary response to the threat of terrorism is a complex question. The U.S. Constitution, as we have pointed out many times in this text, is designed to carve up power between three branches of government and to place important limits on the power of the federal government vis-à-vis the states and individual citizens. The framers were skeptical about the wisdom of power concentrated in the hands of a centralized authority and so placed carefully defined limits on the power of the federal government. One of these limits concerns the use of the military in domestic law enforcement. The Constitution prohibits the use of armed forces in civilian law enforcement except under a state of emergency with the declaration of **martial law**.

Historically Americans have overreacted in times of war or crisis: consider the treatment of more than 100,000 loyal Japanese Americans interned in war camps during World War II.[32] The American government has since apologized to the Japanese American community for the hysteria that occurred during wartime. But once the war was over, these extraordinary measures were no longer legal. As many have pointed out, a state of emergency associated with the war is a temporary condition that ends when a declaration of peace is made with a former enemy state.

Like the war on drugs, the war on terror is very different from an actual conflict with a sovereign power. In his speech on September 20, G.W. Bush stated that "Our war on terror begins with al Qaeda, but it does not end there. It will not end until every terrorist group of global reach has been found, stopped and defeated." Terrorism however is a tactic that can be used by any group or individual. As a threat it has no natural end point: it is always possible that U.S.

MARTIAL LAW
replacing civil law with military law, albeit on an emergency basis.

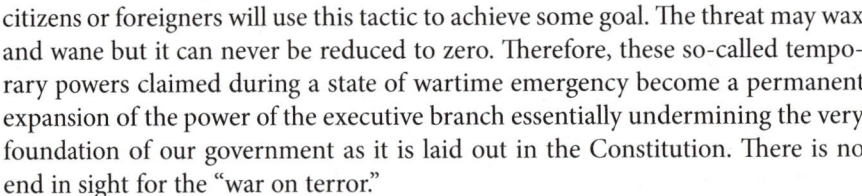

citizens or foreigners will use this tactic to achieve some goal. The threat may wax and wane but it can never be reduced to zero. Therefore, these so-called temporary powers claimed during a state of wartime emergency become a permanent expansion of the power of the executive branch essentially undermining the very foundation of our government as it is laid out in the Constitution. There is no end in sight for the "war on terror."

The act of violence on September 11, 2001, was unprecedented in scale and impact. Other than those who died on 9/11, the actual number of deaths from acts of terrorism on American soil is small: in the last 38 years only 340 Americans have been killed by terrorism. The actual risk of Americans dying from a terrorist act is lower than the risk of being killed by lightning, deer, bee stings, or flammable sleepwear.[33] Many observers note that the U.S. response to 9/11 has produced a higher level of violence than the original attack on 9/11. By waging an actual military operation, the U.S. response has led to a much greater loss of American life than originally taken by terrorists. The response has also involved the deaths of many thousands of innocent Iraqi and Afghan citizens, a rate of lethality many times greater than those killed by jihadist terrorists.

Even small children are subject to routine body screening by the TSA for airport security.

Security versus Liberty: Are We Safer If We Are Less Free?

The fear associated with terrorism is sufficiently high that many Americans feel the trade-off of their **civil liberties** and **right to privacy** is worth the cost of higher security. But just because we have given up our liberties does not necessarily mean that we are actually more secure from the threat of politically motivated violence. Consider the threat of bombings on public transportation systems. Horrific attacks on trains and buses in the bustling cities of Madrid and London led the NYC transit system to institute random checks of backpacks for passengers heading into the subway in 2005. Anyone was free to refuse the search but they would not be allowed onto the subway. Nothing, however, could prevent a determined individual from entering a different station where a checkpoint was not in operation. It is not possible to monitor all possible entrances to the massive New York City transit system.

Yet most NYC citizens reported that they nonetheless "felt" safer with the checkpoints in place. On the one side is the argument that since terrorism targets the ordinary infrastructure of everyday life, the protection of our security necessitates surveillance of everyday life. Most Americans willingly exchange their right to be let alone for the security of believing that the airplane they are traveling on is not going to explode mid-air.

The counter argument is that by destroying these boundaries we compromise the very qualities of civil liberty that make American citizens free. In the immediate aftermath of 9/11 the late Senator Russ Feingold (D-Wis.) was the only senator to vote against the U.S.A. Patriot Act of 2001. He expressed his opposition in the following statement on the Senate floor:

> If we lived in a country that allowed the police to search your home at any time for any reason; if we lived in a country that allowed the government to open your mail; eavesdrop on your phone conversations, or intercept your email communications; if we lived in a country that allowed the government to hold people in jail indefinitely based on what they write or think, or based on mere suspicion that they are up to no good, then the government would no doubt discover and arrest more terrorists. But that probably would not be a country in which we would want to live. And that would not be a country for which we could, in good conscience, ask our young people to fight and die. In short, that would not be America.

terrorism (p. 247)   the unlawful use of force or violence against a target to create fear or coercion for the purpose of obtaining some political concession or reward or other goal.

profiling (p. 249)   a tool used by law enforcement to narrow offender characteristics to assist in prevention or apprehension.

reign of terror (p. 249)   coined by Edmund Burke, the term described the massive number of executions of formerly powerful members of the nobility and church by the new government in the aftermath of the French Revolution; the source of the term "terrorism."

anarchist (p. 250)   a political philosophy that rejects the state and opposes hierarchy.

propaganda by deed (p. 250)   actions, including tossing bombs at important persons in public places, used by anarchists in the nineteenth century to bring attention to their cause.

nationalists (p. 250)   unconventional soldiers fighting for fellow countrymen.

white supremacy (p. 250)   the belief that "white" people are superior to other races.

eco-terrorism (p. 251)   people who use violence to draw public attention to practices related to animal welfare or the environment that they believe are immoral and unjust.

mujahideen (p. 251)   Muslim holy warriors.

suicide mission (p. 252)   a task that is so dangerous that the person performing the act is not expected to survive.

jihad (p. 254)   an internal journey of purification and the willingness to carry arms to defend your community.

militant jihadism (p. 249)   a term used to describe a movement claiming to be rooted in Islam and perceived to be devoted to the destruction of "the west."

Patriot Act (p. 254)   an act of Congress passed in the immediate aftermath of the September 11 attacks, the main goal of which is to enhance the ability of the government to collect intelligence inside the United States by removing the "wall" or legal prohibition on information shared between national intelligence and law enforcement agencies.

terrorist organizations (p. 254)   organizations designated by the president, pursuant to the authority of the Patriot Act, as funders or supporters of "terrorism."

material supporter (p. 254)   anyone who makes a charitable contribution to an organization designated as "terrorist organization."

criminal intelligence (p. 255)   law enforcement surveillance of those believed to have engaged in illegal activities, typically responding to such activities; constrained by the Fourth Amendment requirements of reasonable suspicion or probable cause.

national security intelligence (p. 255)   preventative clandestine surveillance by the government designed to gather information about potential threats to national security.

fusion centers (p. 255)   centers across the country, administered by the Department of Homeland Security, where information is collected and stored.

suspicious activity reports (p. 255)   any report of individual suspicious activity reported to Homeland Security by a citizen or local police; also referred to as SAR.

COINTELPRO (p. 256)   an FBI program in the 1950s and 1960s that engaged in, often illegal, infiltration and disruption of domestic political organizations.

Counterterrorism (p. 256)   a government tactic for responding to terrorist threats.

martial law (p. 257)   replacing civil law with military law, albeit on an emergency basis.

civil liberties (p. 258)   the rights and freedoms provided for by the U. S. Constitution and especially the Bill of Rights.

right to privacy (p. 258)   though not explicitly defined in the U.S. Constitution, the courts have found a right to be let alone from surveillance or interference by the government unless there is evidence one has violated the law.

REVIEW AND STUDY QUESTIONS

1. How can we define the act of terrorism? Are there common goals?

2. What characteristics do people who commit acts of terrorism have in common?

3. Describe three types of domestic terrorists, using examples from the recent news to illustrate.

4. Explain the role the federal government plays in combating terrorism. And also explain the role of local law enforcement in combating terrorism. In what ways do they assist one another? Are there conflicts between their respective functions?

5. Has the U.S. government ever used martial law? What do you believe will happen if they did?

6. In what ways has the Patriot Act affected the Constitution? Are we safer as a result?

7. If there were best practices for responding to terrorism, what do you think these would be?

8. Describe the conflicts between liberty and safety. Which do you believe is more important, and why?

CHECK IT OUT

Websites

Department of Homeland Security, http://www.dhs. gov. Check out web site for the DHS with links to all relevant agencies within the department.

Federal Bureau of Investigation, http://www.fbi. gov/about-us/investigate/terrorism. Check out FBI counterterrorism agenda and current priorities.

National Counterterrorism Center, https://www. nctc.gov. The National Counterterrorism Center (NCTC) was established by Presidential Executive Order 13354 in August 2004, and codified by the Intelligence Reform and Terrorism Prevention Act of 2004 (IRTPA). NCTC implements a key recommendation of the 9/11 Commission for a coordinating body to direct national counterterrorism activities.

Videos

The McVeigh Tapes: Confessions of an American Terrorist—1 hour and 35 minutes. The documentary employs state-of-the-art computer recreations of the interview with McVeigh and his actions on and leading up to the day of the bombing. Available at: http://www.nbcnews.com/id/36135258/ns/msnbc_tv/t/mcveigh-tapes-confessions-american-terrorist/#.WLMe3jszLLc

Beyond 9/11 - Portraits of Resilience—50 minutes. See the faces and hear the stories of survivors, first responders, and others as they reflect on the events of 9/11 a decade later. Available at http://www.youtube.com/watch?v=Vzkk0J8QObA

Brothers on Holy Ground—53 minutes. This documentary film by a New York City firefighter tells about the experiences of New York's Bravest before, during, and after 9/11.

9/12: From Chaos to Community—2 hours and 50 minutes. Follows the lives of people, who had volunteered at ground zero in the days just after the attacks, including the ways their lives were forever changed. Available at: https://www.youtube.com/watch?v=2oGzRPDIoTs

On Native Soil—1 hour, and 25 minutes. A story about national security in the United States: why the attacks of 9/11 were possible and the state of security since that day. Available at: https://www.youtube.com/watch?v=toxUFNFLMUs

Inside Islam: What a Billion Muslims Really Think—56 minutes. This video investigates the findings of Gallup researchers, who asked tens of thousands of residents in thirty-five primarily Muslim nations questions like these: Why is there so much anti-Americanism in the Muslim world? Who are the extremists and how do Muslims feel about them? What do Muslims like and dislike about the West? What do Muslim women really want? Available at: https://vimeo.com/14121737

NOTES

[1] Noam Chomsky, "Who are the Global Terrorists?," in *Worlds in Collision, Terror and the Future of Global Order*, eds. Ken Booth and Tim Dunne (New York: Palgrave Macmillan, 2002).

[2] Jonathan R. White, *Terrorism and Homeland Security* (Belmont, CA: Wadsworth, 2006), 22.

[3] White, *Terrorism and Homeland Security*, 30–35.

[4] White, *Terrorism and Homeland Security*, 39–40.

[5] Jessica Stern, *Terror in the Name of God: Why Religious Militants Kill* (New York: Harper Collins, 2003).

[6] Steven Pinker, *The Better Angels of our Nature: Why Violence has Declined* (New York: Viking, 2011), 347–353.

[7] Jonathan R. White, *Terrorism and Homeland Security* (Belmont, CA: Wadsworth, 2006), 6.

[8] Steven Pinker, *The Better Angels of our Nature: Why Violence has Declined* (New York: Viking, 2011), 347.

[9] Pinker, *The Better Angels of our Nature*, 345.

[10] Robert Gibson, *The Negro Holocaust: Lynching and Race Riots in the United States, 1880–1950* (New Haven, CT: New Haven Teachers Institute, 1979).

[11] Ted Gurr, "Some Characteristics of Political Terrorism in the 1960s," in *The Politics of Terrorism*, ed. M. Stohl (New York: Dekker, 1988).

[12] Jonathan R. White, *Terrorism and Homeland Security* (Belmont, CA: Wadsworth, 2006), 354.

[13] Stephen Jones, *Others Unknown: The Oklahoma City Bombing Case and Conspiracy* (New York: Public Affairs, 1998).

[14] Jonathan R. White, *Terrorism and Homeland Security* (Belmont, CA: Wadsworth, 2006), 266–272.

[15] "Final Report of the National Commission on Terrorist Attacks upon the United States," *9/11 Commission Report* (New York: W.W. Norton& Co, 2004), 59–63.

[16] "Final Report of the National Commission on Terrorist Attacks upon the United States," *9/11 Commission Report* (New York: W.W. Norton& Co, 2004), 1–14.

[17] Final Report of the National Commission on Terrorist Attacks upon the United States, 326.

[18] Peter Baker, Helen Cooper and Mark Mazzetti, "Bin Laden is Dead, Obama Says," *New York Times* (May 1, 2011), A1.

[19] Jonathan R. White, *Terrorism and Homeland Security* (Belmont, CA: Wadsworth, 2006), 263.

[20] David Cole and James X. Dempsey, *Terrorism and the Constitution: Sacrificing Civil Liberties in the Name of National Security* (New York: The New Press, 2006).

[21] Susan N. Herman, *Taking Liberties: The War on Terror and the Erosion of American Democracy* (New York: Oxford University Press, 2011).

[22] "Final Report of the National Commission on Terrorist Attacks upon the United States," *9/11 Commission Report* (New York: W.W. Norton& Co, 2004), 78.

[23] Jonathan R. White, *Terrorism and Homeland Security* (Belmont, CA: Wadsworth, 2006), 411–412.

[24] Dana Priest and William Arkin, "Monitoring America," *Washington Post* (December 20, 2010).

[25] PBS Online, "Are We Safer?," *Frontline* http://www.pbs.org/wgbh/pages/frontline/are-we-safer/

[26] Susan N. Herman, *Taking Liberties: The War on Terror and the Erosion of American Democracy* (New York: Oxford University Press, 2011), 9.

[27] "Final Report of the National Commission on Terrorist Attacks upon the United States," *9/11 Commission Report* (New York: W.W. Norton& Co, 2004), 74–75; Jonathan R. White. *Terrorism and Homeland Security* (Belmont, CA: Wadsworth, 2006), 412–413.

[28] Michael Powell, "Police Monitoring and a Climate of Fear," *New York Times* (February 28, 2012), A17.

[29] PBS Online, "Are We Safer?," *Frontline* http://www.pbs.org/wgbh/pages/frontline/are-we-safer/

[30] Jonathan R. White, *Terrorism and Homeland Security* (Belmont, CA: Wadsworth, 2006), 482.

[31] Richard Zabel and James Benjamin, *In Pursuit of Justice: Prosecuting Terrorism Cases in Federal Court* (Washington, DC: Human Rights First, 2008). https://www.humanrightsfirst.org/wp-content/uploads/pdf/080521-USLS-pursuit-justice.pdf

[32] Susan N. Herman, *Taking Liberties: The War on Terror and the Erosion of American Democracy* (New York: Oxford University Press, 2011), 11.

[33] Steven Pinker, *The Better Angels of our Nature: Why Violence has Declined* (New York: Viking, 2011), 345.

FOCUS QUESTIONS

- **HOW** do voters think about contending alternatives when they are voting?
- **HOW** does the number of alternatives affect voting?
- **WHAT** considerations contend for attention in the minds of voters? How might they cooperate to support a particular choice?
- **HOW** does voters' identification with a political party affect voting?
- **HOW** do parties and candidates maneuver to gain votes?
- **WHAT** does it mean for voter choice to be meaningful?

This chapter presents a well-known case of violence aimed at civil rights workers in the early 1960s. As we follow the case through the legal system, you will be exposed to concepts such as jurisdiction and appeals. The content that follows provides general information about the range of courts in the U.S. legal system, and the roles each plays.

LEARNING OBJECTIVES

After reading this chapter you should be able to:

- Describe the basic structure of the courts and explain the key differences between the lower courts, trial courts, and appellate courts.
- Express the difference between the state and federal court systems.
- Explain how jurisdiction is defined for the various courts.
- Explain why it is important to have a record of court proceedings and explain the right of appeal.
- Describe the composition of the U.S. Supreme Court.
- Present the process by which cases get to the Supreme Court.
- Describe the unique function of the U.S. Supreme Court and describe how these proceedings are different from trial court and state appellate court proceedings.

Case #10: It's Never Too Late for Justice: The Prosecution of Edgar Ray Killen

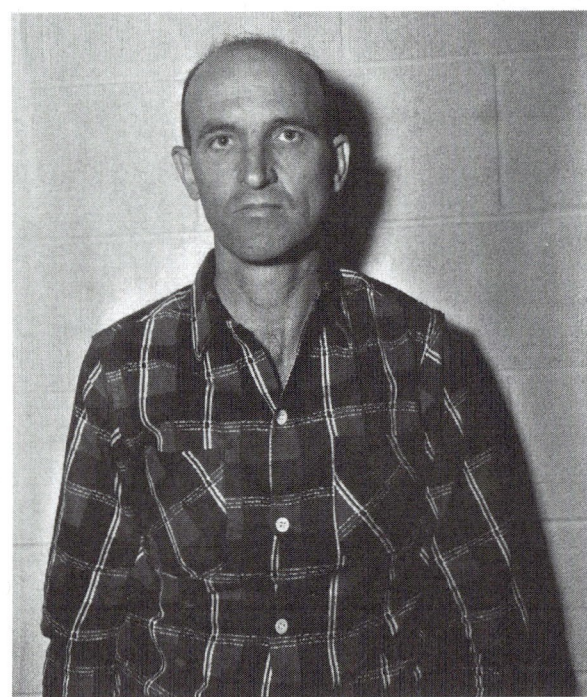

A young Edgar Ray Killen was acquitted at a federal trial for conspiring to deprive the victims of their civil rights but forty years later was found guilty at the state trial for planning the murder of three civil rights workers in 1964. (Getty Images)

In 1964 a haunting image captured the nation's imagination: three boys in a blue Ford station wagon driving down a deserted highway flanked by acres of empty piney woods see the ominous sight of headlights coming up fast in the rear view mirror. Michael, Andrew, and James would have known who was following them that night and when they saw flashing lights of the local sheriff's car they would have been very scared. Their bodies were found forty-four days later buried deep in the earth on a local farm.

There was nothing spontaneous about the murder of three young men on the night of June 21, 1964. Plans were carefully laid at secret meetings with detailed orders about who should do what, to whom, exactly when, how, and where. This was a conspiracy in the truest sense of the word and like most conspiracies those at the top were the last to be held accountable. But finally in June of 2005, Edgar Ray Killen, otherwise known as "the Preacher," stood trial for directing fellow Klansmen to trap, hunt, and kill three young men in the Deep South. At the age of eighty,

Edgar Ray Killen was convicted and sentenced to sixty years in prison—forty-one years after the crime was committed.

The Victims

Michael Schwerner, age twenty-four, loved basketball, his young wife, and his job working with inner city teens in lower Manhattan. After graduating from Cornell University, he and his wife closely followed the fierce battle for civil rights raging in the South on national television. When four young girls perished in a church fire lit by the Ku Klux Klan, they decided they had to join the fight. In his application to work for the Congress of Racial Equality, Michael explained, "I have an emotional need to be of service." Rita, an English major, was more eloquent. She wrote, "My hope is to some day pass on to the children we may have a world containing more respect for the dignity and worth of all men than the world which was willed to us." They waited until Rita finished school and then packed their VW beetle and headed for Meridian Mississippi, ground zero for the struggle for civil rights. Their job was to educate black citizens about their rights, help black citizens register to vote, and organize nonviolent resistance to segregationist laws.

Andrew Goodman, 20, always thought he would be a theater major in college: handsome and talented, he held leading roles in high school and had even performed in an off-Broadway production. He loved music and went often to hear Miles Davis and Ray Charles. But in college his interests took a more serious turn and he decided to major in anthropology. It was through one of his professors that he learned about the "Mississippi Project," an effort by hundreds of students, lawyers, artists, social workers, and teachers to travel South for the summer and establish "freedom schools," which would register Negroes to vote and educate them about their legal rights. He begged his parents to allow him to go the summer between his sophomore and junior year. His mother was not so keen: she too watched the nightly news and worried he might get roughed up by a mob of angry whites. Still she was proud of his idealism and believed in the cause of racial equality. She reluctantly signed the parental permission form on the firm condition that Andrew keep her and his father informed of his whereabouts at all times.

James Earl Chaney, 21, was born and bred in Meridian, Mississippi. As a young black in the South, J. E., knew all too well the bitter truth about life as a second-class citizen in the segregationist South. No one had to convince him to join the struggle for his civil rights. At age sixteen he had been suspended from his blacks-only high school for refusing to remove the NAACP button from his shirt lapel. Now working for civil rights was his full-time occupation. He helped Michael open the Meridian Community Center, where black children barred from whites-only schools and whites-only public libraries could have access to a children's library. At Rita and Michael's suggestion, CORE hired J. E. as a full-time worker to help Michael organize the voter registration drive.

The Crime: How it Happened

In January of 1964, sixty-four burning crosses announced the resurgence of the Klan across the state of Mississippi. Inactive for decades, the return of this secretive and violent organization was instigated by the gathering steam of the civil disobedience marches led by a young minister named Martin Luther King Jr. across the South. Although the courts had overturned the legal principle of "separate but equal" in its landmark 1954 *Brown v. Board of Education* decision, the Deep South resisted any effort to dismantle the system of legal segregation that maintained separate lives for whites and blacks in every aspect of daily life.

For ten years this resistance had been successful: but the clock was ticking on the old South and its way of life. Now, black students and black ministers from the South joined with white northern college students, social workers, and progressive lawyers in a coalition that was determined to end legal segregation through protest, litigation, and direct nonviolent action. The summer of 1964 was designated the "summer of freedom" in which one thousand volunteers were planning to descend upon the Deep South. The state of Mississippi was targeted as the heart of it all. According to one volunteer, "If we can crack Mississippi, we can crack segregation anywhere."

To the southern establishment this was an "invasion" that threatened their settled way of life. The Klan put out the call across the state: "The issue is one of personal, physical self-defense or death for the American Anglo-Saxon." In February of 1964, there were only 300 members of the Klan within the state of Mississippi; by June 1964, that number had swelled

to nearly 6,000. That summer alone the KKK in Mississippi were responsible for thirty-five shootings; thirty-seven church burnings; firebombing of thirty homes; the beating of eighty civil rights workers; over a thousand arrests of civil rights workers and countless threatening phone calls, burning crosses, and other forms of intimidation targeting anyone who spoke out in favor of the protesters. Although only a tiny minority of white Mississippians joined the Klan, almost everyone was terrorized into a complicit silence.

In April, a recruiter for the KKK came to city of Meridian. Posters plastered around the city urged young men to come to the meeting and learn about the White Knights of the Ku Klux Klan. The recruiter or Kleagle was named Edgar Ray Killen, a sawmill operator and part-time Baptist minister, whom everyone called "The Preacher."

It was Michael who was targeted by the KKK. Talking about what was going on in Meridian at the meeting, locals identified Michael Schwerner as someone who needed to be taught a lesson. They referred to him as "Jew-boy" or "Goatee" in reference to the small beard he wore: "We should go and beat him up," they suggested. But Killen told them not to, explaining that plans to handle Schwerner were already in place. According to an FBI informant present that night, Killen informed the boys that Sam Bowers himself, the Imperial Wizard of the KKK, had given orders for the Goatee to be executed. Bowers had put Killen in charge of the plan and Killen did not want anything to go wrong. He pulled a piece of paper from his pocket and waved it in their faces: "If you go over there now, you may mess things up."

The Freedom workers knew to expect trouble. In mid-June, Rita, Michael, and J. E. traveled north to a college in Oxford, Ohio, where they trained fresh volunteers, including Andrew Goodman, in techniques on how to handle the challenging work that lay ahead. Volunteers were taught how to deal with an angry mob that might taunt, intimidate, threaten, and even beat them as they participated in protests. They were prepared for harassment, name-calling, false arrests, beatings, scary phone calls, and the ominous threat of burning crosses. Volunteers were advised to have someone who could post bond for them if they were arrested; and white volunteers were forewarned that the color of their skin would offer no protection for them. Quite the opposite—the Klan hated "nigger-lovers"—whites who believed in equal rights for blacks—most of all.

But nothing could have prepared them for the sheer viciousness of the KKK. On June 16, thirty Klansmen gathered outside the Mount Zion Methodist Church during services, the sounds of the arriving trucks muffled by the singing voices inside. Ten church members, eight adults and two children, leaving church found themselves surrounded by men wearing hoods and carrying bats. They were looking for Schwerner but settled for chasing and beating the terrified men, women, and children, who scattered like rabbits into the surrounding woods. Later the Klansmen returned to burn the church to the ground.

This was all part of Killen's master plan. The church was targeted because Schwerner had asked church members to consider it to serve as a site for a "freedom school," a place where children could be educated and adults could register to vote. Killen expected Schwerner to be there but he did not need to wait long for his prey to walk into his trap. When Michael heard of the attack a few days later, he and J. E. immediately wanted to return to Meridian. They took several volunteers with them, including the new and eager volunteer Andy Goodman. On June 19 Andy called his parents and told them he was heading down to Mississippi. He promised he would send them a postcard as soon as he arrived.

In the early hours of the morning Michel kissed Rita goodbye and the three jumped in the station wagon. After resting at the local CORE organization for a few hours, they set out around 10 a.m. on the morning of June 21 to visit the site. Michael and J. E. wanted to apologize to the church deacon for the beatings and the loss of their beloved church. True to his word, on the morning of the day he died, Andy got up early to scribble a postcard to his parents. "Dear Mom and Dad, I have arrived safely in Meridian, Mississippi. This is a wonderful town, and the weather is fine. I wish you were here. The people in this city are wonderful, and our reception was very good. All my love, Andy." They told Louise the coordinator to expect them back by 4 p.m.

Deputy Sheriff Cecil Price was idly sitting in his patrol car when he saw the unmistakable blue station wagon with a license plate he knew by heart drive through the town of Philadelphia en route to Meridian around 2 in the afternoon. Law enforcement across the state of Mississippi knew a great deal about the civil rights organizers. A state-funded entity called the Mississippi Sovereignty Commission employed hundreds of investigators, spies, and informants. It had been created in 1956 "for the maintenance of racial segregation" and was part of the southern establishment's effort to resist all efforts at integration. The Commission was charged with gathering covert intelligence on anyone organizing protests in the state. This information was routinely conveyed to local law enforcement, many of whom were also active members of the KKK.

The Mississippi Sovereignty Commission often deployed undercover spies or moles, who relayed names, dates, and detailed plans of the civil rights workers. One of these spies had infiltrated the training up in Ohio and had alerted law enforcement that the volunteers were on their way back to Mississippi. When Sheriff Price saw the station wagon, he turned on his siren, and promptly arrested the boys for speeding and then jailed them on suspicion of arson in the church fire. His first phone call was to Edgar Ray Killen, who immediately convened an emergency meeting of the Klan.

While the three boys were locked up in jail, Killen spent the next six hours giving specific instructions to the dozen or so men gathered at the meeting. One man was told to purchase six pairs of brown cloth gloves; others to go home and get their guns. They met again near the courthouse and Killen instructed them where to wait for the trio once they were released from jail; he told them what to do with the car after they were apprehended; and where to bring the bodies for burial. He arranged for someone to be waiting with a bulldozer to cover the bodies with fresh earth. His final instruction was to drop him off at a local funeral home so later he would have an airtight alibi preaching holy words over a deceased body.

At 10 p.m. Deputy Price released the trio and told them, "See how quick y'all can get out Neshoba County." They headed out on Mississippi 19 and almost immediately found they were being followed by three cars. The boys hit the gas but pull over when they see flashing lights. Deputy Price ordered them to get into his squad car. They head down a gravel road to a meeting point where others were waiting. Altogether there are eighteen Klansmen present. First Michael and then Andy are shot, point blank. J. E. tried to make a run for it but was caught, severely beaten, and finally shot. One of the Klansmen complained, "You didn't leave me nothing but a nigger, but at least I killed me a nigger." The bodies were transported to a wealthy farm owner's property for burial and the abandoned blue station wagon was driven to the Choctaw reservation and torched on the deserted edge of a swampy creek.

The final words that night to the Klansmen on their return to town come from the Sheriff Rainey:

> Well boys you've done a good job. You've struck a blow for the White Man. Mississippi can be proud of you. You've let those agitating outsiders know where this state stands. Go home now and forget it. But before you go, I'm looking each one of you in the eye and telling you this: the first man who talks is dead. If anybody who knows anything about this ever opens his mouth to any outsider about it, then the rest of us are going to kill him just as dead as we killed those three sonofbitches tonight. Does everybody understand what I'm saying? The man who talks is dead, dead, dead. [1]

The Hunt for the Bodies

It turned out there was a hitch in Killen's carefully laid plans. His instructions to the Klansmen were to drive the car to Birmingham Alabama and torch it there but the Klansmen drove it only 25 miles to edge of the Choctaw Indian reservation believing it could never be found in such a remote location. Yet the following day, Monday, June 22, several Choctaw Indians noticed the still smoldering vehicle in the Bogue Chitto Swamp and reported it to federal Indian Agency on the reservation. They immediately notified the FBI. Had Killen's original instructions been followed, it is doubtful that the car or the bodies would ever have been found.

Four days later, on June 25, Walter Cronkite's lead story on the national six o'clock news was the disappearance was the three civil rights workers and the discovery of the charred vehicle in Philadelphia, Mississippi. Calls flood the White House demanding the president mobilize the FBI to find the missing boys. Southern officials scoffed at the suggestion that the boys might have been murdered and claimed the disappearance was most likely a "publicity stunt" or a hoax set up to look like a crime. U.S. Senator Jim Eastland called President Lyndon Johnson, "I believe this is a hoax. There's no KKK in the area. . . . Who could possibly harm them?"

Attorney General Robert Kennedy and President Lyndon Johnson order a massive search for the bodies. The FBI sent over 150 agents to the area to scour the murky swamps of the Choctaw reservation joined by hundreds of sailors from the nearby naval station in Meridian. For weeks, nearly four hundred federal agents and U.S. troops searched for the missing boys amid the alligators and snakes of the boggy swamp.

They found two bodies but these were young black men also in their early twenties. Years later it was discovered that these young men had also been killed by the KKK, who mistakenly suspected they were involved in the civil rights crusade. But in the summer of 1964, the eyes of the nation were on the search for the three missing civil rights workers and no one paid any attention to the discovery of those bodies except for their grieving families. Of course, southern law enforcement made no effort to investigate the murders of two black males.

Although FBI agents flooded the county and interviewed thousands of Mississippians about the disappearance they found no one, not a single person, who had seen or heard anything. The words of Sheriff Rainey don't need repeating: the terrorist tactics of the Klan had cowed most citizens into an uncomfortable but unshakeable silence. In the end, the bodies we not found through the laborious efforts of the searchers. Instead an informant revealed the location of the three bodies beneath the fresh earthen dam on "Old Jolly Farm" owned by wealthy farmer Oren Burrage. According to unofficial reports, an informant broke under the illegal but effective violence exerted by a mafia mobster sent down to Mississippi by J. Edgar Hoover himself. The official line is that the informant was offered a reward for the information but no one believed it. To this day, no one knows who the informant was but the information supplied proved accurate: the bodies are found and the names of eighteen Klansmen who participated in the execution we given to the FBI.

The Federal or State? Who Has Jurisdiction in this Case?

Meanwhile Mississippians were complaining bitterly about the federal intrusion into a state criminal investigation. Under what legal authority were federal agents investigating an alleged state crime of murder? What federal statute had been violated that would justify a federal investigation? Robert Kennedy, U.S. attorney general, provided an answer: once the vehicle was discovered, he invoked the federal Lindbergh Kidnapping law, which enables the FBI to enter any state and take any action necessary to apprehend suspected kidnappers.

Now that the bodies had been found, federal prosecutors from the Department of Justice (DOJ) were determined not to hand this case over to the authorities in the state of Mississippi. In the history of the state's criminal justice system, not a single white Mississippian had ever been convicted of murdering a black person, or any person, white or black, engaged in civil rights work. On most occasions there was no legal response at all but even when there was an indictment and a trial these invariably ended in acquittals, mistrials, or dismissals by an all-white jury and judiciary.

But the charge is murder, which is a state crime, not kidnapping, which is a federal offense. It was unclear whether the federal government has statutory authority to prosecute. At the time, there was no federal statute for murder. Because the U.S. attorney general did not trust that the state of Mississippi would prosecute this case, the only solution was to get creative. Turning to an obscure nineteenth-century federal statute which prohibits conspiring to deprive someone of their civil rights without "due process of law," prosecutors proceeded to gather evidence for an indictment under that statute. Although the federal charge carries a much lower punishment than the crime of murder, prosecuting under federal law means at least there would be some hope for accountability for the three dead men. If convicted, the maximum penalty was a $5,000 fine and ten years in federal prison.

Federal investigators made a major breakthrough in the case when one of the named Klansmen who committed the murder confesses. James Jordon (the man who had complained about only getting to shoot a nigger) turned state's evidence. Armed with his confession, they also manage to pressure another Klansman, Horace Barnette, to serve as a witness for the prosecution. Both tell the same story. The DOJ arrest twenty-one Klansmen, including Sheriff Rainey, Deputy Price, Edgar Ray Killen, Sam Bowers, and all others present that night.

The accused we brought into the court of the U.S. commissioner from Meridian for a preliminary hearing. At first, federal prosecutors we shocked at how jovial and unconcerned the accused seemed to be. They are joking and laughing. But when the judge, a local woman named Esther Carter, issued her ruling, federal prosecutors realized why the atmosphere in the courtroom was so lighthearted. Although tried in federal court, the judge, juries, and attorneys were all still citizens of the state of Mississippi subject to the same local pressures and prejudices. Judge Carter instantly dismissed the charges ruling that the written confessions were "hearsay" and therefore inadmissible as evidence in court.

Undaunted, federal prosecutors convened a federal grand jury and presented the evidence of the signed confessions to the jury. The jury handed down indictments charging eighteen Klansmen with conspiring to violate sections 241 and 242 of the federal code. The jurisdictional challenges, however, were considerable. The relatively obscure statute was part of the Civil Rights Act of 1866 in an amendment passed in 1870 after the passage of the Fourteenth Amendment in 1868. The Fourteenth Amendment entitles all U.S. citizens to "due process of law" regardless of the particular state in which they reside. Section 241 of the 18 U.S.C. makes it a federal felony to conspire to deny any individual the free exercise or enjoyment of any right or privilege secured by the Constitution or laws of the United States. Section 242 of the 18 U.S.C. makes it a misdemeanor offense to do this "under the color of law"—that is, acting as officers of the law to deprive someone of their legal rights.

The question was whether this statute should be broadly interpreted to mean all rights as a citizen or narrowly defined as only those rights that are conferred by federal law itself. The U.S. District Court judge to hear the case was Harold Cox, an ardent and vocal supporter of segregation. A former college roommate and close friend of Senator Eastland, Judge Cox was even more hostile to the case than Judge Carter. An unapologetic racist, the *New York Times* had Cox on record as referring to black voters as a "bunch of chimpanzees" causing several senators to initiate impeachment proceedings to have him removed from the federal bench.

Not surprising, Judge Cox dismissed the conspiracy charge under section 241 claiming that the statute only refers to federal law and since the crime of murder is not a violation of federal law but state law, the statute simply did not apply. The federal government therefore did not have jurisdiction to prosecute this case. As far as section 242 was concerned, Cox claimed that only three of the accused were officers of the law, and therefore this misdemeanor charge would not apply to the other fifteen defendants.

Prosecutors appealed the case to the Supreme Court. In *U.S. v. Price*, the Supreme Court overruled the decision by Cox allowing for the federal trial of all eighteen accused Klansmen. By a vote of 9-0 the justices reinstated the indictments against the Klansmen. The Court made it clear that the statute covered conspiracies to deprive citizens of all their rights guaranteed by the Constitution and by U.S. law—whether those laws be state or federal.

The case was remanded back to U.S. District Court presided over by Judge Cox. This time he found an even more outrageous reason to dismiss the indictments by ruling stating that they were in violation of the Constitution because there had been no women or blacks on the federal grand jury. Federal prosecutors fought back again. They didn't bother to challenge the ruling but instead convened another grand jury, this time with adequate representation by blacks and women. The grand jury again indicted all eighteen Klansmen.

The Federal Trial: *U.S. v. Price*

Having run out of legal evasions, the trial of the Klansmen began on May 26, 1967, with Judge Cox presiding, three years, two months, and five days after the murders in the city of Meridian, Mississippi. Surprisingly, the judge allowed the jury pool to be drawn from the entire southern Mississippi District encompassing six counties instead of just Neshoba County. An all-white jury of seven men and five women hear the case over nine days. Most are working-class individuals: secretaries, mechanics, electricians, housewives, and chicken farmers.

The prosecutor knew he had to address the sense, among the citizens of Mississippi, that this trial was an invasion of state's rights by the federal government. He explained to the jury, "when local law enforcement officials become involved as participants in violent crime and use their position, power, and authority to accomplish this, there is very little to be hoped for except with the assistance of the federal government." Still he pointed out that the case is being tried before a Mississippi judge, in a Mississippi courtroom before twelve men and women from the state of Mississippi. "The guilt or innocence of these men is where it belongs: in your hands."

Witnesses for the prosecution include two former Klansmen who had attended several of the earlier meetings but were disgusted by plans to execute civil rights workers. Both quit the Klan but had been persuaded by the FBI to rejoin and become informants. The star witness was Jim Jordan, one of the shooters who had made a full confession of all that happened that night. They all tell the same story.

Most of the 160 defense witnesses either provide alibis for one of the defendants or serve as character witnesses testifying that as upright moral individuals the defendants were incapable of such acts of barbarism. The defense reiterated the earlier claim that the boys may have been murdered "by their own" as a publicity stunt to help their cause. Either way the defense argues there is reasonable doubt and "it is so much better that . . . a thousand guilty go free than one innocent defendant here be convicted."

When the jury went out to deliberate, most court observers expected a full acquittal for all the defendants. A reporter for the *New York Herald* covering the trial observed, "These are little people . . . some live out in small communities on the edge of the piney woods. How can they afford to take such risks?" Decades later, transcripts of interviews with jurors reveal the reporter was right to suspect Klansmen would try to intimidate the jury if they failed to "turn those boys a-loose." During the trial and for weeks afterward, U.S. marshals were posted at the homes of jurors for protection. Many jurors were afraid to let their children walk home from school or be picked up by another's child's parent. Others obsessively checked under the hood of their cars for years before starting the ignition. There were late night phone calls and burning crosses on front lawns. The worst part was that jurors often recognized the threatening voices on those late night calls: these were people they knew.

Even so, the jury returned a surprising verdict. Seven men are found guilty: Sam Bowers, the Imperial Wizard, and Deputy Price among them. Seven men are acquitted, including Sheriff Rainey. For three defendants the jury could come to an agreement. Among these was Edgar Ray Killen, the organizer and mastermind of the crime. Eleven jurors vote to convict but one lone holdout refuses: she simply does not believe that a man of god, preacher, would ever lie. Edgar Ray Killen walks out the courtroom a free man.

Is it Ever Too Late for Justice? The State Trial of Edgar Ray Killen

In 1967 Judge Cox sentenced those found guilty to federal prison: none of them served longer than six years. Commenting later on his sentencing, Cox shrugs, "They killed one nigger, one Jew and white man. I gave them all what I thought they deserved." By 1970, all those convicted are free and living in Neshoba County. Of course those who were acquitted, like Edgar Ray and Sheriff Rainey, swaggered out of the courtroom with big grins secure in their right to use violence against blacks, Jews, northerners, nigger-lovers, "outside agitators," and anyone else who dared challenge the racial codes of the South. For twenty-five years, no one in Philadelphia dared to mention the murders of Goodman, Schwerner, and Chaney. In a small town in the Deep South no one wanted to bring the wrath of the Klan to their front door. A culture of impunity—rooted in fear—protected the killers and they knew it.

The year 1989 was a turning point for dismantling this "culture of impunity" in the state of Mississippi. It started when secretary of state, Dick Molpus, born and raised in Philadelphia himself, offered a passionate and heartfelt public apology for the murders at the twenty-fifth memorial service held on June 21, 1989. Goodman's mother and brother, Schwerner's widow Rita, and Chaney's brother and daughter traveled to the state for the first time since 1967 to hear a state official offer an apology and assert that "every decent person" in Mississippi felt this way too.

The memorial was organized by a group of local citizens—black, white, and Choctaw—who formed an organization called the Philadelphia Coalition. The mission of the organization is to break the silence that covers these events and promote racial reconciliation through a full acknowledgment and accounting of the past.

Thats same year a young investigative reporter, Jerry Mitchell, working for the Jackson Clarion-Ledger also began to write about this and other civil rights killings from that era. Like many across the nation, the 1988 Hollywood film, *Mississippi Burning*, opened Mitchell's eyes to what went on in his own community and to the unfinished business of bringing those responsible for murder to justice. Mitchell along with the small band of citizens of the Philadelphia Coalition and the families of the victims began a relentless call for the state to re-open the case against Edgar Ray.

There is no statute of limitations on the crime of murder. Between 1989 and 2005 twenty-six murders cases from the 1950s to 1960s civil rights era were reopened by state prosecutors in seven southern states. There were twenty-five trials; twenty-one murder convictions; two acquittals and one mistrial. The trial of Edgar Ray was the fifth cold case prosecution in the state of Mississippi. More cases were pending including a prosecution for the murders of the two boys whose bodies were uncovered in the search for the missing trio way back in 1964.

A defiant Edgar Ray, now in his eighties, sneered from his wheelchair in the Neshoba County courthouse. He had his supporters in the crowd: a large family and friends, and even in 2005, an active Klan that raised money for his defense on the internet. Most of the evidence consisted of transcripts from the original trial of 1967: so many witnesses had died there are few people to offer live testimony. The prosecution hired actors to read the transcripts but they know that this was less than persuasive for any jury. The defense was the same as in 1967: Killen had an alibi for that night, he was a man of God with an upstanding character and they scoff at the evidence that he masterminded the crime as unsubstantiated rumors by people motivated to shift blame elsewhere. Although Killen was eager to take the stand in his own defense, his lawyers were not willing to put the virulent preacher in the public eye. He remained an unrepentant believer in racial separatism and his lawyers feared his testimony would clinch the case for the prosecution.

By a strange twist of fate, the day the jury delivered its verdict was Tuesday, June 21, 2005, exactly forty-one years to the day that Michael Schwerner, James Chaney, and Andrew Goodman were murdered. The jury found Edgar Ray Killen guilty of three counts of manslaughter: one for each victim. Two days later, Mississippi judge Marcus Gordon born and raised in the same tiny hamlet as Edgar Ray himself, sentences Edgar Ray Killen to the maximum penalty on each count: twenty years for each victim to run consecutively for a total of sixty years. Having exhausted all appeals, Killen remains in Parchment state prison. As of this writing he is ninety-one years old.

THINKING CRITICALLY ABOUT THIS CASE

1. Do you believe that "justice" was finally served in this case? Why or why not?

2. Why was it necessary for the justice department to bring a federal charge in the original trials in 1967? Was this justice or was the federal government interfering with the state of Mississippi?

3. The jury verdict in the 1967 trial convicted seven prominent members of the local community for violating the civil rights of three people includ-

ing one African American. What is your view of the decision made by the jury in this case? Was this a just verdict in your view? Explain your answer.

4. Edgar Ray Killen was eighty years old when he was convicted and sent to prison. What purpose does this trial and sentence serve? Do you believe it was the right thing to do? Why or why not?

5. The citizens who formed the Philadelphia Coalition believed that it was important to uncover the truth about a crime that happened forty years ago. To whom is this important and why?

6. The killer of the two black young men found dead forty years ago has also been recently tried and convicted of the crime. Why is it important to prosecute these cases? To whom it is important?

REFERENCES

Case adapted from:

Howard Ball, *Murder in Mississippi: United States v. Price and the Struggle for Civil Rights* (Kansas: University Press of Kansas, 2004).

Shaila Dewan, "Former Klansman Guilty of Manslaughter in 1964 Deaths," *The New York Times*, June 22, 2005.

Darryl Fears, "Justice Dept. to Revisit Civil-Rights-Era Killings," *The Washington Post*, February 28, 2007.

Suzanne Goldenberg, "Still burning: Scores of civil-rights activists were murdered in the American south in the 1950s and 60s. Their killers mostly went unpunished. But now cases are being reopened, as a new generation resolves to see justice done at last," *The Guardian*, April 11, 2007.

Jerry Mitchell, " 44 Days: Jurors faced death threats, ostracism," *The Clarion-Ledger*, May 7, 2000.

Scott Turow, "Still Guilty After All These Years," *The New York Times*, April 8, 2007.

Over the doors of any courthouse one finds inspirational words carved in stone or marble that proclaim the awesome responsibility of the institution to deliver justice. Courthouses are usually elaborate public buildings with fancy facades, graceful columns, and intricate marble. The splendor of the outside of the building is meant to reflect the importance of what takes place inside the building. It is in these hallowed spaces that the mysterious and majestic process of "justice" unfolds before the public.

Trials are public ceremonies bound by ritual and solemn dignity. Where else in modern society do public officials sit on a high platform and wear long black robes? Where else does an audience "all rise" to mark the hushed entrance of the main speaker? And where else, in modern society, do we still use such words as "hear ye, hear ye," "to wit," or address a public official as "your honor"? If you are thinking that the courthouse reminds you of the ceremony one might find in church on Sunday, then you are right in seeing that courts, like religious institutions, are places where ritual and ceremony symbolize an important social function in our society. For better or worse, the courts are where people most often look to "see" how the American justice system works.

Historically, in the American colonies, each colony had its own court system both criminal and civil for resolving disputes, which formed the basis for the state court system we have today. As the nation grew, the local courthouse emerged as an integral and central public space within the community. It was there that local disputes were resolved, public announcements were made, and people gathered to meet in times of crisis or celebrate in times of joy. The courthouse stood at

The courtroom is ornate and somber to reflect the symbolic importance of the trial in our culture.

the center of the town, and like the church it was a place where news and gossip were exchanged.[2]

Indeed, before the rise of a professional body of trained lawyers at the end of the nineteenth century, local justices of the peace settled many matters of civil disputes and minor criminal matters in an informal way. Once a month on "court day," a visiting judge with higher authority would visit to hear more serious criminal cases. The more serious the crime, the more likely that on the day of the trial the courthouse would be packed with spectators eager to "see" justice done. And as we have seen in the case of the Salem witch trials, before the rise of prisons as the main form of criminal sanction, the meting out of physical punishment was also a public ceremony attended by young and old alike.

Tremendous changes in the state court system took place in the nineteenth and twentieth centuries as society became more complex. In addition to local and county courts run by a magistrates and justices of the peace and higher courts for more serious matters, there developed police courts, mayors' courts, municipal courts, night courts, probate courts, juvenile courts, family courts, traffic courts, and drug courts. Each state devised their own system for naming and organizing the courts and assigning them different forms of **jurisdiction** or authority over various bodies of the law. In addition, of course, the federal court system evolved operating in a parallel track with its own complex system of administrative, specialized, lower and higher courts. By the end of the nineteenth century, a growing army of trained lawyers was needed to simply understand which court held jurisdiction for a given legal matter. The trained practitioner increasingly became a "necessity" to navigate the complex system of procedures and processes for bringing a case to the court for **adjudication**.

STRUCTURE OF THE COURTS

While many countries have a single national court system, the United States has a highly decentralized, complex, and diverse system of many different types of courts with jurisdiction over different types of legal issues. Courts have jurisdiction based on a number of different criteria: political boundaries, geography, subject matter, or function. Court jurisdiction is defined by geography because certain courts have jurisdiction to hear cases for crimes that have taken place within a particular city, county, or state. Courts may also be authorized to hear only certain types of cases: there may be a traffic court to deal with violations of the traffic laws; a family court to deal with divorce and custody proceedings; or a probate court to settle the handling of wills and estates.

Courts are always differentiated according to their specific procedural function within the hierarchy of the court system itself: courts may have **limited, general,** or **appellate jurisdiction**. Courts of limited jurisdiction do not try felony cases and are restricted in scope and do not have appellate authority. Courts with general jurisdiction are the major trial courts. These courts have the power and authority to try and decide any case, including appeals from the lower courts. **Trial courts** have the power to hear a case from the start, examine the evidence, and apply the law to those facts, whereas courts with appellate jurisdiction have the specific function of only hearing cases on appeal and settling matters of legal procedure.

Broadly speaking, two types of courts function within the American criminal justice system: the state court system and the federal court system. The U.S. Constitution, Section 1 of Article III created the federal system by establishing

JURISDICTION
the geographical district or subject matter over which the authority of a court extends.

ADJUDICATION
the process whereby the court arrives at a decision regarding a particular case.

LIMITED JURISDICTION
the restricted geographical district or subject matter over which the authority of a court extends and is authorized to handle criminal and civil proceedings.

GENERAL JURISDICTION
the geographical district or subject matter over which the authority of a court extends and is authorized to handle criminal and civil proceedings.

APPELLATE JURISDICTION
the jurisdiction of these courts is restricted to matters of appeal and review.

TRIAL COURTS
courts with the power to hear a case from the start, examine the evidence, and apply the law to those facts.

"one supreme Court, and . . . such inferior courts as the Congress may from time to time ordain and establish" with jurisdiction over constitutional issues, federal laws, and disputes between states and treaties. State courts within each individual state have jurisdiction over state law. For every criminal case filed in federal court, nearly three hundred are filed in state courts because most crimes are violations of state law.[3]

Jurisdiction is not always easy to determine, and as we see in the *Edgar Ray Killen* case, who has jurisdiction is often a political decision as much as a legal one. The federal prosecutors in the *Killen* case weren't confident that the state would conduct an effective prosecution because of southern political views regarding civil rights laws. Some crimes carry different punishments, and there may be pressure, for instance, to pursue a case in federal court if a particular state does not allow the imposition of the death penalty. In still other instances, there may be compelling reason to change jurisdictions in order to tap into a different jury pool.

Three- or Four-Tier System

Each state has organized its court system in a unique structure that reflects the particular history and politics of that state. Some have specialized lower courts for different areas of the law while others do not; some have only three levels while others have four or even five distinct levels of courts. Not only are no two state court systems exactly the same, but even more confusing is the fact that all the states use different terminology to label the different courts. For example, all states have major trial courts, but in Massachusetts, these are called "superior court," in New York, they are labeled "supreme courts," and in Florida, they are called "district courts."

Despite the labels, all state court systems and the federal system share in common a fundamental structure that consists of three or four basic tiers: courts with limited jurisdiction at the bottom, courts of general jurisdiction at the next level, and then the appellate courts at the top, usually divided into the intermediate appellate courts and final appellate courts.[4]

Lower Courts: Courts of Limited Jurisdiction

Courts with limited jurisdiction, often referred to as the lower courts or inferior courts, have limited authority over the criminal justice process. There are

TABLE 10.1	Structure of Courts in the United States	
State Courts	**Jurisdiction**	**Federal Courts**
Courts of last resort	Appellate	U.S. Supreme Court
Intermediate appellate	Appellate	U.S. Courts of Appeals
General trial courts	General	U.S. District Courts
Lower or inferior courts	Limited	U.S. Magistrates Courts

more than 13,000 lower courts across the nation. Generally speaking, they do not try felony cases and cannot hear appeals. Most civil cases are heard in lower courts.

In urban areas, the lower courts are often called **municipal**, **magistrate**, or **police courts**. These courtrooms are the busiest of all courts because the amount of cases they handle is most numerous. They hear thousands of misdemeanor and petty offenses cases, such as prostitution, drunkenness, disorderly conduct, petty larceny, and traffic offenses. Television programs like *Judge Judy* depict some of the flavor of the lower court where the offenses are minor, juries are rare, and the atmosphere of the court is relatively informal. Judges generally dispense "justice" in quick fashion leading many to characterize these courts as a form of inferior or "**rough**" **justice**.[5]

Lower courts are also the point of entry into the courts for more serious felony offenses. For defendants charged with felonies, lower courts have the authority to hold initial appearances and preliminary hearings and to make bail decisions. In rural areas, justice of the peace courts handle an array of criminal and civil matters, most commonly performing marriage ceremonies. In many remote jurisdictions, justices of the peace are not attorneys and may have no legal training at all.

Ultimately the lower courts actually process about 90 percent of all criminal cases: they are noisy, crowded places with little trappings of pomp and ceremony. Some refer to these courts as **assembly-line justice** because cases are decided in matters of minutes or even seconds, with quick consultations between attorneys and judges. It is not unusual for a public defender to meet their client for the first time, examine the file, advise their client, and argue the case before the judge all in a space of five minutes or less. Then it is on to the next client and the next case. The courtroom, particularly in the busy urban courts, is jam-packed with defendants, victims, mothers, fathers, spouses, children, attorneys, police officers, probation officers, parole officers, and other social service workers. No one is listening to the activity that is taking place at the bench, and even if they wanted to listen, most of the discussion takes place quietly among the attorneys and the judge.[6] Crowded dockets mean that many cases scheduled for that day will not be heard so all the people standing around will be expected back the next day and often the day after that as well. Cases are frequently postponed because one or the other party is not present.

Trial Courts: Courts of General Jurisdiction

Courts with general jurisdiction are the major trial courts authorized to try all civil and criminal cases. As noted above, these courts may be referred to as high courts, circuit courts, superior courts, courts of common pleas, or supreme courts. They have original jurisdiction to try any case including those that involve less serious offenses and they have authority to hear cases on appeal from the lower courts. About 10 percent of the defendants originally brought into the lower court have cases tried in the higher court. These are also known as **courts of record** because a court recorder will keep a transcript of the trial proceedings that forms the legal basis for further proceedings and appeals.

In most states a defendant tried in the lower court system has an automatic right to have a new trial in the trial court system. At the lower level a detailed record of the proceedings is not kept: case files will include information on the

MUNICIPAL, MAGISTRATE, OR POLICE COURTS
busy lower courts where a large number of misdemeanor cases are handled.

ROUGH JUSTICE
informal proceedings within the lower courts that do not conform to formal due process.

ASSEMBLY-LINE JUSTICE
another term for describing the lower court proceedings where cases are decided in matters of minutes or even seconds, with quick consultations between attorneys and judges.

COURTS OF RECORD
courts in which a full transcript of the proceedings is made for all cases.

charge, the plea, the finding of the court and the sentence. Lower courts are often criticized for being loose with a defendant's rights and a safeguard has been the **trial de novo system** which affords the defendant an automatic right to have a new trial in the general court system if they are convicted in the lower courts. For many critics, however, the trial de nova system has been a perfect example of unnecessary duplication in the system and some states, such as Massachusetts, have eliminated the trial de nova system as part of court unification and reform.

Appellate Courts and the Right of Appeal

All jurisdictions give defendants the right to have the proceedings of lower courts and trial courts reviewed by a higher court. In most states, the **right of appeal** is exclusively a defendant's right. The prosecution is not able to **appeal** a verdict or judgment of an acquittal. Appellate courts, which include intermediate appellate courts in thirty-eight states and the courts of last resort in every state, are distinct from trial courts because they have jurisdiction only to review the record of cases on appeal from the lower and trial courts. An appeal by a convicted defendant asks a higher court to review the proceedings that took place in the lower court. Generally, appellants claim that there was an error in procedure.

These courts examine the written transcript of the lower court proceedings and may hear brief oral arguments from the attorneys. There is no jury in the appellate process. The appellate court does not conduct a new trial or re-examine the facts of the case. The focus is on the legality of the proceedings. If the appellate court finds no legal error or if it finds that the legal error was "harmless" and did not affect the verdict, the court will affirm the conviction or the court may reverse the decision and remand it back to the lower court for some modified legal proceeding.

An **intermediate court of appeals** (the third tier) exists to reduce the burden for the highest state court. Usually, it consists of a panel of judges who review all cases that are appealed in a legal manner. The vast majority of these are civil cases involving child custody, property disputes, alimony, and child support. At the highest level are the **courts of last resort**, which operate as the final word within that particular hierarchy of courts. We have seen the extraordinary impact of the U.S. Supreme Court with its ultimate power to be the final arbiter of the interpretation of constitutional law. Each state has its own court of last resort, referred to by various names such as the Supreme Court, Supreme Court of Appeals, Court of Appeals, or Supreme Judicial Court. The highest court in the state is not required to review all cases that are appealed after an unfavorable decision in the intermediate appellate court. Like the U.S. Supreme Court, the justices sitting on the state court of last resort are given the power to choose which cases it will hear except in cases involving capital punishment.

The push for states to reform and unify their court systems had been a major effort across the nation in the last thirty years. Reformers have called on states to reduce the number of courts, standardize their names, and clarify their respective jurisdictions. Eliminating the "de nova system" has been a major push of court reform. As caseloads have multiplied and backlogs mushroomed, the inefficiency, duplication, and sheer waste of time of the courts have been sharply criticized by those in state government. Yet the pace of change has been very slow. Political interests, power struggles, control, and funding issues favor the status quo and resist the overhaul of a system that the public often does not really understand.

TRIAL *DE NOVO*
statutory right of the defendant to a new trial in the general court system if convicted in a lower court.

RIGHT OF APPEAL
the right of the defendant to have the proceedings of lower courts and trial courts reviewed by a higher court.

APPEAL
a request by a convicted defendant to have a higher court review the proceedings claiming an error in due process proceedings which significantly impacted the outcome of the case.

INTERMEDIATE COURT OF APPEALS
courts charged with automatic review of all appeals by defendants whose decisions are subject to review by a court of last resort.

COURT OF LAST RESORT
a court whose ruling has final authority within a given jurisdiction.

THE FEDERAL COURT SYSTEM

The federal court system is structured into the same basic four-tier system. At the lowest level are the **U.S. Magistrates Courts** with very limited powers to try lesser misdemeanors, setting bail in more serious cases, issuing search and arrest warrants, and other legal matters. The courts of general jurisdiction within the federal system are the **U.S. District Courts** created by the federal Judiciary Act passed by Congress on September 24, 1789. U.S. District Courts have original jurisdiction over all cases involving alleged violations of federal statutes. Therefore the trial of the eighteen Klansmen accused of violating the Federal Codes 241 and 242 in 1967 was heard in the U.S. District Court located within the state of Mississippi. Cases heard in the U.S. District Court generally involve violations of federal law, including bank robbery, civil rights abuses, mail fraud, counterfeiting, smuggling, kidnapping, drug trafficking, national security issues such as treason, sedition, and espionage, violations of the many federal regulatory codes such as the SEC, IRS, and so forth.

The next tier in the federal judicial hierarchy is the intermediate appellate level called the **U.S. Court of Appeals**. There are thirteen of these courts covering a defined geographical portion of the United States. For example, the U.S. Court of Appeals for the 6th Circuit handles federal appeals that arise from district court cases in Michigan, Ohio, Kentucky, and Tennessee. The court of appeals have mandatory jurisdiction for cases heard in the district court: defendants who are disappointed in the conviction in the federal district court have the right to have their appeal heard by the circuit court.

U.S. MAGISTRATES COURTS
federal courts with limited powers to try lesser misdemeanors, setting bail in more serious cases, issuing search and arrest warrants, and other legal matters.

U.S. DISTRICT COURTS
courts of general jurisdiction in the federal court system.

U.S. COURT OF APPEALS
thirteen intermediate appellate-level federal courts.

This ornate facade houses the U.S. Supreme Court, the highest court in the land.

The U.S. Supreme Court

At the pinnacle of the federal system and state court system sits the ultimate court of last resort, the U.S. Supreme Court. The jurisdiction of the Supreme Court is spelled out in Article III, Section 2 of the Constitution. The highest court of the land has original general jurisdiction over suits between states, constitutionality of state laws, and matters relating to ambassadors. For these matters, the Supreme Court may function like a trial court.[7]

The Supreme Court has appellate jurisdiction over all federal issues that primarily concern the constitutionality of a lower court ruling or procedure. Defendants do not have the right to have their cases heard in the ultimate court of last resort and out of the thousands of cases filed each year, only a tiny percentage are granted a review or **writ of certiorari**. The Supreme Court does not concern itself with protecting the rights of individual defendants: a case that showed such a violation would not be heard before the Supreme Court. The highest court of the land agrees to hear only cases that will settle ambiguous areas of the law that need clarification.

Procedurally, a request for review is made by petitioning for a writ of certiorari, and granting of review is signaled by the courts issuance of the writ. The phrase comes from the Latin *certiorari volumus* that means we "wish to be certified" or we wish to be heard.[8] Out of almost 6,000 cases on the docket in 2010, Supreme Court justices granted review in only 165 cases.[9]

The selection of cases heard by the Supreme Court in each individual state and in the U.S. Supreme Court, known as its **certiorari power** is a matter of judicial discretion and utmost importance. Unlike the intermediate appellate division that must hear all appeals regardless of their merits, the court of last resort is highly selective about which cases it will hear. Since the mission of the lower appellate court is to protect the rights of individual defendants, it must hear all cases since every defendant has the right to appeal a criminal conviction or civil judgment. If an error has been made in the trial court, it is the function of the appellate court to correct that error by ordering a new trial or procedure.

The purpose of Supreme Court deliberations, however, is not to protect rights of individuals; indeed, the Supreme Court will not grant a writ even in cases where there has been a mere error because, in the words of Chief Justice Hughes, "Review by the Supreme Court is in the interest of the law . . . not in the mere interest of the litigants."[10] The **Rule of Four** is the requirement that at least four of the Supreme Court justices approve a case for consideration for the full Court. Cases that are selected for review, therefore, are of major significance in settling serious confusion about the correct interpretation of the law.

Gideon v. Wainwright

The U.S. Supreme Court does not have jurisdiction over all the decisions made in civil and criminal matters in the state court system but it does have the final word on the constitutionality of state laws and criminal procedures as they operate in the thousands of courts, police departments, and correctional institutions across the land. In a case memorialized in print and screen, Clarence Earl Gideon, a

WRIT OF CERTIORARI
a document issued by a higher court directing the lower court to prepare the record of a case and send it to the higher court for review.

CERTIORARI POWER
the judicial discretion of Supreme Court to select cases for review.

RULE OF FOUR
the requirement that a minimum of four U.S. Supreme Court justices must consent to issue a writ of certiorari.

poor uneducated man challenged the constitutionality of his conviction and won a hearing before the U.S. Supreme Court by sending a petition for a writ of certiorari from a prison cell.

The year was 1961. Gideon was accused of breaking and entering the Bay Harbor Poolroom to steal 25 dollars in coins from the cigarette machine, a bottle of wine, and twelve cans of beer. Gideon had four prior felony convictions, so was no stranger to the court and its procedures. He asked the judge to appoint him an attorney because he could not afford to pay for one himself. He claimed that it was his Sixth Amendment right to have a defense attorney at his trial. The judge told Gideon that the state is only required to pay for an attorney if he is being tried for a capital offense. So the trial proceeded with Gideon representing himself and not surprisingly Gideon is quickly convicted and sentenced to five years in a Florida State penitentiary.

According to established law at the time, the judge was correct to deny Gideon a state-appointed attorney. A Supreme Court ruling on this question, *Betts v. Brady*[11] in 1942, stated that in all non-capital trials the necessity of appointed defense counsel depended upon special circumstances of the case such as age, illiteracy, mental illness, capital sentence, or unusual complexity of the evidence. However, Gideon believed that he was constitutionally correct in asking to be represented by a lawyer. Once inside prison, Gideon pursued his case by filing a petition handwritten in pencil on ordinary lined prison-issue yellow paper requesting the Supreme Court to review the constitutionality of the judge's decision in his case. He basically asked the Court to overturn its previous interpretation of the law decided twenty-one years earlier.

In the decision now known as *Gideon v. Wainwright* (Wainwright was the director of the Florida Division of Corrections), the Court unanimously overturned the decision in *Betts. v. Brady*. With a single stroke of the pen, the nine sitting justices from that time on forward put forth the legal constitutional requirement that each and every state provide adequate legal representation for each and every poor criminal defendant facing a felony conviction.

When the Supreme Court decides a case, there are several possible outcomes of the review. It may **affirm** the lower court decision, that is, the conviction remains in force. It may **reverse** the decision or overturn the conviction and **remand** the case back to the original jurisdiction, which in this case was Panama City, for a new trial under the new set of legal standards. When an appellate court issues a reverse and remand ruling, the state prosecutor faces several options. In some cases, the state's attorney may decide not to try the defendant again for a variety of reasons. Or it may retry the case under the new guidelines by appointing defense counsel for the defendant. In some cases, the Supreme Court may order a reversal of the original decision with prejudice specifically requiring a trial court judge to re-sentence a defendant, or ordering prison conditions found to be unconstitutional to be corrected.

In Gideon's case, when the Supreme Court ruled that lawyers in the courtroom were a necessity for every defendant, poor or rich, the case was remanded back to the original trial court in Panama City, Florida. A new trial took place, only this time Gideon was not struggling to represent himself. A local defense attorney paid for by the state of Florida proved to a jury that Gideon was indeed innocent of the charges that he had stolen 25 dollars, a bottle of wine, and a twelve pack of beer from the Bay Harbor Poolroom.

AFFIRM
the ruling by an appellate court to uphold the decision of the lower court.

REVERSE
the ruling by an appellate court to overturn the decision of the lower court.

REMAND
the ruling of the higher court directing the lower court to rehear the case with a new set of proceedings.

The Impact of the Supreme Court on Criminal Justice Policy

The Supreme Court is composed of nine justices, one chief justice, and eight associates. Each justice is nominated by the president of the United States, confirmed by the Senate and appointed for life. For most of our nation's history, the composition of the highest court has been exclusively white, wealthy, male, and Protestant.[12] It was not until the mid-nineteenth century, that the Court broke with religious tradition to include a Roman Catholic and not until the early twentieth century that a Jew, Justice Louis Brandeis, was appointed to the Court. The inclusion of minorities and women have come even more recently: the first African American justice was Thurgood Marshall appointed by President Lyndon B. Johnson in 1967 and the first women justice appointment, Justice Sandra Day O'Connor, was made by Ronald Reagan in 1981. Out of 112 Supreme Court justices in our nation's history, four have been women, two have been African Americans, and one has been a Latina.

Today the Court is more diverse than it ever has been in the past. As we entered the twenty-first century, there were three women, Ruth Bader Ginsburg, Sonia Sotomayor, and Elena Kagan, one African American, Clarence Thomas, three Jewish justices, Ruth Bader Ginsburg, Stephen Breyer, and Elena Kagan, and three Catholics, John Roberts, Anthony M. Kennedy, and Samuel Alito. In many other respects, however, the Supreme Court is very homogenous. Most Supreme Court justices spent years working within the federal judiciary and other top-level governmental jobs.[13] Most are graduates of elite Ivy League law schools, predominantly, Harvard, Yale, Stanford, Columbia, or Northwestern. Most are substantially wealthy before they are appointed to the Court and hail from upper or upper-middle-class social backgrounds. The one exception to this homogenous social background was the former justice Thurgood Marshall, who graduated from Howard University and whose father was a steward on a passenger train. Marshall achieved prominence as civil rights lawyer serving as chief counsel to the NAACP, then as a federal judge and solicitor general of the United States before being appointed to the Supreme Court.

Before the 1960s, it would have been extremely unusual for the Supreme Court to grant a writ to rule on state criminal procedure. Except in extreme cases, the Supreme Court preferred to leave states to operate their own criminal justice systems as they saw fit. The Supreme Court involvement in state criminal justice systems begins dramatically with the Mapp decision[14] in 1961 under the leadership of Chief Justice Earl Warren, a former prosecutor. By 1969, most of the provisions of the Bill of Rights related to criminal violations were "incorporated" into the due process clause of the Fourteenth Amendment. During the 1970s and 1980s under the leadership of Chief Justice Burger, the Supreme Court moved more toward the crime control model of the criminal justice system. The 1980s saw the "good faith" exception to the Mapp rule that gave police the opportunity to violate a citizen's civil liberties as long as they could show that they made a good faith effort to respect their civil liberties. Exceptions to the Miranda ruling also loosened the court's interference with police interrogation practices. Both the public safety exception and the inevitable discovery exception allow police to ignore Miranda when there is an overriding concern with public safety or when it is likely they would have uncovered the information from sources other than the suspect's confession. In the 1990s, under the leadership of another conservative, William Rehnquist, the court had continued to value the crime control philosophy. As we saw in the *Montoya de Hernandez* case in chapter 7, the majority opinion favored the preservation and expansion of the prerogative of law enforcement to fight the war on crime.

Despite the so-called political leanings of individual justices at the time of their appointment, however, the history of the court tells us that Supreme Court justices often surprise observers by their rulings. The lifetime appointment of justices to the bench is designed to offer the justices an independence from the pressures of political affiliations. The future direction of the court on criminal justice matters appears to follow the conservative emphasis on crime control but that is by no means a certain outcome.

We turn in our next two chapters to the role of the various courtroom players and the way the business of the court is conducted every day. In the process we will explore the process of a trial and the courtroom participants' contributions.

jurisdiction (p. 275)   the geographical district or subject matter over which the authority of a court extends.

adjudication (p. 275)   the process whereby the court arrives at a decision regarding a particular case.

limited jurisdiction (p. 275)   the restricted geographical district or subject matter over which the authority of a court extends and is authorized to handle criminal and civil proceedings.

general jurisdiction (p. 275)   the geographical district or subject matter over which the authority of a court extends and is authorized to handle criminal and civil proceedings.

appellate jurisdiction (p. 275)   the jurisdiction of these courts is restricted to matters of appeal and review.

trial courts (p. 275)   courts with the power to hear a case from the start, examine the evidence and apply the law to those facts.

municipal, magistrate, or police courts (p. 277) busy, lower courts where a large number of misdemeanor cases are handled.

rough justice (p. 277)   informal proceedings within the lower courts that do not conform to formal due process.

assembly-line justice (p. 277)   another term for describing the lower court proceedings where cases are decided in matters of minutes or even seconds, with quick consultations between attorneys and judges.

courts of record (p. 277)   courts in which a full transcript of the proceedings is made for all cases.

trial *de novo* (p. 278)   statutory right of the defendant to a new trial in the general court system if convicted in a lower court.

right of appeal (p. 278)   the right of the defendant to have the proceedings of lower courts and trial courts reviewed by a higher court.

appeal (p. 278)   a request by a convicted defendant to have a higher court review the proceedings claiming an error in due process proceedings which significantly impacted the outcome of the case.

intermediate court of appeals (p. 278)   courts charged with automatic review of all appeals by defendants whose decisions are subject to review by a court of last resort.

court of last resort (p. 278)   a court whose ruling has final authority within a given jurisdiction.

U.S. Magistrates Courts (p. 278)   federal courts with limited powers to try lesser misdemeanors, setting bail in more serious cases, issuing search and arrest warrants, and other legal matters.

U.S. District Courts (p. 278)   courts of general jurisdiction in the federal court system.

U.S. Court of Appeals (p. 278)   thirteen intermediate appellate-level federal courts.

writ of certiorari (p. 280)   a document issued by a higher court directing the lower court to prepare the record of a case and send it to the higher court for review.

certiorari power (p. 280)   the judicial discretion of Supreme Court to select cases for review.

Rule of Four (p. 280)   the requirement that a minimum of four U.S. Supreme Court justices must consent to issue a writ of certiorari.

affirm (p. 281)   the ruling by an appellate court to uphold the decision of the lower court.

reverse (p. 281)   the ruling by an appellate court to overturn the decision of the lower court.

remand (p. 281)   the ruling of the higher court directing the lower court to rehear the case with a new set of proceedings.

REVIEW AND STUDY QUESTIONS

1. Explain how state courts differ from federal courts. Why do we have so many different court systems?

2. What is the jurisdiction of limited, general, and appellate courts?

3. What is the jurisdiction of the Supreme Court? How does a case get to the Supreme Court? Does the Supreme Court hear every case that reaches it?

4. Explain why the *Gideon* case was important.

5. What is meant by "rough justice"? Is this real justice?

6. Most district courts are said to deliver assembly-line justice. What does this mean? Why do you think this is the justice delivered? Is this justice?

7. Describe the composition of the Supreme Court. How important is the background—race, class, gender, and religion—of the justices? Explain your answer.

CHECK IT OUT

Websites

The Supreme Court, https://www.supremecourt. gov. Go to the web site of the U.S. Supreme Court and click on "About the Court" to learn more about Supreme Court justices, past and present, and the history of the Court.

Federal Court, http://www.uscourts.gov/about-federal-courts. Visit this site for all the information you want about the federal court system.

National Center for State Courts, http://www.ncsc. org. Browse by state, or search for career ideas.

Landmark Cases, www.landmarkcases.org/. Click on *Gideon v. Wainwright* to get information about this decision and other information about this case.

The Civil Rights Cold Case Project, http://cold-cases.org/. The Civil Rights Cold Case Project uses investigative reporting techniques to compile information on unsolved civil rights cases. The Project provides information to prosecutions and offers reconciliation and healing to victims of unsolved crimes. Check out current cold cases under the "Cases" tab.

Videos

Mississippi Cold Case—60 minutes. This documentary focuses on the two bodies found during the search for the three civil rights activists. As a result of the evidence collected by Director David Ridgen, the case was reopened in 2005, concluding in a conviction in 2007. Available at: http://www.nbcnews.com/id/19236422/ns/msnbc-documentaries/t/mississippi-cold-case/#.WLM2WzszLLc

Movies

Gideon's Trumpet—105 minutes. A 1979 Hollywood film starring Henry Fonda as Clarence Earl Gideon and John Houseman as Chief Justice Earl Warren.

Mississippi Burning—128 minutes. This film follows two FBI agents investigating the 1964 disappearance of the three civil rights activists in Mississippi and provides an accurate portrayal of the atmosphere in the South during this time.

NOTES

[1] Howard Ball, *Justice in Mississippi: The Murder Trial of Edgar Ray Killen* (Lawrence, KS: University of Kansas Press, 2006), 62.

[2] Samuel Walker, *Popular Justice: A History of Criminal Justice* (New York: Oxford University Press, 1980), 21–22;

Howard Abadinsky, *Law and Justice: An Introduction to the American Legal System* (Chicago: Nelson Hall Publishers, 1995), 55.

[3] U.S. Administrative Office of the U.S. Courts, *Judicial Business of the U.S. Courts, 1994* (Washington, DC: Administrative Office of the U.S. Courts, 1995), 7–9.

[4] Henry R. Glick, *Courts, Politics and Justice* (New York: McGraw-Hill, 1993), 24–27.

[5] Malcolm Feeley, *The Process is Punishment: Handling Cases in a Lower Court* (New York: Russell Sage Foundation, 1979).

[6] John A. Jenkins, "The Lobster Shift: One Night in the Nation's Busiest Court," *ABA Journal* 56 (1986), 76.

[7] Robert G. McCloskey, *The American Supreme Court* (Chicago: University of Chicago Press, 1960).

[8] Anthony Lewis, *Gideon's Trumpet* (New York: Vintage Books, 1964), 26.

[9] Ann L. Pastore and Kathleen Maguire, eds., "Petitions for Review on Writ of Certiorari to the U.S. Supreme Court Filed, Terminated, and Pending," *Sourcebook of Criminal Justice Statistics Online;* http://www.albany.edu/sourcebook/pdf/t5702010.pdfTable 5.70.2010; retrieved August 18, 2012.

[10] Anthony Lewis, *Gideon's Trumpet* (New York: Vintage Books, 1964), 26.

[11] 316 U.S. 455, 462 1942.

[12] Henry R. Glick, *Courts, Politics and Justice* (New York: McGraw-Hill, 1993), 149.

[13] Glick, *Courts, Politics and Justice*, 151.

[14] *Mapp v. Ohio*, 367 U.S. 643 (1961).

In this chapter you will read about one of the most covered cases in the last fifty years, the trial of O. J. Simpson. You will read about the judicial processes and examine how and why they lead to judgment at trial. The chapter content describes the process of trials, with a particular focus on juries.

LEARNING OBJECTIVES

After reading this chapter you should be able to:

- Identify and define pretrial motions, types of evidence, and witnesses presented at trial.
- Describe the key steps of the trial process.
- Explain the origins of the jury system and the role of the jury in the justice system.
- Distinguish the role of the grand jury and the petit jury.
- Articulate the process of jury selection and the issues of discrimination such as those raised by the use of peremptory challenges.
- Explain the historical significance of jury nullification and discuss the current issues of jury nullification.

Case #11: America in Black and White: The Celebrity Trial of O. J. Simpson

O. J. Simpson, celebrity football player, on trial for the murder of his ex-wife, Nicole Simpson, and her friend Ron Goldman.

On June 17, 1994, roughly ninety-five million Americans watched the spectacle of a white Ford Bronco traveling slowly down the Los Angeles freeway followed by dozens of law enforcement vehicles. Three days earlier, shortly after midnight on June 12, the bodies of Nicole Brown-Simpson and Ron Goldman were discovered just outside her upscale home. Both victims had been viciously stabbed and beaten. Everyone knew who was inside the Ford Bronco as television crews filmed the bizarre slow-speed chase from over twenty helicopters hovering above the freeway.

In the backseat of the Bronco sat the main suspect in the double murder: Orenthal James Simpson, estranged husband of Nicole Simpson and well-known football legend, television personality, movie actor, and corporate spokesperson. Handsome, wealthy, and famous, O. J. or "The Juice" was a national celebrity whose face and nickname was known and beloved across America. With a warrant out for his arrest, O. J. Simpson had agreed to voluntarily turn himself in to the LAPD that day at 11 a.m. A crowd of over one thousand reporters awaited his arrival at the police station.

When he failed to show up, the news instantly hit the airwaves. The drama intensified further when he was spotted in the backseat of a car driving south on Interstate 405. When approached by law enforcement, the driver Al Cowlings yelled that Simpson had a gun to his own head and was threatening to kill himself. So, for five hours of live coverage, the Bronco slowly made its way back to Simpson's estates at 35 mph as pleas for him to turn himself in were broadcast over the radio. Cars, spectators, and camera crews lined the route and watched in wonder as Simpson was arrested by the waiting LAPD. It was one of the largest television audiences in American history.

So began one of the most celebrated and media-driven trials in American history. For nine months, cameras in the courtroom televised 134 days of testimony replayed and rehashed endlessly by "talking heads" on news and radio programs. Print media in newspapers and magazines, and eventually books covered the trial from every conceivable angle. Public opinion on the trial, its outcomes, and its many players was tracked by polls which parsed the views of whites, blacks, men and women, young and old. On October 3, 1995, sixteen months after the murder, much of America stopped what it was doing to listen to the verdict announced on television. After less than four hours of deliberation, a jury of nine blacks, two whites, and one Latino acquitted Simpson of the charge of double homicide. An estimated 150 million Americans heard these verdicts read live on national television.

The Case Begins

A team of twenty-five prosecutors, twelve full-time and thirteen part-time, under the leadership of Marcia Clark, a short, no-nonsense white woman with years of experience, faced an equally large defense team composed of a set of attorneys the media dubbed the "Dream Team." Costing Simpson an estimated six million dollars, this set of attorneys, many celebrities in their own right, succeeded in raising reasonable doubt in the minds of the jury. By the end of the trial the prosecution had outspent the defense, mounting a nine-million-dollar prosecution at taxpayer expense.

From the outset, the celebrityhood of the defendant and the media spotlight on every aspect of this trial presented enormous challenges for the legal proceedings. The grand jury that heard evidence to produce an indictment was dismissed due to excessive media coverage of the case. Two key witnesses who testified at that hearing, the only eyewitness to place Simpson at the scene and a witness who testified that he had sold Simpson a knife three weeks earlier, both undermined their credibility by selling their stories to the tabloid press for a hefty fee. Neither was ever called to testify in the criminal trial. In the end, the DA's office filed criminal charges in California Superior Court where a judge agreed that there was sufficient evidence to charge Simpson with double homicide.

The Defense Strategy: It's All about Race

The defendant was a celebrity but he was also a black celebrity. From the early stages of the trial, Johnny Cochran, one of the lead defense attorneys, recognized the potential to raise reasonable doubt in the minds of a jury likely to be sympathetic to the plight of a black man on trial in racist America. Almost immediately, public opinion about Simpson divided along racial lines. A nationwide survey conducted one month after the murders showed a glaring discrepancy between blacks and whites on the subject of Simpson's guilt. While persons of both races admitted that they did not know enough to comment on the case, 34 percent of white respondents believed Simpson was "probably guilty" (versus 18 percent who felt he was "probably not guilty") while the reverse was true for black respondents. Among blacks 33 percent felt Simpson was "probably not-guilty" versus 11 percent who felt he was "probably guilty." Sympathy for Simpson was also racially divided: 39 percent of blacks felt a great deal of sympathy for O. J. compared to only 8 percent of whites.

Given these widely reported public opinion polls and the more broadly recognized discrepancy in attitudes about the fairness of the criminal justice system (blacks are more than twice as likely to believe the criminal justice system is unfair toward blacks while whites are three times more likely than blacks to think the system is fair to all races), the decision on the part of the prosecution to hold the trial in downtown LA was seen as one of the most significant strategic mistakes in the trial.

According to the Constitution, defendants are entitled to be tried within the district in which crime was committed. It is possible to file a motion for a change of venue, and in this case, the natural party to request such a change would have been the defense. The crime was committed in the nearly all-white wealthy neighborhood where O. J. Simpson and Nicole Brown-Simpson lived. For the prosecution, a jury pool with relatively few black potential jurors reduced the likelihood of jurors with racial sympathies for Simpson. Yet it was the prosecution who decided to change the venue from the very white Santa Monica to the nearly all-minority district of downtown Los Angeles. According to the prosecution, the decision was administratively pragmatic; to critics, it was a huge blunder that gave the defense the opportunity to go on the offensive and "play the race card."

Jury selection is a key element in any trial and is especially important in a trial fraught with the loaded issues of race, gender, and class. Simpson was a black man who grew up poor in the projects. But his lifestyle no longer reflected that background. Rich, famous, and well-heeled, O. J. Simpson moved in predominantly white social circles. He divorced his first African American wife and married Nicole Brown, a glamorous blonde. The defense made ample use of the highly skilled jury consultants who use targeted market research to help select jurors likely to be sympathetic to their arguments.

For this trial, the most sympathetic jurors to O. J. Simpson were, surprisingly, black women. Contrary to the assumption that women would be sympathetic to Nicole as a victim of domestic violence, the data indicated that women were more likely to accept and forgive this behavior than would men, white or black. Prosecutor Marcia Clark, however, did not agree with the advice of the jury consultants, preferring to follow her gut belief that women of color would be outraged by the violence Simpson committed against his former wife. The jury that returned the verdict had ten women and two men: eight were black, two Hispanic, one was half Native American, and one was white.

The Case against O. J.

For many in the legal community, this case was a slam dunk. O. J. Simpson's blood was found at the scene of the crime and the blood of his ex-wife and her male companion, Ron Goldman, were found in Simpson's car, driveway, and home. The motive was simple: Simpson had been a violent husband who beat and threatened his wife repeatedly over the course of their seventeen-year relationship. The prosecution opened its case by playing a 911 tape from January 1, 1989 in which a terrified Nicole Brown-Simpson can be heard expressing her fear of an angry Simpson yelling in the background. The prosecution claimed that O. J., acting in a violent rage, slashed Nicole's throat and shortly afterward killed Goldman, the only eyewitness to the murder. A bloody shoeprint matching the size and make of Simpson's exclusive footwear was found inside his car and a bloody left-hand glove was also found at the scene. The match to this glove was later found at Simpson's home, the same exclusive brand and color purchased for him by Nicole years earlier at Bloomingdales in New York City.

In the end the case rested on the scientific analysis of the blood samples found at the scene, which established a DNA match with a sample of blood drawn from Simpson shortly after he was taken into custody by the LAPD. Prosecution experts testified that the likelihood the blood found at the scene belonged to someone other than Simpson was one in 170 million. These experts also testified that the odds the blood found on Simpson's socks inside his home belonged to someone other than Nicole Brown was one in 9.7 billion.

DNA analysis was relatively new at the time of the trials. It had been used for the first time in the United States in 1987. And it was certainly new to the jury. While DNA evidence is specific to individuals, uniquely identifying single persons, it was easy for the jury to confuse this type of evidence with the classification of blood type, which consists of broad categories inclusive of many individuals. What the prosecution relied on as its most powerful evidence would become the greatest source of doubt for the jury. The key strategy for the defense was to challenge the competence and honesty of the police investigators and detectives,

who handled the evidence and provided the analysis. These doubts once raised outweighed the scientific testimony presented by the prosecution.

Putting the LAPD on Trial

Two individuals claimed the constitutional privilege against self-incrimination during this trial. The first was the defendant himself. O. J. Simpson did not take the stand in his own defense. By claiming this privilege, Simpson was never subject to cross-examination.

But there was another person who later claimed the Fifth during the trial. Mark Fuhrman was the LAPD detective who found the highly incriminating evidence of blood on the driveway at Simpson's home and Simpson's right-hand glove that found to have traces of blood belonging to both victims. Fuhrman became the lightning rod for charges of racism in the investigation and for the central defense claim that Fuhrman had planted the evidence against Simpson, who was being framed by a racist LAPD.

In a pretrial hearing, the issue of whether or not it was admissible to ask Fuhrman on cross-examination if he had ever used the term "nigger" to refer to African Americans came before the presiding judge. The defense was arguing that it was relevant to show that Fuhrman was racist in order to show that he had a motive for framing Simpson by removing the bloody glove from the crime scene and planting the highly incriminating evidence in Simpson's home. Christopher Darden, arguing for the prosecution, said introducing the term "nigger" was highly inflammatory and likely to prejudice the jury against the prosecution in a way that would affect the entire case, not only their attitudes toward a particular witness. Even though it was a relatively slim reed upon which to tie a motive for framing Simpson, Judge Ito allowed the line of questioning to occur.

What transformed the charge from slim reed to a strong allegation was the failure of Fuhrman to answer truthfully when asked if he had used the term "nigger" to refer to black criminals at least once in the last ten years. When asked this question, on cross-examination by F. Lee Bailey, Fuhrman replied no. The defense then entered into evidence an hour-long audio tape made ten years earlier by a young reporter from North Carolina who interviewed Fuhrman and caught him using the term to refer to blacks thirty-nine times. By lying on the stand, Fuhrman destroyed his own credibility, and with it the credibility of the entire police investigation. Although most African Americans did not believe that Simpson had been framed at the start of the trial, by the end, polls showed that the majority of African Americans in the nation, Los Angeles, and, most significantly, on the jury, believed Simpson had been framed by the LAPD because of his race.

The heart of the defense's case, therefore, was to raise reasonable doubt through the possibility that the LAPD had planted evidence against him. This combined with aggressive cross-examination of all DNA experts raising doubts about the timing of evidence and the extent to which it might have been tampered with or contaminated through malicious intent or incompetence. The final doubt was to suggest that blood evidence was inconclusive regarding the possibility that there might have been another individual at the scene that night.

The Civil Trial

In the wake of the acquittal, the Brown and Goldman families had another legal recourse. They sued O. J. Simpson in a wrongful death suit for damages through the civil system. In the civil trial, the standard of proof is lower than in the criminal trial because what is at stake is merely money rather than a defendant's life or liberty. Instead of "beyond a reasonable doubt" standard in criminal trials, the civil verdict depends on the "preponderance of the evidence" or "clear and convincing" evidence. This generally means that jurors are instructed to return a guilty verdict if they feel there is a 50 percent probability that the defendant is guilty of the charge. Nor does the verdict need to be unanimous in the civil trial. Only nine of the twelve jurors must agree in order for a verdict to be reached.

In the civil trial, the verdict of the all-white jury was unanimous: Simpson was responsible for the deaths and therefore owed damages to compensate for their loss. They awarded the Goldman family 8.5 million dollars in compensatory damages.

The defense case presented in the civil trial was the same as that presented by the "Dream Team" in the criminal trial three years earlier. Simpson had been framed by a corrupt and racist police department, which ignored other potential killers to focus exclusively on Simpson. The defense again presented the arguments that the evidence had been contaminated, tampered with, or planted by police to build a case against Simpson.

This time, however, there were significant differences in the key elements of the legal proceedings. The first difference was the composition of the jury and the location of the trial. The civil case was tried in Santa Monica and the jury, drawn from that judicial district, was nearly all-white in composition. Another important difference was the absence of cameras. Unlike the criminal trial, the judge in the civil trial banned cameras and even photographers from his courtroom. He ordered lawyers and witnesses not to discuss the case with the media.

The plaintiff's case in the civil trial focused more attention on the history of domestic abuse between Simpson and Nicole. Key pieces of evidence not presented at the criminal trial were entered in at the civil trial. Foremost among these was the letter that Simpson wrote after the murders, which many believe to be a suicide note more or less admitting his guilt. The prosecution also focused on the lack of an alibi for Simpson during the crucial time in which the murders were committed. Both Simpson's housemate and limousine driver testified that they did not see Simpson between the hours of 9:30 and 11:00 p.m. The driver buzzed the intercom at 10:30 for over fifteen minutes with no response until he saw someone that looked like Simpson entering his front door. Both witnesses testified that Simpson appeared agitated as they helped him put his suitcases in the limo to catch a flight to Chicago.

On February 5, 1997, an all-white jury found Simpson liable for damages and he was ordered to pay an additional 25 million in punitive damages for a total of 33.5 million to the Goldman family. Collecting this money, however, was another issue. California law forbids the use of pensions for punitive damages; so Simpson continued to receive his $22,000/month pension.

In the years following the case, Simpson continued to seek media attention to restore his public image and tell his side of the story. In 2006, the Goldman family took Simpson back to court to prevent him from reaping financial reward from a book and TV deal allegedly confessing to the crime. The book, which was highly controversial, provided a hypothetical account in which Simpson claimed to explain why he did it if he did it. A Florida bankruptcy court awarded the rights to the book to the Goldman family as partial payment for the mostly unpaid civil judgment in the 1997 lawsuit.

Whose Story Do We Believe and Why?

What is the truth of the Simpson case? That is not possible to say. Do we "know" what really happened? People have different beliefs about what happened and what we believe to be true tells us a great deal about ourselves. The narratives we find convincing about the *Simpson* case tells us a great deal about who we are within the social structure of American society. For many within white America, the acquittal of O. J. Simpson was a travesty of justice. They believed that he was guilty according to two dominant narratives or theories. The first is domestic violence narrative. One-third of female homicide victims killed within the United States are victims of their intimate partners: husbands and boyfriends who regularly beat, stalk, and too often, eventually kill them. This narrative is especially convincing given the highly macho world of American football stars.

The second narrative concerns racialized images of the black male sexuality. For many white Americans, it was highly plausible to imagine a black man to be a violent predator of a white woman. This image taps into powerful racial stereotypes of the black man as hyper-sexualized and physically dangerous. Underneath the calm and smiling face Simpson presented to the public lurked a monster.

The acquittal by a predominantly black jury also fit the stereotype held by whites that blacks are intellectually and morally inferior to whites. Many whites believed that the jury was not intelligent enough to comprehend the scientific evidence presented to them and that they substituted emotion for reason when they responded to the "race card" played by the defense.

For black Americans who thought the acquittal was a just decision, there was a different narrative, in which this verdict made sense. Blacks and whites have very different views about the ongoing fairness of American society. For whites, egregious racism is an historical fact eradicated by the civil rights movement and other changes within American society. For blacks, the picture is not so rosy. Quite simply, there is a strong belief that the institutions of American society continue to be highly racist. This is especially true of the institutions of the criminal justice system. Blacks are only 12 percent of the population but comprise 30 percent of all arrests and 45 percent of all people incarcerated.

Police are one of the most visible and notorious institutions that treat minority citizens differently from white citizens. The Los Angeles police department was infamous for routinely disregarding the law in its treatment of black citizens. The phrase "testilying" was coined to refer to the habit of police to lie on the witness stand. Police were widely believed to routinely lie and manipulate in order to win a conviction. Furthermore, the "code of silence" among police officers, white and non white alike, was seen as a shield for unethical and zealous officers like Fuhrman who were willing to plant evidence. It is also widely believed that police officers are unwilling to publicly condemn a fellow officer for fear of swift and often severe retaliation from their peers.

Given this context it is not surprising that it was highly credible for black Americans on the jury to believe that the case against Simpson had been manufactured through the illegal conduct of the LAPD. The evidence presented at trial showed detectives entering Simpson's home the night of the murders without a search warrant; it showed them violating procedures by bringing Simpson's blood with them to his house giving them the opportunity to plant the evidence. These suspicious practices combined with the trace chemicals from police labs found in the blood supposedly from the crime scene added up to a picture of police misconduct that black Americans find highly plausible. Of course, the crowning blow was the testimony of Mark Fuhrman who pleaded the Fifth in response to a series of questions, including the all-important one about whether he manufactured and planted evidence at Simpson's home on the night of the murders.

A Sorry Legacy

Exactly thirteen years after his acquittal, a jury found O. J. Simpson guilty of twelve counts of robbery, conspiracy to commit a crime, assault, and kidnapping with a deadly weapon. He and a co-conspirator kidnapped two sports memorabilia dealers and robbed them at gunpoint. Simpson was sentenced to nine years in state prison.

REFERENCES

This case is based on the following sources:

Alan Dershowitz, *Reasonable Doubt: The O. J. Simpson Case and the Criminal Justice System* (New York: Simon and Schuster, 1996).

Darnell M. Hunt, *O. J. Simpson: Facts and Fictions* (Cambridge: Cambridge University Press, 1999).

Jeffrey Abramson (ed.), *Postmortem: The O. J. Simpson Case* (New York: Basic Books, 1996).

Marcia Clark, *Without a Doubt* (New York: Viking, 1997); Christopher Darden, *In Contempt* (New York: Regan Books, 1996).

Toni Morrison and Claudia Brodsky Lacour (eds.), *Birth of a Nation'hood* (New York: Pantheon Books, 1997).

Vincent Buliosi, *Outrage: The Five Reasons O. J. Simpson Got Away with Murder* (New York: Norton, 1996).

This chapter provides an overview of the trial process from pretrial activity through the judgment, with a special emphasis on the role and institution of the jury. The jury is the key decision-making body at the public trial. Trial by jury is one of the central pillars of the ideal of democracy. The Sixth Amendment in the Bill of Rights affords all citizens the right to a public trial before a jury of one's peers. An essential element of fairness is the presentation of evidence for both sides by zealous advocates in a public forum where the ultimate judgment lies in the common wisdom of one's fellow citizens. In a jury trial, it is the collection of ordinary folk who are the "fact-finders" of the case: they decide whom to believe, which evidence is credible, and what "really" happened. As we have seen with the dramatic acquittal of O. J. Simpson, as long as the judicial procedure has conformed to the standards of due process, the legal "truth" is what the jury decides.

The Trial Process

Sometimes what takes place before the trial is more important than what happens during the trial itself. The first interaction that a defendant has with the court and often with their attorney, appointed or privately hired, is the **bail hearing**. Bail serves two functions: it prevents us from incarcerating a person who has not yet been determined to be guilty, and it assures that defendants will appear in court. The bail hearing therefore determines if a defendant stays in lock up or retains their freedom until a judge or jury determines guilt. So important is a bail hearing that the Supreme Court found that a criminal defendant's initial appearance before a magistrate or judge is an "adversarial" proceeding triggering

BAIL HEARING
the first interaction with the court, where terms of interim release are established.

The role of the jury is to come to a unanimous decision regarding the truth of the evidence and the application of law to facts.

PRETRIAL MOTIONS
a written or oral request to a judge by the prosecution or defense before the trial begins.

CHANGE OF VENUE
a written request to the judge to change the jurisdiction from the location where the crime was committed to a different jurisdiction.

MOTION TO SUPPRESS
a pretrial motion that requests the judge to deny that certain evidence be used in the trial.

MOTION FOR DISCOVERY
a written or oral request to the opposing side to inform their opponent about evidence that will be produced during the trial.

MOTION FOR CONTINUANCE
a written or oral request to the judge by the defense or prosecution to delay trial proceedings.

MOTION TO DISMISS
a written or oral request to the judge to dismiss the charges against the accused.

TRIAL BY JURY
the examination of the facts and law in a court before a jury authorized to give the verdict according to the evidence as to the guilt or innocence of the accused.

IMPANELING THE JURY
the process of selecting individuals to serve on a jury from the jury pool.

OPENING STATEMENT
introduction to the jury by the prosecution and the defense of the evidence and arguments that will be presented in the trial.

the Sixth Amendment's right to counsel.[1] Bail itself can be in the form of cash, a bail bond or cash deposit, property, or a set of requirements placed upon the defendant.

The next step toward trial is **pretrial motions** that are written or oral requests by the attorney to the judge before the actual trial begins. In the Simpson trial, the success of the defense in having the judge allow evidence about racist attitudes on the part of police was critical to the story they wished to present to the jury. In the Ford Motor trial, the success in getting the judge to disallow evidence about company crash tests was also critical to their ultimate success because the jury only hears evidence the judge allows them to hear at trial. As we have seen several times, a request for a **change of venue** alters the jury pool, and therefore the composition of the jury for a trial that also has a significant impact on the outcome of the trial itself. Recall that the Ford Motor Company was granted a change of venue to move from a location where potential jurors might have known the victims and their families to one where that kind of personal connection was unlikely. Prosecutor Marcia Clark in the O.J. Simpson trial was also granted a change of venue, presumably for administrative reasons, and was criticized for creating a jury pool more sympathetic to Simpson as a result. Other common pretrial motions concern the investigatory process and the strength of the evidence against the defendant. A **motion to suppress** the evidence asks that certain evidence not be allowed in court; a **motion for discovery** is a request by defense counsel to see the evidence, including the list of witnesses, that the prosecution intends to present at trial; a **motion for continuance** is a request for more time before the start of the trial. Though they didn't prevail, the Ford Motor Company filed a **motion to dismiss,** requesting the judge to dismiss the case.

A formal **trial by jury** begins with the **impaneling of the jury.** Although the formal presentation of the evidence is supposed to begin at opening statements, attorneys begin to present their case to prospective jurors long before the bailiff calls the court to order during the process of questioning potential jurors about the case.

The judge begins the formal presentations by the attorneys by signaling the prosecution to make its **opening statement** followed by the opening statement of the opposing side. This is one of two times that each side has the opportunity to directly address the jury without interruption from the opposing side. The opening statement presents the jury with an "overview" of the evidence and arguments that will come in the hours and days to follow. Like the jury selection process itself, the opening statement is an important moment to gain the sympathy and support of the jury. The skill of the attorneys lies often in their ability to make a personal connection with the jury: the Ford Motor Company knew that in addition to all the legal power of the major national law firm, it was essential to put a very friendly and folksy attorney in front of the jury.

The presentation of the evidence begins with the prosecution who will first present all its evidence to the jury. There are several different types of evidence but it is necessary that all evidence offered in the trial be relevant to the material elements of the case. **Direct evidence** refers to the testimonial of eyewitnesses who actually saw or heard the crime itself. **Circumstantial evidence** requires a jury to make some inferences from the facts: if a person is coming out of a building where a robbery occurred, the jury must infer about the actions that took place inside the building.

Demonstrative evidence refers to physical objects like the bloody glove, photos of the burnt-out Pinto vehicle, or videotape of the police officers beating Rodney King. These are forms of evidence that can actually be shown to the jury at the trial. The jury relies on its own eyes and ears to evaluate this evidence. **Testimonial evidence** refers to the statements offered under oath in depositions outside the courtroom or by testifying in court as to what they saw or heard. The jury must evaluate the credibility of the witness (are they telling the truth?), or the quality of what they say they saw (could they really see inside the windows of the pool hall?), in order to evaluate the evidence. In **hearsay evidence,** a person testifies as to what another person saw or said and it is generally not permissible as evidence in criminal trials except under certain circumstances such as a **dying declaration** when the last words of a deceased witness may be relayed in court by a third party.

In addition to **eyewitnesses,** who testify about what they themselves saw and heard, each side may hire **expert witnesses** who offer their opinion about the evidence based on expert knowledge. Criminal defendants who are poor and represented by public defenders are often at a disadvantage because they lack funds to hire expert witnesses. Expert witnesses can be very persuasive to juries, especially in the area of scientific evidence. Due to what is sometimes referred to as "the CSI effect," named after the CSI television syndicate, juries now have heightened expectations that they will be presented with scientific evidence in criminal cases.

Character witnesses know the defendant and offer information about the defendant as a person beyond their actions in the crime itself. According to the rules of evidence, if one side calls either a character or expert witness, the other side is also permitted to call expert and character witnesses who present opposing opinions. It is the prerogative of the defense to offer character witnesses that is often seen as a risky choice since it offers the prosecution the opportunity to introduce negative character witnesses and evidence of misconduct in the defendant's past. This type of witness generally benefits higher status defendants who may have many people able to come forward with glowing tales about their character. In his first trial, Edgar Ray Killen clearly benefited from the testimony about his upstanding moral character, which convinced one crucial member of the jury, who refused to believe that Killen was capable of committing a terrible crime.

When an attorney questions his or her own witness, the questioning is referred to as **direct examination.** On direct examination, attorneys are required to ask open-ended questions such as, "What did you observe that night on Highway 33?" When examining their own witnesses, attorneys are prohibited from "leading" the witness with questions, such as "Isn't it true that you saw the Pinto instantly burst into flames?" After each direct examination, however, the opposing attorney is given an opportunity to cross-examine the witness. On **cross-examination,** leading questions are permissible and generally necessary to undermine the testimony supporting the opposing side. The skillful trial lawyer will use his or her own words to force "yes" or "no" questions from the witness which will raise some degree of doubt in the mind of the jury about their previous testimony. On cross-examination, witnesses are not generally permitted to explain their answers and are subject to manipulative questions from the attorney who is seeking to recast their testimony in a light that is favorable to their client.

DIRECT EVIDENCE
firsthand accounts of relevant facts of the case.

CIRCUMSTANTIAL EVIDENCE
evidence that requires a jury or judge to infer a fact about the case.

DEMONSTRATIVE EVIDENCE
evidence such as a photograph or physical object which demonstrates a fact about the case for the judge or jury.

TESTIMONIAL EVIDENCE
statements offered under oath as to what a witness saw or heard.

HEARSAY EVIDENCE
testimonial regarding what another person saw or heard which is generally not permissible as a criminal evidence.

DYING DECLARATION
the last words of a dying witness which may be entered as hearsay evidence in a criminal trial.

EYEWITNESS TESTIMONY
a testimony based upon direct observation.

EXPERT WITNESS
a person with specialized education, training, or qualifications in a particular field who testifies on behalf of the prosecution or defense.

CHARACTER WITNESS
persons who offer testimony regarding the defendant unrelated to the facts of the case.

Once the prosecution and the defense have presented their cases and had the opportunity to challenge each other's evidence, each side offers a **closing statement** before the jury. Like the opening statement, this is a chance to address the jury directly without interruption. Closing statements can run for many hours and oftentimes do depending upon the style and rhetorical skill of the attorney. Even more than opening statements, closing statements are the chance to tie the case together for the jury, to pull all the pieces of evidence presented in the trial and put all the facts together for the jury to see and accept. Although the closing statement is highly charged and emotional, attorneys may not make statements that extend beyond the evidence or make inferences based on that evidence. They may not hint to the jury that other evidence still exists out there or make reference to the refusal of a defendant to testify as evidence of guilt. In many jurisdictions, but not all, the defense presents their closing arguments first and the prosecution is given the privilege of the having the last word before the jury.

Before they go out to make their deliberations, the jury is subject to **instructions from the judge.** The judge actually has the final word on the legal criteria relevant to the case. It is the job of the judge to explain to the jury the type of evidence needed to support the charges and the possible alternate verdicts they may choose from. Judge's instructions can also be very influential in any given case and can also be grounds for an appeal. In the Rodney King trial, for instance, the judge instructed the jury that they should consider what a "reasonable *police officer*" would have done in this case rather than the usual "reasonable person" standard. This led the jury to rely on the testimony of other police who all testified that they found the use of force to be "reasonable" under the circumstances. Without those instructions, it is likely the jury would have applied a different set of criteria when assessing the conduct they viewed on the videotape.

Jury deliberations may range anywhere from a few minutes to many weeks to come to a decision. Most jurisdictions require a unanimous verdict for felony convictions. If the jury is unable to reach a verdict, it is called a **hung jury**. The judge may require them to continue deliberating but may not continue this indefinitely. The one lone holdout is important to the defense since a conviction cannot occur without a unanimous verdict. If there is a hung jury, the judge must declare a **mistrial**. A mistrial is different from an acquittal. An acquittal is a finding of not guilty. The constitutional prohibition against double jeopardy prevents the state from prosecuting the defendant again on the same charges. The defendant is free of all further prosecutions although often prosecutors are able to bring different charges against a defendant. However, they cannot try an individual on the same charges without violating the Constitution if they have been acquitted. In the event of a mistrial, the prosecution may decide to retry the defendant all over again with a new jury. In the first King trial, the jury deadlocked on one of the charges against Laurence Powell. If the federal trial had not ensued, it is likely that prosecutors would have retried Powell to seek a conviction on that charge. This is not a case of double jeopardy because a verdict was not reached in the first trial.

But the jury has a broader function than determining the facts. In the *Ford Pinto* case, there was no dispute that Judy, Lyn, and Donna died from the burns received when the car they were in was rear-ended by Duggar's van. It is the job of the jury to determine the moral guilt of the defendant. What role did the Ford

DIRECT EXAMINATION when counsel questions its own witnesses during the trial.

CROSS EXAMINATION when counsel questions witnesses called by the opposing side.

CLOSING STATEMENT a summary statement made by each attorney to the judge and the jury reviewing the main arguments and facts of the case.

JURY INSTRUCTIONS the judicial responsibility to lay out the law which the jury should follow in making its verdict.

HUNG JURY a jury unable to come to a unanimous decision for a legal verdict.

MISTRIAL judicial ruling that the trial was invalid because it was terminated without a verdict or because of substantial error in due process proceedings.

Motor Company play? To what extent did they willingly and knowingly cause harm to others? Did they take these actions with a cold act of premeditation or wanton disregard for human life? Did they act with malicious and evil intent when they caused harm? These are important questions that underlie our criminal law. It is the job of the jury to deliberate on the culpability of the person being tried by the state. Juries may determine "truth" about the facts but they are also given the responsibility to fit those facts to the law and determine the "justice" of the case.

At this point, we will take a careful and critical look at the institution of the jury itself. The jury system takes a collection of total strangers, throws them together for a relatively brief period of time giving them no training in law or any real background about the defendants, victims, and their lives, and then asks them to make an impartial and objective determination of "truth" and "justice." Is this a realistic expectation? Many countries have no jury system at all; Japan instituted one in the 1920s and then abolished it twenty years later; and although the jury system exists in both England and France, it is rarely used. Today too, some argue that we have abandoned the jury system given that so few cases are ever heard at trial; for some observers the American criminal justice system has also abandoned the institution of the jury in favor of plea bargaining.

The jury verdict in the Rodney King trial led to massive riots. The jury verdict at the O. J. Simpson case generated a great deal of public skepticism about the objectivity and neutrality of the jury. The juries in the Scottsboro trial and the Peairs trial made decisions that many people in our society felt were unjust. Yet juries have also been important in our history in resisting unjust laws. Today people doubt that juries are above the prejudices and passions that govern society. But is it really possible, or even desirable, that juries rise above the everyday opinions of ordinary citizens? How do we guarantee a "jury of one's peers" in a diverse society? How do we guarantee that juries are "objective" and what does this mean? Why do we have a jury system today? Are there alternatives that may be more satisfying to the determination of justice?

THE INSTITUTION OF THE JURY

There are two kinds of juries that serve two different functions. The **grand jury** is a body of twenty-three citizens who serve as protection against excessive prosecution by the government. The purpose of the grand jury is to hand down criminal indictments. The government must present evidence to the grand jury and show probable cause that the accused is guilty as charged. Prosecutor Clark went before a grand jury to seek indictments against O. J. Simpson on two counts of murder; Cosentino too had to convince a grand jury that he had probable cause to criminally prosecute the Ford Motor Company for reckless homicide.

The **petit jury** is composed of twelve or six citizens who hear the evidence in trial itself. In theory, the role of the jury is to determine the "facts" of the case and then apply the law as determined by the judge. Juries listen to witnesses, examine the evidence, view the videotapes, hear the experts on both sides, and ultimately decide who is telling the truth, which evidence is more believable, and what inferences are more likely than others.

In practice, the distinction between the "facts" of the case and the application of the "law" is far from crystal clear. The job of the jury is far more complex

GRAND JURY
a group of, usually twenty-three, citizens assembled to determine whether sufficient evidence exists to support the prosecution of the accused.

PETIT JURY
a panel of citizens charged with determining the defendant's guilt or innocence in a trial.

than simply evaluating evidence. In the *King* case, the jury was grappling with the issue of intent: What was in the mind of Powell when he was beating King? Was he "justified" in being fearful or angry? Which law applies to his actions and where does justice lie in this matter?

The jury is also a **deliberative** body. This means that the twelve or six persons on the jury must discuss, debate, argue, cajole, and eventually come to a unanimous decision. Unlike legislatures that rely upon majority voting, the jury is unique in its requirement that these twelve or six individuals come to an agreement with each other about what is just. In 1972 the Supreme Court ruled it constitutional for states to permit juries to split by 10-2 or 9-3 in non-capital cases, but only two states, Louisiana and Oregon, authorize non-unanimous verdicts.[2]

The deliberative process requires people to come to a consensus. It also creates the possibility that a single holdout may derail the entire process. A hung jury does not reach consensus and therefore is unable to deliver a verdict. The result is a mistrial: the prosecution must begin all over again with a new trial or the case must be dismissed. Judges try hard to avoid a mistrial since it is a waste of resources expended in the trial.

DELIBERATIVE
as with juries, individuals come to an agreement with each other about what is just through a process of discussion, argument, and debate.

The Bill of Rights gives every citizen the right to be judged by a jury of their peers. Historically, however, blacks and women have been excluded from the jury in law and in practice.

Why Does the Jury Exist?

Historically the role of the petit jury has been understood to be about judging the justice of the law itself and ensuring that it remains true to the conscience of the community. The purpose of the jury system is to protect the rights of the accused against governmental tyranny. In the Magna Carta of 1215, King John promised that "no free man shall be taken or imprisoned or in any way destroyed except by the lawful judgment of his peers." In the Bill of Rights, the Sixth Amendment guarantees citizens the right to a public trial before a jury of one's peers. Who constitute one's "peers," how those individuals are chosen, and what their responsibilities are have evolved historically and continue to be a central concern in the justice system.

At the time of framing the Constitution, colonists were concerned about the power of the British monarchy to impose unjust laws on the people.[3] Mindful of the many times that colonists had been sent back to England to be tried before British juries who knew nothing of life in the colonies, the founding fathers explicitly formulated the jury as an institution of local justice. The American jury system was intentionally designed so that local people, neighbors, friends, and relatives of the accused were the ones to sit in judgment at the trial. The jury was to be a pillar of democracy because ordinary citizens were to rely upon their own consciences rather than the letter of the law. The jury was the means to ensure that the law

accurately reflected the morals, values, and common sense of the people being asked to obey the law.

An amusing story illustrates the ideal of common sense justice. Back in the wilder days of West, a woman, Maude, was on trial for pistol-whipping her neighbor.[4] She had done this in retaliation for his act of sewing up her horse's mouth, because the horse was eating his hay. After hearing all the facts, the judge clearly and firmly instructed the jury that no matter what the justification, it is illegal to take the law into one's own hand. He sternly told the jury that it was their duty to uphold the law and determine only if she was guilty of the fact of striking a man with a pistol. The jury politely listened to the judge and his explanation of their responsibilities and then proceeded to find Maude not guilty of a crime she had clearly committed. The foreman explained, "The judge trusted us to do justice. . . . That judge knew we wouldn't go along with all that legal horseshit as he was readin' us."[5]

The power of **jury nullification** refers to the right of the jury to ignore the formal requirements of the law and rely upon their conscience and values to acquit the defendant. In 1735, John Peter Zenger was put on trial for violating the laws against seditious libel, when he published criticisms about the royal governor.[6] The law of the land prohibited the publication of any negative information about any public figures whether or not the information was true. According to the letter of the law, Zenger was guilty. All the jury needed to do was to determine whether or not Zenger had, in fact, written and published the newsletter.

Andrew Hamilton, Zenger's lawyer, appealed to the conscience of the jury. He urged them to disobey the judge's instructions telling them that they had the duty and the power to determine the law as well as the facts. Hamilton told the jury "to see with their own eyes, to hear with their own ears, and to make use of their consciences and understanding in judging of the lives, liberties or estate of their fellow subjects."[7] The jury responded and acquitted Zenger.

Time and again, in our history, juries have used the power of jury nullification to oppose unjust laws. The Fugitive Slave Law of 1850 passed by Congress was enacted to stem the flow of fugitives from slave states to free states.[8] People who aided the slaves were subject to prosecution and punishment. Time and again, however, northern juries acquitted defendants based on their rejection of the law itself rather than on the facts of the case. They relied upon a higher sense of justice that they found to be in conflict with the law, and by their actions they declared the law null and void.

The dark side of the power of jury nullification can be seen in the willingness of all-white southern juries to excuse white violence against blacks. The letter of the law declared all citizens equal regardless of race but community norms of the South upheld vigilante justice against blacks who violated the racial codes of white supremacy. As late as the 1960s, the power of nullification allowed all-white juries in the South to acquit whites who used violence to "punish" blacks for crossing the color line.[9] One of the most infamous examples was the acquittal of two men who shot fourteen-year-old Emmet Till through the head for the "crime" of talking fresh to the wife of one of the men. Despite eyewitnesses who saw the men kidnap Till on the night of the murder, an all-white jury took only one hour and seven minutes to acquit the defendants.[10]

Ideal of Objectivity

The purpose of a jury composed of local citizens who know the accused and the victims also served another purpose. Like the case of Maude above, local juries

JURY NULLIFICATION
a jury verdict that is made without regard to the evidence or the law.

brought to the courtroom their knowledge about a person's character, history, and relationships within the community. Rather than having total strangers pass judgment on a given case, the definition of "peers" was conceived in terms of "those near him . . . who are well acquainted with his character and situation in life." Local juries would be aware of the case, know the facts surrounding it, and circumstances that led up to it. In the eighteenth and nineteenth centuries, it was likely to be one's neighbor who is on the jury, not a complete stranger.

Our contemporary vision of the impartial and objective juror is very different from this earlier notion of neighbor as juror. In the nineteenth century, the ideal vision of the jury shifted from one which relied on local and specific knowledge about the defendant and the victim to an ideal in which jurors were total strangers, with no prior knowledge or connection to anyone involved. The ideal shifted toward the stranger rather than the neighbor. Today, jurors will be removed if they have any personal connection to any of the parties in the case.

The ideal of the impartial juror can be seen in our attempts to find potential jurors in the highly publicized trials of Simpson or King who are unfamiliar with the facts of the case. Typically people who have read about a case, or have heard about it, are routinely excluded from the jury in the search for the "perfect stranger" who will come to the trial as a blank slate with no prior knowledge about the case. Mark Twain remarked in the nineteenth century that the search for the impartial juror often leads us to seat the ignorant juror who doesn't read or talk with others in the community: "The jury system puts a ban upon intelligence and honesty and a premium upon ignorance, stupidity and perjury."[11] Are these the individuals we should be trusting to deliver "justice," as Twain wonders? In the media-saturated world of today, people who are disconnected from the media often lead atypical or strange lives: does this ensure impartiality or does it ensure ignorance?

Issue of Representation

Along with the ideal of impartiality is the ideal that the jury should represent a cross-section of the community. Like so many of our democratic institutions, the jury rolls of the eighteenth and nineteenth, and twentieth centuries have systematically excluded many of our citizens from participation. Blacks, women, non-property owners, and other ethnic minorities were seen as intellectually, morally, and emotionally unfit to serve on the jury. In the colonies, it was only white males who were eligible to serve. No black person sat on a jury until 1860.[12] Before the Civil War the only state to permit blacks to serve on juries was Massachusetts.[13] The first state law ever struck down as unconstitutional by the U.S. Supreme Court concerned the racial composition of the jury. In the 1879 decision of *Strauder v. West Virginia*,[14] the Court ruled that a West Virginia statute limiting jury service to white males violated the equal protection clause of the Fourteenth Amendment and was therefore unconstitutional.

The first state to legally permit women to serve on juries was Utah in 1898, but it was not until the 1940s, that a majority of states made women eligible as jurors.[15] As we saw in the *Scottsboro* case, blacks were systemically excluded from jury rolls on the assumption that they were unqualified to serve as intelligent or educated jurors. No blacks could be called for jury duty because they were not included on the master lists created by jury commissioners. The key-man system that was still in operation until the 1970s gave the power to a prominent man or group of men in the community to select the pool of jurors. In theory, the **key-man system** was to ensure the insertion of community values in the justice process; in reality, this system sometimes only ensured that the values of privileged white males were carried into the courtroom.

The goal to have juries that reflect a true cross-section of the community has centered on the way to construct jury rolls inclusive of all members of the community. In the 1968 the Jury Selection and Service Act, Congress specified the use of voter registration lists as a source for prospective juror names for the selection of federal juries. Yet voter registration lists leave out many potential jurors.[16] African Americans, Hispanics, younger citizens, and the poor are far less likely to be registered to vote than white, middle-class Americans. In the 1990s in North Dakota, for instance, only 17 percent of the eligible Native Americans registered to vote.[17] Not surprisingly, therefore, only a handful of Native Americans appeared on the jury rolls despite the fact that Native Americans constituted 4.9 percent of the population of the entire state.[18] Today, in the effort to construct a truly representative jury pool, most states supplement voter registration lists with other sources such as driver's license lists, telephone directories, tax rolls, and utility customers lists.

But should the jury pool be "representative" of the ethnic diversity of the community or should the specific jury itself reflect the ethnicity of the defendant and victim? How important is gender, class, and racial composition of the jury to render verdicts which are fair, impartial, and just? This is a key question facing the institution of the jury. In the 1940s, Gunnar Myrdal noted that the institution of the jury as a form of local democracy only works when people are judging others who are like themselves.[19] People are able to be fair when the victim and defendant are similar to themselves in terms of race, class, and gender. However, when an all-white jury is asked to judge a black defendant accused of harming a white victim, the jury becomes an institution of oppression. Similarly, we have seen juries composed of all men who are unable to empathize with women as victims in rape or domestic violence cases. The absence of women on the jury undermined the ability of all-male juries to be impartial: data show that all-male juries in the 1950s and 1960s failed to convict males accused of rape and acquitted them even when the evidence was strong.[20] Mock juries' studies demonstrate that all-white juries are more likely to convict black defendants than white defendants.[21]

Jury Selection

In England, there is typically no **voir dire** or jury selection process: at the start of the trial, twelve citizens are chosen at random from the jury pool and that is the jury.[22] Attorneys rarely try to unseat any particular juror. In England, the trial is said to begin after jury selection takes place; in the United States, the trial is said to be over after jury selection has taken place.[23] As we have seen, the process of impaneling a particular jury for a given trial in the United States involves an elaborate process of jury selection in which the opposing attorneys attempt to seat a jury predisposed to their side. Attorneys may **challenge for cause** any potential juror who expresses attitudes and opinions prejudicial to their case. If the attorney is successful in seating a jury favorable to their case, they may have effectively won the trial before it has begun.

KEY-MAN SYSTEM
an eligibility process for serving on jury, based on recommendations from key persons of high character and reputation within the community.

VOIR DIRE
a process by which lawyers and judge question potential jurors for a given case.

CHALLENGE FOR CAUSE
removal of jurors for stated reasons.

The defense in both the King trial and Simpson trial hired jury consultants to assist in the jury selection process. In the *Simpson* case the prosecution also hired a jury consultant, and it is notable that the consultant's advice was ignored—to the detriment of the prosecution. According to jury consultants, a trial is like a play: whether or not it is a hit will depend on how receptive the audience is. Juries are seen as passive bystanders to the drama of justice staged by the two opposing attorneys. Scientific jury selection became popular in the 1970s and has become a routine part of trial preparation for well-funded clients. The jury consultant uses standard social science techniques like opinion surveys and focus groups to assess views that are correlated or associated with various demographic attributes. They will construct an ideal juror for the attorney according to age, occupation, hobbies, marital status, religion, race, political views, and social attitudes. They devise the questions that attorneys should ask on the questionnaire and during the voir dire and analyze the answers to rank the prospective jurors. In addition, consultants are looking for people who will be able to either persuade others to come over to their point of view or hold out against the viewpoint of others on the jury.

The use of **peremptory challenges** to influence the gender or racial composition of the jury is a long-established practice among attorneys. Attorneys do not required highly paid jury consultants to get the message that race and gender of the jury will influence their response to the defendant. Because peremptory challenges require no reason, attorneys have long used these to strike minorities from the jury. This strategy is easily successful because the number of minorities in any jury pool is small, even those that are cross-sectional representations of the community. Removing all blacks or Hispanics from the panel is possible especially when there are only a handful in the pool to begin with.

In 1986, in *Batson v. Kentucky*,[24] the Supreme Court ruled that attorneys could not legitimately use the peremptory challenge to strike jurors solely because of their group membership. While the Court ruled that a black defendant did not have the right to a jury that reflected his race, the jury selection process could not systematically exclude blacks either from the pool or from the individual jury. From 1986 on, if there is a racial pattern in the use of peremptory challenges, the attorneys must offer a nondiscriminatory reason for the dismissals. In 1994, the Supreme Court extended this rule to the use of peremptory challenges to exclude jurors on the basis of gender.

Although it is laudable that the Supreme Court has banned race and gender-based peremptory challenges, it is also the case that attorneys are adept at coming up with legitimate reasons for their choices when challenged. In the Simi Valley trial, the defense had fourteen peremptory challenges. Aware that they could not legally strike for reasons of race alone, the defense grilled potential black jurors for attitudes, opinions, or connections that would constitute cause for dismissal. Most people agree that if attorneys look hard enough, it is always possible to find some legitimate reason to excuse a candidate.

PEREMPTORY CHALLENGES
removal of a certain number of jurors by counsel for each side without reason.

Jury Nullification Today

The power of jury nullification has existed in the United States since pre-revolutionary times.[25] At times it has played a noble role in upholding the conscience of the community against unjust laws, and at other times, it has played an ignoble part in maintaining oppression and inequality within the wider society. The courts have upheld the ultimate power of the jury to acquit defendants by recognizing that it is a power that cannot be taken away from juries. "We recognize the undisputed power of the jury to acquit even if its verdict is contrary to the law as given by the judge and contrary to the evidence."[26]

Yet the courts have decided that juries should not be fully informed of this power either in the judge's instructions or by statements of defense counsel. Although it is recognized that the "court cannot search the minds of jurors" and prevent them from relying upon their conscience when they decide a verdict, to tell jurors that they may nullify the law would be to invite anarchy. Thus, the courts have generally refused to permit defense attorneys to tell juries that they may disregard the law in making their decision: "By clearly stating to the jury that they may disregard the law . . . we would indeed be negating the rule of law in favor of the rule of lawlessness."[27]

The Fully Informed Jury Association is promoting legislation that would require the courts to instruct juries of their power to vote their conscience. Supporters range from members of the NRA, pro-life groups, groups in favor of legalization of marijuana, militia groups, abortion rights supporters, and gun control advocates. This organization advocates the passage of the "Fully Informed Jury Act" which would require judges to instruct jurors that they can determine both facts and the law. Others believe that the promotion of jury nullification would create anarchy by encouraging juries to decide cases based on their own perceptions and beliefs rather than the requirements of the law.

Today, the power of jury nullification technically continues to exist. Judges do not tell juries, however, that they literally hold the legitimate power to question or overrule the law itself. But some observers argue that juries in some jurisdictions have become more inclined to nullify the law especially in the prosecution of drug offenses. The enactment of three-strikes laws and mandatory sentencing, the widespread perception of racial inequities in the administration of justice, and the increasing recognition of complex factors that contribute to criminal conduct, such as battered women's syndrome, has led juries to return decisions which are based on a broader view of justice than simply applying the strict interpretation of the law to the facts of the case.

Did the Simpson jury "nullify" the law when they acquitted him of the double homicide? Was this jury attempting to come up with a fair decision by taking into account the bias evidenced by the Los Angeles police? Was the jury decision in the O. J. Simpson trial an instance of nullification in which the jury ignored the facts and the law to "send a message" to the LAPD about its long-standing history of racist behavior toward minority citizens? Or, were both of these verdicts simply the fair application of the legal principles in which the juror legitimately found reasonable doubt in the prosecution's case?

Professor Paul Butler, Associate Professor of law at George Washington University Law School, argues that African American jurors should nullify the law and acquit black defendants who are guilty of nonviolent crimes in order to stop the flow of black men into the prison system.[28] Butler and others observe that juries are increasingly unwilling to convict clearly guilty defendants under harsh mandatory sentencing laws that they may view as excessive or unjust. The power of jury nullification may serve to act as a check on governmental oppression of minorities through the power of the jury to say "no" to unjust laws.[29] On the other hand, jurists such as Supreme Court justice Clarence Thomas take the position that nullification is a danger to the rule of the law.

The simple reality of the court system is that only a tiny fraction of criminal cases ever go to trial. The dramatic presentation of evidence and the cross-examination of witnesses, which relies so heavily on the skill and preparation of talented advocates, almost never happens in criminal convictions. In more than 94 percent of the cases, defendants plead guilty to the charge. The practice of plea bargaining, which we will examine in depth in the next chapter, is an alternative and routine judicial proceeding far more common than the public trial. It involves the same cast of characters—the judge, prosecutor, and defense attorney—all of whom play major roles in a complex process of give and take to produce a criminal conviction. Although it is less public and dramatic, the process of plea negotiations affects the fate of most criminal defendants, especially those who are poor, to a far greater extent than the adversarial trial process.

bail hearing (p. 293)   the first interaction with the court, where terms of interim release are established.

pretrial motions (p. 294)   a written or oral request to a judge by the prosecution or defense before the trial begins.

change of venue (p. 294)   a written request to the judge to change the jurisdiction from the location where the crime was committed to a different jurisdiction.

motion to suppress (p. 294)   a pretrial motion that requests the judge to deny that certain evidence be used in the trial.

motion for discovery (p. 294)   a written or oral request to the opposing side to inform their opponent about evidence that will be produced during the trial.

motion for continuance (p. 294)   a written or oral request to the judge by the defense or prosecution to delay trial proceedings.

motion to dismiss (p. 294)   a written or oral request to the judge to dismiss the charges against the accused.

trial by jury (p. 294)   the examination of the facts and law in a court before a jury authorized to give the verdict according to the evidence as to the guilt or innocence of the accused.

impaneling the jury (p. 294)   the process of selecting individuals to serve on a jury from the jury pool.

opening statement (p. 294)   introduction to the jury by the prosecution and the defense of the evidence and arguments that will be presented in the trial.

direct evidence (p. 295)   firsthand accounts of relevant facts of the case.

circumstantial evidence (p. 295)   evidence that requires a jury or judge to infer a fact about the case.

demonstrative evidence (p. 295)   evidence such as a photograph or physical object which demonstrates a fact about the case for the judge or jury.

testimonial evidence (p. 295)   statements offered under oath as to what a witness saw or heard.

hearsay evidence (p. 295)   testimonial regarding what another person saw or heard which is generally not permissible as a criminal evidence.

dying declaration (p. 295)   the last words of a dying witness which may be entered as hearsay evidence in a criminal trial.

eyewitness testimony (p. 295)   a testimony based upon direct observation.

expert witness (p. 295)   a person with specialized education, training, or qualifications in a particular field who testifies on behalf of the prosecution or defense.

character witness (p. 295)   persons who offer testimony regarding the defendant unrelated to the facts of the case.

direct examination (p. 296)   when counsel questions its own witnesses during the trial.

cross-examination (p. 296) when counsel questions witnesses called by the opposing side.

closing statement (p. 296) a summary statement made by each attorney to the judge and the jury reviewing the main arguments and facts of the case.

jury instructions (p. 296) the judicial responsibility to lay out the law which the jury should follow in making its verdict.

hung jury (p. 296) a jury unable to come to a unanimous decision for a legal verdict.

mistrial (p. 296) judicial ruling that the trial was invalid because it was terminated without a verdict or because of substantial error in due process proceedings.

grand jury (p. 297) a group of, usually twenty-three, citizens assembled to determine whether sufficient evidence exists to support the prosecution of the accused.

petit jury (p. 297) a panel of citizens charged with determining the defendant's guilt or innocence in a trial.

deliberative (p. 298) as with juries, individuals come to an agreement with each other about what is just through a process of discussion, argument, and debate.

jury nullification (p. 299) a jury verdict that is made without regard to the evidence or the law.

key-man system (p. 301) an eligibility process for serving on jury, based on recommendations from key persons of high character and reputation within the community.

voir dire (p. 301) a process by which lawyers and judge question potential jurors for a given case.

challenge for cause (p. 301) removal of jurors for stated reasons.

peremptory challenges (p. 302) removal of a certain number of jurors by counsel for each side without reason.

expert witness? What is "hearsay" and under what special circumstances is it permissible in court? What is the difference between the process of examination and cross-examination?

3. What is the purpose of the jury in our justice system? How has the jury acted as the "conscience of the community" in U.S. history?

4. What is the specific function of the grand jury? What is the specific function of the petit jury?

5. Describe the process of impaneling the jury. What is the voir dire? What are challenges for cause and peremptory challenges and how does each of these function in the process of jury selection?

6. What does it mean to say that the jury is a deliberative institution? Why is the process of deliberation important to the jury? What is hung jury and why does it lead to a mistrial?

7. What is the ideal of objectivity? What is the ideal of representation? What are the processes in place to create an impartial jury of peers for a defendant?

8. What are the mechanisms by which blacks and women have been excluded from the jury? What did the Supreme Court rule in *Batson v. Kentucky*? Does this ruling prevent the systematic exclusion of minorities and women from the jury? Why or why not?

9. What is the power of jury nullification? What is the position of the courts on the right of a jury to effectively nullify the law by acquitting a defendant despite the facts and the law? What is the position of the Fully Informed Jury Association?

10. State the positions for and against the power of jury nullification. Why does Butler believe African Americans should use the power of jury nullification for nonviolent offenses committed by blacks? Why does Supreme Court justice Clarence Thomas oppose this power?

REVIEW AND STUDY QUESTIONS

1. What is a pretrial motion? Give examples of the motions made before a trial.

2. Describe the different types of evidence admissible at a criminal trial. What is the difference between an eyewitness, character witness, and

CHECK IT OUT

Websites

CNN: O. J. Simpson Main Page, http://www.cnn.com/US/OJ/. For further details about the Simpson trial, explore CNN's record of the evidence, the players, and the trial.

Videos

The Jury System on Trial—twenty-nine minutes. Attorney Mark Zauderer, chair of a special New York commission on the jury, discusses the system of the trial by jury. Available at: *http://video.pbs.org/video/2155424787/*

Movies

12 Angry Men (1957). See the original 1957 classic film starring Henry Fonda as the one lone holdout and honest juror in the deliberations for a murder trial dedicated to the pursuit of the facts while prejudices and weaknesses cloud the judgment of the other eleven men.

OJ: Made in America (2016). Winner of the Academy Award for Best Documentary, this film (actually a mini-series at eight hours) traces the life and career of O. J. Simpson while exploring race and celebrityhood in America.

NOTES

[1] *Rothgery v. Gillespie County*, 554 U.S. 191 (2008).

[2] Jeffrey Abramson, *We, The Jury: The Jury System and the Ideal of Democracy* (New York: Basic Books, 1994), 180–181.

[3] Abramson, *We, The Jury*, 28.

[4] Stephen J. Adler, *The Jury: Disorder in the Court* (New York: Doubleday, 1994).

[5] Adler, *The Jury*, 3.

[6] Jeffrey Abramson, *We, The Jury*, 73–75.

[7] Abramson, *We, The Jury*, 74.

[8] Abramson, *We, The Jury*, 80–82.

[9] Randall Kennedy, *Race, Crime and the Law* (New York: Vintage Books, 1997), 65.

[10] Jeffrey Abramson, *We, The Jury: The Jury System and the Ideal of Democracy* (New York: Basic Books, 1994), 111–112.

[11] Mark Twain, *Roughing It* (New York: Harper and Brothers, 1913), 55–58.

[12] David Cole, *No Equal Justice* (New Yorks: The New Press, 1999), 105.

[13] Randall Kennedy, *Race, Crime and the Law* (New York: Vintage Books, 1997), 169.

[14] 100 U.S. 303 1880.

[15] Jeffrey Abramson, *We, The Jury: The Jury System and the Ideal of Democracy* (New York: Basic Books, 1994), 112–113.

[16] Hiroshi Fukurai, Edgar Butler and Richard Krooth, "Where Did Black Jurors Go," in *Reading Racism and the Criminal Justice System*, ed. David Baker (Toronto, Canada: Canadians Scholars Press, 1994), 88.

[17] Jeffrey Abramson, *We, The Jury: The Jury System and the Ideal of Democracy* (New York: Basic Books, 1994), 129.

[18] North Dakota Data Center, Census 2000 Profiles, Table DP-1. Profile of General Demographic Characteristics: 2000, http://www.ndsu.nodak.edu/sdc/data/profiles/profilesDP1to4/ND.pdf, retrieved August 18, 2012.

[19] Gunnar Myrdal, *An American Dilemma: The Negro Problem and Modern Democracy* (New York: Harper, 1944), 552–553.

[20] Jeffrey Abramson, *We, The Jury: The Jury System and the Ideal of Democracy* (New York: Basic Books, 1994), 113.

[21] Sherri Lynn Johnson, "Black Innocence and the White Jury," *University of Michigan Law Review* 83 (1985).

[22] James Q. Wilson, "Criminal Justice in England and America," *The Public Interest* (1997), 3–14.

[23] Jeffrey Abramson, *We, The Jury: The Jury System and the Ideal of Democracy* (New York: Basic Books, 1994), 145.

[24] 476 U.S. 79, 1986.

[25] Lawrence W. Crispo, Jill M. Slansky and Geanene M. Yriate, "Jury Nullification: Law Versus Anarchy," *Loyola of Los Angeles Law Review* 31 (1997).

[26] *Horning v. District of Columbia*, 254 U.S. 135, 138 (1920) 1006.

[27] *Horning v. District of Columbia*.

[28] Paul Butler, "Racially Based Jury Nullification: Black Power in the Criminal Justice System," *Yale Law Journal* 105 (1995).

[29] Alan W. Scheflin, "Jury Nullification: The Right to Say No," *Southern California Law Review* 45, (1972).

This chapter begins with the case of Paul Lewis Hayes, which illustrates the conflicting role that plea bargains have in our legal system. The chapter presents the roles and responsibilities of the participants in the courtroom work group, then delves deeper into the topics of right to counsel. The chapter concludes by returning to the topic of plea bargains.

LEARNING OBJECTIVES

After reading this chapter you should be able to:

- Define the courtroom work group and describe the primary functions of the judge, prosecutor, and defense attorney.
- Explain the unique role of the prosecutor in the American justice system.
- Present the issues that are unique in the prosecution of "white collar" crime.
- Describe the role of the defense attorney and identify the different segments of the defense bar.
- Understand the significance of representation in the criminal court system.
- Define the process of plea negotiations and define the different forms of plea bargaining.
- Discuss the advantages and disadvantages of plea bargaining.
- Explain the role of the courtroom work group in the plea bargaining process.
- Weigh the issues of justice raised by plea bargaining with the goals of the criminal justice system.

Case #12: Bargaining for Justice: *Bordenkircher v. Hayes*[1]

Attorneys offer advice to their clients in the plea negotiation process, but it is the right of the defendant to have their case heard at trial before a jury of their peers. (Getty Images)

The Crime

On a cool day late in November 1973, Paul Lewis Hayes and his friend, Larry Frazier, entered the Pic-Pac Grocery store on South Upper Street in Lexington Kentucky.[2] The pair roamed the store picking up a few items, some dog food, and a carton of cigarettes and placing them on the counter along with a check from the Brown Machine Shop several blocks away on West street. Clerk Robin Grey eyed Paul Lewis suspiciously and picked up the check to examine it. Later Paul would claim the check belonged to Larry who had headed away from the counter to collect more groceries, but at that moment, Hayes stood at the counter offering the check as payment to the clerk. Robin said she needed to talk to the manager before she could cash the check.

Store manager, Gayle Bourne, came forward from the backroom. Only last Sunday another man had come into the store with a check stolen from the Brown Machine Shop. Bourne recognized the check and phoned the police to come as quickly as they could. A nearby patrol car arrived within minutes and Paul Lewis Hayes, still standing at the counter, found himself staring down the barrel of a thirty-eight revolver. His companion, Larry disappeared out the back door. The officers informed Hayes that he was being arrested for breaking and entering the Brown Machine Shop. Hayes protested, "But it's not my check. You got the wrong guy!"[3] Later, Larry Frazier would be arrested

and charged with the break-in. Paul Lewis Hayes, age 29, was arrested, booked, and ultimately charged with uttering a forged check in the amount of eighty-eight dollars and thirty cents.

A Good Deal?

The state of Kentucky had been providing counsel for its poor citizens even before the Supreme Court ruling in *Gideon v. Wainwright* (see chapter 10). Paul Hayes certainly qualified as indigent. The sixth child in a family of sixteen, Hayes had made it only to the ninth grade before being sent to reform school.[4] His father, an alcoholic, died from heavy drinking. His mother, diabetic, and sickly, raised the family and was the only person in the world Hayes thought cared whether he lived or died. He had been briefly married for only six or seven weeks, and had a child by another woman but she lived in Florida with his son. At age twenty-nine, Hayes lived with his mother, two sisters, and two brothers and earned a meager living working as a horse groom at the Koto Horse Transport Company. Hayes's small salary together with the welfare check from the local office of public assistance supported his mother and siblings. When the judge set bail at one thousand dollars, Hayes was unable to meet the bond and began a long wait in jail to await trial.

Five weeks later, on January 8, Assistant District Attorney Glen Bagby asked the grand jury to return an indictment against Hayes on the charge of check forgery.[5] After arraignment, at a pretrial conference held between Hayes, his publically appointed defense attorney, the state prosecutor, and the clerk of the court on February 2, Bagby offered Hayes what he believes to be a very good deal: the charge of forgery in Kentucky carries a penalty of two to ten years. Bagby put on the table an offer of five years in state prison in exchange for an immediate guilty plea.

Raising the Stakes

For an eighty-eight dollar forgery, five years in prison does not sound like much of a bargain. But the real deal here was not the sentence for the forgery charge. Paul Lewis Hayes had been in trouble before. When he was still a juvenile, he had pled guilty to "detaining a female against her will with intent to have carnal knowledge."[6] As a minor, he had served five years in a state reformatory while his co-defendant, an adult, got a life sentence. In his early twenties, Hayes pled guilty to a robbery for which he was given a five-year suspended sentence. Paul was still on probation for that offense three years later when he was charged with the check forgery. Now he faced his third felony conviction, the third strike. On his record were the two prior felony convictions and under the Kentucky Habitual Criminal Act,[7] a person convicted of a third felony was subject to prosecution as a habitual offender. If convicted as a Habitual Criminal, the penalty was much more than five years. In fact, the mandatory punishment was life imprisonment. The real deal being offered to Hayes was the prosecutor's offer not to charge Hayes under the Habitual Criminal statute.

A Devastating Gamble

Hayes listened as his defense attorney, Anthony Todd, explained the situation. Given his record of offenses, it is in the district attorney's power to go back before the grand jury and seek a second indictment under Kentucky's Habitual Criminal Offender statute, which carries a mandatory life sentence. If Hayes was going to make the state go to all the trouble, expense, and inconvenience of a trial, the prosecutor was going to raise the stakes. If Hayes loses, he would lose big: on the line was his freedom for the rest of his natural life. The choice is yours said the state prosecutor, save the state the time and inconvenience of a trial by pleading guilty to this offense or risk spending the rest of your life locked away in Kentucky state prison. The choice was laid out for Paul Hayes in plain language.

Kentucky law requires all defendants charged under the Habitual Offender Act to undergo psychiatric evaluation. Dr. German Gutierrez interviewed Hayes on February 7, 1973[8] and found no intellectual impairment or emotional disorder, which would interfere with his ability to understand the legal charges or make responsible decisions for himself. In the view of the psychiatrist, Paul Hayes was intellectually competent but emotionally he was consumed with anger and hostility over a sense of injustice toward his treatment in life. As a poor black man, he felt that he had been subjected to negative treatment all his life. Once before he felt that he had been pressured by the advice of his defense attorney and his mother to admit guilt to avoid going to jail. In his mind, he had once before admitted to guilt when he believed he was innocent.

No one knows what went through Paul's mind in making the decision to ignore the advice of his defense counsel and his mother this time. Maybe those five years in the reformatory had something to do with his choice. Going inside prison for any length of time might have been just too hard to face. If he took his chances at trial, even with the stakes raised so high, there was still a chance he could go free. The hope he might avoid prison may have blinded him to the risk of being stuck there forever. Maybe Hayes was truly innocent of the charge and wanted the chance to go to trial to prove it. Or maybe Hayes was too angry or upset to understand the magnitude of the choice he was making.

Whatever the rationale, Paul Lewis Hayes turned down the bargain and entered a plea of "not guilty." Once before he had abandoned his right to a trial: this time he was determined "to fight" rather than admit to being guilty to get a lesser sentence. The district attorney did as he said he would: he returned to the grand jury and obtained a second indictment against Mr. Hayes charging him on two counts: first of uttering a forged instrument and for being a habitual criminal.[9] Bail again was set at one thousand dollars, again, much too high for Lewis to pay. Paul Lewis Hayes remained locked up in the Kentucky County jail until trial set for April 19, 1973.

Losing Big Time

On Thursday, April 19, twelve jurors listened to testimony from the owner of the machine shop, the store manager, store clerk, Paul Hayes, and Larry Frazier, who was now serving time at the Kentucky state reformatory for theft of the stolen checks. Despite his protestation of innocence, the jury firmly believed that Paul Hayes "did willfully, unlawfully, fraudulently, knowingly and feloniously utter and publish to Robin Gray of the Pic-Pac Food Store, as true, the check of the Brown Machine Works in the amount of 88.30."[10]

The jury also was charged with finding Hayes guilty or not guilty on the second charge of being a habitual offender. According to the judge's instructions, if the jury found, beyond a reasonable doubt, that Hayes had been convicted of a felony in 1962 and again of a felony in 1971 and finally of the third charge of uttering a forged instrument, "then you shall fix the defendant's punishment at imprisonment in the penitentiary during his life."[11] If the jury had reasonable doubt about either of the two previous charges, then they were charged with fixing his punishment at ten to fourteen years. If they found reasonable doubt about whether or not he had been convicted of both of the prior felony charges, then they were charged with fixing a sentence between two and ten years.

But there was no reasonable doubt in the two prior convictions: Paul Lewis Hayes had pled guilty to both prior felony convictions. And the jury had just found him guilty on the third count. The jury decision was inevitable. The jury returned a verdict exactly one sentence in length: "We, the jury fix the defendant's punishment at imprisonment in the state penitentiary for life."

Cruel and Unusual Punishment?

Appellate attorneys from the public defender's office filed a writ of habeas corpus on behalf of Paul Lewis Hayes to the U.S. District Court claiming his imprisonment by the state of Kentucky was a violation of his constitutional rights.[12] A writ of habeas corpus is a request to the courts to review the reasons the state is imprisoning a citizen. In essence, the writ of habeas corpus claims to the courts that the individual is being held illegally and asks the courts to order their release from prison.

Hayes's attorneys claimed that the penalty of life in imprisonment for a writing a bad check for eighty-eight dollars and thirty cents was so disproportionate to the crime as to constitute "cruel and unusual punishment" prohibited by the Eighth Amendment. The Habitual Criminal was repealed two years after Lewis was convicted and replaced by a new statute

which imposed life only if the defendant has been over 18 when he committed each offense and only if he had actually served time for the subsequent offenses. Under the terms of the new statute enacted in 1975, Paul Lewis Hayes would not have been eligible for a life sentence. Keeping Hayes locked up for the rest of his life would be out of keeping with the punishments meted out to other Kentuckians for their crimes.

The Right to Trial or the Right to Deal?

Hayes also raised another constitutional issue in his habeas corpus petition to U.S. District Court. The Fourteenth Amendment states that no state may abridge a citizen's right to due process as specified in the Bill of Rights. It was Hayes's contention that prosecutors had robbed him of his right to a trial by threatening him with the Habitual Offender statute. The prosecutor brought that second indictment against Hayes for the sole purpose of dissuading him from exercising his constitutional right to a fair trial before a jury of his peers.

Plea bargaining has a long and not very noble history in the American court system.[13] Despite the fact that attorneys and judges have been negotiating deals in the courts since the nineteenth century, for most of our nation's history there was no official recognition by the courts that the practice was taking place. Attorneys and their clients would broker deals in quiet backrooms while no one ever admitted that such conversations and agreements had taken place. Plea bargaining came out of the closet, so to speak, in the 1970s when many influential groups began to argue that the practice should be abolished. In one state, Alaska, the state's chief prosecutor banned the practice of plea bargaining for all state's district attorneys effecting an end to the process.[14]

But the Supreme Court affirmed plea bargaining ruling in 1970 that plea bargains were an acceptable and pragmatic process for the efficient administration of justice provided the defendant voluntarily and knowingly agrees to the bargain.[15] The Supreme Court qualified their approval of plea bargaining by stating that certain conditions must be met to ensure the process of plea bargaining complies with the Constitution.[16] First, defendants must never be coerced, tricked, or deceived into agreements. They must fully understand and agree to the terms on a voluntary basis. Second, prosecutors and judges must hold up their end of the bargain: the state cannot promise one sentence and then impose another once the defendant has entered a guilty plea. Third, and most relevant for this case, it is unconstitutional for judges or prosecutors to use their power to vindictively punish someone for choosing not to plea bargain. The charge of either judicial or prosecutorial vindictiveness refers to the abuse of power in cases where defendants opt to exercise their rights to due process.

Vindictive Prosecution? Challenging the Motives of the Prosecution

The issue in the *Hayes's* case focused on whether or not the decision to seek the second indictment under the Habitual Criminal Act was an act of prosecutorial vindictiveness and on whether life imprisonment for his crimes was "cruel and unusual punishment." The U.S. District Court flatly rejected both of these arguments. Hayes's mandatory life imprisonment was neither cruel nor unusual in their view. Nor did the U.S. District Court agree that the prosecutor had acted unconstitutionally by choosing to raise the more serious charges once Lewis insisted upon his right to trial. The right to choose which charge to bring against a defendant is well within the discretionary power of the prosecutor. The prosecutor was merely exercising his power to make a deal: the law gave the state certain advantages and he used them.

But the U.S. 6th Circuit Court of Appeals saw the matter very differently.[17] They believed that Hayes was right to claim his due process rights had been violated. In their assessment, the sole reason Hayes was charged under the Habitual Criminal Act was because he was choosing to exercise his right to a jury trial. The prosecutor openly admitted that the only reason he sought the second indictment was to induce Hayes to plead guilty. During the trial, on cross-examination of the defendant, he reminded the accused, "isn't it a fact that I told you if you did not intend to save the court the inconvenience and necessity of a trial and taking up this time that I intended to return to the grand jury and ask them to indict you based upon these prior felony convictions?"[18]

For the court it was significant that the state attorney chose to file the habitual criminal charges after Hayes insisted upon a trial. Without a doubt, the sole purpose of the more serious charge was to dissuade him from exercising due process. Since the prosecutor did not opt to charge Hayes as a habitual offender on the first indictment, the state prosecutor must have decided that the interests of justice were not served by a habitual offender charge for this defendant. If this was true, then it was clear to the justices that the prosecutors were using their power only to prevent Hayes from claiming his right to a trial. If there were no other purposes for the second indictment than to prevent Hayes from going to trial, then he was being denied his due process rights under the Fourteenth Amendment. The Court of Appeals decided this case was a clear-cut example of prosecutorial vindictiveness.

When a prosecutor obtains an indictment less severe than the facts known to him at the time might permit, he makes a discretionary determination that the interests of the state are served by not seeking more serious charges. Accordingly, if after plea negotiations fail, he then procures an indictment charging a more serious crime, a strong inference is created that the only reason for the more serious charges is vindictiveness. Under these circumstances, the prosecutor should be required to justify his action. In this case, a vindictive motive need not be inferred. The prosecutor has admitted it.[19]

The court reversed the district court decision and remanded the case back to the Circuit Court with instructions that the petitioner (Hayes) should only serve a lawful sentence for the crime of forgery which may range from two to ten years. It would be up to the judge to set the terms of that sentence.

Hope and Frustration for Hayes

Like many prisoners locked away and forgotten by society, Hayes's entire existence revolved around his "case" and the hope that he would someday persuade the court to reduce his sentence and set him free. Hayes wrote again and again from behind the prison walls to the judge, defense attorneys, clerks, and anyone who might have the power to issue an order for his release. In July of 1973, Hayes filed a motion on his own behalf requesting the court to suspend further execution of his sentence. Hayes petitioned the court to show him and his family some mercy: he promised to abide by the rules and violate no further laws; his employer was willing to have him back and his income was crucial for the welfare of his siblings and ailing mother. His motions for suspension were denied; most of his letters went unanswered.

On February 9, 1977, the Fayette Circuit Court issued an order to move Hayes from the state penitentiary to the custody of the county jail awaiting a new hearing ordered for 9 a.m. on March 8, 1977. Hayes must have been filled with hope believing the transfer was bringing him one step closer to freedom but the news he received at the hearing on March 8 was not good. The attorney general of the state of Kentucky told the court that he had filed a motion to stay the release of Hayes pending appeal of the decision to the U.S. Supreme Court.

Hayes's attorney requested a bond, which would release Hayes while the case went before the nation's highest court. Everyone doubted that the Supreme Court would agree to review the case. Hayes had already served three and half years of hard time and his attorneys asked that he at least be freed on bond until the Supreme Court ruled on whether or not it would hear the case. The motion to release Hayes pending the appeal to the Supreme Court was denied and in what must have been a crushing defeat for Hayes, he was transported back to the Kentucky State Penitentiary on May 16, 1977.

Lawful Discretion or Prosecutorial Vindictiveness

In 1978, the question of when and how plea bargaining was to be consistent with the Constitution and the rules of due process was a powerful and important issue in the courts. The Supreme Court had stated that it is better that plea bargaining be recognized and regulated than be driven "back into the shadows from which it had so recently emerged." The justices recognized the need to clarify and define more precisely the boundaries of permissible conduct on the part of prosecutors, judges, and defense attorneys during the plea bargaining process.

Just as the timing favored the issue brought forward by Gideon about the right to counsel, so too the luckless Paul Hayes was pushed into the spotlight to serve the "higher interests of the law." Much to the surprise of the local attorneys, the U.S. Supreme Court granted certiorari in what was now the U.S. Supreme Court case, *Bordenkircher v Hayes*.[20]

Plea Bargains Are Different from Trials

By a slim 5-4 majority, the U.S. Supreme Court reversed the ruling of the 6th Circuit Court of Appeals extinguishing the last glimmer of hope for prisoner #28862. According to the majority, Hayes had been fully informed at the pretrial conference of the intention of the prosecutor to charge him under the more

serious statute if he chose to plead not guilty. In fact, the justices argued, this case is no different from if the state attorney had first indicted Hayes under the Habitual Offender statute and then offered at the negotiations to drop the charges. Either way, this kind of "give and take" is the nature of plea negotiations and it is in the very nature of plea negotiations that each side use whatever it legally can to make the other side give in.

Justice Stewart wrote the opinion for the majority stating that "as long as the accused is free to accept or reject the prosecutor's offer" this does not constitute an instance of punishment or retribution. Furthermore, it is constitutionally legitimate for the prosecutor to have as his or her main goal at the bargaining table to dissuade the defendant from pleading not guilty. Realistically, the justice said, that is precisely what plea bargaining is about: inducing defendants to cooperate in order to save the state the time and money of a formal trial. Prosecutors are free to use whatever legitimate sentencing options at their disposal in order to achieve this end, including the Habitual Offender statute.

In two previous cases, *North Carolina v. Pearce*,[21] and *Blackledge v. Perry*,[22] the Supreme Court found evidence of vindictiveness in the plea bargaining process.[23] In both those cases, the defendant had been subject to additional and more serious charge or sentence in retaliation for exercising due process rights. In *North Carolina v. Pearce* the defendant had been granted a new trial after a successful appeal on constitutional grounds. At that second trial, however, he received a more serious sentence than he had in the original trial. In this case, the Supreme Court reasoned that the sole reason for the longer sentence was judicial vindictiveness or punishment of the defendant for exercising his right to appeal.

In *Blackledge v. Perry*, Perry had been given a six-month sentence on a misdemeanor charge in lower court. After he appealed the case and sought his right to a second trial de nova in the Superior Court, the prosecutor filed felony charges rather than misdemeanor charges. These charges carried a much higher penalty and in the second trial, the defendant was convicted and sentenced to a much longer period of time, five to seven years. The Supreme Court concluded in both these cases that the defendants had been maliciously punished by the state for having "done what the law plainly allows them to do."

But in the *Hayes's* case, the justices argued that the plea bargaining situation was different from the trial process. In plea bargaining, the defendant still has the option of accepting or rejecting the prosecution's offer. Hayes could have accepted the deal and served the five years. Prosecutors always have a wide range of legitimate charging alternatives, "so long as the prosecutor has probable cause to believe that the accused committed an offense defined by statute, the decision whether or not to prosecute, and what charge to file or bring before a grand jury, generally rests entirely in his discretion.[24]" Sure the motive was to dissuade him from going to trial, but that is always the motive for the prosecution when it comes to plea bargaining. Whether the state is offering a defendant a more lenient charge or threatening them with one that is more severe, the overall goal is to influence the decision of the defendant to plead guilty to the charge.

Putting Justice above Efficiency: The Dissenting Opinion

Four Supreme Court justices strongly dissented from the majority opinion. In their view, the interests of efficiency, the central reasoning behind the practice of plea bargaining, was a distant second to the paramount interests of justice. In their view the 6th Circuit was totally correct. Prosecutorial vindictiveness is defined as those actions where the state seeks to discourage a citizen from the exercise of his right to trial. To use one's discretionary power as a state prosecutor to file excessively harsh charges or to use one's power as a judge to sentence a defendant harshly because a defendant is protesting innocence constitutes an abuse of that power. "Prosecutorial vindictiveness in any context is still prosecutorial vindictiveness" whether it takes place at the bargaining table or in the courtroom.

The justices acknowledged that in the real world of the courtroom, boosting the charges for the purposes of bargaining, a practice known as overcharging, is common among prosecutors. But just because it is common does not mean that it is fair, constitutional, or legitimate. When charging a defendant, prosecutors should make their decision based solely on the interests of justice encompassing such considerations as public safety, seriousness of the offense, and prior criminal conduct of the individual. The decision of what to charge should not be based on whether or not they are trying to "win" a deal from the defendant. Prosecutors should reach their own decision about what to charge independent of the defendant's

willingness to plead guilty; otherwise, defendants who believe themselves to be innocent will be forced to take "devastating gambles" to maintain their innocence.

Whatever Happened to Hayes?

Paul Lewis Hayes tried to appeal his life sentence one last time. He and his attorneys filed for a writ of habeas corpus in the U.S. District Court again on the grounds that his sentence constituted "cruel and unusual" punishment for the crime committed. The U.S. District Court rejected his claim and when the matter went to the U.S. Court of Appeals, they too rejected the argument that life imprisonment for the offense of forgery was a violation of the Eighth Amendment. A previous Supreme Court ruling in *Rummel v. Estelle*, had stated that American citizens do not have an Eighth Amendment constitutional right to have punishment proportionate to the severity of the crime. What constitutes "usual" punishment for any given crime is totally up to the state legislatures to decide. When the *Hayes's* case was appealed to the Supreme Court, a writ of certiorari was denied. When last heard from, Paul Lewis Hayes remained serving a life sentence in a Kentucky state prison.

THINKING CRITICALLY ABOUT THIS CASE

1. Do you agree with the majority of opinion in this case or the dissenting opinion? Was this a case of prosecutorial vindictiveness or fair and lawful exercise of prosecutorial discretion?

2. When Paul Lewis Hayes was asked to choose between taking the prosecutor's offer or going to trial under the Habitual Offender Act, was this a fair choice for Hayes to make? Why or why not?

3. If you were a defendant facing the choice of pleading guilty to a crime you did not commit or going to trial under the Habitual Offender statute, what choice would you make? What factors would you consider? How would you feel about the justice system?

4. If Hayes had been offered a suspended sentence for the charge, do you believe he would have been willing to plead guilty? Would you plead guilty to an offense you know you did not

commit if you were offered probation or would you maintain your innocence and risk conviction at trial and a prison sentence?

5. Mandatory sentencing statutes increase the power of prosecutors within the plea bargaining process. Explain how this case illustrates that enhanced prosecutorial power. Does this advance the interests of justice in your opinion? Why or why not?

6. Most convictions are the result of guilty pleas entered by defendants. Is it possible that innocent defendants enter guilty pleas in order to receive lenient treatment? What are the implications of this reality for the "three-strikes" statutes which seek to severely punish repeat offenders?

7. Does plea bargaining undermine the legitimacy of the legal system? Why or why not? Is there a viable alternative? What safeguards do you think need to be put in place to ensure that plea bargaining does not undermine the interests of justice?

REFERENCES

Case based on primary documents:

Bordenkircher v. Hayes, 434 U.S. 357 (1978).
Paul Lewis Hayes v. Henry Cowan, United States District Court, Eastern District of Kentucky, No. 75–61, October 9, 1975
Commonwealth of Kentucky v. Paul Lewis Hayes, 73 C-29, April 19, 1973

This chapter examines the courtroom work group, the process of the trial, and the role of plea bargaining in the legal process. The chapter begins with a close look at the "players" of the courtroom and what they do in the array of proceedings that constitute the adjudication phase of the criminal justice system. Lawyers dominate the proceedings in the courthouse but there is a cast of "supporting" roles played by non-lawyers. Clerks, secretaries, guards, bailiffs, stenographers, victim advocates, probation officers, social workers, and mediators are a growing army of non-legal personnel who are engaged in the "business of the court."

The trial is about "truth" according to the rules of due process. As we have seen, the spectacle of the trial is the exception, not the rule in the adjudication process. Even so, the trial remains one of the central institutions where most of our society sees "justice" being performed. With television, the courtroom as an arena for the delivery of justice has become even more central in the public imagination with celebrated trials witnessed by millions of American citizens.

Judges, prosecutors, and defense attorneys work together closely in the courtroom on a daily basis.

COURTROOM WORK GROUP

The **courtroom work group** refers to the professional occupational roles whose primary mission is the administration of criminal justice. It includes judges, prosecuting attorneys, defense attorneys, public defenders, and others, who earn their living serving the court. In a sense, defendants, victims, witnesses, and members of the jury are all "outsiders" to the world of the courthouse. When a criminal prosecution proceeds to adjudication, ordinary citizens temporarily penetrate the boundaries of the strange world of the court with its own language, customs, and rules. Typically victims, offenders, witnesses, and their families feel completely lost in this world without the assistance and representation by "insiders"—the criminal justice personnel who earn their living by serving the court and administering the judicial process.

The **adversarial system** formally pits one side against the other in the battle for truth and justice. Formally, the prosecuting and defense attorney fight vigorously in accordance with the rules of due process to win the case for their client. A very different version of the facts may emerge when testimony and evidence is tested in the presence of a skilled and experienced advocate. For a trial to be genuinely fair, both sides must be evenly matched with skilled advocates to prosecute and to defend in a formal contest of opposing sides. As the court noted in *Gideon v. Wainwright*, "Lawyers are necessities not luxuries."

Informally, however, the defense attorney, prosecutor, and judge are all part of single system.[25] They are colleagues who work together day in and day out disposing of thousands of cases over the course of long careers. While they may act out adversarial roles in front of the public, behind the scenes, they share coffee in the judge's chambers, eat lunch together, play squash, have attended the same schools, live in similar neighborhoods, and belong to the same clubs and associations. Many judges are former prosecutors or defense attorneys, many public prosecutors go on to become private defense attorneys, public defenders join the judiciary, and so forth. The members of the courthouse work group generally have more in common with each other, both professionally and personally, than they do with the defendants and victims whom they represent.

Despite the importance of the adversarial system, most cases processed by the criminal justice system are not resolved by a formal trial.[26] What appears to be an adversarial process is often more a cooperative process. The informal reality is that courtroom work groups arrange settlements on cases through plea bargaining and other forms of negotiation in the vast majority of cases.[27] In a purely adversarial system, one side is the winner and the other is the loser but in the real world of criminal justice, justice is most often a compromise between the two sides negotiated in the judge's chambers, in the hall, on the phone, over lunch, and even in the restroom. In the view of Abraham Blumberg, the reality of the criminal law is that the adversarial system operates only a facade or "con game" concealing a kind of conspiracy to induce defendants to plead guilty in order to meet the organizational needs of the courtroom work group.[28]

The Legal Profession

Harvard University established the first law school in 1817 but attendance at law school through most of the century was rare.[29] Until the late nineteenth century, most lawyers gained their knowledge and skill simply by apprenticing

COURTROOM WORK GROUP
criminal justice professionals who conduct the daily business of the criminal courts.

ADVERSARIAL SYSTEM
a system in which the prosecution and the defense are each on opposing sides seeking to persuade the judge and the jury to accept their version of the truth.

to practicing attorneys. The American Bar Association was formed in 1878 to regulate standards for law schools and help establish statewide bar examinations to control the standards of the profession and who was permitted to practice it.

The profession of lawyering has historically been segregated by class, race, and gender. In England, the occupation divided into two segments: barristers of high noble birth wore white wigs and black robes to argue the case before the court while solicitors from more modest middle-class backgrounds prepared the briefs and advised the clients outside of the court. In the United States, the occupation of lawyer functioned like a "gentlemen's club" dominated by white Protestant males from wealthy classes.[30] Law schools were costly and refused to admit worthy candidates from less privileged backgrounds. Catholics, Jews, blacks, women, and other ethnic minorities were barred from access to the elite institutions of legal education, such as Harvard, Yale, Columbia, and so forth.

The first female to be admitted to the bar was Arabella A. Mansfield in 1869, the same year that the first female law student, Ada Kepley, graduated from University of Chicago Law School.[31] Despite her degree, however, Ada Kepley was denied admission to the Illinois Bar because of her status as a woman. In *Bradwell v. Illinois*[32] in 1873, the Supreme Court ruled that women did not have a constitutional right to engage in all of the professional occupations within civic society because, as the Court said, "The natural and proper timidity and delicacy which belongs to the female sex evidently unfits it for many of the occupations of civil life."

For many in the nineteenth century, the courtroom and profession of law were deemed "unsuitable" for the feminine character. According to the chief justice of Wisconsin Supreme Court which rejected the application of women to the bar in 1876: "The peculiar qualities of womanhood, its gentle graces, its quick sensibility, its tender susceptibility, its purity, its delicacy, its emotional impulses, its subordination of hard reasoning to sympathetic feeling, are surely no qualifications for forensic strife."[33] In the 1880s, there were only about two hundred women attorneys practicing in the United States. By 1900, thirty-four states permitted women to practice law, and by 1920, all states had admitted women to the bar. Yale Law School accepted women in 1918, Columbia Law School in 1927, but Harvard Law School refused to admit women until 1950. As late as 1971, only 5 percent of all the students involved in law were female.

The 1970s and 1980s saw a dramatic influx of women into the profession. By the mid-1990s, half of all law school students were women. By 2015, women constituted about 35 percent of all practicing attorneys.[34] But women still earn significantly less than male lawyers (78.9 percent in 2013)[35] and are more likely to work in less lucrative public agencies or solo practice. While women make up about 22 percent of the partners in private practice law firms, they only represent 4 percent of the managing partners in the largest firms. Women are still underrepresented on the faculty of law schools, in leadership positions within bar associations, and on the bench, but they have made tremendous progress in a short period of time. In 1990, only 6 to 8 percent of state judges and 9 percent of federal judges were women.[36] Twenty-two years later in 2012 women represented 32 percent of state judges and 24 percent of federal judges.[37]

The status of racial and ethnic minorities within the law is considerably bleaker than it is for women. In 2010, African Americans made up 5 percent of U.S. lawyers while Hispanics accounted for 4 percent of practicing attorneys.[38] And of a total of 73,000 judges nationwide, approximately 3,500 or 4.8 percent are African American and 5,100 or 7 percent are Hispanic.[39] Despite the fact that Hispanic and African Americans citizens are disproportionately targeted by criminal justice prosecution and punishment, few of these groups are represented in the occupational roles of the courthouse work group.

The Role of the Judge

Judges are public officials who preside over courts of law. The judge is umpire, referee, coach, adviser, and teacher all rolled into one. The judge is responsible for the legal conduct within the courtroom and administrative flow of cases through the courtroom. The role of the judge is to uphold the rights of the accused and to ensure that the law of criminal procedure is upheld in all the proceedings. Gideon asked the judge to appoint him an attorney because it is the judicial obligation to see that defendants' rights are duly protected. Administratively, especially in the lower courts, the job of the judge expands to include management of the court itself, evaluation of the court personnel, the budget, and even responsibilities for the physical building of the courthouse itself.

Before the trial, the judge rules on all motions concerning the **venue** of the trial, the granting of bail, jury selection, submission of evidence, and the like. During the trial, it is the responsibility of the judge to manage the conduct of the attorneys and to guarantee that what the jury hears and sees during the proceedings is in accordance with the law. It is also the duty of the judge to explain the relevant law to the jury and to give them legal guidance as they begin their deliberations. Any judicial decision during a felony proceeding in a trial court may be the basis for an appeal by the defendant arguing that they had been denied a fair trial according to the law.

From pretrial proceedings through sentencing, the judge is also charged with assessing the strength of the prosecution's case against the accused. The judge retains the power to dismiss the charges against the defendant at any point in the judicial process if he or she believes that sufficient evidence to convict is lacking. Substantively, the judicial role is to protect the accused against frivolous or malicious prosecution. In superior court proceedings, defendants may waive their right to a jury trial and choose a **bench trial**, in which the judge is both neutral arbiter of the process and the person who must decide if witnesses are telling the truth, what the evidence really means, and whether or not the defendant is guilty as charged beyond a reasonable doubt.

In the lower court proceedings where juries are rare, judges are the ultimate decision-makers interpreting the evidence and evaluating the credibility of witnesses.[40] In these busy courts, most cases are dispensed with through guilty pleas negotiated on the spot in routine exchanges between the courtroom work groups. Here the job of the judge is closer to that of a kind of justice broker helping sides come to agreement, offering quick deals one after the other in routine cases that repeat themselves in mind-numbing succession.

The Manhattan Criminal Court is one of the busiest courts in the nation and the only one in the country that actually operates twenty-four hours a day, three hundred and sixty-five days of the year.[41] Prostitutes, addicts, drug dealers, car thieves, angry spouses, and drunks parade in front of the judicial bench in a steady stream of human misery and confusion. This is "assembly-line justice" where juries are non-existent. Police officers round up defendants who are signed over to court officers and taken to holding cells just off the courtroom. There each prisoner, most of whom are indigent, will be briefly interviewed

JUDGES
public officials who preside over courts of law.

VENUE
the place where a case is heard.

BENCH TRIAL
a trial in which the judge hears the fact and issues a verdict on the guilt or innocence of the defendants.

in preparation for arraignment. Standing in front of the bench, the pubic defender, the assistant defense attorney, and the judge will quickly negotiate the deal to be offered to the defendant waiting in the pen. Judges settle most cases at the time of arraignment, entering charges, hearing the facts, and delivering the sentence in a matter of minutes.[42] The majority of defendants charged with misdemeanor offenses will appear before the judge without an attorney.

Even during a **jury trial** the judge plays an important role. Judges routinely rule on what evidence can be presented at trial. In the criminal trial of the Ford Motor Company the judge's ruling that evidence about the details of the girls' deaths could not be presented to the jury likely played a part in shaping the emotional content of the trial and probably contributed to the jury decision to find the Ford Motor Company not guilty.

Appellate judges play a very different role from either lower court or trial court judges. Appellate judges neither examine evidence nor hear from witnesses; they don't assess credibility or make inferences from the facts of the case; rather the job of the appellate judge is to analyze the legality of the proceedings, review legal briefs written by the opposing attorneys, listen to oral arguments made by both sides, and determine if the law has been properly executed. If there has been an error in procedure, the appellate court may order a new trial or order a sentence to be revoked. But an appellate judge will never second-guess a lower court judge's assessment of the evidence or credibility of the witnesses; the appellate court monitors the legality of the proceedings rather than the veracity of the evidence.

One of the most important judicial functions is sentencing of criminal defendants. In most criminal statutes, there is a wide range of sentencing alternatives for a given charge. Historically, the discretion of judges in making this important decision has been very broad. Judges are assisted in this decision by pre-sentence reports written by probation officers and by recommendations from defense attorney and prosecuting attorneys. Criminal statutes such as the Kentucky Habitual Offenders Act that specify a mandatory sentence remove the judge from the key role in sentencing. Under this form of sentencing, there is far less discretionary decision-making required of the judge.

Judicial Selection

Judges are either appointed or selected.[43] Federal judges are nominated by the president and then confirmed by the Senate. Most appointments are confirmed unanimously but occasionally there are heated disputes over a presidential nomination, particularly for Supreme Court justices. For lower court federal judges, senators have tremendous influence in promoting or resisting particular candidates to the U.S. District and Appeals Courts within their state. All federal judges hold their offices for life, and the appointment onto the Supreme Court, as we have seen, can be highly influential in shaping the law of the nation. Indeed, the issue of judicial appointment to the U.S. Supreme Court is a significant factor in the political election of the president of the United States since the influence of the Supreme Court lasts far beyond the term of any individual presidency.

At the state level the selection of judges is determined by state law. One method of selection is via regular party politics: judges campaign for election just like any other politician, by securing a party nomination and running on the party ticket. The major concern of judicial elections is that politics erodes

JURY TRIAL
evidence is presented to a panel of citizens who are required to determine the defendant's guilt or innocence of the charges.

impartiality of those on the bench who must think about re-election and returning political favors rather than upholding the law. States where judges are simply appointed by the governor of the state are also subject to the criticism that such a method of selection fosters favoritism and corruption in the courts that should be above political influence and bias.

In an effort to overcome the drawbacks of both elections and appointments, the **Missouri merit selection plan** was devised in 1940. This is a hybrid system that relies upon an independent commission of lawyers to draw up a list of qualified nominees for the bench. The governor then selects a nominee from this list, who is then provisionally appointed for probationary term subject to voter approval. According to the American Judicature Society, currently two-thirds of the states use some version of the Missouri plan to select some or all of their judges.[44]

The Prosecuting Attorney

The **prosecutor** has become the most powerful figure in the criminal justice system exercising enormous discretion and power in the decision to prosecute. The prosecutor is a government lawyer charged with the responsibility of enforcing the law by investigating the accused and representing the state at trial. As an advocate in the adversarial process, the prosecutor pursues conviction of the accused in accordance with the rules of due process and champions the state in courtroom combat.

The functions of the prosecutor are extremely broad and span the entire criminal justice process. They begin with the investigation of criminal suspects when the prosecutor works with the police to prepare search and arrest warrants. In some cases prosecutors may initiate an investigation on their own. Following an arrest, the prosecutor screens a case at the intake phase to assess the evidence and to determine the charge. The prosecutor is also responsible for preparing the information report that establishes probable cause and, in jurisdictions that require it, for bringing the evidence before the grand jury to obtain an indictment.

The prosecutor participates in all pretrial proceedings as the state's attorney and is responsible for giving formal notice of the charges to the defendant. If the case should go to trial, the prosecutor is the state advocate who prepares and presents the evidence to argue the case for the state. The prosecutor also makes recommendations for sentencing, responds to appeals made by the defendant, and participates in parole hearings by making recommendations for or against early release of the inmate.

Federal prosecutors, known as U.S. attorneys, are appointed by the president and confirmed by the Senate. There are federal prosecutors in each of the ninety-four U.S. judicial districts. They work hand in hand with the FBI to investigate and prosecute federal crimes. The attorney general of the Department of Justice formally supervises the U.S. attorneys and their assistants but in practice each U.S. attorney is relatively independent and free to decide which case will be investigated and prosecuted. The position of U.S. attorney is very prestigious and public and is frequently a stepping-stone to political office or appointment to a federal judgeship.

The office of state prosecutor is also a highly public role and integrally connected to the political arena. State prosecutors (referred to as district attorney, county attorney, commonwealth attorney, or state's attorney) are almost all elected officials answerable to the electorate. The office of state prosecutor is very

MISSOURI MERIT SELECTION PLAN a judicial selection plan devised in 1940 which relies upon an independent commission of lawyers to nominate candidates for final appointment by the governor of the state subject to voter approval.

PROSECUTORS a government attorney who instigates the prosecution of an accused and represents the interests of the state at trial.

often a first step on the ladder of a career in state politics. As political figures, state attorneys are frequently in the media and these professionals typically have close ties with political parties and political circles.

Across the United States, about 2,300 state prosecutors employ approximately 21,000 assistant district attorneys (A.D.As) who carry out the actual duties of the prosecutor.[45] The elected prosecutor acts as an office administrator setting policy within the office for the disposition of cases. The average state prosecutor's office has a staff of only eight employees, but within urban districts with population exceeding half a million, employees may number in the thousands. Los Angeles County has the largest state prosecutor's office in the nation, with a total staff of approximately 2,256, including 1,056 prosecutors.

The typical assistant prosecutor is a recent law school graduate seeking to gain some trial experience for three or four years before moving into private legal practice. Turnover is high, pay is low, and the hours are long. Like public defenders, public prosecutors often experience "burnout" from the grueling endless processing of human misery, incompetence, failure, anger, and pain. Some assistant prosecutors stay on to become career prosecutors and a select few seek the office of state chief prosecutor as a stepping-stone to higher public office within the judiciary, legislature, or executive branches.

Prosecutorial Discretion

According to Supreme Court Justice Robert H. Jackson, "The prosecutor has more control over life, liberty, and reputation than any other person in America."[46] The police may act as gatekeepers to the criminal justice system by bringing most suspects in through the power of arrest but it is the prosecutor who has the power to re-open that gate and allow them to leave the system. It is the prosecutor, more than any other player, who has a highly influential role in determining the pathway through the system a particular defendant must take: Are they charged with misdemeanor or a felony? Is it a serious felony or not? How many counts? These decisions affect how long the individual will be in the system, where they will be in the system, and how they will be treated. Like the selective pattern of law enforcement operated by the police, **selective prosecution** is the unrestricted discretion to choose who is prosecuted and who is not.

The sphere of prosecutorial discretion over the justice system has expanded largely at the expense of the judiciary.[47] In a largely administrative system of justice, it is the prosecutor who makes most of the decisions about the fate of a given defendant. Discretion begins with the decision to investigate. Commonly, prosecutors face the decision to investigate and prosecute suspects who have been arrested by the police, although prosecutors can, and do, initiate investigations. Like the decision to investigate, the decision to file charges is entirely in the realm of prosecutorial judgment. Michael Consentino chose to pursue the Ford Motor Company and prosecute them for this crime; he could have decided to prosecute the driver of the van; or he could have decided not to prosecute anyone at all. The power to decide whether or not to prosecute and, if so, which charges to file is probably the most significant discretionary authority held by the office of the prosecutor.

The policy decision by the district attorney's office to aggressively prosecute certain kinds of crimes, such as drug offenses, while devoting fewer resources to other types of crimes, such as gambling or prostitution, has a significant impact on other parts of the system. The screening prosecutor may decide to divert the

SELECTIVE PROSECUTION
the authority held by prosecutors to use discretion in choosing whom to prosecute.

individual to a social service agency or specific program or dismiss the case for a variety of reasons.

Once the case has been formally entered in the court record through arraignment, prosecutors still have the power to terminate the proceedings. The entry of a **nolle prosequi** also known as *nol. pros* or simply *nolle* is a formal entry of record that simply declares an unwillingness to prosecute a case. The prosecutor may do this without explaining the reasons for this decision to any other party in the criminal justice system.[48]

The most common reasons for dismissing cases are witness problems and other evidentiary reasons.[49] Witnesses may be reluctant to testify, lack credibility or be unavailable, errors may have been made by the police in the arrest or search phase, or the lab may have damaged crucial forensic evidence needed to successfully try the case. Other reasons for dismissal include conserving resources for more serious cases, dropping the charges in exchange for information and cooperation on a more serious offense, the petty nature of the crime, or the fact that it a first offense of an otherwise, well-behaved individual.

Dismissals from prosecution are also often based on the prosecutor's quick judgments and stereotypes about the credibility of the victim. Young black males, young women who are engaged in questionable occupations such as exotic dancing or prostitution, and victims who are in intimate relationships with the suspect are all seen by prosecutors as risky foundations upon which to build an effective case. Prosecutors often exercise a double standard depending upon the status, background, and behavior of the victim rather than the evidence and actions of the perpetrator. Many victims of crime, especially in cases of domestic violence, rape, and sexual assault find their cases are dismissed by prosecutors despite the victim's willingness to testify because prosecutors do not believe they will make a convincing case to a judge or jury.[50]

In addition to deciding whether to prosecute or not, it is also within the realm of prosecutorial discretion to determine what to charge a defendant with. For most criminal acts, there is a range of possible statutes that may be applied to the facts. Prosecutors often prefer to seek multiple charges in order to increase their chances of conviction if the case goes to trial or to gain leverage in plea negotiations. The power to drop, reduce, or, in some cases, enhance the charges at any point in the process gives the prosecutor enormous leverage in the negotiation process of plea bargaining as we will see in later cases.

Prosecuting Corporations

Special problems arise when trying to prosecute businesses or corporations that discourage prosecutors from even attempting to do so. The *Ford Motor* case (chapter 4) is a good illustration, and even though the case raised the possibility of criminally prosecuting a corporation, it continues to be a rare event. Recall that the district attorney in that case first had to overcome the presumption that corporations are something different from the individuals that are employed to act on their behalf: Who exactly should be prosecuted when criminal charges are filed against a company or institution? The chairman of the board? The CEO? Or the actual employee who made a specific decision? In most corporations, many people are involved at some level in decision-making, so it becomes difficult to determine who is responsible for the act itself.

NOLLE PROSEQUI
a formal entry in the record by which a prosecutor declares he or she will not prosecute the case.

That is merely the first prosecutorial challenge. The process of investigating, gathering evidence, and showing intent are more of a challenge when the "defendant" is a really a legal entity not a live human being. Corporations are generally located far from the geographic location where the harmful act takes place: for example, the headquarters for the Ford Motor Company where decisions were made was far from the state of Indiana where the cause of action arose. Furthermore, how could the prosecutor obtain vital documents from the company with evidence of decisions if the company was allowed to exercise its Fifth Amendment rights? Of course, the question of punishment also presents a challenge. If found guilty, how would the state go about "punishing" a legal entity?

In the *Ford Motor* case the victims of corporate misconduct were clear: the people who died driving their defective product. But the issue of victimization is also sometimes harder to define in the prosecution of corporate criminal conduct than in other kinds of crime. Think about an oil spill that kills fish and birds and also gets into the drinking water of an entire county or municipality. How do we determine who the victims are and bring those responsible to justice? Criminal charges? Sometimes the actions of a business result in damages that aren't apparent for years, and by then different people are in charge or the company has been sold. Who should be held responsible? It is also a common perception among the public that corporate crime just isn't as important or harmful as street crime; that it is a question of financial harm, not physical injury. But as we saw in the *Ford* case, the actions of corporations can cause death and significant personal injury.

Another illustration of all these challenges can be found in the suffering of the community called Love Canal, a small village located in upstate New York. In the mid-1970s numerous unusual birth defects and more than expected number of miscarriages were noticed among the local community. It was then discovered that the site that now held a school, and mixed income housing was used by Hooker Chemical Company to illegally dump toxic waste. Twenty years had gone by since the company owned the site, and the company was now part of Occidental Petroleum. How would one even begin to prosecute such a case? Should we even consider the use of the criminal law to hold corporations accountable for the physical harm and injury they do when they violate the law in order to enhance their profits? If so, how do we prove intent especially when those who made decisions and took certain actions are no longer employed by the company?

The final challenge in the prosecution of corporate crime is that often businesses have resources that far exceed the prosecution and they are able to outspend the state. Even more than wealthy individuals who are able to hire teams of highly visible defense attorneys, corporations can afford the utmost talent and resources to mount a legal defense, and can eventually pass that cost along in consumer products.

The Defense Attorney

The highest priority of the **defense attorney** in the criminal case is to advocate for the interests of the accused. Within the adversarial system of justice, counsel for the defense has a singular purpose: acquittal or the least punitive sanctions possible for their client. Unlike the prosecutor who is sworn to uphold "justice" for all parties, the job of the defense attorney is to zealously represent and advocate for the defendant regardless of their innocence or guilt. It is only the government's lawyer who is sworn to pursue the truth. According to the

DEFENSE ATTORNEY an attorney whose ethical duty is to zealously represents the interests of the defendant before the court.

ABA General Standards, "The basic duty the lawyer for the accused owes to the administration of justice is to serve as the accused's counselor and advocate with courage, devotion, and to the utmost of his or her learning and ability and according to the law."

According to Alan Dershowitz, one of the most famous private criminal defense attorneys, "The zealous defense attorney is the last bastion of liberty—the final barrier between an overreaching government and its citizens"[51] It is not the responsibility of the defense to assess the guilt of the accused; to do that would be to usurp the function of the judge or the jury. The function of the defense is to challenge the government at every turn in order to act as a check on the power of the state to prosecute its citizens. Justice Jackson acknowledges the awesome power of the prosecution to use the resources of the state to proceed against an individual citizen. To protect the right of all citizens, it is essential for the defense attorney to zealously advocate for and defend regardless of their guilt or innocence.

The responsibilities of the defense attorney are to represent the interests of the accused as soon as possible after arrest. *Miranda v. Arizona*[52] established the right of the accused to be represented by counsel as soon as he or she is identified as a formal suspect by the state. Defense counsel may be present at interrogations to ensure that the defendant's civil rights are protected by police and the courts. Defense attorneys file pretrial motions on behalf of the accused, represent him or her at all bail hearings, review police reports, interview the witnesses, examine evidence collected by the state in the discovery process, and collect additional evidence and witnesses on behalf of the accused. If the case goes to trial, the defense prepares the case for trial, represents the accused, and provides assistance and advice in sentencing and appeal. Defense counsel pursues appropriate bases for appeals and prepares briefs and oral arguments at appeal.

The practice of criminal law, however, is the least prestigious and least lucrative of all the types of legal practice.[53] Out of approximately 820,000 licensed attorneys in 1994, only 30,000 to 40,000 practice criminal law on a regular basis.[54] Most of these are either solo practitioners or operate in small two or three-person firms in big cities where the number of criminal arrests and prosecutions is high. The typical low status of the average criminal defendant parallels the relative low status of the criminal attorney within the hierarchy of law.

The criminal defense bar can be divided into three general types: elite private defense attorneys; ordinary private criminal lawyers; and indigent counsel systems. The practice of each of these defense attorneys is quite different from one another along with the outcome. Despite the implementation of the public defender systems and the noble and famous Gideon ruling, the quality of the criminal defense and the outcome of a criminal prosecution are often predicated on the size of the defendant's bank account.

ELITE PRIVATE COUNSEL
a small percentage of criminal defense attorneys who have lucrative practices which specialize in representation of the rich and famous.

Private Defense Counsel

Elite private defense attorneys such as Alan Dershowitz, F. Lee Bailey, Johnny Cochran, Leslie Abramson, and Harvey Silvergate form the famous "dream teams" retained in celebrated wedding cake cases of the rich and famous. Celebrities such as O.J. Simpson can afford to bankroll this kind of criminal defense. The Ford Motor Company also hired a large firm to prepare and provide the best defense money could buy. Counsel for defense in these cases spare no expense in advocating for their clients: pretrial motions are filed, one at a time

Inside a federal courtroom.

to slow the judicial process down, large sums are spent on investigations, finding witnesses and preparing them, scientific jury selection, specialized consultants, DNA analysis, and expert testimony. When the rich and powerful are on trial the amount of money spent on the defense can easily outspend the state's budget to prosecute.

But few defense attorneys ever perform this full range of advocate functions. The typical private defense attorney performs their job far from the spotlight and glamour of the celebrated trials.[55] Most practice criminal law by necessity rather than choice: usually criminal cases are a part of a larger general practice of civil law. Some attorneys pick up criminal cases by hanging around the courthouse and finding clients who are desperate and need a lawyer immediately. There is little prestige or glory in the gritty world of the criminal defense attorney who spends a large amount of time in jails, prisons, and station houses meeting with defendants. The typical defense attorney's clients are not the rich and famous but society's misfits and unfortunates who have hurt and damaged others as they may have been hurt and damaged themselves.

The private criminal attorney must also face the challenge of getting paid by clients who may refuse to pay once a case is over, especially if he loses the case. It is common practice for criminal attorneys to require an up-front retainer for at least part of the fee in advance. By necessity, quantity takes precedence over quality—criminal attorneys spend small amounts of time on many cases to eke out a living wage. Since court appearances often result in continuances or waiting for witnesses or defendants or police officers who do not appear, defense attorneys typically overbook their own schedules. The result is even more delays when the defense attorney fails to appear in the courtroom. Most of the members of the courtroom work group understand that when a defense attorney appears before the judge asking for a continuance because the client has not yet appeared, what the attorney is really saying is that the client has not yet paid his fee.[56]

Indigent Defense

The vast majority of criminal defendants are poor and cannot afford even the modest fees of ordinary private counsel. In 1996, 80 percent of criminal defendants relied upon public defenders or court-appointed attorneys whose legal fees are paid by the court or by the state.[57] There are three main systems for delivering **indigent defense**: assigned counsel, public defenders, and voluntary defender systems.

Assigned counsel systems are the oldest and most widely used system for providing defense counsel for the poor. Judges appoint counsel from a list of volunteers or from a list of all available attorneys; attorneys are paid by the court on a fixed fee basis. About 60 percent of the counties, mostly rural counties, in the United States use court-appointed private attorneys to represent the poor. Fees paid to private counsel are considerably lower than that of private defense attorney, although they do have the advantage that they are guaranteed to be paid by the court. In New York City, for example, attorneys hired by the courts are paid 75 dollars an hour,[58] fees much lower than the typical 500–600 dollars an hour charged by private attorneys.[59]

Voluntary defender programs are staffed by full-time attorneys who work for legal aid offices that provide a wide array of legal services to the poor including criminal defense services, although most concentrate primarily on civil and family issues.

During the mid-1960s, federal funds supported legal services within poor communities as part of Lyndon Johnson's war on poverty. The Legal Services Corporation was established in 1974, and federal funding for legal aid services continued into the 1980s when their budgets were slashed by the Reagan administration. A more recent method of delivering these services is the contract system in which individual attorneys or law firms contract with the court to provide legal services to poor defendants for a specified fee.

The major system of indigent defense is the **public defender office**. Public defender offices are funded by the county, state, or federal government; public defenders are government employees who earn a fixed salary and specialize in criminal defense.[60] When Gideon filed his case in 1961, only 3 percent of the nation's counties, serving only a quarter of the U.S. population had public defender systems in place. Most counties and states relied upon private counsel who were appointed and compensated by the court. The Gideon decision came like a "wake-up call" galvanizing the states to provide legal counsel to low-income Americans, not only in criminal but also in civil cases. In 2007 a total of 957 public defender offices in forty-nine states and the District of Columbia received more than 5.5 million cases. Maine is the only state to rely completely upon private attorneys for indigent defense services.[61]

Like the job of assistant state prosecutor, the job of public defender is typically a stepping-stone in the legal career of a young graduate from law school. Most are paid quite low salaries with heavy caseloads. The people they represent are drug dealers, muggers, thieves, pimps, prostitutes, rapists, murderers, and swindlers. While some are innocent of the charges, many more are guilty of harming other people. Public defenders must present an ethical defense regardless of the guilt or innocence of their clients. Although most realize that they are performing an important social function, they are tainted by their association with those who are at the bottom of the heap within society.

Furthermore, defendants often take a dim view of the quality of legal representation offered by public defenders.[62] A common streetwise quip is "Did you have a lawyer when you went to court? No, I had a public defender." There are good reasons for many criminal defendants to feel this way. Most meet their lawyers for the first time in the court hallway of the jail lockup for five or ten minutes. The public defender rifles through the stack of files and quickly gets to the point stating what deal they think they can get for them if they plead guilty. For many defendants, it appears that the public defender is part of the system itself working as an agent for the prosecution with a strong interest in closing the deal as quickly as possible. Many defendants do not realize the enormous burdens on the individual attorney nor do they realize the futility of taking their particular case to court.

Davis describes the working conditions in her own office known as the top public defender office in the entire nation. There are few resources to hire investigators, social workers, or expert witnesses to help their client win a case. Some offices cannot afford to pay for collect calls so attorneys are forced to refuse calls from their own clients. In Kentucky, public defenders carry caseloads of 120 felony cases per defense attorney and the attorneys are so poorly paid that in one jurisdiction, public defenders were found to be moonlighting in another county to pay their bills.[63] The quality and quantity of resources devoted to supporting competent legal services for the poor suggest that we continue to have a two-tiered system of justice within this country.

Frequently, public defenders feel the best they can do for their client is to convince them to plead guilty. Some systems even have financial incentives that favor guilty pleas. For example, some jurisdictions pay the same flat fee to a court-appointed attorney or public defender whether they enter a guilty plea that requires about a half hour worth of work or take the case to trial that may require a hundred or more hours of work. Whether their client pleads guilty or they work to defend their client's presumption of innocence at trial, either way, the fee is a set amount: $300 for a misdemeanor offense and $750 for a felony.[64]

Did Gideon "Work"?

Four Supreme Court cases form the cornerstone of the **right to counsel.** In 1928, the Supreme Court ruled in *Johnson v. Zerbst*[65] that a poor defendant is entitled to counsel in federal criminal prosecution; in 1932 *Powell v. Alabama*[66] ruled that state must provide "competent counsel" for indigent defendant accused of a capital offense; *Gideon v. Wainwright*[67] in 1963 ruled that all indigent defendants accused of felonies are entitled to counsel at state expense; and in 1972 in *Argerslinger v. Hamlin*[68] extended that right to poor defendants accused of misdemeanors if the penalty includes loss of liberty. The result of these decisions, particularly *Gideon*, was to require all of the states and counties across the nation to provide defense counsel for indigent defendants.

RIGHT TO COUNSEL a defendant's constitutional right to the assistance of an attorney during prosecution.

The vision of the justice implied in the *Gideon's* case was that all American citizens, regardless of their station in life, are equal before the law. Every person, rich or poor, has the right to be presumed innocent unless proven guilty beyond a reasonable doubt through a fair and public trial. Providing poor people with publically paid-for lawyers is an important milestone and monumental achievement in the struggle to establish a criminal justice system that treats all citizens alike. More than 80 percent of criminal defendants in our nation's courts are poor; therefore, the vast majority of criminal defendants today are represented by publically appointed counsel.[69]

Yet, despite the massive infrastructure in legal aid, assigned counsel, and public defenders, do poor people receive equal justice in court? In 1990 federal, state, and local governments spent 1.3 billion to provide legal representation for criminal defendants, but that same year, federal, state, and local governments spent about 5.5 billion to prosecute criminal defendants.[70] In recent years that gap has been closing; in 2005 federal, state, and local governments spent $4.1 billion to provide legal representation for criminal defendants and $4.9 billion on prosecuting criminal defendants.[71]

Still, according to the director of the Public Defender Service in Washington DC, the promise of indigent defense is not what many had hoped in the heady and idealistic days of 1963.

> Imagine practicing law in the basement of an old, dilapidated building with peeling paint, asbestos, broken toilets. Imagine sharing a small office cluttered with broken furniture with one, maybe two other lawyers. Envision having to consult with your office mates before you meet with your client just to get some privacy. Imagine sharing a secretary with seven or eight other lawyers. And imagine working in these conditions sixty to seventy hours per week making onehalf, perhaps onethird of what other lawyers with your same experience are making.[72]

As we will see in the next chapter, the absence of adequate defense counsel is most egregious in capital cases. Defendants facing death penalty too often have publically appointed defense counsel who are drunk, who fall asleep, who never meet with them, are completely unprepared, or who may be grossly inexperienced in the legal complexities of capital defense. While incompetent counsel is technically a basis for an appeal, the burden of proof rests upon the defendant to "prove" the incompetence of their counsel on appeal. Anthony Lewis describes the difficulty of this burden by sarcastically calling the legal standard of competence the "spoon test": "if you hold a spoon up to a defense lawyer's mouth and it shows he is breathing, he is competent."[73]

PLEA BARGAINING AND JUSTICE

Do Poor and Rich Defendants Receive "Equal" Justice Within Our Courtrooms?

Paul Lewis Hayes and Clarence Earl Gideon have a lot in common. Both are poor men with a long and troubled history with the criminal justice system. Both found themselves locked up as young teens followed by a life spent in and out of prison. Clarence Gideon knew from bitter experience that the rules, customs, and procedures of the court were confusing, strange, and incomprehensible to ordinary folk like himself. Because of his determination, the Supreme Court acknowledged that even highly intelligent and educated persons unfamiliar with the culture and norms of the law are lost and bewildered inside a courtroom. Gideon's triumph in securing the right to an attorney for all poor criminal defendants benefited those who came after him like Paul Hayes, who was afforded legal representation in all of the proceedings against him.

But Hayes's case illustrates a different reality about the halls of justice within American society. Despite the symbolic importance of the trial where Americans can see "justice" happen, few criminal convictions are the result of these types of proceedings. Over 90 percent of all felony convictions are the result of guilty pleas.[74] In one study recently conducted by the U.S. Department of Justice, the data revealed that for every hundred felony arrests, fifty-six resulted in convictions. Of those fifty-six convictions, fifty-four were the result of guilty pleas.[75] Clearly, other types of proceedings, such as pretrial conferences, informal negotiations, and other forms of "deal making" are far more important to the justice process than the formal trial.

The court in *Gideon v. Wainwright* attempted to ensure equal justice before the law by providing funds for poor person's defense. At the start of the second trial for Clarence Gideon, the state attorneys observed that had Clarence been represented by defense counsel from the start, there would probably have never been a trial. A competent defense attorney would probably have advised Gideon to plead guilty in exchange for a "deal."

This observation refers to the fact that, most of the time, criminal defense attorneys mount no formal defense: their main contribution is negotiating on behalf of their client with the prosecutor and the judge. Had Gideon had a defense attorney and had he pled guilty, it is likely his sentence would have been far less than five years. In plea negotiations, it is the job of the defense attorney to get the best deal for their client. Clarence Gideon realized that poor defendants without the benefit of counsel were not only more likely to be convicted but were also likely to be serving long sentences for relatively minor crimes. In this chapter, we look at the informal reality of plea bargaining, the prospects of poor defendants in the informal process of plea negotiations, and the impact of these proceedings on the goal of "justice for all."

The Process of Plea Negotiation

The hidden secret of the American justice system is that the adjudication process is rarely the celebrated adversarial trial. Plea negotiation or **plea bargaining** has operated within the U.S. court system for more than one hundred years.[76] It was not until the late 1960s that the practice came out into the open and launched a heated political debate within scholarly and judicial circles. In 1972, the National Advisory Commission on Criminal Justice Standards and Goals recommended that plea bargaining be abolished by 1978.[77] Alaska, initiated a no-plea-bargaining policy to force the criminal justice system to conduct itself professionally without reliance upon "deals" and "shortcuts."[78] During the same period, however, the Supreme Court ruled that plea bargaining was both constitutional and necessary for an efficient system of justice.[79]

PLEA BARGAINING the negotiation of an agreement among the prosecutor, judge, and the defense counsel as to the charge and/or sentence to be imposed if the defendant enters a guilty plea.

In plea negotiations, it is the job of the defense attorney to get the best deal for their client.

There are three major kinds of plea bargaining: implicit expectations of leniency in sentencing or straight pleas; explicit sentence bargaining; and explicit charge bargaining. Bargains may also be made by exchanging a guilty plea for release on bail or for the benefit of dropping a charge in another jurisdiction for a different offense. The preferred system of bargaining and an implicit understanding of the **"going rate"** for guilty pleas are largely determined by the local norms of the particular court or jurisdiction.[80] Although not all the details of the agreement are ever made explicit, most states now require the final agreement to be in writing and signed by all parties involved. By signing an agreement, in theory, defendants are acknowledging that they are voluntarily and knowingly entering into the agreement.

The first form of plea negotiations known as the **straight plea** is probably the most common and does not really involve overt bargaining at all. Because so many defendants are guilty and there is ample evidence to support a conviction against them, some kind of "reward" is implied to criminal defendants who do not contest their guilt and thereby make the justice process more efficient for everyone. Without any explicit offer or deal, a defendant pleads guilty with the informal or tacit understanding that his or her sentence will be far more lenient than if he or she were to be convicted at trial.

Fulfilling this expectation is entirely within the realm of judicial discretion—judges exercise the latitude they have in sentencing to "reward" the guilty defendant, who enters a plea and saves the state the expense and time of criminal

GOING RATE
local informal norms concerning the typical sentence for a given crime within a particular court or jurisdiction.

STRAIGHT PLEAS
a defendant's formal entry of a guilty plea without explicit negotiation by the courthouse work group.

prosecution. Although Supreme Court has ruled that judges who sentence defendants at trial too severely are engaging in judicial vindictiveness, empirical studies show that judges consistently dispense harsher sentences to people convicted through jury trials than those who opt for a bench trial or those who negotiate plea agreements.[81] A recent national study confirmed that felons who pled guilty to violent offenses were sentenced to less than half the time as were those who went to trial.[82]

Explicit **sentence bargaining** involves more overt exchange agreements between the parties to arrive at an agreeable sentence. This is precisely what Prosecutor Bagby did during the first round of negotiations with Hayes: the statute had a range of two to ten years and he made an offer of five. Sentence bargaining may be initiated by the judge, the prosecution, or the defense, although all sides have to come to an agreement.

Charge bargaining is exclusively within the control of the prosecution. An initial charge may be reduced to a lower offense or some of the counts on a multiple charge may be dropped. If one man beats up another on the street, the prosecutor may charge him with anything from assault to attempted murder. **Vertical overcharging** refers to charging a single offense at the most serious level possible in order to maximize the advantage at the bargaining table. This is the strategy the district attorney adopted the second time he charged defendant Hayes; Bagby expected this serious charge to bring Hayes to the table.

Prosecutors also routinely overcharge by bringing the defendant up on as many charges as possible in a process known as **horizontal overcharging**. These "multiple count" indictments include the major offense as well as any additional crimes, often known as "lesser and included offenses" committed in association with the offense. This gives the prosecutor the option to drop some of the lesser charges that reduce the amount of punishment the defendant must face upon conviction.

With the rise of Habitual Offender laws, mandatory sentencing laws, and "three strikes" laws, charge bargaining gives prosecutors far more leverage than other players in the courtroom work group. Once convicted, the judge must sentence according to the statutory prescription for the charge chosen by the prosecutor. Under these types of sentencing laws, the charging decision is synonymous with the sentencing decision.

The Courtroom Work Group and Plea Bargaining

There are strong organizational pressures to forego the formal adversarial system in favor of this system of informal exchanges among the courtroom players who process case after case day after day.[83] Members of the courtroom work group share a common and strong interest in seeing cases dispensed with efficiently and swiftly. Attorneys are often pressured to cooperate in order to preserve informal standing as a team player within the courtroom work group. Failure to cooperate often leads to retaliation and lack of cooperation from others in future cases.

Just as police cannot arrest every person who they find is violating the law, prosecutors must be selective about which cases to prosecute. The sheer volume of cases leads prosecutors to seek to plea bargain rather than go to trial. Court calendars are full and trials may be set months or years in advance. Rather than engage in a lengthy process or simply dismiss a case, prosecutors prefer to strike

SENTENCING BARGAINING
plea negotiations which agree on the type of sentence to be imposed in exchange for a guilty plea on a given charge.

CHARGE BARGAINING
plea negotiations that agree on the charges to be filed in exchange for a guilty plea by the defendant.

VERTICAL OVERCHARGING
charging a single offense at the most serious level possible to maximize the state's advantage in plea negotiations.

HORIZONTAL OVERCHARGING
multiple count indictments to maximize the state's advantage in plea negotiations.

a deal which gets them a speedy conviction and avoids the possibility of either a dismissal or acquittal. When the case is weak prosecutors are also more willing to come to the table with a reduced charge or sentence. This is particularly true in the types of serious cases such as sexual assault or child abuse that rely upon the word of the victim and are hard to win at trial. Rather than lose the case at trial, the prosecutor may reduce the charges to get some kind of conviction. The agreement enables them to at least get the person whom they may believe is guilty, on some charge, even if it is not the one they believe most accurately fits the offense.

Prosecutors are also operating under organizational and career pressures to demonstrate high conviction rates.[84] Successfully negotiated guilty pleas add to their tally of convictions that boost the efficiency of their office and their personal reputation as a prosecutor. Plea bargaining can be a very efficient means to a high conviction record. Bringing weak cases to trial and losing is a black mark for prosecutors and discouraged by judges and their superiors within the district attorney's office.

Defense attorneys also have reasons to negotiate rather than go to trial. The goal of the defense attorney is to act in the best interests of their client. The prevalence of plea bargaining means that the most valuable skill of the defense attorney is not necessarily about what happens in the courtroom but what happens at the negotiating table. An experienced defense attorney is trusted by the judge and prosecutors to make reasonable assessments about their client's options, to advise their client well, and to be a shrewd, realistic, and efficient bargainer at the table. If a defense attorney insists on going to trial despite what the judge and prosecutors want, they are likely to lose the cooperation of these colleagues in future cases. For most private defense attorneys, fees are earned by the ability to strike quiet deals behind the scenes, rather than the ability to win the hearts of juries through showy speeches at contentious trials. Through plea negotiations, many more cases can be efficiently handled, and for the defense attorney this also means that many more fees collected.

Judges too want to see cases negotiated, and increasingly judges are taking a major role in the process. Judges may even order the prosecutor and defense counsel to meet and see if they can work out an agreement prior to trial. In the interest of efficient administration the judge is trying to avoid the time and expense of a trial. The courtroom work group prefers a predictable and efficient outcome to the case.[85] What may happen when a case comes before a jury is relatively uncertain and unpredictable. The everyday workers in the courtroom have a shared interest in routinizing the administration of justice.

Given the pressure by all parties to resolve cases through plea bargaining, one might ask how critical is the defense attorney to the process. The Supreme Court says they are vital. In a pair of 2012 cases, the Court said that not only does a defendant have the right to assistance of counsel in bargaining, but that counsel must also be ethical and competent.[86]

The Interests of Justice

The question before the Supreme Court in the *Hayes'* case concerns the motives and ethical conduct of the prosecutor. Prosecutor Glenn Bagby diligently interviewed witnesses and victims in the *Hayes's* case. He reviewed the police report, decided a charge, and presented evidence of probable cause to the grand jury. He made a pretrial offer to the defendant and his attorney for a plea agreement with a sentence he felt was just. Once the defendant decided to go to trial, Bagby again sought and won a new indictment against Hayes and then successfully argued and won the case before a jury who found Hayes guilty as charged. There is little doubt that Bagby fulfilled his duties as an advocate for the state of Kentucky.

But the job of the prosecutor is broader and more ambiguous than simply representing one side in an adversarial battle. As public servant and chief law enforcement officer of the state, the prosecutor is also charged with the responsibility of upholding the **interests of justice** in the name of the whole community. As an elected official, the prosecutor is ethically sworn to administer justice for all. On taking office, prosecutors take an oath that requires them to "seek justice."

According to the American Bar Association General Standards, "A prosecutor should not institute, cause to be instituted, or permit the continued pendency of criminal charges in the absence of sufficient evidence to support a conviction."[87] A prosecutor is ethically barred from advocating for any fact or position that he or she knows is untrue and prosecutors should only pursue cases when they believe the evidence is sufficient "beyond reasonable doubt." The ABA Standard for Criminal Justice 3-1.1 describes the prosecutor's duty this way: "The duty of the prosecutor is to seek justice, not merely to convict." Prosecutorial discretion is ideally guided by a commitment to justice rather than a desire to win a conviction at all costs.

Inequality and Plea Bargaining

Gideon v. Wainwright was a triumph for the struggle for justice—a real accomplishment in bringing equal justice to the forefront. The theory of the American justice system rests upon the zealous advocacy of opposing sides played out according to the fair rules of evidence before a neutral judge and a jury of one's peers. The process of plea bargaining contradicts that mythology, replacing it with a process that bears little resemblance to that formal process. Much of this reality may be hidden from the public by forms of various kinds of impression management—suggestions that it is a necessary part of the process, that it conserves resources, and even that it furthers the ends of justice.

The process of plea bargaining, like all forms of exchange, depends upon the amount of resources each side brings to the table. In such a process, those who have more resources get more while those with less can expect to receive less. Not surprisingly, then, plea bargaining heightens the advantages that wealthy defendants with competent counsel have in the justice process, while at the same time compounds the disadvantages of those represented by public counsel.

Plea bargaining, particularly for wealthy white collar offenses, is routine and requires the tremendous skill on the part of defense and the prosecution. In these cases, the private defense attorney advises the client through a complex series of negotiations calibrated to undermine the prosecution's case and serve the best interests of their client. White collar criminals and others, such as those involved in organized crime or drug trafficking operations often have information and assets that can be exchanged in the plea negotiation process. In exchange for dropped or reduced charges, a defendant may agree to cooperate with the prosecution of a partner or accomplice.

Asset forfeiture laws also enhance the bargaining power of some criminal defendants and provide another incentive for the prosecution to engage in

INTERESTS OF JUSTICE
ethical duty of the prosecutor to administer justice for all rather than seek conviction.

ASSET FORFEITURE LAWS
statutes which authorize the confiscation of cash, vehicles, property, and other assets used in the commission of crime or purchased with criminal profits.

plea bargaining. Asset forfeiture laws allow the confiscation of cash and other property used in the commission of crime or purchased with criminal profits. The practice of seizing the assets of criminal suspects occurs principally in the prosecution of drug cases. Through a **contingent plea agreement**, prosecutors can stipulate that defendants forfeit or surrender specific financial assets before a deal can be struck. The possession of these assets is another bargaining tool for the defense attorney and another incentive to prosecutors to strike a favorable deal in exchange for the forfeiture of the property.

For a defendant like Paul Lewis Hayes, too poor to afford a private defense attorney, the negative impact of being socially disadvantaged begins early in the process. Poor defendants like Hayes can rarely even make bail. The prospect of going to jail for three to six months just to await trial is often enough to encourage a poor defendant to trade a guilty plea in exchange for a suspended sentence. The conviction goes on record as a guilty plea, but the immediate advantage of going home often is more attractive than the future costs of a conviction on their criminal record.

Defense attorneys also know that poor defendants who come to trial from county jail wearing a prison jumpsuit in handcuffs and leg irons are deeply disadvantaged when they appear in court compared to the wealthier client, who can afford bail and will appear neat and respectable in a suit and tie. Even though the poor defendant from the county jail has come to court to prove their innocence, the jury "sees" a convicted felon. Competent defense counsel will therefore try hard to persuade a poor defendant to accept a plea bargain rather than risk conviction at trial that inevitably carries a harsher punishment.

Is Plea Bargaining Just?

The central argument for the existence of plea bargaining has always been expediency: if every case were to go through the trial process, the justice system would grind to a halt. Many people, including Supreme Court justices, believe that there is no point in banning plea bargaining because it will simply re-emerge surreptitiously in the backrooms and hallways as it has done for over a century. It is better, therefore, that the practice be conducted out in the open and be monitored to ensure fairness. Fairly executed, the practice of plea bargaining will increase efficiency and therefore the overall effectiveness of the justice system. Plea bargaining should be encouraged since it enhances the capacity of the court to administer justice to a large volume of cases.

On the other side of the debate, plea bargaining has been criticized for seriously undermining the "justice" of our system by creating an administrative structure which only appears to go through the motions of due process.[88] Quite simply, plea negotiations undermine the rule of law by permitting authorities to cut special deals for certain defendants. Plea bargaining increases the advantages of wealthy criminal defendants and multiplies the disadvantages of the poor. It denies constitutional rights to thousands of defendants who are pressured to waive their rights and corrupts our system of justice beyond recognition. It also leads to excessive leniency for some and inconsistent or unfair outcomes for others. Recall the plea agreement made by Keith Riddick: in exchange for testifying against Garner, Riddick—the one who organized the crime—got off easy. In that case, truth was far less important to the defense counsel than getting an advantageous deal for their client.

CONTINGENT PLEA AGREEMENT
an agreement that the defendant forfeit specific assets prior to the start of plea negotiations.

William Stuntz believes that the replacement of the process of the simple jury trial with the routine of plea bargaining is a serious loss for democratic governance. District attorneys respond to political pressure from suburban voters who reside in the communities far removed from the urban streets where much of the crime that is handled by our courts takes place creating a disconnect between those who have influence over the making of the law and those who have to live with its consequences. Jury trials with juries that come from the local community would allow the system to better meet the needs of victims and the community than a process such as plea negotiations that takes place behind closed doors in hushed conversations among professionals.

Hayes's insistence that he was innocent angered the courtroom work group. In the business of processing hundreds of these cases the situation of Paul Lewis Hayes to the attorneys was a **dead bang case**, in which the evidence against him was solid. Although we do not have a record of what took place in the pretrial conference between the attorneys, it is likely that the public defender agreed with the prosecution and urged Hayes "to cop a plea." A competent defense attorney would have advised Hayes that the risk of going to trial was too high, given his prior record and the evidence against him in this case. Hayes's refusal to plead guilty was probably against the advice of counsel who, as a member of the courtroom work group, was more apt to agree with the prosecutor than the defendant about how justice should happen.

The challenge to the practice of plea bargaining often comes from citizens such as victims' groups or advocates for minorities and the poor, who do not share the organizational interests and pressures of the courtroom work group and who perceive this form of delivering justice as inherently unfair to defendants, victims, and the wider community. From the perspective of "insiders" or the courtroom work group, however, plea bargaining is a necessary accommodation to the overwhelming demands placed on the justice system. From the perspective of "outsiders," the citizens who come into the system as defendants, victims, witnesses, and bystanders, the informal process raises many doubts about the quality of the day-to-day justice we routinely practice within our courtrooms.

DEAD BANG CASE
a case in which the evidence to convict is strong.

KEY TERMS

courtroom work group (p. 316)   criminal justice professionals who conduct the daily business of the criminal courts.

adversarial system (p. 316)   a system in which the prosecution and the defense are each on opposing sides seeking to persuade the judge and the jury to accept their version of the truth.

judges (p. 318)   public officials who preside over courts of law.

venue (p. 318)   the place where a case is heard.

bench trial (p. 318)   a trial in which the judge hears the fact and issues a verdict on the guilt or innocence of the defendants.

jury trial (p. 319)   evidence is presented to a panel of citizens who are required to determine the defendant's guilt or innocence of the charges.

Missouri merit selection plan (p. 320)   a judicial selection plan devised in 1940 which relies upon an independent commission of lawyers to nominate candidates for final appointment by the governor of the state subject to voter approval.

prosecutors (p. 320)   a government attorney who instigates the prosecution of an accused and represents the interests of the state at trial.

selective prosecution (p. 321) the authority held by prosecutors to use discretion in choosing whom to prosecute.

nolle prosequi (p. 322) a formal entry in the record by which a prosecutor declares he or she will not prosecute the case.

defense attorney (p. 323) an attorney whose ethical duty is to zealously represents the interests of the defendant before the court.

elite private counsel (p. 324) a small percentage of criminal defense attorneys who have lucrative practices which specialize in representation of the rich and famous.

indigent defense (p. 326) state-funded systems for providing defense counsel for the poor.

assigned counsel systems (p. 326) appointment of private defense counsel by the trial judge compensated on a fixed fee basis by the court.

voluntary defender programs (p. 326) full-time attorneys who work for legal aid officers funded by federal or state governments who provide a full range of civil and criminal legal aid for poor citizens.

public defender offices (p. 326) full-time attorneys funded by state or federal governments who specialized in criminal defense for the poor.

right to counsel (p. 327) a defendant's constitutional right to the assistance of an attorney during prosecution.

plea bargaining (p. 330) the negotiation of an agreement among the prosecutor, judge, and the defense counsel as to the charge and/or sentence to be imposed if the defendant enters a guilty plea.

going rate (p. 331) local informal norms concerning the typical sentence for a given crime within a particular court or jurisdiction.

straight pleas (p. 331) a defendant's formal entry of a guilty plea without explicit negotiation by the courthouse work group.

sentencing bargaining (p. 331) plea negotiations which agree on the type of sentence to be imposed in exchange for a guilty plea on a given charge.

charge bargaining (p. 331) plea negotiations that agree on the charges to be filed in exchange for a guilty plea by the defendant.

vertical overcharging (p. 331) charging a single offense at the most serious level possible to maximize the state's advantage in plea negotiations.

horizontal overcharging (p. 331) multiple count indictments to maximize the state's advantage in plea negotiations.

Interests of justice (p. 333) ethical duty of the prosecutor to administer justice for all rather than seek conviction.

asset forfeiture laws (p. 334) statutes which authorize the confiscation of cash, vehicles, property, and other assets used in the commission of crime or purchased with criminal profits.

contingent plea agreement (p. 334) an agreement that the defendant forfeit specific assets prior to the start of plea negotiations.

dead bang case (p. 335) a case in which the evidence to convict is strong.

REVIEW AND STUDY QUESTIONS

1. What is the courtroom work group? Who are the "insiders" to the courtroom process and who are the "outsiders"?

2. Describe the role of the judge. What are the main methods of judicial selection?

3. Explain the formal role of the prosecutor. Identify key areas of discretion for the public prosecutor. What is the "interest of justice" and how does this define the unique role of the prosecutor?

4. Why does Justice Jackson refer to prosecutors as the "most powerful player" in the criminal justice process?

5. What are the reasons the prosecutor might use to explain dismissing a case?

6. Describe the issues that are unique in prosecuting white collar crimes. How do these issues impact prosecution?

7. Describe the role and responsibilities of the defense attorney. How does the role of the defense attorney differ from the role of the prosecutor? Why does Alan Dershowitz refer to the criminal defense attorney as the "last bastion of freedom"?

8. Identify the different segments of the criminal defense bar. What are the factors that may affect each segment's ability to best represent their client?

9. Explain the three main systems of indigent defense. What are the constraints that face the various indigent counsels?

10. What is plea bargaining? Define a straight plea, sentencing bargaining, and charge bargaining.

11. How is plea bargaining different from the formal trial? How does this process change the roles of the defense, prosecution, and judge?

12. Identify some of the organizational pressures on prosecutors to participate in plea bargaining. Identify organizational pressures on defense attorneys to participate in plea bargaining.

13. What are the advantages of engaging in negotiations—plea bargaining—over the formal adversarial process?

14. Identify the shortcomings in the use of plea negotiations instead of formal trials.

15. Stuntz says that plea bargaining represents a serious loss for democratic governance. Why would he make this claim? Do you agree? Explain.

CHECK IT OUT

Websites

Lawyer Jokes, http://www.iciclesoftware.com/Law Jokes/IcicleLawJokes.html. Law is the one profession everyone loves to rag on: even lawyers love to make fun of lawyers. Check out this web site for all the lawyer jokes you could ever want!

American Judicature Society, http://www.judicialselection.us/. The premier organization for judicial independence and ethics. Click on judicial selection methods to find out how judges are appointed and selected in your state. Read about codes of ethics for judges and other useful information.

Prosecutors Directory, http://www.eatoncounty.org/departments/prosecuting-attorney/144-departments/prosecuting-attorney/prosecutorinfocom/466-prosecuting-attorney-web-sites. Go to this web site and click on your state to get see web site for state and federal office in your county and state. Find out about local programs, victims assistance, and witness programs, community prosecutions, and much more in your local district attorney's office.

National District Attorney's Association, http://www.ndaa.org. Check out this site to find out useful information about salaries for district attorneys nationwide; see results from the latest DOJ survey on State Prosecutors. Click on the link to National Center for Community Prosecution to find out about innovative programs across the country.

National Legal Aid & Defender Association http://www.nlada.org. Great site to explore both the criminal and the civil sides of public law. Articles, events, and a directory.

The Plea http://www.pbs.org/wgbh/pages/frontline/shows/plea/. This *Frontline* presentation includes four stories along with interviews, discussion questions, and links to additional readings.

Videos

Plea Bargains: Dealing for Justice—28 minutes. This film deals with the vast majority of criminal cases and takes a hard "behind the scenes" look at who gets out of jail, who doesn't, and who decides what kind of deal to make. Emmy Award Nominee. Currently available at: https://mvcc-video.mvcc.edu/app/plugin/plugin.aspx?insideIFrame=true&style SheetUrl=http%3A%2F%2Fmvcc-video.mvcc.edu%2Fapp%2Fplugin%2Fcss%2Fensemble Plugin.css&q=www.mvcc.edu&destinationID=no0t7hZkV0eZoP1_7oMeIw&contentID=Hsh_PWVzW0KVzl7xzA4aPA&pageIndex=83&page Size=10

And Justice for Some—57 minutes. On the anniversary of *Gideon v. Wainwright* Bill Moyers sits down with legal scholar Bryan Stevenson to look at the legal systems failures regarding "justice for all." http://billmoyers.com/episode/and-justice-for-some-2/

Movies

...And Justice for All (1979). Al Pacino stars in this courtroom movie, in which an idealistic lawyer tries to win cases for clients but realizes that they are trapped in a hypocritical and corrupt legal system.

The Verdict (1982). A powerful courtroom drama in which an alcoholic lawyer (Paul Newman) takes on the legal establishment.

NOTES

[1] *Bordenkircher v. Hayes* 434 U.S. 357, 363 (1978).

[2] *Commonwealth of Kentucky v. Paul Lewis Hayes* 73-C-29, (April 19, 1973).

[3] *Commonwealth of Kentucky v. Paul Lewis Hayes*, 103.

[4] German Gutierrez, M.D. Court-ordered Psychiatric Evaluation, Paul Lewis Hayes, Eastern State Hospital (February 6, 1973).

[5] Indictment No. 73-C-26, Indictment for uttering a Forged Instrument KRS 434.130.

[6] Indictment No. 73-C-26.

[7] KRS 431.190–434 130.

[8] German Gutierrez, M.D. Psychiatric Evaluation, Paul Lewis Hayes, Eastern State Hospital, (February 6, 1973).

[9] Indictment No. 73-C-29, Count 1: Indictment for uttering a Forged Instrument KRS 434.130; Count 2: Indictment for Habitual Criminal KRS 431.190 (January 29, 1973).

[10] *Commonwealth of Kentucky v. Paul Lewis Hayes* 73-C-29 (April 19, 1973), 156.

[11] *Commonwealth of Kentucky v. Paul Lewis Hayes,* Instructions to the Jury, James J. Park Jr., Presiding Judge, Fayette Circuit Court.

[12] *Paul Lewis Hayes v. Henry Cowan,* U.S. District Court, Eastern District of Kentucky, No. 75–61 (October 9, 1975).

[13] Alschuler, "Plea Bargaining and Its History," *Columbia Law Review* 79 (1978).

[14] Howard Abidinsky, *Law and Justice: An Introduction to the American Legal System* (Chicago: Nelson Hall, 1995), 349.

[15] *Brady v. United States* 397 U.S. 742.

[16] Rule 11 (c) *Federal Rules of Criminal Procedure* requires judges to determine that defendants understand the nature of the charges, voluntarily agrees to waive his or her right to a jury trial, and to accept the terms of the plea negotiation.

[17] *Hayes v. Cowan* 547 F2d 42 1976.

[18] *Hayes v. Cowan*, n.2.

[19] *Hayes v. Cowan*.

[20] *Bordenkircher v. Hayes* 434 U.S. 357, 1977.

[21] 395 U.S. 711,725, 1969.

[22] 417 U.S. 21,25 1974.

[23] C. Peter Erlinder and David C. Thomas, "Criminal Law: Prohibiting Prosecutorial Vindictiveness While Protecting Prosecutorial Discretion," *Journal of Criminal Law and Criminology* 76 (1985), 341.

[24] Justice Stewart, Majority, *Bordenkircher v. Hayes* 434 U.S. 357, 1977.

[25] Peter F. Nardulli, *The Courtroom Elite* (Cambridge MA: Ballinger Publishing Company, 1978).

[26] Arthur Rossett and Donald R. Cressay, *Justice by Consent: Plea Bargains in the American Courts* (Philadelphia: J. Lippincott, 1976); Roy B. Fleming, Peter F. Nardulli and James Eisenstein, *The Craft of Justice* (Philadelphia: University of Pennsylvania Press, 1992).

[27] Donald Newman, *Conviction: The Determination of Guilt or Innocence Without Trial* (Boston, MA: Little Brown, 1966).

[28] Abraham S. Blumberg, "The Practice of Law as a Confidence Game: Organizational Cooptation of a Profession," *Law and Society Review* 1 (1967), 15–39.

[29] Howard Abidinsky, *Law and Justice: An Introduction to the American Legal System* (Chicago: Nelson Hall, 1995), 89–104.

[30] Lawrence M. Friedman, *A History of American Law* (New York: Simon and Schuster, 1973).

[31] Jocelyn M. Pollock and Barbara Ramirez, "Women in the Legal Profession," in *Women, Law and Social Control*, eds. Alida V. Merlo and Joycelyn M. Pollock (Boston, MA: Allyn and Bacon, 1995), 83.

[32] 83 U.S. 130,140 1873.

[33] Jocelyn M. Pollock and Barbara Ramirez, "Women in the Legal Profession," in *Women, Law and Social Control*, eds. Alida V. Merlo and Joycelyn M. Pollock (Boston, MA: Allyn and Bacon, 1995), 80.

[34] American Bar Association, "Lawyer Demographics, Year 2015," https://www.americanbar.org/content/dam/aba/administrative/market_research/lawyer-demographics-tables-2015.authcheckdam.pdf; retrieved January 4, 2017.

[35] Commission on Women in the Profession, American Bar Association, "A Current Glance at Women in the Law 2014" (January 2014), http://www.americanbar.org/content/dam/aba/marketing/women/current_glance_statistics_july2014.authcheckdam.pdf; retrieved January 4, 2017.

[36] Jocelyn M. Pollock and Barbara Ramirez, "Women in the Legal Profession," in *Women, Law and Social Control*, eds. Alida V. Merlo and Joycelyn M. Pollock (Boston, MA: Allyn and Bacon, 1995), 91.

[37] Commission on Women in the Profession, American Bar Association "A Current Glance at Women in the Law 2014" (January 2014), http://www.americanbar.org/content/dam/aba/marketing/women/current_glance_

statistics_july2014.authcheckdam.pdf; retrieved January 4, 2017.

38 American Bar Association, "Lawyer Demographics, Year 2015," https://www.americanbar.org/content/dam/aba/administrative/market_research/lawyer-demographics-tables-2015.authcheckdam.pdf; retrieved January 4, 2017.

39 Elizabeth Chambliss, "The Demographics of the Profession," *IILP Review 2011: The State of Diversity and Inclusion in the Legal Profession.* http://www.theiilp.com/resources/Documents/IILP2011_Review_final.pdf, accessed August 18, 2012.

40 Stephen R. Bing and S. Stephen Rosenfeld, "The Quality of Justice in the Lower Criminal Courts in Metropolitan Boston," in *Rough Justice: Perspectives on Lower Criminal Courts*, ed. John Robertson (Boston: Little Brown and Company, 1974), 259–285.

41 John A. Jenkins, "The Lobster Shift: One Nights in the Nation's Busiest Court," *American Bar Association Journal* 72, 56 (1986).

42 Maureen Mileski, "Courtroom Encounters: An Observation of a Lower Criminal Court," *Law And Society Review* 5 (1971), 473–533.

43 Henry R. Glick, *Courts, Politics and Justice* (New York: McGraw-Hill, 1993), 112–155.

44 AJS, "Merit Selection: The Best Way to Choose the Best Judges," http://www.judicialselection.us/uploads/documents/ms_descrip_1185462202120.pdf, accessed August 18, 2012.

45 Carol J. DeFrancis and Greg W. Steadman, "Prosecutors in State Courts, 1996" *BJS Bulletin* (Washington, DC: National Institute of Justice, 1998).

46 Kenneth Culp Davis, *Discretionary Justice* (Baton Rouge: Louisiana State University Press, 1969), 190.

47 William. F. McDonald, "The Prosecutor's Domain," in *The Prosecutor*, ed. W.F. McDonald (Beverly Hills, CA: Sage Publication, 1979), 15–59.

48 Howard Abidinsky, *Law and Justice: An Introduction to the American Legal System* (Chicago, IL: Nelson Hall, 1995), 209.

49 Kathleen B. Brosi, *A Cross-City Comparison of Felony Case Processing* (Washington, DC: U.S. Government Printing Office, 1979).

50 Susan Estrich, *Real Rape* (Cambridge, MA: Harvard University Press, 1987).

51 Alan Dershowitz, *The Best Defense* (New York: Random House, 1982).

52 384 U.S. 436, 1966.

53 Henry R. Glick, *Courts, Politics and Justice* (New York: McGraw-Hill, 1993), 212.

54 American Bar Foundation, *Lawyer Statistic Report: The U.S. Legal Profession in the 1990s* (Chicago: American Bar Association, 1994).

55 Paul B. Wice, *Criminal Lawyers: An Endangered Species* (Beverly Hills, CA: Sage, 1978).

56 Wice, *Criminal Lawyers*, 111.

57 Bureau of Justice Statistics. "Indigent Defense" *Bureau of Justice Statistics: Selected Findings* (Washington, DC: National Institute of Justice, 1996), 1–4.

58 Alan Feuer, *The Defense Can't Afford to Rest*, New York Times (May 20, 2011), accessed September 2, 2012.

59 Vanessa O'Connell, "Big Law's $1000-Plus an Hour Club," *The Wall Street Journal* (February 23, 2011), accessed September 2, 2012.

60 Lisa McIntyre, *The Public Defender: The Practice of Law in the Shadows of Repute* (Chicago: University of Chicago Press, 1987).

61 Lynn Langton and Donald J. Farole Jr., Census of Public Defender Offices, 2007, revised 6/7/2010, Bureau of Justice Statistics, US. Department of Justice, Office of Justice Programs. (NCJ 228538, November 2009).

62 Jonathan Casper, *Criminal Courts: The Defendants Perspective* (Washington, DC: U.S. Government Printing Office, 1978).

63 Casper, *Criminal Courts*.

64 Casper, *Criminal Courts*.

65 304 U.S. 458 1938.

66 287 U.S. 45 1932.

67 372 U.S. 335 1963.

68 407 U.S. 25 1972.

69 Bureau of Justice Statistics. "Indigent Defense" *Bureau of Justice Statistics: Selected Findings* (Washington, DC: National Institute of Justice, 1996), 1–4.

70 Steven K. Smith and Carol J. Defrancis, *Indigent Defense* (Washington, DC: U.S. Department of Justice, 1996).

71 Matthew J. Hickman and Brian A. Reaves, *Sheriffs' Offices 2003*, Bureau of Justice Statistics (Washington, DC: Government Printing Office, May 2006).

72 Angela Jordan Davis, "Remarks at Conference on 30th Anniversary of the U.S. Supreme Court's Decision in Gideon v. Wainright: Gideon and the Public Service Role of Lawyers in Advancing Equal Justice," *American University Law Review* 43 (1993).

73 Anthony Lewis, "Keynote Address, Conference on 30th Anniversary of the U.S. Supreme Court's Decision in Gideon v. Wainright: Gideon and the Public Service Role of Lawyers in Advancing Equal Justice," *American University Law Review* 43 (1993).

74 Jodi M. Brown and Patrick A. Langan, *State Court Sentencing of Convicted Felons, 1994* (Washington, DC: U.S. Department of Justice, 1998).

[75] Bureau of Justice Statistics, *The Prosecution of Felony Arrests* (Washington, DC: U.S. Department of Justice, 1990).

[76] Joseph Sanborn, "A Historical Sketch of Plea Bargaining," *Justice Quarterly* 3 (1986), 111–138; Lawrence Friedman, "Plea Bargaining in Historical Perspective," *Law and Society Review* 7 (1979), 247–59.

[77] National Advisory Commission on Criminal Justice Standards and Goals, *Courts, Standard 3.1* (Washington, DC: U.S. Government Printing Office, 1973), 46.

[78] Michael Rubinstein, Stevens H. Clarke and Teresa J. White, *Alaska Bans Plea Bargaining* (Washington, DC: U.S. Government Printing Office, 1980).

[79] *Santobello v. New York* , 92 S.Ct. 495, 273n, 354 (1971).

[80] Milton Heumann, "Thinking About Plea Bargaining," in *The Study of the Criminal Courts*, ed. Peter F. Nardulli (Cambridge, MA: Ballinger Publishing Company, 1979), 208–210.

[81] Thomas Uhlman and N. Darlene Walker, "He Takes Some of My Time and I Take Some of His," *Law and Society Review* 14 (1980), 323–341.

[82] Matthew R. Durose. "State Court Sentencing of Convicted Felons, 2004-Statistical Tables," *Bureau of Justice Statistics Bulletin NCJ 217995* (Washington, DC: Department of Justice, July 1, 2007).

[83] Peter F. Nardulli, James Eisenstein and Roy B. Flemming, *The Tenor of Justice: Criminal Courts and the Guilty Plea* (Urbana, IL: University of Illinois Press, 1988); Herbert S. Miller et al., *Plea Bargaining in the United States* (Washington, DC: National Institute of Law Enforcement and Criminal Justice, 1978).

[84] Henry N. Pontell, *A Capacity to Punish* (Bloomington, IN: Indiana University Press, 1984).

[85] Malcolm Feeley, *The Process is the Punishment: Handling Cases in a Lower Court* (New York: Russell Sage Foundation, 1979).

[86] *Lafler v. Cooper,* 566 U. S. (2012); *Missouri v. Frey,* 566 U. S. (2012).

[87] "American Bar Association General Standards" (Chicago: American Bar Association, 1999).

[88] George P. Fletcher, *With Justice for Some: Victims' Rights in Criminal Trials* (Reading, MA: Addison-Wesley, 1995).

FOCUS QUESTIONS

- **HOW** do voters think about contending alternatives when they are voting?
- **HOW** does the number of alternatives affect voting?
- **WHAT** considerations contend for attention in the minds of voters? How might they cooperate to support a particular choice?
- **HOW** does voters' identification with a political party affect voting?
- **HOW** do parties and candidates maneuver to gain votes?
- **WHAT** does it mean for voter choice to be meaningful?

In this chapter, the case tells the story of Kemba Smith, a college student convicted and incarcerated for transporting drugs. Many people challenged the fairness of her sentence. The chapter explores the justifications for criminal sanctions, and the often discriminatory manner that punishment is delivered in our society. We examine the War on Drugs and its effect on sentencing as well as the evolving use of the death penalty in the United States.

LEARNING OBJECTIVES

After reading this chapter you should be able to:

- Identify and explain the five goals of sentencing.
- Describe three models of sentencing and identify key decision-makers in each model of sentencing.
- Understand sentencing reforms which have limited judicial discretion in sentencing.
- Explain the impact of key Supreme Court decisions on the constitutionality of capital punishment.
- Identify changes in the rate of incarceration from 1970 to 2012 and know the contrast between the rates of incarceration for white and nonwhites.
- Discuss changes in drug sentencing policies within the past twenty years, including the crack cocaine disparity in federal law and the impact of drug sentencing on the minority community.

Case #13: The Crime of Punishment: The Story of Kemba Smith

Gus and Odessa Smith, parents of Kemba Smith, holding her young son, speak at a rally to oppose lengthy mandatory sentencing for drug offenses. (Associated Press)

In 1994 Kemba Smith, a twenty-four-year-old woman, seven months pregnant, pled guilty in federal court to charges of conspiracy to distribute cocaine, lying to federal authorities, and conspiracy to launder drug money.[1] For over three years Kemba was the girlfriend of Peter Michael Hall, an alleged drug dealer under federal indictment for running a cocaine distribution ring. During this time Kemba carried and concealed illegal weapons for Peter; rode in a van carrying drugs from New York to North Carolina; carried drug money for him strapped to her body; purchased a vehicle and rented apartments for him in her name; and denied any knowledge of Peter's whereabouts on at least two occasions, when questioned by federal agents. Kemba Smith admitted guilt and responsibility for these actions and was held in jail without bail until sentencing.[2]

At the sentencing hearing, U.S. district judge Richard B. Kellam announced the sentence to a packed courtroom: 294 months on the drug conspiracy charge, 60 months for lying to authorities, and 60 months on the money laundering charge—the latter two sentences to run concurrently with the first. A stunned hush filled the courtroom as the reality sunk in that twenty-four-year-old Kemba Smith had been sentenced to twenty-four years in prison: one year for each year of her life with no chance for parole.[3] Four months earlier, Kemba had given birth to a son who was immediately taken from her. She was allowed to breast-feed him only once and see him for only two days after he was born.

From Debutante to Mule

Kemba Smith grew up the cherished only child of a professional middle-class couple in a comfortable suburb in Richmond, Virginia.[4] Born in 1971, she spent her childhood attending Brownie and Girl Scout meetings, gymnastic, piano, and ballet lessons. Her dad, an accountant, and her mom, a business education teacher, were college sweethearts, who gave their only daughter all they felt she needed to follow in their footsteps. In high school, she played flute in the marching band while her father volunteered as the club treasurer to fund out of town trips. She was active in clubs such as Students Against Drunk Driving and belonged to the Future Homemakers of America just as her mother had during her high school years. At age sixteen, she came out as a debutante dressed in white organza and pearls at the Alpha Kappa Alpha sorority ball.

By any standards, Kemba had a loving but sheltered upbringing. Because her parents were raised by strict parents, they imposed similar rules for Kemba. She had to obey a curfew, dress conservatively, and be responsible for her schoolwork. Although Kemba admits she sometimes snuck out without her parents' knowledge, she did not really date until her senior year in high school. By the time Kemba was entering college, she had little exposure to the world beyond her parents and childhood friends.

The decision to attend Hampton College seventy-three miles from home was the first independent decision Kemba ever made. Her parents were against the idea of her being so far away and preferred her to attend a local college in Virginia. But Kemba wanted to go to a historically black college. In her childhood, Kemba had been the minority in her middle-class community with largely white friends. Now she decided she wanted the "black experience" and chose Hampton despite her parents, desire to keep her close to home. In the fall of 1989, her mother and father helped her move into the dormitory, setting up a microwave and television to make the room feel just like home.

Like many young people living away from home for the first time in her life, Kemba had difficulty adjusting to the new social scene at Hampton.[5] In her world at home, she had always felt attractive and popular; here, she was a little fish lost in a big sea. She felt awkward and unappealing and worried about being hip. She wanted a boyfriend badly so she could feel like she fit in and belonged.

The turmoil in her social life was quickly reflected in her academic performance. The B average Kemba had maintained before college plummeted and by the end of her first semester she had failed two of her five classes. She started smoking the marijuana that seemed to always be around the dorms. Alarmed by her failing grades, her parents asked Kemba to see a counselor, but Kemba believed her parents were overreacting. She refused to see the psychologist beyond a few sessions and continued to cultivate her new image as a party girl on campus.

Girls like Kemba are easy targets for men like Peter Michael Hall. She met him at a party. Eight years older with a lilting Jamaican accent, he was not a student but seemed to know all the college kids. There was much about him to impress the young Kemba: he had money and spent it lavishly on expensive cars, clothes, restaurants, and apartments filled with high-tech equipment and luxurious furniture. He had style, charm, and personality, holding the spotlight at any gathering usually surrounded by the prettiest and most popular girls. Kemba was flattered when, one spring night in her sophomore year in college, Peter called her and asked her to meet him. That night he took her, blindfolded, to his apartment for an overnight stay and thus began their stormy three-year relationship.

Battered Woman: Standing by her Man

It was naive of Kemba to believe she was Peter's "main girl" but she did. Shortly after their affair began Peter demonstrated his "love" for her when he saw her hold hands briefly with another man. In a jealous rage, he beat her, choked her, and hit her so badly she wore

shades the next day to hide her swollen eyes. He did this, he claimed, because she had betrayed him and he needed to teach her a lesson. In the aftermath of the violence, he cried and apologized, promised never to hurt her again. He told her he loved her and needed her. Kemba shouldn't have believed him, but she did. He asked for forgiveness and she gave it.[6]

By summer she had moved in with Peter, spending almost all her time with him and losing contact with most of her former friends at Hampton. Their life together steadily went downhill over the next two years, as gradually Kemba became aware of the extent of Peter's illegal drug activities. Once he was arrested and jailed for four months on state drug and fake ID charges. Peter's brother called Kemba and gave her money to give to a lawyer to get Peter out of jail. She did as she was told not realizing that the money was from the cocaine business or that Peter's brother was also wanted by the federal authorities as his co-conspirator in the drug business. She believed Peter when he said this was mainly about immigration problems and she believed him when he said he was going to change his lifestyle.

Kemba's parents met Peter shortly after he was released from jail on bail. They lied to her parents and told them the lockup had been for reasons of immigration, a mistake that had finally been cleared up. He put on a good performance for Gus and Odessa Smith and they were pleased their daughter was dating such a well-mannered young man. But that good impression was fleeting. Shortly afterward, federal agents in search of Peter Hall contacted the Smith home looking for Kemba. Gus called the Drug Enforcement Administration (DEA) to find out why they wanted to talk with his daughter.

As agents circled around Kemba and her parents asking questions about Peter and all those who worked for him, Peter began to beat Kemba again, this time with a belt and a brush accusing her of ratting on him and lying to him. Like so many battered women, Kemba protested that she was loyal, but she cowered and suffered his humiliations and tortures. And like so many other battered women, Kemba comforted him when he wept afterward, believed his promises, excuses, and apologies, and forgave him yet again. Whatever he asked her to do, she did. She felt trapped. She was both afraid of losing him and afraid of him.

Their life together went from bad to worse as Peter began to run from the federal authorities. Again Peter was caught and arrested, this time in New York for carrying ten ounces of crack in a taxicab. This time, a different friend contacted Kemba and asked her to help him get out of jail and again she dutifully did as she was asked, traveling to New York to deliver an envelope to a man in Brooklyn rescuing her man yet again.

Peter was released from jail for a large sum of cash. Again he skipped town before trial returning to Virginia with Kemba, who he accused of not caring about him at all. Kemba almost left him this time when one of the beatings caused her to miscarry a pregnancy. She called her father to wire her a bus ticket so she could come home but Peter followed her onto the Greyhound bus begging forgiveness and weeping with despair. She called her father and told him she was staying with Peter.

A few months later, one of the many associates hanging around Peter was found dead from bullet wounds to the neck and the head. Peter had gone to Atlanta and phoned Kemba to join him there. When she arrived, he told her he had killed the street dealer whom he said was ratting on him to the federal government. Kemba believed that if he would kill Derrick for betraying him, there was little doubt what he would do to her if she did the same. Finally, in the summer, after an investigation that had begun the year Kemba had finished high school, federal agents filed a sixteen-count indictment against Peter Michael Hall and his brother. Added to the charge of running a drug ring that had moved as much as four million dollars' worth of cocaine and crack cocaine between New York and Virginia was a murder warrant for the death of Derrick Taylor. Federal agents believed that Peter ran the operations in Virginia and that his modus operandi was to recruit college students, males to sell drugs and young women like Kemba to act as "mules" for the transport of drugs, money, and weapons.

Kemba may have believed that she was Peter's "main girl" but he had several such girlfriends in different cities performing a variety of services out of a sad mixture of love, fear, and devotion. Not all of them were as loyal or as fearful as Kemba.[7] Several of them had provided information that led to the jailing of members of the drug ring. In exchange for this information, most were released from jail without charges, including one girlfriend originally charged with being an accomplice in the murder of Derrick Taylor, who was subsequently placed in the federal witness protection program.[8]

When Kemba returned home from school that summer she was apprehended by federal agents in the middle of the night. Held on $50,000 bail, Kemba was asked to give information about Peter's whereabouts and his operation. Kemba's lawyer urged her to cooperate warning her that they could put her away for a long time if she refused. Kemba talked but it was all lies. She remembered the warnings Peter had given her about telling things to the police; she remembered his rage when he suspected he was betrayed, and she remembered what happened to Derrick Taylor. Claiming she did not know where Peter was, Kemba was released and sent home.

After she was released, her parents begged her to stay away from Peter but Kemba felt her place was with her man. She joined him in hiding in Atlanta but he feared that the authorities would find him through her and he sent her home. For a few months, Kemba lived at home and began to return to the life she had always known. She enrolled in a local college, got a job, and began to lead the kind of life she had known before Peter. But Peter still needed her, especially now that he no longer had access to cash from his drug operation. She sent him money by cleaning out a joint account she held with her mother. Rather than face her mother and explain the missing money, Kemba left home suddenly one day to join Peter on the run again.

The Truth: Too Little Too Late

This time Kemba and Peter were truly down and out. Kemba found herself pregnant again and penniless. They reached the West Coast living on the streets, sleeping in bus stations, and pawning whatever possessions they still had from the high-living days. Kemba was afraid to go back home fearful her parents would be too angry to take her back. At last Kemba returned home worried for her unborn child and unable to live on the streets anymore. She was welcomed with open arms by her desperately worried parents and on September 1, 1993, with her father beside her, she turned herself in to federal authorities.

Still Kemba would not give Peter up. Was it loyalty or fear that kept her revealing his location? Kemba says it was both. She still loved him but she was also scared— for what he might do to her, to her parents, or her child if she betrayed him to the police. While she was still in jail and trying to decide if she should turn her lover in, Seattle police found Peter Michael Hall dead of a gunshot wound to the head. No one knows who killed Peter. His death remains an open case for the Seattle police. Now Kemba had no reason not to be truthful with the federal authorities and she immediately told everything she knew. Upon advice of her lawyers she pled guilty to all the federal charges against her.

The Conspiracy

Although the government acknowledged that Kemba had never touched, used, or sold cocaine nor did she ever personally benefit from the proceeds of the drug ring, they claimed that she knowingly and willingly aided and abetted the activities of the organization. For this she deserved the full punishment of the mandatory drug sentence. Although Kemba confessed to transporting approximately $15,000 between New York and Charlotte, North Carolina, four times, she was ultimately sentenced for trafficking more than five hundred and sixty pounds of cocaine worth four million dollars. Kemba was held responsible for the entire amount of drugs distributed by the operation from 1989 to 1993.[9]

Kemba's lawyers argued for the judge to show mercy in sentencing Kemba for her crimes. While Kemba admitted all the conduct that brought her here, her attorneys argued she was acting under the influence of coercion and duress. They believed that these psychological pressures merited a reduction in the mandatory sentence under the guidelines that set the penalties for people involved in the sale and distribution of illegal, controlled substances. Under certain circumstances, the sentencing guidelines permit a judge to reduce the length of the mandatory sentence.

The government argued that Kemba's actions allowed drugs to plague the streets and endanger the lives of innocent citizens. Because of the evils of the drug trade on society, Kemba Smith needed to be punished without mercy. Fernando Groene, assistant U.S. attorney handling the drug ring cases, declared in court, "Judge, the real tragedy of this case is that this is a drug case and that the distribution of drugs by the people who the defendant assisted, those lives are also ruined. She hasn't expressed remorse for the lives that those drugs have destroyed. . . . She turned her back on her parents, on the laws, on society, on the people who were being threatened . . . people who were being killed . . . and the only possible explanation is she did it willingly for the love of Mr. Hall, not because she was afraid of him."[10]

Despite massive show of public support for Kemba and her family, which included requests for leniency from the former mayor and the former director of corrections for the state of Virginia, and despite testimony at the trial about her emotional state as a battered woman, the federal judge stated, "I think there isn't a soul alive that can understand how any woman or girl would permit some man to beat on her and then continue to live with him and to love him. . . .[11] I am not willing to say that her actions and conduct were controlled by her love for Peter Hall or her fear of Peter Hall. It went on too long a period of time for that to have existed."[12]

In the judge's opinion, Kemba Smith knew what she was doing when she lied. While he recognized that Kemba was not a danger to society nor was she likely to ever pursue these activities again, the purpose of locking Kemba up for almost twenty-five years was to send a message to others not to get mixed up with the other Peter Halls out there. According to Judge Kellam, "Putting the defendant in incarceration will certainly not benefit her tremendously. I think that the purpose of it is, and the only purpose of it, is a deterrent to others, so that everyone knows that if they violate the law, they must pay the penalty."[13] According to the sentence, Kemba Smith would be released from federal prison at the age of forty-eight when her baby son would be twenty-four years old.

Fighting for an Appeal

Gus and Odessa spent their entire savings and took out a second mortgage on their home to pay for legal expenses to challenge Kemba's severe sentence. By the time Kemba was sentenced they had spent more than $25,000 in legal fees. After twenty-two years with a company, Gus lost his job as the chief financial officer because of the public notoriety about his daughter. Within two years, the couple filed for federal bankruptcy protection to avoid being thrown out onto the street with their young grandson.[14] Gus and Odessa receive public assistance of $131 per month to support him.[15]

When the article about Kemba was featured in a popular news magazine, the response was overwhelming. The magazine was flooded with letters about Kemba. A high school in Dayton, Ohio, was motivated to begin a "Free Kemba" campaign, first writing to Kemba Smith and then to black legislators, Oprah Winfrey, the NAACP, and President Clinton to advocate for a reduction in her sentence. The youth strongly identified with Kemba realizing that they too could make a similar mistake. The students formed a club that raised money to support a protest on the steps of the Capitol Hill with signs "Let the punishment fit the crime" and "24.5 Years, Too Harsh."

The students also joined forces with groups mobilized to oppose harsh mandatory sentencing and its impact on young blacks in America. Families Against Mandatory Minimums (FAMM) was formed in 1988 by Julie Stewart, sister of a man convicted for five years in federal prison for growing marijuana plants. Says Julie, "I had enormous outrage at the system. Judges who had been on the bench 25 years had been told they were not able to make a judgment because Congress had already issued a sentence."[16] Particularly vulnerable are young people between the ages of eighteen and twenty-five, who constitute over half of those convicted of federal drug trafficking. Over the past twenty-five years FAMM has been at the forefront of the sentencing reform movement. Membership in FAMM now exceeds 70,000 family members and others who have been affected by harsh prison sentences, and FAMM claims that over 312,000 people have benefited from the reforms they advocate.

In April 1997, the NAACP legal defense asked the U.S. court to vacate, set aside, or correct Kemba's sentence claiming that the judge had never correctly received expert testimony about her status as a battered woman. Judge Kellam declared in his opinion that he simply did not believe that Kemba was afraid of Peter Hall. Yet traditional notions about self-defense don't always apply to the threatening relationship between a woman and her batterer. Battered women often believe their batterer will hunt them down wherever they hide and are powerful enough to hurt them despite restraining orders and other forms of protection from the courts. Sadly, these women are often correct in these perceptions.

The NAACP also maintained that there had been legal errors, including a failure by the attorneys for Kemba to adequately inform her of the implications of entering a guilty plea to the drug conspiracy. But a federal district court judge rejected the petition on a technicality even while he stated that in his own personal opinion that he had a hard time finding this particular application of the law fair.[17] Judge Robert Doumar wrote, "The court is indeed sympathetic to the plight of petitioner Smith. She is the recipient of a truly heavy sentence—an occurrence that has become standard practice under the Sentencing Guidelines. . . . In the opinion of the undersigned, the Guidelines represent a prime example of how Congress is sometimes unaware of the unintended consequences of its legislation."[18]

Yet Judge Doumar refused to grant her a new hearing or reduce her sentence. A federal appeals court upheld the district court ruling ending legal avenues within the courts.[19]

One Last Hope

Kemba's last and final hope was a presidential pardon from Bill Clinton. The NAACP submitted the petition and a coalition of more than 650 clergy appealed to him to commute the sentence of Kemba, along with several others serving lengthy sentences for minor roles in the drug trade. Kemba's supporters included Congresswoman Maxine Waters, who advocated on her behalf by pointing out that before mandatory minimums for crack cocaine went into effect the racial disparity between white and black drug offenders in federal prisons was about 11 percent. After Congress passed stiffer mandatory sentences specifically for crack cocaine, the number of African Americans serving hard time in federal prison soared 49 percent higher than whites.[20]

Waters and others kept steady pressure on President Clinton to grant Kemba clemency as one of his last presidential acts. In his last hours in office, Clinton added Kemba to the two hundred and thirty-eight federal prisoners granted a presidential pardon. After six and half years in federal prison, Kemba was reunited with her parents and six-year-old son.

Gus and Odessa Smith have been at the heart of this activism. Their anger and despair had been channeled into the hope that one day the sentence would be overturned and the draconian laws would be repealed. Upon her release, Kemba pledged to publicly apologize for what she has put her parents through and to make them proud of her once more.[21] Married now, with children, she has written a book and speaks publicly about domestic abuse, and her own experiences with the law. In 2014 she was appointed as a member of the Virginia Criminal Sentencing Commission. She continues to advocate for sentencing and criminal justice reform and has testified before Congress and spoken at the White House.

THINKING CRITICALLY ABOUT THIS CASE

1. Does this punishment fit the crime? Why or why not? Outline the position of the prosecutor and

the position of the defense attorney on a just sentence. Which do you agree with and why?

2. If you were given the power to create an alternate sentence, what sentence do you believe would be appropriate and why?

3. Should a judge take into consideration elements of Kemba's past, such as her upbringing, education, the support of her parents, and the community? Why or why not? Should the judge consider her status as new mother? Why or why not?

4. Should the psychological state of Kemba during her years with Peter be a factor in the sentencing process? Why or why not?

5. If President Clinton had not pardoned Kemba as his last act in office, she would still be in federal prison in Danbury Connecticut. Write an imaginary letter from Kemba to her son at age sixteen explaining the reasons for her incarceration hoping to guide him in his own future behavior.

6. If you were parents of a college-age student involved with a drug dealing crowd, would you counsel your child to turn him or herself in to the authorities as Gus and Odessa did? Why or why not?

7. Is drug trafficking a "victimless crime" in your opinion? Why or why not? Who are the victims of the drug trade and who are the offenders?

REFERENCES

Case adapted from:

Libby Copeland, "Kemba Smith's Hard Time," *The Washington Post,* February 13, 2000.

Rhonda Chriss Lokeman, "When Smart Women Make Foolish Choices," *Kansas City Star,* April 22, 2001.

Anthony Lewis, "Abroad at Home: A Christmas Carol," *The New York Times,* December 23, 2000.

Mark Morris, "Pardoned Woman Backs Drug Law Change," *the Kansas City Star,* April 20, 2001.

E.R. Shipp, "Gone Too For Too Long," *Daily News,* January 28, 2001.

Reginald Stuart, "Kemba's Nightmare," *Emerge* 7(7) May, 1996 pp. 28–48.

Reginald Stuart, "Kemba's Nightmare II: Justice Denied," *Emerge* 9(7), May, 1998.

If the trial is the symbolic center of the criminal justice process where "justice" is seen and heard, the most dramatic moment in the process comes with the pronouncement of the sentence. The question of how to respond to the offender after they have been convicted is the most controversial and troubling decision point for the justice system. Consider the sentence given to Kemba Smith: What purpose would her twenty-four years in prison serve for society? Safer streets? Deterring crime? Retribution? Will it prevent others from committing the same crime? Or is it simply her just deserts for repeatedly and deliberately lying to federal authorities?

SENTENCING GUIDELINES
a standardized set of penalty options based on key characteristics of the offense and offender.

This chapter begins our examination of the fifth stage of criminal justice processing: corrections and punishment. When someone violates a common code of conduct, all societies feel it is important to respond in some fashion. We resent the harmful conduct of drug dealers like Peter Michael Hall and those like Kemba Smith who support and protect them. Our sense of justice leads us to desire some kind of societal reaction toward a person who acts unjustly toward others. And we usually want the response to reflect the seriousness of the crime and the degree of harm it brings to the wider community. In the **sentencing** of Kemba Smith, we see the tremendous power of the criminal justice system to respond to crime by depriving citizens of their liberty for years, sometimes their entire life, and in the case of capital punishment, even life itself.

Sentencing of convicted offenders has traditionally been a responsibility of the judge, who considers the seriousness of the offense, past criminal history, level of remorsefulness, and victim impact to determine the appropriate sentence.

Yet how we respond to those who have violated our criminal laws is also a reflection of who we are and what we value as a society. Winston Churchill observed that "The mood and temper of the public in regard to the treatment of crime and criminals is one of the most unfailing tests of the civilization of any country . . . the treatment of crime and criminal mark and measure the stored-up strength of a nation, and are a sign and proof of the living virtue in it."[22] At the time of the Salem witch trials, an acceptable punishment was to hang people in public or crush them beneath giant rocks. Today we no longer permit such painful methods of punishment and even attempt to put people to death in a "humane" act of killing through lethal injection. The use of incarceration has replaced corporeal punishment and restitution as the main response to crime. Is this more "humane" than earlier modes of punishment? Why have we invested so much public resources to warehouse millions of American citizens who have committed crime?

This chapter examines the history of criminal sentencing, shifting sensibilities about forms of punishment and the varying rationales used to justify different responses to crime.[23]

What is the purpose of criminal sentencing? Are we hoping to rehabilitate the offender? Avenge society? Deter others from crime? Teach our children a lesson? Heal the victim? Repair the damage caused by crime? Prevent future crime? What are our priorities in imposing a criminal sanction on a citizen who has violated the law?

This chapter also looks at who in the justice system is charged with the responsibility of handing down a just sentence. Who determines the appropriate sentence for a given individual who has been convicted of a crime? Is it the judge, jury, prosecutor, probation officer, prison warden, parole board, psychiatrist, politician, victim, or community? Who should play this crucial role? Should the victim have a significant voice in the sentencing process? What about the community? And what about the case of drug crimes such as Kemba's? Who are the "victims" in the crime of drug trafficking?

We begin the chapter by looking carefully at the specific rationale for the punishment of Kemba Smith. Kemba is a casualty in the war on drugs. By voluntarily engaging in the drug trade with her boyfriend, Kemba Smith made herself a target of the tactics the government uses to fight that war. But the burden and costs of incarceration do not fall only on the individual behind bars. Increasingly researchers are assessing the impact of imprisonment on families especially children of inmates and the impact on the overall economic and social health of the community. We close the chapter by examining the unintended or **collateral consequences** of incarceration.

FIVE GOALS OF SENTENCING

There are five recognized philosophies of punishment that guide our response to criminal conduct: **retribution**, **incapacitation**, **deterrence**, **rehabilitation**, and **restitution**. Common everyday expressions we are all familiar with capture some of the widely held sentiments about how offenders should be treated and why. To a certain extent, the modern criminal justice system embraces all of these goals. Yet these goals compete with one another, and throughout history, the justice system has generally embraced one or two above the rest. Let us examine each one in turn.

Retribution

"You do the crime, you do the time" expresses a philosophy of "just deserts."[24] The infliction of some type of suffering or pain on an offender is a just and legitimate response provided it is proportionate to the degree of suffering he or she chose to inflict on a victim. A crime violates our sense of "justice." A criminal act imposes some kind of injury on a victim and on the rest of the community. This injury evokes feelings of anger and outrage. In most of us, to some degree, an unjust action provokes the desire for vengeance. We feel that some equivalent action must be taken toward the individual in order to correct the imbalance created by their wrongdoing, and even more important, we feel entitled to inflict suffering upon that person. In fact, we feel we are in the right and it is our obligation to impose some kind of suffering or burden. This is the essence of the goal of retribution: the retaliatory infliction of harm back upon the offender. We punish in order to avenge the harm suffered by the victim.

The biblical passage from the Old Testament is often cited in support of the goal of retribution. Leviticus (24:17–22) states, "When one man strikes another and kills him, he shall be put to death" and Exodus (21:23–24) states "Whosoever sheds blood shall have his blood be shed. A life for life; eye for an eye; tooth for tooth; hand for hand, foot for foot, burning for burning, wound for wound." Under Mosaic law the punishment that should fall upon the offender is what was done to his or her neighbor.

COLLATERAL CONSEQUENCES the outcome of an action that is neither planned nor anticipated.

RETRIBUTION a sentencing philosophy that prioritizes punishment commensurate to the seriousness of the offense.

INCAPACITATION the elimination of the capacity to commit future crimes within society usually through incarceration.

DETERRENCE the imposition of punishment in order to discourage the commission of future crimes by the offender and others within society.

REHABILITATION the process of changing the attitudes and behavior of the offender through training, education, treatment, or vocational programming to produce law-abiding conduct in the future.

RESTITUTION the obligation on the part of the offender to repay the victim or the community with money services or symbolic gestures commensurate with the harm caused.

The principle of an "eye for an eye" expresses a retributive goal in response to wrongdoing but it also demands proportionality and moderation in claiming revenge. The biblical passage recognizes that the human desire for vengeance can become unjust. When punishment goes too far, it is no longer justice. We only need to look at our history to know that the emotion of vengeance often leads to a cycle of violence or blood feud when the victim exacts excessive revenge which spurs the "victim" to retaliate in turn. Most wars are fought in the name of "justice" on both sides.

Retribution through legal punishment therefore is only justified in equal measure to the crime. The biblical passage tells us that if an eye has been lost, it is only an eye that one is entitled to claim, not the life of the offender. If it is a life, it is only one life in response and not the death and destruction of an entire family or village. In ancient times, the principle of retribution was an important principle of restraint designed to prevent war between families or clans if one member committed a crime against another.

In modern times the legitimate act of retribution may only be performed by the state in part to prevent vigilante violence on the part of private citizens. Committing harm against a person even in response to an illegal act is itself illegal. It is only the state that holds the legitimate right to punish. Under the modern system of administration, it is the state that imposes proportionate retributive punishment on the offender in the name of the victim and society as well. Due process exists to ensure that the process of accusation and conviction is fair and truthful and only then is the state justified in inflicting harm in proportion to the harm of the crime.

The judge who imposes sentencing under a retributive philosophy seeks to create "just" punishment proportionate to the crime, the culpability of the offender, and the extent of the harmfulness of the criminal behavior. Victim-impact statements are submitted to the judge at the time of sentencing to describe the suffering endured by the victim and their families, to assist the judge in determining the extent of punishment under a retributive philosophy. The goal of the sentence is to do unto the offender in equal measure what they have done unto others.

Incapacitation

"Lock em up and throw away the key" suggests society needs to be protected from persons who are dangerous to others. The goal of incapacitation seeks to protect society by physically restraining the person so they are unable to commit offenses again. We might lock an offender up in order to make is impossible for them to repeat their behavior or we might physically disable the offender in some way which makes it impossible for them to repeat their behavior in the future through chemical castration, for example. Alternatively we might place an electronic bracelet on a person's ankle that monitors their movements 24 hours a day and signals an alarm if they leave a designated restricted area. All of these sanctions are designed to keep the public safe by literally taking away an offender's capacity to commit crime.

The death penalty is the ultimate form of incapacitation. We might justify the use of capital punishment on the grounds that it at least achieves this goal: once we have put someone to death, we can be certain the person will never hurt someone again. It is one clearly recognized benefit of capital punishment over life in prison which still holds open the possibility of harm inflicted by the offender upon their fellow prisoners.

Today our dominant means of incapacitation is through imprisonment.[25] When we talk about "getting people off the streets" we acknowledge our goal is to protect society. Protection of the community from dangerous offenders is a key criterion for locking people in prison, particularly in institutions where little attempt is made to provide any treatment, counseling, or education. The warehousing of prisoners, at the very least, incapacitates the offender by preventing them from committing more crimes against members of the community during the time they are locked in that prison cell.

Deterrence

"Next time they will think twice" or "we need to teach them a lesson" expresses the belief that the penal sentence will prevent or deter the person from repeating the same behavior in the future.[26] In the goal of deterrence we hope to influence the future conduct of a person who is tempted to commit crime. The goal of deterrence is to prevent future wrongdoing, not through physical restraint, but by influencing the mind of the offender and other potential offenders in society. This is, along with retribution, the most widely held justification for punishment today. We believe that by imposing some kind of punishment on a person who commits a wrongful act, we will influence their choices in the future. When the next opportunity to commit crime arises, we expect they will remember the pains of punishment and choose to refrain from crime to avoid this suffering happening again.

Specific deterrence refers to the effect of the sanction on the particular individual who committed the crime. When we punish an individual in the expectation that next time he or she will behave differently in future, we are attempting to attain the goal of specific deterrent. **General deterrence** is the effect we hope the punishment will have on others who are yet to commit the crime. We use the expression "send a message" to refer to the goal of general deterrence. The goal of general deterrence states that we punish offenders to prevent others from committing crimes. By making the "costs of crime" (in the form of punishment) greater than the "benefits" or rewards from violating the law, we hope to achieve an overall effect of reducing the amount of crime within the wider society. The person who is punished is used as an "example" to others of what will happen if they choose to commit crime.

The goal of deterrence was first articulated in the eighteenth century, as the image of man as rational actor began to gain dominance among intellectuals and policymakers.[27] Crime was no longer seen as an act of sin brought on by the Devil or the result of innate evil on the part of the criminal, but a calculated act designed to bring about maximum reward. By this logic, Enlightenment philosophers reasoned that it made sense to raise the cost of crime above its rewards. Once people experienced the reality that "crime does not pay" they will stop committing crime. The goal of deterrence seeks to reduce the overall amount of crime in society by raising the stakes for doing crime.

Rehabilitation

"They're sick, they need treatment" implies that the purpose of sentencing is to address the psychological, sociological, or personal problems that led to the crime. The goal of rehabilitation seeks to reform the offender through the interventions provided by the "correctional" system.[28] Like deterrence, the goal of rehabilitation has its eye on the future behavior of the convicted offender.

SPECIFIC DETERRENCE the imposition of punishment to discourage the individual from committing crimes in the future. Also known as special or individual deterrence.

GENERAL DETERRENCE the imposition of punishment in order to set an example to others contemplating crime.

By offering the offender some form of treatment, training, counseling, or education, it is believed that whatever led the person to commit crime in the first place can be altered. The goal of rehabilitation is to improve the offender, to transform him or her, and to correct the flaw that led him down the path to criminal conduct. Most states call their agencies responsible for operating prisons and criminal sanctions *correctional departments* reflecting one of the key underlying philosophies of modern punishment.

The discipline of corrections bears close alliance with a medical model of criminal offending. Rooted in nineteenth-century science of positivism in which it is believed that all effects have a cause we can understand through science, all human behavior including criminal conduct is believed to be the result of environmental, psychological, or biological forces acting upon the offender.[29] Just as physical disease is caused by bacteria or viruses, so too is criminal behavior caused by various "pathologies" of social life. These pathologies include dysfunctional nuclear families, disorganized communities, poverty, lack of education, poor diet and nutrition, brain injuries, fetal alcohol syndrome, substance abuse, child abuse, and so forth. While the causes vary and may differ from individual to individual, the goal of criminal justice sanctioning should be to correct the "root causes" so that the offender can return to society and be able to lead a productive and law-abiding life.

Restitution

"Make amends and say you are sorry" focuses on the victim and on the need for the offender to restore what was lost, financially, emotionally, or symbolically, directly to those who suffered the loss. The principle of restitution is as fundamental to the human experience as the emotion of revenge. When something has been broken or taken away, the goal of restitution demands that it be fixed or returned: the money should be paid back, the broken window repaired, the graffiti on the fence wiped clean, or stolen property returned.

Today, the state collects fines from offenders and dispenses a tiny portion of this to victim compensation funds. In the so-called golden age of the victim before the rise of state systems of justice, criminal sentences centered around compensatory punishments that focused attention on restoration of the victim.[30] In addition to some degree of entitlement to express revenge against the offender, victims were offered restitution for their losses. The community required the offender, as well as their extended family, to pay the victim back. Early legal systems spelled out the precise amount to redress different types of wrongs. In Roman law, for example, thieves were required to pay victims double restitution for what was stolen unless the property was taken from inside their house in which case they were required to pay three times the value of the property.

The principle of restitution in early law operated for violent crimes as well as property crimes. In Mosaic law, if two men were involved in a fight with the result that one person was badly injured but did not die, the perpetrator was required to pay the family for the loss of the injured man's time and support until he was thoroughly healed.[31] Some legal codes spelled out the precise compensation for different types of injuries: in the law of eighth- and ninth-century Anglo Saxons, if a man knocked out the front teeth of another man he had to pay eight shillings; if it was an eye tooth, he had to only pay four shillings; but if he knocked out a molar, which is far more valuable for chewing, he owed fifteen shillings.[32]

The payment of a death fine was found in many different pre-Western and non-Western codes of law requiring the murderer and his kin to compensate the victim's family for the loss of the murdered relative. Among the ancient Germans, homicide was atoned for by compensation in cattle and sheep to assuage the family and prevent the start of a dangerous spiral of retaliatory violence. In Anglo Saxon times, the law states that if anyone slayed a man he is subject to the vengeance unless he compensates the family within twelve months the full worth of the man's estate: the amount of compensation depended upon the age, rank, gender, and prestige of the injured party.[33]

Restitution is not only about the material loss suffered by the victim but also includes various forms of emotional and psychological restitution. Recall the Serrell family's desire for justice in chapter 6. They knew there was no way Susan could bring their loved one back to life. Yet they wanted the offender to take positive actions in her life that would, to some degree, give them the emotional satisfaction that their loved one had not died in vain. Recall the sentiments of the Hattori family. Above all else, they desired an honest act of taking moral responsibility and expression of genuine remorse from Rodney Peairs and his wife. The emotional acts of repentance, remorse, and apology that help restore a victim's faith in humanity are significant elements of the goal of restitution.

RANGE OF MODERN SENTENCES

The modern criminal justice system is an offender-focused system that relies upon the state to formulate criminal laws, specify sentences, and administer sanctions. The victim is no longer central to that process. Nor are many of the pre-modern forms of penalties in use today: offenders cannot be paraded down the main square covered in tar and feathers; nor are they hoisted on a scaffold to be stoned by the community. At the time of the Salem witch trials there were a host of penal sanctions, such as whipping posts, ducking stools, branding, and stoning, that are no longer a part of our justice system.[34] Nor can a judge order an offender to care for a victim's family for the rest of his or her life. The range of penalties available to the criminal justice practitioners is established by legal codes, which reflect shifting social norms about the nature of legitimate criminal justice sanctioning.

Modern sanctions range from the imposition of death, through incarceration in various types of institutions and for differing lengths of time, to a host of community-based sanctions and financial sanctions.[35] Thirty-one states and the federal governments administer capital punishment for specific offenses. Since reinstating the death penalty in 1976, there have been 1,445 executions. Seventy-five percent of these executions have taken place in six southern states: Texas, Oklahoma, Virginia, Florida, Missouri, and Georgia.[36]

The use of incarceration as a form of punishment is largely a nineteenth-century invention. To an extent, the shift toward incarceration as the predominant form of punishment was the result of a change in the attitudes of society toward physical violence.[37] Over the course of centuries, modern societies abandoned corporeal punishments of whipping, beatings, branding, mutilation, and torture in favor of imprisonment.[38] The "spectacle of suffering" was no longer socially tolerable in our public streets, and punishment began to disappear from public spaces to behind the prison wall.

In the past twenty years, the United States has seen an explosive growth in the use of incarceration as a form of punishment. The number of people in prison and jail increased 500 percent over the thirty years from 1970 till the peak population in 2008. In 1970 there were about 330,000 people incarcerated. That number reached 2.3 million by the end of 2008, and by the end of 2013, the number of people incarcerated dropped slightly to about 2.2 million.[39] As a whole, the United States has an incarceration rate of about 716 inmates per 100,000 citizens, the highest rate of incarceration in the entire world.[40]

Offenders may also be given split sentences that combine periods of incarceration followed by periods of community-based supervision on probation or parole or intermittent sentences that combine periods of freedom; for instance, during the work week with periods of confinement, say, during the weekend. Boot camps for juveniles and other less serious offenders became an alternative form of incarceration in the 1980s, combining a shorter period of incarceration with intensive military discipline and correctional treatment.[41]

A sentence of probation retains an offender within the community but may carry a wide range of conditions. House arrest accompanied by some form of electronic surveillance maintains an individual within their own housing but severely restricts their movements beyond the home. Conditions of probation or parole may include hours of community work service, mandatory drug treatment, mandatory counseling, anger management, or drunk-driving classes. In addition, offenders may be ordered to pay a fine to the court or pay restitution to a victim compensation fund or directly to their individual victim.

Who Decides?

The parties that determine a criminal sanction range from legislatures who write the criminal laws to judges, prosecutors, parole boards, juries, probation officers, victims, and communities.[42] There are three key sentencing models that emphasize discretion of different players within the criminal justice system.

The **judicial model of sentencing** relies upon the wisdom and experience of the judge to craft a sentence that fits a given offender within the parameters set by the statutory code. When legislatures craft a criminal statute, the principle of legality requires that the punishment for violating the code be specified within the statute. But the scope of legal sanctions for a given offense may be extremely broad ranging from probation to many years in prison. Statutes vary widely on the latitude of sanctions for a given crime, but in this model, it is the judge who has the legal responsibility to set a specific sentence for a given offender.

It is the responsibility of probation officers in most jurisdictions to prepare **pre-sentencing reports** based on interviews with offenders and their families.[43] The purpose of the **pre-sentence investigation** (PSI) is to help the judge select an appropriate sentence within the statutory framework. In some jurisdictions, a PSI is mandatory for all felonies, in others it may be done at the request of the judge. Pre-sentencing investigations are rarely conducted for misdemeanor offenses and are generally required in cases where probation is being considered as a sanction.

The quality of reports vary: in some jurisdictions the report is highly detailed including extensive information about the offenders' past history, including facts about his or her childhood, current family life, extended family, work relationships, and so forth; in other jurisdictions, the facts in the report do not extend much beyond what is known about the offender by his prior record and details of the current offense. Pre-sentence investigations have been known to contain subjective impressions and opinions about the offender that are sometimes based on racial stereotypes, baseless rumors, or unsupported inferences about the offender's personality and future criminality.

JUDICIAL MODEL OF SENTENCING sentencing decisions that rely upon the broad discretion of the judge to craft the individual sentence within parameters set by statute.

PRE-SENTENCE INVESTIGATION/ REPORT an investigation and summary report of the background of a convicted offender prepared to help the judge decide on an appropriate sentence for the individual.

The PSI also contains a recommendation for sentencing based on the information gathered in the investigation. In theory, this recommendation and background information is intended as a guide to the judge to assist him or her in making the sentencing decision. In practice, studies have found a high correspondence between the recommendation in the PSI and the judicial sentence.[44] In one study in California, researchers found that judges accepted 86 percent of the recommendations made by probation officers in the PSI.[45] Thus in the judicial model of sentencing, probation officers play a substantial role in the sentencing decision.

The **administrative model of sentencing** depends upon parole boards, wardens, and other administrators of the correctional system to determine when an offender has completed his or her sentence. An offender may be sentenced by a judge to a term in prison bounded by a minimum and maximum length of time. The actual period served is "indeterminate," with the release date determined by the professionals within the correctional system. An offender enters the prison system not knowing when they will be released. Their release date will depend upon their behavior in the correctional system and their ability to demonstrate they have been rehabilitated.

The **legislative model of sentencing** fixes specific sentences through mandatory sentences. These statutes require a precise sentence if the person is convicted. The judge plays little or no role in the sentencing process. Mandatory minimum statutes does not eliminate or even reduce discretion in the criminal justice system. These laws may tie the hands of judges in determining sentences for convicted offenders, but they increase the discretionary power of the prosecutors who may choose to charge an individual under the mandatory statutes or not. In the investigation and conviction of drug offenses, prosecutors often reduce charges if the suspect is willing to become an informant or able to forfeit substantial property assets to the justice department.

In addition to these three sources of sentencing authority, there is also the power of governors and presidents to alter or negate sentences of convicted criminals through the **executive clemency,** which is the power to pardon or forgive or commute a sentence to a reduced form. President Clinton, as we saw, reduced Kemba's sentence to the time already served. Executive authority is usually one of the last resorts for inmates on death row seeking to commute their death sentence to life imprisonment.

The simple fact is that we cannot eliminate discretionary decision-making from the criminal justice system. The decision-making of criminal justice personnel is an essential and necessary element of the justice system. We can change how and when in the justice process discretionary decisions are made and we can change who has discretion over a given part of the process, but we cannot eliminate human decision-making and judgment from the justice system.

Determinate sentencing systems specify a precise sentence for the crime, whether it is set by legislatures or judges at the time of sentence, hence the saying "you do the crime, you do the time." Adhering to the goal of retribution and deterrence, determinate sentencing is calibrated to fit the crime as retribution and it is believed to offer a predictable consequence for wrongdoing. According to the theory of deterrence, when punishment is swift, certain, and proportionate to the crime, rational human beings respond by refraining from crime.

Indeterminate sentencing systems function differently. A judge will set a maximum amount of time to be served as well as a minimum, but the actual

ADMINISTRATIVE MODEL OF SENTENCING
the use of parole boards, wardens, and other correctional officials to determine when an offender is to be granted conditional release from incarceration.

LEGISLATIVE MODEL OF SENTENCING
the setting of mandatory sentences for specific crimes established within criminal statutes passed by legislative bodies.

EXECUTIVE CLEMENCY
the power to pardon (forgive) a criminal conviction or commute a sentence, held by the chief executive officer.

DETERMINATE SENTENCING
the imposition of a fixed or set amount of time in prison.

INDETERMINATE SENTENCING
the imposition of an unspecified amount of time in prison somewhere between a statutory minimum and maximum term.

amount of time served will depend upon the individual conduct and reformation within the correctional system. From the end of the nineteenth century until the late 1970s, most state criminal justice systems operated on an indeterminate sentencing structure. Indeterminate sentencing is compatible with the goal of rehabilitation: the sentence is individualized to fit the criminal rather than the crime.

The theory of rehabilitation suggested that if correctional systems were able to "correct" or cure the offender, it was best left up to the practitioners of the correctional system to determine which individuals had been reformed and could be safely paroled to the community and which ones needed to remain behind bars. Prisoners could earn early release from prison through earned and statutory "good time" for conduct inside the facility. Indeterminate sentencing was sometimes called "bark and bite sentencing": the bark was the threat of the maximum; the bite was the minimum. No one in the system expected the maximum to be served or even thought it was in society's best interest. The threat of a long sentence hanging over the inmate was seen as a powerful motivational tool inducing them to cooperate with the prison regime and to participate in correctional treatment and programming. Only the worst inmates who were so angry, out of control, hostile, or unmanageable would be retained to serve their full sentence. The carrot of early release was seen as a key motivational and management tool for correctional systems.

The return to determinate sentencing largely through a rise in mandatory sentencing statutes, the abolition of parole in some jurisdictions, and the passage of **truth in sentencing laws** was driven by discontent with the judicial model which resulted in wide **sentencing disparities** for similar offenses.[46] The era of judicial discretion that allowed one judge to give an offender convicted of a rape twenty-five years in prison and a different judge to give an offender convicted under the same statute only two years' probation led to a political movement to reduce judicial discretion in sentencing. Critics argued that judicial discretion led to excessive leniency for some and excessive harshness for others. Critics also complained that parole boards operated in a discriminatory and inconsistent manner: white offenders were more likely to make parole than blacks and other minorities, when they faced predominantly white parole boards.

Today critics of fairness in sentencing argue that prosecutors are now the most powerful players in the criminal justice system in deciding criminal sanctions through the discretionary choice to prosecute and to choose specific charges. Discrimination based on race and class is a key concern in mandatory sentencing set by legislatures because of the discretionary decisions made in any given case by local prosecutors.

TRUTH IN SENTENCING LAWS
statutes which require that most or all of the sentence be actually served.

SENTENCING DISPARITIES
the imposition of widely different sentences for offenders convicted of the same offense.

DECIDING DEATH: THE ISSUE OF CAPITAL PUNISHMENT

At the time of the Salem witch trials, the execution of offenders was a public affair for all to witness as the victim suffered a painful and torturous demise. By 1845 most states had outlawed public hangings and replaced them by discreet hangings behind prison walls. Today, the execution is a sanitized bureaucratic procedure carried out in the middle of the night in the deepest recesses of the penal system. Clinical, dispassionate, and efficient, the modern execution in its effort to hide the cruelty may intensify it.

The use of capital punishment has declined as part of the overall modern shift away from brutal and violent forms of punishment. Many nations have abolished the death penalty altogether while it persists in about ninety-five countries around the world. The United States is the only advanced democratic nation among the list of nations that sanctions the use of death as punishment for ordinary crimes.[47] The list includes China, Cuba, Iran, Iraq, Libya, and Russia. The federal government began collecting data on the death penalty in 1930. From that time until the end of 2016, 5,301 people have been executed, more than half of them in eight southern states.[48]

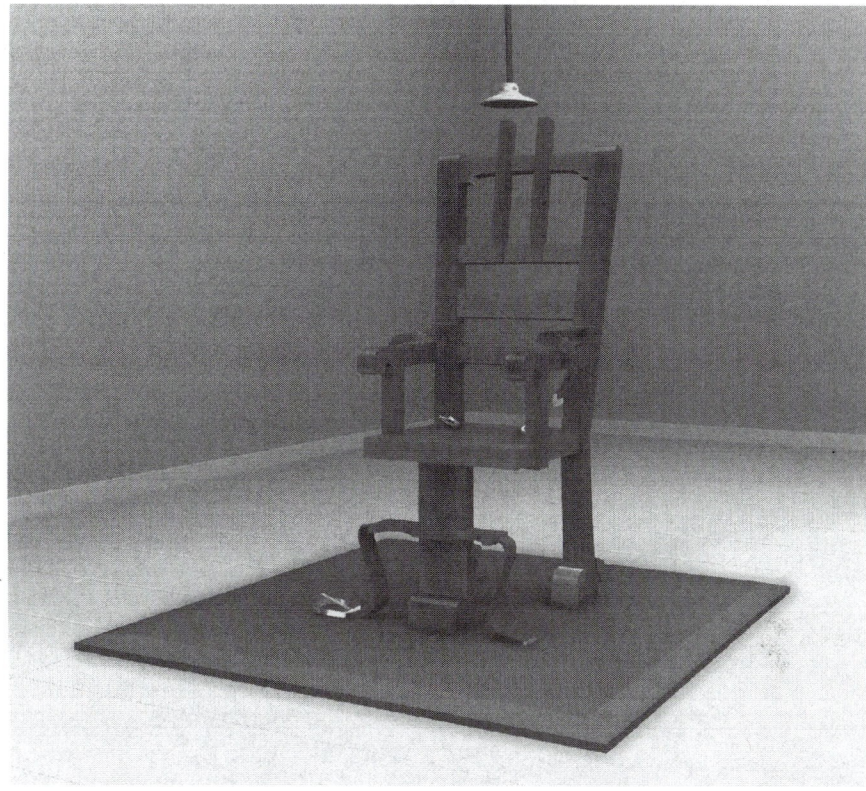

The electric chair is a widely recognized symbol of capital punishment, but the actual use of the electric chair has declined in favor of lethal injection, a method that is believed to be more humane.

In 1972, the Supreme Court ruling in *Furman v. Georgia*[49] called a halt to executions in this country by declaring that capital punishment as it was then applied violated the Eighth Amendment prohibition against cruel and unusual punishment. In a 5-4 decision, the court did not declare the death penalty itself unconstitutional but declared the absence of clear standards a violation of the Eighth Amendment. Without standards for juries and judges to guide them in deciding when the death penalty is appropriate, punishment by death was tantamount to being "struck by lightning." The justices also found that the lack of clear guidelines resulted in blatant discrimination against minorities who were more likely to be given the death penalty than non-minorities.

In 1976, in *Greggs v. Georgia*,[50] the Supreme Court effectively reinstated the use of capital punishment by approving a state statute that addressed the concerns expressed in the Furman decision. In the wake of Furman, new death penalty laws were passed by thirty-five states. States that enacted a mandatory death penalty for a particularly heinous crime were seen as meeting the constitutional standard for fairness and consistency, although a mandatory statute for the crime of rape was later struck down. Also constitutional were statutes that offered a **bifurcated trial** process and **guided discretion** statutes.

The bifurcated process established a two-part proceeding in which a separate sentencing hearing was held after the trial to establish guilt. The jury would then hear arguments from the prosecution and the defense as to the specific reasons why this particular crime deserved or did not merit a sentence

BIFURCATED TRIAL
the constitutional requirement that the imposition of the death penalty be subject to a separate hearing after the adjudication of guilt or innocence has taken place.

GUIDED DISCRETION STATUTES
capital statutes which specify the mitigating and aggravating circumstances juries should consider in the penalty phase of the capital trial.

of death. The guided discretion statutes are laws that specify the **aggravating** or **mitigating circumstances** that juries and judges should consider in making their decision. As long as the jury or judge focuses on the particularized circumstances of the crime, there no longer is a wanton use of the death penalty and its use meets constitutional standards. The first execution under the new constitutional requirements was the execution of Gary Gilmore in 1977. Since that time, by 2010, 1,188 executions have taken place, 447 in the state of Texas alone.[51] In 2010, an additional 3,113 inmates were on death row.[52]

The justification for the death penalty is often a deterrence. The argument is that the death penalty saves lives because it deters the crime of homicide. Research shows no evidence that there is a deterrent effect from the use of capital punishment. Indeed, on the contrary, some argue that the use of the death penalty by the state has a **brutalization effect** increasing the incidence of homicide instead of lowering it.[53]

Other justifications include incapacitation and retribution. A person who is executed is incapable of ever harming another person even behind the walls of the prison. Life imprisonment still leaves open the possibility of escape or inside violence, so the most secure form of protection is execution. The retributive rationale rests on the simple proposition that the taking of life in such a heinous manner requires an equal and proportionate response. By embracing the use of capital punishment, society acknowledges the sanctity of life.

Opponents to the death penalty reject the belief that the way to show respect for life is to sanction state murder. Opponents including family members of murder victims believe that their personal or religious values prohibit the taking of a human life except in self-defense. Members of Murder Victims Families for Reconciliation, an anti–death penalty group of family member survivors, asks the state not to execute people in their name. Critics of the death penalty point out that the death sentence is the ultimate rejection of the belief in redemption or rehabilitation.

The use of the death penalty has long been criticized for being discriminatory, and the evidence strongly suggests that this remains as true today as it was in the past. There are few women and few middle-class people sitting on death row. As of 2009, over 40 percent of those under the sentence of death were black[54] and nearly all people on death row are too poor to pay for private counsel.[55] Many defendants were represented by poorly prepared defense counsels, who fail to adequately present mitigating factors to the jury or to investigate witnesses and gather evidence that might acquit their clients. Nowhere is the inequality around the importance of legal representation more evident than when a person is facing death.[56]

Data clearly show the continued influence of racism in the use of the death penalty. It appears that the race of the victim as well as the offender has shown to strongly determine whether or not the death penalty is applied. Statistically, black offenders who kill white victims are more likely to be executed than any other offender-victim combination.[57] In a classic study, David Baldus and his colleagues found that controlling for thirty-nine non-racial variables, the likelihood of being executed was 4.3 times greater for defendants who killed whites than for defendants who killed blacks. Historically, in the United States, out of more than 18,000 documented executions, only forty-two have involved a white person sentenced to death for killing a black person.[58] In recent times, the NAACP project confirmed a similar pattern: between 1977 and 2012, of the 994 executions

AGGRAVATING CIRCUMSTANCES facts about the heinous nature of the criminal act specified by law that guide a jury decision to apply the death penalty.

MITIGATING CIRCUMSTANCES facts about the offender and circumstances of the crime specified by law that guide a jury decision to apply the death penalty

BRUTALIZATION EFFECT the theory that capital punishment contributes to greater violence within society by increasing the tolerance for violence within society.

that took place, 18 involved white offenders who killed black victims while 262 involved black offenders who killed white victims.[59]

In 1986 the Supreme Court rejected these data as evidence that the use of the death penalty violated the Eighth Amendment ban against cruel and unusual punishment and the Equal Protection Clause of the Constitution. Robert McClesky was an African American man who shot a white police officer in Georgia in 1978. While acknowledging that the statistical data clearly demonstrated a statistical pattern of racial disparity in the criminal justice system of the state of Georgia, the Court ruled in the 5-4 decision that it was nevertheless necessary to provide evidence of actual jury discrimination in this particular case. The ruling in *McClesky v. Kemp*[60] is widely seen as severely limiting the ability to turn to the courts to address the problem of racial disparities, not just in the administration of capital punishment but throughout the many stages of the criminal justice processing where such disparities exist.

One of the key arguments marshaled against the death penalty is the irreversibility of the sentence. The criminal justice system is notorious for making errors. Even a perfect system cannot be infallible. Mistakes will be made. The justice system fails to offer equal protection of due process to those who are poor, minority, or otherwise marginal to society. Eyewitnesses lie, prosecutors withhold evidence, informers misinform, and juries make mistakes. But once the death penalty has been imposed, nothing can be done to redress the wrongful conviction.

In 2000, the pro death penalty republican governor of Illinois became the first governor to declare a moratorium on the use of the death penalty after thirteen people on death row in his state were found to be innocent.[61] The science of **DNA testing** has begun to offer reliable evidence to exonerate a growing number of convicted individuals serving prison sentences, including a number who are on death row. A nationwide study found over four hundred wrongful convictions in death penalty cases since 1992.[62] Currently only seven states give inmates the right to have their DNA tested, and in four states, it is only in cases where the offender is facing the death penalty or life imprisonment.[63]

Proponents of the death penalty often decry the lengthy proceedings and appeals for death row inmates because they believe that executions must be swift to have a true deterrent effect. The average death row inmate may sit on death row for as long as ten years. The time spent on death row is far more dehumanizing and alienating than the worst experiences of the general inmate. Inmates on death row are isolated from the rest of the prison and each other. They are rarely allowed to participate in any programs or engage in any recreational activities. Their time is spent alone with the knowledge of their future walk down that "green mile." In the words of Albert Camus,

> Many laws consider a pre-mediated crime more serious than a crime of pure violence. . . . For there to be equivalence, the death penalty would have to punish a criminal who had warned his victim of the date at which he would inflict a horrible death on him and who, from that moment onward, had confined him at his mercy for months. Such a monster is not encountered in private life.[64]

How do Americans feel about the death penalty? Public opinion polls show that, in 1994, 80 percent of American citizens favored the death penalty as compared to 59 percent in 1973 and only 42 percent in 1966.[65] Since the 1990s the numbers of Americans in support of the death penalty have been declining. A survey conducted in 2016 found that only about 49 percent of Americans favor the death penalty, the

DNA TESTING
a broad field of science that has begun to offer reliable evidence to exonerate a growing number of convicted individuals serving prison sentences including a number who are on death row.

first time it has fallen below half of the population since the 1960s.[66] Lawmakers and judges use this kind of polling data to infer that the conscience of our society finds the imposition of death by the state morally justifiable and acceptable.

But what does public support in opinion polls really mean? Would Americans be willing to witness the imposition of death as people did in the eighteenth century? Would the majority of citizens themselves choose the death penalty for a given offender if they were sitting on a jury? Sister Helen Prejean who serves as a spiritual adviser to death row inmates, and who has witnessed many executions, believes most Americans would "vomit" if they were forced to witness an execution.[67] In her view, we carry out the executions at the darkest hour of midnight in the deepest bowels of the prison system because we, as a society, are not comfortable with the sight of killing a person "in cold blood." Some opinion polls and research show that support for the death penalty substantially diminishes when people are offered an alternative of life imprisonment without parole and required restitution to the victim's family.[68]

RETHINKING THE WAR ON DRUGS AND DRUG LAWS

Kemba's sentence of twenty-four and a half years with no eligibility for parole shocked her parents and other members of the community unfamiliar with the shift in sentencing structures toward longer and determinate forms of sentencing. This final section of this chapter briefly examines the impact of our drug laws on the criminal justice system. In the effort to control rising prison costs and overcrowding, states have begun to seek ways to reduce the prison population by releasing nonviolent drug offenders and increasing the use of alternatives to incarceration, such as drug courts, which divert offenders into community-based treatment under court supervision. Concerns about fairness have also led to changes in the federal sentencing structures for cocaine to reduce the disparity in sentencing for different forms of the drug. Lastly, several states, including California, Massachusetts, Colorado, Maine, Washington, Oregon, and Alaska have legalized the sale and use of marijuana for recreational purposes, and many more states have laws allowing the sale and distribution for medical purposes. These state laws were the result of state wide referendums reflecting a change in the public attitude about the dangers of marijuana and about the efficacy of the war on drugs itself. Currently, these state laws are in conflict with federal law that continues to classify marijuana as a Schedule I drug and prohibits its distribution, sale, and use for any purpose.

A Brief History of U.S. Drug Laws: Moral Panics and Moral Entrepreneurs

Americans have long had conflicting attitudes toward the use of drugs of all kinds. Alcohol has been viewed both as a healthy staple and as an evil substance capable of destroying lives with a single drop. What is true of alcohol is also the case with drugs such as heroin, cocaine, tobacco, and marijuana: changes in our drug laws reflect conflicting attitudes and beliefs. Between 1890 and 1920 it was legal to purchase heroin or cocaine but the sale of alcoholic beverages and cigarettes was prohibited; today an adult can legally purchase alcohol on every street corner but it is not legal, under any circumstances, to buy, sell, or use heroin or cocaine. Time and again American drug laws moved through periods of tolerance and intolerance for the use of specific drugs for recreational and medicinal purposes.[69]

Our laws reflect the distribution of power within society: some groups are better able to project their views through the media and pass legislation that reflects their interests and point of view. Historian David Musto argues that each time the United States has passed laws prohibiting the use of a particular substance it is because the use of the drug is associated with a stigmatized and less powerful group.[70] The crusade against alcohol was a campaign against the millions of immigrants, with habits of drinking that others found distasteful and dangerous. The first U.S. laws against opium targeted the cultural practices of Chinese immigrants, who threatened to take jobs away from white workers; cocaine was linked with the threat of crazed blacks lusting after white women; and the first laws against marijuana focused on the threat of Mexican laborers high on dope roaming the countryside.[71]

Sociologists have coined the term **moral crusade,** to refer to the process by which a particular set of behaviors, in this case, the use of a particular drug, is constructed as a widespread threat to the public welfare.[72] Prominent activists, newspapers, politicians, clergy, educators, and professionals/experts of all kinds help to "construct" the image of a substantial danger posed by the use of the drug with narratives that are usually well beyond objective reality. This "panic" generates public support for legislation prohibiting the drug. Generally, there are multiple political agendas and interests associated with any given drug crusade.[73] Politicians gain votes, certain industries profit, and bureaucracies created to enforce the law see their budgets grow as a result. These actors become powerful interest groups committed to the eradication of that particular drug use within American society.

Key Developments in the Modern War on Drugs

To understand the origins of the modern "war on drugs," it is necessary to look at the development of drug laws during the Nixon administration. The use of the term "war" became a powerful image in the 1960s and 1970s in the battle against a host of social ills, including poverty, hunger, then crime and drugs, and later terrorism. But the term is much more than a fancy use of language: as we have seen in chapter 9, the war metaphor in policing has shaped the culture and practice of policing through the use of military weapons, strategies, and tactics.[74]

The federal Controlled Substances Act (CSA), Title II of the Comprehensive Drug Abuse Prevention and Control Act of 1970 consolidated many laws regulating the manufacture and distribution of narcotics, stimulants, depressants, hallucinogens, steroids, and chemicals used in the illicit production of controlled substances. It established five drug schedules through its CSA and remains the basic classification in use today.[75] This legislation also allowed for **civil asset forfeiture** of money, property, houses, land, or any other asset that was gained through the trafficking in illegal drugs.

Schedule I drugs are those drugs deemed to have a high potential for abuse and has no currently acceptable medical purpose for treatment. These drugs include heroin, LSD, and marijuana. Schedule II are drugs with high potential for abuse but with accepted medical use. These include morphine, PCP, cocaine, methamphetamine, and methadone. Schedule III through V classified remaining drugs from Tylenol to codeine based on two characteristics: their potential for abuse and their utility in medical treatment. The higher the level, the more vigorously its prohibition is enforced.

MORAL CRUSADE
the process by which a particular set of behaviors is constructed as a widespread threat to the public welfare.

CIVIL ASSET FORFEITURE
legal process that allows officials to confiscate any money, houses, vehicles, land or other property that was gained through trafficking in illegal drugs.

Although the "war on drugs" is most commonly associated with the Reagan administration, it was President Nixon who declared drugs to be "public enemy #1" in 1971.[76] One of the central concerns of the Nixon administration was the high level of heroin addiction among returning Vietnam veterans. This era was the only time when there was substantial federal investment in treatment strategies, primarily the use of methadone clinics to treat those with an addiction to heroin. Under the administration of Ronald Reagan most of these treatment dollars were diverted to **interdiction** efforts and law enforcement.[77]

In 1973, the DEA was formed. The DEA is the primary federal agency involved in drug seizures and federal drug busts. It also assists in the development of interdiction and eradication measures. The creation of the DEA signaled a major shift from treatment to a law and order approach. In 1978 the Comprehensive Drug Abuse Prevention and Control Act authorized information about illicit drugs in the United States to be collected through the creation of the main sources of drug use, including the National Household Survey on Drug Abuse (NHSDA) and Monitoring the Future (MTF) surveys of high school students.

During the 1960s and 1970s, the rediscovery of marijuana and other mind-altering drugs by middle-class youth led to a relaxation of criminal penalties known as decriminalization. Between 1973 and 1978 eleven states reclassified marijuana possession as a misdemeanor offense punishable by no more than a small fine. This development ended with the shift in attitude toward zero-tolerance policies of the 1980s and 1990s, assisted by a moral panic and moral crusade associated with the cocaine epidemic.

The Crack Cocaine Epidemic of 1980s

The war on drugs intensified greatly with a modern-day moral panic concerning the use of crack cocaine.[78] During the 1980s, the use of cocaine as a recreational drug rose in popularity. The innovation of crack was to convert the powder form of the drug into smokeable nuggets easily sold in small quantities. This made the cocaine affordable to low-income users at the same time that it opened up a lucrative drug trade. Competing gangs fought openly with guns creating elevated levels of violence on urban streets. Furthermore, cocaine, as an earlier generation had discovered in the era of patent medicines, is highly addictive.

Drug coverage within the television and print media of the problem of cocaine rose dramatically during this decade.[79] In 1986 both *Time* and *Newsweek* featured the problem on the cover of their magazines five times in just one year. In one month that year, the three major news networks ran seventy-four drug stories on their nightly newscasts. Not surprisingly, by the mid-1980s, public opinion polls found that Americans believed drugs to be the number one problem in America.

As is typical of most moral panics, the media's coverage of the so-called epidemic was sensationalized, overblown, and inaccurate. One of the most lurid stories concerned the fate of the so-called crack babies thought to be permanently damaged by fetal exposure to mothers' ingestion of cocaine; these accounts turned out to be wildly overstated, as many of the babies were of low birth weight due to poor maternal nutrition, alcohol consumption, and cigarette smoking rather than maternal use of cocaine. The claim that these babies were permanently damaged was also grossly exaggerated.[80]

The passage of federal drug laws in the 1980s reflects the high levels of concern about the threat of crack cocaine. The Anti-Drug Abuse Act of 1986 created

INTERDICTION
to prohibit through intervention

the 100:1 disparity in penalties for crack versus powder cocaine that made punishment for five grams of crack equal to the punishment for five hundred grams of powder. The Anti-Drug Abuse Act of 1988 also created the Office of National Drug Control Policy; enhanced penalties associated with the sale of drugs anywhere within a hundred feet of a school or playground; and allowed federal, state, and local authorities to deny benefits, including public housing to anyone convicted of a drug offense, including simple possession.[81] Finally, the law created an Asset Forfeiture Fund that legalized seizing of the fruits of criminal activity for federal agencies.

By the end of the decade, both violence of the drug business and levels of cocaine consumption, both crack and powder, had declined; the number of new users dropped, as people came to understand the drugs' addictive potential. Much of the violence associated with the crack epidemic subsided. A combination of aggressive law enforcement and market consolidation helped reduce the level of street violence. By the 1990s, the so-called crack epidemic was over, but the laws and polices passed during the panic remain.

Racial Disparities in Sentencing for Drugs

Many observers point out that minorities, particularly poor minorities, are bearing the cost of punitive drug laws. Although self-report surveys do not show any difference in drug use by race, African Americans are more likely to be arrested for drug use. Minority citizens are subject to higher levels of surveillance through traffic stops, frisks, searches, and seizures than white citizens who reside outside the inner city neighborhoods. Data from 2005 show that even when there is no difference in the rate at which white, black, and Hispanic drivers are stopped on the highway, black and Hispanic drivers are more than twice as likely to be searched by police.[82] In 1980, African Americans constituted 21 percent of all drug arrests; this rose to 36 percent in 1992 before declining to 27 percent in 2015.[83] Racial disparities in arrests translate into racial disparities in sentencing. This is exacerbated by sentencing policies, such as **mandatory minimums** and school zone enhancements, that appear to be race neutral but in practice have a disparate impact on African Americans. Of the more than 200,000 people serving state prison sentences in 2014 on convictions involving drugs, 33 percent were non-Latino white, 33 percent were non-Latino African American, and 7 percent were Latino (note that no race/ethnicity data were available for 20 percent of state prisoners.)[84]

The disparity in federal sentences for crack cocaine and power cocaine passed by Congress at the height of the moral panic of the 1980s is one clear example of a policy that appears race neutral but has had a disparate impact on African Americans. Because 80 percent of those arrested and charged with a crack offense are African Americans, blacks are serving much harsher sentences than whites.[85] In 2010, President Obama signed the Fair Sentencing Act that reduced the sentencing disparity to some extent by raising the threshold for a five-year mandatory minimum sentence from five grams of crack to twenty-eight grams, and for a ten-year sentence from fifty grams to two hundred and eighty grams. The law did not change the threshold for a ten-year mandatory sentence for powder cocaine, however, which remains at 500 grams, a disparity of about 18:1.

Citizens within poor neighborhoods are also those who are most vulnerable to the ravages of drug addiction and the systemic violence associated with the illegal

MANDATORY MINIMUM
the minimum penalty that must be imposed and carried out for all cases convicted of a given offense.

drug business. The scarcity of treatment programs, which have been shown to reduce demand, is most problematic in the poorer communities without resources for private treatment options. While the price tag for the criminal justice system is borne by the general public, the negative unintended consequences of the war falls heaviest on citizens living in the most vulnerable communities. There is also a tendency to ignore the social and economic reasons behind the problems of addiction. The war on drugs is massively expensive: public money invested in law enforcement efforts is therefore not available for many other kinds of public spending on education, health care, and other basic societal needs.

Revising Marijuana Laws

Beginning with the passage of Proposition 215 in California in 1996, many states have passed laws allowing the distribution and use of smoking marijuana for medical purposes. A total of twenty-eight states, the District of Columbia, Guam, and Puerto Rico now allow for comprehensive public medical marijuana and cannabis programs. Seven states and the District of Columbia have adopted more expansive laws legalizing marijuana for recreational use. In November 2016 California, Massachusetts, Maine, and Nevada had public referendums legalizing recreational marijuana for adults over the age of twenty-one.

The Department of Justice continues to enforce the federal law which classifies marijuana as a dangerous illegal substance under the CSA. The priorities of the current federal drug law enforcement as outlined by the DOJ is to prevent the sale and distribution to minors; the trafficking of drugs from states where it is legal to those where it is not legal; the incidence of drugged driving; the use of violence, and firearms in the sale; the use of federal lands or public lands in the growing of the drug; and the diversion of the revenues from the drug to support illegal criminal enterprises.[86]

COLLATERAL CONSEQUENCES OF INCARCERATION

Kemba's punishment of twenty-four and a half years in prison is shocking but even more staggering are the human and social costs associated with these lengthy sentences.[87] In addition to the estimated cost of thirty-one thousand dollars per year to keep locked up in a federal prison, if Kemba had served her full sentence, there would have been many additional financial costs. Who would have raised her little boy? Kemba would have earned nothing during those years in prison to help contribute to the cost of raising her son or for her own future. Nor would she have been able to contribute to the tax base as a productive member of society. When released at age forty-eight, her earning capacity would be severely diminished by her lengthy period of incarceration and her status as an ex-con. It would be very difficult for her to obtain gainful employment and she would likely end up dependent upon some form of public assistance.

For the wider community, there is both the financial loss of a constructive taxpaying member of the workforce during the prime earning years between twenty-four and forty-eight and the added cost of incarceration as a prisoner sits in forced idleness behind bars. Gus and Odessa, two productive and contributing citizens within the community, must also care for their daughter's child. They had been forced to declare bankruptcy to pay for legal fees and Gus had lost his job because of the negative publicity.

Studies estimate that for each person incarcerated, $12,000 worth of economic activity is removed from the local economy: Kemba's incarceration hurts not only her immediate family but also the neighborhood, where she would buy her morning coffee, groceries, have her hair done, hire babysitters, or have her clothes cleaned.[88]

The financial costs are high but we should not neglect to account for the human and social costs of this sentence that impact not only Kemba but also her young son, who will grow up with a mother in prison. In 2015, about 2.7 million American children had at least one parent in prison. Of these children with incarcerated parents, 45 percent were black, 28 percent were white, and 21 percent were Latino.[89] One study found that of black children born in the United States in 1990, 25 percent would have a parent incarcerated by the time they reached fourteen years of age.[90]

What will Kemba's son tell his friends and teachers about his mother as he goes to school and people ask questions? How will he maintain a relationship with her over the long years of separation? Gus and Odessa can look forward to twenty-four years of depressing visits to the federal prison as they struggle to raise their grandson and keep him connected to his incarcerated mother. Like so many parents of incarcerated men and women, Gus and Odessa will not enjoy the sympathy and support of the wider community: having an incarcerated daughter will be a hidden shame they will most likely keep to themselves.

Given all these costs to the taxpayer, to the community, to Kemba's family, and to Kemba herself, what is the justification for this sentence? What does society gain by imposing a sentence of this magnitude for a crime of this nature? What is the rationale that leads the federal government to imprison a young woman for a quarter of a century for playing a small part in a criminal activity of her faithless boyfriend?

The reasoning behind the judge's sentence of Kemba is clearly articulated and rooted in the just deserts philosophy that has dominated sentencing in the past twenty years. The judge stated that the sole benefit of her incarceration was to send a message to other young girls not to trust men like Peter Michael Hall. The prosecutor in asking for the sentence had a different rationale: drug dealing was bad and the source of much harm and suffering in the community. Kemba chose to support the man she loved despite the knowledge of his activities. She chose to lie to federal investigators on several occasions. The sentence is an act of retribution: you do the crime, you do the time.

The mid-1970s saw a shift away from rehabilitation as a justification for punishment toward the "just deserts" philosophy of punishment that prioritized the twin goals of retribution and deterrence over the previously dominant philosophy of rehabilitation. In the next chapter on prisons, we will explain why there is such a strong association between rehabilitation and prisons such that most states call their penal system the Department of Corrections rather than the Department of Punishment. For most of the twentieth century, the goal of rehabilitation was an ideal for correctional professionals and systems.

Let us return to the question of the purpose of punishment. Kemba Smith was imprisoned so that others will learn from her mistake. We feel morally justified in using her in this way because she voluntarily chose to break the law and harm others through her conduct. To an extent, therefore, she "deserves" to suffer. There is no need to incapacitate Kemba—no one believes that she will resume involvement in the drug business since her involvement depended upon the romantic link to her boyfriend. There is no public safety rationale for locking her up.

368 \ PART V • Punishment and Social Inequality

If we were to prioritize one of the other five goals of sentencing, it is easy to imagine a different kind of sentence for Kemba Smith. The goal of rehabilitation would stress the need to understand what drove Kemba to this behavior. Many of the women who find themselves in positions like Kemba are drug addicted. An alternative sentence based on the goal of rehabilitation would be to offer them treatment for their addiction. In Kemba's case, she did receive counseling inside of prison to address issues of low self-esteem and gender inequality, which contributed to her willingness to remain in an abusive relationship. Upon her release, Kemba has devoted herself to speaking out to young women about the dangers of "standing by" men who are violent and abusive.

If we shift our attention to the goal of restitution, we need to ask many serious questions about the genuine victims of the crime of drug trafficking. According to the prosecution, the real victims in this case are the people in the neighborhoods where drug use is rampant. They are the ones whose children become addicted, streets riddled with violence, homes robbed by addicts, and whose parks are littered with discarded needles.

But is the community served by the punishment of Kemba Smith? In the "war on drugs," the "collateral" damages fall heavily on the victims themselves. These are also communities whose sons and daughters are going to jail for long periods of time, leaving young children in the care of grandparents draining the community of its valuable human resources.

If the community is the genuine victim, can we imagine alternative sentences where Kemba could be required to serve the community and help to undo some of the harm she had a part in creating? In the final chapter of this book we will return to an examination of alternative sentencing and the use of innovations such as drug courts that are beginning to slow down the rate of incarceration, particularly for drug offenses. Before we look at these community-based responses to crime, we must first take a closer look at the institution of the prison and try to gain some understanding of the place Kemba nearly spent twenty-four years of her life in.

PUTTING INCARCERATION IN A SOCIAL, POLITICAL, AND RACIAL CONTEXT

Before we turn to an examination of prisons themselves, it is useful to put our growing reliance on incarceration in context. If you recall the discussion of Jim Crow laws in chapter 3, you will recall that some scholars argue that our criminal justice system has been used to perpetuate a system of racism. The Thirteenth Amendment to the Constitution, which banned the institution of "involuntary servitude" retained criminalization as the one legal exception. As long as people of color comprise a disproportionate percent of those incarcerated, the claim can be made that prisons are little more than a modern-day system of slavery.

PRISON INDUSTRIAL COMPLEX
a web of government and industry interests that profit or otherwise benefit from the perpetuation of surveillance, policing, and incarceration.

Another charge brought against our system of incarceration is found in the term "**Prison Industrial Complex**." Like the Military Industrial Complex of the 1950s, the Prison Industrial Complex is seen as a web of government and industry interests that profit or otherwise benefit from the perpetuation of surveillance, policing, and incarceration. Private prisons, which are discussed in the next chapter, are a prime example of the way in which profit can be made by feeding and housing a never-ending supply of bodies. Whether either of these arguments fully explains our excessive reliance on imprisonment, it is important for us to consider the evidence in support of these propositions. It is also important to raise questions about the legitimacy and effectiveness of a system that is widely seen as racist and unfair.

---

sentencing guidelines (p. 350)   a standardized set of penalty options based on key characteristics of the offense and offender.

collateral consequences (p. 351)   the outcome of an action that is neither planned nor anticipated.

retribution (p. 351)   a sentencing philosophy that prioritizes punishment commensurate to the seriousness of the offense.

incapacitation (p. 351)   the elimination of the capacity to commit future crimes within society usually through incarceration.

deterrence (p. 351)   the imposition of punishment in order to discourage the commission of future crimes by the offender and others within society.

rehabilitation (p. 351)   the process of changing the attitudes and behavior of the offender through training, education, treatment, or vocational programming to produce law-abiding conduct in the future.

restitution (p. 351)   the obligation on the part of the offender to repay the victim or the community with money services or symbolic gestures commensurate with the harm caused.

specific deterrence (p. 353)   the imposition of punishment to discourage the individual from committing crimes in the future. Also known as special or individual deterrence.

general deterrence (p. 353)   the imposition of punishment in order to set an example to others contemplating crime.

judicial model of sentencing (p. 356)   sentencing decisions that rely upon the broad discretion of the judge to craft the individual sentence within parameters set by statute.

pre-sentence investigation/report (p. 356)   an investigation and summary report of the background of a convicted offender prepared to help the judge decide on an appropriate sentence for the individual.

administrative model of sentencing (p. 357)   the use of parole boards, wardens, and other correctional officials to determine when an offender is to be granted conditional release from incarceration.

legislative model of sentencing (p. 357)   the setting of mandatory sentences for specific crimes established within criminal statutes passed by legislative bodies.

executive clemency (p. 357)   the power to pardon (forgive) a criminal conviction or commute a sentence, held by the chief executive officer.

determinate sentencing (p. 357)   the imposition of a fixed or set amount of time in prison.

indeterminate sentencing (p. 357)   the imposition of an unspecified amount of time in prison somewhere between a statutory minimum and maximum term.

sentencing disparities (p. 358)   the imposition of widely different sentences for offenders convicted of the same offense.

truth in sentencing laws (p. 358)   statutes which require that most or all of the sentence be actually served.

bifurcated trial (p. 359)   the constitutional requirement that the imposition of the death penalty be subject to a separate hearing after the adjudication of guilt or innocence has taken place.

guided discretion statutes (p. 359)   capital statutes which specify the mitigating and aggravating circumstances juries should consider in the penalty phase of the capital trial.

aggravating circumstances (p. 360)   facts about the heinous nature of the criminal act specified by law that guide a jury decision to apply the death penalty.

mitigating circumstances (p. 360)   facts about the offender and circumstances of the crime specified by law that guide a jury decision to apply the death penalty

brutalization effect (p. 360)   the theory that capital punishment contributes to greater violence within society by increasing the tolerance for violence within society.

DNA testing (p. 361)   a broad field of science that has begun to offer reliable evidence to exonerate a growing number of convicted individuals serving prison sentences including a number who are on death row.

Moral crusade (p. 363)   the process by which a particular set of behaviors is constructed as a widespread threat to the public welfare.

Civil asset forfeiture (p. 363)   legal process that allows officials to confiscate any money, houses, vehicles, land or other property that was gained through trafficking in illegal drugs.

Interdiction (p. 364)   to prohibit through intervention.

mandatory minimum (p. 365)   the minimum penalty that must be imposed and carried out for all cases convicted of a given offense.

Prison Industrial Complex (p. 368)   a web of government and industry interests that profit or otherwise benefit from the perpetuation of surveillance, policing, and incarceration.

REVIEW AND STUDY QUESTIONS

1. Identify and describe the five goals of sentencing. What is the common phrase that expresses each goal of sentencing?

2. Explain the difference between general and specific deterrence. How does the goal of restitution differ from the goal of rehabilitation?

3. Describe the three central models of sentencing. Identify which goal of sentencing is associated with each model. Identify who holds discretionary power in each model.

4. Contrast determinate sentencing and indeterminate sentencing. Which goals are associated with each form of sentencing and why?

5. What is sentencing disparity? Explain liberal and conservative positions against indeterminate sentencing.

6. Identify at least three ways that judicial discretion has been limited through sentencing reforms. How does each reform limit judicial discretion?

7. What were the impacts of *Furman v. Georgia* and *Greggs v. Georgia* on the constitutionality of capital punishment? Describe the bifurcated trial and guided discretion statutes.

8. Identify changes in the rate and use of incarceration from 1970 to 2000. How have these changes impacted African American and Hispanic males?

9. Explain the change in U.S. sentencing policy for drug offenses within the past twenty years. What is the 100:1 ratio? How have these changes impacted minorities and women?

10. Explain the rationale for Kemba Smith's sentence under the federal sentencing guidelines. Describe the collateral damages this form of justice could have on the minority community.

CHECK IT OUT

Websites

United States Sentencing Commissions, http://www.ussc.gov. Check out sentencing guidelines, statistics, and more.

The Sentencing Project, http://www.sentencing-project.org. Check out this web site to access statistics on sentencing and race; and to learn about alternative sentencing programs across the nation.

Gallup Poll, http://www.pollingreport.com. Check out the latest public opinion polls on public views on the death penalty drug policy, and mandatory sentencing. Find out what the American public feels today and how opinions are changing toward sentencing and punishment.

Death Penalty Information Center (DPIC), http://www.deathpenaltyinfo.org. This site is an award-winning site, which provides a wealth of information on the death penalty, including up-to-date statistics on executions, state by state, including those which are scheduled to take place; the history of the death penalty; issues of race; public opinion; women; and mental retardation. Click on the DPIC Quiz and test your own knowledge about the facts of the death penalty.

Videos

Crime Seen: Advances in DNA Testing—26 minutes. After being identified in a lineup, Edward Honaker was convicted and sent to prison for rape. Ten years later, he was exonerated through advances in DNA analysis. This video spotlights the advances in DNA testing and explores the issue of wrongful convictions based on eyewitness identification. Available from Films for the Humanities and Sciences at www.films.com

Judgment At Midnight—47 minutes. ABC takes the viewer inside death row and the mind of the condemned and his executioners as the film follows the final preparation and execution of convicted murderer Antonio James. It chronicles the experience and feelings of his victims as well as his own family and explores the feelings of the warden responsible for carrying out the task of execution. Available at: https://vimeo.com/86677969

How Executions Go Wrong—2 and 16 minutes. CNN looks at forms of execution used in United States and how they can go wrong. http://www.cnn.com/videos/justice/2015/08/12/death-penalty-execution-methods-orig-mg.cnn

Movies

Dead Man Walking (1995). Based upon a true story, Sister Helen Prejean establishes a special relationship with a prisoner on death row in Louisiana, acting as his spiritual adviser after carrying on correspondence with him.

NOTES

[1] Reginald Stuart, "Kemba's Nightmare," *Emerge* 7(7) (May, 1996), 28–48; Libby Copeland, "Kemba Smith's Hard Time," *The Washington Post* (February 13, 2000), F-1.

[2] Stuart, Kemba's Nightmare, 45.

[3] Stuart, Kemba's Nightmare, 48.

[4] Stuart, Kemba's Nightmare, 32.

[5] Stuart, Kemba's Nightmare, 34–35.

[6] Stuart, Kemba's Nightmare, 38.

[7] Stuart, Kemba's Nightmare, 42.

[8] Libby Copeland, "Kemba Smith's Hard Time," *The Washington Post* (February 13, 2000), F–10.

[9] Mark Morris, "Pardoned Woman Backs Drug Law Change," *The Kansas City Star* (April 20, 2001), B2.

[10] Reginald Stuart, "Kemba's Nightmare," *Emerge* 7(7) (May, 1996), 46.

[11] Anthony Lewis, "Abroad at Home; A Christmas Carol," *The New York Times* (December 23, 2000), A-19.

[12] Reginald Stuart, "Kemba's Nightmare," *Emerge* 7(7) (May, 1996), 48.

[13] Stuart, Kemba's Nightmare, p. 46.

[14] Reginald Stuart, "Kemba's Nightmare II: Justice Denied," *Emerge*, 9(7) (May, 1998), 43.

[15] Stuart, Kemba's Nightmare II, p. 46.

[16] Betsy Peoples, "Advocates Fight a War on Drug Sentencing," *Emerge*, 9(7) (May, 1998), 50.

[17] Reginald Stuart, "Kemba's Nightmare," *Emerge* 7(7) (May, 1996), 48.

[18] Libby Copeland, "Kemba Smith's Hard Time," *The Washington Post* (February 13, 2000), F-1.

[19] Tom Campbell, "Kemba Smith's Appeal Dismissed," *Times-Dispatch* (August 20, 2012).

[20] Rhonda Chriss Lokeman, "When Smart Women Make Foolish Choices," *Kansas City Star* (April 22, 2001), B9.

[21] E.R. Shipp, "Gone Too Far For Too Long," *Daily News* (January 28, 2001), 33.

[22] Robert James, ed., *Winston S. Churchill: His Complete Speeches, 1897–1903* (New York: Chelsea House Publishers, 1974), 1598.

[23] David Garland, *Punishment and Modern Society: A Study in Social Theory* (Chicago: University of Chicago Press, 1990).

[24] Andrew von Hirsch, *Doing Justice: The Choice of Punishments* (New York: Hill and Wang, 1976).

[25] Jacqueline Cohen, "Incapacitation as a Strategy for Crime Control: Possibilities and Pitfalls" in *Crime and Justice: An Annual Review of Research*, eds. Michael Tonry and Norval Morris, (Chicago: University of Chicago Press, 1983), 1–84.

[26] Hugo Adam Bedau, "Retributivism and the Theory of Punishment," *Journal of Philosophy* 75 (1978), 601–620.

[27] Cesare Beccaria, trans., Edward D. Ingraham, *On Crimes and Punishment* (Philadelphia: Philip N. Nicklin, 1819); Jeremy Bentham, *An Introduction to the Principles of Morals and Legislation* (New York: Hafner, 1948).

[28] Karl Menninger, *The Crime of Punishment* (New York: AuthorHouse, 1968).

[29] David Garland, *Punishment and Welfare: A History of Penal Strategies* (UK: Aldershot, 1985).

[30] Stephen Schafter, *Victimology: The Victim and his Criminal* (Virginia: Reston 1977), 5–15.

[31] Schafter, *Victimology*, 8.

[32] Schafter, *Victimology*, 12.

[33] Daniel W. Van Ness, *Crime and Its Victims* (Downers Grove, IL: InterVarsity Press, 1986), 64–66.

[34] William Andrews, *Old Time Punishments* (London: Tabard Press, 1890).

[35] Joan Petersilia, *Expanding Options for Criminal Sentencing* (Santa Monica, CA: Rand, 1987).

[36] Death Penalty Information Center, *Facts about the Death Penalty* (Washington, DC: 2017). http://www.deathpenaltyinfo.org/documents/FactSheet.pdf; retrieved January 28, 2017.

[37] Michael Ignatieff, *A Just Measure of Pain: The Penitentiary in the Industrial Revolution* (London, UK: Peregrine, 1978).

[38] Pieter Spierenburg, *The Spectacle of Suffering* (Cambridge, UK: Cambridge University Press, 1984).

[39] Lauren E. Glaze and Danielle Kaeble, *Correctional Populations in the United States, 2013* (Washington, DC: U.S. Bureau of Justice Statistics, December 2014).

[40] Glaze and Kaeble, *Correctional Populations*.

[41] Doris Layton Mackenzie and Eugene E. Hebert, eds., *Correctional Boot Camps: A Tough Intermediate Sanction* (Washington, DC: U.S. Department of Justice, 1996).

[42] Michael H. Tonry, "Sentencing," *Encyclopedia of Crime and Justice,* Sanford Kadish, ed. (New York: Free Press, 1983).

[43] Anthony Walsh, "The Role of the Probation Officer in the Sentencing Process: Independent Professional or Judicial Hack?," *Criminal Justice and Behavior* 12 (1985), 289–303.

[44] Charles E. Frazier and E. Wilbur Bock, "Effects of Court Officials on Sentence Severity," *Criminology* 20 (1982), 257–272.

[45] Robert M. Carter and Leslie T. Wilkins, "Some Factors in Sentencing Policy," *Journal of Criminal Law, Criminology and Police Science* 58 (1967), 503–514.

[46] Sandra Shane Du-Bow, Alice P. Brown and Erik Olsen, *Sentencing Reform in the United States: History, Content, and Effect* (Washington, DC: National Institute of Justice, 1985).

[47] Amnesty International, "The Death Penalty: list of Abolitionist and Retentionist Countries" February, 1999. http://www.amnesty.org/ailib/intcam/dp/abrelist.htm

[48] Death Penalty Information Center, *Facts about the Death Penalty* (Washington, DC: 2017). http://www.deathpenaltyinfo.org/documents/FactSheet.pdf; retrieved January 28, 2017.

[49] 408 U.S. 238 (1972).

[50] 96 S. Ct. 2726 1972.

[51] Tracy L. Snell, "Table 17. Number of persons executed by jurisdiction, 1930–2009," *Capital Punishment 2009* (Washington, DC: Bureau of Justice Statistics, December 2010).

[52] Tracy L. Snell, "Persons Under Sentence of Death, by Sex, Race, and Hispanic Origin, December 31, 2009," *Capital Punishment, 2009* (Washington, DC: Bureau of Justice Statistics, December 2010).

[53] William J. Bowers, "The Effect of Executions is Brutalization, Not Deterrence" in *Capital Punishment: Legal and Social Science Approaches*, eds. Kenneth C. Hess and James A. Inciardi (Newbury Park, CA: Sage, 1988).

[54] Tracy L. Snell, "Prisoners Under Sentence of Death, by Region, Jurisdiction, and Race, 2008 and 2009," *Capital Punishment 2009* (Washington, DC: Department of Justice, December 2010).

[55] NAACP Legal Defense, *Death Row, USA* (New York: National Association for the Advancement of Colored People, 2012).

[56] Stephen B. Bright, "Counsel for the Poor: The Death Sentence Not for the Worst Crime but for the Worst Lawyer," *Yale Law Journal* 103 (1994), 1835.

[57] David Baldus, Charles Pulaski, and G. Woodworth, *Equal Justice and the Death Penalty* (Boston: Northeastern University Press, 1990).

[58] Campaign To End the Death Penalty, "Five Reasons to Oppose the Death Penalty," http://www.nodeathpenalty.org/get-the-facts/five-reasons-oppose-death-penalty

[59] Deborah Fins, "A Quarterly Report by the Criminal Justice Project of the NAACP Legal Defense and Educational Fund," *Death Row, U.S.A.* (Spring 2012).

[60] *McCleskey v. Kemp*, 481 U.S. 279 (1987).

[61] Henry Weinstein, "Death Penalty Moratorium Attracting Unlikely Adherents," *Los Angeles Times* (October 17, 2000), A-5.

[62] Michael L. Radelet, Hugo Adam Bedau and Constance E. Putnam, *In Spite of Innocence: Erroneous Convictions in Capital Cases* (Boston, MA: Northeastern University Press, 1992).

[63] Robert Tanner, "States are Slow to Grant DNA Testing to People Seeking to Prove Innocence," *St. Louis Post-Dispatch* (June 22, 2000), A10.

[64] Albert Camus, trans. Justin O'Brien, *Resistance, Rebellion and Death* (New York: Vintage Books, 1974), 199.

[65] Hugo Adam Bedau, *The Death Penalty in America* (New York: Oxford University Press, 1982).

[66] Oliphant, Baxter, *Support for the Death Penalty Lowest in More than Four Decades*, (Pew Research Center: September 29, 2016). http://www.pewresearch.org/fact-tank/2016/09/29/support-for-death-penalty-lowest-in-more-than-four-decades/; retrieved January 28, 2017.

[67] Sister Helen Prejean, *Dead Man Walking: An Eyewitness Account of the Death Penalty in the United States* (New York: Vintage Books, 1994).

[68] William J. Bowers, "Capital Punishment and Contemporary Values: People's Misgivings and the Courts Misperceptions," *Law and Society Review* 27 (1993).

[69] David Musto, *The American Disease: Origins of Narcotic Control* (New York: Oxford University Press, 1987).

[70] Musto, *The American Disease*, 4–5.

[71] Musto, *The American Disease*, 219–221.

[72] Howard Becker, *Outsiders* (New York: Free Press, 1963.).

[73] Matthew B. Robinson and Renee G. Scherlen, *Lies, Damned Lies, and Drug War Statistics: A Critical Analysis of Claims Made by the Office of National Drug Control Policy* State (New York: University of New York Press, 2010), 426–435.

[74] Matthew B. Robinson and Renee G. Scherlen, *Lies, Damned Lies, and Drug War Statistics: A Critical Analysis of Claims Made by the Office of National Drug Control Policy* State (New York: University of New York Press, 2010), 332–340.

[75] "Office of Diversion Control: Drug Enforcement Administration," *U.S. Department of Justice* accessed September 26, 2012 http://www.deadiversion.usdoj.gov/schedules/index.html.

[76] Matthew B. Robinson and Renee G. Scherlen, *Lies, Damned Lies, and Drug War Statistics: A Critical Analysis of Claims Made by the Office of National Drug Control Policy* State (New York: University of New York Press, 2010), 749–752.

[77] Peter Kraska, "The Unmentionable Alternative: The Need For and the Argument Against Decriminalization of Drug Laws," in *Drugs, Crime and the Criminal Justice System*, ed. R. Weisheit (Cincinnati: Anderson, 1990), 117.

[78] C. Reinarman, "Crack Attack: America's Latest Drug Scare," in *Typifying Contemporary Social Problems*, ed. J. Best (New York: Aldine de Gruyter, 1995).

[79] S. Belenko, *Crack and the Evolution of the Anti-Drug Policy* (Westport, CT: Greenwood Press, 1993), 9.

[80] Susan Okie, "The Epidemic that Wasn't," *New York Times*, January 26, 2009, D1.

[81] Matthew B. Robinson and Renee G. Scherlen, *Lies, Damned Lies, and Drug War Statistics: A Critical Analysis of Claims Made by the Office of National Drug Control Policy State* (New York: University of New York Press, 2010), 802–806.

[82] M. Durose, R. Smith and P. Lanagan, *Contacts Between Police and the Public, 2005* (Washington, DC: Bureau of Justice Statistics, 2005).

[83] Crime in the United States, 2015. (Washington, DC: U.S. Department of Justice, 2016) Appendix Table 43.

[84] E. Ann Carson, PhD, and Elizabeth Anderson. *Prisoners In 2015*. (Washington, DC: US Dept of Justice Bureau of Justice Statistics, Dec. 2016) Appendix Table 5.

[85] Marc Mauer, "Addressing Racial Disparities in Incarceration," *The Prison Journal* 91 (August 25, 2011), 95.

[86] James Cole. "Guidance Regarding Marijuana Enforcement." *Memorandum for all U.S. Attorneys.* (August, 29, 2013). https://www.justice.gov/iso/opa/resources/3052013829132756857467.pdf

[87] Dina Rose and Todd Clear, "Incarceration, Social Capital and Crime: Implications for Social Disorganization Theory," *Criminology* 36 (1998).

[88] Todd Clear, *Imprisoning Communities: How Mass Incarceration Makes Poor Neighborhoods Worse* (New York: Oxford University Press, 2007).

[89] Sarah D. Sparks, *Parents' Incarceration Takes Toll on Children, Studies Say*, Education Week (February 24, 2017). http://www.edweek.org/ew/articles/2015/02/25/parents-incarceration-takes-toll-on-children-studies.html; retrieved January 28, 2017.

[90] Sara Wakefield and Christopher Wildeman, *Children of the Prison Boom: Mass Incarceration and the Future of American Inequality* (New York: Oxford University Press, 2013).

In this chapter we read the case of one individual who spent twenty years in prison for a crime he didn't commit. The case illustrates both the conditions inside our prison system and the challenging process for correcting a wrong. The chapter discusses the history and goals of incarceration, life behind bars, including time spent in isolation, as well as issues unique to women in prison.

LEARNING OBJECTIVES

After reading this chapter you should be able to:

- Recognize the origins of and goals of the penitentiary, explain why the penitentiary differed from earlier forms of punishment, and contrast the penitentiary with the later reformatory movement.
- Identify and describe different types of penal institutions within modern correctional systems.
- Define the concept of a "total institution" and give an example of a "status degradation ceremony" within the institution.
- Describe the "pains of imprisonment."
- Contrast the "importation" and "deprivation" theory of inmate subcultures.
- Identify the status of prisoners' rights within the institution.
- Name the key dilemmas facing correctional administrators today in the areas of health care, incarceration of women, and prison violence.

Case #14: Surviving Time: The Case of Rubin "Hurricane" Carter

A mature Rubin Carter speaking to an audience about the problem of wrongful convictions. After being released from prison, Carter headed the Association in Defense of the Wrongly Convicted for twelve years and founded Innocence International in 2004. (Getty Images)

Rubin "Hurricane" Carter spent almost twenty years of his life serving time for a crime he did not commit. In 1967 he was found guilty of a triple homicide. The conviction was overturned in 1976 but he was retried and convicted again in 1977. This conviction was overturned by a federal court in 1988 and Rubin Carter was finally released from the New Jersey state prison system.[1]

A Young Fighter Is Born

As a young boy, Rubin Carter was no angel. A severe speech impediment that impaired his ability to communicate led Carter to use his fists instead of speech. By the age of eleven Rubin had been booted out of school and was sent to a disciplinary school, where his fellow schoolmates placed high value on his willingness to use his fists.[2]

Rubin Carter's trouble with the law also began at an early age, when he was running with a gang of youth controlling their precious few blocks of neighborhood from other gangs just like themselves. Responding to a dare, Carter led a parade of young thieves on a swooping raid on an outdoor clothing vendor. Swift of feet, Carter would never have been caught if it weren't for the stern reaction of his God-fearing and law-abiding father, who found the stolen clothes, beat him soundly, and carted him down to the local police station. This

was the first time Carter was alone in an interrogation room with white police officers. Carter, as usual, was silent, and for this, he received a beating from a tough white cop who would have it in for him for the rest of his life.[3]

Carter was sentenced to probation for the theft, but the justice system was not so lenient the second time he came before a judge; this time on a charge of assaulting and cutting a prominent white man, who had the habit of preying on young boys deep in the woods. The judge spared no words in his disgust for Carter: "I only wish you were older so I could send you to State Prison . . . where they have cages for animals like you."[4] At the age of eleven, Carter was sentenced to Jamesburg State Home for Boys until the age of twenty-one.

The World of the Reformatory[5]

The Jamesburg State Home for Boys was nestled in the rural landscape of southern New Jersey far from the dense city streets of places like Paterson and Newark. It resembled a tranquil college campus with its three-story red-brick buildings arranged in cottages around a bucolic green parade ground. Each residential "cottage," eight in all, housed about fifty to sixty boys, who slept in a dormitory on the second floor; the basement housed the recreation room and showers while the third floor was reserved for the couple known as the cottage "mother" and "father." The Jamesburg Home for Boys had been built in the era of the reformatory when the hope was to provide a wholesome and family-like environment for wayward delinquents. The "cottage" system with its homey architecture reflected this lofty aspiration. But when young Carter arrived, he soon discovered the reality behind the red-brick facade of the Jamesburg State Home for Boys.

The juvenile system lumped all kinds of juvenile offenders together: some were there for truancy while others had robbed, raped, and killed. Whites and blacks were segregated into separate cottages, with boys as young as age eight thrown in with maturing young men of seventeen, eighteen, and older. The "reformatory" operated on a mixture of military-style discipline and viciously delegated authority in which the older boys in the cottage controlled the younger boys through sheer brutality and perverse forms of enslavement and domination. The cottage "father" and "mother" had little to do with the discipline inside the cottage. They were local white residents who despised their urban charges and kept them in line through the liberal use of blackjacks.

But the staff preferred not to discipline the boys at all. Instead, they appointed two line sergeants chosen from among the inmates—generally the toughest and most aggressive among the inmates—to keep discipline among the boys. These head boys, in turn, appointed their own lieutenants relying upon fear, humiliation, and violence to keep others in line. It was a pecking order of the most vicious kind. At the bottom were the youngest and the most vulnerable, who were forced to serve as "wives" or sexual servants on a relentless nightly tour of routinized gang rape.

The reformatory made little attempt to "reform" inmates. The inmates cleaned their own cottages, performed chores for the institution, and were contracted out as cheap labor to local farmers. The line "sergeants" within each cottage put the other boys to work—watching as they scrubbed the floors or cleaned the toilets. If someone faltered, brutal violence kept them at the task. Fear ran the social system of the cottage, as it ran the wider institution. And when someone really stepped out of line, there was always the hole: a small isolated building deep in the woods: sixteen cells with nothing inside but a hard cement floor. Carter whose explosive temper and willingness to fight soon made him top dog in the world of the cottage also led him into many confrontations with the white staff. Carter

spent many days and nights alone in those stinking isolation cells.

Escaping the System

At the age of seventeen, the warden made Carter a sudden and surprising offer. With three years left until his twenty-first birthday, the warden offered to reduce his time at Jamesburg to three short months provided Carter stayed completely out of trouble during that period.[6] If he got a single disciplinary report, even for failing to tie his shoelaces properly, he would be shipped out to a harsher institution, Annandale, whose reputation was even worse than Jamesburg. "Why would you do this?" Carter asked. The reason, the warden explained, was that he could see Carter was getting too used to the vicious world of the reformatory. Soon it would be too late for Carter. This was his one last chance to be free from the kind of "reform" that really took place within the state system for wayward boys.

Carter completed his three months with a perfect record but on the last day, of the last week, of the third month, while the warden was away for the day, his second in command, who disapproved of the warden's decision to release Carter, issued a disciplinary report for Carter's use of bad language to a cottage supervisor.[7] The report wasn't true but it wouldn't matter: the power was all in the hands of the system. Carter was helpless.

He decided the only thing in his power was to run. At the age of seventeen Carter escaped from the Jamesburg State home and ran home to Paterson, New Jersey, where his family hid him from the police and shipped him off to Philadelphia where he enlisted in the paratroopers and was sent to Fort Jackson to train for combat in the Korean War. It was in the military that Carter discovered a constructive use for his pugilistic gifts. By the time he was discharged from the army in 1956, he had won the European Welterweight Champion title and returned to Paterson, New Jersey, a prizefighter and a champion.[8]

Back Inside

Carter's dreams of launching his professional career were put on hold, when he was immediately arrested for the escape from Jamesburg and sentenced to Annandale Reformatory for ten months as punishment.[9] Annandale made Jamesburg look like Sunday school.[10] This was where they sent the really tough juveniles. Annandale functioned more like a penitentiary than Jamesburg did. On the first day, Rubin, a proud ex-serviceman and prizefighter, at age twenty-one, had his head shaved, was told to strip, and put on prison garb that consisted of short pants. In Rubin's memoir he said, "These [short pants], like the shave they gave your head when you entered the place, were designed to strip away your manhood and make you feel like a kid again, to wipe out whatever remained of your personal identity."[11] Rubin tried to resist wearing those clothes and landed in the Graveyard, the prison that exists within all prisons where the difficult prisoners go.

Ten months later Carter was released from Annandale:

> Finally my day came—that bright, beautiful morning when it was time for me to go home. A brutal, ugly year of wasted energy had gone out of my life. Ten long worthless months of bitter frustration had blown everything I had achieved, and had tickled my old animosity back to life. On that Tuesday morning when Annandale set me free, they might not have known it . . . but they had just unleashed a walking, ticking, short-fused time bomb set to explode on contact with an unsuspecting public. A society that fooled itself into believing that this miniature penitentiary sitting in the hills of its community was really an honest-to-God rehabilitation center.[12]

Within five weeks of his release, Carter, in an act of pure aggression, snatched the purse of an elderly black woman passing by him early one evening.[13] Not for money, just for fun. He ran down the street laughing, assaulting another man, and then another, both of them black. The crimes didn't make any sense: Carter had a good job working for a plastics manufacturer, plenty of money in his pockets, and he had his freedom. He hated whites and the justice system which had just locked him up for ten months, but he had nothing against these innocent black folks just minding their own business. Carter's actions were irrational.

It was only a matter of time before the Paterson police arrested Carter for the crimes witnessed by many who knew Carter. In the eyes of the police, these crimes confirmed what they had believed about Carter since he was eleven years old: Rubin Carter was a good for nothing "nigger punk" who was destined, sooner or later, to be locked up for the rest of his life. Carter pled guilty to the charges of assault and robbery. This time he was spared the niceties of the youth reformatory system and sent straight to Trenton State Prison.

Up to the Big House

Trenton State Prison was built in 1836 by famed British architect John Haviland, who adorned the building with pink limestone and Egyptian symbols.[14] The Quaker vision for the penitentiary was a place of redemption and monk-like prayer and industry. The cells were designed for prisoners to live in contemplative isolation alone with their Bible and individual piecework. In the oldest part of the Trenton Prison, the original cells had oak doors purposely set low so that upon entering the cell each prisoner was forced to bow his head in penance. Inside the cell, the Quakers believed that genuine reform would take place as each prisoner was kept away from the corrupting influences of temptation and was able to commune with God and their own soul.

But the dream was an illusion. Oak doors quickly gave way to iron cages built in rows or tiers so a few guards could keep watch on the hundreds of imprisoned bodies.[15] The prison was organized around a huge and dusty yard ringed by razor wire and surrounded by towers with armed guards looking down. The vision that inspired the Quakers had little in common with the giant maze of human warehouses.

In one corner of the yard, right next to the hospital was the Death House, a one-story cement block building that held the electric chair and all those sentenced to end their life there.[16] Designed to hold nineteen men, two tiers of cells ran along one side of the building. The "last mile" to the dark green door led to the execution chamber itself: a windowless room with three or four wooden benches for spectators to witness the act. A waist-high barrier separated onlookers from the chair itself sitting in the middle of the room elevated on a platform in all its grisly splendor.

A constant cacophony of sound surrounded life inside the prison: shrill bells, cell counts, whistles, the clanking of steel gates, the plumbing of hundreds of sinks and toilets flushing, and the noisy locking contraptions of steel grating upon steel. The ancient building of stone and brick heated up like an oven in the summer: the smallest cells were only seven and a half feet long and four or four and a half feet wide and seven feet high. The largest cells were less than twice that size and held up to four occupants.[17]

According to the handbook for inmates, each inmate was required to walk in line as they moved at the sound of the bell from the mess hall to the industrial shop. They were to "maintain good posture with their face held forward." [18] Stepping out of line was a violation of the rules and grounds for a disciplinary report. The prison routine was regulated by bells: six o'clock sharp was the morning bell; another bell for inmates to be at their jobs making license plates or sewing clothes, or lying idle in their cells; another bell to be back for a count.

Working in the tag shop making license plates, an inmate could earn about eleven cents a day. After a month or so they might earn enough money to buy some candy, cigarettes, razor blades, or bars of soap from the commissary. These items were the currency of life inside prison. Traded and labored for, these luxuries acquired value of enormous proportion among the inmates. Cigarettes, soap, toilet paper, books, lights, food, newspapers, visits—the minutia of life outside the prison, became the all-important focus of everyday life inside. And the all-powerful prison authorities held the absolute prerogative to take away these amenities for any reason at any time.

The dark economy of prison life operated through a violent sexual hierarchy among the inmates. The real currency of the prison involved the trade of petty privileges, toiletries, personal grudges, and sexual favors. The prison administration relied upon this system to control the inmates, allowing the tough to prey upon the weak knowing that at least it kept the men occupied. The shower house was an open building with fifty stalls. Inside the cell, inmates were given a bucket for washing themselves and herded into the shower house every few days. There the guard on duty would calmly smoke a cigarette willfully oblivious to the violence happening among the men. "Everyday . . . some poor unsuspecting fool would get ripped off in the dense clouds of concealing steam. He would be stabbed in his back, then humped in his backside while the shower cop had his smoke, butt pressed against the wall and his senses shut off from the anguished cries."[19]

During this period in prison, Carter made a decision about his life. Fighting was all he knew how to do and all he was good at. He didn't want to die in prison like so many around him. He knew his temper and rage would lead him back to prison along with many of the boys he grew up with. Already familiar faces from the gangs of his youth showed up at Trenton State Prison and a few of Carter's old pals from Jamesburg were already entombed in the Death House waiting to be executed. Carter made a decision to focus all his energies on building the physical and mental capacity to get out of prison and become a professional prizefighter.

A Dream Pursued and Lost

On September 1961, after four years and two months, Rubin Carter was released from prison ready to make good on his dream to join the world of boxing. Within a year he had acquired the nickname "Hurricane": an unstoppable force of nature inside the rink. By the end of 1963, Carter was a contender for the U.S. middleweight championship. A successful Carter married, bought a house in Paterson, and began a family.[20]

On the night of June 17, 1966, two armed black men entered an all-white bar room and opened fire on the patrons killing three and wounding one more. The shooting was believed to have been in retaliation for an earlier shooting death of a black bar owner by a white gunman. When Rubin "Hurricane" Carter was picked up for questioning late that same night, he was a celebrity earning 100,000 dollars a year. But to the Paterson police officers who arrested him and interrogated him in the same windowless room he had sat in at age eleven, Rubin Carter was the same punk they had sent off to prison three times before. Carter's nemesis, Lieutenant DeSimone, was placed in charge of the investigation.

Released after questioning, Carter went off to fight a match in Argentina. When he returned, he was arrested and charged with the murder. Two eyewitnesses had come forward to testify that it was Carter and a young man with him in the car, John Artis, who had walked into the bar and opened fire on three white patrons. At the trial, the testimony of these eyewitnesses, obtained through a plea agreement engineered by DeSimone, convicted Carter and the twenty-year-old passenger in his car. Later, the veracity of these eyewitnesses, their motives for deciding to come forward, and the shady role played by the police investigators would be grounds for appeal.[21] The judge noting Carter's "anti-social history" sentenced him to three life sentences.[22]

Resisting Prison

The first stop in any prison is the moment of transition where the prisoner is forced to let go of his possessions and clothing and adopt the status and identity of the inmate. A person gives the prison guard his name, age, crime, and sentence, and, in exchange, is assigned a number, in Carter's case, number 45,472, meaning he was the 45,472nd prisoner to be interred behind the thick stone walls of Trenton State Prison. Carter watched as the man ahead of him went through the drill.[23] The man removed all his clothing, watches, and jewelry placing these belongings into a cardboard box to be carted away. Next he was handed his drinking cup, spoon, blanket, and prison-issue khaki uniform stamped with the NJSP on the back. The trousers had thick black stripes about the same width as the bar cells.

When it was Carter's turn, he suddenly balked. On previous occasions he had cooperated but Carter knew the loss of self-respect that accompanied this stripping away of his outside self. Carter understood prison life and what it did to the spirit of the men there. No matter what the cost, Carter refused to become what the prison told him he was. He refused to remove his suit. On his first day, Rubin "Hurricane" Carter was sent to the hole still wearing his expensive gray suit, diamond ring on his finger, gold watch, and black patent leather shoes.

At Trenton, the "hole" was literally cut into the wall itself.[24] About thirty-five cells ran along the deepest tier. The cells were deeper than graves. There were no sinks, no faucets, and no toilets. A concrete slab and a bucket were the only "furnishings." There was no light, no books, and no contact with other inmates or guards. Inmates were fed through an opening at the bottom of the door: one cup of water three times a day and four slices of bread. After several months in the deepest level of Trenton's system of solitary confinement, Rubin "Hurricane" Carter was still unwilling to change into prison clothing.

Every fifteen days Carter, still wearing his own clothes, was allowed out to take a shower and every thirty days he received a medical inspection. One of these inspections landed Carter in the prison hospital for an operation that would eventually take his right eye: with the loss of that eye went Carter's hopes of ever returning to professional boxing. Still refusing to wear the same prison outfits as others, Carter proposed a compromise he could live with. If the warden permitted him to wear the white scrubs of the hospital, he would be willing to take off his now ragged and tattered clothing. The administration agreed and upon release from the hospital, Carter was sent to 7 Wing,

the cellblock reserved for "incorrigibles" like him who refused to go along with the internal prison regime.

Refusal continued to be Rubin Carter's main weapon of psychological survival in prison. He took his punishments in solitary rather than submit to the degradation of the routine of prison life. Carter understood that the psychological harm of incarceration was far more damaging to him than any of the physical threats. He was prepared to die rather than lose his sense of himself as a human being. He refused to be interviewed by prison psychologists or to meet with a parole officer to discuss his participation in his own "rehabilitation." Carter felt disdainful of his fellow inmates who seemed to accept the degradation of their lives and did all they could to live up to the prison's view of them as animals. Drugs and booze flowed freely inside the walls: a steady supply of dope and prison-made hooch, a kind of sugary foul-tasting wine, meant that many continued the destructive life that had brought them to prison in the first place.

Carter remained aloof from the prison scene—working on his appeals, studying the law, and writing an autobiography that was published to much acclaim in 1974. Although Carter had ended his formal schooling at the eighth grade, he educated himself as a jailhouse lawyer learning the law and moved on to tackle erudite reading material of Freud, Jung, Malcolm X, Nelson Mandela, and many others.

Standing Up for Prisoners Rights at Rahway State Prison

Prison administrators rarely give reasons to prisoners when they move them, and they move them often. In 1971, Carter was transferred to Rahway State Prison.[25] Originally built in 1896 as a youth reformatory, the physical layout resembled the less oppressive architecture of the Jamesburg institution. But the social structure of the prison was the same as Trenton and other institutions.

In the 1970s, tensions among inmates were running high. A growing political consciousness was infecting black and other minority prisoners. Black Muslims and other militant prisoners were growing incensed by the indeterminate sentencing system that relied upon the parole system for release and seemed to favor white inmates over black inmates. The inmate population at both Trenton State Prison and Rahway was 80 percent black, 5 percent Hispanic, and 15 percent white. With the exception of few black guards, the entire prison administration was white.

Attica, a maximum-security prison in upstate New York, exploded in violence in 1971 when inmates rebelled against the inhumane conditions of their confinement. Forty-three people were killed before the National Guard fought to take the prison away from inmate control. Shortly afterward, Rahway State Prison too erupted in violence for many of the same reasons. Conditions were abysmal with overcrowding, brutality, poor food, unsanitary conditions, and few programs.

In the midst of the tensions, Rubin Carter found himself in a leadership role counseling his fellow prisoners to avoid violence and try to make their demands through peaceful channels. When a riot erupted at Rahway, Carter led a group of inmates to wait it out in a separate wing of the prison. The riot lasted twenty-seven hours with seven guards, including the warden, beaten and held hostage by about two hundred inmates.

After the riots, Carter became active in a growing movement among the inmates to organize peacefully for their rights.[26] He joined the Rahway Inmate Committee that expressed demands about medical conditions, overcrowding, recreation, telephone privileges, and the right to wear civilian clothing. He was elected chairman of the Rahway Inmate Committee which he renamed the Rahway People's Council. Within the prison different ethnic groups formed various factions: the blacks were the largest but there were also the Hispanics, Italians, and Muslims. Carter sought support from the toughest leader in each group promising to improve conditions and expand their rights.

The more outspoken Carter became the more the prison administration sought ways to limit his power. Carter was brought before a prison tribunal composed of prison staff and was told that he was being punished for inciting a riot and holding an illegal meeting. As punishment Carter was transferred to the "Vroom Readjustment Unit," the institution within the New Jersey corrections system for the criminally insane and other incorrigibles.[27] The Vroom building was more than hundred years old and had been designed entirely for isolation. Inmates rarely left their cells except for a brief trip every few days to the yard. Meals were served in cells, and the cells were designed to prevent communication between adjacent inmates.

Carter, by now well educated and connected to growing network of writers, reporters, lawyers, activists, and celebrities on the outside, who believed he had been unjustly convicted, filed a suit in federal court alleging he had been illegally transferred to the VRU. A federal District Court judge ordered Carter to be released from the VRU on the grounds that his due process rights had been violated and that "inciting" was not a recognizable offense under the disciplinary rules of the prison.[28] After ninety-two days in the VRU, Carter was transferred away from Rahway and back to Trenton State Prison. `

A Taste of Freedom

By the time Carter's appeal was heard for the first time he was a national celebrity. His autobiography was a bestseller. Bob Dylan came to prison to meet Carter and wrote a song about his plight that further enhanced his growing support among liberal activists and radical reformers. The NAACP and other organizations became involved as it became clear that Carter had been framed by the two eyewitnesses who lied to protect themselves from criminal prosecution on other charges. Muhammad Ali and many other celebrities joined the bandwagon to free Hurricane Carter.[29]

On March 17, 1976, the conviction of Carter and Artis was overturned by the New Jersey Supreme Court in a 7-0 decision.[30] The Supreme Court agreed that they had been denied a fair trial. The case was remanded back to state court on the grounds that the prosecution had failed to inform the defense and the jury of the plea agreement it had made with the two key eyewitnesses in exchange for their testimony. Even more significant was the fact that both of the eyewitnesses, now in prison, were saying they had lied in order to avoid going to prison and in response to serious pressure from the investigators.[31] Such information might surely persuade the jury that these witnesses were less than credible.

The prosecution began immediate proceedings for a new trial against Carter and Artis. Both men were released from jail on bond posted by heavyweight champion Muhammad Ali. Now 38, Carter had spent about half of his life, eighteen years, locked up in prison. With the vision in his right eye gone, Carter would never return to professional boxing.

In a trial watched by the world, Artis and Carter were convicted a second time by a second jury. One of the key witnesses took the stand again, recanted the statements he had made about lying, and repeated his original testimony.[32] Despite information given to the jury about the plea agreement, the all-white jury believed the two white men, when they testified, were telling the truth.

Race played an important factor in this trial.[33] The white victims drinking in an all-white part of town had been gunned down by two black men in an act thought to be in retaliation for a shooting of a local black bar owner by a white man. All the witnesses, victims, and jury in the courtroom were white. Although Carter was only a passing acquaintance of the bar owner's son, and did not personally know any of the people who were killed, the prosecutor nonetheless argued that the motive for the killing was racial revenge. The prosecutor put forth the theory that Carter and Artis, out of deep-seated black rage, were willing to kill four innocent strangers on behalf of a black man they barely knew, in front of many witnesses for the simple reason that they were consumed with a desire for revenge against the white society. According to the prosecution, it made also sense that Artis and Carter would then drive around the neighborhood all night making no effort to run or hide. The prosecution presented no particular evidence that either Artis or Carter held negative feelings toward whites or had even acted or expressed any desire to seek revenge against whites. The theory was based on racist assumptions about black criminality and black rage and the all-white jury bought it.

Reformation on the Inside

After nine short months of freedom, Rubin Carter was sent back to Trenton State Prison. This time the anger and hope that had sustained him in his struggle to clear his name was gone. He divorced his wife and cut off ties with the outside world. This time Carter would have to find a different way to survive.

Now Carter retreated to the inner life of his spirit and his mind. He read a book about a concentration camp survivor who had come to the realization that prisons could control you physically but not spiritually. Carter looked around him and saw so many men whose spirit had been broken and destroyed by the prison system. Indeed the entire system was designed to do just that. But true freedom, he came to understand, was about the inner life, and here, even in prison with all the suffering it imposed, was the opportunity for growth and even freedom.[34]

Carter began to study classics in philosophy, religion, the civil rights movement, and the theory of non-violence. Carter came to the understanding that his moral system based on "giving as good as you got" was the equivalent of the corrupt moral system of the prison itself. Carter wrote in his journal: "A real revelation is not 'an eye for an eye' or 'do as others do, just do it first,' but a revelation is to change worse to better; hate to love; war to peace; it means turning things around; a total change from the opposite of what it is now."[35]

Carter's language changed as did his demeanor. He continued to oppose the prison's assault on his dignity and selfhood and he took the punishment they doled out rather than give in to being a mere number warehoused like so much junk to be thrown away. The system locked him in the hole, kept him in administrative segregation, and sent him back to the dreaded Vroom at least once more before his final release. But Carter nourished his soul with the new understandings about the world and the human condition. Locked away in the deepest and darkest prisons, Carter liberated himself to a level of freedom he had never experienced before in his life.

Seeking Physical Freedom One Last Time

At this point, Carter may have disappeared inside the system forever as he attempted to lead the ascetic life of a monk inside the bowels of the system. Forgotten by the outside world and cut off from everyone, Carter would have simply disappeared along with the many thousands, now millions, of Americans who are locked away. But a twist of fate created a tie between Carter and the outside world. A young black man from Brooklyn, Lester Martin, had been adopted by an unconventional group of liberal Canadians.[36] Lester read Carter's book and wrote to him. For some reason, the young man touched something in Carter and he wrote back to Lester. Soon afterward, Lester came down to Trenton State Prison for Carter's first visit with someone from the outside world in many years. Thus began a friendship between Carter and Lester and the group of young adults who were raising him that would ultimately lead to the release of Artis and Carter.

It took nine years. If it weren't for the passionate dedication of these Canadians who revived the legal battle for Carter's appeals, Rubin probably would have remained behind bars for the rest of his life. Their enthusiasm and energy renewed his own commitment to try to fight for his physical freedom again. This time, the Canadians and Carter's lawyers abandoned the New Jersey state court system and filed an appeal in federal court. The appeal argued that the prosecutor had illegally appealed to racist beliefs without any evidence that either Carter or Artis personally was vengeful toward whites and that the prosecution and the police had illegally concealed evidence of a failed polygraph by the key eyewitness in the case.

The moment of victory came suddenly and completely when a federal court overturned the conviction and ordered their immediate release from prison. Judge Sarokin stated that "To not throw out these convictions would be to commit a crime as heinous as those for which they were unjustly convicted. . . . I cannot, in the face of the conclusions reached in my opinion and the injustices found, permit Mr. Carter to spend another day or even an hour in prison, particularly considering that he has spent almost twenty years in confinement based upon a conviction which I have found to be constitutionally faulty."[37] After losing an appeal, the district attorney's office decided to forego a third trial for Carter and Artis.

Together the two men had collectively served thirty-four years in prison. Carter lost nineteen years of his life, his boxing career, his wife, and his two children. Neither the state of New Jersey nor the attorney general offices ever offered Carter, Artis, or their families an apology or compensation of any kind for their loss. At a press conference two years after his release, at the age of fifty, Carter talked about what he had felt and learned from his tragic experience:

> The State of NJ has just now seen fit to dismiss the charges and the indictment—the same indictment that they used 22 years ago to take my life by seeking the death penalty. But they failed to get the death penalty . . . instead they sentenced me to a life of living death—and there is no other way to describe the nature of prison. Prison destroys everything that is valuable in a human being. It destroys families—it destroyed mine. It destroys one's dignity and self-respect in too many ways to even mention here. It got to me and I knew I was innocent. It gets to everybody. I was locked away in an iron cage for not one but three of my lifetimes. I was a prisoner, a number, a thing to be guarded with a maximum of security and a minimum of compassion. Not a person. Not a human being. But a body to be counted fifteen or twenty times a day. . . . After all that has been said and done—the fact that the most productive years of my life between the ages of twenty nine and fifty have been stolen; the fact that I was deprived of seeing my children grow up—wouldn't you think I have the right to be bitter? Wouldn't anyone under those circumstances have a right to be bitter. . . . If I have learned nothing else in life, I've learned that bitterness only consumes the vessel that contains it. And for me to permit bitterness to control or infect my life in any way whatsoever, would be to allow those who imprisoned me to take even more than the twenty two years they've already taken . . . that would make me an accomplice to their crime.[38]

Carter went to live in Canada as he re-adjusted to life on the outside. After a few years, he returned to the United States and became executive director of an organization, Association in Defense of the Wrongly Convicted, to assist prisoners and Death Row inmates in their struggle for justice.

THINKING CRITICALLY ABOUT THIS CASE

1. Why did Rubin Carter refuse to wear the prison uniform? Does his refusal make "sense" to you? Why or why not?

2. Is the prison a place for rehabilitation? Why or why not? What would need to change for prisons to genuinely reform inmates?

3. Rubin Carter learned violence on the street but he learned it even better behind the walls, first in juvenile reformatory, and then in prison. Why are prisons such violent environments? Are prisons violent because they hold violent inmates or are the inmates violent because they are in prison?

4. What should conditions be like inside of a prison? Should prisoners have access to education including college? Why or why not? Should prisoners have access to recreation? Why or why not? Treatment? Why or why not?

5. Should prisoners enjoy a degree of civil rights inside the prison? Why or why not? Do you support the prisoners' right to vote? Why or why not?

6. The absence of contact with the opposite sex is a major deprivation for incarcerated men and

women. Would you support the implementation of conjugal visits in which married partners or couples are permitted to have overnight visits on the prison facility? Why or why not?

7. Carter once observed that released prisoners who have been inside for so long "have so much anger that they have to swallow that the first person who looks at them the wrong way, they lose it. There comes a point where the prison should never set you free." What are the implications of this observation? What needs to change so prisoners can be safely released back into the community?

8. Carter used to tell his fellow inmates, "Don't leave your manhood at the front gates and expect to pick it up on your way out." What is the meaning of this statement?

REFERENCES

Case adapted from:

James S. Hirsch, *Hurricane: The Miraculous Journey of Rubin Carter* (Boston: Houghton Mifflin Co., 2000).

Paul B. Wice, *Rubin "Hurricane" Carter and the American Justice System* (New Brunswick: Rutgers University Press, 2000).

Rubin "Hurricane" Carter, *The Sixteenth Round* (New York: Viking Press, 1974).

Check Out This Case

Find out more about the trials and the legal issues involved in Rubin Carter case at http://www.lawbuzz.com/justice/hurricane/hurricane.htm

The Hurricane

This award-winning film by Norman Jewison starring Denzel Washington gives an entertaining and accurate portrayal of the life of Rubin "Hurricane" Carter.

At the heart of the correctional system that supervises more than 6.89 million American citizens[39] is a vast network of jails and prisons housing more than two million convicted adults, juveniles, and defendants awaiting trial. For most Americans the daily lives of these imprisoned persons are both out of sight and out of mind. Unlike the trial that takes place in a public setting and may even be broadcast on television, the process of punishment takes place behind thick fortress-like walls far from the center of everyday life. While colonial Americans doled out punishment in the bright light of day for all to see, the process of punishment for Kemba Smith and Rubin Carter, day after day and year after year, is not witnessed by the general public. It is easy for the public to believe that prisons are like "country clubs" offering inmates free room and board, weightlifting rooms and color television. The reality is far different.

The thirty-year odyssey of Rubin Carter through the penal institutions of the state of New Jersey offers us an insider's view of the prison world. Like layers in geological rock, we can detect traces of penal history preserved in prison practices, such as the wearing of striped uniforms, the chain gang, lockstep marching, individual cells, shaved heads, the use of bells and enforced silence, solitary confinement, the ubiquitous inmate hierarchy of violence and sexual assault, the sheer idleness and boredom, racial tensions among the inmates, riots, prisoners' rights, and the ever-present hostility between the guards and inmates. All these features tell us something about the hopes, intentions, and failures of the prison system in our society.

The use of incarceration as a form of punishment is a nineteenth-century innovation. Imprisonment is a costly response to crime. A society must have substantial resources to be able to create specialized institutions whose sole function is to deprive people of their liberty. The institution must provide for all the necessities to maintain them by housing, feeding, and clothing those held within their walls. Even higher is the cost of guarding them to prevent escape, rioting, or fighting back. Incarceration is an act of state coercion that must be continually maintained in order to keep people inside. The most costly item on the bill is the custodial staff and technology to maintain constant surveillance and vigilance over those who are imprisoned.

But we expect something more from our prison system than merely locking people away from society. The goal of rehabilitation is one key founding aspirations of the prison system. In Carter's view, "prison destroys everything that is valuable in a human being." The pains of imprisonment described by Rubin Carter suggest that incarceration is more destructive than rehabilitative; less about correction and more about retribution. Is that what we intend? Are prisons intended to be destructive institutions that destroy human beings and their families? Why then do we call them "correctional systems"?

In this chapter, we continue our exploration of the goals of sentencing by looking at the purpose incarceration serves in our search for justice. What is the purpose of the prison and why have we, as a society, come to rely upon imprisonment as the dominant response to crime?

Prisons exact a heavy price on inmates, their families, and communities but they take a huge toll on the "keepers" as well. What is the work of corrections today? And what does the future hold?

ORIGINS OF THE PRISON: ENLIGHTENMENT AND REFORM

Before the nineteenth century, jails and prisons were typically used to hold the accused awaiting trial and the convicted awaiting punishment. The accused and convicted "witches" of the seventeenth century languished in jail while they waited for trials or the scaffold. Their confinement itself was not conceived of as punishment. In the teeming jails and dungeons of Europe, men, women, and children were thrown together in huge stockades or pits. In the seventeenth and eighteenth centuries, transportation and banishment to the vast wild spaces was a cost-effective means of dealing with the growing number of petty thieves, pickpockets, and prostitutes overwhelming cities like London and Paris.[40] The only other use of incarceration was debtor's prison that confined people until they could pay their debts, usually by their extended family or some other benefactor. Apart from keeping the iron gates locked, there was little attention given to what went on inside among the prisoners.

One of the problems with the system of punishment between the twelfth and eighteenth centuries was its heavy reliance on the threat of the gallows for almost all felony offenses.[41] In England, the nobles of Parliament passed a series of statutes that punished crimes of poaching, petty theft, pickpocketing, and setting fires in the forest with death by hanging. Known as the infamous "**bloody codes**," the nobles of Parliament passed nearly two hundred capital offenses. But the use of hanging for these crimes was both too extreme and too erratic to serve as a rational deterrent. The sight of a servant swinging from the gallows for the theft of silver from his master's kitchen angered the crowd who had far more sympathy for the servant than for his master. Yet, letting people go with a pardon of mercy undermined the rule of law that protected private property.

The same logic that gave birth to the institution of the modern police force also was a foundational ideal for the modern prison.[42] The concept of deterrence, as we have seen, relies upon the belief that all people are rational and that the decision to commit crime is a calculated decision based on weighing costs and benefits. According to Enlightenment thinkers, the solution to crime was to devise a rational form of punishment that would be both certain and proportionate to the crime. A system based on fines and deprivation of one's liberty through incarceration seemed a logical and rational alternative to the messy gallows.

Another contributing factor to the rise of prisons was the decline in the use of **corporeal punishment**. Whipping, branding, mutilation, dunking, public humiliation, stoning, and banishment all focused on the body of the offender. These public punishments took place before raucous crowds who witnessed the punishment with mixture of vengeful satisfaction and gleeful relief. By the nineteenth century, the growing bourgeois middle class no longer approved of the violent spectacle of punishment in the city streets. There was a shift in sensibilities away from the brutality of corporeal punishments and more value was placed on impersonal and bureaucratic forms of governance and social control.[43]

BLOODY CODES
a system of laws in eighteenth-century England that permitted capital punishment for a wide range of property and minor offenses.

CORPOREAL PUNISHMENT
punishment inflicted on the body through whipping, branding, mutilation, or torture.

Penitentiary: Redemption and Reform

Before the shift to incarceration, whippings, brandings, and executions were popular public spectacles held in the town market square and attended by members of the community.

The nineteenth century was the golden age of the asylum.[44] Large-scale institutions for the poor, orphans, the mentally ill, the criminal, and the juvenile delinquent were invented to care for dependent and troublesome populations. The modern penitentiary is a peculiarly American invention owing as much to the religious philosophy and understanding of the Quakers as to the rationality of European classicists. Observers from Europe flocked to the New World to study these new penal innovations.[45]

The ideal of rehabilitation, originally conceived as a form of religious redemption through monastic silence, contemplation, and hard labor, was at the heart of the American vision of the penitentiary. Quakers believed that everyone had God within them and everyone could be redeemed. Prisoners had been corrupted by the evil influences of alcohol, the city, and sin. But they could be reformed as acceptable members of society through the contemplative power of the penitentiary.

The **Walnut Street Jail** was the first American **penitentiary** in Philadelphia in 1790 and the first penal institution to adopt the monastic structure of individual cells for solitary confinement of inmates.[46] Less serious offenders were held in larger cells, where they worked together at various trades. The solitary system developed at the Walnut Street Jail was adopted by the first major large-scale American institutions called the Eastern and Western Penitentiaries built in 1826

WALNUT STREET JAIL
the first American penitentiary.

PENITENTIARY
an institution intended to isolate prisoners from society and from one another so they could reflect on their past, repent, and emerge as reformed sinners.

and 1829, respectively, in different parts of the state of Pennsylvania. The architecture of these vast and hugely expensive institutions was based on the concept that prisoners needed complete isolation from their corrupting environment in the city and from the influences of their fellow prisoners.

In the **separate system**, individual cells were built with individual exercise yards attached to them. The prisoner washed, ate, worked, and slept in his cell seeing no one other than the guard who brought meals and who was forbidden to speak. Europeans flocked to America to see and praise this new innovative design described in glowing terms as prisoners gained peace and serenity through religious contemplation and mediation. Others, however, noted the intense cruelty of this form of imprisonment where a man could be confined in a twelve by eight cell, with no human contact, for three, ten, or even twenty years. According to Charles Dickens, who visited Eastern Penitentiary in 1842, "very few men are capable of estimating the immense amount of torture and agony which this dreadful punishment, prolonged for years, inflicts upon the sufferers."[47]

The separate system was soon supplanted by another model that was far more economical to administer. The **congregate system** was developed in the Auburn Prison in upstate New York in 1823. Also known as the silent system, the Auburn Prison held prisoners at night in individual cells, but put them together in large work groups during the day to perform manual labor. The use of group labor supported the institution financially but shielded against corruption via the strict enforcement of silence among the prisoners. Auburn invented the "hole" or the use of **punitive solitary confinement** for those who violated the rules of silence, the **lockstep**, a peculiar form of marching for prisoners, and the wearing of striped uniforms to degrade inmates and make it more difficult for them to escape.

The penitentiary was considered a noble experiment in human reform. The use of solitary confinement as a form of punishment was a humane and civilized alternative to whipping, beatings, and other forms of corporeal punishments. Each prisoner, in theory, was a soul that could be saved. But the reality of the prison never came close to the dreams of the reformers. Institutions in the North became the dumping grounds for poor immigrants who flooded the cities during the nineteenth century. What characterized most of the inmates was not a perverse degradation of the soul but economic dislocation and poverty. The silence, isolation, and the "hole" were perhaps even more inhumane than the previous system of whipping and beatings for crimes of property. And despite the intentions of the reformers, brutality by the guards flourished behind the walls without the watchful eye of the public crowd to keep it in check.

On a practical level, prisons were expensive to operate. The economic need to run the institution itself led to the efficient use of the convict labor. For much of the nineteenth century, Auburn-style prisons operated like a "factory or industrial prisons" making use of the unskilled labor force for work in industries such as textile mills turning handsome profits for the institution.[48] In some states, cheap inmate labor was leased out to private businesses under the **contract system**. Private employers bid for control of the labor force at the same time generating profits for the warden. In the agricultural regions, prison labor was used for farming on plantation prisons generating revenue and resources for the warden to support the institution.[49]

SEPARATE SYSTEM
complete solitary confinement in an individual cell to encourage redemption and prevent social contamination via association with others in the prison first used in the Walnut Street jail.

CONGREGATE SYSTEM
a penitentiary system developed in Auburn, New York, in which inmates were held in solitary confinement at night but worked with fellow prisoners during the day under a rule of complete silence.

PUNITIVE SOLITARY CONFINEMENT
the use of solitary confinement under conditions of extreme deprivation as a punishment for disciplinary infractions.

LOCKSTEP
a peculiar form of marching for prisoners in which they were required to move in unison with their hands on each other's shoulders.

CONTRACT SYSTEM
a form of prison industry in which the labor of inmates was leased to an outside contractor or business for a fee.

Reformatory Movement

By the close of the nineteenth century, the state of these penitentiaries had become a national scandal, sparking a wave of prison reform. Far from the contemplative vision of the founders, these institutions were brutal environments with a heavy emphasis on forced labor and custody. Beginning in 1870, a treatment philosophy began to supplant the religious ideals of the earlier prison regimes.[50] Treatment professionals, social workers, psychologists, and probation officers became the new personnel to genuinely reform the criminals held within the institution. The reformatory movement advocated the use of vocational preparation, treatment interventions, education, and an internal system of privileges or rewards to motivate offenders to earn their way toward rehabilitation and release back to society as a productive member of society.

At the heart of the **reformatory model** was the indeterminate sentence: confinement should not be allocated for a set period of time but should be based on his or her behavior within the system. The concept of parole or conditional release was developed in Ireland in the 1850s in one of the first reformatory systems where prisoners were able to earn early release or have their privileges taken away from them depending on whether their conduct met the specified criteria.[51]

The first American reformatory opened in 1876 in Elmira, New York, primarily for youth and first-time offenders.[52] The reformatory movement coincided with the establishment of a juvenile justice system and the philosophy was the dominant ideal adopted by the juvenile correctional authorities.[53] When Rubin was sent to Jamesburg State Home for Boys, the institution was authorized to hold him until his twenty-first birthday but at their discretion they could release him at any time before that date. The warden, who offered Rubin a release almost three years before his twenty-first birthday, held complete legal discretion in these matters. Under the administrative model of sentencing, prison officials held enormous power over the actual length of prisoners' sentences. They used this release authority as a carrot to induce cooperation on the part of the prisoners.

The reformatories were designed primarily for the young first-time offenders or for females whose primary crimes were prostitution or promiscuity beyond the bounds of marriage.[54] Until 1870, most women prisoners were housed in leftover rooms within prisons built for men. Between 1860 and 1935 twenty-one institutions for women were built in the United States. These reformatories were designed and built specifically for women reflecting the belief that women were in need of a gentler, more homelike environment. These institutions sought to prepare women for domestic life as wives or servants. Women reformatories largely served minor offenders, often young white working-class women, while black women continued to be shunted off to custodial-type institutions.

Before long, these institutions, for males or females, devolved to the pure custodial model relying primarily upon constant surveillance, brutality, and solitary confinement to contain the inmates.[55] The inmate population was made up of poor immigrants. Middle-class reformers treated their charges harshly and with far more discipline than love. There was nothing "homelike" inside the cottages with their tidy brick facades and deceptively tranquil green lawns. The problem of inmates constantly escaping from the institutions increased reliance upon force, physical restraint, and punishment. As we can see in Jamesburg State Home for Boys, there was little in that experience which would "reform" young boys like Rubin Carter into law-abiding citizens. Reformatories became the proverbial "schools for crime" and the first step toward doing time in the penitentiary.

REFORMATORY MODEL
a nineteenth-century prison reform movement generally reserved for youth and women that focused on rehabilitation, reform, and the use of indeterminate sentencing.

Big House

The penitentiary and reformatory designed by the passionate and educated reformers to transform the "criminal" into a model citizen did not survive beyond the early years of enthusiastic experimentation and reform. The physical buildings remained with their thick walls and hundreds of individual cells and practices persisted such as solitary confinement, the marching in single-line formation, and the wearing of the prison stripes, but the goals of redemption and rehabilitation were rapidly subordinated to the practical agenda of confinement for thousands upon thousands of young, poor, uneducated European immigrants and southern blacks.

The term "**Big House**" refers to the maximum-security prison noted for its harshness and reserved for the really tough criminals.[56] The prison regime that survived into the twentieth century had less idealistic reform and more sheer boredom for the inmate. The profitable use of prison labor diminished in the twentieth century because of opposition from labor unions who fought for laws that prevented unfair labor competition from cheap inmate workers. Many states passed **state-use laws**, which forbade the use of prison labor for market goods requiring that convict labor be utilized only for the prison needs or state needs, such as making of license plates.

Work became less productive and more a tool for punishment. The image of the Big House where convicts are forced to bust rocks, for no apparent purpose other than to maintain order and to impose misery, was the prototype for the early twentieth-century maximum-security prison. In the South, plantation prisons with hard field labor and chain gangs were commonplace both for black men and black women. Prisoners spent their time sitting in their cells, engaged in some kind of menial work such as prison laundry, busting rocks, making license plates, or milling about the yard. As Carter noted, boredom is the "inmate's worst enemy."[57]

Modern Correctional System

By the mid-twentieth century, most states had a centralized department of corrections to oversee all the penal institutions within the state with the Federal Bureau of Prisons responsible for the federal penal system. Many states prefer the term "correctional institution" instead of prison, penitentiary, or reform school. From the late twentieth into the twenty-first century, prisons have been a growth industry. Between 1985 and 2009, annual correctional expenditures increased 700 percent, from $6.7 billion to more than $47 billion.[58] In 1995, for the first time in history, the state of California spent more money on building prisons than it did on financing the state college system.[59] By 2010, annual state correctional costs were estimated at $52 billion nationally.[60]

The trend appears to be shifting though. Nationwide, between 2009 and 2014 state prison rates decreased by 8 percent. The decline in prison population varies from state to state; in California, for example, the rate fell from 342 per 100,000 in 2007 to 257 per 100,000 in 2014,[61] while in other states the decline was much slower. For the first time in decades, the U.S. Bureau of Labor Statistics predicts that new job growth for correctional officers will be 5 percent, slower than average industry growth.

Today institutions are categorized by the level of custody associated with the facility.[62] **Maximum-security** prisons are designed to hold the most dangerous,

BIG HOUSE
slang for maximum-security prisons infamous for harsh conditions and tough inmate populations.

STATE-USE LAWS
laws that require prison industry to produce goods solely for use in state institutions.

MAXIMUM SECURITY
a facility designed to impose maximal restriction on inmates in order to contain the most incorrigible and violent offenders.

aggressive, and incorrigible inmates. They are typically surrounded by massive walls supplemented by armed guard towers and layers of razor wire. The prison regime in a maximum-security facility is heavily focused on custody and control. Inmates may be locked down in their cells much of the time and movement is heavily restricted and monitored.

Modern cells resemble cages for human beings who are being warehoused in overcrowded conditions as punishment for their crimes.

Medium-security prisons are less fortress-like and inmates have a higher degree of mobility within the facility, although there is generally a maximum-security wing inside the facility for inmates who violate the rules. **Minimum-security prisons** have the least degree of internal restrictions on inmates, dormitory living is common, and the external structure of the building may be surrounded by a simple high fence.

Most correctional systems have all three types of facilities as well as an array of supplemental correctional facilities, such as boot camps, forestry camps, prison farms, halfway houses, or ranches, which function more as open institutions with greater interaction with the life outside the facility than prisons which operate as closed total institutions. We will look at some of these alternatives to prison when we examine community corrections.

MEDIUM SECURITY
a prison designed to impose less restrictive conditions on inmates allowing for greater visitation, programming, and recreation for inmates.

MINIMUM SECURITY
an institution designed to permit the least dangerous inmates allowing relative freedom of movement within the confines of a locked perimeter.

The contemporary maximum- and medium-security facility is composed of many tiers of cells stacked one on the top of the other to facilitate efficient surveillance by correctional personnel.

SUPER-MAX PRISON
a new generation of maximum-security facility which relies upon technology and high levels of supervision and restriction of inmate movement.

CLASSIFICATION
the process through which the custodial, educational, sand treatment needs of the offender are assessed in order to ascertain placement within the correctional system.

A third wave of building of prisons has occurred in recent decades with a fourth style of prison design known as the **super-max prison** or maxi-maxi prison. Designed to address the rampant violence within the maximum-security prison, the super-max aims to achieve order and control through technology and design as well as correctional supervision. The first super-max was the U.S. Penitentiary in Marion, Illinois. Other institutions have copied the high-tech super-controlled regime giving rise to the term "marionization" to refer to the creation of the super-maximum-security facilities in which movement by inmates is severely restricted.[63]

In most modern correctional systems today, there is a complex process of **classification** that determines the type of institution where an inmate will serve their time. The idea of classification is to determine the security level, educational, vocational, and treatment needs of the offender. The classification may depend upon the offense, the prior history of the offender, their psychological or educational needs, and their behavioral record within the institution. System-wide classification determines where a particular inmate will serve and classification within the institution determines which wing or cellblock they will be assigned to. Prisoners typically are continually reclassified as they move them around the system.

Rubin Carter refused to cooperate in the classification process when he declined to be interviewed by the staff social workers or psychologists. Despite the custodial regime of the Trenton State Prison, the facility nonetheless maintained a treatment staff to offer some kind of rehabilitation or correctional programming for qualified inmates. In most correctional settings, there is a constant tension between the custodial staff that includes the correctional officers or guards and the treatment staff of social workers, psychologists, and medical workers. This tension between those who view the prisoners as objects of punishment and those who view them as recipients of services reflects the contradictory aims of the system itself.

In recent decades, there has been substantial growth in the use of **private correctional facilities,** such as Corrections Corporation of America, the largest private company, Wackenhut Corporation, and Esmor Corporation. In 1983, there were no privately operated facilities; by 1994, private beds were up to about 45,000 across the nation;[64] by the end of 2010 that number had reached 128,195 beds.[65] The pressure from overcrowding has led many states to contract out their prisoners to private facilities or in some cases send prisoners to other states. In addition, private companies contract with state prison systems to provide goods such as furniture, clothing, and security systems and services such as medical care or food service.

As private companies, these are for-profit businesses that claim to offer correctional facilities to states at competitive prices saving taxpayers millions of dollars.[66] To the critics, however, profit-making on our incarcerated population is highly problematic: companies are likely to cut corners wherever possible and to avoid costly state unions to control costs. For-profit prisons also have an incentive to keep people locked up: release of an inmate is loss of revenue. The economic incentive for the prison business is to run a full occupancy institution. Critics are also concerned about the absence of oversight and regulation of private prisons and the serious possibility for abuse of the highly vulnerable and neglected criminal population.

In addition to state and federal prisons, there is also a network of **jails** operated by local authorities, usually the county. Jails serve a distinct purpose from prison. Jails are designed as short-term detention facilities for defendants awaiting trial or for short-term stays of incarceration on minor offenses. Jails range in size from small-town lockups that can house only a few occupants at a time to modern facilities that house thousands of inmates for periods of up to five years or more.

Jails have a notorious history of being neglected, vermin-ridden, decrepit places where inmates are housed in large cage-like rooms containing a number of offenders ranging from the drunk who needs to sleep it off to the shoplifter to the dangerous predator.[67] Sanitary facilities are often very poor, facilities are old, and staffing is minimal. Many jails lack any recreational or educational facilities, so inmates remain idle and in their cells for most of their stay. On the other hand, there are some jail facilities that are run according to the best of modern standards in both physical and correctional programming.[68]

Structure of Correctional Management Today

The management of modern correctional facilities is a highly specialized professional occupation requiring skills not dissimilar to the management of other large organizations. Historically, the warden was an autocratic figure appointed through political connections to the governor with the power to run the institution according to his or her own rules. After World War II, most states established "departments of correction" run by a commissioner and supported by

PRIVATE CORRECTIONAL FACILITIES
corporate-owned and run facilities that contract with local, state, and federal governments to house inmates.

JAIL
a facility authorized to hold persons awaiting trial and those sentenced for misdemeanors and minor felony offenses.

an executive bureaucracy that set policy for the correctional system as a whole. These policies are carried out by superintendents or wardens who, in turn, are supported by numerous layers of deputies or middle managers responsible for key administrative functions within the institution. Since the 1960s, there is also a large support staff in most institutions: doctors, nurses, chaplains, psychologists, teachers, counselors, clerks, and secretaries, with specific jobs associated with the needs of the incarcerated population.

The most difficult job and the one with the greatest degree of direct contact with the inmates is that of the correctional officer. The job of the modern correctional officers is largely focused on the custodial function of maintaining security, order, and discipline among the inmate population. In the jargon of prison culture, correctional officers are referred to as "hacks," "pigs," or "screws": there is little about the job of the line officer that deals with treatment or rehabilitation.

While not always in direct conflict with each other, the nature of the prison means that there is constant tension between guards and inmates that can erupt into violence at any time. Like the police officers, prison guards face a constant challenge to their authority among those who are constantly seeking to undermine it. Similar to the war model of policing, where police come to view citizens as "enemies," prison guards are structured to view inmates as dangerous, threatening, and less than human.

These are social conditions highly conducive to abuse of authority through violence on the part of a minority of guards who choose to use violence to exert control over inmates. In a classic social psychological experiment, researcher Phillip Zimbardo of Stanford University set up a mock prison environment, with college students randomly assigned to play the roles of guards and inmates.[69] The experiment elicited substantially aggressive and sadistic behavior on the part of a few of the "guards" as well as disturbing signs of psychological deterioration on the part of those assigned to play "inmates" and had to be called off after only a few days to protect the participants. This experiment illustrates the power of the "structured conflict" to bring out negative behaviors in people who occupy those roles.

There are some ironic similarities between the working environment of the correctional guard and conditions of life for the inmate. Guards are subject to constant threat of danger, and experience tremendous isolation, boredom, loneliness, and distrust in an environment in which no one can be trusted. Correctional staff is isolated from management and often feel disrespected in their status as guards. They are also vulnerable to informants or prison snitches who might relay any rule violations or infractions to their superiors. Many guards refer to themselves as the "other inmates" and refer to their job as "doing life" eight hours at a time.

Inside the Prison World

TOTAL INSTITUTION a term coined by Erving Goffman to refer to institutions organized so that those who work in the institution exercise total control over every aspect of the lives of those who are inmates within the institution.

Regardless of the prevailing philosophy or the type of facility where a person is incarcerated, prisons and jails are coercive institutions that maintain complete control over the inmate's existence. Segregated from society, the entire life of the inmate is regulated by the institution: they live, eat, work, sleep, wash, and recreate in one environment totally controlled by their "keepers." Erving Goffman, a sociologist who studied concentration camps, mental asylums, and prisons, coined the term "**total institution**" to describe the social structure of these types of organizations.[70] A total institution is one that maintains complete control over the entire lives of the inmates.

Most of us in modern society occupy a wide range of social roles: we are simultaneously sons and daughters, classmates, baseball players, lovers, spouses, customers, employees, students, friends, siblings, and parents. We possess not one social identity but many. The complexity of modern society and the separation of different parts of life allow us, as social actors, to have considerable amount of control over our presentation of ourselves to others in order to "manage" the impression we project. We use clothing, hairstyle, jewelry, speech, cars, and demeanor to control how we want others to see us. The process of "impression management" is a natural part of how we maintain a sense of our own identity within any given social setting.

The total institution stands in sharp contrast to the outside society. Within the world of the "total institution" there are only two social roles: that of the "keeper" or prison staff and that of the "kept" or inmate. The inmate is forced to occupy a single social role, that of a convict, twenty-four hours a day. The relationship between the guard and the inmate is one of **structured conflict**: inmates are locked up against their will and are subordinate to the domination of the institution; guards are the personnel who represent that authority and must enforce it as part of their job.[71]

The process of entering the institution involves a deliberate "stripping away" of all the markers of a person's outside identities. Goffman called this a **status degradation ceremony** because it marks a downward social transition into the lowly status of an inmate. A person's head is shaven, their rings, necklaces, earrings, and watches taken away; their naked bodies are searched, often brutally and in a dehumanizing fashion; and they may be required to stand naked while they are washed down, examined, or deloused. Literally stripped of all that represented their former identity, the prisoner is now handed the markings of their new all-encompassing social status as an inmate.

Recall the clothing selected in the congregate system: the striped pajamas were intentionally designed to identify incarcerated persons as convicts and to humiliate them. The short pants put on the men at Annandale symbolically marked them as inferior beings like children dependent upon the institution for their every need, big and small. The final insult of all is the taking away of one's name and its replacement with a number. The institutional ritual told Carter he was no longer Mr. Rubin Carter but inmate # 45,472.

Rubin Carter resisted the "status degradation" ceremony when he entered Trenton State Prison for the second time. He had experienced it before when he had been incarcerated and he knew the psychological pain of being stripped of his identity and his dignity. Although he paid dearly for his resistance, he refused to submit to this assault on his sense of self.

What Carter feared most was the possibility that he might become socialized to his status as an inmate and come to accept his position as so many did around him. Donald Clemmer uses the term "**prisonization**" to refer to the process of assimilation whereby inmates became accustomed to their life as inmates.[72] Prisonization is the taking on of the folkways, mores, customs, and general culture of the penitentiary. The longer they are in the institution, the more inmates become "prisonized" to the rules of the institution and the values of the inmate subculture. Clemmer believed that at some point a person internalizes these values and they became a permanent part of their value system. Others argue that inmates

STRUCTURED CONFLICT
the relationship between inmates and guards within the institution in which inmates are confined against their will and guards are charged with the responsibility of enforcing their detention.

STATUS DEGRADATION CEREMONY
rituals which mark the transition from a citizen to the lower status of an inmate.

PRISONIZATION
the process whereby a new inmate becomes socialized to the inmate subculture and adapts to prison life.

adopt the values during their period in prison but return to the norms of the outside world when they are released.

Pains of Imprisonment

In 1958, sociologist Gresham Sykes studied the Trenton State Prison where Rubin Carter later spent so many years of his life.[73] Sykes argued that the prison experience is shaped by deprivations of a profound and deeply shameful nature that he called the **pains of imprisonment.** The deprivation of liberty does not even begin to describe what is really taken away from the person who is incarcerated. Sykes describes the utter dependence upon the institution for all the goods and services of daily life. If the prison does not provide a place to relieve oneself, the inmate is utterly powerless to maintain even basic personal hygiene. Humans are reduced to the status of animals. In the hole, Carter lived with only a bucket for his bodily needs. The prison controlled toilet paper, soap, clothing, food, water, light, and even air to breathe. An adult is forced to become completely dependent upon guards and prison management for every last detail of their basic physical needs, reducing grown men and women to the state of infantile dependency.

Inmates are deprived of heterosexual interactions. This is far more significant than merely the absence of sexual contact. Gender identity represents a significant part of one's personal sense of self: being masculine or feminine is a social role that depends upon the presence of the opposite sex. Just as it is impossible to be a parent without a child or a teacher without a student, it is psychologically difficult to maintain an identity as masculine without the presence of women. According to Sykes, the perverse nature of homosexual sex in prison, in which weak inmates are forced to take on feminine roles of "wives" or "ladies," is the result of this deprivation.

The form of sexual intimidation and violent sexual assault that Carter witnessed in all of the institutions he was confined is ubiquitous in most maximum- and medium-security prisons and jails. The hidden secret of the prison system is that some unknown number of men are systematically and continually subjected to rape. There is little available data on this topic given its sensitive nature. Some believe prison rape to be ubiquitous while others believe it is relatively rare. In 2003, the Prison Rape Elimination mandated that the Bureau of Justice Statistics collect data on the incidence of sexual violence within the nation's prisons, jails, and community treatment facilities. The first-ever National Former Prisoner Survey conducted in 2008 shows that an estimated 9.6 percent of former state prisoners reported one or more incidents of sexual victimization during the most recent period of incarceration. Of these, 5.4 percent reported the incident involved another inmate while 5.3 percent reported that the incident involved facility staff.[74]

Most agree that prison rape, like rape in the outside culture, is more about violence and control than it is about sexual relationships or bonding. Older inmates often called "wolves" offer protection to young inmates, "punks," who trade sex for security and goods from the commissary. The punks are treated like sexual slaves who are owned and may be lent or traded to other inmates. Only the men who have been forced to be "ladies" are seen as homosexuals and are generally despised for it. The "wolves" are seen as real men who rely upon their toughness and willingness to use violence to protect their status.

The prison also deprives the inmate of their autonomy. Every decision is made for them by the institution. As Rubin Carter observed, along with the absence of

PAINS OF IMPRISONMENT deprivations of prison life, including absence of goods, autonomy, heterosexual interaction, and security.

women, the other most difficult pain of imprisonment is the complete absence of control.

> Two of the hardest things about being in jail are, first that you can never make a decision for yourself—every one, from the time to eat or sleep, walk, talk or even breathe, is already made up for you; the only thing that is yours to decide which requires no deep concentration, is whether or not to stand up or sit down in your cell. . . . The other . . . is the unreasonable absence of women.[75]

Inmates are told when to eat, when to shower, when to walk, where to stand, when to sleep and when to wake; lights go out at a certain time and they must wake at a certain time. They are often moved around from cell to cell or institution to institution like so many boxes in a giant storehouse. They have no control over what happens to them.

Finally, the prison deprives inmates of security over their own personal safety. Men in prison exist in a constant state of fear of assault from fellow inmates. It is impossible to let one's guard down so everyone wears the "mask" of toughness as a form of protection. As long-time prisoner Jack Abbott wrote, "Everyone is afraid. It is not an emotional, psychological fear. It is a practical manner. If you do not threaten someone at the very least someone will threaten you." The ability to protect oneself by locking one's doors or moving away from dangerous people is not an option for a person held under these conditions. The prison deprives inmates of the peace of mind that comes from being safe.

The impact of these deprivations is difficult for people outside of prison to truly comprehend. The pains of imprisonment are assaults on one's sense of self-respect, dignity, and self-esteem. Animals might be quite content to be warehoused if they are adequately fed and exercised. But human beings are not animals, and the indignities, humiliations, and frustrations of prison life generate enormous rage and attack the very spirit of the inmates. Carter believed that the real danger of prison life was its impact on his own psychological well-being and he resisted taking on the inmate role as much as he could. He was willing to endure physical suffering over this kind of social death. When Carter refused to enter a cell in the VRU unit littered with rat droppings, his words of resistance were very telling: "My name is Rubin, not Fido."[76]

PRISON SUBCULTURE: IMPORTATION VERSUS DEPRIVATION

The inmate social system was heavily studied between 1940s and 1960s describing many different "roles" within the subculture of the inmates. A common thread in all the different descriptions is the predominance of violence, the value placed on physical strength, the aggressive pattern of sexual activity, and the proscription against "snitching" to the guards or prison administration. Sykes and others believe that the psychological harms of deprivation are responsible for much of the violence and pathology of the prison subculture. The frustration and degradation generates the continual atmosphere of violence that erupts between inmates over petty issues. Lives may be lost over a pack of cigarettes, a second dessert, a sexual favor, an offhand comment, or a careless glance.

IMPORTATION THEORY
the theory that inmate subculture is brought inside the institution from criminal subcultures within outside society.

The **importation theory** of prison violence argues that the inmate culture is the result of values and norms that are imported from street culture. In their classic research, Irwin and Cressey found many of the same "social types" inside the prison as on the outside.[77] The current dominance of gangs inside the prison provides strong support for the idea that much of what takes place inside the prison has strong connections to the patterns of interaction in the outside world. Patterns of race relations inside the prison mirror and intensify existing historical patterns of segregation and hostility within the wider society.

Beginning in the 1960s, the influence of racially or ethnically homogenous gangs operating inside the prison has grown in significance in the internal dynamics of the prison.[78] Opposing gangs, segregated by racial and ethnic affiliation, compete for dominance within the inmate population. Sexual assault and gang rape is often committed across racial lines to assert dominance of blacks over whites in an intentional form of racial revenge for historical oppression within the outside world.[79]

Some researchers argue that gang activity is the result of the breakdown in earlier authoritarian systems of control in which powerful white inmates within the unit were delegated substantial power and control by autocratic administrations. Known in southern prisons as the **building tender system**, this type of management system is similar to the structure at Jamesburg in which the administration appointed certain inmates to keep order within their own units. This system was dismantled during the era of increased civil rights for prisoners for a secure environment. The **paradox of reform,** some believe, is that the prisoners' rights movement, legal mandates, and shifts in management philosophies which were intended to improve prison conditions have actually unleashed even more virulent forms of violence than during the repressive days of the "Big House."[80] On the other hand, others believe that the source of violence and risk of assault has merely shifted from the building tenders and guards of the old-style regime to the violent gangs and aggressive inmates of today.[81]

There is also a great deal of drug and alcohol use and abuse behind the walls. In fact, some believe that it is as easy to obtain drugs in prison as it is to get them on the outside. Drugs are smuggled into the institution partly by visitors but principally through prison staff who are blackmailed or enticed by financial reward. Gangs control the terrain of the prison in the same way they control parts of the city streets claiming a portion of the yard or a particular recreation room. They also control the drug trade and sex trade that operate on the inside as they do on the outside.[82]

Both the importation theory of prison violence and the **deprivation theory** of prison violence point to important causal factors of prison violence. In prisons where the "pains of imprisonment" are lessened through a more enlightened or genuinely rehabilitative regime, there is significantly less violence among the inmates. A brutal and punitive prison administration, on the other hand, stokes tension and rage among the inmates and allows the worst abuses to occur unchecked. On the other hand, the racial tension within the institution and the impact of gangs are clearly factors beyond the control of the prison authorities. These dynamics originate within the wider society and are brought into the prison.

PRISONERS' RIGHTS MOVEMENT

When Rubin Carter was disciplined for refusing to take a prison job and transferred to the VRU as punishment, he knew he had rights within the prison

BUILDING TENDER SYSTEM
a system of inmate control whereby the most violent and intimidating inmates were chosen as "building tender" by guards to control their fellow inmates by violence and coercion.

PARADOX OF REFORM
theory that legal interventions designed to improve the conditions of incarceration may have contributed to more serious violent conditions within the prison.

DEPRIVATION THEORY
the theory that the inmate subculture is formed as a adaptation to and reaction to the deprivations of prison life.

system even though he was an inmate. After nearly ten years behind walls, Carter had educated himself in the laws governing his conditions of confinement. Not only was Carter able to understand the law as it pertained to his own circumstances, but he also knew that the courts had ruled that as a **jailhouse lawyer**, he was permitted to advise other inmates on their own legal issues.

The recognition that prisoners retain some degree of their rights as citizens did not occur until the 1960s and 1970s. In 1871, in *Ruffin v. Commonwealth*,[83] the courts ruled that a convicted felon "has as a consequence of his crime, not only forfeited his liberty but all his personal rights. . . . He is for the time being a slave of the state." The Ruffin doctrine declared that prisoners, while they were behind bars, were, in the eyes of the law, "civilly dead."

Although this legal theory was amended in the twentieth century stating that prisoners retained some rights while incarcerated, the courts maintained a **hands-off doctrine** deferring to prison administrators preferring to leave matters of correctional policy in the hands of legislators and executive branch of government. Courts also feared an avalanche of prisoner litigation if they set the precedent of interfering with the prerogatives of the penal authority. But in 1964 in *Cooper v. Pate*[84] the Supreme Court ruled that inmates could file lawsuits under the federal Civil Rights Act, Section 1983, against public officials for alleged violations of the prisoners' civil rights. This case involved the First Amendment rights of black Muslims to practice their religion by having access to the Koran.

The prisoner rights movement coincided with increased political consciousness within the prison system and the wider society.[85] Black and Hispanic prisoners became increasingly militant and angry over the injustices of the indeterminate sentencing system. Rubin Carter lived through this period while in Rahway State Prison. The civil rights movement and the Black Power Movement laid the groundwork for a growing political consciousness among inmates, especially inmates of color.

On September 9, 1971, a riot broke out in Attica prison in upstate New York.[86] The riot lasted for four days. Prisoners led by the militant black Muslims took over large portions of the prison and presented the administration with a list of demands largely for more due process in discipline and grievance, better food, and more treatment programs. Negotiations began with outside civil rights attorneys and journalist observers. But Governor Rockefeller decided not to cooperate and stormed the prison with state police and correctional guards. Of the forty-three individuals who were killed in that riot, thirty-nine were killed by state officers in the retaking of the prison. In the aftermath, prisoners were brutally and violently beaten by the guards.

In 1974, the Supreme Court ruled in *Wolff v. McDonald*[87] that there was "no iron curtain drawn between the Constitution and the prisons of this country" signaling an end to the hands-off doctrine on the part of the courts. Since *Cooper* there is a recognition that prisoners retain some civil rights inside prison, although not equal to a free citizen. The role of the court is to strike a balance between security needs of the administration and the civil rights of the inmates.

During the 1970s, the federal courts became willing to more actively assert and defend the constitutional rights of prisoners. The entire prison system of several states, Arkansas, Alabama, Rhode Island, and Mississippi, was declared to be unconstitutional. By 1980, one out of every five cases filed in federal court was on behalf of prisoners. Most of the issues concerned the detail of everyday life within the prison. The key issues concerned overcrowding, brutality,

JAILHOUSE LAWYER
a prisoner who gives legal advice and assistance to other prisoners.

HANDS-OFF DOCTRINE
the refusal of the courts to hear inmates' cases regarding conditions of confinement and constitutional deprivations within the institution.

poor medical care, inadequate or unhygienic living conditions, access to lawyers, access to mail, religious freedom particularly led by the black Muslims, and due process in disciplinary transfers and good time forfeiture. By 1988, thirty-five states were under court order to improve their conditions of confinement. In the 1990s, the courts had, to an extent, returned to a reliance on the hands-off doctrine by ruling against a number of due process protections for inmates in disciplinary matters signaling reluctance on the part of the courts to interfere with the discretion of state administrators.[88] That changed in 2011 when the U.S. Supreme Court found that the overcrowding in California prisons violated the Eight Amendment ban on cruel and unusual punishment, and ordered the state to reduce the prison population by 30,000. The state was given two years to comply.[89] Three years later and California has indeed reduced its prison population by about 30,000. This was accomplished through a series of reforms which included sentencing certain kinds of felonies to local jails or diversionary programs rather than prison, keeping low-level offenders out of jail, and treating mental illnesses and addiction in less "restrictive settings."

Despite the downward trend in population, along with some decline in prison overcrowding, conditions in the country's jails and prisons have not improved significantly, and prison actions continue. In 2016 and early 2017 there were several uprisings (called riots in the press), including that in Holmes Correctional in Florida, where more than 400 inmates protested what they contend is inhumane and violent treatment; Holman Correctional Facility in Alabama, where about 100 inmates in a segregated unit attacked a warden; at the Souza-Baranowski Correctional Facility, a maximum-security prison in Massachusetts, after prisoners refused to be locked in their cells; and at the James T. Vaughn Correctional Center in Smyrna, Delaware, where one prisoner told the a news reporter, "Education, we want education first and foremost. We want a rehabilitation program that works for everybody. We want the money to be allocated so we can know exactly what is going on in the prison budget."[90]

CONTEMPORARY PRISON ISSUES

Women in Prison

Women constitute about 7 percent of the prison population and women's institutions have both been neglected by administrators and been ignored by researchers for most of the twentieth century. Although men vastly outnumber women in the prison system, in recent decades the number of women being sent to prison has been accelerating even faster than the number of men.[91] Between 1977 and 2005, the women's prison population rose by 757 percent.[92] Since the 1960s, prison litigation on behalf of women has focused on the inferiority of programming for women, the absence of different levels of incarceration, which exists for men resulting in the over-classification of many women in secure facilities, and the right to have equal treatment to that available to men.[93]

Life behind the walls for Kemba Smith most likely was very different from it was for Rubin Carter. Research has found that the women's inmate subculture differs from the male subculture, although in some respects there are similarities. Giallombardo found women inmates tended to form pseudo-families with extended kin roles to provide support, protection, emotional sustenance, and shared resources.[94] While homosexuality was prohibited within these families, women also formed stable and consensual relationships within prison based on consensual sex. The pattern of exploitation and assault typical of male prisons is not commonly found within women's institutions. Gang activity within women's prison is also different from men's prisons. Although younger women are joining gangs today, there is little evidence of substantial gang activity within women's prisons. Women's prisons are less violent so there is less need for group protection and the pseudo-families serve this function to some extent.

Kemba Smith is, in some respects, very typical of the female prison population. The average female inmate is black or Hispanic, between the ages of thirty and forty-four, and a single parent with one to three children.[95] She is typically serving time on drug offense or for non violent property crime. Most incarcerated women leave children behind and are the primary caregivers for those children. When women are put behind bars, there is a profound loss for ther children who are punished by the loss of their mother. When a father is incarcerated, care for children is usually assumed by the mother, but when a mother goes to prison, her children have usually lost their sole caregiver. The separation from their children and the attempt to maintain contact with their children while they are behind the wall is a key issue for women. Children generally are dependent upon relatives or foster care.

Many women enter into the system already pregnant. Women generally are allowed to deliver their babies in an outside hospital although they will be separated from the infant within days of the birth. In the Bedford Hills Correctional Center in New York state where nearly 80 percent of the inmates have children, there is a prison nursery on a floor of the prison hospital in which mother and baby share a room for the first year of the child's life. Older children are permitted to come for longer stays and there is even a camp near the facility for inmates' children. According to Sister Elaine, "The kids have done nothing wrong to cause this painful separation. We need to do all we can to strengthen bonds so the kids don't come back to prison later in a different way."

The Dangers of Solitary Confinement

Isolating prisoners to manage and punish inmates is a long-standing feature of prisons. Rubin Carter spent many months in the "hole" for his refusal to cooperate with the prison rules and regulations. Prison systems refer to solitary confinement by a number of different names: SHU (special or secure housing units), administrative segregation, voluntary or involuntary protective custody, isolation, the hole, STGMU (security threat groups, i.e., gang-management units), or permanent lockdown.

According to the Bureau of Justice Statistics, in 2011–2012 on any given day, about 4.4 percent, or 75,000 inmates, are confined in disciplinary or administrative segregation; nearly 20 percent of all inmates have spent time in isolation during the past twelve months; and 10 percent of all prison inmates were held for thirty days or longer. Young inmates, inmates without a high school diploma, and lesbian, gay, and bisexual inmates were more likely to spend time in segregation or solitary confinement than older inmates, inmates with at least a high school education, and heterosexual inmates.[96]

Although the specific conditions vary, the common features include confinement behind a solid steel door between 22 and 24 hours per day, severely limited contact with other people, extremely limited access to phone calls, family visits, and programming along with restricted reading materials and personal property. The psychological impacts of this kind of human and sensory deprivation have been well documented by prison psychologist Craig Haney.[97] These impacts include visual and auditory hallucinations, hypersensitivity to touch and noise, insomnia, paranoia, uncontrollable feelings of rage and fear, increased risk of suicide, and PTSD. These conditions are particularly harmful for younger inmates, who are more likely to end up in solitary than older inmates.

The dangers of solitary confinement to mental health are exacerbated by preexisting mental health conditions of many inmates. About a quarter of prisoners and jail inmates diagnosed with a mental health disorder spent time in segregation or solitary confinement. Many prisoners are released directly to the streets after spending years in isolation returning to the street with severe mental health issues.

Overcrowding and Violence

The modern correctional administrator faces an enormous number of challenges, and overcrowding is often at the top of the list.[98] Sentencing policies of the previous three decades have led to huge increases in the volume of inmates. The judicial process continues to funnel people to prison despite the limited capacity of institutions to adequately house them. Double and triple bunking of inmates in cells designed for single occupancy heightens stress, increases vulnerability to assaults, and raises tensions between inmates and guards. Studies show a strong relationship between overcrowding and inmate rule violations.[99] In addition, the density of housing adds to the spread of infectious diseases within the institution as well as adding to a range of stress-related illnesses, such as high blood pressure.

As noted earlier, violence in prison, particularly inmate on inmate violence as well as inmate assault of guards, has increased significantly in the post-rights era.[100] The largest single contributor to the increase in prison populations is drug sentencing that has fallen disproportionately on minorities. The disparity in sentencing of racial minorities has increased racial hostility, as minority gangs assert power and control over whites within the institution. Race has become the key feature of the inmate subculture. Even in women's prisons where racial dynamics have been less prominent, the recent influx of new female prisoners has been predominantly African American and there are signs of increasing racial tensions.

Overcrowding exacerbates the problem by both increasing the incidence of violence and making violence harder to control. The condition of overcrowding, in turn, leads to a heavier reliance upon solitary confinement and punitive disciplinary segregation to maintain order. Inmates come to prison from violent subcultures on the street and are maintained in an environment that also relies on violence as a means of survival. It is not surprising, therefore, that the many prisoners who are initially arrested for nonviolent offenses are later rearrested for violent offenses.[101]

Health Care and Special Needs Inmates

Another major challenge facing prison administrators today concerns the growing crisis of long-term health problems among prisoners with AIDS, drug-resistant TB, age-related illnesses, and mental illness. The rate of confirmed AIDS among prisoners is estimated to be at least six times higher than that among the general population.[102] By 1995, one-third of all inmate deaths in state prisons across the nation was due to AIDS.[103] As we have found better ways to treat AIDS, the number of inmate deaths has dropped, from 194 per 10,000 in 2001 to 146 per 10,000 in 2010. The number of male inmates known to have AIDS in state or federal prisons was 18,337 at the end of 2010.[104] The actual number may be substantially higher. Many of the inmates entering prison are IV drug users and are entering the institution already infected. Among the inmates, the rate of transmission is not known given the hidden nature of prison sexual activity but, by all estimates, there is a growing epidemic inside our nation's prison which will be felt in the near future, as the incubation period comes to an end and more inmates with HIV will be in need of medical attention.

Other infectious diseases are also spreading rapidly within modern prison system. The transmission of drug-resistant strains of tuberculosis, hepatitis, and other infectious diseases are exacerbated by conditions of overcrowding and the lack of adequate medical attention within many institutions. Given that approximately ten million persons are released back to the community each year after spending some time, either in jail or prison, the public health of the wider society is also in jeopardy, as prisons become breeding grounds for serious disease.[105]

Caring for elderly inmates is the third looming crisis facing correctional administrators in the twenty-first century. A natural consequence of the shift toward longer sentences is the aging of the inmate population: although few elderly people are convicted of crime, changes in sentencing practices has meant that many more inmates are growing old behind bars. In the state of California alone, the number of geriatric inmates will rise from 5,000 in 1994 to about 126,400 in the year 2020.[106]

As inmates age, their health needs skyrocket compounded by the unhealthy conditions of confinement. The need for special "geriatric" wards is emerging requiring more intensive health care and the purchase of equipment such as wheelchairs and walkers and replacing stairs with ramps. While the cost of incarceration for the average inmate hovers between 20 and 30,000 per year, the cost of confining the elderly inmates soars to 69,000 per year.[107] As the inmate population ages, the need to care for these inmates will continue to stress the resources of state budgets and prison systems.

Further compounding the management of inmate populations is the crisis of caring for mentally ill inmates. In 2005 approximately 56 percent of state prisoners, 73 percent of female inmates, and 55 percent of male inmates were found to have mental health problems.[108] Rollbacks in state mental health systems in the 1970s led to a corresponding rise in the number of the mentally ill inside the prison system. The mentally ill are often homeless and end up in the penal system for lack of an alternative system of care. Some estimate that 40 percent of all seriously mentally ill people in the United States are currently behind bars. In most states, jails and prisons function as the largest mental health provider in the state.

But the delivery of psychiatric services is extremely difficult inside of the prison system. Prisons are intended to deliver punishment through custodial confinement, not psychiatric treatment. Inmates on medication are not monitored to ensure they are taking the medication to prevent psychotic outbreaks, and frequent transfers between institutions leads to disruptions in the provision of medication. Inmates with serious mental illnesses are difficult to manage behaviorally. Correctional officers are not trained to distinguish between psychotic behavior and outward signs of disobedience and so they usually respond punitively. Psychotic inmates are routinely placed in disciplinary solitary confinement or administrative segregation, which tends to deteriorate their mental condition even further.

WHAT ABOUT REHABILITATION?

In 1974, Robert Martinson was asked the question of "what works?" in prison rehabilitation programs. Martinson reported that "With few and isolated exceptions, the rehabilitative efforts that have been reported so far have no appreciable effects on **recidivism**."[109] This answer led many people to declare that the ideal of rehabilitation was dead. Since prisons had never been successful at changing people from criminals to model citizens, the purpose of prisons is punishment, nothing more.

There are, however, many advocates of the belief that "some-things-do-work-some-of-the-time" within the field of correctional treatment and programming. Ted Palmer, Paul Gendreau, and Robert Ross, and many others believe the evidence clearly shows that some programs work when they are appropriately matched with the right offender.[110]

Yet, the fact remains that the **correctional treatment model** has problems which prevent the kind of optimistic results that the researchers often claim they can produce. First of all, most criminal conduct is not the result of some kind of sickness or personal flaw inside the offender that can simply be "cured" or "corrected." The commission of crime is a socially embedded activity involving a whole set of social relationships. Many offenders return to friends and a criminal lifestyle, and despite what they may have learned while inside the prison, they find it easier to go back to the old habits and patterns of behavior.

Programming inside of prisons remains a vital element of the prison world regardless of its long-term impact on recidivism or future criminal activity of inmates. Work programs relieve the stress of boredom and sometimes help build a person's work skills; religious programs offer inmates access to services for various denominations, mentor programs, and spiritual guidance and counseling. Recreational programs focus on physical activity that relieves the stress of incarceration. Basketball, softball, and weightlifting are often criticized by the public who are offended by the idea of inmates enjoying themselves. But correctional administrators value these programs since they assist them in managing the inmate population on a day-to-day basis providing a healthy alternative to using drugs or making trouble.

The single exception to the disappointing effect of prison programs on recidivism is the impact of earning a college education behind the walls on future criminal behavior. Research has found that college-level education significantly lowers inmate recidivism.[111] Among the most well-known and arguably successful programs are the Prison Education Project, which provides educational opportunities for inmates in eleven facilities in California; the BU Prison Education Program providing college courses to prisoners in state facilities in Massachusetts; the Bard Prison Initiative, which serves New York prisoners; and the Inside-Out Prison Exchange Program. The Inside-Out Prison Exchange Program is unique in that it has trained teachers throughout the United States (and even some internationally) and, rather than sending educators alone into facilities, Inside-Out brings entire college courses, including college-based students, into the facility where college students and incarcerated men and women learn side by side. Despite these varied successes, college programs are increasingly rare in prison, partly because few inmates have completed high school and many have serious learning problems but also because of political pressure from those opposed to offering a free college education for people who have committed crime.

RECIDIVISM
the repetition of criminal conduct.

CORRECTIONAL TREATMENT MODEL
reliance on prison rehabilitation programs.

Drug treatment is one of the most common treatment programs behind the wall. The most prevalent system is self-help groups, such as AA and NA, which offer mutual support for people suffering from addiction. Inmates can continue to participate in these programs once they leave the prison since every town and community has AA groups that are free and open to anyone who wishes to attend. Other common treatment programs behind the wall include anger management, parenting classes, life skills groups, individual and group counseling, and specialized treatment for sex offenders. Approximately two-thirds of entering prisoners are believed to have some substance abuse issues. Nearly half of these prisoners receive some treatment services while incarcerated. Ten months after release about one-quarter are still receiving services.[112]

Can prisons change a person? Here the answer from the evidence is probably negative. Prison treatment programs cannot *make* a person change how they think and how they act in the future. We can ask the question differently: Can prison programs help a person who wants to lead a different life when they leave the institution change? Here the answer is a most definite yes. Rubin Carter found that personal change and growth was possible even in the worst possible circumstances. Carter made constructive use of his time in prison to educate himself, shift his values, attitudes, and ultimately, his behavior. The prison did not assist Carter in making these changes; just the opposite, the prison did everything possible to make it hard for Carter to develop constructive attitudes and ideas. Rubin Carter was able to find peace despite the prison, not because of it.

It is possible, however, for prisons to offer those who want to change the opportunity to use their time behind the walls constructively to build new lives for themselves and their families. Ninety-five percent of people in prison will return to the community at some point. This is often cited as a compelling reason to emphasize vocational, educational, and treatment programs in prison. But there is another reason to be concerned about penal institutions which do nothing more than warehouse human beings in conditions of indignity and violence. As Winston Churchill remarked, how we treat criminals tells us a great deal about who we are as a society and as a nation. In the words of Victor Hassein, a lifer in the Pennsylvania prison system: "Today in prison I find myself longing for any glimpse of an attempt to rehabilitate, not because I believe in rehabilitation but because I worry about a society that no longer bothers to consider its possibility."[113]

---

bloody codes (p. 386) a system of laws in eighteenth-century England that permitted capital punishment for a wide range of property and minor offenses.

corporeal punishment (p. 386) punishment inflicted on the body through whipping, branding, mutilation, or torture.

Walnut Street Jail (p. 387) the first American penitentiary.

penitentiary (p. 387) an institution intended to isolate prisoners from society and from one another so they could reflect on their past, repent, and emerge as reformed sinners.

separate system (p. 388) complete solitary confinement in an individual cell to encourage redemption and prevent social contamination via association with others in the prison first used in the Walnut Street jail.

congregate system (p. 388) a penitentiary system developed in Auburn, New York, in which inmates, were held in solitary confinement at night but worked with fellow prisoners during the day under a rule of complete silence.

punitive solitary confinement (p. 388)   the use of solitary confinement under conditions of extreme deprivation as a punishment for disciplinary infractions.

lockstep (p. 388)   a peculiar form of marching for prisoners in which they were required to move in unison with their hands on each other's shoulders.

contract system (p. 388)   a form of prison industry in which the labor of inmates was leased to an outside contractor or business for a fee.

reformatory model (p. 389)   a nineteenth-century prison reform movement generally reserved for youth and women that focused on rehabilitation, reform, and the use of indeterminate sentencing.

Big House (p. 390)   slang for maximum-security prisons infamous for harsh conditions and tough inmate populations.

state-use laws (p. 390)   laws that require prison industry to produce goods solely for use in state institutions.

maximum security (p. 390)   a facility designed to impose maximal restriction on inmates in order to contain the most incorrigible and violent offenders.

medium security (p. 391)   a prison designed to impose less restrictive conditions on inmates allowing for greater visitation, programming, and recreation for inmates.

minimum security (p. 391)   an institution designed to permit the least dangerous inmates allowing relative freedom of movement within the confines of a locked perimeter.

super-max prison (p. 392)   a new generation of maximum-security facility which relies upon technology and high levels of supervision and restriction of inmate movement.

classification (p. 392)   the process through which the custodial, educational, and treatment needs of the offender are assessed in order to ascertain placement within the correctional system.

private correctional facilities (p. 393)   corporate-owned and run facilities that contract with local, state, and federal governments to house inmates.

jail (p. 393)   a facility authorized to hold persons awaiting trial and those sentenced for misdemeanors and minor felony offenses.

total institution (p. 394)   a term coined by Erving Goffman to refer to institutions organized so that those who work in the institution exercise total control over every aspect of the lives of those who are inmates within the institution.

structured conflict (p. 395)   the relationship between inmates and guards within the institution in which inmates are confined against their will and guards are charged with the responsibility of enforcing their detention.

status degradation ceremony (p. 395)   rituals which mark the transition from a citizen to the lower status of an inmate.

prisonization (p. 395)   the process whereby a new inmate becomes socialized to the inmate subculture and adapts to prison life.

pains of imprisonment (p. 396)   deprivations of prison life, including absence of goods, autonomy, heterosexual interaction, and security.

importation theory (p. 397)   the theory that inmate subculture is brought inside the institution from criminal subcultures within outside society.

deprivation theory (p. 398)   the theory that the inmate subculture is formed as a adaptation to and reaction to the deprivations of prison life.

building tender system (p. 398)   a system of inmate control whereby the most violent and intimidating inmates were chosen as "building tender" by guards to control their fellow inmates by violence and coercion.

paradox of reform (p. 398)   theory that legal interventions designed to improve the conditions of incarceration may have contributed to more serious violent conditions within the prison.

jailhouse lawyer (p. 399)   a prisoner who gives legal advice and assistance to other prisoners.

hands-off doctrine (p. 399)   the refusal of the courts to hear inmates' cases regarding conditions of confinement and constitutional deprivations within the institution.

recidivism (p. 404)   the repetition of criminal conduct.

correctional treatment model (p. 404)   reliance on prison rehabilitation programs.

REVIEW AND STUDY QUESTIONS

1. Describe the intentions of the reformers who invented the penitentiary. How did the use of the penitentiary differ from previous forms of punishment?

2. Define and describe the separate and congregate system of confinement. Where was each practiced? What were the significant differences between these two? Which one was ultimately successful and why?

3. Describe the reformatory model of incarceration. What form of sentencing is associated with this era of penal reform?

4. Identify and describe the different types of institutions found with most state correctional systems.

5. What is a "total institution"? Define and illustrate the concept of a "status degradation ceremony" within the prison setting.

6. Describe the four key deprivations associated with imprisonment. Why does Sykes refer to these as the "pains" of imprisonment? Define the concept of "prisonization."

7. Explain the importation theory of prison culture. Contrast this theory with the deprivation theory.

8. To what extent do prisoners have constitutional rights? Explain the "paradox of reform."

9. Explain the relationship between overcrowding, race, and violence within the prison.

10. What are the health care challenges facing the modern prison?

CHECK IT OUT

Websites

National Criminal Justice Reference Service, https://www.ncjrs.gov/App/Topics/Topic.aspx?TopicID=1. Excellent web site with access to full text publications on all matters related to corrections. Read recent NIJ research reports on AIDS-HIV, health care, inmate programs, jail, women in prison, and lots more.

Federal Bureau of Prisons, https://www.bop.gov/. Check out this site for a great deal of information about federal prisons, including the latest figures on gender, race, age, and offense for federal prisoners.

ACLU Prisoners' Rights, https://www.aclu.org/issues/prisoners-rights. Excellent web site for all learning more about prisoners' rights.

Just Detention International, https://justdetention.org. This non-profit human rights organization is dedicated to end sexual violence committed against men, women, and youth in all forms of detention.

Videos

Let the Doors Be Made of Iron: 19th Century Prison Reform—23 minutes. Academy Award–nominated documentary using dramatic re-enactments, photographs, and lithographs to trace the story of the Eastern State Penitentiary. Brings the hopes and reality of the so-called humane experiment to life. Available from https://www.easternstate.org/shop/dvds/let-doors-be-iron

Quiet Rage: The Stanford Prison Experiment—50 minutes. The video documents the classic landmark study of a mock prison which demonstrates the effect of the roles of the prison environment on the psyche of the subjects and their treatment of fellow human beings. Classic black and white footage from the original experiment is interspersed with a current group of college students on tour of the mock prison. Available from http://www.prisonexp.org/quiet-rage/

Women Doing Time—48 minutes. The video goes inside New York's Bedford Hills Correctional Facility, one of the oldest prisons for women, to examine what it means for women to be serving time. Available on VHS from https://www.amazon.com/48-Hours-Women-Doing-Time/dp/B012MLU4NC

Criminal Injustice: Death and Politics at Attica—60 minutes. Forty years after the Attica prison uprising, this video raises new questions about the deaths and the corrupting power of politics. Trailer at: http://www.usatoday.com/story/news/nation/2013/02/09/documentary-raises-questions-attica-prison-riot/1905655/ Full video available from Blue Sky Project, http://

bspfilms.org/films/criminal-injustice-death-and-politics-at-attica/

Supermax, a Prison Within a Prison—40 minutes. ABC news anchor Ted Koppel takes us inside the world of the solitary confinement in today's super-max security prisons and the effect of this confinement on the inmates and the correctional officers as well. Available from FilmsMediaGroup at http://www.films.com/id/10991

Prison Gangs and Racism Behind Bars—40 minutes. Ted Koppel explores the racist hatred within the prison between ethnic and white supremacist gangs. He interviews those who are put in solitary confinement because of their gang affiliations, spends a night inside a cell, and explores the impact of this confinement on the psychological and emotional health of inmates who will one day return to the public streets. Available from FilmsMediaGroup at http://www.films.com/id/10992

NOTES

[1] Paul B. Wice, *Rubin "Hurricane" Carter and the American Justice System* (New Brunswick: Rutgers University Press, 2000).

[2] Rubin "Hurricane" Carter, *The Sixteenth Round* (New York: Viking Press, 1974).

[3] Carter, *The Sixteenth Round*, 25.

[4] Carter, *The Sixteenth Round*, 41.

[5] Carter, *The Sixteenth Round*, 43–76.

[6] Carter, *The Sixteenth Round*, 82.

[7] Carter, *The Sixteenth Round*, 87.

[8] James S. Hirsch, *Hurricane: The Miraculous Journey of Rubin Carter* (Boston, MA: Houghton Mifflin Co, 2000), 75.

[9] Paul B. Wice, *Rubin "Hurricane" Carter and the American Justice System* (New Brunswick: Rutgers University Press, 2000), 30.

[10] Rubin "Hurricane" Carter, *The Sixteenth Round* (New York: Viking Press, 1974), 139.

[11] Carter, *The Sixteenth Round*, 141.

[12] Carter, *The Sixteenth Round*, 156.

[13] James S. Hirsch, *Hurricane: The Miraculous Journey of Rubin Carter* (Boston, MA: Houghton Mifflin Co, 2000), 76.

[14] Hirsch, *Hurricane*, 4.

[15] Hirsch, *Hurricane*, 88.

[16] Rubin "Hurricane" Carter, *The Sixteenth Round* (New York: Viking Press, 1974), 180–181.

[17] Carter, *The Sixteenth Round*, 88.

[18] Carter, *The Sixteenth Round*, 89.

[19] Carter, *The Sixteenth Round*, p.162.

[20] James S. Hirsch, *Hurricane: The Miraculous Journey of Rubin Carter* (Boston, MA: Houghton Mifflin Co, 2000), 19–20.

[21] Paul B. Wice, *Rubin "Hurricane" Carter and the American Justice System* (New Brunswick: Rutgers University Press, 2000), 67.

[22] Rubin "Hurricane" Carter, *The Sixteenth Round* (New York: Viking Press, 1974), 307.

[23] Carter, *The Sixteenth Round*, 89–91.

[24] James S. Hirsch, *Hurricane: The Miraculous Journey of Rubin Carter* (Boston, MA: Houghton Mifflin Co, 2000, 91–92.

[25] Hirsch, *Hurricane*, 98.

[26] Hirsch, *Hurricane*, 102–104.

[27] Hirsch, *Hurricane*, 105–106.

[28] Hirsch, *Hurricane*, 107.

[29] Hirsch, *Hurricane*, 114–132.

[30] Hirsch, *Hurricane*, 132.

[31] Paul B. Wice, *Rubin "Hurricane" Carter and the American Justice System* (New Brunswick: Rutgers University Press, 2000), 80.

[32] Wice, *Rubin "Hurricane" Carter*, 115–118.

[33] Wice, *Rubin "Hurricane" Carter*, 129–130.

[34] James S. Hirsch, *Hurricane: The Miraculous Journey of Rubin Carter* (Boston, MA: Houghton Mifflin Co, 2000), 169.

[35] Hirsch, *Hurricane*, 171.

[36] Hirsch, *Hurricane*, 189–197.

[37] Paul B. Wice, *Rubin "Hurricane" Carter and the American Justice System* (New Brunswick: Rutgers University Press, 2000), 184–185.

[38] Wice, *Rubin "Hurricane" Carter*, 190–191.

[39] Lauren E. Glaze and Danielle Kaeble, "Correctional Populations in the United States, 2013," *Bureau of Justice Statistics, No. NCJ 2484799* (Washington, DC, December 19, 2014).

[40] Thorstein Sellin, *Slavery and the Penal System* (New York, Elsevier, 1976).

[41] Georg Rusche and Otto Kirchheimer, *Punishment and Social Structure* (New York, Russell and Russell, 1939).

[42] Michael Ignatieff, *A Just Measure of Pain* (New York, Pantheon, 1978).

CHAPTER 14 • Inside the Prison World / 409

43 Pieter C. Spierenburg, *The Spectacle of Suffering* (Cambridge, UK: Cambridge University Press, 1985).

44 David Rothman, *The Discovery of the Asylum* (Boston, MA: Little Brown, 1971).

45 Gustave de Beaumone and Alexis de Toqueville, *On the Penitentiary System of the United States and Its Application in France* (Philadelphia: Carey, Lea and Blanchard, 1833).

46 Paul Takagi, "The Walnut Street Jail: A Penal Reform to Centralize the Powers of the State," *Federal Probation* December (1975).

47 Charles Dickens, *American Notes*, Vol.1 (London: Chapman and Hall, 1842), 238.

48 Dario Melossi and Massimo Pavarini, *The Prison and the Factory: Origins of the Penitentiary System* (London. UK: Macmillan, 1981).

49 Thorstein Sellin, *Slavery and the Penal System* (New York: Elsevier, 1976).

50 David J. Rothman, *Conscience and Convenience: The Asylum and its Alternatives in Progressive America* (Boston: Little, Brown and Company, 1980).

51 Elizabeth Eileen Dooley, "Sir Walter Crofton and the Irish or Intermediate System of Prison Discipline," *New England Journal of Prison Law* 575 (1981).

52 Zebulon Brockway, *Fifty years of Prison Service* (Montclair, NJ: Patterson Smith, 1969).

53 Anthony Platt, *The Child-Savers: The Invention of Delinquency* (Chicago: University of Chicago Press, 1970).

54 Estelle B. Freedman, *Their Sisters' Keepers: Women's Prison Reform in America, 1830-1930* (Ann Arbor: University of Michigan Press, 1981); Nicole Hahn Rafter, "Chastizing the Unchaste: Social Control Functions of a Women's Reformatory, 1894-1931" in *Social Control and the State*, eds. Stanley Cohen and Andrew Scull (Oxford: Martin Robertson, 1983), 288–310.

55 David J. Rothman, *Conscience and Convenience: The Asylum and its Alternatives in Progressive America* (Boston, MA: Little, Brown and Company, 1980).

56 John Irwin, *Prisons in Turmoil* (Boston, MA: Little Brown and Company, 1980).

57 Rubin "Hurricane" Carter, *The Sixteenth Round* (New York: Viking Press, 1974), 165.

58 National Association of State Budget Officers, *The State Expenditure Report* (Washington, DC: 1987), 8; National Association of State Budget Officers, *The State Expenditure Report* (Washington, DC: 2009), 54.

59 Elizabeth Alexander, "The Care and Feeding of the Correctional-Industrial Complex" in *Building Violence: How America's Rush to Incarcerate Creates More Violence*, ed. John P. May (Thousand Oaks, CA: Sage, 2000), 53.

60 Christian Henrichson and Ruth Delaney, *The Price of Prisons: What Incarceration Costs Taxpayers* (New York: Vera Institute of Justice, 2012).

61 E. Ann Carson, Prisoners in 2014, (Department of Justice: Bureau of Justice Statistics, 2015), NCJ 248955.

62 Richard G. Singer, "Prisons: Typologies and Classifications," *Encyclopedia of Crime and Justice* (New York: The Free Press, 1983).

63 Raymond Holt, "Marion: Separating Fact from Fiction," *Federal Prisons Journal* 2 (1991), 33–34.

64 Ken Silverstein, "America's Private Gulag," in *The Celling of America: An Inside Look at the U.S. Prison Industry*, ed. Daniel Burton-Rose (Monroe, ME: Common Courage Press, 1998), 156–163.

65 Suevon Lee, "By the Numbers: The U.S.'s Growing For-Profit Detention Industry," *Pro Publica* (June 20, 2012).

66 Charles H. Logan, *Private Prisons: Cons and Pros* (New York: Oxford University Press, 1990).

67 Ronald Goldfarb, *Jails: The Ultimate Ghetto* (New York: Archer Press, 1975).

68 Stephen H. Gettinger, *New Generation Jails: An Innovative Approach to an Age-Old Problem* (Washington, DC: National Institute of Corrections, 1984).

69 Philip G. Zimbardo, "The Pathology of Imprisonment," *Society* 9 (1972), 4–8.

70 Erving Goffman, *Asylums* (New York: Bantam Books, 1987).

71 James Jacob and Lawrence Kraft, "Integrating the Keepers: A Comparison of Black and White Prison Guards in Illinois," *Social Problems* 25 (1978), 304–318.

72 Donald Clemmer, *The Prison Community* (New York: Holt, Rinehart & Winston, 1940).

73 Gresham M. Sykes, *The Society of Captives: A Study of a Maximum Security Prison*, (Princeton: Princeton University Press, 1958).

74 Allen J. Beck and Candace Johnson. *Sexual Victimization Reported by Former State Prisoners, 2008*, (Department of Justice: Bureau of Justice Statistics, 2012), NCJ 237363.

75 Rubin "Hurricane" Carter, *The Sixteenth Round* (New York: Viking Press, 1974), 170.

76 James S. Hirsch, *Hurricane: The Miraculous Journey of Rubin Carter* (Boston, MA: Houghton Mifflin Co, 2000), 210.

77 John Irwin and Donald R. Cressey, "Thieves, Convicts and the Inmate Culture," *Social Problems* 10 (1962), 142–55.

78 Leo Carrol, *Hacks, Blacks and Cons: Race Relations in a Maximum Security Prison*, (Princeton, NJ: Princeton University Press, 1974).

79 James B. Jacobs, "Race Relations and the Prisoner Subculture," in *Crime and Justice: An Annual Review of Research*, eds. Norval Morris and Michael Tonry (Chicago: University of Chicago Press, 1980).

[80] Robert Johnson, *Hard Time: Understanding and Reforming the Prison* (Belmont, CA: Wadsworth, 1996).

[81] Ben M. Crouch and James W. Marquart, "Resolving the Paradox of Reform: Litigation, Prisoner Violence and the Perceptions of Risk," *Justice Quarterly* 7 (1990), 103–122.

[82] Paige H. Ralph, "From Self-Preservation to Organized Crime: The Evolution of Inmates Gangs" in *Correctional Contexts*, eds. James W. Marquart and Jonathan R. Sorensen (CA: Roxbury Publishing Company, 1997), 182–186.

[83] 62 Va. 790, (1871), 88, 341.

[84] 378 U.S. 546 (1964), 343.

[85] James B. Jacobs, *New Perspectives on Prisons and Imprisonment* (Ithaca, New York: Cornell University Press, 1983).

[86] Burt Useem and Peter Kimball, *States of Siege: U.S. Prison Riots, 1971–1986* (NY: Oxford University Press, 1989).

[87] 94 S.Ct. 2963 (1974).

[88] John McLaren, "Prisoners' Rights: The Pendulum Swings," in *Prisons Today and Tomorrow*, ed. Joycelyn M. Pollack (Gaithersburg, MD: Aspen, 1997), 377.

[89] *Brown v. Plata*, 131 S.Ct. 1910 (2011).

[90] Josh Keefe, *Delaware Prison Riot Latest" Corrections Officer Killed in Anti-Trump Prisoner Uprising.* (International Business Times, 02/02/17). http://www.ibtimes.com/delaware-prison-riot-latest-corrections-officer-killed-anti-trump-prisoner-uprising-2485196; retrieved February 3, 2017.

[91] Bureau of Justice Statistics, *Women in Prison* (Washington, DC: U.S. Department of Justice, 1994).

[92] Natasha Frost, Judith Greene and Kevin Pranis, "The Punitiveness Report-HARD HIT: The Growth in Imprisonment of Women, 1977–2004," Women's Prison Association. http://www.wpaonline.org/institute/hardhit/HardHit Report4.pdf; accessed September 20, 2012.

[93] Lawrence Bershad, "Discriminatory Treatment of the Female Offenders in the Criminal Justice System," *Boston College Law Review* 26 (1985).

[94] Rose Giallombardo, *Society of Women: A Study of a Women's Prison* (New York: Wiley, 1966).

[95] "Quick Facts: Women & Criminal Justice—2009," Institute on Women & Criminal Justice. http://www.wpaonline.org/pdf/Quick%20Facts%20Women%20and%20 CJ%202009.pdf; accessed September 20, 2012..

[96] Allen J. Beck, Use of Restrictive Housing in U.S. Prisons and Jails, 2011–12. (U.S. Department of Justice Office of Justice Programs Bureau of Justice Statistics Special Report, October 2015.)

[97] Haney, C. "Mental Health Issues in Long-Term Solitary and 'Supermax' Confinement." *Crime and Delinquency*, 49(1), 124–156. Retrieved from http://www.supermaxed.com/NewSupermaxMaterials/Haney-MentalHealthIssues.pdf

[98] Alida V. Merlo, "The Crisis and Consequences of Prison Overcrowding," in *Prisons: Today and Tomorrow*, ed. Jocelyn M. Pollack (Gaithersburg, MD: Aspen Publications, 1997), 52–74.

[99] Merlo, The Crisis and Consequences of Prison Overcrowding, 65.

[100] Robert Johnson, *Hard Time: Understanding and Reforming the Prison* (Belmont, CA: Wadsworth, 1996).

[101] John P. May, "Feeding a Public Health Epidemic," in *Building Violence: How America's Rush to Incarcerate Creates More Violence*, eds. John P. May and Khalid R. Pitts (Thousand Oaks, CA: Sage, 2000), 134.

[102] Laura Maruschak, "HIV in Prisons and Jail, 1995," *Bureau of Justice Statistics Bulletin* (Washington, DC: Department of Justice, Bureau of Justice Statistics, 1997), 1–12.

[103] Maruschak, HIV in Prisons and Jail, 1995, 10.

[104] Laura Maruschak, "HIV in Prisons, 2001–2010," *Bureau of Justice Statistics Special Report No. NCJ 238877* (Washington, DC, September 13, 2012). http://bjs.ojp.usdoj.gov/index.cfm?ty=pbdetail&iid=4452; accessed September 20, 2012.

[105] John P. May, "Feeding a Public Health Epidemic," in *Building Violence: How America's Rush to Incarcerate Creates More Violence*, eds. John P. May and Khalid R. Pitts (Thousand Oaks, CA: Sage, 2000), 134.

[106] May, Feeding a Public Health Epidemic, 53.

[107] Stephen Donzinger, ed., *The Real War on Crime: The Report of the National Criminal Justice Commission* (New York: Harper Collins, 1996), 54.

[108] Lauren E. Glaze and Doris J. James, "Mental Health Problems of Prison and Jail Inmates," *Bureau of Justice Statistics Special Report No. NCJ 213600* (Washington, DC, September 6, 2006). http://bjs.ojp.usdoj.gov/index.cfm?ty=pbdetail&iid=789; accessed September 20, 2012.

[109] Robert Martinson, "What Works? - Questions and Answers About Prison Reform," *The Public Interest* 35 (1974), 54.

[110] Daniel Antonowicz and Robert Ross, "Essential Components of Successful Rehabilitation Programs for Offenders," *International Journal of Offender Therapy and Comparative Criminology* 38 (1994), 97–104; Paul Gendreau and Robert Ross, "Revivification of Rehabilitation: Evidence for the 1980s," *Justice Quarterly* 4 (1987), 349–407; Ted Palmer. *A Profile of Correctional Effectiveness and New Directions for Research*, (Albany, NY: SUNY Press, 1994).

[111] David Clark, *Analysis of Return Rates of Inmate College Program Participants* (Albany, NY: New York State Department of Correctional Services, 1991).

[112] Kamala Mallik-Kane and Christy A. Visher, "Health and Prisoner Reentry: How Physical, Mental, and Substance Abuse Conditions Shape the Process of Reintegration," (Washington, DC: Urban Institute: Justice Policy Center, 2008).

[113] Victor Hassine, *Life Without Parole: Living in Prison Today* (Los Angeles, CA: Roxbury Publishing, 1996), 84.

In this chapter we follow the story of a California man's efforts to get paroled from a life sentence, as well as the challenges he faces after parole is granted. The chapter presents the history of probation and parole, as well as other diversion models along with the unintended consequences of community-based programs. The more recent concept of restorative justice is presented. The chapter concludes with the challenges of addressing criminal justice reform in an era of mass incarceration.

LEARNING OBJECTIVES

After reading this chapter students should be able to:

- Identify the historical origins of probation and parole.
- Describe the functions of probation and parole today.
- Identify the three periods of community corrections; identify goals and philosophy of each period and identify specific programs developed within each period.
- Define the concept of "net-widening" and show how it undermines goals of community corrections
- Describe restorative and community justice and explain how they offer an alternative to traditional community corrections.

Case #15: Making Parole in California

At a parole hearing an offender must present convincing evidence of rehabilitation and remorse to members of the parole board.

In 2007 when her producer asked reporter Nancy Mullane to prepare a radio broadcast on the scale and scope of mass incarceration, she realized she had never really given much thought to the nearly 1.7 million people locked up inside our nation's prisons. Faced with alarming statistics, Mullane decided she wanted to talk with the real human beings behind those numbers and ask the questions that so quickly came to her mind: What did you do to get here? What kind of person are you? What does it feel like to be locked inside for years on end? How does your family cope with what has happened? How on earth do you survive?

With a reporter's persistence Mullane achieved the impossible and got herself and her tape recorder inside San Quentin, one of California's largest prisons. Face to face with a small group of men serving life with the possibility of parole, she got to know them, their life stories, and the story of their crime. Eventually one question more than any other rose in her mind: "How does one go from a relatively normal person to a monster and then back to who you really are?"[1] Is it possible for people to change their behavior? And if they do will society allow them to come back? Is it safe? Can we be sure?

For nearly five years Mullane interviewed five men serving life sentences for homicide as they did everything they could to convince the parole board and governor of the state of California that they could be trusted to live back in the community. When she met them, they were no longer the young men who had used and sold drugs, committed armed robberies, or thought it was cool to take a drunken joyride in someone else's car. Each one had served at least fifteen to twenty-seven years before they were even eligible for parole. Inside California state prison system they spent those long years as constructively as they could: getting degrees; engaging in religious activities; participating in programs; learning a trade; and working at any kind of job for thirty cents an hour.

The court had sentenced them to "life with the possibility of parole." That is only a possibility—not a guarantee. Only a glimmer of hope, a slim reed that maybe, once they have served fifteen, seventeen, twenty-five, or twenty-seven years, and can prove that they are now rehabilitated and if they managed to avoid even a single disciplinary report for the tiniest of infractions, and if they win approval from countless officials in distant offices, then, maybe, one day—they might again—walk on carpet, take a bath, ride a bike, walk to town, climb a mountain, or eat a meal at their own kitchen table.

The questions that led Mullane to talk with the real human beings who were living in steel mesh cages not all that different from the kennels found at the dog pound—How on earth do you cope?—gave way to a different kind of curiosity. Now Mullane focused on one question above all others: How does one convince a distant board of professionals and an even more distant governor of the state of California, that you are no longer a threat to society? How do you prove a negative—that you won't do harm, that you won't violate the law? What can you say or do to demonstrate to a set of skeptical strangers that you are no longer the same person as the one who was brought here decades earlier? And what do you do if they refuse to believe you? How do you cope when they say no?

One Man's Story

Phillip Jay Seiler was convicted of second-degree murder in 1988. Sentenced to seventeen years to life with the possibility of parole, he eventually served twenty years and thirty-four days before being released on parole. These bare facts, which are often all we hear about the lives of convicted criminals, tell us almost nothing about who Phillip is, what he actually did to deserve such a sentence, and how he lived his life before and after committing the act that so profoundly changed everything for him, his family, and everyone connected to the man he killed.

These are the stories that the prison walls keep from the rest of society. Those thick walls perform double duty when they close shut on the life of a convicted criminal. They lock those who have done harm far from the rest of society but they also keep society apart from the details that led them there, the reality of the penal system and the lives we force them to endure behind those walls. There is a silence that shrouds crime: beyond the lurid stories told in the media, rarely do we hear from those who commit crime about what they did, why they did it, and how they feel about it many years later.

Nancy Mullane asks Phillip Seiler, as she did all the rest of the men interviewed in her book, to tell her about his crime. She asks him while her tape recorder is running knowing the story will find its way into a book for the world to read. She wonders if she herself really wants to know—sitting across from her is a forty-five-year-old mild-mannered man wearing spectacles and a button-down shirt. Does she really want to know the circumstances under which he violently took another person's life? Even more, she wonders why any of these men would share this hard truth about their past with a public that is likely to see them as nothing more than a murderer? Why open yourself up to that especially when you are on the verge of finally coming back to live with ordinary citizens? Why take a chance that people will not accept you as their neighbor, co-worker, or friend once they know about the past? Wouldn't anyone prefer to keep those secrets to themselves?

Yet each of the men Mullane interviewes for this book agrees to tell her the full story of their crime for the book using their real names. They accept the risk of societal censure as part of the cost of the crime itself: the truth of the past is the truth of who they were and what they did, not who they are now and what they will do tomorrow. Prison has taught them to deal with the truth as it is, not as they wish it to be. Being a lifer eligible for parole in the state of California has taught them a thing or two about the nature of reality: wishful thinking is luxury they cannot afford.

In Phillip's case Mullane pops the million-dollar question at the oddest time and place. Phillip has just won a long and heartbreaking legal battle to be released on parole; to get out he had to fight his way up to California Court of Appeals. It is the actual day of his release and he is in the administrative office waiting for his parole officer, dressed and ready to go. He and Mullane are not alone: the room is full of officers who have known Phillip for decades but never heard him (or any other prisoner, for that matter) talk about what they did. Mullane knows it is not the best time to ask but since it may be her only chance she blurts it out, not really expecting Phillip to respond before an audience of stone-faced correctional officers. "So, twenty years ago, what did you do?" Once the question is out there, the room goes silent. Heads down, everyone pretends to be busy as Phillip begins to talk. For twenty minutes, only the sound of his voice fills the room. The audio on the recording is perfect.

It was a really bad day during a really bad time in Phillip's marriage. Twenty-seven-year-old, Phillip was working long hours in construction doing pretty well—he had a house, four cars, and two young sons, aged four and eight. His wife though had started using meth again despite having tried drug programs and was now hanging around with a guy she liked to do drugs with. The marriage was coming apart at the seams. Phillip now sees that his first mistake was putting one of the rifles he used for target practice into the backseat of his car: his wife's new boyfriend was a tough guy, who threatened to send his boys after Phillip if he interfered with their affair. It was a dumb move which paved the way for even worse decisions down the road. But the steam was building inside Phillip.

On this particular day things went from bad to worse: he unexpectedly got laid off from his job and came home early to find his wife and her new boyfriend setting out in one of his four cars. He jumped in his car intending to chase them out of the neighborhood. At a stop sign the cars rear-ended and both men got out, Phillip grabbing his gun from the back seat. The first words out of this man's mouth included the words, "She's mine," and without another thought, Phillip fired, point blank at his chest killing him instantly. Leaving the scene, Phillip drove to his mother's house where holding his sons on his lap sobbing, he called the police and turned himself in.

Phillip makes no excuses for himself as he relates the story. He points out, to no one in particular, that there were many choices he could have made other than the ones he did make. He points out, to no one in particular, the mistakes he made every step of the way. He had options—he could have left his wife, sued for divorce, told the police about the threats, and found a new life with his young sons. He shakes his head and tries to explain that at twenty-seven the last thing Phillip knew was how to deal with the emotions churning inside him at that time. None of this diminishes his responsibility for what he did—he states that as clearly as he can.

Following the advice of his attorney, Phillip pled guilty to second-degree murder and was sentenced to fifteen years to life with possibility of parole, with two additional years' enhancement for using the gun. According to state law, Phillip would be eligible for parole after serving 80 percent of his sentence: just under fifteen years of his seventeen-year sentence.

The Long and Winding Road to Parole

Parole eligibility is set by statute, but once the time is served, the process to determine if a person will be released on parole begins. When a prisoner reaches his minimum eligibility date, he is automatically brought before at least two or three members of the state's Adult Board of Parole Hearings, who decide if the inmate is "suitable" for parole.

Suitability requires demonstrating a lot of tangible facts to these commissioners: the inmate has to prove that he has a place to live when he returns, that this living arrangement is stable and affordable and that no one else living there has a criminal record or is involved in crime. The inmate will also have to show that he has a full-time job waiting for him and it must

be one that will pay him a living wage. He will present the record of all that he did while inside the facility; letters from people on the inside and on the outside attesting to his progress; and must display a spotless disciplinary history showing that he has never violated any of the countless rules and regulations that dominate day to day life inside the prison.

As hard as all this is, these requirements are easy compared with what else Phillip must prove to the parole board. In addition to all those tangible achievements, Phillip must demonstrate that he is remorseful for his crime, that he truly understands the impact of his actions on others, that he has made serious effort to change during his time in prison and—perhaps the hardest of all—that he will no longer pose a threat to the public in the future. For this there are no documents or letters to produce: Phillip simply appears in person before the board and does his best to answer their questions as truthfully as he can.

Once the commissioners make their decision, the case goes to the California Department of Corrections and Rehabilitation where they will have 120 days or four months to review all the information and verify the facts by sending out parole officers to check out the information supplied by the inmate. Does he really have a job offer? Is the pay what he says it is? Does anyone with a criminal record live at the place he says he will live? Even the tiniest discrepancy between the inmate's statements and the facts are grounds for denial. If the review is successful, however, the file heads to the governor's office for the final determination. The governor then has thirty days to approve or deny the decision.

The Marathon Begins

In Phillip's case, his first hearing before the parole board, called an initial hearing, comes after he has served ten years behind bars. By this time, Phillip had earned his GED, and was taking college-level courses. He was an avid participant in a program called IMPACT (Incarcerated Men Putting Away Childish Things) and Squires, a program in which inmates speak with troubled teens. Fairly routinely, the parole board denied his parole and issues a two-year period before he can return again.

In two years, he tries again but has to wait an additional year because they are backlogged. They again issue a two-year denial.

Now, a third time, five years from his original hearing, Phillip goes before the board again. By this time he has accumulated dozens of letters from chaplains, volunteers, program directors, and teachers about his conduct and progress. His disciplinary record is flawless: not a single disciplinary report in fifteen years. This time the board changes its mind: Phillips is determined "suitable" for parole.

The Marathon Continues

Now his case goes to the CDRC for a grueling 120-day wait while the department checks out every reference and letter in his file. If the department finds any reason to question the living arrangements on the outside, it will rescind the offer of parole. If all seems ship shape, the final stage is the governor's desk—the governor has thirty days to review the file and approve or deny parole.

Phillip's file goes up to the governor. The governor's office sends a one-sentence-long fax to the prison warden: the parole board decision is reversed. That is all. No explanation is required or provided. Phillip will need to wait two years before being allowed to start the whole process all over again.

Phillip's experience is highly typical. Even a model prisoner found "suitable" by the skeptical hard-to-impress parole board and scrutinized by the CDRC can be summarily turned down by a negative nod from the governor's office with no rationale or explanation. There is no hearing, chance to explain, or opportunity to find out why they are turned down. A simple fax with a one-line decision. The impact on inmates and their families is devastating. Phillip is no exception. One month after his denial, his eldest son is arrested for drugs and sent to jail. Phillip sinks into depression.

A fellow inmate, a jailhouse lawyer, comes to his aid. He encourages Phillip to file a lawsuit challenging the governor's constitutional power to deny him parole. With his help, Phillip files a writ of habeas corpus claiming that the governor has overstepped his legal authority by denying parole without any evidentiary reasons to do so. A California Superior Court agrees with Phillip and demands the governor show a reason for the denial. The case is appealed and another state appellate court agrees with Phillip. The case now goes to the California Supreme Court which sides with the governor claiming that the seriousness of Phillip's original crime is sufficient cause to deny parole. Now Phillip, filing his briefs from inside San Quentin takes his appeals to the federal courts: to the U.S. District Court and then to the 9th Circuit Court of Appeals

both of which uphold the California Supreme Court decision.

And Continues

By now, two years have gone by and Phillip is scheduled to appear before the parole board yet again. He goes again with the mountains of evidence of his stellar record, his endless determination to make something of himself with whatever opportunities are available to him. He provides, yet again, meticulous proof of his wide network of support on the outside. He shows, again, that in all his years of incarceration he has never failed to comply with the demanding regimen of prison: never failed to fall in line or get to his knees on daily yard count; never fought with a fellow inmate or possessed any contraband in his cell; always spoke courteously to correctional officers.

The board again finds him "suitable" and yet again the case moves to the CDRC and then onto a new governor's desk for final approval. After 150 days, another fax is sent. The decision is reversed, parole is denied. Phillip does not lose heart but begins filing his appeals all over again. His argument is simple: the governor needs a reason for the denial based on something he did or failed to do while he has been incarcerated: denying him based on the facts of his original offense is not the correct basis for deciding parole status.

And Continues

While his case is working its way through the maze of state courts, the march of appearances before the Parole board also goes on: Phillip is scheduled to be heard yet again before members of the parole board which has now twice denied him and twice found him "suitable" for release. It is his fifth appearance in eight years. This time, with nearly four hundred letters of recommendation from everyone connected with him inside and outside the prison, Phillip makes his case before the board. This time, for no apparent reason, the board denies him parole and he is told to wait two years before coming up again.

Now Phillip files a different set of lawsuits directed at the board itself. A judge in the Sacramento Superior Court orders the prison system to release Phillip; the governor refuses. An appeal to a higher court in California sends the matter back to the original judge who again orders Phillip to be released. Again the governor refuses to back down. His case is scheduled to be heard by an appellate court when a decision by the California Supreme Court on someone else's case settles Phillip's fate once and for all.

And Is Over

On August 21, 2008, in re *Lawrence*, a landmark 4-3 decision, the California Supreme Court ruled that the facts from a prisoner's original crime are not sufficient as evidence for a denial of parole. The reality is that the past cannot be changed: nothing Phillip, or any other prisoner, can do will undo his original offense. The courts already sentenced him based on the facts of his crime: the decision of the parole board needs to be based on a different set of facts.

The purpose of parole is to evaluate what Phillip has done since the crime and to use that information to make a prediction about what he may or may not do in the future. A finding that a prisoner still poses a threat to public safety must be based on evidence of his behavior other than the crime he was originally sentenced for. By those criteria, prisoners like Phillip, with a flawless record for conduct inside the prison system and with extraordinary levels of support within the community, meet the criteria set by law for parole. Without evidence of his current dangerousness to the community, Phillip must be released.

Why Is It So Hard to Make Parole?

Three times a governor of the state of California overrode the decision of the parole board that Phillip was suitable for release and denied his release. There was nothing special about Phillip: such denials from the governor are standard. If anything, what is unusual is that Phillip was found suitable for release by the parole board in the first place. In California most inmates sentenced to fifteen years to life with the possibility of parole are never found suitable for parole. A person sentenced to life in prison with the possibility of parole has a far greater chance of dying in prison than being released on parole. In 2007 out of 6,181 parole board hearings, only 119 lifers were deemed "suitable" for parole, and as Phillip learns, being found suitable at a parole hearing is a very long way from actually making parole.

Two questions arise: first, why are distant governors who never see or hear from the prisoners, inmates, or anyone else, given the final power to approve or reverse parole decision? And second, why are they so likely to reverse rather than approve the decisions made by their own appointed parole commissioners?

The answer, according to most observers, is simple: politics and Willie Horton. In 1988, the presidential hopes—and indeed, political career—of Michael Dukakis, then governor of Massachusetts, were dashed forever by a television ad that blamed him for the release of a convicted murderer who went on to commit a violent rape and home invasion. Although Horton was not technically released on parole, he was released on a furlough program existing in most states at that time that allowed prisoners out on supervised visits. The program was highly successful: very few inmates ever tried to escape. But Horton was an exception and the political fallout from a system that released a dangerous criminal back into the community landed on the governor, with disastrous consequences for his political career. This lesson was not lost on every other sitting and future governor in every state across the country. Any release of an inmate on parole was a potential political calamity: the safe decision is to deny.

When the citizens of California approved Proposition 89 in 1988 giving the governor the authority to approve or deny any parole decision, the stage was set for a drastic reduction in the actual granting of parole. As of 2011, of the more than 17,000 lifers in California prisons serving sentences with parole eligibility, more than 10,000 had served enough of their sentences to meet their minimum eligible parole date. The likelihood of being paroled was slim until Governor Jerry Brown took office that year. Since that time he has approved parole for just over 1,300 individuals serving "life" sentences.[2] And nearly thirty years after the possibility of parole was almost closed down in California, voters overwhelmingly passed a measure, backed by the governor, to loosen parole rules for those convicted of felonies.

The Challenge of Staying Out

Now that he is on parole, Phillip like all parolees must walk the straight and narrow with no deviations and no exceptions. The rules he must follow are explained by his parole officer: Phillip must not violate these rules—even the smallest infraction could send him back to prison for the rest of his life. On the day of his release before going home, the parole officer explains the invisible boundaries that will define his life for the next five years. He must check in every week; he cannot travel beyond a fifty-mile radius from his home without advance permission; he cannot change jobs or move without permission; he cannot drink alcohol and will be randomly tested for drugs; he cannot associate with anyone who has a criminal record; must not have any contact with law enforcement for any reason—traffic ticket, jaywalking—nothing; the parole officer may stop by his house at any time unannounced—if it is after his 10 p.m. curfew he better be there. No exceptions. If there is a violation of any kind it will be up to the parole officer whether or not to file for a revocation of parole. Phillip fully understands what is at stake.

Yet even for someone as fortunate as Phillip the re-entry to the free world is tough. He deeply misses the close friends from the past fifteen years. He can write to them but is forbidden from phoning or visiting. He lives with his parents at first but that soon becomes a problem for them: they are not used to having their grown son live with them, and after about a year or so, they want him to leave. His boss who had known him as a young man, attended his trial, and faithfully written many letters to the parole board over the years, bailed him out by providing a rent-free apartment until Phillip could save some money for his own place. Renting an apartment from landlords understandably reluctant to take on a tenant who is out on parole for murder is one challenge Phillip will not yet have to face. Two years into his parole, Phillip falls in love and wants to move to live near his fiancé. Now he faces the challenge of finding a job from employers who don't know him from the days before he committed his crime. He is turned down many times before landing a job in a construction company. Engaged, living with his fiancé, Phillip has landed on his feet: working full time and volunteering at the program to help young teens stay out of trouble.

Phillip is one of the lucky ones. After more than twenty years in prison he still had his parents' home to come back to and an old boss from his plumbing days holding a good job for him. Phillip also had a marketable set of skills as a plumber and a carpenter and many friends and family ready to give the emotional and material help to transition to life on the outside. This was not all luck: for all those years, Phillip worked hard to stay in touch with law-abiding people on the outside. Now that effort paid off.

Few parolees are as diligent or as fortunate as Phillip. Many come from homes and neighborhoods where large numbers of people have some kind of criminal record and lots are involved in illegal activities. Most do not have a skilled trade to fall back on. Many more have long since lost contact or burned bridges with family and friends, who might be able to help them; the majority never had that kind of support in their lives to begin with.

For the typical parolee walking the line is nearly impossible and the statistics on parole revocations bear that out. Each year approximately one-third of the prison admissions in the state of California are for people who have had their parole revoked for crossing the line in some way. Almost none, however, are the tiny handful of lifers who have managed to get out on parole: for them, the stakes are way too high: one mistake and they know they will stay behind bars for the rest of their life.

THINKING CRITICALLY ABOUT THIS CASE

1. If you were serving on a parole board what kinds of information would you consider most important in determining whether to release someone on parole? Explain your answer.

2. Do you believe that Phillip was treated fairly by the parole process in the state of California? Why or why not?

3. Should the governor of a state have the final approval of parole decision? Does this policy allow politics to distort the parole process or is this an appropriate response to the demands of the voters?

4. Do you believe it is safer for society to release an inmate for a period of parole supervision or to have them serve their entire sentence without any period of conditional release? Explain your answer.

5. Phillip was lucky to have much support in his life on the outside. Most inmates do not. Is the requirement of having a steady job and secure home a reasonable requirement for the majority of inmates? Is it a fair requirement?

6. What kinds of support do people need to successfully transition to life in the community? Who should provide that support?

7. A large percentage of the prison population in the state of California is there because they have violated non-criminal conditions of parole or probation, such as curfew. Should minor violations be grounds for revocation? Why or why not?

REFERENCE

Case adapted from:

Mullane, Nancy, *Life After Murder: Five Men in Search of Redemption* (New York: Perseus Book Group, 2012).

In the previous chapter we learned that over two million American citizens are serving a criminal sentence behind the bars of a locked correctional facility. But even more Americans are serving a criminal sentence while they are living and working within the community. Alongside the sharp rise in imprisonment has been a parallel growth in the numbers of persons living under the supervision of the justice system. In 2015, approximately 4.65 million citizens were under the supervision of state or federal probation and parole authorities.[3] Most Americans are surprised to discover that the vast majority of people under correctional supervision reside within the community. Phillip is one of millions of Americans whose freedom within society is conditional upon their rigorous adherence to a set of rules and conditions that pertain only to those Americans under supervision.

The final chapter of this text takes a careful look at the system of community corrections. The pendulum of criminal justice policy has begun to swing back to community-based alternatives, as states come to terms with the social and economic costs of mass incarceration. Within the past decade politicians on the left and the right have been arguing for the need to reduce prison populations and to fund more effective strategies for treatment and rehabilitation, particularly for nonviolent and first-time offenders. Drug treatment, halfway houses, re-entry programs, and alternative forms of supervision in the community are now beginning to be reviewed as viable alternatives to incarceration.

For many, the sentence of probation is the proverbial "slap on the wrist." In some counties even high-risk adult offenders receive less than an hour of probation supervision time per month. The minimal nature of this "supervision" angers the public who are concerned about public safety and feel that offenders placed on probation have not been adequately punished for their crimes. For many citizens the granting of parole is also seen as a form of leniency that puts the public at risk from dangerous criminals who deserve to be behind bars serving their entire sentence.

Yet many justice professionals believe community-based corrections has enormous potential for enhancing public safety, satisfying victims, and holding offenders accountable for their crimes in a way that is constructive. The use of alternatives to incarceration dates back to the nineteenth century when the first experiments in community supervision began in the city of Boston, Massachusetts. Parole as an institution was also invented at the end of the nineteenth century and until the end of the 1970s was a standard element in nearly all sentences.

The 1960s and 1970s saw an explosion of community-based alternatives to incarceration with a great deal of failures along with some success; in the 1980s and 1990s, technology such as drug testing and electronic monitoring enhanced the ability of the system to "supervise" the offenders and control their movements within the wider community along with the creation of a network of day-reporting centers in some states. In the first decade of the twenty-first century, the challenge of **re-entry**—how to help reintegrate the more than 700,000 of offenders who exit prison each year[4]—reemerged as a central concern of criminal justice policy.

Many questions remain concerning the effectiveness of community corrections, the impact on public safety, and the role of the community in the process. We can see the importance of the community in Phillip's case: a place to live and a stable job are essential for remaining crime free back in the community.

RE-ENTRY
refers to the process of returning to society after being incarcerated.

Preparing inmates to be released on parole supervision in the community. (McClatchy-Tribune via Getty Images)

Ex-offenders also need a host of social supports to transition back to freedom after time behind bars, where even the smallest decision had been taken out of their hands. Being out in a society after years of incarceration can be an overwhelming, terrifying, and often, debilitating psychological experience for offenders.

Then there is the question of public safety. Can offenders be safely monitored while living in the community? What services and resources are available for people on probation and parole? Do these improve the likelihood of offender rehabilitation and reform? What about victims? Should community correction deal with the needs of victim? And what about the community? Should the community be involved in the process of supervising, sentencing, sanctioning, or helping the offender?

The term "community justice" is increasingly used to refer to criminal justice innovations that seek to involve the community in areas such as community policing, community courts, and community corrections. For the most part, traditional community correction programs have been physically located within the community but have not actually involved the community in the supervision or rehabilitation of the offender.[5] Increasingly community corrections are seeking ways to bring the "community" back into the justice process.

Here the issue of fairness, legitimacy, and trust between the community and the criminal justice system emerges again. Offenders returning to the community after a period of incarceration are subject to a range of penalties and restrictions that undermine their ability to reintegrate back into the community. Having paid their "debt" to society, ex-offenders continue to face significant obstacles in housing, employment, access to education, and other benefits in the community.

Approximately 5.85 million American citizens are denied the right to vote through felony disenfranchisement laws.[6] State laws vary whether a person is prohibited from voting during incarceration; probation and parole, or if it is lifetime disenfranchisement. For African Americans, one out of thirteen black males are denied the right to vote because of these laws; in states such as Florida, Virginia, Tennessee, and Kentucky, more than one out of five black adults have lost the right to vote due to a felony conviction—across the United States approximately 2.2 million black citizens are barred from voting under these laws.

Is it fair to continue to deny an individual basic citizenship rights, including the right to vote, once they have been released from prison? Is the community refusing to give people who have been convicted of crime a second chance? How can someone avoid future crime if all pathways to a legitimate life style are blocked based on what they have done in the past?

What is the community role and responsibility in community justice? Can the community effectively partner with criminal justice agencies, such as the police, corrections, or the courts? What would these partnerships look like? We close this chapter by considering the restorative justice movement and its commitment to engaging the victims, offenders, their families, and communities in partnership with the criminal justice system. Is there sufficient trust on both sides, for such partnerships to take place?

PROBATION AND PAROLE

The Origins

The founding ideals of probation and parole are to provide individualized justice to those offenders ready and willing to undergo reform. The term **probation** comes from the Latin word *probare* that means "to test or to prove." The probationer is given a second chance to "prove" they are able to conform to societal laws. Offenders placed on probation are at the "front end" of the system usually at the time of sentencing by the courts. These offenders tend to be first time, juvenile, or low-level criminals.

Parole is the practice of permitting the final portion of a criminal sentence to be served within the community under the supervision of the parole authority. The word parole derives from the French for "word of honor" signifying the pledge to behave as a law-abiding citizen. Parole occurs at the "back end" of the justice process: offenders have already served a significant portion of their sentence within the prison system. Parolees, therefore, have been convicted of more serious offenses, are older and have been inside the prison system, and are coping with re-adjustment and reintegration back into the community after a period of time behind bars.

Probation and parole have their roots in the discretionary decision-making power of the justice system to respond to individual offenders with leniency in recognition of their willingness to reform. The capacity of courts to exercise a degree of mercy for individual offenders reaches back to the thirteenth century in England when convicted criminals were permitted to plead for leniency by reading the text of the Fifty-First Psalm in court.[7] Called the "**benefit of clergy**," this practice gave the judge the option of saving the convicted person

PROBATION
a sentence the offender serves in the community under correctional supervision.

PAROLE
the conditional release of an inmate from incarceration under supervision after a portion of the prison sentence has been served.

BENEFIT OF CLERGY
a medieval privilege which allowed clergy and other offenders to avoid the gallows at the judge's discretion.

from the gallows. Similarly, the practice of **judicial reprieve** allowed judges to indefinitely suspend imposition of punishment on a convicted criminal provided they continued to refrain from crime. The power of judicial reprieve was declared unconstitutional in the United States in 1916,[8] but the concept of court supervision under a suspended sentence has continued under the authority of the probation service which formalized court supervision of convicted offenders.

The first person to conceive of a formal function of court supervision and the first volunteer probation officer himself was a modest philanthropist named John Augustus.[9] A Boston boot maker by trade, Augustus had modest financial resources but chose to devote them to the humanitarian goal of assisting those who had fallen on hard times through the evils of alcohol. The invention of probation began with his plea to the Boston Police court in 1841 when he posted bail for a man charged with being a common drunkard.[10] The judge granted bail and was willing to defer sentencing for three weeks under the condition that the man be released into the custody of Augustus. Augustus took on the task of assisting the man in taking positive steps toward his own reform and re-appeared with him before the judge at the appointed time as a testimonial of his good efforts at sobriety.

Thus began Augustus's lifework that ultimately led him to bail out 1,152 men and 794 women charged with temperance and other offenses, such as prostitution, theft, and minor assaults, in the Boston courts. Augustus was selective in whom he chose to assist, screening them for good character and positive influences in their lives. He accompanied them to court, posted bail, paid their fines, assisted them in finding lodging, employment, worked with their family, and helped them find confidence in themselves to live responsible and sober.

Augustus offered his services to the courts on a volunteer basis. But as judges grew more familiar with Augustus, they were eager to have an alternative sentence for individual offenders who were ripe for rehabilitation. The practice coincided with the emerging dominant ideology of rehabilitation and reform of the Progressive Era: individual criminals who could be "saved" from a life of crime should be treated differently by the correctional system and given the chance for reform. The first official probation officer was Edward Savage who resigned his post as chief of police in the city of Boston in 1878 to take the job.[11] By 1891, the state of Massachusetts has legislated a statewide probation system under the formal authority of the courts.

The institutionalization of parole was a key component to the reformatory movement in penal reform. The "father of parole" is Captain Alexander Maconochie of Norfolk Island in the United Kingdom, who created a system where inmates could earn early release, known as a **ticket of leave** through hard work and good behavior.[12] The practice of parole was then adopted within the Irish penal system by Sir Walter Crafton who implemented it as a part of a complete system of graduated confinements, including spending time in a kind of halfway house before finally earning the "ticket of leave."

In the United States "**good time**" **laws** were first passed in 1817 to enable prison wardens to reward compliant inmates and to offer incentives for working hard in prison industries and outside contract labor sites. With the reformatory movement and the growing popularity of indeterminate sentencing laws, conditional release through parole became more closely tied to the goal of rehabilitation. By the end of the nineteenth century, more than half the states had some kind of parole authority to make the release decision for individual inmates and to supervise them to some extent during the remainder of their legal sentence.[13]

JUDICIAL REPRIEVE
the postponement of the execution of a sentence by a judge.

TICKET OF LEAVE
a system of conditional release from prison started by Sir Walter Crofton of Ireland in the nineteenth century.

GOOD TIME LAWS
first passed in 1817, these authorize wardens to release inmates before full completion of their sentence as reward for good behavior.

The Board of Parole for the federal prison system was created by Congress in 1930; by 1932, forty-four states and the federal system relied upon parole as the key system of release for prisoners.[14]

Probation Today

Probation is the most common sentence given to offenders in the United States. In most jurisdictions, probation is a statutory alternative to imprisonment for the majority of felony convictions, although offenders convicted of very serious crimes, such as murder, rape, or robbery, are generally ineligible for probation in most state penal codes. Of the 4.65 million citizens residing within community under the legal supervision of the correctional system in 2015, 3.7 million or 80 percent are on probation.[15] About 31 percent of felons convicted in state court are sentenced to "straight probation."[16]

Although probation originated in the judicial branch of government, in some jurisdictions it is under the executive branch as a part of the correctional agency of state government. In some states it is unified as one central agency across the state while in others it is highly de-centralized and operates independently at the county or local level. Those who argue that probation should remain a judicial function feel that probation officers should work closely with sentencing judges, extending the authority of the judge to exercise discretion and supervise offenders within the community. Others argue that the human service function of probation is best administered by correctional agencies. Many states combine probation and parole into a single agency, arguing that the professionalization of community supervision is best served by unification. Within the federal system probation is administered by the district courts.

Job of the Probation Officer

Probation is a sentence but it is also a job. The two primary functions of the probation officer are investigation and recommendation through the **pre-sentence investigation** (PSI) **and report** and the actual supervision of the offender until the legal sentence is terminated. The PSI process includes a more or less thorough examination of the offender, their history, including past crimes, employment, education, their family, and close associates, their mental and physical health, and history of drug abuse. In some jurisdictions, PSI reports are very thorough and detailed; in others, they offer only a brief sketch of the basic facts. The purpose of the PSI is to assist the judge in the formulation of the sentence. The PSI generally includes a sentencing recommendation that details specific conditions of probation for the offender and how intensive the supervision should be.

The second function is the job of supervision itself. Probation is a sentence of conditional release into the community. The **conditions of probation** vary but the basic concept is that for the duration of the sentence the offender is neither a free citizen nor are they locked up. Rather probationers' status in the community is conditional: they may remain out of jail as long as they abide by certain rules and conditions. Failure to comply with the conditions of probation is grounds for revocation of this conditional freedom and the imposition of the jail sentence. It is the legal authority of the probation officer to ensure the probationer is meeting the conditions of probation.

Thus, one of the central duties of probation is the protection of public safety and enforcement of the rules. Probation officers may be required to visit the

PRE-SENTENCE INVESTIGATION AND REPORT collection of information by a probation officer about an offender's character, family life, work habits, and prior record to assist and guide the judge in sentencing.

CONDITIONS OF PROBATION court-ordered conditions which must be met by probationers and are enforced by probation officers.

probationer in their home; administer daily urine screens for drug use; or they may use electronic monitoring technology, such as electronic bracelets or other tracking devices, to monitor the offender. Violating the conditions of probation through the commission of new crimes or breaking the technical rules of probation may be grounds for the revocation of probation and imprisonment of the offender.

Standard conditions of probation are fairly common across all the states. These conditions require the probationer to refrain from any further violations of the law, hold down regular employment or course of study, participate in any specified treatment plan, support any dependents, remain within the geographical jurisdiction of the court, and maintain regular contact with the probation officer. In addition to these standard conditions, judges may add on any special conditions that are relevant to the particular offender. These special conditions may include payment of restitution to the victim or victim compensation fund, performance of community work service, mandatory treatment for alcohol or drug abuse, anger management counseling, completion of a GED, abstention from the use of alcohol, and even participation in religious services for the period of probation. As long as the condition is related to the offense, the courts have upheld novel requirements of probation devised by the courts. More than half of states exact a fee from probationers to help defray the cost of supervision.

The issue of heavy caseloads is one key factor that negatively affects the quality of probation supervision. Caseloads often run high reaching as high as three hundred per officer in some jurisdictions. Under these conditions, the job of maintaining supervision and helping the offender is a highly perfunctory bureaucratic task that may mean little more than simply receiving a postcard or making a phone call once a month.

Conflicting Philosophy of Probation

Inherent in the job of the modern probation officer is a tension between the two basic components of the probation supervision function.[17] On the one hand, probation has its origins in the humanitarian desire to assist convicted persons in rehabilitation. In this sense, the work of probation has much in common with the job of social work: helping offenders get counseling and treatment, offering vocational and employment assistance, and providing constant guidance and support for the individual and their family. But the job of the probation officer also involves supervision of the offender, a function that has more in common with law enforcement, where offenders must be monitored to assure they do not commit additional crimes and to protect public safety.

These two functions are often incompatible and lead to **role strain** for probation officers, who find themselves torn between conflicting goals. The social worker function may require a probation officer to offer sympathetic support to an offender who has violated technical conditions of their probation or even committed a minor crime. The social worker function prioritizes the desire to offer continual chances for the offender. The supervisory function leads to the adoption of a more hardline attitude toward the probationer who violates the terms of the agreement. Some probation officers see enforcement of legal rules as the prime component of their job and believe their central obligation is to protect the public by ensuring that probationers comply with the legal requirements of the court order while others prioritize the social worker function.

ROLE STRAIN
tension between two facets of the job of probation and parole: rule enforcement and rehabilitation.

The tension between these two philosophical positions often erupts most acutely around the issue of **revocation of probation** for rule violations. The "law enforcer" prioritizes the rules. From this perspective, the issue of revocation is straightforward: if the rules are violated, the individual should be brought back to court for re-sentencing. For the probation officer whose central priority is to assist an offender toward rehabilitation, revoking probation status particularly for technical violations, such as breaking curfew, is seen as undermining the more important goal of rehabilitation. Being in an enforcement role also undermines trust that reduces the ability of the probation officer to genuinely help the offender deal effectively with his or her problems. As we will see below, in some programs, these roles are divided between two different probation officers to help each perform their functions more effectively without the inherent conflict.

Parole Today

Like probation, parole is a form of conditional release from incarceration. A person on parole is neither free nor are they behind bars; rather, they remain within the legal custody of the state and must conform to specified conditions in order to remain within the community. Failure to comply with the rules will lead to the revocation of parole and a return to imprisonment.

Unlike probation that is generally a judicial function, parole is an administrative function located in an independent state agency or operates as part of the correctional system.

There was a time in this country when the majority of prisoners went to prison not knowing the date they would be released. As we saw in chapter 13, before 1977 most criminals were sentenced for an indeterminate amount of time. A judge would sentence someone to a term that stretched from a minimum amount of time, six months for example, or two years, or five years to life. Every person convicted for a felony offense was potentially serving a life sentence and it was up to the parole board to determine how much time beyond the minimum that they would actually serve.

To many Americans, this system was problematic: it was too lenient for some and way too harsh for others. People lost faith in the ideal of rehabilitation and the system stopped believing that it was its responsibility to rehabilitate inmates. Changes in the laws after 1977 replaced most indeterminate sentencing structures with determinate sentences: inmates do not need to appear before the parole board to prove they had changed. They simply do their time. When their time is served, they are handed $200 at the gate and released without any follow-up or supervision.

The vast majority of felons locked up in the enormous prison system are serving determinate sentences: nothing they do while on the inside will shorten their sentence. With no incentive to engage in programming and with relatively few programs available anyway, most wait out their time without making any effort to change the habits and attitudes that brought them there in the first place. Not surprisingly recidivism rates rose during the 1980s and remain high today: in a survey of fifteen states just over two-thirds of the prisoners released were rearrested within three years, an increase of 5 percent from a decade earlier.

Why did the American public lose faith in the system of parole and parole supervision? The answer is complex but one dynamic more than any other contributed to this loss of faith. Known as the Horton effect is refers to the political impact of

REVOCATION OF PROBATION
return of offender to court for sentencing for failure to meet conditions of probation.

high-profile crimes committed by parolees. As we saw in Phillip's marathon struggle to make parole, the governor of the state of California was extremely reluctant to endorse the discretionary decision of his own appointed parole commissioners who had carefully reviewed Phillip's case and decided he was a good candidate for conditional release. Yet the political fallout in the event of a parolee committing another serious crime, as Willie Horton did, could be catastrophic—and few governors, anywhere in the country, are willing to take that political risk. More than any other factor, the politics of crime affect the dynamics of parole.[18]

Parole Board

Parole refers both to the decision to release a person before their complete sentence has been served and a period of community-based supervision. Under indeterminate sentencing systems, the release decision is made by a **parole board** that may be part of the department of corrections or an autonomous body whose members are appointed by the governor. As we saw in the case of Phillip, the parole board considers a host of factors in determining parole release for an individual offender, including their own record of performance within the institution, their prospects for work and non-criminal lifestyle upon release, victims, preferences, needs of the institution for available beds, and the wider politics of the community.

Parole eligibility defined by various statutes is the earliest date for which an inmate may be considered for conditional release. Offenders do not apply for parole but are automatically considered for parole when they become eligible. Nearly all jurisdictions have **statutory good time** laws which automatically reduce an inmate's sentence by a specified number of days for each month of time served without disciplinary problems. These range from more than thirty days for every month of "good time" served to as few as five days for each "good time" month served in the federal prison system. In addition to statutory good time, there may also be **earned good time** statutes that credit an inmate time off their full sentence for participation in work, educational, or treatment programs. Accumulation of good time credits (statutory and earned) may result in **unconditional mandatory release** from prison without parole supervision.

Parole release is a reduction in the sentence in addition to good time reductions. The parole board reviews the inmate's record, interviews the inmate, solicits recommendations from the prosecutor's office, and hears testimony from victims, family members, and other witnesses to assist them in making their decision. Criticism of the discretionary parole decision was a key factor in the political movement to end indeterminate sentencing. Parole boards held broad discretion and offenders believe that they are treated arbitrarily with substantial discrimination based on race and class of the offender. When Rubin Carter was in Rahway State Prison, one of the demands of the 1972 riot was the abolition of parole.[19] Inmates were demoralized by never knowing when they would be released and felt it unfair to rely upon the judgment of a group of strangers who held such power over their lives.

Since 1975, most states' legislative codes have shifted toward determinate sentencing reducing reliance upon parole release. Under determinate sentencing systems parole serves as a mandatory period of community supervision structured as part of the sentence itself. Once the offender has served the required portion of the sentence behind bars, the offender is released to a period of community supervision. By 2010 about 25 percent of prisoners were released from

PAROLE BOARD
an administrative agency charged with the authority to grant conditional release for prisoners eligible for parole.

PAROLE ELIGIBILITY
determined by statute and the amount of time an inmate has served.

STATUTORY GOOD TIME
the number of days deducted from a sentence determined by statute for a time served without disciplinary reports.

EARNED GOOD TIME
the number of days deducted from a sentence for participation in specified programs while in prison.

UNCONDITIONAL MANDATORY RELEASE
release from prison required by statute when a criminal has served his or her full sentence minus statutory and earned good time.

prison unconditionally while the remaining 75 percent were released under some kind of community correctional supervision.[20]

In jurisdictions where parole decision-making still exists, parole hearings have become more formalized. In about half of the states, offenders are permitted to have a counsel present, call witnesses, and a transcript of the proceedings is maintained. Today, most parole authorities provide a written and oral explanation of the decision, although the courts have refused to concede equivalent due process rights to the offender in a parole hearing as are granted to a defendant in court proceedings.[21]

Parole Supervision

The job of the parole officer is similar to that of the probation officer. Parolees constitute about 11 percent of the population under correctional supervision.[22] Similar to probation officers, the job of parole officers is to monitor compliance of the parolee within the conditions of parole. Standards conditions of parole include the same requirements to maintain contact with the parole officer, to continue employment or education, and to refrain from any further criminal activity or associations. Parolees must contact their parole officer if they change jobs, residence, or marital status. In addition, parolee contracts may include individualized conditions tailored to the particular circumstances. Failure to comply with the conditions of parole may lead to the **revocation of parole** status resulting in a return to incarceration for the offender.

Parole officers are charged with assisting parolees adjust to community life and continue to pursue a non-criminal lifestyle. Officers make referrals to community agencies and to employment agencies and work with the family of the offender to assist in the transition to life outside of prison. Like probation, however, the job of parole is heavily weighted toward supervision and policing. This is more acute in the parole than it is in probation because the offenses are more serious than those that are sentenced to probation. Parole officers, therefore, stress the law enforcement aspect of their work more than probation and are armed peace officers in many states. Like probation, however, individual officers appear to emphasize different aspects of the job according to their personal preferences for control versus assistance as well as on the overall philosophy of the agency.[23]

HISTORY OF COMMUNITY CORRECTIONS

For decades community corrections were synonymous with probation or parole. Beginning in the 1960s, three distinct periods of expansion and development in community corrections took place. The first began with the community corrections movement of the 1960s centered around the concept of **diversion**; the second started in the 1980s focused on the provision of a continuum of graduated intermediate sanctions and closer supervision within the community; and the third arose in the 1990s with the concept of community/restorative justice and the growing inclusion of victims and the community as stakeholders in the justice process.

Each of these periods impacted the work of probation and parole creating new programs, techniques, and approaches within the field. Like many criminal justice policies, different periods of community corrections overlap with one

REVOCATION OF PAROLE
administrative removal of an offender from parole status for failure to comply with parole conditions usually requiring the return of the offender to incarceration.

DIVERSION
the removal of offenders from the criminal justice process at any stage prior to criminal conviction.

another and many programs share features in common. Although each period of growth within community corrections has been based on a distinctive philosophy, each has also built upon the innovations of earlier periods.[24]

Diversion Movement of 1960s and 1970s

In 1967, the President's Crime Commission endorsed the concept of **formal diversion** programs designed to rehabilitate and treat offenders in order to reduce the negative impact of incarceration and to reduce reliance upon costly incarceration.[25] Incarcerating less serious offenders with violent or chronic offenders was seen as likely to socialize offenders to hardened criminal lifestyles rather than preventing future crimes. The federal government urged states to seek the "least restrictive" option for first-time or young offenders and to set up social service programs for referrals from the justice system to deal with the underlying problems driving crime.

The concept of diversion refers to the decision to remove a particular offender from the formal mechanics of the system at some stage in criminal justice processing. Informal diversionary practices are inherent in the discretionary authority of police, prosecutors, and judges, whereas formal diversion requires an offender to attend a particular type of alternative programs, such as drug treatment or job training. During the 1960s, community corrections were driven by the goal to keep people out of the formal system and to provide rehabilitative community-based interventions as an alternative to incarceration.

During the 1970s, an estimated 1,200 diversion programs were established throughout the nation to provide treatment and services as an alternative to the traditional criminal justice processing.[26] This might include diversion to an employment training program, drug treatment, education, or counseling program. The hope was that these programs would reduce recidivism at the same time they reduced costs of correctional supervision.

A key criticism of the expanding diversion programs of the 1960s and 1970s was the problem known as **net-widening**.[27] The traditional forms of diversion, often referred to as "old" or "**true**" **diversion**, literally kept people out of the criminal justice system altogether. When a police officer drives a teenaged shoplifter home to his parents rather than bringing him to the station house for booking and arrest or a prosecutor enters a *nolle pros* for a minor theft, these justice professionals are informally "diverting" particular low-level offenders away from the formal sequence of events. Informally, diversion may take place any time before a person is convicted. Individuals seen as "low-risk" offenders and therefore likely to cease from all future criminal conduct are determined not to need any criminal justice supervision at all.

But once formal diversion programs became established, criminal justice professionals tended to refer these kinds of cases to formal diversion programs rather than simply letting low-risk offenders go. Individuals previously dropped from the system were now assigned to programs thus increasing the overall number of people under correctional supervision and driving up costs rather than saving money. Although the recidivism rate of many diversion programs initially appeared low compared to the recidivism rates among those going to jail, researchers discovered that their success was due to "widening the net" to include low-risk participants, who were unlikely to commit crimes in the future even without the benefit of a program.[28]

FORMAL DIVERSION
the removal of eligible offender from the routine criminal justice process to an alternative program.

NET-WIDENING
the increase in the correctional population by the diversion of less serious offenders into program intended for more serious offenders thus expanding the overall correctional population.

TRUE DIVERSION PROGRAMS
traditional forms of diversion that kept people out of the criminal justice system.

Diversion programs, many of which still exist today in many jurisdictions particularly for juveniles, were seen as a panacea for the criminal justice system during the 1960s and 1970s. The hope was that these programs would effectively rehabilitate offenders at the same time that they would also be considerably cheaper than prison. The expectations were so high that the results were bound to be disappointing: diversion did not reduce the overall size of the prison population or reduce costs because of net-widening, and many diversion programs failed to demonstrate high rates of success with more serious offenders.[29]

Intermediate Sanctions Movement

Motivation for the second wave of expansion of community-based corrections in the 1980s shared much in common with the diversion movement. State systems struggled with prison overcrowding and the need to lower the high cost of imprisonment. As prisons came under legal pressure to reduce overcrowding, state judicial systems were seeking alternative punishments that were less extreme than incarceration but more punitive than traditional probation. During the 1980s and 1990s, the **intermediate sanctions** movement led to a wide array of alterative sentences ranging from shock incarceration, intensive probation, house arrest, electronic monitoring, and more. The goal had been to create a continuum of graduated sanctions between probation and prison tailored to the seriousness of the crime.

The general disillusionment with the rehabilitative promise of diversion programs coincided with the demand for greater surveillance for offenders on probation and a tougher approach to probation as a form of punishment; at the same time, the pressure to control costs of imprisonment became even more acute. In the mid-1980s, there was serious effort to control the skyrocketing costs of imprisonment in several states. Intervention by the courts which ordered states to reduce overcrowding left them with one of two choices: build more prison beds at a hefty price tag or find less expensive alternatives. The alternative sanctions movement was an effort to increase the correctional supervision of probation while avoiding the full-scale costs of incarceration. Judges were searching for a wider range of punishment options in between the leniency of probation and the extreme deprivation of incarceration. State correctional systems began to explore a more extensive use of community service, restitution, fines, and intensive supervision similar to programs within European countries.[30]

During the 1980s and 1990s, several key types of community-based correctional programs emerged: **ISP or IPS or intensive supervision probation** (or intensive probation supervision); **boot camps or shock incarceration**; **house arrest** or degrees of confinement with the use of **electronic monitoring**; and **day-reporting centers** combined with drug testing, treatment, and intensive supervision. These programs were often combined or overlapped with one another but the common denominator among them was an enhanced close supervision by the correctional system. During this period, every major probation and parole agency in the nation experimented with the establishment of programs of intensive surveillance using enhanced probation supervision through reduced caseloads, electronic monitoring, house arrest, drug testing, day-reporting centers, and boot camps. By 1998, all states were operating some kind of ISP programs; all states reported use of some electronic monitoring; about thirty-five states were operating boot camps, and across the nation there were about 125 operating day-reporting centers.[31] An estimated 10 percent of

INTERMEDIATE SANCTIONS
a variety of punishments that are more restrictive than traditional probation but less extreme than incarceration.

INTENSIVE SUPERVISION PROBATION
a program of closer surveillance and more intensive programming for higher risk juvenile and adult offenders.

SHOCK INCARCERATION
the use of shorter but more intense periods of incarceration designed to have a deeper impact on the offender.

HOUSE ARREST
a sentence requiring the convicted offender to remain within his or her house during specified periods.

BOOT CAMP
short-term incarceration that relies on intensive military drill, physical exercise, and correctional treatment.

ELECTRONIC MONITORING
the use of monitoring technology to trigger alarms if an offender moves beyond prescribed physical locations.

DAY-REPORTING CENTERS
programs of community-based supervision to which offenders must report daily and where their activities are monitored and structured throughout most of the day.

probationers across the nation were assigned to these forms of community-based correctional supervision by the end of the 1990s. While reliance on some forms of intermediate sanctions, such as boot camps, has decreased in the past decade, other forms, such as day-reporting centers, have increased in popularity.

Intensive Supervised Probation

ISP programs, sometimes standing for intensive supervision programs or intensive surveillance programs, also known as intensive probation supervision, flourished between 1985 and 1995. Hundreds of programs emerged to correct the looseness of probation and enable more serious offenders to be sentenced within the community.[32] ISP programs offer much greater supervision than traditional probation. This typically involves daily face-to-face contact five times a week, mandatory alcohol and drug testing, mandatory curfews, and other special conditions designed to offer close supervision and enhanced levels of treatment for more serious offenders. Caseloads for officers in these programs are reduced to facilitate tighter control.

Day-Reporting Centers

A day-reporting center (DRC) is a nonresidential program providing intensive supervision for offenders who would otherwise have been incarcerated.[33] The first center opened in the Massachusetts in 1986 modeled after "probation centers" in England and Wales. They may be used at the front end as an alternative to imprisonment or they may be used at the back end for offenders on parole. The purpose of the center is to provide high levels of structure and supervision without twenty-four hours a day incarceration. Offenders live within their own homes but are required to report to the center seven days a week and provide an itinerary of their movements with the case manager for the entire twenty-four-hour period of the day. Centers vary in the degree and nature of the supervision. Random drug testing is generally utilized to monitor offenders, and case managers use telephone contact and home visits to maintain surveillance over offenders. Offenders are required to be either employed or in school, to participate in treatment programs offered at the center, and may be required to perform community service.

Monitoring through Technology

The use of electronic technology to extend the reach of correctional surveillance emerged through the application of defense industry technology to the problem of community supervision in the mid-1980s.[34] These technologies enable the enforcement of house arrest using the home as a detention center during specified hours of the day. There are two major types of systems of electronic monitoring: one based on a computer-programmed telephone system that contacts the offender at random intervals at home. The verification that the offender is at home is achieved through various methods, including video images, voice verification systems, or electronic devices or "keys" strapped to the offender. The alternative method of electronic surveillance uses an electronic bracelet locked onto the offender that emits radio frequencies monitored by the telephone unit connected to a computer. Drive-by systems enable probation officers to confirm a person's presence at home by passing by in an automobile.[35] The basic objective of all of these systems is to enforce home detention through the ability to detect the failure to comply with the court order for house arrest.

Shock Incarceration and Boot Camps

A key innovation of the 1980s was the use of intensified periods of confinement known as shock incarceration.[36] Although these are institutionally based, the boot camp innovation is part of the impulse to provide an alternative to lengthy periods of imprisonment for relatively serious offenders and to include short but intense periods of incarceration as part of a graduated continuum of sanctions.[37] According to underlying theory of shock incarceration, shorter but more intense experiences of incarceration have a greater impact upon the offender at the same time that shorter periods reduce the costs of incarceration. These programs typically rely upon the military model of boot camp to impose a rigorous routine of mandatory physical exercise, drill, and hard labor on youthful offenders. In most programs, the day is highly structured beginning before sunrise requiring almost constant activity until lights out sixteen hours later. These forms of confinement are a stark contrast to the enforced idleness of the typical prison routine.

Boot camp programs vary in the degree to which they also offer treatment, educational, and other type of programming in addition to military discipline and routine. They also vary in the extent to which they supervise offenders within the community after the program and the intensity of that supervision. The popularity of boot camps with the public derives from the sense that discipline and rigor are helpful structures for offenders, although there does not appear to be sufficient evidence that the boot camp experience changes offenders' behavior once they are living back in the community. The concept of shorter but more intense forms of incarceration relies on the research finding that the period of time when inmates are most willing to embark on personal rehabilitation programs is relatively early on in their incarceration, usually within the first three months, when the stress of incarceration and adjusting to the pains of imprisonment is felt most acutely by the inmate. It is at this time that the inmate expresses the greatest willingness to participate in programming. Over time, as inmates adjust to the daily routine of prison life, they lose the motivation to engage in rehabilitative programming to change their lives.

Like all intermediate punishments, one of the key criteria for the success of boot camps is to reduce prison populations and control costs. Yet, research shows that the net-widening effect remains an obstacle for boot camps: there is only a cost-saving outcome if the offenders sent to boot camps are those who would have been sentenced to longer prison terms.[38] If those sentenced to boot camps would have been sentenced to probation, then boot camps actually increase rather than decrease state costs, as boot camps cost more to operate than probation or even traditional prison systems.

RESTORATIVE/COMMUNITY JUSTICE MOVEMENT

The new wave of community corrections variously referred to as community justice or restorative justice focuses on a new set of objectives beyond offender rehabilitation or supervision. Diversion and intermediate sanctions programs prioritize the rehabilitation and close supervision of the offender exclusively by the justice professionals. The primary goal is to rehabilitate or effectively punish the offender within a community setting. Much of the innovation is focused on finding the right combination of programs, services, and intensive supervision that will "work" with a given offender. These community corrections programs do not rely on actual involvement of the community and none of these programs aims to meet the needs of victims of crime.

Community and restorative justice, by contrast, is not merely community based, but it is also victim-centered and community-engaged. Restorative justice is a philosophical approach to justice that seeks to promote maximum involvement of the victim, the offender, and the community in the justice process. The goal of sentencing in restorative justice is to provide restitution for victims, promote accountability for offenders, and facilitate reintegration and reconciliation of the offender into positive relationship with the community. Emerging from the victim's movement, restorative innovations within community corrections have emphasized direct encounters between victims and offenders through mediation, family group conferences, and Native American circles. Programs have attempted to develop genuine partnerships between the community and the justice system with direct accountability of offenders to the community and victims through community service and restitution.

Community Service

Community service is a court-ordered sanction that requires the offender to perform unpaid labor within the community. The use of unpaid labor as a form of criminal sanction has a long history in the prison system, including chain gangs, picking up trash on the highway, and busting rocks. Community-based service orders first appeared in this country in the 1960s and became more common during the 1980s as either a condition of probation or a standalone form of intermediate sanction. Unpaid work was an attractive alternative to the imposition of fines for offenders too poor to pay fines, as a mild form of restitution for "respectable" white collar offenders, and as a cost-effective alternative to incarceration which provides value to the community. One of the drawbacks to the use of community service, however, has been the perception that it is a lenient sanction.

In the 1990s, the use of community service as a means of providing reparation directly to those who have been vandalized or victimized emerged with new vigor within the restorative justice model.[39] Rather than pay a fine to the courts or sit in jail at the taxpayers' expense, the restorative paradigm calls for direct accountability between offenders and the people they have harmed. Rather than using community service orders merely to impose punishment, community service orders in restorative approach require offenders to give back to the victim and community, promoting reconciliation between the offenders and the community. People convicted of DUI may be required to speak about drunk driving to high school audiences or work at a trauma center for accident victims.

Dennis Maloney refers to community work service as "earned redemption" for offenders: by doing good for the community, they are able to literally "pay back" those they have harmed. By working to do something positive for those they have hurt in the past, the social bonds between the victim and the offender are sometimes repaired

Community Courts

The shift toward a community-based justice has also brought innovation in the courts that seek greater involvement of the community and victims. The Midtown Community Court was launched in 1991 to bring the community and the

COMMUNITY JUSTICE criminal justice activities that explicitly include the community and volve prevention and enhancement of the quality of life and the health of the community as part of their goals.

RESTORATIVE JUSTICE a response to crime that seeks to restore the well-being of victims and the larger community while promoting responsible and productive behavior in offenders.

COMMUNITY SERVICE performance of a unpaid work for the community as compensation for an injury or harm to the community.

court closer together and to deal with the thousands of misdemeanors, property crimes, and drug offenses that were undermining the quality of life within the city.[40] The key principle of the community court is to act in partnership with the community and at the same time bring together all resources of the system to help constructively address the problem of crime. A community advisory committee provides input from the community; police regularly hold community meetings at the court; and mediation, counseling, treatment, and education are all available under one roof monitored by frequent interaction with the judge. The community court prioritizes the goal of restoration and helping offenders and the community address problems that cause crime. The Manhattan Midtown relies upon community service as the primary punishment.

The drug court is another example of a problem-solving community court. The first drug court was launched in 1989 in Dade County, Florida. Since that time there has been a rapid increase in the use of this alternative model. There are currently over 2,500 drug courts operating in all fifty states, the District of Columbia, Northern Mariana Islands, Puerto Rico, and Guam. Of these about half serve adults and the other half serve juveniles.[41] The purpose of the drug court is to provide addicts with direct access to treatment closely monitored by the court. These courts partner with a range of community agencies to provide comprehensive services in order to address the underlying issues such as unemployment, illiteracy, and lack of adequate housing. The drug court judge is personally involved in monitoring the offenders' progress through the treatment program; failure to cooperate results in short jail stays but there is a willingness to give participants a second, third, or fourth chance as they struggle to overcome addiction. The primary goal of these courts is to help the drug user rather than to punish them.

Extensive evaluations have been conducted about the effectiveness of drug courts to reduce recidivism; however, the variations between the courts make them difficult to research. Some studies indicate that re-arrest data for individuals who complete the drug court program decline significantly, with research indicating those individuals are 12 percent to 58 percent less likely than a comparison group who were not involved with drug court.[42] But the numbers who actually complete the program varies widely, and their continued success is uncertain. Overall, there does appear to be a slight reduction in the rate of recidivism for those who have participated in drug court as compared to those similarly charged who have not, but that varies significantly and, as with program retention, studies have only recently begun to isolate the program factors that impact this variation.[43]

Victim-Offender Mediation, Conferencing, Boards, and Circles

In traditional justice processes decisions are made by professionals—judges, probation officers, police, or parole authorities. In restorative processes, decision-making is shared between justice professionals and the parties most directly affected by the crime: victims, offenders, their families, and others who are impacted by the event are included in the decision-making process.

Victim-offender mediation programs offer the victim a direct voice in the criminal justice process: victims and offenders negotiate a restitution agreement that is perceived as fair by both sides. Many mediation programs today include family members in the mediation resembling a conferencing model. As we saw

VICTIM-OFFENDER MEDIATION face-to-face facilitated meetings between victims and offenders to promote victim healing, restitution, and offender accountability.

REPARATIVE BOARDS community volunteer boards supervised by the justice system which provide supervision and support for juveniles and adults on probation and for those re-integrating back into the community from prison or jail.

FAMILY GROUP CONFERENCING a form of restorative justice originating in New Zealand in which offenders, victims, and their families meet under the authority of the justice system to discuss the impact of the harm and negotiate accountability by the offender to the victim and the community.

CIRCLE SENTENCING An alternative process involving victims, offenders, the community and the justice system derived from the aboriginal forms of justice used to promote victim's healing, offender accountability and rehabilitation, and to alternative forms of sentencing with input from all stakeholders.

JUSTICE REINVESTMENT is a data-driven approach to improve public safety, reduce corrections and related criminal justice spending, and reinvest savings in strategies that can decrease crime and strengthen neighborhoods.

in chapter 7, the Serrell family wanted specific forms of restitution from Suzanne Cooper that included talking publically about her crime and taking better care of her own children. VOM resulted in an agreement that held Suzanne directly accountable to those she had most seriously harmed.

Communities have also set up **reparative boards** and community account-ability panels staffed by community volunteers to provide supervision for offenders on probation and for offenders returning to the community from incarceration similar to traditional parole supervision. Reparative boards orig-inated in the state of Vermont in the mid-1990s and are used for supervision of both juveniles and adults on probation. The boards work with victims and offenders to examine the harm of the offense, develop a restitution agreement, and monitor the behavior of the offender in the completion of that agreement. These community boards are staffed by probation officers, who provide adminis-trative support, training, and input from the justice system.[44]

In **family group conference** and **circle programs**, an even wider circle of participants take part in the dialogue and contribute to the agreement and monitoring of the agreement in partnership with the justice system. Participants include offenders and their support systems, victims and their support systems, other individuals who have also been impacted by the crime, such as secondary or indirect victims, and wider community members with an interest in the pos-itive resolution of the case. In addition to the direct parties, an array of justice professionals may be present at a circle process. These include justice profes-sionals, such as probation officers, the judge, prosecuting and defense counsels, arresting police officers, and professionals such as teachers, guidance counselors, or social service agencies.

The process can be quite complex: some of the circles are dedicated to healing of the victim; others may focus on the offender and the problems that led to the behavior, while still others focus on preventative changes within the community, which will help to reduce the problem in the first place. In some programs, circles are held as part of the preparation process for release of an offender back into the community. Victims are given an opportunity to meet with offenders to talk about the impact of the crime on their life, ask questions, and gain reassurance about the future of living in the community with the offender. The offender and their family are offered support for living a crime-free lifestyle in the community.

The Challenge of Dismantling Mass Incarceration

Mass incarceration entails massive costs heavily burdening the budgets of states and local county governments. After three decades of steady growth in the prison system, legislators on both sides of the political aisle are seeking to reduce incarcer-ation in order to reduce the costly burden of the correctional system. After decades of being "tough on crime," politicians are now looking to be "smart" on crime. The idea of "**justice reinvestment**" is to reduce spending on prisons and re-invest those funds into practices that have been empirically demonstrated to improve offender behavior in such a way that there is a positive benefit to public safety.

The Justice Reinvestment Initiative is a collaboration between state and federal governments to educate politicians about the costs of mass incarceration and to encourage states to pass legislation designed to reduce prison expenditure and shift spending to community-based alternatives. In some states this has translated into an effort to reduce the prison population by releasing nonviolent offenders, such as drug offenders, for community-based treatment and supervision, while in other states the goal is to slow the rate of prison growth by offering alternatives to incarceration without actually reducing the numbers behind bars.

A key motive for this agenda is to reduce the impact of harsh punishment on the communities of color. As we saw with Kemba Smith, the collateral consequences of incarceration devastate families and neighborhoods and seriously impact the children of those who are behind bars. The aspiration is that funds that are not spent on prison will be re-invested into community-based programs, including treatment, jobs, and housing that will benefit all members of the community.

In other states there has been a concerted effort to reduce prison populations by releasing non violent drug offenders back into the community. In 2013, California passed Proposition 47, a law that made simple possession of any drug—including cocaine and heroin—a misdemeanor offense. The law allowed any inmate to petition to have their sentences reduced based on the change in the law and be released early from prison. In 2016, California also passed Proposition 57 which supported increasing parole and good behavior opportunities for felons convicted of non violent crimes and allowing judges, not prosecutors, to decide whether to try certain juveniles as adults in court. Finally, the current governor of California, Jerry Brown, reversed the policy of the previous governor, Gray Davis, regarding the granting of parole for lifers. Under Brown, roughly 2,700 inmates convicted of murder and lesser offenses have been approved for parole. This number is in stark contrast to the record of his predecessor, Governor Davis, who approved only two lifers for parole during his entire four-year term. By 2016 the prison population in the state of California had dropped by 50,000 inmates since 2006, one of the largest drops in the nation.

RETHINKING THE ROLE OF THE COMMUNITY

Community/restorative justice creates new roles for the community, victims, and offenders. Ironically, the earliest form of community corrections through the efforts of John Augustus relied upon the voluntary efforts of a member of the community willing to supervise wayward members of the community as they struggled to get sober and reform their bad behaviors. But in the twentieth century most community corrections programs have been operated by justice professionals with little involvement by the community in the process.

The dilemma of modern probation and parole systems is the enormous burden of caseloads which preclude adequate relationship building between the overburdened justice professional and any given offender. Offenders are unsupervised and therefore less accountable for meeting the conditions of probation or parole. They are also unable to receive the kind of services they need. Victims are given even less attention. Many probation and parole officers point out that meeting the need of victims stretches their limited resources even further.

In community/restorative justice, the natural capacity of people in the community to provide supervision and support for both victims and offenders is an untapped resource for the justice system. The benefit of community involvement is to lighten the load for probation by bringing the resources of community into the supervision and counseling process. Within the circle are probation officers but there are many other individuals as well—guidance counselors, grandmas, neighbors, and ministers—who might have much to offer the probationer. These additional community members also serve a supervisory function, when they see a probationer walking the streets whom they know should be either in school or at work. More people are aware of the conditions of probation and it is far more difficult for the probationer to avoid detection than on traditional probation. The future of community-based corrections and restorative justice is uncertain. For some, community-based restorative justice is the most constructive option for the future. With two million Americans sitting idly behind bars, and another five million under the supervision of probation or parole authorities, many believe the justice system must seek to engage the community in a problem-solving approach to crime, with the aim to create healthier communities. The trends we have examined suggest that the criminal justice system is turning to the community more and more as it seeks to find a better solution to crime than incarceration.

On the other hand, the militarization of law enforcement, punitive sentencing, and decades of under-investment in housing, employment, education, vocational training, healthcare, and other basic services in the black, Latino, and poor neighborhoods within our major cities represent a persistent challenge to the formation of these partnerships. The issue of racial and economic justice undermines a basic sense of fairness that in turn undermines belief and faith in the legitimacy of the law and the system itself. This breeds resentment and resistance, making it difficult for communities and the criminal justice system to work together.

LOOKING TOWARD THE FUTURE

Winston Churchill believed that the treatment of crime and the criminal by a society was a mark of the stored-up strength and virtue of a nation. The criminal justice system rests upon certain values concerning the rule of law and equality fundamental to our legal system and the highest ideals of American culture. The ideal of equality before the law, the wisdom of due process, the rules of fundamental fairness, standards of dignity for all, the hope of rehabilitation, and faith in redemption are enduring principles which have guided efforts to create a system that truly delivers "justice for all."

In this text, we have seen the tireless campaign to bring the daily practice of the criminal justice system in alignment with the high ideals of the system. There have been many achievements in the justice system: the criminalization of violence against women; the inclusion of minorities and women as justice professionals; the struggle for equal enforcement and protection of the law for minorities; and the achievement of rights for victims to be heard and to be treated with dignity and respect, and have basic rights within the judicial process. Many believe that the push for sweeping reform in the criminal justice system to reduce the disparate impact on communities of color is the key civil rights issue of this century.

The one prediction we can make for sure is that the criminal justice system will continue to change. With the election of Donald Trump, an avowed "law and order" candidate, new priorities and policies will emerge at the federal level, which will influence criminal justice policy across the nation. Social movements of the twenty-first century will extend efforts of the past and we can be certain that new movements will emerge to seek renewal and transformation of the justice system. As citizens and future justice professionals, every reader of this text can choose to participate in defining what justice will mean for this generation and the next.

re-entry (p. 421)   refers to the process of returning to society after being incarcerated.

probation (p. 423)   a sentence the offender serves in the community under correctional supervision.

parole (p. 423)   the conditional release of an inmate from incarceration under supervision after a portion of the prison sentence has been served.

benefit of clergy (p. 423)   a medieval privilege which allowed clergy and other offenders to avoid the gallows at the judge's discretion.

judicial reprieve (p. 424)   the postponement of the execution of a sentence by a judge.

ticket of leave (p. 424)   a system of conditional release from prison started by Sir Walter Crofton of Ireland in the nineteenth century.

good time laws (p. 424)   first passed in 1817, these authorize wardens to release inmates before full completion of their sentence as reward for good behavior.

pre-sentence investigation and report (p. 425) collection of information by a probation officer about an offender's character, family life, work habits, and prior record to assist and guide the judge in sentencing.

conditions of probation (p. 425)   court-ordered conditions which must be met by probationers and are enforced by probation officers.

role strain (p. 426)   tension between two facets of the job of probation and parole: rule enforcement and rehabilitation.

revocation of probation (p. 427)   return of offender to court for sentencing for failure to meet conditions of probation.

parole board (p. 428)   an administrative agency charged with the authority to grant conditional release for prisoners eligible for parole.

parole eligibility (p. 428)   determined by statute and the amount of time an inmate has served.

statutory good time (p. 428)   the number of days deducted from a sentence determined by statute for a time served without disciplinary reports.

earned good time (p. 428)   the number of days deducted from a sentence for participation in specified programs while in prison.

unconditional mandatory release (p. 428)   release from prison required by statute when a criminal has served his or her full sentence minus statutory and earned good time.

revocation of parole (p. 429)   administrative removal of an offender from parole status for failure to comply with parole conditions usually requiring the return of the offender to incarceration.

diversion (p. 429)   the removal of offenders from the criminal justice process at any stage prior to criminal conviction.

formal diversion (p. 430)   the removal of eligible offender from the routine criminal justice process to an alternative program.

net-widening (p. 430)   the increase in the correctional population by the diversion of less serious offenders into program intended for more serious offenders thus expanding the overall correctional population.

true diversion programs (p. 430)   traditional forms of diversion that kept people out of the criminal justice system.

intermediate sanctions (p. 431)   a variety of punishments that are more restrictive than traditional probation but less extreme than incarceration.

intensive supervision probation (p. 431)   a program of closer surveillance and more intensive programming for higher risk juvenile and adult offenders.

day-reporting centers (p. 431)   programs of community-based supervision to which offenders must report daily and where their activities are monitored and structured throughout most of the day.

house arrest (p. 431)   a sentence requiring the convicted offender to remain within his or her house during specified periods.

electronic monitoring (p. 431)   the use of monitoring technology to trigger alarms if an offender moves beyond prescribed physical locations.

shock incarceration   the use of shorter but more intense periods of incarceration designed to have a deeper impact on the offender.

boot camp (p. 431)   short-term incarceration that relies on intensive military drill, physical exercise, and correctional treatment.

restorative justice (p. 434)   a response to crime that seeks to restore the well-being of victims and the larger community while promoting responsible and productive behavior in offenders.

community justice (p. 434)   criminal justice activities that explicitly include the community and include prevention and enhancement of the quality of life and the health of the community as part of their goals.

community service (p. 434)   performance of a unpaid work for the community as compensation for an injury or harm to the community.

victim-offender mediation (p. 435)   face-to-face facilitated meetings between victims and offenders to promote victim healing, restitution, and offender accountability.

reparative boards (p. 436)   community volunteer boards supervised by the justice system which provide supervision and support for juveniles and adults on probation and for those re-integrating back into the community from prison or jail.

family group conferencing (p. 436)   a form of restorative justice originating in New Zealand in which offenders, victims, and their families meet under the authority of the justice system to discuss the impact of the harm and negotiate accountability by the offender to the victim and the community.

circle sentencing (p. 436)   An alternative process involving victims, offenders, the community and the justice system derived from the aboriginal forms of justice used to promote victim's healing, offender accountability and rehabilitation, and to alternative forms of sentencing with input from all stakeholders.

Justice reinvestment (p. 436)   is a data-driven approach to improve public safety, reduce corrections and related criminal justice spending, and reinvest savings in strategies that can decrease crime and strengthen neighborhoods.

3. Describe the two key functions of the probation officer's job. Define the concept of role strain and explain why there is an inherent conflict within the probation officer's job. Describe the key functions of the parole officer today. What is the job of the parole board?

4. Define standard conditions of probation and parole. What does "revocation" of parole or probation mean?

5. Identify the three distinct periods of expansion and development in community corrections. Identify the key goals for community corrections in each period.

6. What is diversion? What is the difference between "true" diversion and "formal" diversion? Explain the concept of net-widening. Explain why net-widening undermines achievement of the goals of community corrections.

7. What are "intermediate sanctions"? Describe the practice of ISP, boot camps, and DRCs. How do these sanctions differ from traditional probation or traditional incarceration?

8. Explain the distinctive goals of community and restorative justice programs compared to the intermediate sanctions movement and the diversion movement. What is community service and how is it related to the philosophy of restorative justice?

9. What is a "community court"? Demonstrate how the community court takes a problem-solving approach to crime.

10. Describe the key practices of restorative justice victim-offender mediation, family group conferencing, boards, and circles. Explain how these practices involve victims and the community in the justice process.

REVIEW AND STUDY QUESTIONS

1. Describe the origins of the probation function. Which Latin term does the word "probation" come from and what does it mean? Identify the primary goal of the founder of the probation function.

2. Describe the origins of the parole function. Which French term does the word derive from? Explain the "ticket of leave" practice.

CHECK IT OUT

Websites

California Department of Corrections and Rehabilitation, http://www.cdcr.ca.gov/Parole/

American Probation and Parole Association, http://www.appa-net.org. A very useful web site with access to free publications, information about best practices in probation and parole, and lots of great links for practitioners.

Prisoner Recidivism Analysis Tool, http://bjs.ojp. usdoj.gov/index.cfm?ty=datool&surl=/recidivism/index.cfm. This tool, provided by the Bureau of Justice Statistics, allows users to calculate recidivism rates using a number of variables. Analysis is based upon a three-year data sample.

Center for Mediation and Restorative Justice, http://www.wiscs.org/programs/court_community_services/justice_center/. Just one of many web sites addressing Restorative Justice, this site offers access to a wide range of information about restorative justice and victim-offender mediation, including recent evaluation and research on programs across the country and around the world. Also has many links other good restorative justice and community justice web sites.

Real Justice, http://www.realjustice.org Non-profit organization devoted to the promotion of the "conferencing" method of restorative justice in North America. A wealth of information about the origins of family group conferencing and its uses within the criminal justice and other settings.

Videos

Blocking the Exit—14 minutes. A documentary which illustrates the profound impact that requiring governor's approval of parole for lifers has had in Maryland. Available at http://www.justicepolicy.org/research/2152

Life After Prison   Success on the Outside—42 minutes. Award-winning program which talks to parolees about success and failure after prison and examines the specific steps needed to successfully transition to life on the outside. Available at FilmsMediaGroup, http://www.films.com/id/10430

High Risk Offender—58 minutes. A powerful look at the relationship between six offenders and their parole officer and therapists as they struggle to remain on the right side of the law. Offenders range from white collar offender to armed robbery to murder, the tough look at the unique problems and situations for the parole officer and his clients. Winner of Gold Apple Award. Available from First Run-Icarus Films www.frif.com

Exploring Alternatives to Prison and Probation—22 minutes. A look at the range of innovative solutions being tried around the country, including community service, house arrest with electronic monitoring, boot camp, and intensive supervised probation. Available from Filmmakers library at www.filmakers.com

NOTES

[1] Nancy Mullane, *Life After Murder: Five Men in Search of Redemption* (New York: Perseus Books Group, 2012).

[2] Christopher Zoukis, "California Lifers Paroled in Record Numbers," Prison Legal News, March 31, 2016. https://www.prisonlegalnews.org/news/2016/mar/31/california-lifers-paroled-record-numbers/; retrieved January 29, 2017.

[3] Danielle Kaeble and Lauren E. Glaze, "Correctional Populations in the United States, 2015," *Bureau of Justice Statistics, Bulletin NCJ250374* (Washington, DC, December 2016).

[4] Paul Guerino, Paige M. Harrison, and William J. Sabol, "Prisoners in 2010 (Revised)," *Bureau of Justice Statistics, Bulletin NCJ-236096* (Washington, DC, December 2011).

[5] Todd R. Clear and David R. Karp, *The Community Justice Ideal: Preventing Crime and Achieving Justice* (Boulder, CO: Westview Press, 1999), 21.

[6] Jean Chung, *Felony Disenfranchisement: A Primer* (Washington, DC: The Sentencing Project 2016). http://www.sentencingproject.org/wp-content/uploads/2015/08/Felony-Disenfranchisement-Primer.pdf

[7] Todd R. Clear and George F. Cole, *American Corrections* (Belmont CA: Wadsworth Publishing Company, 1994), 173–175.

[8] Ex parte United States, 242 U.S. 1916.

[9] Samuel Walker, *Popular Justice: A History of American Criminal Justice* (New York: Oxford University Press, 1980), 87–89.

[10] John Augustus, *A Report of the Labors of John Augustus (1852)* (Montclair, NJ: Patterson Smith Publishing Co, 1972).

[11] Augustus, *A Report of the Labors of John Augustus*, 88.

[12] Augustus, *A Report of the Labors of John Augustus*, 95.

[13] Lawrence M. Friedman, *Crime and Punishment in American History* (New York: Basic Books, 1993), 161–162.

[14] Todd R. Clear and George F. Cole, *American Corrections* (Belmont, CA: Wadsworth Publishing Company, 1994), 407.

[15] Danielle Kaeble and Lauren E. Glaze, "Correctional Populations in the United States, 2015," *Bureau of Justice Statistics, Bulletin NCJ250374* (Washington, DC, December 2016).

[16] Matthew R. Durose, Donald J. Farole, Jr., and Sean P. Rosenmerkel, "Felony Sentences in State Courts, 2006 – Statistical Tables," *Bureau of Justice Statistics Bulletin NCJ-226846* (Washington, DC: Department of Justice, December 2009).

[17] Carl B. Klockars, Jr., "A Theory of Probation Supervision," *The Journal of Criminal Law, Criminology and Police Science* 63 (1972), 550–557.

[18] David Anderson, *Crime and the Politics of Hysteria: How the Willie Horton Story Changed American Justice* (New York: Random House, 1995).

[19] Todd R. Clear and George F. Cole, *American Corrections* (Belmont, CA: Wadsworth Publishing Company, 1994), 411.

[20] Paul Guerino, Paige M. Harrison, and William J. Sabol, "Prisoners in 2010 (Revised)," *Bureau of Justice Statistics, Bulletin NCJ-236096* (Washington, DC, December 2011).

[21] *Greenholtz v. Inmates of Nebraska Penal and Correctional Complex,* 422 U.S. 1 (1979).

[22] Ann L. Pastore and Kathleen Maguire, eds. "Adults on Probation, in Jail or Prison and on Parole, United States 1980–99" *Sourcebook on Criminal Justice Statistics, 1999* (Washington, DC: USGPO, 2000), 484.

[23] Todd R. Clear and Edward E. Latessa, "Surveillance v. Control: Probation Officers Roles in Intensive Supervision," *Justice Quarterly* 10 (1993), 441–462.

[24] Robert B. Coates, Mark Umbreit, and Betty Vos, "Restorative Justice Cirlces in South St. Paul, Minnesota," *Research Monograph* (Minneapolis, MN: Center for Restorative Justice and Peacemaking, University of Minnesota, August 2000), 15.

[25] "The Challenge of Crime in a Free Society," *President's Crime Commission* (Washington, DC: USGPO, 1967).

[26] Samuel Walker, *Sense and Nonsense about Crime and Drugs* (Belmont, CA: Wadsworth 1998), 207.

[27] Stanley Cohen, *Visions of Social Control* (Cambridge: Polity Press, 1985), 50–56.

[28] Thomas G. Blomberg, "Widening the Net: An Anomaly in the Evaluation of Diversion Programs," in Malcom Klein and K.S. Teilman, eds., *Handbook of Criminal Justice Evaluation* (Beverly Hills, CA: Sage, 1980).

[29] Andrew Scull, "Community Corrections: Panacea, Progress or Pretence?" in *The Power to Punish*, eds. David Garland and Peter Young (London: Heinemann, 1983).

[30] Norval Morris and Michael Tonry, *Between Prison and Probation: Intermediate Punishments in a Rational Sentencing System* (Oxford: Oxford University Press, 1990).

[31] Morris and Tonry, *Between Prison and Probation*, 6.

[32] Joan Petersilia, "A Decade of Experimenting with Intermediate Sanctions: What Have We Learned?," *Federal Probation* (1998), 3–9.

[33] John F. Larivee, "Day-Reporting in Massachusetts," in *Intermediate Sanctions in Overcrowded Times*, eds. Michael Tonry and Kate Hamilton (Boston, MA: Northeastern University Press, 1995), 128–130.

[34] Terry L. Baumer and Michael G. Maxfield, "Electronically Monitored Home Detention," in *Intermediate Sanctions in Overcrowded Times*, eds. Michael Tonry and Kate Hamilton (Boston, MA: Northeastern University Press, 1995), 104–108.

[35] J. Robert Lilly, "Electronic Monitoring in the U.S." in *Intermediate Sanctions in Overcrowded Times*, eds. Michael Tonry and Kate Hamilton (Boston, MA: Northeastern University Press, 1995), 113–114.

[36] Doris Layton MacKenzie and Claire Souryal, "Multisite Evaluation of Shock Incarceration," *National Institute of Justice Research Report* (Washington, DC: USGPO, 1994).

[37] J. Robert Lilly, "Electronic Monitoring in the U.S." in *Intermediate Sanctions in Overcrowded Times*, eds. Michael Tonry and Kate Hamilton (Boston, MA: Northeastern University Press, 1995), 121.

[38] Dale G. Parent, "Boot Camps Failing to Achieve Goals," in *Intermediate Sanctions in Overcrowded Times*, eds. Michael Tonry and Kate Hamilton (Boston, MA: Northeastern University Press, 1995), 139–147.

[39] Gordon Bazemore and Dennis Malony, "Rehabilitating Community Service: Toward Restorative Service Sanctions in a Balanced Justice System," *Federal Probation* 58 (1999), 24–35.

[40] John Feinblatt and Michele Sviridoff, "The Mid-town Community Court Experiment" in *Sex, Scams and Street Life: The Sociology of New York City's Times Square*, ed. Robert P. McNamara (Westport, CN: Praeger, 1995).

[41] Office of Justice Programs, *Drug Courts, Bulletin NCJ 236074* (Washington, DC, October 2011). https://ncjrs.gov/pdffiles1/nij/236074.pdf; accessed September 23, 2012.

[42] Government Accountability Office, *Adult Drug Courts: Studies Show Courts Reduce Recidivism, but DOJ Could Enhance Future Performance Measure Revision Efforts'*, Report to Congress GAO 12–53 (Washington, DC, December 2011.) http://www.gao.gov/new.items/d1253.pdf, accessed September 23, 2012.

[43] Susan T. Krumholz, "Problem Solving Courts," in *U.S. Criminal Justice Policy: A Contemporary Reader*, ed. K. Ismaili (Boston, MA: Jones and Bartlett, 2010).

[44] Michael E. Smith "What Future for "Public Safety" and "Restorative Justice" in Community Corrections?," *Sentencing and Corrections: Issues for the 21st Century* 11 (2001).

GLOSSARY

A

actus reus the physical element of the criminal act.

adjudication the process whereby the court arrives at a decision regarding a particular case.

administrative model of sentencing the use of parole boards, wardens, and other correctional officials to determine when an offender is to be granted conditional release from incarceration.

adversarial system a system in which the prosecution and the defense are each on opposing sides seeking to persuade the judge and the jury to accept their version of the truth.

affirm the ruling by an appellate court to uphold the decision of the lower court.

affirmative defenses a category of defense raised by the defendant's counsel who had the burden of proof to prove beyond a reasonable doubt.

aggravated assault the intent to commit serious bodily injury.

aggravating circumstances facts about the heinous nature of the criminal act specified by law that guide a jury decision to apply the death penalty.

anarchist a political philosophy that rejects the state and opposes hierarchy.

appeal a request by a convicted defendant to have a higher court review the proceedings claiming an error in due process proceedings which significantly impacted the outcome of the case.

appellate jurisdiction the jurisdiction of these courts is restricted to matters of appeal and review.

arraignment a hearing before the court in which the defendant is formally informed of the charges and is required to enter a plea.

arrest the action of taking a person into custody for the purpose of charging them with a crime.

arrest warrant a written order, based on probable cause and issued by a judge or magistrate, commanding that the person named on the warrant be arrested by the police.

arson the willful or malicious burning or attempt to burn any dwelling, building, vehicle, or personal property.

assault the intentional attempt or threat to physically injure another.

assembly line justice another term for describing the lower court proceedings where cases are decided in matters of minutes or even seconds, with quick consultations between attorneys and judges.

assembly line model a model of the justice process which depicts the system processing cases as swiftly and efficiently as possible in a standard manner.

asset forfeiture laws statutes which authorize the confiscation of cash, vehicles, property, and other assets used in the commission of crime or purchased with criminal profits.

assigned counsel systems appointment of private defense counsel by the trial judge compensated on a fixed fee basis by the court.

authority a specific form of power which is seen as legitimate by those subject to it.

B

bail money or other security placed in custody of the court in order to insure the return of a defendant to stand trial.

bail hearing the first interaction with the court, where terms of interim release are established.

Battered Women's Syndrome a constellation of symptoms similar to those experienced by someone with post-traumatic stress.

battery the non-lethal culmination of an assault.

bench trial a trial in which the judge hears the fact and issues a verdict on the guilt or innocence of the defendants.

benefit of clergy a medieval privilege which allowed clergy and other offenders to avoid the gallows at the judge's discretion.

beyond a reasonable doubt the standard of proof necessary for a conviction in criminal trials; the highest possible standard.

bifurcated trial the constitutional requirement that the imposition of the death penalty be subject to a separate hearing after the adjudication of guilt or innocence has taken place.

Big House slang for maximum-security prisons infamous for harsh conditions and tough inmate populations.

bloody codes a system of laws in eighteenth-century England that permitted capital punishment for a wide range of property and minor offenses.

blue curtain social isolation of police and their families from civilians in society.

Bobbies the nickname for the first formal municipal police unit in London founded by Sir Robert Peel.

boot camp short-term incarceration that relies on intensive military drill, physical exercise, and correctional treatment.

border exception all persons, citizens and non-citizens, may have their luggage and persons searched by law enforcement without probable cause.

broken windows theory of crime minor crimes such as vandalism and graffiti are early signs of a neighborhood in decline which lead to more serious criminal conduct in that location.

brutalization effect the theory that capital punishment contributes to greater violence within society by increasing the tolerance for violence within society.

building tender system a system of inmate control whereby the most violent and intimidating inmates were chosen as "building tender" by guards to control their fellow inmates by violence and coercion.

burglary the trespass through breaking and entering of a personal or commercial property with the intent to commit a crime.

"but for" standard a standard for determining causality which holds that "but for" the conduct of the accused, the harm in question would not have occurred.

C

causation a causal link between an actor's conduct and a harm.

certiorari power the judicial discretion of Supreme Court to select cases for review.

challenge for cause removal of jurors for stated reasons.

change of venue a written request to the judge to change the jurisdiction from the location where the crime was committed to a different jurisdiction.

character witness persons who offer testimony regarding the defendant unrelated to the facts of the case.

charge bargaining plea negotiations that agree on the charges to be filed in exchange for a guilty plea by the defendant.

circle sentencing An alternative process involving victims, offenders, the community, and the justice system derived from the aboriginal forms of justice used to promote victim healing, offender accountability and rehabilitation, and alternative forms of sentencing with input from all stakeholders.

circumstantial evidence evidence that requires a jury or judge to infer a fact about the case.

Civil asset forfeiture legal process that allows officials to confiscate any money, houses, vehicles, land or other property that was gained through trafficking in illegal drugs.

civil liberties the rights and freedoms provided for by the U. S. Constitution and especially the Bill of Rights.

classification the process through which the custodial, educational, and treatment needs of the offender are assessed in order to ascertain placement within the correctional system.

clearance rate the proportion of crimes that result in arrest.

closing statement a summary statement made by each attorney to the judge and the jury reviewing the main arguments and facts of the case.

code of silence the unwritten norm to support fellow officers by not revealing problems and illegal conduct to outsiders.

COINTELPRO an FBI program in the 1950s and 1960s that engaged in often illegal, infiltration, and disruption of domestic political organizations.

collateral consequences the outcome of an action that is neither planned nor anticipated.

community justice criminal justice activities that explicitly include the community and include prevention and enhancement of the quality of life and the health of the community as part of their goals.

community policing a pro-active policing strategy which relies upon problem-solving in close collaboration with the citizens within the community.

community service performance of a unpaid work for the community as compensation for an injury or harm to the community.

concurrence the simultaneous coexistence of an act in violation of the law and a criminal intent.

conditions of probation court-ordered conditions which must be met by probationers and are enforced by probation officers.

conflict model of law law that reflects the values, beliefs, and interests of powerful elites within any given society and serves to help those in power preserve their position within society.

congregate system a penitentiary system developed in Auburn New York in which inmates were held in solitary confinement at night but worked with fellow prisoners during the day under a rule of complete silence.

consensus theory of law law that reflects the collective conscience or widely shared values and beliefs of any given society.

consent search warrantless search conducted when the party to the search provides voluntary and intelligent consent to law enforcement.

consent positive cooperation in act or attitude.

constructive intent the actor doesn't intend harm but their conduct violates basic standards of responsible conduct.

contingent plea agreement an agreement that the defendant forfeit specific assets prior to the start of plea negotiations.

contract system a form of prison industry in which the labor of inmates was leased to an outside contractor or business for a fee.

conviction the judgment of a court based on the verdict of a jury or judicial officer that the defendant is guilty of the offense charged.

corporate crime criminal conduct of employees of an organization committed for the benefit of the organization.

corporeal punishment punishment inflicted on the body through whipping, branding, mutilation, or torture.

correctional treatment model reliance on prison rehabilitation programs.

counterterrorism a government tactic for responding to terrorist threats.

court of last resort a court whose ruling has final authority within a given jurisdiction.

courtroom work group criminal justice professionals who conduct the daily business of the criminal courts.

courts of last resort the power of the state Supreme Court to be the final interpreter of the state constitution and the power of the U.S. Supreme Court to be the final interpreter of the U.S. Constitution.

courts of record courts in which a full transcript of the proceedings is made for all cases.

coverture the wife's legal status was subsumed under her husband's identity as a citizen.

crime as social construction behaviors defined as crime are the result of the beliefs, values, and institutions of that society.

crime clock a form of display used in the UCR to illustrate the annual ratio of specific crimes to fixed time intervals.

crime control function detection and apprehension of law violators.

crime control model of justice it prioritizes the efficient and effective enforcement of the law as a basic precondition for a free society.

crime control formal and informal processes that respond to violations of legal norms.

crime rate the number of crimes known to the police for a given year divided by the population for that year and multiplied by 100,000.

crimes of omission failure of governments to provide decent opportunities for housing, education, jobs, and citizenship rights for its citizenry.

criminal homicide the unlawful killing of one human being by another.

criminal intelligence law enforcement surveillance of those believed to have engaged in illegal activities, typically responding to such activities; constrained by the Fourth Amendment requirements of reasonable suspicion or probable cause.

criminal liability the degree of blameworthiness assigned to the defendants based on legal adjudication.

criminal negligence unconscious creation of high risk of harm.

criminal recklessness knowing creation of high risk of harm to others.

cross examination when counsel questions witnesses called by the opposing side.

cycle of violence a pattern of behaviors experienced in abusive relationships that moves from tension, to action, to apology or remorse.

D

dark figure of crime crimes that do not become part of the official police record.

date rape non-consensual intercourse where the victim knows the attacker socially.

DAWN or Drug Abuse Warning Network a program which compiles data on drug overdoses and deaths reported within hospital emergency rooms.

day-reporting centers programs of community-based supervision to which offenders must report daily and where their activities are monitored and structured throughout most of the day.

de facto rights or practices which exist in fact although not in law.

de jure rights or practices which are established by law.

dead bang case a case in which the evidence to convict is strong.

defense attorney an attorney whose ethical duty is to zealously represents the interests of the defendant before the court.

defense of alibi a legal defense in which a defendant claims to be in a different location when the crime was committed.

defense of duress a defense to a criminal charge that the defendant was forced to act against one's will.

defense of excuse a category of legal defense in which the defendant claims a personal condition at the time of the act that excuses them from criminal liability under the law.

defense of infancy a defense that claims that individuals below a certain age should not be held criminally liable for their actions by virtue of their young age.

defense of justification a category of legal defense in which the defendant admits committing the act in question but claims it was necessary to avoid some greater evil.

defenses of insanity an affirmative defense seeking to prove a mental state that prevents an individual from comprehending the nature and consequences of actions or from distinguishing right from wrong.

deliberative as with juries, individuals come to an agreement with each other about what is just through a process of discussion, argument, and debate.

demonstrative evidence evidence such as a photograph or physical object which demonstrates a fact about the case for the judge or jury.

deprivation theory the theory that the inmate subculture is formed as a adaptation to and reaction to the deprivations of prison life.

determinate sentencing the imposition of a fixed or set amount of time in prison.

deterrence the imposition of punishment in order to discourage the commission of future crimes by the offender and others within society.

deviance conduct which is contrary to the norms of conduct or social expectations of the group.

the dilemma of discretion discretionary decision-making is both essential for justice and creates the possibilities for discrimination and bias in the justice process.

diminished capacity an affirmative defense that an individual could not have developed the requisite intent; usually resulting in conviction on a lesser offense.

direct evidence firsthand accounts of relevant facts of the case.

direct examination when counsel questions its own witnesses during the trial.

discretion the authority to choose between alternative actions.

disproportionate minority confinement it refers to the high levels of racial and ethnic minorities behind bars relative to their numbers in the population.

disproportionate minority contact it refers to the over-representation of minorities at all stages of the criminal justice process.

diversion the removal of offenders from the criminal justice process at any stage prior to criminal conviction.

DNA testing a broad field of science that has begun to offer reliable evidence to exonerate a growing number of convicted individuals serving prison sentences including a number who are on death row.

domestic violence a pattern of violence and/or abuse used by one person against another in an intimate relationship such as marriage or dating.

domestic violence restraining orders legal remedies created for abused women which can be sought at the discretion of the complaining party to prohibit or restrict contact with an abusing spouse or partner.

due process model of justice it prioritizes rules of due process which guarantee and protect individual civil liberty and fairness in the enforcement of the criminal law.

DUF or Drug Use Forecasting a Department of Justice program which compiles data on drug use by people arrested in selected cities.

dying declaration the last words of a dying witness which may be entered as hearsay evidence in a criminal trial.

E

earned good time the number of days deducted from a sentence for participation in specified programs while in prison.

eco-terrorism people who use violence to draw public attention to practices related to animal welfare or the environment that they believe are immoral and unjust.

electronic monitoring the use of monitoring technology to trigger alarms if an offender moves beyond prescribed physical locations.

elements of the crime the five key elements common to almost all criminal statutes which must be proven within a court of law beyond a reasonable doubt according to the rules of criminal procedure and evidence to establish legal guilt.

elite private counsel a small percentage of criminal defense attorneys who have lucrative practices which specialize in representation of the rich and famous.

entrapment the inducement of an individual to commit a crime not contemplated by him or her.

exclusionary rule the constitutional prohibition of the use of illegally obtained evidence in court.

excusable homicide homicide that is committed by persons without legal liability for their conduct or in a manner that the criminal law does not prohibit, for example, accidentally.

executive clemency the power to pardon (forgive) a criminal conviction or commute a sentence, held by the chief executive officer.

expert witness a person with specialized education, training, or qualifications in a particular field who testifies on behalf of the prosecution or defense.

eyewitness testimony a testimony based upon direct observation.

F

factual guilt guilty based upon the facts, though not necessarily legally guilty.

family group conferencing a form of restorative justice originating in New Zealand in which offenders, victims, and their respective families meet under the authority of the justice system to discuss the impact of the harm and negotiate accountability by the offender to the victim and the community.

felony an offense punishable by more than one year in state or federal prison.

felony murder if a death occurs during the commission of a felony, the person committing the primary offense can also be charged with first-degree murder.

first degree a premeditated, deliberate and clear conscious intention on the part of an individual to carry out a homicide

five stages of the criminal justice system entry, pretrial, and investigation; adjudication, sentencing and corrections.

fleeing felon doctrine a now-defunct law enforcement rule which permitted officers to shoot a suspected felon attempting to flee from a lawful arrest.

folkways unplanned but expected ways of behaving within any given culture.

forcible rape the unlawful sexual intercourse with a female without her consent and against her will.

formal diversion the removal of eligible offender from the routine criminal justice process to an alternative program.

founding decision a decision made by police that a particular incident should be treated as a crime (founded) or not treated as a crime (unfounded).

frankpledge a system of law enforcement in medieval societies where every male member of the community over the age of 12 was bound by a pledge to keep peace and assist in delivering offenders to court.

fruit of a poisonous tree doctrine evidence obtained through other illegally obtained evidence, inadmissible because it is tainted by the illegality of the initial search, arrest or confession.

fundamental fairness doctrine the definition of due process which focuses on the substantive fairness in the application of the law.

fusion centers centers across the country, administered by the Department of Homeland Security, where information is collected and stored.

G

gender neutral modern rape laws do not specify gender, applying to either male or female victims.

general deterrence the imposition of punishment in order to set an example to others contemplating crime.

general intent state of mind inferred from the behavior or conduct itself to commit the act.

general jurisdiction the geographical district or subject matter over which the authority of a court extends and is authorized to handle criminal and civil proceedings.

genocide an international crime consisting of specific acts of violence committed with intent to destroy, in whole or in part, a national, ethnic, racial, or religious group.

going rate local informal norms concerning the typical sentence for a given crime within a particular court or jurisdiction.

good faith exception exception to the exclusionary rule in which evidence obtained by police acting in good faith with a search warrant issued by a judge is admissible even though the warrant is ultimately found invalid.

good time laws first passed in 1817, these authorize wardens to release inmates before full completion of their sentence as reward for good behavior.

grand jury a group of, usually twenty-three, citizens, assembled to determine whether sufficient evidence exists to support the prosecution of the accused.

grass eaters police officers who accept payoffs for rendering police services or who look the other way when police action is called in exchange for a goods and services.

guided discretion statutes capital statutes which specify the mitigating and aggravating circumstances juries should consider in the penalty phase of the capital trial.

H

Hands-off doctrine the refusal of the courts to hear inmates, cases regarding conditions of confinement and constitutional deprivations within the institution.

harm loss, disadvantage, or injury to victim.

hearsay evidence testimonial regarding what another person saw or heard which is generally not permissible as a criminal evidence.

hegemonic masculinity the cultural ideal of masculine gender characteristics.

High School Senior Survey an annual survey of a representative sample of high school seniors which asks questions about use of drugs and alcohol and attitudes and

values toward these behaviors conducted by the National Institute of Drug Abuse.

Homeland Security Act of 2002 massive reorganization of federal law enforcement, creating the Department of Homeland Security.

homicide the killing of a human being by the act, procurement or omission, of another human being.

horizontal overcharging multiple count indictments to maximize the state's advantage in plea negotiations.

house arrest a sentence requiring the convicted offender to remain within his or her house during specified periods.

hue and cry an old English call for assistance in the pursuit of felons

human conduct rule the requirement that some human action is required for criminal liability; thought is not sufficient.

human rights the concept that there are basic inalienable rights universal to all people by virtue of their humanity.

hung jury a jury unable to come to a unanimous decision for a legal verdict.

I

ideal of expressive justice the use of heavy and harsh punishments to express moral outrage at the injustice of crime.

ignorance of law a lack of knowledge of the law or the existence of the law

impact techniques techniques for use of coercive force designed to subdue a combative suspect without resorting to lethal force.

impaneling a jury the process of selecting individuals to serve on a jury from the jury pool.

importation theory the theory that inmate subculture is brought inside the institution from criminal subcultures within outside society.

incapacitation the elimination of the capacity to commit future crimes within society usually through incarceration.

incorporation doctrine the legal principle that all the procedural protections of the Bill of Rights applies to state courts under the due process and equal protection clause of the Fourteenth Amendment.

indeterminate sentencing the imposition of an unspecified amount of time in prison somewhere between a statutory minimum and maximum term.

indigent defense state-funded systems for providing defense counsel for the poor.

individualization the value that each case be treated on the basis of its own unique and specific facts.

initial appearance the first court processing stage after arrest in which the accused is brought before a judge or magistrate to hear the formal charges.

inquisitorial system the state represented by the judge has the power to investigate, interrogate, adjudicate, convict, and sanction the accused.

intensive supervision probation a program of closer surveillance and more intensive programming for higher risk juvenile and adult offenders.

interests of justice ethical duty of the prosecutor to administer justice for all rather than seek conviction.

intermediate appellate court courts charged with automatic review of all appeals by defendants whose decisions are subject to review by a court of last resort.

intermediate sanctions a variety of punishments that are more restrictive than traditional probation but less extreme than incarceration.

Interdiction to prohibit through intervention

interrogation explicit questioning or actions by law enforcement that may elicit an incriminating statement from a suspect.

intersectionality a variety of demographic characteristics, such as race, gender, and sexual identity, that collude or intersect when we try to understand the influence that social structures have on our lives.

involuntary intoxication intoxication that is not willful.

involuntary manslaughter an unintentional killing for which criminal liability is imposed.

J

jail a facility authorized to hold persons awaiting trial and those sentenced for misdemeanors and minor felony offenses.

jailhouse lawyer a prisoner who gives legal advice and assistance to other prisoners.

jihad an internal journey of purification and to the willingness to carry arms to defend your community.

Jim Crow laws state and local laws passed in the aftermath of the Civil War that reinforced racial segregation, marked by the concept of "separate but equal."

judges public officials who preside over courts of law.

judicial affirmation of probable cause judicial review and agreement with the facts establishing probable cause for an arrest or search.

judicial model of sentencing sentencing decisions that rely upon the broad discretion of the judge to craft the individual sentence within parameters set by statute.

judicial reprieve the postponement of the execution of a sentence by a judge.

judicial review the power of the judicial branch to declare acts of the executive or legislative branch unconstitutional.

jurisdiction the geographical district or subject matter over which the authority of a court extends.

jury instructions the judicial responsibility to lay out the law which the jury should follow in making its verdict.

jury nullification a jury verdict that is made without regard to the evidence or the law.

jury trial evidence is presented to a panel of citizens who are required to determine the defendant's guilt or innocence of the charges.

the justice funnel a model of the justice process which depicts the impact of discretionary decision-making by criminal justice personnel as they sort and filter defendants through the five stages.

justifiable homicide homicide that is permitted under the law either through self-defense, necessity or through the execution of a public duty.

Justice reinvestment is a data-driven approach to improve public safety, reduce corrections and related criminal justice spending, and reinvest savings in strategies that can decrease crime and strengthen neighborhoods.

K

Kansas City experiment a 1973 experiment which compared the deterrent effect of three different modes of police patrol.

key-man system an eligibility process for serving on jury, based on recommendations from key persons of high character and reputation within the community.

L

larceny the taking and carrying away of personal property of another with intent to deprive them of the property permanently.

latent function of law a by-product of law which is to define the identity and strengthen social bonds among members of a group.

laws social norms which are codified and enforced through the authority of the state.

learned helplessness the point at which a victim of domestic abuse believes they are entirely powerless to change their situation.

legal guilt proof of criminal liability beyond a reasonable doubt by admissible evidence within a court of law.

legislative model of sentencing the setting of mandatory sentences for specific crimes established within criminal statutes passed by legislative bodies.

lethal force a force likely to cause death or great bodily harm; also known as deadly force.

limited jurisdiction the restricted geographical district or subject matter over which the authority of a court extends and is authorized to handle criminal and civil proceedings.

lockstep a peculiar form of marching for prisoners in which they were required to move in unison with their hands on each other's shoulders.

lynching an act of violence used as terrorism and social control typically by vigilantes, and often in the form of hanging.

M

mandatory arrest a policy requiring police to make an arrest in the case of an allegation of domestic violence.

mandatory minimum the minimum penalty that must be imposed and carried out for all cases convicted of a given offense.

manslaughter the unlawful killing of a human being without malice or premeditation.

martial law replacing civil law with military law, albeit on an emergency basis.

masculinity all the gender characteristics assigned to males within a society.

mass incarceration it refers to the rapid increase in incarceration in the United States between 1970s and 2010, resulting in record high numbers of Americans in jails and prisons.

material supporter anyone who makes a charitable contribution to an organization designated as "terrorist organization."

maximum security a facility designed to impose maximal restriction on inmates in order to contain the most incorrigible and violent offenders.

mean world syndrome the belief that the world is full of predators waiting to assault innocent strangers.

meat eaters police officers who actively and systematically solicit bribes or conspire with criminals in criminal activity.

medium security a prison designed to impose less restrictive conditions on inmates allowing for greater visitation, programming, and recreation for inmates.

mens rea the mental element in crime or criminal intent or the guilty mind.

Militant Jihadism a term used to describe a movement claiming to be rooted in Islam and perceived to be devoted to the destruction of "the west."

military model of policing the use of the military metaphor for the structure and mission of policing.

minimum security an institution designed to permit the least dangerous inmates allowing relative freedom of movement within the confines of a locked perimeter.

Miranda warnings warnings that explain the rights of an arrestee which police are required to recite at the time of arrest or prior to interrogation.

misdemeanor a relatively minor offense punishable by fine or up to one year in jail.

Missouri merit selection plan a judicial selection plan devised in 1940 which relies upon an independent commission of lawyers to nominate candidates for final appointment by the governor of the state subject to voter approval.

mistake of fact a defense claiming an error or misunderstanding of fact or circumstances resulting in an act that would otherwise not have been undertaken.

mistrial judicial ruling that the trial was invalid because it was terminated without a verdict or because of substantial error in due process proceedings.

mitigating circumstances facts about the offender and circumstances of the crime specified by law that guide a jury decision to apply the death penalty

moral crusade the process by which a particular set of behaviors is constructed as a widespread threat to the public welfare.

moral entrepreneurs people who identify certain forms of conduct as dangerous to society and mobilize others to exert social control over those who engage in the conduct.

moral panic shared belief that a particular behavior is significant threat to the well being of the entire society.

morality beliefs about the rightness and wrongness of human conduct.

mores important rules of conduct within a society which define right and wrong.

motion for continuance a written to oral request to the judge by the defense or prosecution to delay trial proceedings.

motion for discovery a written or oral request to the opposing side to inform their opponent about evidence that will be produced during the trial.

motion to dismiss a written or oral request to the judge to dismiss the charges against the accused.

motion to suppress a pretrial motion that requests the judge to deny that certain evidence be used in the trial.

motive a reason a person commits a particular action.

mujahideen Muslim holy warriors.

multiple marginalities the combined impact of low status in more than one aspect of identity.

municipal, magistrate or police courts busy lower courts where a large number of misdemeanor cases are handled.

murder the killing of one human being by another with malice or premeditation.

N

National Crime Victimization survey an annual survey of 100,000 people aged 12 and older to determine the nature and extent of their victimization of crime administered by the U.S. Census Bureau.

national security intelligence preventative clandestine surveillance by the government designed to gather information about potential threats to national security.

National Youth Survey A longitudinal survey of adolescents interviewed each year from 1978 to 1981 and then four more times as adults through 1993.

nationalists unconventional soldiers fighting for fellow countrymen.

natural law the belief that law is grounded in a higher set of moral principles universal to all human societies.

necessity justification a defense to a criminal charge that claims it was necessary to commit some unlawful act in order to prevent or avoid a greater harm.

net-widening the increase in the correctional population by the diversion of less serious offenders into program intended for more serious offenders thus expanding the overall correctional population.

NIBRS or National Incident Based Reporting System new system for recording criminal statistics to replace the UCR based on twenty-four types of crimes with expanded data on victims and offenders.

No knock warrant is: a warrant that allows officers to enter a property without notifying residents immediately prior to such entry.

nolle prosequi a formal entry in the record by which a prosecutor declares he or she will not prosecute the case.

norm expected behavior for a member of a group within a specific set of circumstances.

notification rights the right of victims to be informed of key decisions and hearings related to their cases, such as plea agreements, parole hearings or early release decisions.

O

obstacle course model a model of the justice process which depicts the system as complex and convoluted deliberately difficult to negotiate in order to protect due process rights of the accused.

occupational crime offenses committed by persons acting in their legitimate occupational roles.

offender-focused all the resources, policies, and personnel of the justice system are devoted to activities which concern the person who is accused of or has been convicted of violating the law.

opening statements introduction to the jury by the prosecution and the defense of the evidence and arguments that will be presented in the trial.

order maintenance function to maintain peace and order, handle disputes, deal with troublemakers and keep the public spaces free from disorder.

organized crime an illegal business which provides illegal goods and services to the public.

P

pains of imprisonment deprivations of prison life, including absence of goods, autonomy, heterosexual interaction, and security.

paradox of coercive power the more a person in authority uses power, the more they lose authority to use power.

paradox of reform theory that legal interventions designed to improve the conditions of incarceration may have contributed to more serious violent conditions within the prison.

para-militarization the use of military equipment, tactics, and weapons in policing.

parole board an administrative agency charged with the authority to grant conditional release for prisoners eligible for parole.

parole eligibility determined by statute and the amount of time an inmate has served.

parole the conditional release of an inmate from incarceration under supervision after a portion of the prison sentence has been served.

Part I Offenses crimes designated by the FBI as most serious.

Part II Offenses crimes designated by the FBI as less serious.

Patriot Act an act of Congress passed in the immediate aftermath of the September 11 attacks, the main goal of which is to enhance the ability of the government to collect intelligence inside the United States by removing the "wall" or legal prohibition on information shared between national intelligence and law enforcement agencies.

patronage a form of corruption in which the political party in power awards jobs and promotion in policing is given out as return for loyalty and favors to politicians.

penitentiary an institution intended to isolate prisoners from society and from one another so they could reflect on their past, repent, and emerge as reformed sinners.

peremptory challenges removal of a certain number of jurors by counsel for each side without reason.

petit jury a panel of citizens charged with determining the defendant's guilt or innocence in a trial.

plain view exception the rule that any evidence police can see or hear in plain view when they are where they have a legal right to be is admissible in court even without a legal warrant or probable cause.

plea bargaining the negotiation of an agreement among the prosecutor, judge, and the defense counsel as to the charge and/or sentence to be imposed if the defendant enters a guilty plea.

police brutality the unlawful use of physical force by officers in the performance of their duties.

police corruption misconduct by police officers through illegal activities for economic gain including the acceptance of payment of services, non-enforcement of the law in exchange for payment and active participation in criminal activities.

political crimes illegal acts committed against the government or other public authorities.

post-traumatic stress disorder a set of psychological symptoms suffered by some victims in response to the trauma of the crime.

power the ability to affect the behavior of others, with or without the use of force.

preponderance of the evidence the standard for determining legal liability in civil trials requiring a certainty of more than 50 percent of defendant's guilt.

pre-sentence investigation/report an investigation and summary report of the background of a convicted offender prepared to help the judge decide on an appropriate sentence for the individual.

presumption of innocence the guiding principle of criminal procedure which places the burden of proof on the state.

presumptive sentence the expected sentence for a given crime and given offender prescribed by the sentencing guidelines.

pretrial motions a written or oral request to a judge by the prosecution or defense before the trial begins.

pretrial phase the second stage of criminal justice processing where numerous decisions about the trial procedure is adjudicated by the lower court.

preventative patrol the use of continuous and visible walking of public streets by police in order to deter crime.

Prison Industrial Complex a web of government and industry interests that profit or otherwise benefit from the perpetuation of surveillance, policing, and incarceration.

prisonization the process whereby a new inmate becomes socialized to the inmate subculture and adapts to prison life.

private correctional facilities corporate-owned and run facilities that contract with local, state, and federal governments to house inmates.

probable cause facts are reliable and generate a reasonable belief that a person has committed, is committing, or is about to commit a crime.

probation a sentence the offender serves in the community under correctional supervision.

problem-oriented policing the identification, analysis, and solution of the source of a crime problem in cooperation with the community.

procedural criminal law the lawful process for creating, enforcing, and implementing the criminal law.

professionalism the master trend in twentieth-century policing which sought to separate policing from politics through civil service examination, education, training, and bureaucratization.

profiling a tool used by law enforcement to narrow offender characteristics to assist in prevention or apprehension.

propaganda by deed actions, including tossing bombs at important persons in public places, used by anarchists in the nineteenth century to bring attention to their cause.

property crime index the sum of four Part I property offenses (burglary, larceny, auto-theft, and arson) reported in a given place for a given period of time.

prosecutors a government attorney who instigates the prosecution of an accused and represents the interests of the state at trial.

public defender offices full-time attorneys funded by state or federal governments who specialized in criminal defense for the poor.

public duty a defense that claims the defendant was lawfully exercising their authority at the time the act was committed.

punitive solitary confinement the use of solitary confinement under conditions of extreme deprivation as a punishment for disciplinary infractions.

Q

quality of life policing aggressive enforcement of public nuisance laws.

R

racial profiling the use of a group characteristic such as race, gender, or ethnicity as a part of the evidence that constitutes reasonable suspicion that a crime has occurred.

rape shield laws laws that bar the introduction of evidence about a victim's prior sexual conduct.

rape forced or coerced sexual assault, usually intercourse.

rapid response an urgent response system of policing based on citizen use of 911, two-way radios and mobile command and control units.

reactive patrol   a police patrol model in which police respond only when there is a call for assistance.

reasonable person standard   the circumstances as they appeared to the defendant would have created the same beliefs in the mind of an average, normal sensible human being.

reasonable suspicion   reliable facts that a person has been or is about to commit a crime.

recidivism   the repetition of criminal conduct.

re-entry   refers to the process of returning to society after being incarcerated.

reformatory movement   a nineteenth-century prison reform movement generally reserved for youth and women that focused on rehabilitation, reform, and the use of indeterminate sentencing.

rehabilitation   the process of changing the attitudes and behavior of the offender through training, education, treatment, or vocational programming to produce law-abiding conduct in the future.

reification   the transformation of a neutral word or concept into a sacred and powerful symbol.

reign of terror   coined by Edmund Burke, the term described the massive number of executions of formerly powerful members of the nobility and church by the new government in the aftermath of the French Revolution; the source of the term "terrorism."

release on recognizance   a nonfinancial release in which the accused promises to appear in court at the required date.

remand   the ruling of the higher court directing the lower court to rehear the case with a new set of proceedings.

reparative boards   community volunteer boards supervised by the justice system which provide supervision and support for juveniles and adults on probation and for those re-integrating back into the community from prison or jail.

restitution   a criminal sanction in which offenders repay victims for their crime or provide work service to the community or the victim.

restorative justice   a response to crime that seeks to restore the well-being of victims and the larger community while promoting responsible and productive behavior in offenders.

retribution   a sentencing philosophy that prioritizes punishment commensurate to the seriousness of the offense.

retributive justice   a response to crime that seeks to inflict punishment on offenders in just proportion to the seriousness of the offense.

reverse   the ruling by an appellate court to overturn the decision of the lower court.

revocation of parole   administrative removal of an offender from parole status for failure to comply with parole conditions usually requiring the return of the offender to incarceration.

revocation of probation   return of offender to court for sentencing for failure to meet conditions of probation.

right of appeal   the right of the defendant to have the proceedings of lower courts and trial courts reviewed by a higher court.

right to counsel   a defendant's constitutional right to the assistance of an attorney during prosecution.

right to privacy   though not explicitly defined in the U.S. Constitution, the courts have found a right to be let alone from surveillance or interference by the government unless there is evidence one has violated the law.

robbery   the felonious taking of money or goods from another person through the threat of force and violence.

role strain   tension between two facets of the job of probation and parole   rule enforcement and rehabilitation.

rotten apple theory   a theory that extra-legal violence by police is the result of few excessively aggressive individuals, or "rotten apples" who spoil the reputation of police as a whole.

rough justice   informal proceedings within the lower courts that do not conform to formal due process.

Rule of Four   the requirement that a minimum of four U.S. Supreme Court justices must consent to issue a writ of certiorari.

rule of law   the basic principle that the exercise of governmental power is regulated by laws formulated by legitimate institutions of representative government.

rule of thumb   the common law doctrine regulating the use of physical force by husbands against their wives.

S

saturation patrolling   increased police presence in "hot spots" known to have high amounts of criminal activity. Also known as problem-oriented patrolling.

search incident to a lawful arrest   search of persons immediately after an arrest specifically for the purpose of seizing weapons or evidence.

search warrant   an order issued by a judge and signed by a police officer indicating where the search will take place and what is expected to be found in the search.

second degree   committing a homicide with malice but without premeditation.

secondary victimization   callous and insensitive treatment by the criminal justice system which inflicts additional psychological harm and emotional trauma on victims.

selective enforcement of the law   when criminal justice personnel enforce some laws and not others or enforce them in some situations and not in other situations.

selective incorporation   the legal principle that only some of the protections in the Bill of Rights applies to state courts under the due process and equal protection clause of the Fourteenth Amendment.

selective prosecution   the authority held by prosecutors to use discretion in choosing whom to prosecute.

self-defense   a defense to a criminal charge based on a person's inherent right to self-protection and to reasonably defend oneself from unlawful attacks.

self-report surveys   surveys that ask people whether they have committed crimes during a given period of time.

sentencing bargaining   plea negotiations which agree on the type of sentence to be imposed in exchange for a guilty plea on a given charge.

sentencing disparities   the imposition of widely different sentences for offenders convicted of the same offense.

sentencing guidelines   a standardized set of penalty options based on key characteristics of the offense and offender.

separate system   complete solitary confinement in an individual cell to encourage redemption and prevent social contamination via association with others in the prison first used in the Walnut Street jail.

separation of powers   the division of the government into three branches: executive, legislative, and judicial.

service function   to provide assistance with a wide array of social problems.

sexual assault   verbal, visual, or any other kind of assault that forces a person to join in unwanted sexual contact or attention, including rape, inappropriate touching, voyeurism, exhibitionism, incest, and sexual harassment.

shock incarceration the use of shorter but more intense periods of incarceration designed to have a deeper impact on the offender.

social construction of reality a process by which members of every society collectively define and interpret the world around them.

social control formal and informal processes that maintain conformity with social norms.

socialization the process of learning the norms, values, and beliefs of a given culture.

specific deterrence the imposition of punishment to discourage the individual from committing crimes in the future. Also known as special or individual deterrence.

specific intent the thoughtful and conscious intention to perform a specific act in order to achieve a particular outcome.

spousal or marital rape rape of one's spouse.

stake in conformity when a person is subject to social controls such as employment or marriage they are believed to have an increased interest in complying with society's rules or laws.

standardization the value that each case be treated according to the same rules regardless of individual circumstances.

state crimes illegal acts committed by governments and other public authorities in violation of domestic and international law.

state-centered justice when crime is defined as primarily an offense against the authority of these powerful institutions rather than a harm to individuals within the community.

state-use laws laws that require prison industry to produce goods solely for use in state institutions.

status degradation ceremony rituals which mark the transition from a citizen to the lower status of an inmate.

statutory good time the number of days deducted from a sentence determined by statute for a time served without disciplinary reports.

statutory rape sexual activities with someone not capable of giving consent, typically because they are too young to give legal consent.

stop and frisk a technique used by police to "pat-down" a person suspected of being armed or in possession of the instrumentalities of crime.

straight pleas a defendant's formal entry of a guilty plea without explicit negotiation by the courthouse work group.

strict liability statutes crimes for which one may incur liability without fault or intention.

structured conflict the relationship between inmates and guards within the institution in which inmates are confined against their will and guards are charged with the responsibility of enforcing their detention.

substantive criminal law actions which are prohibited or prescribed by the criminal law.

suicide mission a task that is so dangerous that the person performing the act is not expected to survive.

super-max prison a new generation of maximum-security facility which relies upon technology and high levels of supervision and restriction of inmate movement.

supremacy clause Article VI, clause 2, of the federal Constitution declares federal law to be the Supreme Law of the Land.

survivors mission sustained efforts by victims to bring about positive legislative or social change that will prevent re-occurrence of the crime to others or will assist victims in dealing with the trauma of crime.

suspicious activity reports any report of individual suspicious activity reported to Homeland Security by a citizen or local police; also referred to as SAR.

symbolic assailants working stereotypes of citizens likely to pose a potential threat to police officer's safety used informally by police in their interactions with citizens on the street.

T

terrorism the unlawful use of force or violence against a target to create fear or coercion for the purpose of obtaining some political concession or reward or other goal.

terrorist organizations organizations designated by the president, pursuant to the authority of the Patriot Act, as funders or supporters of "terrorism."

testimonial evidence statements offered under oath as to what a witness saw or heard.

thief-takers eighteenth-century mercenaries who offered to pursue felons for a fee.

three-strikes laws statutes that mandate life in prison if convicted of a third felony.

ticket of leave an early system first created in the United Kingdom, whereby inmates could earn early release.

total crime index the sum of Part I offenses reported in a given place for a given period of time.

total institution a term coined by Erving Goffman to refer to institutions organized so that those who work in the institution exercise total control over every aspect of the lives of those who are inmates within the institution.

totality of circumstances while each piece of information alone might not satisfy probable cause, when put together, they will create a reasonable set of facts to justify an arrest.

trial by jury the examination of the facts and law in a court before a jury authorized to give the verdict according to the evidence as to the guilt or innocence of the accused.

trial courts courts with the power to hear a case from the start, examine the evidence and apply the law to those facts.

trial de novo statutory right of the defendant to a new trial in the general court system if convicted in a lower court.

true diversion programs traditional forms of diversion that kept people out of the criminal justice system.

truth in sentencing laws statutes which require that most or all of the sentence be actually served.

tything In Anglo-Saxon law, an association of ten families bound together by a frankpledge.

U

U.S. Court of Appeals thirteen intermediate appellate-level federal courts.

U.S. district courts courts of general jurisdiction in the federal court system.

U.S. Magistrate Courts federal courts with limited powers to try lesser misdemeanors, setting bail in more serious cases, issuing search and arrest warrants, and other legal matters.

unconditional mandatory release release from prison required by statute when a criminal has served his or her full sentence minus statutory and earned good time.

under-enforcement of the law when the criminal justice system fails to enforce the law and respond to certain kinds of victimization.

Uniform Crime Reports the collection and dissemination of national data on crimes known to the police and arrest operated by the FBI.

V

vehicular homicide the killing of a human being by the operation of a motor vehicle by another in a reckless manner likely to cause the death of, or great bodily harm to, another.

venue the place where a case is heard.

vertical overcharging charging a single offense at the most serious level possible to maximize the state's advantage in plea negotiations.

victim compensation funds money collected by the state from criminal fines and awarded to victims for medical bills, counseling and to compensate for financial losses.

victim witness and advocacy programs an organized program with specialized personnel housed within district attorneys' offices or victims assistance agencies who assist victims throughout the justice process.

victim-blaming the responsibility for the crime is shifted from the perpetrator to the victim.

victim-impact statement a report to the sentencing judge listing the effects of the crime on the victim.

victimization surveys surveys that ask people whether they have been victims of crime during a given period of time.

victimless crimes illegal activities that involve willing participants, such as drug use, prostitution, and gambling.

victim-offender mediation face-to-face facilitated meetings between victims and offenders to promote victim healing, restitution and offender accountability.

victim-offender reconciliation programs programs which bring victims and offenders in a face-to-face dialogue to discuss the impact of the harm and to negotiate restitution by the offender to the victim and the community.

victimology the scientific study of the physical, psychological, and financial harm people suffer because of crime and the handling of crime by the criminal justice system itself.

victim-precipitation behavior of individuals that increases the likelihood of criminal victimization.

victims' rights movement a social movement started in the 1970s to increase awareness of victims issues and to advocate for the right of victims in the criminal justice process.

vigilantism illegal violence conducted by groups or individuals who believe they are enforcing justice despite the actual content of the law.

violent crime index the sum of four Part I violent offenses (homicide, forcible rape, robbery, aggravated assault) reported in a given place for a given period of time.

voir dire a process by which lawyers and judge question potential jurors for a given case.

voluntary defender programs full-time attorneys who work for legal aid officers funded by federal or state governments who provide a full range of civil and criminal legal aid for poor citizens.

voluntary intoxication intoxication that is the result of willful personal choice.

voluntary manslaughter the unlawful killing of a human being without malice which is done intentionally upon a sudden quarrel or in the heat of passion.

W

Walnut Street jail the first American penitentiary.

warrant a writ issued by a judicial officer ordering law enforcement to perform a specific action such as a search or an arrest.

warrantless arrest an arrest made without first seeking a warrant based on probable cause and permissible under specified circumstances.

wedding cake model a model of the justice process which describes the public's and media focus on a few extraordinary and exceptional crimes.

white collar crime a general term which encompasses crimes committed by "respectable" persons.

white supremacy the belief that "white" people are superior to other races.

Wickersham Commission a panel of national experts convened in 1929 to conduct the first comprehensive national report on the criminal justice system. Evidence of systematic corruption and abuses within policing in the Wickersham Report generated public support for reform.

working personality the effect of daily police work on officers' view of the world characterized by cynicism and suspicion. The key features of police work to generate this view are the response to danger and the obligation to exercise authority.

writ of certiorari a document issued by a higher court directing the lower court to prepare the record of a case and send it to the higher court for review.

writ of habeas corpus a petition to the court contesting the legality of imprisonment.

INDEX

CAROLYN BOYES-WATSON is professor of sociology at Suffolk University, where she serves as founding director of the Center for Restorative Justice (CRJ). She is coauthor of the textbook *Youth, Crime, and Justice: Learning through Cases* with Erika Gebo and coeditor of the series Learning through Cases with Susan Krumholtz. She has published extensively in the field of restorative justice and has published two manuals, *Circle Forward: Building a Restorative School* and *Heart of Hope*, with Kay Pranis. In the sociology department Dr. Boyes-Watson has taught a range of undergraduate and graduate courses about the criminal, juvenile justice, and restorative justice systems and now directs the work of the CRJ in developing the capacity of schools, juvenile justice, and criminal justice organizations to effectively implement restorative justice practices.

SUSAN T. KRUMHOLZ received her J.D. from Seattle University and her Ph.D. in Law, Policy and Society from Northeastern University. She is currently professor in the Department of Crime and Justice Studies.

Her research/publication interests include intimate violence, alternatives to the criminal/legal system, and women as students and practitioners of the law. Dr. Krumholz is most passionate about the classes she teaches at the Bristol County House of Corrections as part of the Inside-Out Prison Exchange Program. These classes bring together students at UMD with incarcerated students for semester-long study. For this work she received the 2008 UMass President's Public Service Award.